THE PAPERS OF
THOMAS JEFFERSON

THE PAPERS OF
Thomas Jefferson

Volume 8
25 February to 31 October 1785

JULIAN P. BOYD, EDITOR

MINA R. BRYAN AND ELIZABETH L. HUTTER,

ASSOCIATE EDITORS

PRINCETON, NEW JERSEY

PRINCETON UNIVERSITY PRESS

1953

Printed in the United States of America by
Princeton University Press, Princeton, New Jersey

DEDICATED TO THE MEMORY OF

ADOLPH S. OCHS

PUBLISHER OF THE NEW YORK TIMES

1896-1935

WHO BY THE EXAMPLE OF A RESPONSIBLE

PRESS ENLARGED AND FORTIFIED

THE JEFFERSONIAN CONCEPT

OF A FREE PRESS

GUIDE TO EDITORIAL
APPARATUS

1. TEXTUAL DEVICES

The following devices are employed throughout the work to clarify the presentation of the text.

[. . .], [. . . .]	One or two words missing and not conjecturable.
[. . .]¹, [. . . .]¹	More than two words missing and not conjecturable; subjoined footnote estimates number of words missing.
[ ]	Number or part of a number missing or illegible.
[roman]	Conjectural reading for missing or illegible matter. A question mark follows when the reading is doubtful.
[*italic*]	Editorial comment inserted in the text.
⟨*italic*⟩	Matter deleted in the MS but restored in our text.
〚 〛	Record entry for letters not found.

2. DESCRIPTIVE SYMBOLS

The following symbols are employed throughout the work to describe the various kinds of manuscript originals. When a series of versions is recorded, *the first to be recorded is the version used for the printed text.*

Dft	draft (usually a composition or rough draft; later drafts, when identifiable as such, are designated "2d Dft," &c.)
Dupl	duplicate
MS	manuscript (arbitrarily applied to most documents other than letters)
N	note, notes (memoranda, fragments, &c.)
PoC	polygraph copy
PrC	press copy
RC	recipient's copy
SC	stylograph copy
Tripl	triplicate

All manuscripts of the above types are assumed to be in the hand of the author of the document to which the descriptive symbol pertains. If not, that fact is stated. On the other hand, the follow-

ing types of manuscripts are assumed *not* to be in the hand of the author, and exceptions will be noted:

FC   file copy (applied to all forms of retained copies, such as letter-book copies, clerks' copies, &c.)

Tr   transcript (applied to both contemporary and later copies; period of transcription, unless clear by implication, will be given when known)

3. *LOCATION SYMBOLS*

The locations of documents printed in this edition from originals in private hands, from originals held by institutions outside the United States, and from printed sources are recorded in self-explanatory form in the descriptive note following each document. The locations of documents printed from originals held by public institutions in the United States are recorded by means of the symbols used in the National Union Catalog in the Library of Congress; an explanation of how these symbols are formed is given above, Vol. 1: xl. The list of symbols appearing in each volume is limited to the institutions represented by documents printed or referred to in that volume.

CLU	William Andrews Clark Memorial Library, University of California at Los Angeles
CSmH	Henry E. Huntington Library, San Marino, California
Ct	Connecticut State Library, Hartford, Connecticut
CtY	Yale University Library
DLC	Library of Congress
DNA	The National Archives
ICHi	Chicago Historical Society, Chicago
IHi	Illinois State Historical Library, Springfield
MB	Boston Public Library, Boston
MHi	Massachusetts Historical Society, Boston
MdAA	Maryland Hall of Records, Annapolis
MeHi	Maine Historical Society, Portland
MHi: AMT	Adams Family Papers, deposited by the Adams Manuscript Trust in Massachusetts Historical Society
MiU-C	William L. Clements Library, University of Michigan

MoSHi Missouri Historical Society, St. Louis
MWA American Antiquarian Society, Worcester
NBu Buffalo Public Library, Buffalo, New York
NHi New-York Historical Society, New York City
NN New York Public Library, New York City
NNC Columbia University Library
NNP Pierpont Morgan Library, New York City
NNS New York Society Library, New York City
NcD Duke University Library
NjP Princeton University Library
PHC Haverford College Library
PHi Historical Society of Pennsylvania, Philadel-
       phia
PPAP American Philosophical Society, Philadelphia
PPL-R Library Company of Philadelphia, Ridgway,
        Branch
PU University of Pennsylvania Library
RPA Rhode Island Department of State, Providence
Vi Virginia State Library, Richmond
ViHi Virginia Historical Society, Richmond
ViU University of Virginia Library
ViW College of William and Mary Library
ViWC Colonial Williamsburg, Inc.
WHi State Historical Society of Wisconsin, Madison

4. OTHER ABBREVIATIONS

The following abbreviations are commonly employed in the annotation throughout the work.

TJ Thomas Jefferson

TJ Editorial Files Photoduplicates and other editorial materials in the office of *The Papers of Thomas Jefferson*, Princeton University Library

TJ Papers Jefferson Papers (Applied to a collection of manuscripts when the precise location of a given document must be furnished, and always preceded by the symbol for the institutional repository; thus "DLC: TJ Papers, 4:628-9" represents a document in the Library of Congress, Jefferson Papers, volume 4, pages 628 and 629.)

PCC Papers of the Continental Congress, in the National Archives

RG   Record Group (Used in designating the location of documents in the National Archives.)

SJL   Jefferson's "Summary Journal of letters" written and received (in DLC: TJ Papers)

SJPL   "Summary Journal of Public Letters," an incomplete list of letters written by TJ from 16 Apr. 1784 to 31 Dec. 1793, with brief summaries, in an amanuensis' hand (in DLC: TJ Papers, at end of SJL).

5. SHORT TITLES

The following list includes only those short titles of works cited with great frequency, and therefore in very abbreviated form, throughout this edition. Their expanded forms are given here only in the degree of fullness needed for unmistakable identification. Since it is impossible to anticipate all the works to be cited in such very abbreviated form, the list is appropriately revised from volume to volume.

Atlas of Amer. Hist., Scribner, 1943.   James Truslow Adams and R. V. Coleman, *Atlas of American History*, N.Y., 1943

Biog. Dir. Cong.   Biographical Directory of Congress, 1774-1927

B.M. Cat.   British Museum, *General Catalogue of Printed Books*, London, 1931—. Also, *The British Museum Catalogue of Printed Books, 1881-1900*, Ann Arbor, 1946

B.N. Cat.   Catalogue général des livres imprimés de la Bibliothèque Nationale. Auteurs.

Burnett, *Letters of Members*   Edmund C. Burnett, ed., *Letters of Members of the Continental Congress*

Cal. Franklin Papers   Calendar of the Papers of Benjamin Franklin in the Library of the American Philosophical Society, ed. I. Minis Hays

CVSP   *Calendar of Virginia State Papers . . . Preserved in the Capitol at Richmond*

DAB   *Dictionary of American Biography*

DAE   *Dictionary of American English*

DAH   *Dictionary of American History*

DNB   *Dictionary of National Biography*

Dipl. Corr., 1783-89   The Diplomatic Correspondence of the United States of America, from the Signing of the Definitive Treaty of Peace . . . to the Adoption of the Constitution, Washington, Blair & Rives, 1837, 3 vol.

Evans   Charles Evans, *American Bibliography*

Ford   Paul Leicester Ford, ed., *The Writings of Thomas Jeffer-son*, "Letterpress Edition," N.Y., 1892-1899

Fry-Jefferson Map   *The Fry & Jefferson Map of Virginia and Maryland: A Facsimile of the First Edition*, Princeton, 1950

Gottschalk, *Lafayette, 1783-89* Louis Gottschalk, *Lafayette between the American Revolution and the French Revolution (1783-1789)*, Chicago, 1950

Gournay   *Tableau général du commerce, des marchands, négocians, armateurs, &c., . . . années 1789 & 1790*, Paris, n.d.

HAW   Henry A. Washington, ed., *The Writings of Thomas Jefferson*, Washington, 1853-1854

Henry, *Henry*   William Wirt Henry, *Patrick Henry, Life, Correspondence and Speeches*

JCC   *Journals of the Continental Congress, 1774-1789*, ed. W. C. Ford and others, Washington, 1904-1937

JHD   *Journal of the House of Delegates of the Commonwealth of Virginia* (cited by session and date of publication)

Jefferson Correspondence, Bixby   *Thomas Jefferson Correspondence Printed from the Originals in the Collections of William K. Bixby*, ed. W. C. Ford, Boston, 1916

Johnston, "Jefferson Bibliography"   Richard H. Johnston, "A Contribution to a Bibliography of Thomas Jefferson," *Writings of Thomas Jefferson*, ed. Lipscomb and Bergh, xx, separately paged following the Index.

L & B   Andrew A. Lipscomb and Albert E. Bergh, eds., *The Writings of Thomas Jefferson*, "Memorial Edition," Washington, 1903-1904

L.C. Cat.   *A Catalogue of Books Represented by Library of Congress Printed Cards*, Ann Arbor, 1942-1946; also *Supplement*, 1948

Library Catalogue, 1783   Jefferson's MS list of books owned and wanted in 1783 (original in Massachusetts Historical Society)

Library Catalogue, 1815   *Catalogue of the Library of the United States*, Washington, 1815

Library Catalogue, 1829   *Catalogue. President Jefferson's Library*, Washington, 1829

MVHR   *Mississippi Valley Historical Review*

OED   *A New English Dictionary on Historical Principles*, Oxford, 1888-1933

PMHB   *The Pennsylvania Magazine of History and Biography*

Randall, *Life*   Henry S. Randall, *The Life of Thomas Jefferson*

Randolph, *Domestic Life*   Sarah N. Randolph, *The Domestic Life of Thomas Jefferson*

Sabin   Joseph Sabin and others, *Bibliotheca Americana. A Dictionary of Books Relating to America*

Sowerby   *Catalogue of the Library of Thomas Jefferson*, compiled with annotations by E. Millicent Sowerby, Washington, 1952-53

Swem, *Index*   E. G. Swem, *Virginia Historical Index*

Swem, "Va. Bibliog." Earl G. Swem, "A Bibliography of Virginia," Virginia State Library, *Bulletin*, VIII, X, XII (1915-1919)

TJR   Thomas Jefferson Randolph, ed., *Memoir, Correspondence, and Miscellanies, from the Papers of Thomas Jefferson*, Charlottesville, 1829

Tucker, *Life*   George Tucker, *The Life of Thomas Jefferson*, Philadelphia, 1837

Tyler, *Va. Biog.*   Lyon G. Tyler, *Encyclopedia of Virginia Biography*

Tyler's Quart.   Tyler's Quarterly Historical and Genealogical Magazine

VMHB   *Virginia Magazine of History and Biography*

Wharton, *Dipl. Corr. Am. Rev.   The Revolutionary Diplomatic Correspondence of the United States*, ed. Francis Wharton

WMQ   *William and Mary Quarterly*

CONTENTS

Guide to Editorial Apparatus   vii
Jefferson Chronology   2

⋅◖ 1 7 8 5 ◗⋅

continued

From George Washington, *25 February*   3
Jefferson's Advertisement of Hopkinson's Invention *[ca. February?]*   6
From Anthony Garvey *[ca. February?]*   8
To John Adams and Benjamin Franklin, *1 March*   8
Proposed Changes in Translation of the Treaty with Prussia
    [ca. 1 March?]   9
To Geismar, *3 March*   10
To Samuel Henley, with a List of Books, *3 March*   11
De Thulemeier to the American Commissioners, *4 March*   14
From Charles Thomson, *6 March*   15
From Alexander Moore, *10 March*   17
To Clouet *[11 March]*   18
John Jay to the American Commissioners *[11] March*   19
From Jean Holker, *12 March*   22
From Eliza House Trist, *12 March*   24
American Commissioners to De Thulemeier, *14 March*   26
From John Jay, *15 March*   33
From John Page, *15 March*   34
From Chevallié, *17 March*   34
American Commissioners to John Jay, *18 March*   36
To James Madison, *18 March*   38
To James Monroe, *18 March*   42
[To Alexander Moore, *19 March*]   45
[To Nathaniel Tracy, *19 March*]   45
John Adams to Franklin and Jefferson, *20 March*   46
From James Buchanan and William Hay, *20 March*   48
From Francis Hopkinson, with Enclosure, *20 March*   50
From Richard Price, *21 March*   52
From John Jay, *22 March*   54
Jefferson's Attestation of Depositions, *22 March*   54
[To Jean Holker, *24 March*]   55
Dorset to the American Commissioners, *26 March*   55

CONTENTS

From Abiel Foster, *26 March*   60
From Anthony Garvey, *26 March*   60
From Siot de St. Pol, *26 March*   60
American Commissioners to Vergennes, *28 March*   61
From Geismar, *28 March*   63
From William Carmichael, *29 March*   64
From Jean Holker, *29 March*   67
From Patrick Henry, *30 March*   67
To William Short, *2 April*   68
From William Carmichael, *4 April*   69
From James Monroe, *6 April*   70
Lafayette to the American Commissioners, *8 April*   70
Notes on Presents made by Foreign Powers to Algiers
    [after 8 April]   72
〚To Thomas Barclay, John Bondfield, and James Carmichael,
    10 April〛   73
From the Rev. James Madison, *10 April*   73
From James Monroe, *12 April*   75
American Commissioners to John Jay, *13 April*   80
〚To Alexander Moore, *14 April*〛   83
William Carmichael to Benjamin Franklin, *15 April*   83
From David Hartley, *15 April*   85
From John Jay, *15 April*   86
From James Milligan, *15 April*   87
To James Monroe, *15 April*   88
To the Governor of Virginia, *15 April*   90
From James Carmichael, *16 April*   92
From the Abbés Arnoux and Chalut, *17 April*   92
〚To William Carmichael, *17 April*〛   93
〚To Jean Holker, *17 April*〛   93
From John Bondfield, *19 April*   93
From William Carmichael, *19 April*   95
From Peter Carr, *20 April*   96
From Madame de Doradour, *20 April*   96
From Francis Hopkinson, *20 April*   98
From Walker Maury, *20 April*   101
From P. Guillibaud & Cie., *22 April*   102
From Jean Holker, *25 April*   103
Favi to the American Commissioners, *26 April*   104
Notes on Alterations Proposed by Favi *[after 26 April]*   105
From James Madison, *27 April*   110

CONTENTS

[From John Bondfield, *28 April*]   116

From John Page, *28 April*   116

Vergennes to the American Commissioners, *28 April*   120

From Jacques Le Maire, *30 April*   120

To William Short, *30 April*   132

From Madame de Doradour, *1 May*   133

To William Short, *2 May*   133

[To William Carmichael, *3 May*]   134

De Thulemeier to the American Commissioners, *3 May*   134

From Eliza House Trist, *4 May*   135

From William Carmichael, *5 April [i.e., May]*   137

[From Martha Jefferson Carr, *6 May*]   139

From Madame de Doradour *[8 May]*   139

From C. W. F. Dumas, *10 May*   140

American Commissioners to John Jay, *11 May*   140

From Madame de Doradour *[11? May]*   141

[To Francis Eppes, *11 May*]   141

To Elbridge Gerry, *11 May*   142

[To George Gilmer, *11 May*]   145

[To Samuel Hardy, *11 May*]   145

To John Jay, *11 May*   145

To John Jay, *11 May*   146

[To Nicholas Lewis, *11 May-3 June*]   147

To James Madison, *11 May*   147

[To James Maury, *11 May*]   148

To James Monroe, *11 May*   148

[To John Walker, *11 May*]   151

[To Edward Burd, *12 May*]   151

From Madame de Doradour *[12 May]*   151

To the Governor of Virginia, *12 May*   151

[To Philip Mazzei, *12 May*]   152

From John Polson, *13 May*   152

American Commissioners to Dorset, *16 May*   153

From Richard Henry Lee, *16 May*   153

From St. John de Crèvecoeur, *18 May*   155

From Madame de Doradour *[18 May]*   156

From John Adams, *19 May*   157

To De Blome, *19 May*   157

From the Ambassador of Venice at the Court of Versailles *[ca. 19 May]*   158

[To John Bondfield, *20 May*]   158

[xv]

CONTENTS

To C. W. F. Dumas, *20 May*   158
[To Jean Holker, *20 May*]   159
From John Adams, *22 May*   159
From John Adams, *23 May*   161
[To Giovanni Fabbroni, *23 May*]   161
From Alexander Learmonth, *23 May*   161
From the Abbés Arnoux and Chalut, *24 May*   162
From Jean Holker, *24 May*   162
From Louis Guillaume Otto, *24 May*   163
To John Adams, *25 May*   163
From Vergennes, *25 May*   164
American Commissioners to De Thulemeier, *26 May*   165
[To Louis Guillaume Otto, *26 May*]   166
From John Adams, *27 May*   166
From John Adams, *27 May*   167
From Samuel Amory, *27 May*   168
From Barré, *28 May*   168
From Samuel House, *28 May*   169
From Louis Guillaume Otto, *28 May*   169
John Adams to Franklin and Jefferson, *29 May*   170
[From John Jay, *30 May*]   171
[From Nathanael Greene, *1 June*]   171
From Louis Guillaume Otto, *1 June*   171
To John Adams, *2 June*   172
From Chastellux, *2 June*   174
[To Anthony Garvey, *2 June*]   175
From John Adams, *3 June*   176
To Barré, *3 June*   176
From Anthony Garvey, *5 June*   177
[From James Jarvis, *5 June*]   178
From Abigail Adams, with Enclosure, *6 June*   178
From Jean François Briet, *6 June*   181
[To Anthony Garvey, *6 June*]   183
From John Adams, *7 June*   183
To Chastellux, *7 June*   184
From C. W. F. Dumas, *7 June*   187
American Commissioners to Favi, with Observations on Treaty
    Project, *8 June*   187
From Ralph Izard, with Reports on the Trade of South Carolina,
    10 June   195
To Jean François Briet, *11 June*   205

[xvi]

CONTENTS

Favi to the American Commissioners, *11 June* 205
From Nathanael Greene, *11 June* 205
From Madame de Doradour, *14 June* 206
From Neil Jamieson, *14 June* 206
〚From John Jay, *14 June*〛 207
From Jean François Briet, *15 June* 207
〚To James Buchanan and William Hay, *15 June*〛 207
Franklin and Jefferson to John Adams, *15 June* 208
From John Jay, *15 June* 209
From David Ramsay, *15 June* 210
To John Banister, *16 June* 211
To the Governor of Virginia, with Enclosure, *16 June* 212
From Patrick Henry, *16 June* 214
From James Monroe, *16 June* 215
From Benjamin Rush, *16 June* 220
To the Governor of Maryland, *16 June* 220
From Louis Alexandre, with Enclosure, *17 June* 221
From John Banister, Jr., *17 June* 224
From David S. Franks, *17 June* 225
To David S. Franks, *17 June* 225
To John Jay, *17 June* 226
To James Milligan, *17 June* 227
To James Monroe, *17 June* 227
From Du Portail, *17 June* 234
De Thulemeier to the American Commissioners, *17 June* 234
American Commissioners to John Jay, *18 June* 235
To Joseph Jones, *19 June* 236
To Adam Stephen, *19 June* 237
John Adams to Franklin and Jefferson, *20 June* 238
John Adams to Franklin and Jefferson, *20 June* 238
From Jean François Briet, *20 June* 238
To Abigail Adams, *21 June* 239
From F. W. Bleibtrear, *21 June* 242
From Katherine Sprowle Douglas, *21 June* 243
From P. & V. French & Nephew, *21 June* 244
To Charles Thomson, *21 June* 245
To John Adams, *22 June* 246
To William Carmichael, *22 June* 247
To William Stephens Smith, *22 June* 249
From John Bondfield, *25 June* 250
From William Carmichael, with Enclosures, *27 June* 251

[xvii]

CONTENTS

From the Abbés Arnoux and Chalut, *28 June*   256
From Barré, *28 July [i.e., June]*   256
To William Short, *28 June*   257
From John Polson, *1 July*   258
From Richard Price, *2 July*   258
〚To Samuel Hardy, James Madison, and James Monroe, *4 July*〛   259
To Katherine Sprowle Douglas, *5 July*   259
From Giovanni Fabbroni, *5 July*   260
To James Monroe, *5 July*   261
To Francis Hopkinson, *6 July*   262
To Abigail Adams, *7 July*   264
To John Adams, *7 July*   265
From Laumoy, *7 July*   268
To Charles Williamos, *7 July*   269
Franklin and Jefferson to Adams, with Proposed Treaty with
     Great Britain, *8 July*   273
From Charles Williamos, *8 July*   275
Castries to the American Commissioners *[9?] July*   277
From Philip Mazzei, *9 July*   277
To Castries, *10 July*   278
〚To Laumoy, *10 July*〛   279
To George Washington, *10 July*   279
To John Adams, *11 July*   281
To Barré, *11 July*   281
From Benjamin Franklin, *11 July*   282
From Benjamin Franklin, *11 July*   282
To the Governor of Virginia, *11 July*   282
To John Jay, *12 July*   284
To Richard Henry Lee, *12 July*   286
To James Monroe, *12 July*   288
To the Virginia Delegates in Congress, *12 July*   289
To Louis Alexandre, *13 July*   290
To Jean François Briet, *13 July*   291
〚To B. Contée, *13 July*〛   291
To P. & V. French & Nephew, *13 July*   291
From John Jay, *13 July*   292
From David Ramsay, *13 July*   293
From John Bondfield *[after 14 July]*   294
To Anthony Garvey, *14 July*   294
〚To Jan Ingenhousz, *14 July*〛   295
To Charles Thomson, *14 July*   295

From Barré, *28 July [i.e., June]*   256

To William Short, *28 June*   257

From John Polson, *1 July*   258

From Richard Price, *2 July*   258

〖To Samuel Hardy, James Madison, and James Monroe, *4 July*〗   259

To Katherine Sprowle Douglas, *5 July*   259

From Giovanni Fabbroni, *5 July*   260

To James Monroe, *5 July*   261

To Francis Hopkinson, *6 July*   262

To Abigail Adams, *7 July*   264

To John Adams, *7 July*   265

From Laumoy, *7 July*   268

To Charles Williamos, *7 July*   269

Franklin and Jefferson to Adams, with Proposed Treaty with Great Britain, *8 July*   273

From Charles Williamos, *8 July*   275

Castries to the American Commissioners *[9?] July*   277

From Philip Mazzei, *9 July*   277

To Castries, *10 July*   278

〖To Laumoy, *10 July*〗   279

To George Washington, *10 July*   279

To John Adams, *11 July*   281

To Barré, *11 July*   281

From Benjamin Franklin, *11 July*   282

From Benjamin Franklin, *11 July*   282

To the Governor of Virginia, *11 July*   282

To John Jay, *12 July*   284

To Richard Henry Lee, *12 July*   286

To James Monroe, *12 July*   288

To the Virginia Delegates in Congress, *12 July*   289

To Louis Alexandre, *13 July*   290

To Jean François Briet, *13 July*   291

〖To B. Contée, *13 July*〗   291

To P. & V. French & Nephew, *13 July*   291

From John Jay, *13 July*   292

From David Ramsay, *13 July*   293

From John Bondfield *[after 14 July]*   294

To Anthony Garvey, *14 July*   294

〖To Jan Ingenhousz, *14 July*〗   295

To Charles Thomson, *14 July*   295

CONTENTS

From James Monroe, *15 July* 296
From John Adams, *16 July* 297
From Plowden Garvey, *16 July* 298
To Ezra Stiles, *17 July* 298
To George Washington, *17 July* 301
From John Adams, *18 July* 301
From B. Contée, *18 July* 303
To Benjamin Franklin, *18 July* 303
From Samuel Henley, *18 July* 304
From Jean Holker, *18 July* 304
From De Thulemeier, *19 July* 305
From William Temple Franklin, *20 July* 306
From Benjamin Franklin, *21 July* 308
From De Pio *[21 July]* 308
To De Pio, *21 July* 309
From Francis Hopkinson, *23 July* 309
From John Adams, *24 July* 310
From Nicolas & Jacob van Staphorst, *25 July* 311
American Commissioners to C. W. F. Dumas *[27 July]* 312
American Commissioners to William Short *[27 July]* 313
To Vergennes, *27 July* 315
To John Adams, with Enclosure, *28 July* 315
From William Carmichael, *28 July* 320
To John Stockdale, *28 July* 322
To De Thulemeier, *28 July* 323
To G. K. van Hogendorp, *29 July* 324
To Jean Holker, *29 July* 325
From John Paul Jones, *29 July* 326
From William Bingham, *30 July* 328
[[From B. Contée, *30 July*]] 329
From Katherine Sprowle Douglas, *30 July* 329
To Nicolas & Jacob van Staphorst, *30 July* 330
To John Adams, *31 July* 332
From John Paul Jones, *31 July* 334
From John Banister, Jr., *1 August* 335
From the Marquis and Marquise de Spinola, *1 August* 336
From Stael de Holstein, *1 August* 336
From John Cooper, *2 August* 336
From C. W. F. Dumas, *2 August* 337
To Castries, *3 August* 337
To John Paul Jones, *3 August* 339

CONTENTS

From Pierrard, *3 August* 339
From John Adams, *4 August* 340
From James Currie, *5 August* 342
To John Adams, with Draft of Treaty Proposed for Barbary
    States, *6 August* 347
From John Adams, *7 August* 354
[[To Wilson Miles Cary, *7 August*]] 356
To Richard Price, *7 August* 356
From William Short, *7 August* 358
[[To William Bingham, *8 August*]] 359
[[From James Gordon, *8 August*]] 359
From David Ramsay, *8 August* 359
To John Adams, *10 August* 361
[[To James Gordon, *10 August*]] 363
To Pierrard, *10 August* 363
To Katherine Sprowle Douglas, *10 August* 364
[[From Abigail Adams, *12 August*]] 364
From Castries, *12 August* 364
From John Stockdale, *12 August* 365
From Thomas Thompson, *12 August* 366
To James Buchanan and William Hay, *13 August* 366
From Plowden Garvey, *13 August* 368
From John Jay, *13 August* 369
From John Jay, *13 August* 371
To John Paul Jones, *13 August* 371
To John Jay, *14 August* 372
To John Jay, *14 August* 375
From Gilles de Lavallée, *14 August* 377
From Jean Holker, *14 August* 379
From Neil Jamieson, *14 August* 380
From Patience Wright, *14 August* 380
From St. John de Crèvecoeur, *15 August* 381
From James Monroe, *15 August* 381
To Vergennes, *15 August* 385
To John Banister, Jr., *16 August* 393
To B. Contée, *16 August* 394
To John Adams, *17 August* 394
To Castries, *17 August* 395
To John Paul Jones, *17 August* 396
From John Paul Jones, *17 August* 397
To Thomas Thompson, *17 August* 398

CONTENTS

To Nathaniel Tracy, *17 August*   398
From John Adams, *18 August*   400
To William Carmichael, *18 August*   401
To Samuel House, *18 August*   402
To Eliza House Trist, *18 August*   403
To Peter Carr, *19 August*   405
From John Paul Jones, *19 August*   409
To Walker Maury, with a List of Books, *19 August*   409
From John Bondfield, *20 August*   412
[To Martha Jefferson Carr, *20 August*]   413
From James Madison, *20 August*   413
To John Page, *20 August*   417
From Abigail Adams, *21 August*   420
To St. John de Crèvecoeur, *22 August*   421
To the Governor of Virginia, with an Account of Expenses,
    22 August   422
From Thomas Thompson, *22 August*   423
From John Adams, *23 August*   423
From C. W. F. Dumas, *23 August*   424
From Elbridge Gerry and Others, *23 August*   425
To John Jay, *23 August*   426
From John Page, *23 August*   428
From William Short, with Enclosure, *23 August*   431
From William Short, with Enclosure, *23 August*   434
Martha Jefferson to Eliza House Trist [*after 24 August*]   436
From John Paul Jones, *24 August*   439
From Richard O'Bryen, *24 August*   440
From William Robeson, *24 August*   441
[From Giovanni Fabbroni, *25 August*]   441
From James Monroe, *25 August*   441
From Stephen Sayre, *25 August*   442
From Castries, *26 August*   443
To James Monroe, *28 August*   444
[To William Robeson, *28 August*]   446
From William Short, *28 August*   446
[From Henry Champion, *29 August*]   448
To John Paul Jones, *29 August*   448
From Miles King, *29 August*   448
From De Ponçins, *29 August*   449
From St. John de Crèvecoeur, *30 August*   450
To Francis Eppes [*30 August*]   451

CONTENTS

To John Jay, *30 August* 452

To John Banister, *31 August* 456

To David Ramsay, *31 August* 457

From Vergennes, *31 August* 458

From Charles Bellini *[ca. August]* 458

To C. W. F. Dumas and William Short, *1 September* 459

To James Madison, with a List of Books, *1 September* 460

From William Carmichael, *2 September* 464

To Chastellux, with Enclosure, *2 September* 467

From David S. Franks *[ca. 2 September]* 470

From Chastellux, *3 September* 471

To Abigail Adams, *4 September* 472

To John Adams, *4 September* 473

To John Adams, *4 September* 475

To John Adams, *4 September* 476

From John Adams, *4 September* 476

From Lafayette, *4 September* 478

From Froullé *[before 5 September]* 480

To Froullé, *5 September* 481

To David Hartley, *5 September* 481

Lease for the Hôtel de Langeac *[5 September]* 485

Private Agreement for Lease of the Hôtel de Langeac
[5 September] 489

From John Paul Jones, *5 September* 492

From Lister Asquith *[ca. 6 September]* 492

From Abigail Adams, *6 September* 498

To Geismar, *6 September* 499

From Lister Asquith, *7 September* 500

From Lister Asquith, *8 September* 501

From G. K. van Hogendorp, *8 September* 501

From William Short, *9 September* 505

From Patrick Henry, *10 September* 507

From Patrick Henry, *10 September* 508

From John Adams, *11 September* 510

From John Adams, *11 September* 510

To Gilles de Lavallée, *11 September* 511

To John Langdon, *11 September* 512

To André Limozin, *11 September* 513

To De Ponçins, *11 September* 514

From William Short, *11 September* 515

From Elbridge Gerry, *12 September* 515

CONTENTS

[From Elizabeth Wayles Eppes, *13 September*] 517

From Mary Jefferson [*ca. 13 September*] 517

To Lister Asquith, *14 September* 517

[From Francis Eppes, *14 September*] 518

From John Jay, *14 September* 518

To William Short, *14 September* 520

From John Adams, *15 September* 521

From Edward Bancroft, *15 September* 522

From Samuel Henley, *15 September* 523

From John Jay, *15 September* 523

From John Adams, *16 September* 525

From James Wilkie, *16 September* 525

From John Adams, *18 September* 525

From André Limozin, *18 September* 526

To John Adams, *19 September* 526

From Lister Asquith, *19 September* 527

From John Banister, Jr., *19 September* 529

From Barré, *19 September* 529

From William McNeill [*19? September*] 530

From Nicolas & Jacob van Staphorst, *19 September* 531

To Mary Jefferson, *20 September* 532

To André Limozin, *20 September* 533

To James Madison, with Account Enclosed, *20 September* 534

To Edmund Randolph, *20 September* 537

To James Buchanan, *22 September* 539

To Elizabeth Wayles Eppes, *22 September* 539

To Neil Jamieson, *22 September* 540

From André Limozin [*ca. 22 September*] 541

From Ferdinand Grand, *23 September* 541

From William Stephens Smith, *23 September* 541

To John Adams, *24 September* 542

To John Adams, *24 September* 545

To Ferdinand Grand, *24 September* 546

To William Short, *24 September* 547

To Abigail Adams, *25 September* 547

From John Adams, *25 September* 550

To Francis Hopkinson, *25 September* 550

To Lister Asquith, *26 September* 551

To Thomas Barclay, *26 September* 552

To Ralph Izard, *26 September* 552

To John Stockdale, *26 September* 554

CONTENTS

To Nathaniel Tracy, *26 September*   554
From George Washington, *26 September*   555
To James Currie, *27 September*   558
[From Dolomieu, *27 September*]   560
From Lister Asquith, *28 September*   560
From C. W. F. Dumas, *28 September*   561
From Francis Hopkinson, *28 September*   562
To the Governor of Virginia, *28 September*   564
To André Limozin, *28 September*   565
From David Rittenhouse, *28 September*   565
From William Carmichael, *29 September*   566
To Richard O'Bryen, *29 September*   567
[To James Wilkie, *29 September*]   568
To Charles Bellini, *30 September*   568
From William Carmichael, *30 September*   570
From André Limozin *[ca. 30 September]*   570
From Benjamin Franklin, *1 October*   571
From John Adams, *2 October*   571
To Barré, *2 October*   573
To the Rev. James Madison, *2 October*   574
From John Adams, *3 October*   577
From Lister Asquith, *3 October*   578
From James Madison, *3 October*   579
To C. W. F. Dumas, *4 October*   582
From C. W. F. Dumas, *4 October*   583
From André Limozin, *4 October*   583
To André Limozin, *4 October*   584
To John Adams, *5 October*   585
To Benjamin Franklin, *5 October*   585
From David Hartley, *5 October*   586
From John Paul Jones, *5 October*   587
To Samuel Osgood, *5 October*   588
To John Jay, *6 October*   592
[From André Limozin, *6? October*]   593
From Abigail Adams, *7 October*   594
From Froullé, *7 October*   596
From John Mehegan, *7 October*   597
From John Paul Jones, *8 October*   597
To John Paul Jones, *8 October*   597
To André Limozin, *8 October*   598
To Charles Thomson, *8 October*   598

CONTENTS

From James Warren, *9 October*   599
⟦From John Adams, *10 October*⟧   600
From James Bowdoin, *10 October*   601
From Ferdinand Grand, *10 October*   601
To Abigail Adams, *11 October*   602
To John Adams, *11 October*   603
To Elbridge Gerry, *11 October*   604
American Commissioners to John Jay, *11 October*   606
To John Jay, *11 October*   606
Documents Pertaining to the Mission of Barclay and Lamb
    to the Barbary States   610
    I. Commission   611
    II. Instructions   613
    III. Supplementary Instructions to John Lamb   616
    IV. Jefferson's "Heads for a letter"   617
    V. American Commissioners to the Emperor of Morocco   619
    VI. Heads of Inquiry   621
    VII. Letter of Credit   622
    VIII. American Commissioners to William Carmichael   623
    IX. Projet of a Treaty with the Barbary States   624
From André Limozin, *11 October*   625
⟦From André Limozin, *11 October*⟧   625
From De Thulemeier, *11 October*   625
American Commissioners to Vergennes, *11 October*   625
To Lister Asquith, *12 October*   627
To Borgnis Desbordes, Frères, *12 October*   627
To Froullé, *12 October*   628
From Froullé, *12 October*   628
To David Ramsay, *12 October*   629
To Nicolas & Jacob van Staphorst, *12 October*   629
To Vergennes, *12 October*   631
To G. K. van Hogendorp, *13 October*   631
To Samuel Henley, *14 October*   634
To John Banister, Jr., *15 October*   635
From André Limozin, *16 October*   638
To De Thulemeier, *16 October*   639
From Lister Asquith, *17 October*   639
From James Currie, *17 October*   640
From Archibald Stuart, *17 October*   644
To John Adams, *18 October*   647
From Borgnis Desbordes, Frères *[18? October]*   647

CONTENTS

From James Buchanan and William Hay, *18 October*   648
To William Carmichael, *18 October*   648
From Madame d'Houdetot, *18 October*   649
From David Ross and Other Virginia Merchants, *18 October*   650
From Abigail Adams, *19 October*   653
From Nicolas & Jacob van Staphorst, *20 October*   655
To Vergennes, *21 October*   656
To D'Aranda, *22 October*   657
From D'Aranda, *22 October*   658
To Ferdinand Grand, *22 October*   658
From David Ross, *22 October*   659
From Lister Asquith, *23 October*   661
From James Bowdoin, *23 October*   662
From John Adams, *24 October*   663
From William Carmichael, *24 October*   665
From Thomas Pleasants, Jr., *24 October*   666
From Richard Price, *24 October*   667
From Abigail Adams, *25 October*   669
To William Carmichael, *25 October*   670
From Thomas Cushing, *25 October*   670
From Francis Hopkinson, *25 October*   671
From William Wenman Seward, *25 October*   672
To Nicolas & Jacob van Staphorst, *25 October*   674
From Philip Mazzei, *26 October*   675
〚From Nicolas & Jacob van Staphorst, *27 October*〛   680
From Vergennes, *27 October*   680
From Castries, *28 October*   680
To James Madison, *28 October*   681
From Richard Henry Lee, *29 October*   683
From Vergennes, *30 October*   685
From Thomas Elder *[ca. October]*   687

ILLUSTRATIONS

PAGE

ABIGAIL ADAMS, PORTRAIT BY RALPH EARL   86

This undated portrait was probably painted in England in 1785, shortly after Mrs. Adams arrived in London and before Earl left England in the summer or early autumn of that year. (Courtesy of Miss Frances J. Eggleston, Oswego, New York; photograph courtesy of Frick Art Reference Library.)

DRAFT FOR THE FIRST PAYMENT ON HOUDON'S STATUE

OF GEORGE WASHINGTON   87

Benjamin Harrison enclosed William Alexander's draft on Laval & Wilfelsheim in his letter of 12 Nov. 1784 (q.v., Vol. 7). See also Jefferson to the Governor of Virginia, 9 Feb. 1785 (Vol. 7), 15 Apr., 12 May 1785. (Courtesy of the Virginia State Library.)

RECEIPT FOR PREMIUM FOR INSURANCE ON HOUDON'S

LIFE DURING THE TIME HE WAS IN AMERICA   87

Jefferson, feeling a keen sense of responsibility for having committed the State of Virginia to a much greater expenditure for the statue of George Washington than was originally intended, began negotiations for insurance on Houdon's life in July. The policy was not actually issued until 12 Oct. 1785—ten days after Houdon reached Mount Vernon—and was drawn for a period of six months. See Jefferson to Adams, 7 July; to the Governor of Virginia, 11 July; to John Adams, 10 Aug. and 24 Sep.; Adams to Jefferson, 3 Oct. 1785. (Courtesy of the Virginia State Library.)

CALLING CARDS AND TRADE CARDS USED AND RECEIVED

BY JEFFERSON IN FRANCE AND ENGLAND   214

These specimens have been selected from a number of similar cards preserved in Jefferson's Papers. It was the custom of the court at Versailles that a new ambassador or minister send formal notice of his first audience with the King to all the other foreign representatives resident at the court, each of whom was expected to pay a formal visit to the new minister, sign his register, and leave a card. See Jefferson to De Blome, 19 May 1785, and the Ambassador of Venice to Jefferson, following. Of the unofficial cards reproduced here, that of Sir John Sinclair may have been received either in France or while Jefferson was in England in 1786. See Sir John Sinclair to Jefferson, 24 Apr. 1786 and note (Vol. 9). The card from Samuel Neele was evidently received in London in the spring of 1786 when Jefferson arranged with Neele to have a map engraved for his *Notes on the State of Virginia*. See Jefferson to William S. Smith, 9 Aug. 1786 (Vol. 10). (Courtesy of the Massachusetts Historical Society and the Library of Congress.)

HOUDON IN HIS STUDIO, PAINTING BY LOUIS BOILLY, 1804   215

This picture of Houdon at work, surrounded by students, is one of several variant canvases painted by his friend, Boilly, almost

twenty years after Houdon was commissioned to make the
statues of Washington, Franklin (in the background to the
right), and Jefferson (in the background, immediately over
Houdon's head). See Jefferson to Benjamin Harrison, 12 Jan.
1785 (Vol. 7); to the Governor of Virginia, 11 July 1785; also,
above, draft for first payment of Houdon's statue of Washington
and receipt for insurance premium. (Courtesy of the Archives
Photographiques from the original in the Musée de Cherbourg,
through Howard C. Rice, Jr.)

JEFFERSON'S PRESENTATION INSCRIPTION IN THE COPY

OF THE *Notes on the State of Virginia* SENT TO

RICHARD PRICE   246

The inscription reproduced here, written on the fly-leaf of Price's
copy of Jefferson's *Notes*, is typical of the inscriptions in most
of the early copies of the first edition which Jefferson sent to
friends in America and Europe. Jefferson sent Price's copy of
the *Notes* by John Adams when he went to London. See Richard
Price to Jefferson, 2 July 1785. For an admirable census of
copies, together with texts of other inscriptions, see Coolie
Verner, "Mr. Jefferson Distributes His *Notes*," N.Y.P.L., *Bull.*,
LVI [1952], 159-86. (Courtesy of Princeton University Library.)

THE GRILLE DE CHAILLOT IN 1779, THE SITE OF JEFFER-

SON'S RESIDENCE IN PARIS FROM 1785 TO 1789   247

Engraving by François-Nicolas Martinet for Béguillet's *Description historique de Paris*, Paris, 1779, looking from the Grille de
Chaillot down the Champs-Elysées toward the Place Louis XV
[Place de la Concorde]. The smaller gate, left, marks the entrance to the Rue Neuve de Berry. The house at the left, between the two gates, is the Hôtel de Langeac where Jefferson
lived from Oct. 1785 until Sep. 1789. The Hôtel de Langeac
was demolished in the 1840's; a memorial tablet recalling Jefferson's residence here was placed on the present building by
alumni of the University of Virginia in 1919. The large building
at the right is the "bureau" of the municipal customs service;
beyond this, a road continuing the Rue Neuve de Berry leads
out to the suburb of Chaillot. About 1787 the Grille de Chaillot
was eliminated and the customs barrier was moved up to the top
of the Champs-Elysées, along the line of the new Farmers-General wall, to a spot where the Arc de Triomphe was later built.
(Courtesy of the Cabinet des Estampes, Bibliothèque Nationale,
through Howard C. Rice, Jr.)

PLAN OF THE SECOND FLOOR OF THE HÔTEL DE LANGEAC,

JEFFERSON'S RESIDENCE SITUATED AT THE GRILLE

DE CHAILLOT   247

This floor, designated on this plan as the "étage d'attique exaucé
[exhaussé]," was above the main ground floor and mezzanine.
In addition to the oval drawing-room overlooking the garden—
which Jefferson perhaps used as his study—there is a series of
bedrooms and adjoining dressing rooms, as well as "lieux à

l'anglaise." The skylight of one of the ground-floor rooms is also indicated here. The windows on the right-hand side of the house look out on the Champs-Elysées, called here the Avenue de Neuilly; those on the western side (along the bottom of the plan) give on the Rue Neuve de Berry. For other floor plans and elevations of the Hôtel de Langeac see Howard C. Rice, Jr., *L'Hôtel de Langeac*, Paris and Monticello, 1947. The Hôtel de Langeac was designed by the architect Jean F.-T. Chalgrin (1739-1811). Work on the house, built by the Comte de Saint-Florentin (later Duc de La Vrillière) for the Marquise de Langeac, began in 1774, was interrupted in 1774, and then resumed after 1778 for the Marquise's son, the Comte de Langeac, from whom Jefferson rented it. (Courtesy of the Cabinet des Estampes, Bibliothèque Nationale, through Howard C. Rice, Jr.)

FINAL PAGE OF THE DEFINITIVE TREATY BETWEEN THE

UNITED STATES AND PRUSSIA   566

The signing of the treaty with Prussia followed a highly unusual procedure in that it was signed in four different places on four separate dates. It was signed and sealed by Franklin, 9 July, before he left Passy; by Jefferson, in Paris, on 28 July; by Adams, in London, on 5 Aug.; and by De Thulemeier, at The Hague, on 10 Sep. 1785. See TJ to Adams, 7 July; American Commissioners to C. W. F. Dumas [27 July 1785] and to William Short, same date; Jefferson to De Thulemeier, 28 July 1785. (Courtesy of the National Archives.)

PASSPORT FOR JOHN LAMB   567

This passport belongs to the group of documents issued in connection with the mission of Barclay and Lamb to the Barbary states (see p. 610-24). The issuance of passports was one of the official routine functions for which Jefferson was responsible while minister to France. There is the following entry in Jefferson's Account Book under 1 Aug. 1785: "Paid Marc . . . for Mons. Pierre [i.e., Pierres, printer of Jefferson's *Notes on the State of Virginia*] . . . printing for Unitd. States, viz. 200 passports 18^{tt}." (Courtesy of the William L. Clements Library, University of Michigan.)

VOLUME 8

25 February to 31 October 1785

JEFFERSON CHRONOLOGY

VOLUME 8 · 1785

10 Mch. TJ elected by Congress to succeed Franklin as minister to France.

10 May. Printing of *Notes on the State of Virginia* completed.

17 May. TJ presented his credentials as minister to France to the King.

20 May. John Adams left Paris to take up his residence as minister to Great Britain.

3 June. Date of first extant press copy of a letter made on TJ's copying press.

11 July. Benjamin Franklin left Paris to return to America.

10 Sep. Definitive Treaty between the United States and Prussia signed by De Thulemeier, and copies formally exchanged at The Hague.

24 Sep. TJ appointed William Short as his secretary.

11 Oct. Commissions and instructions issued to Thomas Barclay and John Lamb to treat with the Barbary states.

17 Oct. TJ took up residence at the Hôtel de Langeac.

THE PAPERS OF
THOMAS JEFFERSON

·《━━━━━》·

From George Washington

DEAR SIR   Mount Vernon 25th. Feb 1785

I had the pleasure to find by the public Gazettes that your passage to France had been short, and pleasant.—I have no doubt but that your reception at the Court has been equally polite and agreeable.

I have the honor to inclose you the copy of an Act which passed the assemblies of Virginia and Maryland at the close of their respective sessions; about the first of last month.—The circumstances of these States, it is said, would not enable them to take the matter up, altogether, on public ground; but they have granted at the joint and equal expence of the two, 6666⅔ dollars for the purpose of opening a road of communication between the highest navigation of the Potomac, and the River Cheat; and have concurred in an application to the State of Pensylvania for leave to open another road from Fort Cumberland, or Wills Creek to the Yohiogany, at the three forks or Turkey foot.

Besides these joint acts of the States of Virginia and Maryland the former has passed a similar law respecting the navigation of James River, and its communication with the Green brier; and have authorized the Executive to appoint Commissioners, who shall carefully examine and fix on the most convenient course for a Canal from the Waters of Elizabeth River in this State, to those passing through the State of North Carolina; and report their proceedings therein, with an estimate of the expence necessary for opening the same, to the next General assembly; and in case they shall find that the best course for such canal will require the concurrence of the State of North Carolina in the opening thereof, they are further authorized and instructed to signify the same to the said State, and to concert with any person or persons who may be appointed on the part thereof, the most convenient and equitable plan for the execution of such work, and to report the result to the General assembly.

With what success the Books will be opened, I cannot at this early stage of the business, inform you; in general the friends of the measure are better stocked with good wishes than money, the former of which unfortunately, goes but a little way in works where the latter is necessary, and is not to be had.—And yet, if this matter could be well understood, it should seem that there would be no deficiency of the latter, any more than of the former; for certain I am, there is no speculation of which I have an idea, that will ensure such *certain* and *ample* returns of the money advanced, with a great, and encreasing interest, as the tolls arising from these navigations; the accomplishment of which, if funds can be obtained, admits of no more doubt in my mind, under proper direction, than that a ship with skilful mariners can be carried from hence to Europe. What a misfortune therefore would it be, if a project which is big with such great political consequences, commercial advantages, and which might be made so productive to private adventurers, should miscarry; either from the inability of the two States to execute it, at the public expence, or for want of means, or the want of spirit or foresight to use them, in their citizens.

Supposing a danger of this do you think, Sir, the monied men of France, Holland, England or any other Country with which you may have intercourse, might be induced to become adventurers in the Scheme? Or if from the remoteness of the object, this should appear ineligable to them, would they incline to lend money to one, or both of these States, if their should be a disposition in them to borrow, for this purpose? Or, to one or more individuals in them, who are able, and would give sufficient security for the repayment? At what interest, and on what conditions respecting time, payment of interest &ca. could it be obtained?

I foresee such extensive political consequences depending on the navigation of these two rivers and communicating them by short and easy roads with the waters of the Western Territory, that I am pained by every doubt of obtaining the means for their accomplishment. For this reason, I also wish you would be so obliging as to direct your enquiries after one or more characters who have skill in this kind of work; that if Companies should be incorporated under the present acts, and should incline to send to France, or England for an Engineer, or Man of practical knowledge in these kind of works, there may be a clue to the application. You will perceive tho', My dear Sir, that no engagement, obligatory or honorary can be entered into at this time, because no person can answer for the determination of the Companies, admitting their formation.

As I have accustomed myself to communicate matters of difficulty to you, and have met forgiveness for it, I will take the liberty, my good Sir, of troubling you with the rehearsal of one more, which has lately occurred to me.

Among the Laws of the last Session of our assembly, there is an act which particularly respects myself; and tho' very flattering, is also very embarrassing to me. This act, after honorable, flattering and delicate recitals, directs the treasurer of the State to subscribe toward each of the Navigations fifty Shares for my use and benefit; which it declares, is to be vested in me and my heirs forever. It has ever been my wish, and it is yet my intention, never to receive any thing from the United States, or any individual State for any Services I have hitherto rendered, or which in the course of events, I may have it in my power to render them hereafter as it is not my design to accept of any appointment from the public, which might make emoluments necessary: but how to decline this act of generosity without incurring the imputation of disrespect to my Country, and a slight of her favors on the one hand, or that of pride, and an ostentatious display of disinterestedness on the other, is the difficulty. As none of these have an existence in my breast, I should be sorry, if any of them should be imputed to me. The assembly, as if determined that I should not act from the first impulse, made this the last act of their Session; without my having the smallest intimation or suspicion of their generous intention. As our assembly is now to be holden once a year only, I shall have time to hit upon some expedient that will enable me to indulge the bent of my own inclinations without incurring any of the imputations before mentioned; and of hearing the sentiments of my friends upon the subject; than whose, none would be more acceptable than yours.

Your friends in our assembly have been able to give you so much better information of what has passed there, and of the general state of matters in this Commonwealth, that a repetition from me is altogether unnecessary, and might be imperfect.

If we are to credit Newspaper accounts the flames of war are again kindled, or are about to be so, in Europe. None of the sparks, it is to be hoped will cross the Atlantic and touch the inflameable matter in these States. I pray you to believe that with sentiments of sincere esteem and regard I have the honor to be Dr. Sir Yr. Most Obed. Hble. Servt.,   GO: WASHINGTON

RC (DLC); endorsed. Recorded in SJL as received 26 Apr. Tr (DLC: Washington Papers); with minor variations from RC in phrasing but not in substance. Enclosure not found, but the Act is printed in Hening, XI, 450-62.

AN ACT . . . VERY EMBARRASSING TO ME: Washington's embarrassment was genuine and acute. Between the two sessions of the General Assembly he sought the advice of several trusted friends in an effort to hit upon some expedient that would solve the difficult dilemma. To Benjamin Harrison he wrote on 22 Jan. 1785: "Not content then with the bare consciousness of my having, in all this navigation business, acted upon the clearest conviction of the political importance of the measure; I would wish that every individual who may hear that it was a favorite plan of mine, may know also that I had no other motive for promoting it, than the advantage I conceived it would be productive of to the Union, and to this State in particular, by cementing the Eastern and Western Territory together, at the same time that it will give vigor and encrease to our commerce, and be a convenience to our Citizens.—How would this matter be viewed then by the eye of the world; and what would be the opinion of it, when it comes to be related that G W——n exerted himself to effect this work, and G W——n has received 20,000 Dollars, and £5,000 Sterling of the public money as an interest therein? Would not this in the estimation of it . . . deprive me of the principal thing which is laudable in my conduct? Would it not, in some respects, be con-

sidered in the same light as a pension? And would not the apprehension of this make me more reluctantly offer my sentiments in future? In a word, under what ever pretence, and however customary these gratuitous gifts are made in other Countries, should I not thence forward be considered as a dependant? One moments thought of which would give me more pain, than I should receive pleasure from the product of all the tolls, was every farthing of them vested in me: altho' I consider it as one of the most certain and increasing Estates in the Country" (Washington to Harrison, 22 Jan. 1785, Writings, ed. Fitzpatrick, XXVIII, 35-6). Stated in much the same form, Washington laid the difficult problem before William Grayson, Lafayette, Patrick Henry, Henry Knox, and Nathanael Greene in addition to TJ (same, XXVIII, 37-8, 72-3, 89-91, 92-3, 146). By late April he had decided to "hold the shares which this State has been pleased to present to me, in trust for the use and benefit of it," and at the opening of the Oct. session of the General Assembly asked that he be permitted "to turn the destination of the fund vested in me, from my private emolument, to objects of a public nature." The result was an Act that the fund should stand appropriated to such objects of a public nature as Washington should determine (Washington to Grayson, 25 Apr. 1784; to Gov. Henry, 29 Oct. 1785; same, XXVIII, 138, 302-4; see also TJ to Washington, 10 July 1785; Washington to TJ, 26 Sep. 1785).

Jefferson's Advertisement of Hopkinson's Invention

[ca. Feb.? 1785]

An improvement in the manner of preparing musical instruments which are keyed and quilled.

The present mode of quilling a harpsichord is subject to this great inconvenience that some of the quills will after a little use, crack and lose their elastic spring, whilst others retain their full vigour, thereby rendering the touch unequal and some tones full and loud whilst others are so faint and weak as scarcely to be heard. The different gradations of strength from a quill absolutely broken to one in full strength are so various and imperceptible that the most nice attention cannot restore the perfect equality which the instrument had when it first came from the hands of the maker: and even to keep the instrument in tolerable order in this respect requires constant examination and frequent repairs. To remedy this many substances have been tried as substitutes for the raven quill; but all without success. They have all been found liable to the same inconvenience, with this additional disadvantage that none of them could draw so pleasing a tone from the string as the crow or raven quill.[1]

After many unsuccessful attempts either to remedy the inconvenience of the quill or to find a substitute, a method perfectly satisfactory has at length been contrived by a person in America which he engages shall have the following properties.[2]

1st. That The instrument shall not want Repair in that Respect, for any reasonable Length of Time—say 4. 5. 6 or more Years: but shall always preserve an equality of Touch, subject only to such Variations as the different States of the Air may occasion, to which all known Substances, are more or less liable.

2d. It shall improve the Touch, rendering it more pleasant, lively and sure.

3d. It shall produce a more sweet and free Tone from the String.

4th. It shall be easily executed and at a small Expence not encreasing the Price of a Harpsichord more than two or three Guineas; if generally practis'd; but if monopolized by Patent, will produce a much greater Price to the Patentee on Account of its demonstrable Advantages.[3]

As the several experiments he has tried have brought on him some expence, not great indeed, yet such as he would be willing to recover, his method shall be communicated to any workman or other person for the small sum he has actually expended in making the trials.[4]

Dft (MHi); without date; partly in TJ's hand and partly in that of Francis Hopkinson. No published copy of this advertisement has been found, but one presumably was enclosed in TJ to Hopkinson, 6 July 1785.

[1] Up to this point Dft is in TJ's hand. This paragraph is drawn verbatim from the introduction of Hopkinson's enclosure to TJ, 25 May 1784.

[2] TJ first began this sentence on recto of leaf (where he employed the

words "devised by a gentleman" instead of "contrived by a person") and then wrote it on verso in substitution for Hopkinson's "By this new method of quilling a Harpsichord it is engaged."

[3] Preceding numbered paragraphs in Hopkinson's hand.
[4] This paragraph in TJ's hand. It is not known when Hopkinson transmitted this text to TJ.

From Anthony Garvey

SIR   [ca. Feb.? 1785]

I received the letter your Excellency honored me with of 29th. December; the China ware is arrived here Some time. The Cases being Plumbed stopped their Expedition, as there was no Cocketts. I wrote some time ago to Mr. Barclay for them. As soon as I receive some, shall load the Ware on the first boat to your Excellency's address and advise you of the departure; I was afraid if delaying longer that you might be uneasy for the fate of the Vessel it was loaded on.

I have the honor to be with great respect Sir Your Excellencys most humble & very obedient Servant,   ANTHONY GARVEY

The thing cant be sent untill Mr. Barclay sends the Cocket; I wish you would drop him a line about it and urge his forwarding it soonest possible.

RC (MHi); undated; endorsed. This letter was written some time before 24 Mch. 1785 when the china was finally shipped, as Garvey notified TJ in his letter of 26 Mch., q.v.

COCKET: A certificate under seal issued by customs officials to merchants signifying that merchandize has been entered and duty has been paid (OED).

To John Adams and Benjamin Franklin

Mar. 1. 1785

Mr. Jefferson's compliments to Mr. Adams and Doctr. Franklin and sends them his notes on the[1] treaty with Prussia. He prays Mr. Adams, when he shall have perused them to send them to Dr. Franklin and proposes to meet them on the subject at Passy on Thursday at 12. o'clock. He sends the Prussian propositions, Mr. Adams's and Dr. Franklin's notes, and the former project and observations which were in the hands of Colo. Humphreys.

RC (PPAP); endorsed. Not recorded in SJL. The "notes" and other papers

were presumably not enclosed, but carried by the messenger who delivered this letter. TJ's comments on the treaty with Prussia may, in fact, have been utilized later as part of the text of the Commissioners' letter to De Thulemeier, 14 Mch. 1785, q.v., notes 4 and 8. See also the following document proposing certain changes in De Thulemeier's translation.

[1] The word "enclosed" is deleted at this point.

Proposed Changes in Translation of the Treaty with Prussia

[ca. 1 Mch.? 1785]

We submit the following passages to the consideration of the Baron De Thulemeyer, collating the English expressions, the French translation and the changes which we think should be made to yeild the true sense.[1]

English expression[2]	Passages in the translation where the sense seems changed[2]	Corrections hazarded[2]
Art. X. shall succeed to their said *personal* goods	succederont à leurs biens	succederont à leur dits biens *personelles*
such care shall be taken of the said goods and for so long a time as would be taken of the goods of a native in like case until the lawful owner may take measures for receiving them.	on prendra pendant ce temps les memes soins des biens qui leur sont echus, qu'on auroit pris en pareille occurrence des biens des natifs du pays: à moins que le proprietaire legitime n'ait pris des arrangemens pour recueiller l'heritage.	on prendra des biens qui leur sont echus les memes soins et pour le meme temps qu'on auroit pris en pareille occurrence des biens des natifs du pays, jusques à ce que le proprietaire legitime aura pris des arrangemens pour recueillir l'heritage.
and where on the death of any person holding real estate within the territories of the one party, such real estate would by the laws of the land descend on a citizen or subject of the other, were he not disqualified by alienage, such subject shall be allowed &c.	et si par la mort de quelque personne possedant des biens-fonds sur le territoire de l'une des parties contractantes, les biens-fonds venoient à passer selon les loix du pays à un citoyen ou sujet de l'autre partie, celui-ci, *s'il est qualifié à aliener les dits biens, obtiendra &c.*	et si par la mort de quelque personne possedant des biens-fonds sur le territoire de l'une des parties contractantes, les biens-fonds *viendroient* à passer selon les loix du pais à un citoyen ou sujet de l'autre partie *s'il n'etoit pas inhabilité comme etranger, celui-ci obtiendra &c.*
17. or by a *pyrate*[3]	ou par un *Armateur*	ou par un *pirate*
19. arrested, searched	ni arretées ni saisies	ni arretées, ni visitées
23.	et en general tous ceux	we concur in adopting this expression as being more extensive than the original and for a good purpose.
private armed vessels	armateurs	vaisseaux armés en course

[9]

24. in some part of their dominions	omitted	assignera 'dans leurs territoires'
and all others	aux simples soldats	à touts les autres
necessaries	douceurs	we like the word 'douceurs' better than the word 'necessaries' which we had proposed and for which we had therefore rather substitute 'comforts'
26. yeilding the compensation where such nation does the same	accordant la meme compensation qu'aura eté agréée pour d'autres nations.	en accordant la même compensation si la concession est conditionelle.

MS (DLC); entirely in TJ's hand. Undated, but certainly done after 24 Jan. and before 28 July 1785. This collation of texts may have been among the notes that TJ sent to Adams and Franklin on 1 Mch. 1785. It is not known when this memorandum was transmitted to De Thulemeier, but it must have been made available to him in some form, for some of the "Corrections hazarded" or modifications of them appeared in the final text of the treaty. Text appears to be a fair copy, though with some alterations made probably after consultation among the Commissioners.

1 This caption was interlined at head of page after the collation of texts had been made; it was done in connection with deletion indicated in note 2.
2 This phrase deleted in connection with the foregoing alteration.
3 The following deleted at this point in the three columns: (1) "public or private *purpose*," (2) "usage public ou particulier," and (3) "*objet* public ou particulier."

To Geismar

Dr. Sir   Paris Mar. 3. 1785.

An unfortunate change in my domestic situation by the loss of a tender connection who joined me in esteeming you, occasioned me to wish a change of scene and to accept an appointment which brought me to this place and will keep me here some time. Since your departure from America I have been altogether uninformed of your subsequent history. I am sure I need not tell you that the regard I entertain for you has rendered that interesting to me. A vague report of your death which was never so authenticated as to command belief, but which has not been authentically contradicted has particularly occasioned me to wish the pleasure of a line from yourself. Till this or some other assurance of your being still on this side the Styx, I shall indulge no further the feelings of friendship which would only render my pen more diffuse, but conclude with an assurance of the esteem and regard with which I have the honr. to be Dr: Sir Your affectte. hble servt.

P.S. Address to me as Min. plen. des E. U. d'Am. à Paris Cul-de-sac Tetebout, and send your letters to the care of Ch. W. Dumas Agent des Etat Unis d'Am. à la Haye.

Dft (DLC); at foot of letter: "A Monsr. Monsr. le Baron de Geismar Capitaine et gentilhomme de la cour au service de S. A. Sme. Monseignr. le Land Grave et Prince Hereditaire de Hesse-cassel, à Hanau par Francfort sur le Main." Entry in SJL reads: "Mar. 3—Baron Geismar. See copy."

This letter, like that to Hogendorp of 20 Nov. 1784, may have been merely another straw thrown into the wind by TJ to try to find out whether peace or war had been determined upon. He had known Geismar when the latter was one of the Convention Troops while they were quartered in Virginia.

To Samuel Henley, with a List of Books

Dear Sir   Paris Mar. 3. 1785.

An expectation of having the pleasure of seeing you myself in England has for a considerable time since my arrival in Europe prevented my writing to you. This expectation having rather lessened, I take the opportunity of sending you this by a gentleman who promises to enquire your residence, and to have it safely delivered. After your departure from Virginia, Mr. Madison, being authorised by you either to dispose of your books generally, or to let me in particular have such as I wished to possess, submitted them to my examination. I selected those mentioned in the catalogue annexed and he set the price on them. A British man of war being then in Hampton road, I wrote you information of this transaction and sent the letter on board this vessel by a flag which happened to be going. Having never received any answer from you, I have doubted whether my letter got to your hands. I have not with me any voucher of his valuation, because when I left my own house to attend Congress, I had no expectation of visiting Europe. Upon receiving their orders, I came directly on from Annapolis, without returning home: and my being able to furnish you with the list inclosed arises from the circumstance of my having with me the catalogue of my library. I am unable to say with certainty at what sum he valued them; but in undertaking to answer your draught for twenty seven guineas, I am sure, from memory alone, that I am near the mark.[1] If this should not be exact, the difference will be small, and may be settled on my return to America. I would have wished at the same time to advertize you that if the valuation should not be satisfactory and you would prefer the books to the money, they should be delivered to your order. But the incertainty of the time of my return to America, the impossibility of having them searched out of my library by any other person, and the injury which some of them sustained in their transportation from Williamsburg to my house, give me to suppose you would not prefer this alternative. However as you know best how far these circumstances might weigh with you, you will be pleased to decide either for the money or books. If you should prefer the latter, I would wish to know it soon, that I may supply myself with the same while here. In either case it gives me pleasure that this circumstance was the means of saving you so much from that general destruction which involved the residue of your books when Mr. Madison's house was burnt. From Miss Digges I purchased Pelloutiere's history of the Celts. 2. vols. 12mo. belonging to Mr. Gwatkin. I shall be obliged to you to add their worth to your draught on me, and to permit me to make you the channel of it's communication to Mr. Gwatkin, together with assurances of my esteem for him, and to accept of the same very cordially yourself. The events which separated us depending on public and national opinion and conduct only, were not of a nature to insinuate themselves between individual connections, or to dissolve the bands of private friendship. I shall be happy to hear that your course of life has been succesful, and that you[2] enjoy health and felicity. I have the honour to be with great regard Dear Sir Your most obedient & most humble servant,   TH: JEFFERSON[3]

Milton's paradise lost. edn.[4] in 10. books. small 4to.
Pierce Plowman 8vo.
Observns. on modern gardening 8vo. patent binding.
Gibson's Saxon chronicle 4to.
Junius. 2. v. 12mo. patent binding.
Connection between price of provisions & size of farms pamphlet.
History of duelling. 12mo. unbound.
Aedes Walpolianae. 4to.
Hoole's Tasso. 12mo.
Dante. 3. v. 12mo.
The Hermit of Warkworth. pamphlet.
Oeuvres de theatre de Diderot. 12mo.
Il Petrarca. 16s. red marocco.
Philips's poems. 12mo.
Garth's Dispensary. 12mo.
Hurd's Cowley. 2. v. 12mo.
Bourne poemata. 12mo.

Clarke's Vegetius 8vo.
Calson's specimens of printing types. pamphlet.
Portroyal Gr. gramm. 8vo.
Portroyal Lat. gram. 2. v. 8vo.
Dict. du vieux language de Lacombe. 2. v. 8vo.
Dictionnaire des monogrammes. 8vo.
Webb on poetry and music
Moor's essay on Tragedy
An essay on design in gardening. } in 1. vol. 12mo.
Jennings on medals.
Harris's Hermes 8vo.
———— three treatises 8vo.
Warton's observns. on Spenser. 2. v. 8vo.
Essay on Shakespeare. 8vo.
Jones poeseos Asiaticae comment. 8vo. unbound.
London catalogue of books. pamphlet
Suidae lexicon. 3. v. fol. injured.
Sallust. Foulis. 12mo.
Wotton's view of Hickes's Thesaurus. 4to.
History of Barbadoes. 12mo.
Taylor's elements of the civil law. 4to.
Dictionnaire de Chymie. 2. v. 12mo.
Tournefort institutiones.[5] 2. v. 4to.
Dacosta's mineralogy.[6]
Linnaei Flora Lapponica. 8vo.
      Critica Botanica. 8vo.
      Philosophia Botanica. 8vo.
      Fauna Suecica. 8vo.
      Genera plantarum. 8vo.
      Species plantarum. 2. v. 8vo.
      Emantissa altera. 8vo.
      Systema naturae. 2. v. 8vo.
Clayton's flora Virginica. 4to.
Clarke on Saxon coins. 4to.
folios.   3.
4tos.   9.
8vos.   28.
12mos. 18.
16s.   1.
pamphlets. 4.

RC (MB); at head of text: "Copy." Technically this was a copy made by TJ to enclose in his to Henley of 14 Oct. 1785, since the text dispatched on 3 Mch. did not reach its destination for reasons there explained; nevertheless it is for convenience considered here as an RC. PrC (DLC); endorsed: "Henley the revd. Saml." Dft (DLC); list of books is separated from Dft and is found in DLC: TJ Papers, 17: 2961; it bears following caption: "Books bought of revd. Saml. Henley"; some of its numerous variations from RC are noted below. Entry in SJL reads: "[Mar. 3.] Saml Henley. See copy."

¹ Instead of the words: "but in undertaking . . . near the mark," Dft reads: "yet I am pretty sure it was about twenty guineas. This was in the year 1778 or 1779, so that including interest I may say that I will answer your draught on me here for twenty seven guineas." TJ had written Henley

about the books on 9 June 1778.

² From this point Dft reads: "yourself and the lady whom I have heard you married and for whom I had all the esteem which her good qualities and your choice commanded, enjoy health and felicity." Evidently TJ had been misinformed about the identity of the lady of Henley's choice, for on 27 Nov. 1785 he wrote: "I have not the happiness of an acquaintance with her."

³ Dft has following postscript not in RC: "P. S. Address to me at Paris cul de sac Tetebout." This was omitted from RC, for by mid Oct., when RC was copied, TJ was planning to move; entry in his Account Book for 17 Oct. 1785 reads: "moved to the house of the Count de Langeac."

⁴ Dft reads: "1st. edn. small quarto."

⁵ Dft reads: "institutiones rei herbariae."

⁶ Following is inserted in Dft at this point: "8vo."

De Thulemeier to the American Commissioners

MESSIEURS   à la Haye le 4. Mars 1785.

Les Ordres du Roi dont je me trouve actuellement muni, me mettent à même de répondre plus amplement à la lettre dont Vous m'avez honoré, Messieurs, en dernier lieu, et dont je Vous ai accusé l'entrée par la mienne du 11. Février. Sa Majesté Se persuade que l'établissement d'un ou de deux ports francs seroit absolument inutile, d'après la réflexion très juste que Messieurs les Plénipotentiares Américains ont faite, que les Articles 2. et 3. du Contre-Projet accordent réciproquement aux deux Nations, dans tous les ports où ils voudront faire le commerce, les avantages dont jouissent les nations les plus favorisées. Cette observation épuise la question, d'autant plus que les intentions du Roi ne sont aucunement de borner le commerce des Citoyens de l'Amérique Confédérée à l'un ou l'autre de Ses ports. Dans le cas où l'établissement d'un port franc paroîtroit cependant de quelque utilité, on s'y prêteroit sans beaucoup de difficulté quant à Emden, mais plusieurs raisons s'opposeroient à une pareille concession à l'égard du port de Stettin. La lettre de Messieurs les Plénipotentiaires ayant été écrite avant l'entrée des Observations sur le dernier Contre-Projet dont la mienne du 24. Janvier de l'année courante étoit accompagnée, il est à présumer que des éclaircissemens ultérieurs paroîtroient plus ou moins inutiles. Je me flatte que la première lettre que j'aurai l'honneur, Messieurs, de recevoir de Votre part, me facilitera les moyens de donner de concert avec Vous à la négociation qui a fait l'objet de nos soins communs, la consistance désirée. Le succés de cette transaction répondra, tant à mes voeux, qu'à l'intérêt commun de nos deux nations.

J'ai l'honneur d'être avec la considération la plus distinguée, Messieurs, Votre très humble et très obéissant Serviteur,

DE THULEMEIER

RC (DNA: PCC, No. 86); in a clerk's hand, except for last phrase of complimentary close and signature, which are in De Thulemeier's hand; endorsed by Humphreys. This letter was enclosed in a covering letter from De Thulemeier to Adams, same date (MHi: Adams Manuscript Trust). It was later enclosed in Commissioners' letter to Jay of 18 Mch. 1785 as item No. 7. Tr (DNA: PCC, No. 116).

From Charles Thomson

DEAR SIR   New York March 6. 1785

I have received your favour of Novr. 11, with the pamphlets, for which I return you my hearty thanks.

The report on animal magnetism gave me great satisfaction. Before I had heard of these experiments and of this report, I was greatly at a loss what to think of the matter.[1] The Marqs. de la Fayette had come over quite an enthusiast in favour of it. He had got a special meeting called of the philosophical Society at Philadelphia and entertained them on the subject for the greater part of an evening. He informed them that he was initiated and let into the secret but was not at liberty to reveal it. He spoke of it as an important discovery which would be of great and wonderful advantage and that he himself had by means of it performed a surprizing cure on his passage. I was not present at the meeting for which I was sorry. Still however it appeared to me surprizing, that there should be a fluid pervading all nature capable of being collected and when collected of producing such wonderous effects as were mentioned and that no trace of it should ever before have been observed or noted in any of the various experiments that had heretofore been made on matter or motion. Having heard of the Shakers in this state, the agitations with which they were affected and with which they affected some who visited them from curiosity, I began to admit the opinion that they had by some means become acquainted with this fluid and that what they ascribed to the influences of the divine spirit was the effect of this unknown agent. The report you sent me has removed this doubt and though it has sufficiently demonstrated that Mr. Mesmer and his disciples have discovered no new property in nature yet it has itself made a very wonderful and very important discovery, namely to what degree the imagination can operate on the human frame.

I am much pleased with your description of the Cylinder lamp and wish for an opportunity of procuring one. The phosphoretic matches I have seen. They are sold in our toy shops. I think them a pretty invention, but am not much disposed to make use of them in the way you hint. I am in general obliged to be so much awake in the day that I sleep sound at night: or if I chance to awake in the night which is but seldom, I find that solemn stillness a good opportunity to revolve some subject which I want to trace through its various relations and probable effects and consequences.

I would willingly subscribe for the Encyclopédie Methodique. But it appears to me as if I must bid adieu to the Sciences. My time and thoughts are so entirely engrossed with the duties and business of my office that I have no leisure to prosecute those philosophical researches I once was fond of. And from what I can see Congress seem disposed rather to encrease than to diminish those duties.

I am made very happy by Mr. Jay's acceptance of the office for the department of foreign affairs. By him you will be supplied with the journals of Congress and regularly informed of their proceedings as well as of the state of our affairs in general, so that I need not trouble you on that head.

I long to see your answer to Mr. M[arbois]'s queries. I hope by this time you have found leisure to revise and compleat that work and have committed it to the press or at least struck off some copies for the satisfaction of your friends, among whom I hope to be ranked. I submit it to your consideration whether you do not owe it to your reputation to publish[2] your work under a more dignified title. In the state in which I saw it I consider it a most excellent Natural history not merely of Virginia but of No. America and possibly equal if not superior to that of any Country yet published.

I thank you for your notice of Mr. Norris[3] and shall be happy in every opportunity of testifying with what sincerity and respect I am Dear Sir Your affectionate friend & humble Servt.,

CHAS. THOMSON

RC (DLC). FC (DLC: Thomson Papers); with endorsement reading "Letters 12 Sept 1783, 11 Nov. 1784 from T. Jefferson answer 6 March 1785." Recorded in SJL as received 2 May 1785. The numerous variations between FC and RC are matters of phraseology only, except for the passages noted below. The reference in endorsement on RC to a letter from TJ of 12 Sep. 1783 is obviously an error; Thomson evidently meant to refer to a letter from John Jay of that date (New-York Hist. Soc., *Colls.*, XI, 175-6).

It is interesting that Thomson should have thought of the SHAKERS in connection with Lafayette and Mesmerism. In Sep. 1784 Lafayette and his party had visited the Shaker mother-community at Nishayuna near Watervliet, New York. To Lafayette the Shakers "furnished a possible example of the workings of animal magnetism, particularly since they healed disease by laying-on of hands. He tried to 'Mesmerize' one of the community but was interrupted by an elder who asked whether he acted in the name of a good or a bad spirit. 'Certainly in the name of a good spirit,' Lafayette replied. Marbois did not think Lafayette had much success, however. Except that the Shakers were as favorably impressed as Marbois was amused that so fine a gentleman should take them so seriously, nothing came from these new observations of Mesmer's disciple" (Gottschalk, *Lafayette, 1783-89*, p. 97-8).

[1] This sentence is not in FC.
[2] FC reads: "revise your work and publish it under a more dignified title than that of 'Notes on the State of Virginia in answer to queries &c.' I think it may deserve the title of 'a Natural history of Virginia.'"
[3] The reference to Norris is not in FC.

From Alexander Moore

DEAR SIR   London, Mar. 10. 1785

Since I had the pleasure to write you the middle of last month, a very particular friend of mine the Revd. Henry Robinson has applyd to me for an introduction to you in case your arrangements should bring you over here. He has some very considerable property in Virginia and I believe the revolution has made it rather precarious. I have used the freedom to give him a line to you and he will take the liberty to inform you the particulars. I am sorry to tell you that the remainder of your game have given up the Ghost. The last on the dead list was a lon solitary hare that broke his heart last night for the want of a Companion. If you embark for America from this place I would recommend you to apply to a Mr. Enderby. He lives on Oxford Road and has always a large Stock by him. Tracy has got from him three brace of Pheasant which I shall take out for him and it would have given me great pleasure to have taken care of some for you had my business carried me to Virginia. The attention they will necessarily require on board has determined me not to send out any by the Spring Ships as I think the only probable chance you can have to carry them safe will be either to take them yourself, or send them under the care of some friend. The Post Chaise is now waiting for me to carry me to Gravesend where I shall embark for the land of Saints and I hope it will not be long before I have the pleasure to take you by the hand in the holy City of Boston. God bless you. Your frd. & Servt.,

ALEXANDR. MOORE

RC (MHi); endorsed. Moore's letter of the MIDDLE OF LAST MONTH and his LINE to TJ introducing the Rev. Henry Robinson are missing.

To Clouet

[11 Mch. 1785]

J'ai reçu Monsr. la lettre que vous m'avez fait l'honneur de m'écrire et je differois d'y repondre en attendant toujours l'arrivée de la caisse renfermant le portrait du Genl. W. afin que je puisse en meme tems vous en annoncer la reception. Je[1] commençois de craindre que quelque malheur l'avoit rencontré chemin faisant, lorsque y reflechissant hier au soir il m'a venu dans l'esprit qu'il pourroit être arrivé a Paris et qu'on en attendoit la demande. J'ai tout de suite ordonné les recherches necessaires, et je suis heureux de vous en annoncer le succès; on l'a trouvé qui etoit arrivé il y avoit plusieures semaines. Je le crois de mon devoir de vous en faire part au plutot et de vous addresser mes remercimens pour toutes les soins que vous avez eu la bonté d'y donner. J'ai l'honneur d'etre avec consideration Monsr. votre tres humble et tres obeissant serviteur.

2d Dft (DLC); undated; at foot of letter: "Clouet." Entry in SJL reads: "[Mar.] 11. Monsr. Clouet Commissaire de la marine à l'Orient, l'instruisant que j'avois reçu le portrait du Gl. Washington." 1st Dft (DLC); also undated; a line has been drawn through the text. Variations in substance between the two drafts are noted below.

The first draft was evidently composed before TJ acted on the assumption that the portrait might already have arrived in Paris and was there to be claimed; he also presumably discarded the first and substituted the second draft after his inquiries had produced results. An entry in his Account Book under 11 Mch. 1785 records payment for "portage of Genl. Washington's picture 13f 8."

[1] 1st Dft reads instead: "Mais comme il n'est pas encore arrivé, et vous avez eu la bonté de m'instruire qu'il devoit partir de l'Orient le 30me. Janvier, je crains où que quelque malheur l'a rencontré chemin faisant, où peutetre qu'il ne soit à Paris dans ce moment, et qu'on n'a pu me trouver. Je vous prie donc Monsr. de me permettre de vous donner encore la peine de m'instruire s'il a eté expedié de l'Orient, comme vous l'avez esperé et au cas qu'il soit, de me donner tous les renseignements dont vous serez vous-meme instruit qui me puissent mettre en etat d'en faire les recherches necessaires." &c.

John Jay to the American Commissioners

Office for foreign affairs
[11] March 1785

GENTLEMEN

On the 7 May 1784 Congress was pleased to Resolve "That Treaties of amity and Commerce be entered into with Morocco, and the Regencies of Algiers Tunis and Tripoly, to continue for the Term of ten Years or for a Term as much longer as can be procured."

They also resolved "That their Ministers to be commissioned for treating with foreign nations, make known to the Emperor of Morrocco the great Satisfaction which Congress feel from the amicable Disposition he has shewn for these States, and his Readiness to enter into Alliance with them: That the occupations of the War and Distance of our Situation have prevented their meeting his Friendship so early as they wished. But that powers are now delegated to them for entering into Treaty with him; in the execution of which they are ready to proceed. That as to the Expences of his minister they do therein what is for the Honor of the United States."

They further Resolved that a Commission be issued to "Mr. J. Adams, Mr. B. Franklin and Mr. T. Jefferson giving Powers to them or the greater Part of them to make and recieve Propositions for such Treaties of amity and Commerce, and to negociate and sign the same, transmitting them to Congress for their final Ratification and that such Commission be in force for a Term not exceeding two years."

I presume Gentlemen that you have received copies of the above Resolutions as well as of a number of others respecting your Department before my coming into this office; and that you have taken such measures in Pursuance of them as were best calculated to promote the Design and objects of them.

On the 14 of Feby. Instant Congress "Resolved that the Ministers of the United States who are directed to form Treaties with the Emperor of Morocco, and the Regencies of Algiers, Tunis, and Tripoly, be empowered to apply so much of the money borrowed in Holland, or any other money in Europe belonging to the United States, to that use as they may deem necessary, not exceeding Eighty Thousand Dollars.

"That they be further empowered, if the Situation of affairs should render it inexpedient for either of them to procede to the above Court, to appoint such Persons as they may deem qualified to execute this Trust.

That the Secretary for foreign affairs be directed to write to the above Ministers, pressing upon them the necessity of prosecuting this important Business, and forwarding to them Commissions and Letters of Credence, with a blank for the name of such Person as may be directed to conclude the said Treaties."

The Secretary of Congress informs me that you have already been furnished with Commissions to treat with these African Powers, so that nothing now remains to be done to enable you to commence your negotiations with them, for Letters of Credence and a commission to enable you to appoint an Agent or Substitute in the Business are herewith transmitted to you.

It also appears to me expedient to send you copies of such Papers in this office on this Subject as may be necessary to give you accurate Information of what has heretofore been done respecting it —a List of which will be subjoined to this Letter.

You will probably meet with Difficulties and Embarrasments of various kinds in the Prosecution of this Business, but Difficulties and Embarrasments are not new to you, and Experience has taught us that there are very few which Talents assiduity and perseverance cannot overcome.

It is the Desire and Expectation of Congress and of the People at large that this Business be immediately earnestly and vigourously undertaken and pursued, and considering to whom the Execution of it is committed the most sanguine Expectations of its being speedily and properly accomplished are entertained. Peace with those States is a most desireable Object, as well on account of its Importance to our Commerce, as because the Continuance of their Hostilities must constantly expose our free Citizens to Captivity and Slavery. The interests therefore of Humanity as well as Commerce urge Congress and the public to provide and to desire that no Time or Pains may be spared to bring this Matter to an advantageous and happy conclusion.

The Readiness which the Court of France has expressed to aid our Negotiations in this affair, will render it proper that these Transactions be communicated to them, and, if Circumstances should render it necessary, that their assistance be requested, for altho the Trouble they have already had with our affairs should render us delicate and modest in our applications, yet Reserve should not be carried so far as to be imputable either to Pride or want of Confidence.

On the 4 Instant Congress received a Letter dated at Cadiz the 16th. Day of Novr. 1784 from Giacomo Francisco Crocco, whom the Emperor of Morrocco had sent to Spain to treat on the Subject of Propositions which Mr. Robert Montgomery had it seems taken the unwarrantable Liberty of making to his Majesty on the part of the United States. This Letter enclosed Copies of two others which he had written on the 15th. day of July and the 25th. Day of Novemr. last to the Honble Doctr. Franklin. A copy of this Letter and of the answer I am directed to return to it are herewith enclosed for your Information.

At Courts where Favoritism as well as Corruption prevails, it is necessary that attention be paid even to Men who may have no other recommendation than their Influence with their Superiors; what the real Characters of Mr. Crocco or Mr. Caille may be, I am not informed; but I think you will find it expedient to purchase the Influence of those whom you may find so circumstanced, as to be able to impede or forward your Views; perhaps Gratuities before the work is done, might tempt them to delay it, in Hopes of exacting Dispatch Money. Would it not therefore be prudent to promise payment on the Completion of the Treaties? These are delicate Subjects which your greater Experience well enables you to manage, and on which I should not venture any Hints, if this Letter was not to be delivered to you by a private and I believe a careful and confidential Hand—vizt. by Capt. Lamb of Connecticut. This Gentleman was recommended by the Governor of Connecticut as a proper Person to be employed in this Business. The Testimonials he has from that State contain the only Information I possess respecting his Character. They are certainly greatly in his favor. In this matter Congress have not thought proper to interfere, and Capt. Lamb has no Encouragement either from them or from me to expect that he will be employed, it being intended to leave you in the full and uninfluenced Exercise of your Discretion in appointing the Agent in Question. But as Capt. Lamb informs me that he means to go to Paris, I have concluded to commit this Letter to his care, because I am persuaded that he will be as faithful a Bearer of it as any other Person. I have the Honor to be with great Respect and Esteem Gent. your most obt. & very hble. Servt.

Dft (DNA: PCC, No. 98). RC (MHi: Adams Manuscript Trust); in clerk's hand, signed by Jay; at head of text: "Duplicate"; endorsed by

Adams: "Secretary of State's Letter to Adams, Franklin, and Jefferson, 11. March 1785." FC (DNA: RG 59); at head of letter: "To the Honorable John Adams, Benjamin Franklin and Thomas Jefferson Esquires Ministers Plenipoteny. &ca." Tr (DNA: PCC, No. 116); in the hand of David Humphreys. The entry in SJL under 17 Sep. 1785 which reads: "received Mr. Jay's of Mar. 11. by Mr. Lambe" may or may not refer to a private letter to TJ; no such private letter has been found. Enclosures: (1) Congress' letters of credence of 11 Mch. 1785 for the American Commissioners or their agents to (a) the Dey and government of Algiers, Tr (DNA: PCC, No. 116); (b) the Emperor of Morocco, Tr (DNA: PCC, No. 116); (c) the lords and governors of Tripoli, MS (DNA: PCC, No. 91), signed by R. H. Lee, John Jay, and Charles Thomson; and (d) the lords, regents, and governors of Tunis, MS (DNA: PCC, No. 91), also signed by Lee, Jay, and Thomson. Except for the letter to the Emperor of Morocco, the above letters of credence are identical, with only minor alterations appropriate to the titles; the full text of that to Morocco is printed in JCC, XXVIII, 143-5, and that to Tunis in same, 142. Duplicates of these letters of credence are in MHi: Adams Manuscript Trust. (2) Engrossed copies of commissions 11 Mch. 1785 empowering the American Commissioners to appoint agents to negotiate with Algiers, Morocco, Tripoli, and Tunis; these, signed by Lee, Jay, and Thomson and to which the Seal of the U.S. is affixed, are all in MHi; duplicates are in MHi: Adams Manuscript Trust. Also in MHi is a Tr (in the hand of David S. Franks) of the commission concerning Algiers, attested by John Adams 21 Jan. 1786. In DNA: PCC, No. 116 is a Tr of the commission concerning Morocco, and in DNA: PCC, No. 98 is a Dft of that concerning Tunis in the hand of Jay. The full text of the latter, to which those concerning the other powers are similar except for minor variations suitable to their respective titles, is printed in JCC, XXVIII, 140-1. (3) Copy of Congress to the Emperor of Morocco, Dec. 1780 (printed in same, 146-7; a Tr is in DNA: PCC, No. 117). (4) Jay's "list . . . subjoined to this letter" has not been found, but see the list of papers to be sent to the Commissioners printed in JCC, XXVIII, 147-8. (5) Giacomo Francisco Crocco to Congress, 16 Nov. 1784 (Tr of translation is in DNA: RG 59). (6) John Jay's reply to Crocco of 11 Mch. 1785 (Tr in DNA: RG 59). Copies of translations of Crocco's letter and Jay's reply are in MHi: Adams Manuscript Trust.

The resolution of Congress ON THE 14 OF FEB. INSTANT was moved by Robert R. Livingston (Dft. in DNA: PCC, No. 36; clerk's copy signed by Thomson is in MHi: Adams Manuscript Trust). MR. CAILLE: D'Audibert Caille, Moroccan consul at Madrid; a copy of his appointment dated 1 Nov. 1779 and also copies of letters between him and Jay in 1780 are in MHi: Adams Manuscript Trust.

From Jean Holker

SIR   Rouen 12 Mars 1785

Youl be surprised their is no doubt not having heard from me Since my last, the Reason was that the Vessel on Board your Box, was only arrived at this port this Morning, and having a favourable occasion to forward it you, I appleyd to Our directure of the farms, to deliver it me which he has don, and send it by my friend Mr. Guilboud who will deliver it, and a letter he has got under my Sons Cover, from the Congres, as I fancy, for you and my friend Mr. Barcley; but as he is not in paris I fancey, If it is necessary, that my Good friend Doctor Franklin will do the needfull for him.

Although I must confes, the affaire is a very disagreeable one indeed.

I shant need to Enter into any detail, as your letter and my Sons will acquaint you of the whole affair, and the leters Mr. Guilboud will present you of the transaction, must convince every honest man that my old friend Samuel Wharton is a bad man indeed.

I am Really sorry for it, as I had the greatest opinion of him, but so it is, and I humble beg youl render Mr. Guilboud every servis in your Power on that head and youl oblige Dear Sir your very humble & Respectful Servant, J HOLKER

I am sorry to Inform you, that It is not in the Power of the Directure of the farms to deliver me the Caise, as all preses or objects of that Nature is visited by the first President here and obliged to be forwarded by water to Paris under an acque so the caise will part this day in a bote and when it arrives in Paris will be sent to his Excelence Doctor Franklin.

RC (MHi); endorsed.

The BOX or CAISE contained TJ's copying press (see TJ to Holker, 15 Dec. 1784; Holker to TJ, 22 and 30 Dec. 1784). On 14 Mch. Holker wrote William Temple Franklin: "Mr. Guilboud my Pardner in the Manufacture at St. Sever will bring the Caise and Deliver it to Mr. Jefferson, as he has a letter he Received under my sons Cover from Philadelpha, Directed for MM. Jefferson and Mr. Barcley conserning some desagreeable Business that concerns Mr. Samul Wharton and Our hous here. It is needles to Enter into any Detaile, as Mr. Guilboud will doe it, having Mr. Whartons leters to justefy the transaction, but as Mr. Barcley is not in Paris I must Intreat you my good friend to doe the Needfull for him, and youl very much oblige me" (Holker to William Temple Franklin, 14 Mch. 1785, PPAP). The letter that Holker fancied was from Congress FOR YOU AND MY FRIEND MR. BARCLEY must have been the covering letter and commission from the Supreme Court of Pennsylvania to TJ and Barclay of 24 Dec. 1784 (see TJ's certification of depositions, De St. Pol to TJ, 26 Mch. 1785). Holker's son's letter on THE WHOLE AFFAIR may have been one addressed to Guillibaud & Cie which reads in part as follows: "Au milieu de tous mes Soins et de mes embarras en ce paÿs, je n'ay point perdu de vue votre reclamation contre Le Sr. Samuel Wharton de cette ville: aprés cent propositions amicales, mais inutiles, je l'ai traduit devant les tribunaux publics, ou j'aurois obtenu Jugement sur sa Personne et ses biens, s'il n'avoit jugé à propos de Contester la Copie translatée de sa lettre que vous m'avés adressée pour former votre titre: J'ai donc eté obligé de solliciter une Commission Juridique pour enquerir sur les faits, sur les Lieux, que J'ay L'honneur de vous adresser sous ce Couvert, afin que Monsr. Guillebaud puisse la presenter en personne aux Commissaires américains actuellement à Paris, et faire avec eux le nécessaire: il n'y aura pas de mal de Joindre L'attestation sur Serment, de L'Extrait des Livres, et la Copie des Lettres du Correspondant dont Le Sr. Wharton a reçu les Marchandises à Nantes où L'Orient, L'une et L'autre Certifiées par les Maires et Echevins des Lieux, comme ayant été faites en leur présence, et en celle du notaire qui y signera également; et le tout, pour être ensuite Légalisé par les Srs. Jefferson et Barclay. Envoyés moy, je vous prie, au plutôt ces pièces, car il n'y a pas un instant à perdre pour se nantir avant qu'une perte totale ne puisse survenir. Je suis actuelement en action Juridique contre notre Sieur Robt. Morris; Le Congrés est intervenu pour solliciter de la Legislature de cet Etat une loi pour faire accelerer le Jugement des Causes pendantes entre lui et moi, sur le chemin public; le quel entrainera les actions particulieres; L'assemblée Générale tiendra le mois prochain, de la quelle J'attends avec quelque fondement, L'accomplissement de mes Voeux à cette occasion, dont J'aurai le plaisir de vous instruire dans le tems. Je pourray alors Juger de L'Epoque absolue de mon retour, pour le quel Je me suis préparé inutilement depuis plus de deux ans sans pouvoir L'Effectuer" (DLC: TJ Papers, 17: 2899; it is dated merely "1785" but evidently was written 12 Jan. 1785). Two days later young Holker wrote Guillibaud: "En addition a Ce que J'ai eu lhonneur de Vous mander par ma lettre du 12 sur des consultations ulterieures avec mon conseil, il nous paroitroit Convenable a l'effet de lever toutes difficultés que Vous fassiez faire une descente Juridique chez Vous pour constater sur le mémorial les offres (faites pour débiter le Sieur Samuel Wharton de Philadelphie) des marchandises a lui Vendues avec la facture d'Icelles, ou que Vous fassiez constater lesdites entrées sur Votre Susdit mémorial a la Jurisdiction consulaire, et que sur Icelles et la prodution de la lettre du Sr Wharton en reponse a Vos lettres qu'il faudra aussi constater légalement, ainsi que la déposition des Commis de la maison a Ce Sujet, afin sur le tout d'obtenir sentence contre Votre débiteur, et nous en envoyer les duplicatas après les avoir fait legaliser par les maires et echevins et ensuite par Mers. Jefferson et Barclay. Il ne serai pas mal non plus [de . . .] faire certifier par lesdits Commissaires sur les Copies des Commissions que Vous recevrez par mon entremise qu'on leur a remis la lettre originale pour etre expediée par eux par les packets boats partant de lorient a l'adresse de M. Burd prothonotaire de la Cour Supreme de Pensilvanie a Philadelphie afin que sur l'arrivée des duplicatas Collationés on puisse en Solliciter jugement [L'exament] et qu'on ne puisse le retarder Sous aucun pretexte; observant que la lettre originale et les deux Copies partent par trois packets boats consecutifs et qu'une des Sentences Consulaires accompagne la lettre originale. Ces formalités sont de rigueur dans la loi anglaise avec tout negociant qui conteste son engagement" (Copy of Holker to Guillibaud & Cie., 14 Jan. 1785; DLC: TJ Papers, 12: 1947; endorsed by TJ: "Guillebaud et al vs. Wharton."). ACQUE: For "acquit à caution," a discharge or receipt.

From Eliza House Trist

Mississippi Acadian Coast
March 12th. 1785

In a very few days, I expect to leave this country having nearly compleated my business, tho not so advantageously as I had reason to expect. Owing to the paper currency, I shall be obliged to give seventy five pr. Cent to get it exchanged into silver, but this loss I must submit to. There is not the most distant prospect that the situation of affairs will be better in the course of another year, and were they to turn out agreeable to my most sanguine wishes, it wou'd be too great a sacrifice for me to make. I have experienced too much pain and anxiety allready in this country and every hour presents something that reminds me of my misfortune.

I have no other expectation of happiness but the company and conversation of my friends. Here I am shut out from all intercourse with them. I was so long deprived of the pleasure of hearing from them that I began to think my self the most miserable of all human beings, forgot by them all at a time when my wounded mind required the aid of friendship to sooth and allay its painfull perturbations. As gloomy Ideas are ever attendant on the wretched my real troubles were constantly augmenting by antisipating other Calamities. I condemn as well as you the harbouring of such thoughts, and have done all in my power to suppress them, but in spite of all my exertions they are too often my superior and allmost over power me. On the 4th. of January I received a letter from my Brother dated 16th. of October 84 enclosing two from Mr. Madison and one from Colonel Wadsworth. They were the first I received since I have been in the country. They gave me the pleasing information of your having wrote to me before you sailed and likewise of your being safe arrived in France. I experienced joy in the extreeme in perusing my letters to find my friends had not been neglectfull of me and their kind sympathy for my unfortunate situation convinces me I had no just cause for suspecting they no longer rememberd me.

Your very friendly letter of the 27th. [*sic*] of May I did not receive until the 22d. of last month. Shall I ever have it in my power to return your many kindnesses? Was I to repeat what I feel it wou'd pain a mind like yours to hear. I can only say I have a heart susceptable of gratitude and a memory faithfull to its trust.

I found Mr. Trist's property unincumberd tho greatly lessen'd since he came to this country owing to the change of Goverment. I shall be able to take with me as many Dollars as he brought Guineas in to it, but it will be sufficient to prevent my being too great a tax upon the generosity of my friends. But my obligation to you is the same as if necessitated to accept your friendly offer.

As there is no Vessel to sail from this to any of the United States I am obliged to go to Jamaica which will be the mean of prolonging my absence from my friends but am in hopes we shall reach Philad. about the 1st. of June. What sort of a sailor I shall make is uncertain never having been at sea. If our voyage shou'd prove more boistrous than coming down the River I flatter my self it will be less tedious and if I have the good fortune to get safe home my desire for traviling will be fully satisfied. When will your embassy be at an end? Shall I ever have the pleasure of seeing you again I mean to give you an account of my peregranation. I fancy your travils will afford much greater entertainment than mine. Miss Patsy will have a fine oppertunity of perfecting her self in the french language and I expect to see her return the accomplish'd lady. Please to present her my best affections and tell her not to let a change of Place customs and manners eradicate from her Remembrance her old friends. Tho they may be less polish'd they may be equally sincere with any new ones she may create. I will write her from Philad. when I expect among other felicitys to hear from you and her. I did my self the pleasure of writing to you some time ago. I sent it to Orleans to take its chance. If it reaches you, it will serve to convince you that I thought of my friends when I doubted of their solicitude for me. I can not give you a very flattering discription of this country. It has been a bubble from the beginning. The poor can live in it, but there are few rich and I fancy tis the policy of the spanish goverment to keep people poor. The climate is not disagreeable. I have seen full as good land in my own country as any on this river but I must conclude for I have not time to enter into a regular detail. You can easily find out that I am not partial to It, but no country wou'd be agreeable to me under the same circumstances that I have labourd under. Wishing you the enjoyment of every erthly happiness I remain your much obliged friend and Humble Servt.,

ELIZA TRIST

RC (MHi); endorsed: "Mrs. Trist. Mar. 12. 1785. recd. Aug. 24." Recorded in SJL under date of receipt. Enclosed in John Bondfield to TJ, 20 Aug. 1785.

American Commissioners to De Thulemeier

SIR   Passy March 14th. 1785

We had the honor of receiving your letter of Janry. 24. covering a translation into French of the Draught of a treaty proposed between his majesty the King of Prussia and the United States of America, together with answers to the several articles. We have considered them with attention, and with all those dispositions to accomodate them to the wishes of his majesty which a respect for his character, and a desire of connecting the two nations in amity and commerce would naturally produce. We will now take the liberty of troubling you with the result of our deliberations article by article.

Art. 2. We agree to add the restriction proposed to the end of this clause, to wit, "submitting[1] themselves nevertheless to the laws and usages there established, and to which are submitted the citizens of the United states, and the citizens and subjects of the most favoured nations."

Art. 3. Agreed to add a like clause, to wit, "submitting[2] themselves nevertheless to the laws and usages there established, and to which are submitted the subjects of his majesty the K. of Prussia, and the subjects and citizens of the most favored nations."

Art. 4. Three effects of this article are objected to.

1. the permission to export and import all the merchandize of either country without exception.
2. the permission to *all persons* to be buyers and sellers.
3. the not extending in express terms the right of transportation beyond the vessels of the two contracting parties.

As to the first we agree to make to the clause the addition proposed, to wit, "Nevertheless the King of Prussia and the United states, and each of them, reserve to themselves the right to prohibit in their respective countries the importation and exportation of all merchandize whatsoever, when reasons of state shall require it. In this case the subjects or citizens of either of the contracting parties shall not import nor export the merchandize prohibited by the other. But if one of the contracting parties permits any other nation to import or export the same merchandize, the subjects or citizens of the other shall immediately enjoy the same liberty."

With respect to the second object, a permission to *all persons* to become buyers and sellers in this intercourse, it does indeed interfere with the practice of some nations of Europe, wherein the right of buying and selling particular articles of merchandize is frequently given to particular persons or descriptions of persons exclusively. The origin of this practice is to be found in a very remote and unenlightened period, when religion, physics, and every other branch of science was sophisticated and abused. The progress of information and of liberal sentiment has led to reformations in those, and in this also seems to have matured principles which should produce a reformation equally wanted.[3] Commerce performs the important office of procuring vent for superfluities, of supplying wants, and of adjusting prices on a reasonable scale. This it does best where it is freest. Casting an eye over the states of Europe, we find them wealthy and populous nearly in proportion to the freedom of their commerce; and we may conclude from thence that were it perfectly free, they would probably attain the highest points of wealth and population of which their other circumstances would admit. A free competition between buyers and sellers, is the most certain means of fixing the true worth of merchandize: on the other hand the restraint of this right to particular persons, which constitutes a monopoly, has been found in experience the most powerful engine ever employed for the suffocation of commerce. It is interesting to both parties therefore to guard against this in their stipulations.[4] The law of Konigsberg which prohibits a foreigner from selling his merchandize to any but native subjects is a monopoly in a certain degree. It would rather seem desireable that foreigners should come into our ports and there transact together all their business of exchange. It is not for us to judge whether under actual circumstances this law of Konigsberg is a proper object of reformation. His Prussian majesty will decide this, who has already so much extended the limits of happiness for his subjects by the removal of other bars to which time and habit had given their sanction. Should it be indispensable to save the force of this law, we would propose to retain the expressions in this article which give freedom to all buyers and sellers, but that at the end of the addition before agreed to a further one should be made in this form. "Nor shall this article derogate from the force of the laws of the city of Konigsberg, which forbid traffic between foreigners within the limits of their jurisdiction." This will guard against monopoly so much of the feild of commerce as is not already occupied by it. We wish however that in this article the word "persons" should be substituted instead of "the subjects or citizens of that other" and again instead of "the said subjects or citizens."

3. The third objection to this article is that it does not extend the right of transportation beyond the vessels of the two countries. It was thought that the securing this right so far was making a valuable step towards the freedom of intercourse. A right would remain to each party of refusing that privilege to vessels foreign to both; a right which probably would never be exercised but in retaliation on any particular nation adopting that narrow principle. We abandon freely the reservation in its general form in pursuit of an object so valuable to mankind as the total emancipation of commerce and the bringing together all nations for a free intercommunication of happiness, and agree after the words "in their own" to insert "or any other."[5] But we still propose it for consideration whether it will be expedient to either party to disarm itself entirely of the power of retaliating on any particular nation which may restrain the loading of vessels to articles of the growth or manufacture of the country to which they belong? Circumstances may be produced which would render the retaliation essential to

the honour and interests of the parties. We therefore propose after the words "reserve to themselves the right" in the amendment before agreed to, to insert these, "where any nation restrains the transportation of merchandize to the vessels of the country of which it is the growth or manufacture, to establish against such nation retaliating regulations; and also the right."⁶

This fourth article with the several amendments which we have proposed or agreed to will stand thus "More especially each party shall have a right to carry their own produce, manufactures and merchandize in their own *or any other* vessels to *any* parts of the dominions of the other where it shall be lawful for all persons freely to purchase them, and thence to take the produce manufactures and merchandize of the other, which all persons shall in like manner be free to sell them, paying in both cases such duties, charges and fees only as are or shall be paid by the most favoured nation. *Nevertheless the King of Prussia and the United States and each of them reserve to themselves the right where any nation restrains the transportation of merchandize to the vessels of the country of which it is the growth or manufacture to establish against such nation retaliating regulations; and also the right to prohibit in their respective countries the importation and exportation of all merchandize whatsoever, when reasons of state shall require it. In this case the subjects or citizens of either of the contracting parties shall not import nor export the merchandize prohibited by the other. But if one of the contracting parties permits any other nation to import or export the same merchandize the citizens or subjects of the other shall immediately enjoy the same liberty. Nor shall this article derogate from the laws of the city of Konigsberg which forbid traffic between foreigners within the limits of their jurisdiction.*"

Art. 5. We agree that the fifth Article shall stand in the form proposed, to wit, "the merchants, commanders of vessels, or other subjects or citizens of either party shall not within the ports or jurisdiction of the other be forced to unload any sort of merchandize into any other vessels, nor to receive them into their own, nor to wait for their being loaded longer than they please."⁷

Art. 8. Agreed to omit the words "and without being obliged to pay any duties charges or fees whatsoever, or to render any account of their cargo" and to substitute those proposed, to wit, "and without being obliged to render account of their cargo, or to pay any duties⁸ charges or fees whatsoever except those established for vessels entered into port and appropriated to the maintenance of the port itself, or of other establishments for the safety and convenience of navigators, which duties, charges and fees shall be the same, and shall be paid on the same footing as in the case of subjects or citizens of the country where they are established."

Art. 9. We agree to the amendment proposed by adding to this article these words "the ancient and barbarous right to wrecks of the sea shall be entirely abolished with respect to the subjects or citizens of the two contracting parties."

Art. 10. By the laws of the United States copied in this instance from those of England, aliens are incapable of holding real estate. When an estate of that nature descends to an alien, it passes on by escheat to the State. The policy of the United States does not permit the giving to the subjects of any other power a capacity to hold lands within their limits, which was proposed by the project formerly delivered to Mr. Adams. But they are perfectly willing to relieve such persons from all loss on this account by permitting them to sell the inheritance and withdraw the proceeds without any detraction. Again, tho' with them it is a fundamental principle that every man has a natural right to quit the country in which either chance or choice has placed him, and to become a member of any other where he thinks he can be happier, and the laws of some of them direct the particular form in which it is to be done, and therefore these States can pass no laws to prevent the emigration of their fellow-citizens, yet they will respect the principles of other governments where the practice is different. We consent therefore to add to the end of this clause, from the 8th. of the project these words "and exempt from all rights of detraction on the part of the government of the respective states. But this article shall not derogate in any manner from the force of the laws already published or hereafter to be published by his Majesty the King of Prussia to prevent the emigrations of his subjects."

Art. 12. Agreed to omit the clause "on the other hand enemy vessels shall make enemy goods" &c. to the end of the article and to leave that question undecided.

Art. 13. The stipulation "to pay a reasonable compensation for the loss such arrest shall occasion to the proprietors" is not so determinate as to save the necessity of a future arrangement. It was thought questionable whether any mode which might now be thought of, might not, by a change of circumstances, before the case should arise, become inapplicable: and that arrangements would then be easily and amicably taken for doing justice to the individuals interested. We are ready however to receive a proposition for defining the mode at this time. We agree also to the addition proposed to this clause, to wit "but in the case supposed of a vessel stopped for articles heretofore deemed contraband, if the master of the vessel stopped will deliver out the goods supposed to be of contraband nature[9] he shall be admitted to do it, and the vessel shall not in that case be carried into any port, nor further detained, but shall be allowed to proceed on her voyage."

Art. 19. A clause in the treaty with France, the first the United States ever entered into, renders necessary the exception subjoined to this Article. It has not been repeated, nor is proposed to be repeated in any subsequent treaty. If any antecedent treaties would require a like exception on the part of his Prussian majesty we shall chearfully concur in its insertion, the case being either particularly specified or generally described. The practice of carrying prizes into neutral ports and there selling them, is admitted by the usage of nations, and can give offence to none where they have not guarded against it by particular contract. Were the clause now under consideration to be so changed as to exclude the prizes made on the enemies of either from being sold in the ports of the other, and that kind of stipulation to take place generally, it would operate very injuriously against the United States in cases wherein it is not presumed his Majesty would wish it. For suppose them to be hereafter in war with any power in Europe, their enemy, tho' excluded from the ports of every other State, will yet have their own ports at hand, into which they may carry and sell the prizes they shall make on the United States. But the United States under a like general exclusion, having no ports of their own in Europe, their prizes in these seas must be hazarded across the ocean to seek a market at home: an incumbrance which would cripple all their efforts on that element, and give to their enemies great advantage over them.

Art. 21. Agreed to add as proposed "but by the judicatures of the place into which the prize shall be conducted."

Art. 25. Agreed to add as proposed "but if any such Consuls shall exercise commerce, they shall be submitted to the same laws and usages to which the private individuals of their nation are submitted in the same place."

Upon the whole it will be seen that we accomodate ourselves to the amendments proposed to the 2d. 3d. 5th. 8th. 9th. 10th. 12th.

13th. 21st. and 25th. articles, that we agree to the amendments proposed to the 4th. article with certain qualifications, and we cannot but hope that the 4th. and the 19th. articles so amended and qualified may be permitted to stand.[10]

We have the honor to be with sentiments of the highest respect Sir Your most obedt. & most hble. Servts.   JOHN ADAMS

B. FRANKLIN

T. JEFFERSON

FC (DNA: PCC, No. 116); in Humphrey's hand. Dft (DLC); in TJ's hand, except for place and date and several marginal notations in French in the hand of David Humphreys. MS includes, in addition to seven numbered pages, one unnumbered page which has been scored out; this, with its verso (page 5), forms the right half of a folded sheet, on the left half of which are pages 1 and 2. Between the halves is an unfolded leaf of different size, whose recto and verso are pages 3 and 4; and pasted on the recto of 3 is a slip with text to be inserted. It is clear from this that the MS is a combination of two drafts; and possibly the present Dft is a revision of TJ's "Notes" of 1 Mch. (see notes 4 and 8). Further, it bears a separate set of alterations in red ink which evidently constitutes another stage of composition. It is not possible to say when these various alterations were made, but they must have been arrived at during various discussions in early Mch. 1785. The more important differences within the draft and between it and FC are indicated below.

[1] Opposite in margin there is a note in Humphreys' hand: "ajoutez a la fin d'art 2." This was probably an instruction to a French copyist concerning this or another treaty; identical notations appear on TJ's draft of a treaty with Great Britain, enclosed in Franklin and TJ to Adams, 8 July 1785.

[2] Opposite in margin there is a similar note in Humphreys' hand: "ajoutez a la fin d'art 3."

[3] TJ first wrote, and then deleted, in Dft: "The office of commerce is to find a vent for all the productions of agriculture and of art, and to supply materials for the."

[4] The beginning of the text of the unnumbered deleted page coincides with the text at approximately this point and reads: "as established in the city of Konigsberg is a monopoly in a certain degree. It prohibits a foreigner to sell to any but native subjects. His majesty, who has already so much extended the limits of happiness for his subjects is the best judge whether under actual circumstances this regulation is a proper object of reformation; and whether it's continuance will be as valuable to the inhabitants of that city as the establishment of the principle that Commerce shall be subject to no monopolies. If he concurs in the expediency of this principle, he will agree instead of the words 'all the subjects or citizens of that other' and again 'the said citizens or subjects' to substitute the words 'persons' as more effectually answering that end than those proposed in our original draught." The final sentence, which is interlined, is obviously addressed to Franklin and Adams rather than to De Thulemeier, and suggests, therefore, that TJ's "notes" as transmitted to them on 1 Mch. were utilized as the basis for the final draft of the actual letter.

[5] The portion of the deleted unnumbered page relating to this paragraph reads: "3. The third objection to this article is the defect of not extending the right of transportation beyond the vessels of the two countries. It was thought that the securing this right to the vessels of the two nations was making a valuable step towards the freedom of intercourse. A right would have remained to each party to refuse that privilege to vessels foreign to both nations. Nevertheless the principle of emancipating commerce is so sound, that we are not afraid of being led too far by it. The right of restraint which would have remained could never have been advantageously exercised but in retaliation on a particular nation. However we willingly abandon it in adherence to a uniform principle, and agree that this article shall be amended

by inserting after the words 'in their own' the words 'or any other.' "

6 Preceding three sentences constitute the inserted text on slip pasted to bottom of page 3 of Dft; they are in red ink, as are several deletions and insertions on page 3.

7 The text of this paragraph as set forth on the unnumbered deleted page reads: "The obligation to use the agency of lighters, porters and others appointed by government is liable to the same observations. It is a monopoly also, a certain description of persons being alone privileged to exercise a certain vocation. A free competition is much more likely to produce to the labourer a just hire, and to the employer faithful and expeditious service."

8 The text of the unnumbered deleted page ends at this point; that part of Article 8 included thereon agrees with the text as given above.

9 At this point in Dft TJ inserted within square brackets the words "and

abandon the same." At the end of the paragraph he added the following explanation for this insertion: "The words 'and abandon the same' are inserted because the case supposing a property of little value, perhaps it will produce less inconvenience on the whole for the owner to abandon it, than for the captor to be embarrassed with the future care of it." He then deleted both insertion and explanation. This, too, has the appearance of a comment made for his colleagues rather than for De Thulemeier.

10 For the latter part of this paragraph Dft reads: ". . . and to two out of three of the amendments proposed to the 4th. article; and we cannot but hope that as to the other amendment of the 4th. and as to the 19th. they may be permitted to stand as we have proposed, or with such qualifying additions as we have herein suggested." The alterations in this paragraph were made in red ink.

From John Jay

DEAR SIR   New York 15th. March 1785

I have the Honor of transmitting to you, herewith enclosed, an Extract from the Journal of Congress respecting your Appointment to represent the United States at the Court of Versailles as their Minister. On which be pleased to accept my sincere Congratulations.

The next Packet will bring you a Letter of Credence, and such other Papers as this Appointment may in the Opinion of Congress render proper.

Mr. Randall, who is the Bearer of this, has also in charge a Packet of Newspapers directed to Mr. Adams, Dr. Franklin and yourself. I have the Honor to be &ca.   JOHN JAY

FC (DNA: RG 59). Entry in SJL under 2 May 1785 reads: "Received Mr. Jay's of N.Y. Mar. 15. inclosing resolution of Congr. of Mar. 10. 1785. for my appointment." The copy of resolution enclosed has not been found, but the entry in Journals of 10 Mch. reads: "Congress proceeded to the election of a Minister plenipotentiary to represent the United States at the Court of Versailles; and, the ballots being taken, the honble. Thomas Jefferson was unanimously elected, having been previously nominated by Mr. [David] Howell"

(JCC, XXVIII, 134).

Vergennes received Marbois' notification of TJ's appointment on 26 Apr., almost a week before Jay's letter arrived. Marbois wrote on 16 Mch. from Philadelphia, where "la situation de ma femme qui est prête d'acoucher, exigeoit ma présence," and informed Vergennes that "Mr. Jepherson a été nommé Ministre plénipotentiaire des Etats unis auprès du Roi: il y avoit huit Etats présents, et l'élection a été unanime" (Arch. Aff. Etr., Corr. Pol., E-U, XXIX, 107; Tr in DLC).

From John Page

My Dear Sir   Rosewell, March. 15th. 1785

I return you many Thanks for your Letter and much valued Packet by Col. Le Maire. I am the more obliged to you as I am conscious I so little deserved your Attention, but I hope when I shall have more Leisure I shall be able to apologise for a long seeming Neglect, give you some Satisfaction respecting several Matters you may wish to be informed of, and demonstrate to you that I can never forget our old Friendship. The Public Business I have been engaged in, added to my own Affairs which have been much involved and deranged by the War, needed not the Additional Load of my Father's and Mr. Burwell's to perplex a Head so easily confused as mine, and to prevent such an one as I am from attending sufficiently to his absent Friends. I have not yet seen Col. Le Maire. I write this in Haste to send by an Opportunity which I am told offers in Wmsburg. that I may not lose one, and that the first to declare to you that I mean to write to you by every good Conveyance which I may hear of. I propose to write by Mazzei more fully. In the mean Time I remain, wishing you and your Daughter every Happiness, most sincerely & affectionately yrs.,   John Page

RC (MHi); addressed: "A Monsr Monsr Jefferson Ministre Plenipotentiaire des Etats unis de l'Amerique a Paris Cul-de-sac Tetebout." Recorded in SJL as received 15 Nov. 1785 by "La Croix."

From Chevallié

Monsieur   Rochefort le 17. Mars 1785.

J'ai vû avec reconnoissance dans les deux lettres que vous avez Ecrit à Mr. Bn. Franklin les 25. 9bre. et 1er. Xbre. dernier, Et que ce Ministre Plénipotentiaire des Treize Etats unis a eû la bonté de me transmettre, à la suite de la Dépêche dont il m'a honnoré le 26 fevrier dernier, tous les renseignements Sur l'objèt de mes demandes auprès de l'Etat de Virginie Et que vous paroissez tenir de Mr. Schort, l'un des membres actuels du Conseil de cet Etat, arrivé en dernier lieu à Paris. Après avoir été aussi bien instruit sur les dispositions où on Etoit de me satisfaire, lorsque Mr. Schort a laissé la Virginie, Je dois avoir l'honneur de vous faire part directement de quelques observations que J'ai à faire sur le contenu de Votre Lettre du 1er. Xbre.

Mes réclamations ne sont du tout point liées avec celles de Mr. de Beaumarchais, Puisqu'elles tiennent à une Comission de 3.P.% que J'ai acquise, à la vérité sur le montant de la Vente des Marchandises qui formoient la Cargaison du Fier Roderigue, Et que je fis moi-même le 8 Juin 1778 à Mr. Peter Henry alors Gouverneur de Virginie (Et non Pas le Sr. Francy, Comme vous l'avez crû), Et pour laquelle Comission il m'a été donné dès le 9. 7bre. 1780. Par ledit Sr. de Francy, comme agent de Mr. de Beaumarchais, deux traîtes à mon ordre Sur Mr. Armstead, ou tout autre agent de Virginie, Payable à dix jours de Vuë, l'une de 5420. Pounds 1 schelin 6 sols avec les intérêts à Compter du 1er. Juillet 1778., tels qu'ils ont étés convenus Etre Payés dans mon Contract de Vente passé avec Mr. Henry, dont Mr. de Franklin a eû une copie que je luy ai envoyé, de L'Expédition que J'ai par devers moi révêtu des Sceaux de la Province Et qu'il est à lieu de vous Communiquer. L'autre Traite est de 46. miliers de Tabac. Il va vous être aisé, Monsieur, de Présumer que ces deux êffets, qui sont en originaux aux mains du Sr. Dominique Cabarrus neveu, Négociant résidant à yorkTown, qui a ma Procuration pour en Solliciter le Payement, portent naturellement sur les fonds qui restent dûs par l'Etat de Virginie à Mr. de Beaumarchais.

Il eut été bien simple, en ordonnant un acompte proportionné au montant de ces deux Effets, le principal et Intérêts, Et de les donner ensuite Pour comptant à celuy qui représente M. de Beaumarchais auprès de l'Etat de Virginie. J'aurois été rempli de mon dû Et tout seroit dans l'ordre aujourd'huy, Aulieu que je me trouve réduit, par le deffaut de Jouissance de mes fonds, à la plus grande détresse. C'est donc sous ce point de Vuë que vous devrez dorénavant envisager mes Justes réclamations, Et que je vous supplie de les appuyer de votre bienveillance en m'envoyant des lettres de recommendation pour mon fils que je vais faire partir tout exprès pour aller solliciter luimême le Payement de ce qui m'est dû, auprès des Puissances de L'Etat de Virginie Et du Congrès. Il s'embarquera dès aussitôt leur réception. Je désirerois beaucoup d'en obtenir par votre moyen de Mr. Schort.

Je dois encore avoir l'honneur de vous observer, qu'au lieu de dépôt de la solde qui restoit duë à Mr. de Beaumarchais quand je Partis de Williamsburg au mois d'Août 1778 dans le Fier Roderigue pour m'en retourner en France, que Je n'avois point traité d'une manière à reçevoir le montant du Produit de ma Vente en monnoye Courante d'Alors, puisqu'il fut expliqué dans mon Contract de Vente qu'on m'allouoit Six pour un du montant de ma

facture de France, Et qu'il me seroit payé en acompte 2000. Boucauds de Tabac fixés à 4. Pounds le Cent, le Surplus Portant
Intérêt sur le Pied de 6.p.% l'an. Faites-vous remettre la Copie
de ce Contract Et du Compte Courant arrêté avec Messrs. Armstead et Henry qui en est dépendant, Et qu'a Mr. de Franklin,
vous aurez la preuve de ce que j'avance, Et de la bonne foi de mon
Traité avec Mr. Henry. Sur ce Principe Je me crois très fondé à
obtenir le Payement de ce qui m'est dû en Dollars, sans quoi je
préférerai de tout Perdre et de rester Ruiné à Jamais. Je le serois
en effêt si on me faisoit Eprouver une Pareille injustice.

Je me conformerai au Surplus, Monsieur, à Tout ce que vous
avez eû la bonté de dire relativement à mes autres Créançes, sur le
Congrès, Mr. Walnay et le Sr. Sans; celuy-cy me doit L'Equivalent de 230. Boucauds de Tabac qu'il est hors d'Etat de me Payer,
à ce que m'a mandé Mr. de Marbois.

J'ai l'honneur d'Etre avec des sentiments aussi distingués que
Respectueux, Monsieur Votre Très humble & très obéissant Serviteur,   CHEVALLIÉ

RC (MoSHi); in a clerk's hand, signed by Chevallié; endorsed: "Chevallié debt
from Virga."

American Commissioners to John Jay

SIR   Paris March 18th. 1785.

We received by the last Packet the favor of your letter of Janry.
14. in which we have the agreeable information of your having
accepted the appointment of Secretary for foreign Affairs. Besides
the general interest we feel in this event as members of the Union
which is to [be] availed of your services, we are particularly happy
that a channel of communication is opened for us with Congress
in whose justice and abilities we so perfectly confide.

In our letter by the Febry. Packet which we addressed to His
Excellency the President of Congress, we had the honor of transmitting a state of our transactions intervening between the date
of that and of our preceding letter. We now beg leave through you
to inform them of our progress since the last period.

No. 1. is a letter from the Popes Nuncio at this court, which
tho' dated at this place as the 15th. of December 1784 was not
delivered to us till late in February. We consider it as definitive of
our commission to the Holy See unless new instructions or circumstances should render a further proceeding under it proper.

No. 2. from the Chargé des Affaires of Tuscany here came also to hand after the closing of our letter by the last Packet.

From Baron de Thulemeier Prussian Minister at the Hague we have received the enclosed letter No. 3. covering a French translation of the Draught of a treaty which we had proposed through him to the court of Berlin as formerly reported to Congress, with observations on the several parts of it. This paper is numbered 4. and has been answered by our letter of which No. 5. is a copy.

We have also received from the Baron de Thulemeier the letters No. 6. and 7. in answer to ours (formerly communicated to Congress) on the subjects of free ports within the territories of his Sovereign.

In consequence of a letter written by Mr. Adams to Mr. Dumas praying his enquiries and information as to the presents, whether periodical or occasional, made by the United Netherlands to the several pyratical States, he has favored us with the enclosed authentic information marked No. 8. We learn from public papers that the Republic of Venice pays annually to Tripoli a tribute of 3500 Sequins. From a comparison of the strength of this with that of the other pyratical States some grounds are furnished for conjecturing what is paid by them to the others when in Peace with them. We have promises of some further information on the subject of these tributes, which the envy or pride of nations endeavours to cover under mystery, the sum of them will serve to form a judgment of the contributions which will be required from us. With great respect We have the honor to be Sir Your most obedient & Most humble Servants,

JOHN ADAMS

B. FRANKLIN

T. JEFFERSON

FC (DNA: PCC, No. 116); in David Humphreys' hand; at head of text: "4th. Report to Congress addressed to Mr. Jay Secry. for Foreign Affairs." Enclosures (all of which are printed above under their respective dates, except for No. 8): No. 1: The Papal Nuncio to Commissioners, 15 Dec. 1784. No. 2: Favi to Commissioners, 10 Feb. 1785. Nos. 3 and 4: De Thulemeier to Commissioners, 24 Jan. 1785, and its enclosure. No. 5: Commissioners' reply to De Thulemeier, 14 Mch. 1785. Nos. 6 and 7: De Thulemeier to Commissioners, 11 Feb. and 4 Mch. 1785. No. 8: a copy of T. C. Van der Hoop to C. W. F. Dumas, 19 Feb. 1785, with a copy attested by Dumas, 22 Feb. 1785, of questions and Van der Hoop's answers respecting the presents given by the Netherlands to the Barbary powers (Tr in DNA: PCC, No. 116; in Humphreys' hand).

IN CONSEQUENCE OF A LETTER WRITTEN BY MR. ADAMS TO MR. DUMAS: On 22 Dec. 1784 Adams wrote Dumas stating that the capture of one or two vessels by the Barbary states had made it necessary for the Commissioners to think seriously of treating with them; that he had been informed that "Mr. Bisdom and Mr. Van der Hope, were perfectly acquainted with the subject"; and that he wished Dumas to obtain information from them (John Adams to C. W. F. Dumas, 22 Dec. 1784,

MHi: AMT). Dumas transmitted the Commissioners' inquiry on 31 Dec. to Van der Hoop, fiscal consular at the College of the Admiralty at Amsterdam, who conferred with Bisdom. The queries and responses, dated at The Hague, 19 Feb. 1785, over the signature of J. C. Van der Hoop, were copied by Dumas in French and transmitted to Adams with the following endorsement: "Copied and collated with the originals, which are in my hands, by me. At the Hague 22 February 1785. C. W. F. Dumas" (Dumas to Adams, 25 Feb. 1785, with queries and answers as described, MHi: AMT). The queries and Van der Hoop's answers thereto are as follows: "1. Quels présens L.H.P. donnèrent l'hiver dernier à l'Empereur de Maroc, et à son Ambassadeur? . . . L.H.P. ont donné à cette occasion, tout l'equippement pour deux Frégattes de guerre; dix Pieces de cannon de bronze, de 24 Livres de balle, et dix de 18 Livres, et ont en outre fait remettre à l'Ambassadeur de Sa Maj. Impe. deux montres, quelques pieces de drap de differentes couleurs, de la Mousseline, du Thé, du sucre, de la porcelaine, et a la disposition de M. l'Ambassadeur; pour avoir de quoi se rendre plus agréable à son retour auprès de l'Empereur. 2. Qu'ont Elles été dans l'usage de donner? . . . L.H.P. ont envoyé de temps en autre une Montre richement montée. Il y a quelque temps qu'Elles ont fait remettre un présent d'un Poignard, enrichi de diamants, de la valeur de 45,000 florins; et en dernier lieu deux-mille fusils, qui avoient coûté environ 18,000 florins. 3. Quelles sont les sommes que la Republique donne annuellement à Alger, à Maroc, à Tunis, à Tripoli, à Tout autre Etat pareil? . . . Il n'y a rien fixé à cet égard par rapport au Maroc, à Tunis, à Tripoli, et d'autres Etats pareils. On y envoie de temps en temps quelques presents pour les obliger.—Quant a Alger, L.H.P. sont dans l'usage d'y envoyer chaque année pour la valeur de cinquante à soixante mille florins en Agrets et en Poudre à canon.—C'est ce qu'on appelle les Presents ordinaire. Les presents extraordinaire s'y envoient outre cela tous les deux et consistent en étoffes, draps, porcelaines, sucre et montent chaque fois a environ 17,000 florins d'Hollande. 4. Quelle est la manier de traiter avec ces Etats-la? . . . Toutes les Négociations avec les Etats susdits se font par les Consuls que la République envoie à ces differentes Puissances, et que y résident constamment: ou bien aussi par les dits Consuls assistés par quelque Capitaine de vaisseau de la Republique: ou bien aussi, en cas de guerre et d'absence des Consuls, par le Commandant d'Escadre ou de vaisseau, qui sont toujours munis dans ce cas-là de Lettres de L.H.P."

For a comparable and detailed list of presents, both ordinary and extraordinary, given by the States General to the Emperor of Morocco in 1784, see *Dipl. Corr., 1783-1789*, I, 635-7. The following comment by John Adams on the subject of treating with the Barbary powers may reflect something of his discussions with TJ: "Some Americans say, that our Mediterranean Trade is not worth the Expense of treating with the Barbary Powers. Others say we had better send Frigates and fight them. I am afraid we shall make a great mistake in regard to these pyratical States. I detest these barbarians as much as any Body, and my Indignation against their Piracies is as hot as that of any Body. But how can we help ourselves? . . . As to fighting of them, what can we do? The Contest is unequal. We have a rich Trade for them to prey upon" (Adams to Gerry, 12 Dec. 1784; MHi: AMT).

To James Madison

DEAR SIR   Paris Mar. 18. 1785.

My last to you was dated Dec. 8. Since that yours of Feb. 1. has come to hand; and I am in hopes I shall shortly receive from you the history of the last session of our assembly. I will pray you always to send your letters by the French packet which sails from N. York the 15th. of every month. I had made Neill Jamieson my postmaster general there, who will always take care of my letters and confide them to passengers when there are any worthy of confidence: since the removal of Congress to that place, you can chuse between N. Jamieson and our delegates there, to which you would rather address my letters. The worst conveyances you can possibly find are private hands, or merchant ships coming from Virginia directly to France. These letters either come not at all, or like the histories of antient times they detail to us events after their influence is spent.

Your *character*[1] of the *M. Fayette*[2] is precisely agreeable to the idea I had formed of *him*. I take *him* to be of *unmeasured ambition* but that the *means he uses* are virtuous. *He is returned fraught with affection to America and disposed* to render every *possible service*. Of the cause which *separated* the *committee* of the *states* we never have had *an explicit account. Hints* and *dark sentences* from newspapers and private letters have *excited* without *satisfying* our *curiosity*. As your *cipher* is safe pray *give me a detail* of it. The navigation of the Scheld had for a great while agitated the politics of Europe and seemed to threaten the involving it in a general war. All of a sudden another subject, infinitely more interesting is brought on the carpet. There is reason to beleive that the Emperor has made an exchange of territories with the Elector of Bavaria, and that while the Scheld has been the ostensible, Bavaria has been the real object of his military preparations. When the proposition was communicated to the *King of Prussia* it is said he declared qu'il mourroit le cul sur la selle rather than see it take effect. *The Dutch* it is thought would be *secretly pleased* with it. And some *think* that certain *places* said to be *reserved* by the *Emperor* on the *borders* of *France* are meant to be *given to the latter* for her *acquiescence*. I am *attending* with *anxiety* to the part she will act on this occasion. I shall change my opinion of *her system* of *policy* if it be not *honorable*. If the Dutch escape a war, they seem still to be in danger of internal revolution. The Stadholder and Aristocracy can carry their differences no further without an appeal to the sword. The people are on the side of the *Stadtholder*. The conduct of the *aristocracy* in pushing *their* measures to such extremity is inexplicable but on the *supposition* that *France* has *promised* to *support them* which it is *thought she* was *obliged* to *do before they* would *enter into* the *late treaty*. We hear nothing from England. This circumstance, with the passage of their N.F.-land bill thro' the house of commons, and the sending a Consul to America (which we hear they have done) sufficiently prove a perseverance in the system of managing for us as well as for themselves in their connection with us. The administration of that country are governed by the people, and the people by their own interested wishes without calculating whether they are just or capable of being effected. Nothing will bring them to reason but physical obstruction, applied to their bodily senses. We must shew that we are capable of foregoing commerce with them, before they will be capable of consenting to an equal commerce. We have all the world besides open to supply us with gew-gaws, and all the world to buy our tobacco, for in such an event England must buy it from Amsterdam, l'Orient or any other place at which we should think proper to deposit it for them. They allow our commodities to be taken from our own ports to the W. Indies in their vessels only. Let us allow their vessels to take them to no port. The transportation of our own produce is worth 750,000£ sterl. annually, will employ 200,000 tonnage of ships, and 12,000 seamen constantly. It will be no misfortune that Gr. Br. obliges us to exclude her from a participation in this business. Our own shipping will grow fast under the exclusion, and till it is equal to the object the Dutch will supply us. The commerce with the Eng. W. I. is valuable and would be worth a sacrifice to us. But the commerce with the British dominions in Europe is a losing one and deserves no sacrifice. Our tobacco they must have from whatever place we make it's deposit, because they can get no other whose quality so well suits the habits of their people. It is not a commodity like wheat, which will not bear a double voyage. Were it so, the privilege of carrying it directly to England might be worth something. I know nothing which would act more powerfully as a sumptuary law with our people than an inhibition of commerce with England. They are habituated to the luxuries of that country and will have them while they can get them. They are unacquainted with those of other countries, and therefore will not very soon bring them so far into fashion as that it shall be thought disreputable not to have them in one's house or on their table.—It is to be considered how far an exemption of Ireland from this inhibition would embarrass the councils of Engld. on the one hand, and defeat the regulation itself on the other. I rather beleive it would do more harm in the latter way than good in the former. In fact a heavy aristocracy and corruption are two bridles in the mouths of the Irish which will prevent them from making any effectual efforts against their masters. We shall now *very soon call* for *decisive answers* to certain points *interesting* to the *United States* and *unconnected* with the *general treaty* which they have a right to *decline*. I mentioned to you in a former letter a very good dictionary of universal law called the Code d'humanité in 13. vols. 4to. Meeting by chance an opportunity of buying a copy, new, and well bound for 104 livres I purchased it for you. It comes to 8 livres a volume which is a fraction over a dollar and a half, and in England costs 15/ sterl. a volume. I shall have an opportunity of sending this and what other books I have bought for you in May. But new information throws me all into doubt what to do with them. Late letters tell us you are *nominated for* the *court of Spain*. I must depend on further intelligence therefore to decide whether to send them or to await your orders. I need not tell you how much I shall be pleased with such an event. Yet it has it's displeasing sides also. *I want you* in the *Virginia Assembly* and also in *Congress* yet we cannot have *you everywhere*. We must therefore be contented to have *you where you chuse*. Adieu, Yours affectionately &c.

RC (DLC: Madison Papers); unsigned; endorsed: "Th. Jefferson. Mar 18. 1785"; partly in code. Entry in SJL reads: "Jas. Madison. Acknowlege receipt of Feb. 1. Send his letters always by Fr. packet to care N. J[amieson] or our delegates in Congress. Private conveiances bad. M. Fay.—exchange Bava. and Austr.—Pruss. against it. Holld. like it. Fr. doubtful. Dutch in danger revolution—people side with Stadtholder. Is thought Fr. must support Aristocracy. Hear nothing from Engld. This and N.F.L. bill and sending Consul to Amer. proves perseverance in their system of managing for both sides. Their ministry governed by the people and these by their interest. We must stop commerce with them. They must buy our tobacco wherever we chuse to deposit it. Transportation of our produce worth 750,000£ sterl. annually, employs 200,000. tons shipping and 12,000 sailors constantly. Worth while to exclude Gr. Br. from participation of this. Their W.I. trade worth a sacrifice, but their Europn. trade injurious to us. Suspension of this will act as sumptuary law in Amer. Query if Ireld. should be privileged. Shall demand decisive answer as to separate articles. Have bought Code d'humanité for him at 104f. I can send his books in May. But hear he is nominated for Spain. Shall decide according to further information whether to send or wait his orders."

YOURS OF FEB. 1: By this TJ clearly meant Madison's letter of 17 Oct. 1784, which arrived on 1 Feb. 1785 and to which the present letter is in part a reply. OF THE CAUSE WHICH SEPARATED THE COMMITTEE OF THE STATES, John Sullivan gave the following estimate: "The Committee of Congress broke up in a most extraordinary manner and (as this goes by a safe hand) I will add that it is much to the dishonor of the states. The locus in quo became a serious question between the Southern and Northern members, and they therefore seperated" (Sullivan to John Adams, 22 Nov. 1784, MHi: AMT).

[1] This and subsequent words in italics were written in code and have been decoded by the editors, employing Code No. 3.

[2] Ford, IV, 35, supplies the following reading for this passage: "Your *character* of the 446. magistrate . . . ," with an accompanying footnote which reads: "Patrick Henry, recently elected Governor of Virginia." But TJ, of course, is commenting here on Madison's characterization of Lafayette in his letter of 17 Oct. 1784.

To James Monroe

DEAR SIR   Paris Mar. 18. 1785.

I wrote you by the packet which sailed from hence in Feb. and then acknoleged the receipt of yours of Dec. 14. which came by the packet arriving here in Jan. That which sailed from N.Y. in Jan. and arrived here in Feb. brings me no letter from any body except from Mr. Jay to Mr. Adams Dr. F. and myself jointly. Since my last the rumour of an exchange proposed between the Emperor and El. of Bavaria has proved to have foundation. What issue it will be permitted to have is doubtful. The K. of Prussia will risk his own annihilation to prevent it. The Dutch would rather be pleased with it; and it is thought by some that it will *not*[1] *be disagreeable to France*. It has even been said that certain *places* are *reserved* by the *Emperor* on the *borders of France* to *give* to *this court* by way of *hush money*. I am *watching* with anxiety the *part* which *this court* will *act*. If the *sordid* one *suspected* by some, I shall *renounce* all *faith* in the *national* rectitude, and beleive that in *public conduct* we are not yet emerged from the *rascality* of the 16th. *century*. There are great numbers of well *enlightened men* in *this nation*. The *ministry* is such. The *King* has an *honest heart*. The *line* of *policy* hitherto *pursued by* them has been such as *virtue* would *dictate* and *wisdom* ap*prove*. Relying on their *wisdom* only I think they will not *accept* the *bribe* supposed. It would be to *relinquish* that *honorable character* of *disinterestedness* and *new faith* which they have *acquired* by *many sacrifices* and which has *put into their hands* the *government* as it were of *Europe*. A wise man, if nature has not formed him honest, will yet act as if he were honest: because he will find it the most advantageous and wise part in the long run. I have *believed* that *this court* possesses this *high species* of *wisdom* even if it's *new faith* be *ostensible only*. If they *trip* on *any occasion* it will be *warning* to *us*. I do not *expect* they will, but it is our *business to be* on the *watch*. The Dutch seem to be on the brink of some internal revolution, even if they escape being engaged in war, as appearances at present seem to indicate. The division between the Stadholder and the aristocracy cannot be greater, and the people are on the side of the former. The fury with which the aristocracy drive their measures is inexplicable but on the supposition *that France has promised to support them* and this *I believe she did* to *induce them to* the *late treaty*. We hear nothing from England. This circumstance, with the passage of their N.F.land bill through the H. of Commons and the sending a Consul to America (which we hear they have done) sufficiently prove a perseverance in the system of managing for both sides in their connection with us. Our people and merchants must consider their business as not yet settled with England. After exercising the self-denial which was requisite to carry us thro' the war, they must push it a little further to obtain proper peace arrangements with them. They can do it the better as all the world is open to them; and it is very extraordinary if the whole world besides cannot supply them with what they may want. I think it essential to exclude them from the carriage of American produce. We wait the arrival of the packet which left you in Feb. in expectation of some instructions on the subject of England. Should none come, we shall immediately press them for an answer on those subjects which were unconnected with a treaty of commerce.[2] It is to be considered how far an exception in favor of Ireland in our commercial regulations might embarrass the councils of England on the one hand, and on the other how far it might give room to an evasion of the regulations. Mr. Carmichael has obtained the interference of the court of Madrid for the vessel and crew taken by the Emperor of Marocco: and I understand there is a prospect of their being restored. A letter on this subject is come to Doctr. Franklin. I have not yet seen it and I doubt whether it will be in time to be copied and communicated by this packet, the post being near it's departure. On the arrival of the packet now expected here, whether she brings us new instructions or not as to those states, we shall proceed to act for the best on the ground before marked out for us. The Marquis Fayette has arrived here in good health, and in the best dispositions towards us. I have had a very bad winter, having been confined the greatest part of it. A seasoning as they call it is the lot of most strangers: and none I beleive have experienced a more severe one than myself. The air is extremely damp, and the waters very unwholesome. We have had for three weeks past a warm visit from the sun (my almighty physician) and I find myself almost reestablished. I begin now to be able to walk 4. or 5. miles a day, and find myself much the better for it. If the state of our business will permit I wish much to take a tour through the South of France for three or four weeks. The climate and exercise would, I think, restore my health. I have used the second cypher in this letter. Either by a gentleman who will go to America in the April packet, or by young Mr. Adams, who will go in May,

I will send you a new cypher which I have prepared on a large and commodious plan. This young gentleman is I think very promising. To a vast thirst after useful knowlege he adds a facility in acquiring it. What his judgment may be I am not well enough acquainted with him to decide: but I expect it is good, and much hope it, as he may become a valuable and useful citizen. I sent you by the former packet the Pour et Contre for the emancipation of the French W. I. trade. I now send you the answer to it. The mass of the nation is with the latter. Adieu. Your's affectionately.

RC (DLC: Monroe Papers); unsigned; partly in code. Entry in SJL under this date reads: "Jas. Monroe. Exchange of Bava. real.—Pruss. will oppose. Dutch be pleased. France doubtful. Said she is to have douceur.—divisions in Holld. extreme. Is beleived Fr. is bound to support the Aristocracy.—nothing from Engld. This with N.F.L. bill and sending Consul to America shews their disinclination to treat.—our people must interdict their commerce. We expect new instructions by next packet. If don't come we shall require answer from Engld. on the separate articles. Query if best to exempt Ireld. from exclusion.—Carmichl. has obtained interest of court of Madrd. with Maroc. for the vessel taken and in prospect of being restored. A letter come but I have not seen it, and will be too late to copy and communicate by this packet. We shall proceed to act for best.—M. Fay. in good dispositions.—had ill health this winter. Begin to walk 4. or 5. mi. a day. I wish a tour into So. of Fr. for 3. or 4. weeks if our business will permit.—have used 2d. cypher.—will send new one by Mr. Adams junr. in May. Hopeful young man—inclose answer to the Pour et Contre." Enclosure: Copy of *Replique à l'auteur du Pour et Contre*, London [i.e., Paris], 1785, Sabin No. 21035. The author was J. B. C. Dubuc St. Olympe, who very probably was encouraged in his efforts by the American Commissioners. En 26 Feb. 1785 young Abigail Adams entered the following in her journal: "To-day Dr. Franklin, Mr. Williams, and a Monsieur St. Olympia, a French West Indian, dined with us; the latter had been writing upon the trade of the Americans with the West Indies; papa breakfasted with him on Thursday. He brought a book on politics for papa to look at, and inquired if the ladies in America talked politics? Papa told him they conversed upon politics, and that the liberties of a country depended upon the ladies" (*Journal and Correspondence of Miss Adams*, p. 50-1). See Frederick L. Nussbaum, "The French Colonial Arret of 1784," *South Atl. Qu.*, XXVII (1928), p. 62-78; Henri See, "Commerce between France and the United States, 1783-1784," *Am. Hist. Rev.*, XXXI (1925), p. 732-52.

ON THE SUPPOSITION THAT FRANCE HAS PROMISED TO SUPPORT THEM AND THIS I BELIEVE SHE DID TO INDUCE THEM TO THE LATE TREATY: It is apparent from this statement that TJ did not at this time have access to the terms of the secret treaty of alliance between France and the Netherlands which had been under discussion for some months, but he acquired a copy of it some time before it was signed on 10 Nov. 1785. In DLC: TJ Papers, 11: 1772-3 there is a copy of this treaty in TJ's hand, marked *"Secret"* and headed: "A [*sic*] Projet d'un traité d'alliance defensive entre la France et les pays-bas Unis remis par M. le Cte. de Vergennes* aux plenipotentiaires de la Repube. a Versailles le 15. Juillet 1784. et envoyé par Courier à L.H.P. qui le reçurent le 21."; the asterisk in this passage is keyed to a marginal note in TJ's hand reading: "C'est les Patriotes qui ont dressé ce plan-ci, et qui l'ont remis à M. le D. de la V." On the last page of this copy of an early text of the projet is the following, also in TJ's hand: "En recevant le projet, ou, comme a dit M. de Vergennes, sa meditation, d'un traité d'alliance pour etre transmise, les plenipotentiaires lui demanderent une explication de l'article 2 [which pledged the contracting parties "de contribuer autant qu'il sera en leur pouvoir à leur sureté respective, de se maintenir et conserver mutuellement la tranquillité, paix et neutralité, ainsi que la possession actuelle de tous leurs etats, domaines, franchises et libertés, et de se preserver l'un l'autre de toute aggression hostile, dans quelques partie du monde que ce puisse etre"], quant aux differents actuels entre la republique et l'Empereur, et il repondit— 'Que d'apres l'opinion reçue des sentiments d'equité de l'Empereur, et des dispositions conciliatoires de L.H.P., il etoit persuadé que les choses n'en viendroient pas a des extremités, que l'objet essentiel de S.M.T.C. en contractant une alliance defensive avec les provinces unies etoit d'assurer, autant qu'il etoit dans son pouvoir, la tranquillité de la republique, tant par terre que par mer.—Que c'est dans cette vue que Sa M. garantira toutes leurs possessions, droits et immunités. Mais qu'il etoit de regle et d'un usage universel et constant que ces sortes de garanties ne sauroient porter sur des objets litigieux, parce qu'elles auroient un caractere offensif a l'egard de la puissance vis-a-vis de laquelle le litige existeroit, que d'ailleurs le roi, ayant promis ses bons offices tant a l'Empereur qu'aux etats Generaux dans le temps meme que la proposition de la republique de faire une alliance avec lui, ne lui etoit pas faite, Sa Maj. ne pouvoit pas s'engager à des promesses qui y etoient directement contraires. Que cependant il pouvoit declarer en meme temps de la part Sa Maj. qu'elle continueroit ses bons offices avec zele aupres de l'Empereur en faveur de L.H.P. et qu'elle feroit tout ce qui pourroit dependre d'elle pour amener les choses à un arrangement amical." (The treaty as ultimately signed is in Martens, *Receuil de Traités*, 1818, IV, p. 65-71.) It is possible that TJ's copy of the projet, with its illuminating explanation of Article 2 by Vergennes, was sent to the Commissioners by Dumas, who occasionally transmitted documents of great secrecy to them (e.g., Dumas to Adams, 24 Sep. 1784, enclosing an unidentified document with the statement that it was entrusted to him under oath of secrecy and directing Adams to enjoin his colleagues "ne temoigner a personne, ou hollandois ou francois de l'avoir vu"; (MHi: AMT). A LETTER ON THIS SUBJECT IS COME TO DOCTR. FRANKLIN: This was Carmichael's letter to Franklin of 27 Feb. 1785 (see Carmichael to TJ, 29 Mch. 1785, and Commissioners to Jay, 13 Apr. 1785).

[1] This and subsequent words in italics were written in code and have been decoded by the editors, employing Code No. 6.

[2] In TJ to Madison, this date, TJ took the precaution of putting a corresponding sentence in code.

To Alexander Moore

[*Paris, 19 Mch. 1785.* Entry in SJL reads: "Alexr. Moore. Lond. Desire him to give me notice before he goes to Virga.—my ill health—introduce Bolling." Not found.]

To Nathaniel Tracy

[*Paris, 19 Mch. 1785.* Entry in SJL reads: "N. Tracy. Letters received by Pickman and West. Intelligence from Marocco. He may give substance of it and say it comes from us, but not print extract verbatim. Compliments to Jackson and Temple. Communicate intelligence to Martin and Shore." Not found. The letters "by Pickman and West" have not been identified.]

John Adams to Franklin and Jefferson

GENTLEMEN   Auteuil March 20. 1785

According to your desire I went early this morning to Versailles and finding the Ct. de Vergennes unembarassed with company, and only attended by his private Secretaries, I soon obtained the honour of a conference, in which I told him that my colleagues were very sorry that indisposition necessarily prevented their paying their respects to him in person, and obliged them to request me alone to wait on him and ask his advice upon a thorny question we had with the Barbary Powers. He asked what it was and I put into his hand all the letters upon the subject in french, spanish, italian and english—all of which he read very attentively and observed that it was obvious what was wanted and what had piqued the Emperor of Morocco, viz, that Congress had not written to him nor sent him a consul with the customary presents, for that he was the most interested man in the world and the most greedy of money. He asked whether we had written to Congress and obtained their instructions. I answered that we had full powers to treat with Morocco, Algiers, Tunis, Tripoli and the rest, but that it was impossible for us to go there and that we had not a power of substitution. He said then we should write to the Emperor. I asked if he would do us the favour to convey a letter for us through the french consul? He said he could not do this himself, because it was not in his department, but if we would make an office of it he would communicate it to the Marquis de Castries and return us his answer.

I told him that in looking over the treaties between the several christian Powers and the Barbary States, we found that the treaty between the crown of France and Algiers of the 25 April 1684 was expired or near expiring, and we were desirous of knowing, if the question were not indiscreet, whether it had been renewed. He smiled upon this and said, it was true that their treaty was upon the point of expiring, but he could not tell me whether it were renewed, as it was not in his department, but if we would insert this Inquiry in our office he would endeavour to obtain the Marshall de Castries's Answer.

I told him, that in order to lay before Congress all the information we could, and to enable them to judge the better what orders to give us or what other course to take we had obtained authentic information from Mr. Bisdom and Mr. Vanderhope, concerning the presents annually given by their high Mightinesses and that we should be very glad to know, if it was not improper, what was the annual amount of the presents made by his Majesty to each of those States, and in what articles they consisted. He said the King never sent them any naval or military stores, but he sent them glasses and other things of value, but that as it was not in his department: he could not give me particular information, but that we might put this into our office with the other things.

I asked if there was not a considerable trade and frequent intercourse between some ports of this Kingdom and the coast of Barbary. He said there was from Marseilles and the other ports upon the Mediterranean: but he thought if we had presents to send it would be more convenient to send them from Cadiz.

I then asked the favour of his advice whether in our letter to the Emperor of Morocco we should leave it to his option to send a Minister here to treat with us, or to wait untill we could write to Congress and recommend it to them to send a consul. He said he would by no means advise us to invite the Emperor to send a Minister here to treat with us because we must maintain him here and bear all the expences of his voyages and journeys which would be much more costly than for Congress to send a Consul.

But the Comte concluded the whole conference by observing that every thing relative to this business was out of his department, and that we must state to him in writing all we desired to know or to have done, and he would convey it to the Minister of the Marine, and communicate to us his answer, and that we might depend upon it that whenever we thought proper to make any office to him it should be carefully attended to.

He added very particular Inquiries concerning the health of Dr. Franklin and Mr. Jefferson which I answered to the best of my knowledge and took my leave. With great respect I have the honor to be Gentlemen Your most obedient & Most humble Servt.,

JOHN ADAMS

Tr (DNA: PCC, No. 86); in David Humphreys' hand; at foot of text: "Their Excellencies Messrs. Franklin & Jefferson"; opposite complimentary close is the notation "No. 5.d." Tr (DNA: PCC, No. 116); also in Humphreys' hand; at head of text: "Report of Mr. Adams to the other Ministers." FC (MHi: AMT). The letter was forwarded by the Commissioners to John Jay as enclosure No. 5d to their letter of 13 Apr. 1785.

There must have been some reason other than illness that caused Franklin and TJ not to join Adams in this conference with Vergennes, for on the preceding day TJ had written that he had been "almost reestablished" in health and had begun "to be able to walk 4. or 5. miles a day and find myself much the better for it" (TJ to Monroe, 18 Mch. 1785). The questions to be asked of Vergennes were of a nature requiring the kind of forthrightness that Adams possessed, and the Commissioners must have agreed that they could be put to the minister more effectively by him than by either of the other two;

Franklin, of course, was so ill as to be confined to his home. Vergennes' inquiry CONCERNING THE HEALTH OF DR. FRANKLIN AND MR. JEFFERSON may indicate that he understood the situation and Adams' reply TO THE BEST OF MY KNOWLEDGE is almost an admission that he confirmed Vergennes' suspicions, if such they were. This conjecture is scarcely dispelled by the following minute in the proceedings of the Commissioners: "Upon receiving the Dispatch from Mr. Carmichael the Ministers plenipotentiary convened at Passy March 19. 1785. and wishing to take the advice of the Court of Versailles in all their transactions with the Barbary Powers, Mr. Adams was requested to have a conference with the Cte. de Vergennes on the subject—Dr. Franklin and Mr. Jefferson being too unwell to go to Versailles on that occasion" (DNA: PCC, No. 116). In brief, though TJ was able to go to Passy on the 19th, he and Franklin were able to foresee that "on that occasion"—the 20th or whenever Adams should be able to obtain a conference with Vergennes—they would not be well enough to make the short trip to Versailles. I PUT INTO HIS HANDS ALL THE LETTERS ON THE SUBJECT: These included an extract of Carmichael's letter to Franklin, 27 Feb. 1785; Franco Chiappe to Franklin, 3 Nov. 1784; Floridablanca to Carmichael, 24 Nov. 1784; Alcaïd Drisse to Carmichael, 23 Dec. 1784; same to Harrison, consul at Cadiz, 23 Dec. 1784; Mordyay de Lamar to Harrison, 3 Jan. 1785; Chiappe to Franklin, 10 Jan. 1785; Emmanuel Salmon to Floridablanca, 15 Jan. 1785 (all are in Arch. Aff. Etr., Paris, Corr. Pol., E.-U., Vol. XXIX, 130-43; filed with Commissioners to Vergennes, 28 Mch. 1785; Tr in DLC). For Adams' account of the Commissioners' meeting, 19 Mch., and his conference with Vergennes, 20 Mch., see his Diary (*Works*, III, 390-1).

From James Buchanan and William Hay

SIR   Richmond March 20th. 1785

The active part which you took before your departure from Virginia, as a director of the public buildings, leads us to believe, that it will not be now unacceptable to you, to cooperate with us as far as your engagements will permit.

We foresee, that in the execution of our commission, the Commonwealth must sustain a heavy expence, and that we can provide no shield so effectual against the censures which await large disbursements of public money, as the propriety of making them. For this purpose we must intreat you to Consult an able Architect on a plan fit for a Capitol, and to assist him with the information of which you are possessed.

You will recollect, Sir, that the first act directed seperate houses for the accommodation of the different departments of government. But fearing that the Assembly would not countenance us in giving sufficient magnificence to distinct buildings, we obtained leave to consolidate the whole under one roof, if it should seem adviseable. The inclosed draught will show that we wish to avail ourselves of this licence. But, altho it contains many particulars it is not intended to confine the architect except as to the number and area of the rooms.

We have not laid down the ground, it being fully in your power to describe it, when we inform You that the Hill on which Gunns yellow house stands and which you favoured as the best situation, continues to be preferd by us and that we have allocated 29 half acre lots, including Marsdon's tenement, and Minzies' lots in front of Gunns. The Legislature have not limited us to any sum; nor can we, as yet at least, resolve to limit ourselves to a precise amount. But we wish to unite œconomy with elegance and dignity. At present the only funds submitted to our order are nearly about £10,000 Virga. Currency.

We have already contract'd with Edward Voss of Culpepper, for the laying of 1500 thousand Bricks. He is a workman of the first reputation here, but skilful in plain and rubbed work alone. We suppose he may commence his undertaking by the beginning of August, and have therefore stipulated with him to be in readiness by that time. This circumstance renders us anxious for expedition in fixing the plans, especially too as the foundation of the Capitol will silence the enimies of Richmond in the next October Session.

Should an assistant be thought necessary whose employment will be either independant of Voss or subordinate to him, we will pay him.

We shall send to Europe for any Stone which may be wanted.

The roof will be covered with lead, as we conceive that to be better than Copper or tiles.

In the remarks, which accompany the plan, we have requested a draught for the Governor's house and prison. But we hope that the Capitol will be first drawn and forwarded to us, as there is no hurry for the other buildings.

We trust Sir, you will excuse the trouble which we now impose on you, and will ascribe it to our belief of your alacrity to serve your Country on this occasion. We have the honour to be very respectfully Sir Your most obt. hble. Servts.,

JAMES BUCHANAN
WM. HAY
on Behalf of the Directors

RC (DLC); in hand of James Buchanan. Recorded in sjl as received 14 June 1785. Enclosures: (1) The "inclosed draught" of a plan for the capitol is in MHi and is reproduced in Fiske Kimball, *Thomas Jefferson and the First Monument of the Classical Re-* *vival in America*, p. 17; (2) the accompanying "remarks" have not been found.

The FIRST ACT concerning the public buildings was, of course, drawn by TJ himself in 1776 and revised in 1779 (see Vol. 1: 598-602 and Vol. 2: 271-

2). The Act by which the Directors were given LEAVE TO CONSOLIDATE THE WHOLE UNDER ONE ROOF was passed at the Oct. 1784 session (Hening, XI, 496). On this subject, see, in addition to the work cited above, Fiske Kimball, "Jefferson and the Public Buildings of Virginia," *Huntington Lib. Qu.*, XII (1949), 115-20, 303-10.

From Francis Hopkinson, with Enclosure

DEAR SIR   Philada. 20th. March 1785

Your Favour of the 11th Novr. came to Hand not long since, for which I thank you. I had, much about the same Time, written to you giving an Account of my further Improvement in the Method of Quilling a Harpsichord and enclosed a Model in my Letter. My Harpsichord quilled in this Way has been freely used by myself and Daughters since its Arrival last fall and not one Quill has failed, the Touch remaining perfect as at first so that I am sure the Discovery is a real One and is certainly of considerable Importance to Performers on that Instrument. About a Year and a half ago, I thought of a Method to improve the Tone of a Harpsichord. The Experiment was easily tried and I had myself little Doubt of the Success. I wrote an Account of it to my Correspondent in London but did not minutely describe the Process. He either did not, or would not understand me. Perhaps it may appear hereafter as a British Discovery. I was discouraged and the Idea remained unnoticed, till lately when it again reviv'd with some Vigour and claim'd my further Attention. I brought it to the Test last Evening. I invited several philosophical Gentlemen to my House, performed the Operation on my new Harpsichord in their Presence, and submitted it to their critical Examination. They declared in Favour of the Experiment. Amongst these Judges were Dr. Moyse the blind philosopher, Mr. Rittenhouse, Mr. Marbois, Mr. Vaughan &c. I will enclose full Directions for performing this Experiment, with a View that you would try it and give me your Opinion of the Result. But I wish you would keep the Secret for a Time at least, as I mean to make further Essays on other Instruments, and when I shall have fully ascertained the Fact, will communicate it to our philos: Society for publication in their next Volume. This Injunction however is not intended with respect to Dr. Franklin. I should be very glad if he would try the Experiment with you, if he thinks it worth his attention. By the Bye, I have not received a Line from him since you left us. Neither have I or Mr. Rittenhouse received the Pamphlets you were so good as to send us, but we have long since heard of the Fate of Animal Magnetism and seen the Report of the Commissioners thereon.

I have mentioned Dr. Moyse. I will now tell you who he is. He is a Scotchman by Birth and a Philosopher by Profession. He came to America from England with the famous Mrs. Haley. He arrived I believe about a Year ago at Boston and has come from thence to this City, giving public Lectures in Natural philosophy all the way. He spent the beginning of this Winter at New York, where he became very popular and a great favourite of the Ladies in particular who crowded to his Lectures, and happy was she who [could] get him to dine or drink Tea at her House. Having gone thro' his Course there and reaped no small Honour and Profit, he is now performing with us. But the Rage for philosophy at New York, is not to be compared with that of Philadelphia. He exhibits three Evenings in a Week in the College Hall, he has already given 10 or a Dozen Lectures to an Audience of not less than 10 and most commonly 1200 Persons. The Ladies are ready to break their Necks after him. They throng to the Hall at 5 o'Clock for places, altho' his Lecture does not begin till 7. He has been blind from his Infancy, has made Philosophy his Study and is well acquainted with the present admitted Systems, adding sometimes Theories of his own, which he does however, with rather too much Arrogance.

Our philos: Society are as dull as ever. There was a large Election of members last January. I took Care that our friend Mr. Maddison should be one of them. The publication of a Second volume of their Transactions is at length thrown into the hands of Mr. Patterson and myself and I do verily believe, it will e'er long be put to the Press.

I say nothing about Congress and their Proceedings. You will receive all Intelligence of that kind either officially or from your political friends.

I had the Misfortune to loose my dear Sister Morgan. She died on the first of January last. My Mother has given up House keeping and for the present lives with Dr. Morgan. They both din'd with me today and join in kind Remembrance to you and Love to your Daughter.

I hope to hear from you before this gets to hand and after too. With respectful Regards to Doctor Franklin I am Dear Sir, as ever Your affectionate friend and very humble Servt.,

FRAS HOPKINSON

I enclose for your Amusement one of my literary Gambols occasioned by a News paper Quarrel between Dr. Ewing and Dr. Rush, in which the broad Bottom of the University was too frequently mentioned. Mr. Bentley the Harpsichord Player and Mr. Brown the flute player have also had a Quarrel which they brought on the public Theatre. The enclosed turned the laugh of the Town upon all the Combatants and put an End to the War.

Since writing the above I have received the Pamphlets from Virginia for which I thank you.

ENCLOSURE

Account of an Experiment made with a View to improve
the Tone of a Harpsichord.

The Octave Stop of the Harpsichord being drawn off, we searched for two Unisons which were quilled as nearly alike as possible. These were perfectly tuned to each other. I then took a pair of strong Steel Magnets and laid them along Side of each other, the North Pole of one to the South Pole of the other. I seperated the lower Extremities of the Bars about an Inch, by Means of a Piece of folded Paper introduced between them; their upper Ends still remaining in Contact. Holding the Magnets in a perpendicular Position I applied their lower or seperated Ends to the steel String of one of the Unisons, and passed it gently along the whole length of the String four or five Times, whereby it became highly Magnetic. We then carefully compared the Tone of the String so magnetised with its Comparison which had not been touch'd and found it manifestly improved. The Vibrations being, or seeming to be, much more uniform and sweet to the Ear. This is a nice Experiment and requires Attention. But I am persuaded a judicious Ear will acknowledge the Effect. At any Rate the operation can do no Harm, and I believe the Idea is original.   F. H.

RC (DLC). TJ's entry in SJL under 10 June 1785, which reads: "received F. Hopkinson's of Philada. Mar. 28.," is undoubtedly an error for this of 20 Mch. (see TJ to Hopkinson, 6 July 1785). Enclosures: (1) Account of an experiment to improve the tone of the harpsichord (MS in MHi). (2) A copy of Hopkinson's "New Sources of Amuse-ment," which had been printed in the *Penna. Packet* of 1 Mch. 1785 and is found in his *Miscellaneous Essays*, Philadelphia, 1792, II, 138-45. Hopkinson's remarks above seem to indicate that two essays were enclosed, but "New Sources of Amusement" includes both the Ewing-Rush and Bentley-Brown affairs.

From Richard Price

DEAR SIR   Newington Green, Mch. 21st. 1785

I received with peculiar pleasure the favour of your letter by Dr. Bancroft, and I return you my best thanks for it. Your favourable reception of the pamphlet which I desired Dr. Franklin to present to you cannot but make me happy; and I am willing to infer from it that this effusion of my zeal will not be ill received in America. The eyes of the friends of liberty and humanity are now fixed on that country. The united States have an open field before them, and advantages for establishing a plan favourable to the improvement of the world which no people ever had in an equal degree. Amidst the accounts of distress and confusion among them which we are often receiving in London, the information which you and Dr. Franklin have communicated to me comforts and encourages me, and determines me to maintain my hopes with respect to them.

Such an enlargement of the powers of Congress as shall, without hazarding too much public liberty, make it capable of preserving peace and of properly conducting and maintaining the union, is an essential point; and the right Settlement of it requires the greatest Wisdom. You have gratify'd me much by acquainting me that a Sense of this is becoming general in America, and by pointing out to me that character of the confederated governments which is likely to preserve and improve them. The character, however, of popular governments depending on the character of the people; if the people deviate from Simplicity of manners into luxury, the love of Shew, and extravagance, the governments must become corrupt and tyrannical. Such a deviation has, I am afraid, taken place along the Sea coast of America and in Some of the principal towns, and nothing can be more threatening. It is promoted by a rage for foreign trade; and there is danger, if some calamity does not give a Salutary check, that it will Spread among the body of the people till the infection becomes general and the new governments are render'd images of our European governments.

There is, I fancy, no probability that Britain can be brought to consent to that reciprocity in trade which the united States expect. This is Sad policy in Britain; but it may turn out to be best for America; and Should the issue be our exclusion from the American ports, we may be ruined, but I do not See that America would Suffer in its true interest. The fixed conviction, however, among us is that such an exclusion cannot take place, and that we are able to Supply America on so much better terms than any other country that, do what we will, we must have its trade. But, Dear Sir, I ask your pardon for detaining you by entering on a Subject of which probably I am not a competent judge. I meant by these lines, when I begun them, only to make my grateful acknowledgments to you for the kind notice you have taken of me by your letter; a notice the agreeableness of which is much increased by the high opinion I have been led to entertain of your character and merit. With great respect and every good wish, I am, Sir, your most obedt. and humble Servt.,   RICHD. PRICE

I have desired Dr. Franklin to convey to you a copy of an edition of my Observations &c. which has been just published here. You will find that I have made considerable additions by inserting a translation of Mr. Turgot's letter and also a translation of a French tract convey'd to me by Dr. Franklin. The Observations are the very Same except two or three corrections of no particular consequence, and an additional note in the Section on the dangers to which the American states are exposed.

RC (DLC); endorsed. Recorded in sjl as received on 4 Apr. 1785. The edition of Price's *Observations on the Importance of the American Revolution* that he sent was the London, 1785, edition (Sabin 65450), which contained the letter from Turgot and an appendix. See Sowerby No. 2993.

From John Jay

DEAR SIR   Office for foreign Affairs 22d. March 1785

The Packet being still here, I have the Honor of transmitting to you herewith enclosed your Commission and Letter of Credence. Mr. Randall who goes as a Passenger in the Packet has my other Letters, and will be the Bearer of this. Permit me to recommend him to your Attention.

I have the Honor to be &ca.,   JOHN JAY

FC (DNA: PCC, No. 80); in clerk's hand, signed by Jay. Entry in sjl of its receipt on 2 May 1785 reads: "received Mr. Jay's of N.Y. . . . Mar. 22. inclosing commission and letter of credence." Enclosures: Engrossed copy of commission (MHi), with paper seal attached and signed by Lee, Jay, and Thomson. Texts of commission and letter of credence are in DNA: PCC, No.

81, endorsed by Thomson: "Form of a commission to Mr. Jefferson and of a Letter of Credence Read and approved March 22. 1785. Referred to the Secy. Foreign Affairs to take order"; printed, with indication of two words deleted by Congress, in jcc, XXVIII, 189-90.

TJ's commission as minister to France ran "for the space of three years from this Day unless sooner revoked."

Jefferson's Attestation of Depositions

Passy in the Kingdom of France to Wit.

In obedience to the Commission hereto annexed (in the absence of Thomas Barclay esq. therein also named), I have diligently examined his Excellency Benjamin Franklin, LeRay de Chaumont and Bouchault on their respective oaths first taken before me on the interrogatories to the said commission annexed, and reduced the said examinations to writing in the preceding depositions; and I do hereby certify that the French copy of the letter shewn to the said Benjamin Franklin and LeRay de Chaumont and declared in their depositions to be a true translated copy of the original letter, is the translated copy to the commission annexed: I do further certify that a letter was produced to me, said to be the original of the translated copy before mentioned, which original letter is that which was exhibited to the several deponents, was declared by them to be of the writing and signature of the said Samuel Wharton, and is the one referred to in their depositions: of which same original letter I have made a copy and hereto annexed the same with the said depositions. Done at Passy aforesaid in the Kingdom of France this 22d. day of March in the y. of our l. 1785. as Witness my hand and seal.

Dft (DLC). Neither the depositions nor TJ's attestation as transmitted in his letter to Holker of 24 Mch. 1785 have been found among the archives of the Prothonotary of the Supreme Court of Pennsylvania.

To Jean Holker

[*Paris, 24 Mch. 1785.* Entry in sjl reads: "John Holker. Rouen. Answer to his letter of Mar. 12. accompanied by letter to Prothonotary of Pennsylva. and depositions." Neither letter nor—with the exception of document preceding—accompanying papers found.]

Dorset to the American Commissioners

GENTLEMEN   Paris 26th. March 1785

Having communicated to my Court the readiness you express'd in your Letter to me of the 9th. of December to remove to London for the purpose of treating upon such points as may materially concern the Interests both political and commercial of Great Britain and America, and having at the same time represented that you declared yourselves to be fully authorized and empowered to negotiate, I have been, in answer thereto, instructed to learn from you, Gentlemen, what is the real nature of the Powers with which you are invested; whether you are merely commission'd by Congress, or whether you have receiv'd seperate Powers from the respective States. A Committee of North American Merchants have waited upon His Majesty's Principal Secretary of State for Foreign Affairs to express how anxiously they wish to be inform'd upon this subject, repeated experience having taught them in particular, as well as the Public in general, how little the authority of Congress could avail in any respect, where the Interests of any one individual State was even concern'd, and particularly so, where the concerns of that particular State might be suppos'd to militate against such resolutions as Congress might think proper to adopt.

The apparent determination of the respective States to regulate their own seperate Interests renders it absolutely necessary, towards forming a permanent system of commerce, that my Court should be inform'd how far the Commissioners can be duly authorized to enter into any engagements with Great Britain which it may not be in the power of any one of the States to render totally fruitless and ineffectual.

I have the honor to be, Gentlemen, with great truth Your most obedient humble Servant, 						DORSET

RC (DNA: PCC, No. 86); in a clerk's hand, signed by Dorset; endorsed by David Humphreys; opposite endorsement is the notation "No. 6." Tr (DNA: PCC, No. 86) and another Tr (DNA: PCC, No. 116), both of which are in Humphreys' hand. The letter was forwarded by the Commissioners to John Jay with theirs of 13 Apr. 1785 as its sixth enclosure.

The immediate background of this letter is shown in a series of communications written and received by John Adams from the time of the Commissioners' letter of THE 9TH. OF DECEMBER to their receipt of Dorset's reply. On 12 Dec. 1784 Adams wrote Gerry: "Dr. Franklin is so bad with the Stone, that he has not been to Versailles nor Paris these twelve months; he has ventured to Auteuil three or four times to dine with me, but the last Time he suffered such cruel Tortures in coming and going, that he seems determined to venture out no more unless in a Sedan. Mr. Jefferson has been a long time ill and confined, so that I have been much employ'd as a go between Passy and Paris. The doctor has appeared to me a long time to wish to go to England whether to see his Friends or to consult Physicians and be cut for the Stone, I know not. Mr. Jefferson is not so fond of going, and I am much averse to the Plague and Fatigue of the Jour-

ney, if it could be avoided. But we are all willing to go if necessary, and the British Ministry insist upon it. Mr. Hayle the Secretary of the British Legation told me at Versailles frankly that his court would never treat here, and this I believe. But whether they will invite us to London, we must wait to see. They have formally made the Proposition that Congress should send a Minister to St. James's. This Congress will consider. Our affairs suffer for Want of somebody in England, but it will be to no Purpose, to send anyone there to starve and be laughed at, on two thousand a Year" (Adams to Gerry, 12 Dec. 1784; MHi: AMT). In a letter to Thomas Barclay Adams assured him in confidence that, if he went to England, Franklin and TJ would go with him and act "all together upon the business of our commission. But whether we shall go or not is yet problematical and depends upon an answer as yet to be received from the British Ministry" (Adams to Barclay, 8 Jan. 1785; MHi: AMT). As the year wore on, the tedious wait became more irritating to Adams: "Dr. F. is wholly confined," he wrote to Francis Dana, ". . . and can no longer take the Exercise in his Chamber, which he used. Mr. Jefferson is as good a co-adjutor as I could desire. But it grieves me to see that his Time as well as mine, and the Expences of us all, are in a manner lost. I hope our Commissions when they expire will never be renewed. We could not do less at separate courts, and I think we might do more. At least I am sure we could do more good at home. The ministers of all the Courts not in hearty Friendship of France seem afraid of us here" (Adams to Dana, 8 Mch. 1785; MHi: AMT). Jonathan Jackson, who had recently been with Adams in Paris, wrote discouragingly from London that he almost despaired "of any Good arising to our country from the Gentlemen in our Commission coming here at all, such is the strange Blindness and Perversion of all ranks of People in this Country whom I meet or can hear the sentiments of" (Jackson to Adams, 25 Feb. 1785; MHi: AMT).

Jackson may indeed have been asked to sound out British opinion on the subject of a commercial treaty with America, but the most illuminating comment from London at this time came from Charles Storer, who reported to Adams that he had been led into conversation with a Mr. Petree, a member of the British committee of merchants respecting American affairs, and that they had discussed the subject of a commercial treaty. The same evening he called upon Jonathan Jackson and asked if he knew Petree, whereupon Jackson informed him that he himself "had had a Conversation upon the same subject with him, but a few days before, and had given him to understand that the reason of a Treaty Commerce's not being made was owing to a disinclination to treat on the part of the American Commissioners: at least that Government had so given it out to the Merchants here; and that in consequence of this information they wished to know where was the obstacle to a treaty, that, if possible, it might be removed." If Storer knew Jackson's answer to what must have been a feeler put out by government, he did not say, but further reported that Petree had called upon him that very morning (his letter is undated) and "asked me if the American Commissioners were not authorized to make a Treaty with this Country and if so why they did not come over here? I told him that I was not authorised to talk with him upon these matters, and that therefore he must take what came from me, as originating with me: that so far as I knew anything it should be at his service. I

told him then, that you were authorized to treat with this Country, and that I was surprised he should put the question to me since the Ministry had been well acquainted with it ever since last Fall and that, so far from the disinclination to treat being upon your side, I believed it laid entirely here. I told him that *Mr. Hartley* had been recalled just when you were empowered to treat and that you have been since amused with having an invitation from this Court to come here, but that you had never had any. He hoped you would not stand upon any etiquette, and ceremony when the business was so important. I told him I was sure you would never suffer any unnecessary etiquette to be any obstacle to you, nor that you would act either unless upon an equal footing and with proper formality: that, however, I knew of no particular objection you had to treat, except the not having an invitation from this Court. He told me that he had waited upon Ld. Carmarthen, the last week, who told him that the only difficulty rested with you, as he had sent the American Commissioners an invitation about a month ago, thro' the D. of Dorset, which you did not incline to accept of: he wondered that you had not been here before this, and said he really wished you would come. I told him I equally wondered at this intelligence being given by Ld. Carmarthen, since he knew that, if he sent a proper invitation you would come here. I asked Mr. Petree if there was any person to treat with you here, if you came. He said that Ld. Carmarthen he believed was authorized, but asked, in his turn, if Congress had power to treat, was this Court inclined to meet them. I told him that other Treaties have been made, but that this would be known when the full powers of each should be exchanged. Upon parting, Mr. Petree said he was glad to hear that the difficulty did not rest with you and, being convinced of this, the Merchants would immediately remonstrance to the Ministry that a proper invitation should be sent to you, in order that Business should be begun. Mr. P. said the Merchants have been alarmed at the appointment of a Consul General, supposing that some Convention had been made. Upon their application to Ld. C. he told them there was no Convention made, and that why a Consul had been appointed he did not know. The merchants have objected to the man.—It seems the Ministry have industriously given it about that the American Commissioners were averse to treating with this Country, wishing to throw all the blame upon them. Whether from a fear of engaging upon an unpopular business, as they must make some concessions, whether from a wish to profit from the monopoly of our carrying trade to the W. Indies, or whether to give time to strengthen the Adventurers in the Whale-fishery is not for me to say. Perhaps they each have weight with them" (Storer to Adams, undated but written during Mch. 1785; MHi: AMT; Storer directed Adams, for safety and privacy, to enclose his reply under cover addressed to John Appleton, No. 11 Spring Garden, or to John Harwood, No. 18 Cullum Street).

Adams replied on 28 Mch. to the effect that he could not enter upon public affairs with Storer or any other private person; that he was joined in the commission with others; and that he therefore had doubts "both of delicacy and Prudence, if not of right," whether he could "communicate opinions Reasoning or even Facts without their Knowledge and Consent." He declared, nevertheless: "We are to Treat with the British Court, not the Royal Exchange, and whatever veneration I might have for this last assembly, I should be thought a mal-adroit Ambassador, if I might be there quoted for things which had not been represented at St. James's. Besides I should look still more unwise if it should appear that Merchants were employed to pump out of me my sentiments by Ministers behind the scene. . . . You may however affirm roundly and with Perfect Truth, that the Disinclination to treat is not in America nor in the American Ministers. We have full Powers to treat and conclude, which we made known to the British Ministry through Mr. Hartly. Instead of being Authorized to treat with us, he was recalled. We then repeated the Communication through the Duke of Dorsett. We were then answered by a Refusall to treat here and an invitation or rather a Proposition that the United States should send a Minister to St. James's. . . . It can hardly be said that we have waited for an invitation. We have rather invited ourselves. I don't see what more we could have done unless we had all three flown over in an Air Balloon, alighted at Lord Carmarthaens House Pour demander a diner of his lordship" (Adams to

Storer, 28 Mch. 1785; MHi: AMT). Despite this disclaimer, it seems evident that, as the Ministry were obviously employing merchants "to pump out . . . sentiments behind the scenes," so the Commissioners, through Storer, were probably attempting to do the same thing. Adams placed confidence in Storer's steadiness and discretion, and when, a few months later, Storer went to New England, Adams gave him letters of introduction to John Hancock, Samuel Adams, and others introducing him as "a Gentleman who has lived some time in my family at the Hague, in Paris, and in London. He will be able to give you, in conversation, an account of the State of our affairs at this Court and in this Country, in greater detail than it would be convenient for me to write. As he has assisted me in copying so many of my papers, he is in confidence well acquainted with their Contents" (Adams to Hancock and others, 2 Sep. 1785; MHi: AMT).

The point advanced in Dorset's letter is one that the British ministry seized upon in support of its policy directed at retention of control over American commerce and at ultimate repossession of the North American colonies. The deliberateness of the strategy of bringing into public view the lack of any coercive power in the Confederation to compel observance of treaty stipulations by the states is apparent and is indicated in particular by the secret instructions to the Governor-General of Canada to retain possession of the northwestern posts, issued 8 Apr. 1784, "the evening before George III proclaimed the treaty of peace to be in effect and enjoined all his subjects to obey its articles" (S. F. Bemis, *Diplomatic History of the United States*, 3rd edn., N.Y., 1951, p. 71) and by the later refusal to abandon these posts during a period of twelve years on the ground that various states had refused to comply with terms of the treaty. But in employing this device to avoid negotiating a commercial treaty, the ministry may have gained an immediate end while sacrificing an ultimate objective. A few weeks after the Commissioners received the present letter, an able American merchant wrote from London to John Jay, who—perhaps not knowing of the secret order—believed the British retention of the northwest posts was not unjustified in view of the actions of some states in failing to live up to treaty obligations: "Every advance on the part of our Gentlemen to begin a Commercial Treaty has been ineffectual and I understand the last Answer given was that 'They could not see the advantage for Security for entering into a Commercial Treaty with Congress, whilst it's Powers if not disputed, were doubted, and that the measures pursuing by different states for restricting Trade with England might strike at the Root of any Treaty made with the Ministers of Congress. That the States reserved to themselves the seperate powers of restraining Laws and therefore unless they would surrender those Powers to Congress, for the purpose of forming a Commercial Treaty, Ministry here could not see the utility of negotiating upon one, which if carried into Effect in Europe, might be rendered ineffectual in America from the opposition of any one of the States'" (Matthew Ridley to John Jay, 2 May 1785; MHi: Ridley Papers). Again, and more emphatically, Ridley reported: "Not a step taken towards forming a Treaty of Commerce; nor until we place a proper Power somewhere and adopt some legal measures to give weight and Dignity to that Power, do I believe this Government will make the least advance towards it. They I believe on the Contrary wish strength to the Party which is against it. Those who have left America leave no measure unassayed to encrease and rivet the popular prejudices against a Connection with us. The Papers teem with abuse and Tradesmen are spurr'd on by insidious Paragraphs to distress and push every Merchant who has the smallest Connection with America; and from this Conduct I really am afraid of consequences to many" (Ridley to Jay, 5 Sep. 1785; MHi: Ridley Papers). "If," John Adams wrote shortly after going to London, "by giving a proper consistency to our Confederation, you mean the making of Congress Souvereign and Supream in the Negotiation of Treaties of Commerce, and in regulation of the Commerce between one State and another, and indeed in regulating the internal commerce of the states, as far as it is necessarily connected with either, I wish it all imaginable success. . . . I hope that neither the Massachusetts, nor any other state, will stop at a Navigation Act. . . . We must and we will have justice from this Country, proud and cunning as it is" (Adams to Mazzei, 23 Aug. 1785; MHi: AMT).

Ridley was correct in observing that the British ministry wished "strength to the Party . . . against" the lodging of a proper power in the Confederation. But the ministry's exploitation of weakness in the Articles of Confederation helped to build strength. It might not be too much to say that the "linch pin of the Constitution" of 1787, Article vi, is in part at least a monument to the British ministry's use of the fact that the Confederation lacked power to compel recognition of treaties as the law of the land. There were, to be sure, many in England who favored liberal commercial relations with America—the younger Pitt, Fox, Lord Lansdowne, David Hartley, Dr. Richard Price, and others, but they were powerless to oppose the contrary policy. In the last analysis it may not be too much to say that the obstacle faced by the Commissioners was the result of the triumph of one book over another— the ascendancy of Lord Sheffield's *Observations on the Commerce of the American States* (1783) over Adam Smith's *Wealth of Nations* (1776). No one put the fact more succinctly than Edmund Burke: "You, Dr. Smith, from your professor's chair, may send forth theories upon freedom of commerce as if you were lecturing upon pure mathematics; but legislators must proceed by slow degrees, impeded as they are in their course by the friction of interest and the friction of prejudice" (for a general discussion of this subject, see S. F. Bemis, *Jay's Treaty: A Study in Commerce and Diplomacy*, N.Y., 1923, p. 21-33; Gerald S. Graham, *Sea Power and British North America*, Cambridge, Mass., 1941, p. 19-35; see also TJ to Adams, 7 July 1785; TJ to Monroe, 17 June 1785; TJ to Lee, 22 Apr. 1786; TJ to Jay, 23 Apr. 1786; also, various letters written by Lafayette to American friends on the importance of strengthening the union in respect to control over commerce, as cited by Gottschalk, *Lafayette, 1783-89*, p. 157-8). But in this instance there is little evidence that British practitioners of the "art of the possible" did not prefer to use rather than guide interest and prejudice (see Richard Price to TJ, 21 Mch. 1785).

From Abiel Foster

Sir   New York 26th. March 1785.

The Honble: Mr: Cook a Member of Congress from the State of Connecticut, from the good opinion he has concieved of Capt. John Lamb, wishes me to enclose a Letter of recommendation address'd to me by my worthy friend Genl. Parsons, at the time Mr. Lamb produced his other credentials to Congress. The Honble. Mr. Jay has so fully stated the opinion of Congress to the Commissioners respecting those other credentials, that I need say nothing on that head. You have my warmest wishes for the success of your negotiations, and for your personal health and prosperity. I am Sir with sentiments of esteem & respect your most obedient & very humble Servt.,   Abiel Foster

RC (DLC). Enclosure: Samuel Holden Parsons to Foster, 1 Jan. 1785 (RC in DLC, endorsed by TJ: "Lambe John"; printed in Burnett, *Letters of Members*, VIII, no. 83, note 2).

From Anthony Garvey

Sir   Rouen the 26 March 1785

Having received from Mr. Barclay the necessary Cockets for the expedition of your China, I retired same out of the King's Stores, and loaded your three Cases to your Excellency's address on board the Dilligence boat Capt. Edme, conducted by Thiebault who parted from this the 24 Inst. I hope you'll receive same in good order; Mr. Barclay has desired I would pass the expences to his account. I shall at all times be very happy to receive your and Friends Commands here, and to be able to convince you of the great respect and true attachement with which I am Sir Your Excellency's most humble & very obedient Servant,

                              Anthony Garvey

RC (MHi); endorsed.

From Siot de St. Pol

Monsieur   Paris ce 26 mars 1785

Voici L'expedition Du proces verbal de prestation de serment pour L'affaire De M. Guillebaud et Compagnie. Je suis tres flatte que cette circonstance me procure Lhonneur de vous presenter Les sentimens respectueux avec lesquels jai celui D'etre De Votre excellence Votre tres humble et tres obeisst. Serviteur,

G Siot de St Pol
avocat aux Conseils du Roy

RC (DLC); without indication of addressee. Enclosure: Copy of the proceedings of 22 Mch. 1785 at Passy for taking the oaths of Benjamin Franklin, Le Ray de Chaumont, and François

Bouchot verifying a letter dated 1 Mch. 1780 from Samuel Wharton to Guillibaud & Co., attested by Siot de St. Pol and Hussy Delahay, 23 Mch. 1785 (MS in DLC).

American Commissioners to Vergennes

Sir   Passy March 28th. 1785

We have the honour to enclose an extract of a letter from the Commissioners of the United States of America to your Excellency dated Augst. 28. 1778, Copy of Your Excellency's answer dated 27 Septr. 1778. and copy of M. de Sartine's letter to your Excellency of the 21st. of Sept. 1778 all relative to a proposed negotiation with the States of Barbary. Not having any particular authority or instructions from Congress at that time to treat with those States, the Commissioners desisted from any further pursuit of the negotiation until Congress should have opportunity to deliberate and decide upon it. We are now able to inform your Excellency that we have received from the United States in Congress assembled special full Powers to treat with each of the Powers of Barbary, Morocco, Algiers, Tunis, Tripoli and the rest, and we have lately received authentic information that one of those Powers at least, the Emperor of Morocco, has commenced hostilities against the United States by the capture of a vessel belonging to Philadelphia by one of his Frigates, which has spread an alarm among the American Merchants and Mariners, raised the premiums of Insurance, and made it necessary for us to do all in our power to prevent the further progress of the war, as well as to procure the liberation of our Countrymen who are made Prisoners. As it is impossible for us to go to Morocco and we have no power of substitution, we can do no more than write a letter to the Emperor and either invite him to send a Minister or authorize his consul in France to treat with us here, or to carry on the negotiation in writing at this distance through the French Consul at Morocco, or propose to him to wait until we can write to America and Congress can send a consul to the Emperor.

We therefore request the honour of your Excellency's advice

which of these measures is the most eligible, and whether your Excellency or the Minister in whose department it is would do us the favour to transmit a letter from us to the Emperor through the French consul.

Looking over several treaties between Christian powers and the Barbary States, we find that the treaty between the crown of France and Algiers of April 1684[1] is upon the point of expiring; and we are desirous of knowing (if it is not improper that we should enquire) whether this treaty is, or is likely to be renewed; because if there is a probability of a war Congress would probably prefer joining in the war, rather than to treat with Nations who so barbarously and inhumanly commence hostilities against others who have done them no injury.

In order to lay before Congress all the information necessary to enable them to judge what is best for them to do, we have obtained from Holland a certain account of the presents given annually and occasionally by the States General to the Barbary Powers, and have taken measures which promise success for procuring similar intelligence from other Christian States. And if there is no impropriety in the request we should desire to be informed what is the annual amount of the presents given by France to each of those States and in what articles they usually consist.

We have the further honour to propose to your Excellency that His Majesty's good offices and interposition may be employed with the Emperor, in order to provide as fully as possible for the convenience and safety of those inhabitants of the United States, their vessels and effects, who are now or may hereafter be in captivity in Morocco, according to the tenor of the eighth article of the treaty of commerce. With the highest respect We have the honor to be Your Excellency's Most obedient and Most humble servants,

JOHN ADAMS
B. FRANKLIN
T. JEFFERSON

FC (DNA: PCC, No. 116). Tr (DNA: PCC, No. 86); at foot of text is notation: "No.5.e." RC (Arch. Aff. Etr., Paris, Corr.-Pol., E.-U., XXIX, 144-5; Tr in DLC). Copies of enclosures are to be found in same and in DNA: PCC, Nos. 86 and 116; all are printed in English in Wharton, *Dipl. Corr. Am. Rev.*, II, 698, 731-2, 746-7. Preceding the texts of enclosures in PCC, No. 116 is the following comment: "The three following papers alluded to in the be- ginning of the preceding letter, are inserted here, because they serve to shew in one point of view all the transactions respecting the Barbary Powers, and because they were made use of on the present occasion as the basis for recommencing a correspondence on the subject with the Court of Versailles." Copies of covering letter and enclosures were forwarded by Commissioners to Jay in theirs of 13 Apr. 1785. In addition to these three documents sent to

Vergennes, Adams had transmitted several others (listed above in note to Adams to Franklin and TJ, 20 Mch. 1785) when he called in person on the minister; at head of text of the present letter is the following note: "à cette lettre etoient jointes 11. pièces qu'on a cotées depuis 1. jusqu'a 11. compris; on croit les devoir laisser avec la pre-

sente lettre, quoique de dates anterieures" (Arch. Aff. Etr., Paris, Corr. Pol., E.-U., Vol. XXIX, 144; Tr in DLC). These, with the present letter, were sent by Vergennes to De Castries for his opinion; see Vergennes to Commissioners, 28 Apr. 1785.

¹ Tr reads, incorrectly, "1784."

From Geismar

Hanau Ce 28 de Mars 1785.

J'ettais on ne peut pas plus flatte Mon Cher Ami de Votre Souvenir par la Votre dont Vous m'honnorés le 3 du Courrant et que je ne tiens que depuis quelques Jours. Je savois par les Gazettes qu'il y avoit un Ministre des Etats d'Amerique qui portait Votre nom à Paris mais j'ignorais si c'ettait Vous; et j'en fus seulement persuadé il y a quelques Semaines par un Baron de Waltersdorff Gentilhomme Danois, qui a passé à notre Cour venant de St. Croix et s'étant arreté quelque tems à Paris. Il a fait Votre Connoissance chés Msr. Franklin. Et il faut que je l'avoue, j'ettais asses fier de croire, et je ne me Suis point trompé dans mon attente, que Si c'ettait Vous Vous disiés un petit Mot à celui au quel Vous aviés temoigné tant d'Amitie et de bonté pendant Son Sejour en Amérique et qui par consequent devait S'interesser le plus vivement de Vous Savoir raproché de Lui. Soiés le bien venu mon Cher dans notre partie du monde; puissiés Vous y etre parfaitement heureux et Content, plus que ma petite Sante ne me permettait de l'etre dans la votre. J'espere que Vous Vous persuaderes aisement de la part sincere que je prens à la perte que Vous venes de faire. J'ai tout lieu de la croire avoir été mon amie et comme telle je la regrette infiniment; mais Vous gardes absolument le silence sur ma petite femme. Il sera bientot tems que je fasse valloir mes droits. Est-elle avec Vous ou l'avés Vous laissée en Virginie! J'ettais fort etonné de voir que Vous n'aves pas eu de mes nouvelles depuis mon depart de l'amerique, tandis que je Vous adressai une lettre de la Nouvelle York et une autre d'abord aprés mon arrivée ici, la quelle j'ai fait passer en Engleterre, et je Vous croiais trop occupé des Affaires politiques pour que Vous patiés [passiez] du tems avec un de ceux qui Vous onts fait bien du mauvais Sang. J'ose le dire à present que j'etois toujours grand Republicain et sur tout bon Americain quoique dans ma Situation alors je n'osai avouer le dernier. Aussi si jámais la Montgolfiere se perfection au point de pouvoir faire un voiage dans l'autre partie du monde je viendrai y voir mes Amis; et je descendrai à Monti Cello mais pour l'Atlantique je n'en ai rien à faire. Dans notre situation presente nous n'avons besoin ni de l'un ni de l'autre pour nous raprocher. Une Voiture commode et des Chevaux de poste valent mieux que tout cela. Ma bourse mon Cher Ami ne me permet cependant pas dans ce moment de faire un voiage à Paris, et comme vous etes en Europe je suppose que Vous desirerés aussi de voir une partie de l'Allemagne. Venés passer quelque tems ches nous. Nous parcourerons alors la meilleure partie de l'allemagne, et comme je sais que Vous aves de tout tems un tendre pour l'Italie nous ferons un Voiage aussi dans ce pays là le quel je n'ai pas vu encore. Je m'interesse beaucoup mon Cher Ami et je souhaite ardement de Vous revoir pour pu[voir] Vous marquer les Sentiments de reconnaisance des bontes Amicals dont Vous m'aves comblé et qui ne s'affaceronts jamais de mon Coeur. Pardonnes que je Vous addresse celle çi en français, mais je Vous avoue que je ne puis plus écrire l'Anglais. Je le comprens, je le parle encore un peu, mais pour l'ecrire je ne m'en mele plus. Si Vos occupations Vous laissent quelques Moments de Loisir et que Vous voullés les employer à me donner de Vos nouvelles, Vous obligeres infiniment celui qui Vous est attaché pour la Vie.

GEISMAR
Major

RC (DLC). Recorded in SJL as received 24 Apr. 1785.

From William Carmichael

SIR   Madrid 29th. March 1785

I had the honor to receive your Letter of the 30th. Jany. the 14th. of Feby. As it was sent me from the Secretary of States Office I presume it came by a Courier from the Ct. D'Aranda. I am happy it passed thro that channel, as the information it contained must have had a good Effect on the Ministry. I easily saw that it had been read from a conversation which I had with the Ct. de Florida Blanca some time after the receipt of it. That Minister having heretofore entertained some doubts of the permanency of the Union of the Confederation, In the conversation alluded to, gave me the Strongest assurances of his entire disbelief of the reports to the Contrary circulated in the Public Prints; as Similar assertions had been [made] here to People of Distinction and Foreign Ministers I took the Liberty of making Translations in French and Spanish of the material part of your Information as intelligence received from America and showed them in Confidence to those who I knew would make in the same manner a communication to Others. The Ct. de Campomanes whose reputation must have reached you, read publicly at his nightly Assemblies, these Translations. As he is Governor of the Council of Castille, his house is frequented by People of all Ranks. He is and has ever been our zealous Partisan and much my Friend.

I have delayed writing because I wished to give you the information you requested with respect to the naval Strength, resources and cruising grounds of the Barbary States respectively, as also of the presents and Tribute They require to keep the Peace. I had obtained and forwarded to Congress the Letter and paper of which I now send you Copies, and am in daily expectation of receiving similar accounts of the Forces of Morrocco, Tunis, Tripoly and Sallee. I have applied to the Secretaries of Different Embassies here for Copies of the accounts of the presents made by their respective courts to these Pirates and they are examining their archives to Satisfy me. As it is sometimes in my power to give their Ministers information a post or two sooner than they would have it, I put them also under contribution on their part. Those Confidences on subjects not connected immediately with the Interests of one's own Country procure good will and sometimes returns proper to be known. The papers I now have the honor to inclose you, were communicated by a Sea Officer of Distinction in this Service and therefore I could not send them by the Post. They were written by a Spy employed by the Spanish Court, a Holy Father of the Order of redemption of Captives &c. &c.

The 27th Ulto. I wrote to Dr. Franklin who no doubt will have communicated to you the Contents of my Letter. I have since received the inclosed copy of a Note from the Ct. de Florida Blanca which you will be pleased to shew to your Colleagues. By a Letter from Gibraltar dated the 11th. Inst., I am advised that orders had been received at Tanger to give up the Vessel to the Captn. and crew and to furnish him with everything he might Stand in need of. I wish this Intelligence may prove true. At all Events some Steps must be taken immediately to pacify the Emperor and the Other States which seem disposed to fall upon our Commerce. The preparations making in Spain for another Expedition against Algiers, lead me to suppose that their negotiations for Peace are not like to be attended with Success.

The intermarriages take up the Attention of the Court at present. The 27th. The Portuguese Ambassador had his public entry and demanded the Infanta. The Evening of the Same Day She was married by Proxy. I have not leisure at present to give you a description of the Ceremony, of which I was a Spectator, if even I knew that you would think it worth your Attention and therefore I shall wait, until I have the honor to hear from you. The Royal Family goes to Aranjuez tomorrow and I shall follow the 10th. of the Month. This Change of Residence is exceedingly Expensive and Troublesome.

Before I execute the Commission you have given me to purchase you a collection of Spanish Voyages &c. I must previously inform you that Most of the Books you mention are very scarce here and consequently very Dear. I have given a list to Sanchez, a famous Bookseller here, with a request that he would note the prices at which they may be procured. I have engaged Bayer, a great Antiquarian, to write to Valentia and Valladolid to know whether they may not be procured on more reasonable terms in these Cities. He also has promised to Add to the List Such others as may be worth your Attention. I have several of the Most curious in my possession, which are at your service. I shall be happy in the continuance of a Correspondence, which has contributed so much to my information and Pleasure and Shall be proud to be employed in any manner that can give you Satisfaction. With respectfull compliments to Messrs. Franklin and Adams I have the honor to be Sir With great Regard & Esteem Your Obliged & Humble Sert.,

WM. CARMICHAEL

RC (DLC); endorsed. Enclosures (missing): Copies of a letter from "a Spy employed by the Spanish Court, a Holy Father of the Order of redemption of Captives"; an account by the same person of the strength of the Algerian naval force, their cruises, and the prizes taken from 1 Feb. 1777 to 8 Sep. 1784 (see enclosure No. 4 to P. R. Randall to TJ, 14 May 1786); Floridablanca to Carmichael, 16 Mch. 1785; and a "Letter from Gibraltar dated the 11th. inst." The first three of these enclosures were forwarded by Commissioners to John Jay with their letter of 13 Apr. 1785.

Young Abigail Adams, in Paris, saw some of the dresses being prepared for the INFANTA; on 9 Mch. 1785 she recorded in her journal: "We went to see Mademoiselle Bertang, who is milliner to the Queen of France and to all Europe. She is now employed in making clothes for l'infante d'Espagne, and the Princess of Portugal. The former is to be demanded the 28th of the present month. in marriage, by the Prince of Portugal; she is now ten years old; the clothes are very rich and superb; but we did not see the best, as they are sent off as soon as finished. . . . Mademoiselle Bertang has lately received orders for unlimited credit upon the court of Spain, for these things; it is said she will not clear less than five or six thousand guineas. She is the first milliner in Europe; every year she sends the fashions to all parts of the world. We went to a large room, where there were twenty girls at work" (*Journal and Correspondence of Miss Adams,* p. 54-5).

From Jean Holker

Sir   Rouen 29 March 1785

I Received the pleaseur of yours of the 24 past which I only got yesterday, am most Sencibly obliged for the affaire you have don for Mr. Guilboud, and shall think my Self happy If ever I may have it in my power to Render you any servis in theise parts, and beg youl most freely command me.

The Caise must be arrived, and youl soon see If your affects air in it. If not you must let me know by what vessel they was sent by, and I shall then be able to find out the Reason they air not come to hand.

If it can be obtaind to have the french Paquits to saill out of Haver, they must be of more use than they ever can be sailing out of Loreant, and If Our Ministers could persaive the advantage it woud bee to tread, they certinly would not heseit[ate] a Moment.

We have seven vessels that saill from London Regularly to this port, on to haver, and they Never was known to be so long on the Rode as they have been this winter. And when you have anething coming from London let your Corrospondont let you Know, by whom they part, and then Il be answerable youl be satisfyed.

I am Sir with Consideration your Most Obed & very humble St.,
                                                    J. Holker

RC (MHi).

From Patrick Henry

Sir   In Council March 30 1785

You will see by the inclosed Advice of Council the nature of the business which I have committed to Mr. Barclay. I could have wished that the Sum to be laid out had been more adequate to our Want of arms. But the pressure of our Debts and the Circumstances of our Country seem to forbid for the present its encrease. However I am to hope that the great Business of laying up arms and military Stores will be invariably prosecuted, and that every year will afford a respectable sum for this purpose till the great object is fully accomplished.

I beg of you sir to be pleased to afford Mr. Barclay your patronage and assistance in fulfilling his Commission and speedily sending to us the articles wanted. And I have hope that your well known Zeal for the safety of our Commonwealth will be my excuse for giving you this trouble.

If I could lay before the assembly favorable proposals for furnishing the residue of the arms and Stores we want, perhaps it would induce them to make an exertion to find the requisite sum of money to complete or nearly accomplish this great work. For this end I have desired Mr. Barclay to look out for such proposals and write me. I am Sir, P. H.

FC (Vi). Recorded in SJL as received 14 June 1785. Enclosure: Advice of Council of 10 Mch. 1785 directing the Governor to authorize Barclay to lay out £10,000 currency in the purchase of "ten tons of Musket powder, two hundred thousand Gun flints, and one hundred ream of Musket cartridge paper," together with so many stand of arms as the remainder would purchase; and advising him to write "to the Marquis Fayette and Mr. Jefferson requesting the interposition of their influence and attention" (MS Va. Council Jour., Vi). Henry wrote Lafayette the same day (Executive Letter Book, Vi).

To William Short

TH: J TO W. S.   Apr. 2. 1785.

I inclose you a letter from l'Orient. When are we to see you? Your letters leave us in doubt whether you mean to protract this odious term of the 4th. of April, or to return to your quarters then and be content to go on with your French at leisure. I am in hopes this will be your choice. You lost much by not attending the Te-deum at Notre dame yesterday. It bids defiance to description. I will only observe to you in general that there were more judges, ecclesiastics and Grands seigneurs present, than Genl. Washington had of simple souldiers in his army, when he took the Hessians at Trenton, beat the British at Princeton, and hemmed up the British army at Brunswick a whole winter. Come home like a good boy and you will always be in the way of these wonders. Adieu

RC (ViW); unsigned; endorsed: "Jeffn. Paris Ap. 2—85 recd. at St. Germain." Enclosure not identified.

TJ was even more impressed by the size of the crowds along the streets than by the numbers of notables in the Cathedral of Notre Dame. Young Abigail Adams recorded in her journal for 1 Apr. 1785: "I believe I may say with truth there were millions of people. Mr. Jefferson, who rode from the Marquis' with us, supposed there were as many people in the streets as there were in the State of Massachusetts, or any other of the States. Every house was full—every window and door, from the bottom to the top" (*Journal and Correspondence of Miss Adams*, p. 66). See also C. F. Adams, ed., *Memoirs of John Quincy Adams*, I, 16-19. The TE-DEUM, of course, was in honor of the birth of the Duke of Normandy.

From William Carmichael

Sir   Madrid 4th. April 1785

On the 29th. Ulto. I had the honor to address you by an expeditious conveyance. Since which I have received the Inclosed paper which may throw some light on the Nature of the presents made to the cheifs of the Piratical States. You will please to observe that as these People are not delicate in their choice the Articles mentioned in the List are generally remnants of unsaleable effects. I expect to receive shortly lists of the Last presents made by Denmark and Sweden to the different Barbary States, which I shall not fail to send to you. By a Letter which I received the 1st. inst. from Doctr. Franklin I find that the Affair of Morrocco had ingaged the Attention of the Commissioners. I shall be happy to know their Sentiments and to follow their Instructions in the correspondence which I entertain with the People About the Emperor. I expect daily answers to Letters which I wrote some time Ago. Not having received any Instruction on this point or indeed on almost any other from Congress since I have had the honor to serve the State here, I have acted to the best of my Judgement for their Interests. In the case of Morrocco I have written nothing that can compromise their Dignity. At the Same time I flatter Myself that I have contributed to a cessation of Hostilities on the part of that Prince. The Expedition proceeded by Spain against the Algereens and the Armaments of the Venetians against Tunis may in some Measure put a Stop to the Depredations of these Pirates during the course of this year and afford an opportunity to Congress to take such measures as they may find Convenient. I know that the Algeriens meant to fall upon our comm[erce] Because some time ago, They captured two English Vessels on a supposition That they were American. These have been released. I have reason to beleive that they have been excited to commit hostilities. I was informed and informed Congress that Curtis the English Agent at Morocco did all in his power to render us bad offices there. The Consuls from Other Nations are instructed not to meddle in the Disputes which may happen between these Pirates and another Country without particular orders from their Respective Courts. This I know to be the case with respect to those of two Nations and am told that the Others are in the same predicament. The intermarriages seem to ingross the Attention of the Public at Present. The Ct. de Campomanes told the King in an harangue which he made his Majesty as

Governor Iterino of the Council of Castille, that he had been destined by Providence to shut for ever the Gates of the Temple of Janus on the Peninsula. Where will England find a port so convenient as Lisbon, or even France, should no regard be paid hereafter to the Family Compact, find a shelter for its fleet on this extended Coast? With respectfull compliments to Mr. Adams I have the honor to be with great Respect & Regard Sir Your Most Obedt. Hble. Sert.,   WM. CARMICHAEL

RC (DLC). Recorded in SJL as received 16 Apr. 1785. Enclosure: A list of presents made to the Dey of Algiers and members of his court (MS in DNA: RG 59; undated; in French; endorsed by TJ: "inclosed in a letter from Mr. Carmichael to T.J. dated Madrid Apr. 4. 1785").

From James Monroe

New York, 6 Apr. 1785. Introducing John Cooper of North Carolina, who intends establishing himself in commerce in London or at the Hague. He was introduced to Monroe by "the gentleman of the No. Carolina delegation and Mr. Hardy as a person of note and probity in his line."

RC (DLC); 2 p.; endorsed. Entered in SJL as received 23 Sep. 1785, "by W. Short." Enclosed in John Cooper to TJ, 2 Aug. 1785, q.v.

Lafayette to the American Commissioners

GENTLEMEN   Paris April the 8th. 1785

In Consequence of Your desire, I Have Endeavoured to Collect informations Relative to the presents which the African powers Usually Receive from European Nations.

By the inclosed Summary, You will get Every intelligences I Could obtain of what Has been done by Holland, Sweden, danemark, Venise, Spain, Portugal, and England. The Returns Nos. 2, 5, 9, 10, 11, 12, 13, are Minuted Accounts of the presents which at Several Periods Have been delivered By those Powers.

As to france, it Has Been More difficult for me to know their Exact Situation. Their Way of transacting Business with the Africans is peculiar to them, and it is a principle with Governement Not to divulge it. I know we are not like the other powers obliged to pay Certain tributes. Our presents are Volontary, with Respect to the time, as well as to the Value, and france is upon a much more decent footing with those pirats than Any other Nation.

It Has Been Avoided to give presents upon fixed Occasions, Like a change of princes. The King of Morocco's Envoys Have not Been Considered as Ambassadors, one excepted who Came to present a Number of french men taken in foreign Vessels Whom that King Had purchased from the Captors. Upon the King's Coronation, He was Complimented By tunis and tripoly. But the permission, I am told, was not Granted Upon the dolphin's Birth.

It is However Costumary that Every french Consul, when first introduced, Makes a present in His own Name. The Last one at Alger, in the Return No. 1 costs 20,000 French livres. Those to tunis and tripoly are much inferior.

In the last treaty of peace with tunis, the present No. 3 was Sent By the late king of france. It did Cost about 50,000 livres, Besides which the french Merchants made a present of about 12,000 livres. The tunisian Ambassador who Came for the king's Coronation Received the present No. 4 which Costs 68,840 livres.

Upon the occasion of the last peace with Morocco, the present to the Emperor was worth 163,708 livres, and to His officers 74,250 livres as appears By the Return No. 6. The Ambassador from that Country, in the Circumstance I Have Mentionned, in the Year 1778, was Complimented with the Articles of the Return No. 8, to the Amount of 129,063 livres.

The Return No. 14th. Contains the present to the Pachà of tripoly, By the Envoy He was permitted to Send for the king's Coronation. It is Worth 34,341 livres.

It is also Costumary to pay the Expenses of those Envoys on the Road, and to Send them Back to their Country in a ship of War.

Such are, Gentlemen, the Intelligences I Could Collect. I am to Apologize for the delay. But Considering the Variety of Articles, and the Reserve of Governement Upon this point, My Exertions Required some time Before I Could gather all the interesting particulars.

With the Highest Respect I Have the Honour to be Your Excellencies's Most obedient Humble Servant,   LAFAYETTE

RC (DNA: PCC, No. 98); at head of text in TJ's hand: "No. 4.a." Enclosures: (1) Summary report, dated Mch. 1785, of the nature and value of presents given to the Barbary powers by Denmark, England, Holland, Portugal, Spain, Sweden, and Venice for protection of their commerce (MS in DNA: PCC, No. 98, in French, in an unidentified hand, and at head of text are the notations in TJ's hand "No. 4.b." and in Lafayette's hand: "This is the footing upon which several European powers now stand with the african princes"; also in PCC, No. 98, is an English translation of the report by John Pintard). (2) Lists of presents given on various occasions to the courts of Algiers, Morocco, Tripoli, and Tunis by Denmark, England, France, Holland, and Sweden; the lists are numbered at head of text from 1 through

14, but these figures were later altered by TJ to read "4.c." and so on through "4.q.," omitting the designation "4.j." (originals and translations are in PCC, No. 98). The covering letter and all of its enclosures were forwarded by Commissioners to Jay in theirs of 13 Apr. 1785. See following document.

Notes on Presents made by Foreign Powers to Algiers

France	Livres	
Algiers. Every French Consul at Algiers. His present on reception	20,027 =	834 Louis
Tunis, on treaty of peace, the king	80,000	
mercht.	12,000	
To the Ambassador	38,840	
	———	
	130,840 =	5451 Louis
Morocco, on treaty of peace,		
to Emperor	163,708	
to his officers	74,250	
to the ambassador	129,063	
	———	
	367,021 =	15,292 Louis
Tripoli, on their kings coronation	34,431[1]=	1430 Louis
England, present in 1774	350,000 =	14,583 Louis
Denmark, with Algiers the peace in 1773	1,000,000 =	41,666 L.
Venice, to Algiers in 1779	187,000 =	7,731 L.
1783	220,000 =	9,166 L.
Sweden to Morocco pays annually	100,000 =	4,166 L.
in 1775 it gave	367,500 =	15,312 L.
Portugal to Morocco on peace of 1773	148,000 =	6,166 L.

MS (DLC); entirely in TJ's hand; undated, but after receipt of the preceding letter from Lafayette. The enclosures that Lafayette had forwarded included lists and descriptions of such gifts as gold and silver, jewels, textiles, furniture, carriages, food, arms, naval stores, &c., and TJ in the present document attempted to summarize values in monetary terms, though clearly some figures (those for France) were exact while others were general estimates; also the gifts from various countries did not cover a uniform period of time.

[1] MS reads "34,341," but TJ erred in transcribing the figure.

To Thomas Barclay, John Bondfield, and James Carmichael

[*Paris, 10 Apr. 1785*. Joint entry in SJL under this date reads: "Mr. Carmichael at Havre. Mr. Barclay. l'Orient and Nantes. Mr. Bonfield. Bourdeaux. Whether any vessels going to Virga. before middle of May or when? To Mr. Barcl. I acknoleged receipt of China. Whether a gentleman with valet could get passage." None of these has been found.]

From the Rev. James Madison

DEAR SIR   Williamsburg April 10th 1785.

Mr. Mazzei affords me an opportunity of expressing the real obligation I feel myself under for the Letter and Packet you were so kind as to favour me with by Col. Le Maire. Nothing can be more desireable to us here than such literary Communications. It is certainly of great Importance to us to know what is done in the Philosophical World; but our Means of Information are confined almost entirely to you. This Circumstance not only increases our Gratitude for every Communication you have been so kind as to make but it will also, I hope, operate as an additional Inducement to continue the good Work you have so generously begun.

The Marq. Le Fayette in his Journey thro' this Town had raised amongst us the highest Anxiety to know the real discoveries made in Animal Magnetism. But the Pamphlet you favoured us with, has effectually quieted our Concern upon that Score. The Matches were the first seen here, and are indeed extremely curious. As soon as I received your Letter I exhibited the Experiment of raising Water by a Rope. The Simplicity of the Method is certainly a great Recommendation. You have probably seen also the new Method of raising Water by Steam of which we have had a very imperfect Account. If that Account however be true, it is probable the Method by Steam will receive a general Use.

The Discovery of the Abbè Rochon in Optics affords altogether a new Feild for Speculation in that Science. It is an Effect which I beleive no Optician before, conceived could be produced by one Lens. If he can apply it to the Purpose you mention it will be a happy Means of solving a Problem which puzzled Euler himself.

Sorry am I that we have no Discoveries to boast of in the American World. The celebrated Boat which received the fullest

Approbation of Gen. W[ashington] and other Gentlemen who saw the Experiment, is not yet exposed to the public Eye. I confess I am still among the No. of the Infidels. The Means by which it is to oppose the Force of the Current downwards depend upon a Support which goes from the Bottom of the Boat and rests upon that of the River. This is all that I have yet heard of it. You will judge better than I can of its Efficacy.

We were engaged last Year in determining the 5 Degrees of Longitude claimed by Pennsa. And I believe few Points on the Globe are better ascertained. Our Instruments were good, the Time peice I carried from this Place exceeded even Mr. Rittenhouses. Our Observations were continued for more than three months. I had some Thoughts at first of sending you the Observations, as they tend not only to establish the Point in Dispute between the two States, but also the Measurement of a greater, or longer Line upon the Globe than has ever yet been effected, and thus shew with more Certainty the real Length of a Degree of Long. in that Lat. It appears to be less than has been hitherto supposed. The Termination of the 5⁰s falls short of the Ohio about 15 or 16 Miles.

We had entrusted a Merchant here to import for us the new Edition of the Encyclopa.; but, since your kind offer, shall endeavour to transfer the Sum paid Viz. £50 stg. to your Hands; and when it shall arrive there, will then beg the Assistance you have offered.

We have received a Present of some valuable Books from the King of France. Among others Buffon in Quo. complete. But unfortunately many of them were ruined before they came to us. We did not however beg for more. But There is one Thing for which I will beg, and that is a Continuance of your Favours whenever sufficient Leisure from more important Concerns will permit. In this I am a sincere Beggar, as well as your other Friends here, whom you mentioned, and by whom I am desired to return their most affectionate wishes for your Happiness.

I am Dr. Sir with the most sincere Respect & Esteem, Yr. Servt. & Friend, J. MADISON

Please to present my best Compliments to Mr. Short.
Since writing what precedes, your Nephew Mr. Peter Carr arrived here. He has entered with Mr. Maury who proposes to give him every Instruction in his Power untill he has arrived at his 16th. Year, agreably to Col. Madison's Advice. Should he then enter the University, my assistance as far as it can extend, shall

not be wanting; on the contrary, I will be happy in rendering him every possible Service in the Prosecution of his Studies. He has been unfortunate hitherto in the Loss of too much Time by Sickness, but he is now perfectly recovered and appears resolved to avail himself of the present Opportunity. His object is at present Latin, Greek, French, Italian.

As I doubt not but you meet with many new and valuable Publications, Should esteem it a particular Favour to be informed of such as you think most worthy of Importation, either in the Philosophical, Historical or Critical Line.

Permit me to add one P.S. more. Has the Abbé Rochon published any Thing upon his new Discovery in optics? How is the Effect produced? What is the specific Gravity of the Chrystal? In what way does it differ from other Rock Chrystals?

RC (DLC); endorsed. Recorded in SJL as received 22 July 1785, "by Mazzei."

On 1 Jan. 1785 Madison wrote to Vergennes thanking him for SOME VALUABLE BOOKS FROM THE KING OF FRANCE: "America can never forget the Hand, which so greatly assisted her in the Acquisition of Liberty and Independence, nor the generous Regard, which would render that Liberty and that Independence the more valuable and permanent, by diffusing amongst her Sons those Rays of Science without which all her other Acquisitions would be vain" ("Signed in behalf of the University"; Arch. Aff. Etr., Paris, Corr. Pol., E.-U., Vol. XXIX, 4-5).

From James Monroe

DEAR SIR   New York April 12th 1785

Since my last I have received yours of the 11th. of Novr. and 10th. of Decr., the former by Col. LeMaire, from whom however I did not receive it altho' I saw him, nor untill after his arrival nearly a month and then I believe by post from Phila. I have had the same difficulty with the cypher but from a different cause. The copy of that I sent by Mr. Short I left in Virga. when I sate out for the westward and have not since been able to command it, but shall most probably by the next post, so that whether you send me one or not our embarrassment will in future be at an end. That you may read my first letter I send you the cypher by which it was wrote. Fully impress'd with the disadvantages which must always arise to the States from a free intercourse with Canada I propos'd an instruction founded on the principles which my letter contains, to the ministers authoriz'd to form the treaty with GB: the committee have reported in favor of it, but the delicacy of our situation with that court, upon *that* of the posts and other subjects, is a consideration which inclines me to decline for the present bringing it to the view of Congress. The restrictions on this intercourse can only be carried into effect by possession of the posts and the more disadvantageous to them their surrender will be, the longer they may delay it.

I enclose you the report of a committee in favor of a change of the first paragraph of the 9th. of the articles of confederation for the purpose of investing Congress with almost the entire regulation of the commerce of the Union, in exclusion of the particular States. I am inclin'd to think it will be best also to postpone this for the present. Its adoption must depend on the several Legislatures and to carry it with them the preferable way perhaps may be to let it stand as it now is. It hath been brought so far without a prejudice against it. If carried farther here prejudices will take place, at least I fear so, and those who oppose it here will in their States. The way then will be to present it to them in its present state, which may be effected by obtaining the permission of Congress for each delegation to take copies for that purpose. If this should be its course I shall have time for your answer and opinion on it. A committee is appointed to revise and report what alterations if any are necessary in the instructions to the commissioners authoriz'd to form commercial treaties. What will be the result I know not, but the object of the appointment was, to change the principle upon which those existing were form'd. To instruct them to make the best bargain they can with each power, such an one as the advantages which they respectively derive from a commercial intercourse with us, intitle us to expect. If the convenience and advantage of the trade of either of these powers with us is equal, the condition upon which it is conducted for commercial and other national purposes, should be equal also. The object is to connect us [with] each power independently of other powers, and to extricate us from the complicated system with which their connections with each other is involv'd—a system which they well understand, have been long accustom'd to the exercise of, and to turn to their particular advantages by every possible means of fraud and chicane. I doubt much the advantage of forming treaties for the present with any of the powers with whom you are authoriz'd to treat (the piratical States excepted) for what advantages can we give here in consideration of advantages there, or rather in consideration that they remove some of the restraints which now exist, which they do not at present possess, or possessing that we can deprive them of. The more I investigate this subject the more I am confirm'd in this opinion. But all these embarrassments in the restrictions laid upon us by other powers, will I am persuaded have a good effect. They will operate more powerfully than the utmost force of argument could do for the strength'ning our government.

From Spain we expect a Mr. Gardoqui in quality of chargé des affaires. All our measures with that court have of course ceasd untill his arrival which is weekly expected. Whatever we have to transact with the Court of G. B. is committed to Mr. Adams, the formation of a commercial treaty only excepted. Upon his removal from the Hague it was resolv'd to appoint a minister in his room: Mr. Rutledge and Mr. R. H. Harrison, C. Justice of Maryld. are in nomination as is likewise Govr. Livingston of Jersey. It is not known whether either will serve. My first letter will advise you of our embarrassment respecting a particular affair upon which you wrote me as you left Phila., an attention to which falls now within your province. It is unfortunate upon this account your cypher would not expose it to you. You will please write me as soon as possible upon this subject. You will receive instructions respecting the piratical states of Barbary. I fear from the information you give me they will not obtain fully the objects which they have in view. From what I have been able to collect here a treaty commencd on our own ground independent of any European power, will be most successful, since I am told they disregard the most powerful among them as much as they do us, and in that instance we might plead ignorance of the presents or amount which would be acceptable to them. It is agreed to raise 700. men for the purposes of guarding the publick stores and giving security to the frontier settlements of the States. At Annapolis Mr. Gerry protested against the right of Congress to *require* men in time of peace; his conduct was approv'd by his State and the delegation instructed to oppose and protest upon all occasions against the exercise of the power. It is agreed that by requisition men cannot be rais'd upon a few States or less than the whole but under particular circumstances of some, and then under a particular modification. It was thought in this instance necessary to have them in the feild, in a short time, to protect the surveyors of the land and as this consideration superseded the propriety of a requisition on the whole it was agreed to recommend it to the States, most contiguous, to raise them.

The land office is not yet open'd. A report drawn principally by Colo. Grayson will be deliver'd in in a few days. It deviates I believe essentially from the one at Annapolis, but in what points I cannot say as I have not compar'd them together. The object of this is to have the lands survey'd previous to the sale, and after the survey to have the lots drawn for in the right of the States and sold in each by the Loan officer at publick vendue for specie or certificates. I shall transmit you the journals of Congress as far as they are printed. They will give you at least the resolutions which determine the erection of buildings at the falls of the Delaware and our intermediate residence here. Our dependence for their erection at Georgetown had been on the southern States and as soon as Congress conven'd we found they had given it up. All further opposition we therefore considerd as useless. One hundred thousand dolrs. are appropriated to it. Between Phila. and this place we were indifferent as a temporary residence; we consider'd our State as no otherwise interested than as it might respect the delegates attending in Congress; upon fœderal principles that this should have the preference. It must have a good appearance for the fœderal government to pay attention to the part which hath suffer'd most, from the depredations of the war; add to this the province of Canada in possession at present of the fur-trade. The first exertion of the States must be to draw it thence and afterwards it may take its direction thro' the Potowmk. or whatever channel is open'd to it. But the 100,000 dolrs are upon no fund. Whether they are to be requir'd from the States or not will become the question. It would be fortunate if a delay could take place. The conduct of our delegation at Trenton was founded upon an acquiessence with the voice of the majority of the Union. We acted together and voted unanimously upon every point respecting these measures. Grayson only was absent. Be the event of this town as it may I think the proportion which will fall to our State will be well dispos'd of if [it] annexes the Idea of stability to our councils and measures. I could wish no more movments untill we take our final position.

I send you this by Colo. Smith, Secry. to the legation for London. Mr. Trumbull only was his competitor. He was formerly an aid de camp to Genl. Washington. He is desirous of being known to you and as I hear from every person who knows him a fair and respectable character, I take the liberty to present these circumstances in his favor to your knowledge.

Be assurd I shall pay particular attention to that circumstance which is more personally interesting to yourself mention'd in your first letter. What can or will be done is incertain but satisfied of the justice of the measure, I shall with the utmost pleasure seek the attainment of it in a manner which will be most delicate and honorable to you. Indeed I think that our ministers should have at least 5. or 600. £ stirl. more annually. I thank you for subscribing for me for the Encyclopedia. I have not at present the money but will send it as soon as possible. I sincerly wish it were in my power to join you this summer but it is impossible. The next I have it in contemplation and shall then be under no necessity to hurry myself so quickly back, and I could wish to remain in Europe if I ever visit at least 12. months. Colo. Smith hath my instructions not to send this by post but some safe hand provided he doth not deliver it himself. Whether Congress will or not adjourn during the summer is incertain. I think they should not, but the fact is our application to business hath been so close during the winter that we wish a relaxation. I think Congress should sit untill our affairs with every foreign power were finally and most amicably settld, and untill the commerce of the Union was properly regulated. The Confedracy might then stand secure and not be expos'd to injury or danger. Mr. Butler, Walcot and A. Lee were on the Indian treaty at fort Stanwix; the State of N. York also held a treaty. They quarrell'd with the commissioners of N. York and disgusted the State. This is attributed to one of those gentlemen only. Mr. Mercer hath been absent since we left Trenton and hath married Miss Sprigg. Mr. Read hath been less active than at Annapolis. He is said to be engag'd to K. Vanhorne of this place. He left this for So. Carolina 2. months since, it is said to prepare matters for this event. A Mr. Carbonneau from the Kaskaskias petition'd Congress to take the people under their protection; a committee hath reported which is so far adopted that a commissioner be appointed to repair thither instructed &c. Mr. A. Lee is in nomination. The three commissioners of the treasury elected at Annapolis declin'd serving, in consequence of which Gervais Osgood and a Walter Livingston were elected. Gervais hath declin'd and Mr. A. Lee who hath upon every occasion been a candidate is again in nomination. Mercer and himself were in nomination at Trenton and we gave the former the preference. The fact is we can get none better than Mr. A. L. and shall upon this occasion vote for him.

Your letters still contain doubts of the event of the interfering claims between the Emperor and the Netherlands. Mr. V. Berkel hath presented a full and able statment of those of the U. Nets. and of the progress of either party to the commenc'ment of the winter

in support of their pretensions. A war between them cannot be injurious to us; provided our merchants have enterprise. As we stand on neutral ground, they may turn it to theirs and the general advantage. Believe me to be dear Sir your affectionate friend & servant,
JAS. MONROE

P.S. The alteration which this report proposes in the whole system of our government will be great. It is in fact a radical change of it. [I] beg of you to write your sentiments fully on it. If it is carried it can only be by thorough investigation and a conviction carried to the minds of every citizen that it is right. The slower it moves on therefore in my opinion the better.

RC (DLC). Entered in sjl as received 14 June 1785. Enclosures: (1) Code No. 5. (2) Copy of report of a committee of Congress of 28 Mch. 1785 recommending that Article ix of the Articles of Confederation be amended so as to give Congress "the sole and exclusive right and power . . . of regulating the trade of the States, as well with foreign Nations, as with each other" (DNA: PCC, No. 24; printed in JCC, XXVIII, 201-205).

It was Monroe's own motion that a committee be appointed TO REVISE AND REPORT WHAT ALTERATIONS IF ANY ARE NECESSARY IN THE INSTRUCTIONS TO THE COMMISSIONERS (4 Apr. 1785, JCC, XXVIII, 229). The report was submitted 2 June 1785; see Monroe to TJ, 16 June and 15 Aug. 1785; TJ to Gerry and TJ to Jay, 11 Oct. 1785.

American Commissioners to John Jay

SIR Paris April 13. 1785.

Our letter to you the 18th. day of March with those preceding that period which had been addressed to the President of Congress have conveyed exact details of our transactions till that time. Since the making out of that dispatch the following proceedings have taken place.

The letter No. 1 from Mr. Carmichael to Dr. Franklin dated Feby. 27. 1784 (instead of 1785) will apprize you that there is a prospect of Mr. Hartwell's regaining his liberty and property tho' not without some delay, and probably some loss.

The same letter will inform you of Mr. Carmichael's proceedings in the case of the brig Betsey taken by the Emperor of Morocco, and the papers which accompanied that letter and which we have marked No. 1. a., b., c., d., e., f., g., will shew the progress in that business to the 15th. of Janry. last; and a subsequent communication from Mr. Carmichael marked No. 2. being a letter from the Ct. de Florida Blanca to him dated March 16th. 1785 will shew its situation at that time.

With this last Mr. Carmichael also sent us the papers No. 3. a. and b. the first being a letter from a spy employed by the Spanish court, a holy father of the order of the redemption of captives; and the second a state made out by the same person of the naval force of the Algerines from Feby. 1. 1777 to Septr. 8. 1783.[1], the revolutions it underwent during that period, the number of cruizes they made, prizes they took, and the nations from whom taken. While these give a smaller idea than had been entertained of this the most formidable of the Pyratical states, the following papers marked No. 4. a. b. c. d. e. f. g. h. i. k. l. m. n. o. p. q. will shew that the price of their peace is higher than the information heretofore communicated, had given us reason to expect. The paper No. 4. a. is a letter from the M. de la Fayette to whose means of access to the depositories of this species of information, and his zeal for the service of the United States we are indebted for the intelligence it contained, as well as for the report No. 4. b. and the details No. 4. c. d. e. f. g. h. i. k. l. m. n. o. p. q. From these it will appear that Powers which, like France and England, can combine the terror of a great naval force with the persuasive of pecuniary tribute, yet give as far as 15,000 guineas to Morocco which holds but the second rank amongst these states. This information is still very incomplete, giving only a view of detached parts of the transactions between the European and African Powers: it will contribute however with what we have formerly laid before Congress, to enable them to form some estimate of what will be required of a people possessing so weak a navy and so rich a commerce as we do. These rovers will calculate the worth of the prizes they may expect to take from us in the Mediterranean and in the Atlantic; and making some allowance for the expence and losses they will incur in these enterprizes, they will adjust their demand by the result regarding little the representations which we may make of our poverty. They count highly too among the motives which will induce us to give a good price the horrors we feel on the idea of our countrymen being reduced to slavery by them. Some of the European merchants and perhaps consuls resident with them will probably not be backward in supplying their want of knowledge as to the extent and nature of our commerce and the degree of protection we are able to afford it.

We have been many days in expectation of the arrival of the French Packet which should have sailed from New York the middle of Feby. Having been informed that as early as Decr. Congress had referred sundry foreign affairs to the consideration of a Committee, and that the Packet arrived at N. York Jany. 17 which conveyed our letter of Novr. with a detail of the situation in which their business was on this side the Atlantic, we hope that the Packet sailing a month afterwards and now expected here will bring us further instructions. In the mean time the situation of our trade rendered it necessary to admit as little delay as possible with the Barbary Powers. We therefore thought it best to put that business in train. For this purpose we resumed a correspondence which had formerly taken place between the American Commissioners and this court, copies of which are herewith given in the papers marked No. 5. a. b. and c. The want of money and the want of powers had discontinued this correspondence. We thought it a proper ground however whereon to found applications to this court for their aid in the treaties which may now be proposed. Mr. Adams accordingly waited on the Count de Vergennes with copies of that correspondence (his colleagues being prevented by indisposition from accompanying him on that occasion). No. 5. d. is his report of what passed, and No. 5. e. a copy of the letter we addressed to the Count de Vergennes according to his desire. To this we have received no answer. We propose to make no actual overtures to the Barbary states till the arrival of the packet now expected, which we suppose will convey us the ultimate will of Congress on this subject.

A similar expectation of new information and instructions from Congress as to our affairs with the British court suspends till the arrival of this packet our taking any measures in consequence of the inclosed letter No. 6. from the Duke of Dorset, the British Ambassador at this court. That their definitive answer must be required to the Articles in our instructions distinct from the treaty of commerce admits of no question: but as to the doubts they pretend and the information they ask with respect to the powers of Congress we do not decide what we shall say or do till we see whether we receive by this conveyance any new instructions. With the highest esteem & regard We have the honor to be Sir Your most obedient & Most humble Servants,   JOHN ADAMS

B. FRANKLIN

TH: JEFFERSON

RC (DNA: PCC, No. 86); in Humphreys' hand, signed by Adams, Franklin, and TJ. Tr (DNA: PCC, No. 116); also in Humphreys' hand; at head of letter: "5th. Report to Congress addressed to Mr. Jay Secry. for foreign Affairs"; Tr varies slightly in phraseology from RC. Enclosures: No. 1:

William Carmichael to Benjamin Franklin, 27 Feb. 1784 [i.e., 1785] (Tr in
DNA: PCC, No. 116; text printed in
Dipl. Corr., *1783-1789*, I, 564-6 and
III, 285-7, under date of "1784"). Nos.
1a-1g: Enclosures to Carmichael's letter to Franklin cited above (these have
not been found, but a notation in Humphreys' hand appended to the covering
letter reads: "N.B. The letters respecting the capture of an American vessel
by a Corsair of Morocco &c. are deposited in the files which comprehend
all the papers relative to the Barbary
powers where are also to be found the
papers referred to under the Nos. 2. 3.
and 4. in the letter addressed April 13.

1785 to Mr. Jay."). Nos. 2, 3a, and
3b: The first three items described as
enclosures to the letter from Carmichael to TJ of 29 Mch. 1785. Nos. 4c-4q:
Lafayette to Commissioners, 8 Apr.
1785, and its fifteen enclosures. Nos.
5a-5c: Letters described as enclosures
to the Commissioners to Vergennes of
28 Mch. 1785. No. 5d: John Adams to
Franklin and TJ, 20 Mch. 1785. No.
5e: Commissioners to Vergennes, 28
Mch. 1785. No. 6: Dorset to Commissioners, 26 Mch. 1785.

¹ Correct date is "1784" (see the
second enclosure described in note to
Carmichael to TJ, 29 Mch. 1785).

To Alexander Moore

[*Paris, 14 Apr. 1785.* Entry in SJL reads: "Alexr. Moore. Answer
to his letter of Mar. 10." Not found.]

William Carmichael to Benjamin Franklin

DEAR SIR   Madrid 15th. April 1785

Since I had the honor to write you on the 4th. Instant I have
received from the Ct. de Rechteren the inclosed copy of a letter
from the Dutch consul in Marocco which I forward for the information of the commissioners. I am also advised by Mr. Harrison that
the Spanish Consul to the Emperor, but now at Cadiz preparing
Presents for that Prince, informed him that he was instructed by
the Ct. de Florida Blanca to make on his Return to Barbary, the
most pressing efforts for the Release of the vessel and People, and
that he flattered himself he shoud succeed.

The Court of Spain is about to send an ambassador to the
Emperor of Morrocco, to conclude as it is Said a Treaty with that
Prince, by which he engages to join this Country against the
algerines. A Nephew of the Ct. de F. B. is destined to this Employment. A Letter which I received from Malaga this day contains
information on this Subject for which Reason I send you a Copy
of it.

It is Said that Lerena Minister of Finance and War department,
declares that he is not able for the Latter and that it Will consequently be given to the Ct. de Fernand Nunez, ambassador at

[83]

present in Portugal. It appears that this court had no Thoughts of Sending one to England.

In Consequence of your advice I have drawn on M. Grand for 5193 Ls. 17s. in favor of Messrs. Drouilhet on account of Salary and for 2075 Ls. 17s. to discharge a ballance due them on the Public account. I inclose the account of these Gentlemen. I have been addressed by Mr. Harrison for money to relieve the distress of the americans in Marrocco, But I cannot take upon me to make any advance on this account without having the approbation of the Commissioners. I think it hard that Mr. Harrison should be constrained to make these disbursements from his private fortune. The Infanta or rather the Princess of Brasils sets out for Portugal the 27th. of this month. The portuguese ambassador has already expended 550000 Ls. Ts. to celebrate this marriage. The actions of the national Bank of St. Charles Sell at 25 pr. Ct. profit. This rapid augmentation arises from manoeuvres, which will make many dupes in france, where the Establishment is puffed by persons interested, in this kind of agiotage. The cedula for the Philippine Company is in the Press. When Public, I will forward a copy by the first courier extraordinary from hence. Should you have in your Possession Colonel Humphreys' Poem or any other american Publications not too Bulky you would oblige me very much by Sending them under cover to the chevalier de otamende, under secretary in the Department for Foreign affairs.

The Ct. D'aranda will readily Send them by one of Mr. del Campas Couriers which pass thro Paris regularly once a Month. With proper compliments to Messrs. Adams and Jefferson and my name Sake I have the honor to be with great Respect & affection, Your Excellency's Most obedient, & most humble Servt.,

W. CARMICHAEL

Tr (DNA: PCC, No. 86); printed in *Dipl. Corr., 1783-1789*, III, 297-8 as to an unidentified person. RC, however, is in PPAP; it was addressed to Franklin but, in event of his absence, was directed to be opened by TJ or Adams (Carmichael to TJ, 19 Apr. 1785). Both in substance and in the manner of address, therefore, it is to be regarded as a letter to the Commissioners. Enclosures: (1) Webster Blount to ———, 4 Mch. 1785 (Tr in DNA: PCC, No. 88); at top of last page is notation in TJ's hand: "No.1.b."; another Tr is in PCC, No. 86, with accompanying English translation by John Pintard. (2) ——— to Carmichael, 8 Apr. 1785 (not found). Both are identified by the entry under 18 July 1785 in the Journal of the Office of Foreign Affairs (DNA: PCC, No. 127) covering Commissioners' letter to Jay of 11 May 1785, with which the present letter and its enclosures were forwarded as enclosures.

From David Hartley

I am infinitely obliged to you for the favour of your letter which contains most interesting information to me who wish to maintain such friendly and candid correspondencies upon American matters for prospects of future times. At present by the public appearance of things the considerations of American matters do not seem to proceed. At least for my part I am not informed or instructed by administration upon any such points. I presume that they will be revived in time, and therefore in the interim I wish to encourage quiescent and conciliatory sentiments between our two Countries. And particularly in my own line of employment, I wish to keep up the chain of information and friendly correspondence as I presume that the consideration of American intercourse must certainly be resumed at some future period. I beg of you to receive my sincerest thanks for all your candid and intelligent communications to me when at Paris, as likewise by letter and I hope you will do me the favour to continue them.

I beg leave to state to you a case of a young gentleman, the Son of a very worthy friend of mine who died a few weeks ago viz. the case of Mr. Francis Upton son of Clotworthy Upton Esqr. (afterwards and at his Death Lord Templeton). I would beg the favour of your advice and assistance if in your power. The case is this. In the year 1764 Clotworthy Upton Esqr. (afterward created Lord Templeton) with the Earl of Ilchester and Lord Holland obtained the King's order in council for a grant of 20,000 acres of land each in the province of New York. About the year 1769 Mr. Upton for the better location of his 20,000 acres joined Colonel Staats Morris, John Butler Esqr. and others in the purchase of a grant from the proprietors of the Country of Aquago Indians of 80,000 acres upon the Sesquehanna and Tiendersah rivers for which a consideration of 2000 Dollars was paid on the 9th. of febry. 1769. Mr. Upton had 20,000 acres of this land located to him accordingly on the Tiendersah river near its confluence with the Sesquehanna as may be seen by the Record of the grants of the Province, upon which Land he expended several sums of money and by Deed of the 3d. of April 1769 conveyed the same in trust for the use of Francis Upton, Clotworthy Upton the younger and Sophia Upton and their heirs for ever. Mr. Francis Upton therefore being just arrived at age is desirous of claiming the said 20000 acres of land in behalf of himself, his Brother and Sister; and hopes that as two of them are still minors and he came of age himself but on the 25 of Febry. 1785 (which prevented their applying to the legislature of New York before) the same may be restored to them, it being their principal dependence. I should be much obliged to you for your opinion and advice upon this case. I hope this will find you in good health and Miss Jefferson the same. Pray Remember me to all friends at Passy and Auteuil and to Mr. Humphries. Pray favour me with any American information, particularly any that may respect Great Britain. I have stated all my Sentiments to the British Ministry previous to the meeting of Parliament in January. You may be assured that every Sentiment of mine ever has and ever will be directed towards the cultivation of amity between Great Britain and the United States of America. I am Dear Sir with great & sincere esteem Ever yours,   D HARTLEY

RC (DLC); addressed: "A Monsieur Monsieur Jefferson Ministre Plenipotentiaire des Etats unis Americains A Paris," with a forwarding address in another hand: "Cul de Sac—Taitbout—sur le Boulevart"; endorsed. Recorded in SJL as received 7 May 1785.

From John Jay

DEAR SIR   Office for foreign Affairs 15th. April 1785

Mr. Randall who sailed in the last french Packet was charged with Dispatches for you, and our other Ministers. Among them were your Commission &ca. to succeed Doctr. Franklin at the Court of Versailles.

The probability of your now being in England renders it less necessary and perhaps expedient, that I should not go into minute Details especially as this Letter would in that Case doubtless pass to you through the british Post Office.

I enclose a "State of the Duties payable by Vessels of the United States in the Ports of Marseilles, Bayonne, L'Orient and Dunkirk." You may find it useful on several Occasions.

Two of the Commissioners lately appointed for the Treasury, Vizt. Mr. Osgood, and Mr. Walter Livingston, have accepted and proceeded to Business. The third Vizt. Mr. Gervais of South Carolina, having declined, another will soon be elected to supply his Place, so that we may hope soon to see the Affairs of that Department again arranged and regulated.

Abigail Adams, portrait by Ralph Earl. (See p. xxvii.)

Draft for the first payment on Houdon's statue
of George Washington. (See p. xxvii.)

Receipt for premium for insurance on Houdon's life during
the time he was in America. (See p. xxvii.)

The making adequate Provision for our Debts, and other Exigencies of Government, has been too long delayed and still meets with Obstacles. An Opinion of the Necessity of it however gains ground, and I flatter myself will eventually become general and operative. I have the Honor to be &ca.,   JOHN JAY

FC (DNA: PCC, No. 121); at head of text: "To the Honorable Thomas Jefferson Esquire—Minister Plenipotentiary of the United States at the Court of France." Recorded in SJL as received 27 July 1785. Enclosure: Printed broadside dated 14 Mch. 1785 entitled "State of the Duties Payable by Vessels of the United States of America, In the Ports of Marseilles, Bayonne, L'Orient, and Dunkirk" (JCC, XXIX, 917, No. 457).

From James Milligan

Treasury of the United States
SIR   Comptroller's Office April 15th. 1785

By a Certificate dated at Passy the 8th. of August 1784 and signed by Doctor Franklin, copy of which I do myself the honor of enclosing, it appears that the Treasury Certificates therein mentioned, of monies due by the United States to General du Portail, General Laumoy and Colo. Gouvion, were at their request lodged in the office of His Excellency, in order to remain there or in the office of the Consul, until Certificates of another form for the whole Sum due to each of the Gentlemen should be transmitted to France for them. In compliance with their request, a new Settlement of their claims has been effected. And as I am uncertain whether Doctor Franklin may be in France when this reaches it, I take the liberty of enclosing to your Excellency the New Certificates for their respective balances, which after adding the Interest that had become due up to the first of January 1784, and deducting the Monies paid here to Colo. Ternant on their respective Accounts, the Certificates are as follows. No. 92 in favor of Major General du Portail for Fifteen thousand Nine hundred and sixty seven $\frac{15}{90}$ Dollars. No. 93 in favor of Brigadier General Laumoy for Ten thousand two hundred and eighty three $\frac{33}{90}$ths. Dollars. And No. 94 in favor of Colo. Gouvion for Seven thousand Nine hundred and Ninety four $\frac{84}{90}$ Dollars, all bearing Interest from the first day of January 1784. I have to request Sir, that you will be pleased to deliver them to the Gentlemen in whose favor they are, And that you will as soon as may be, procure and transmit the old ones that were lodged with Doctor Franklin, to the Treasury here, in order that they may be by me Cancelled. I have the honor to be with Sentiments of great respect Sir Your Most Obt. Hume. Servant,

JAS. MILLIGAN
Comptr. of the Treasy.

RC (ViWC); endorsed. Recorded in SJL as received 10 June 1785. Enclosures: (1) Benjamin Franklin's receipt dated 8 Aug. 1784 for U.S. Treasury certificates to du Portail, Gouvion, and Laumoy (MS in ViWC in the hand of William Temple Franklin, signed by Benjamin Franklin, and endorsed by TJ as follows: "Copy of Dr. Franklin's receipt for certificates. These were de-livered to me, and by me inclosed to Jas. Millegan [by Mr. Otto] and instead thereof I gave to the parties those I had received from Millegan viz Duportail 15967 15/90 D. Gouvion 7994 84/90 D Laumoy 10283 33/90 D dated Nov. 16 1784"; also Tr in ViWC). (2) Treasury certificates Nos. 92, 93, and 94 dated 16 Nov. 1784.

To James Monroe

DEAR SIR   Paris Apr. 15. 1785.

We wrote a public letter to Mr. Jay the day before yesterday. We were induced to hasten it, because young Mr. Chaumont was to set out yesterday for l'Orient to go to N. York in the packet, and a private conveyance is alone to be depended on for secrecy. I have put off writing any letters as long as I could, expecting the arrival of the packet. She is arrived, as the packet of the last month did without bringing a scrip of a pen public or private to any American here. This perplexes us extremely. From your letter of Dec. 14. and from one written at the same time by Mr. Jay to Dr. Franklin we have reason to beleive *Congress*[1] *have done something* in the *affairs* with *England and Spain*. We also thought something would be said to *us* on the *subject* of the *Barbary States*. *We* therefore deferred *moving* lest *we* should *have* to *change our move* which is always *dishonourable*. *We* particularly *expected instructions* as to the *posts still held* by the *English*. *We* shall do the *best we can* under *our old instructions*. The letter from *the Duke of Dorset* will I dare say *surprise you all*. It is a folly above the highest that could have been expected. *I know* from *one* who saw *his instructions* that *he softened* them *much* in the *letter to us*. The following paragraph is from a letter *I recieved from Doctor Price* about *ten days ago*. 'There is, I fancy, *no probability* that *Britain can be brought* to *consent* to that *reciprocity* in *trade* which the *United States expect*. This is *sad policy* for *Britain but* it may *turn out* to be best *for America* and should the issue be *our exclusion* from the *American ports we* may be *ruined* but I do not see *that America* would *suffer* in it's true *interest*. The fixed conviction however is that *we are able to supply America* on so much *better terms than any other country that* do *what we* will *we* must have *its trade.*' It is *dated March twenty first. He* is said to be in great *intimacy with Mr. Pitt* and I verily beleive *this paragraph contains* the *genuine creed* of the *nation and ministry*. You will observe that the 4th. article of our original draught of a treaty transmitted to *the several courts was contrary to a right reserved by the states* in the *confederation. We shall correct* it in every *instance*. War and peace still doubtful. It rather seems that the peace may continue a while yet. But not very long. The Emperor has a head too combustible to be quiet. He is an eccentric character. All enterprize, without calculation, without principle, without feelings. Ambitious in the extreme, but too unsteady to surmount difficulties. He has had in view at one time to open the Scheld, to get Maestricht from the Dutch, to take a large district from the Turks, to exchange some of his Austrian dominions for Bavaria, to create a ninth electorate, to make his nephew king of the Romans, and to change totally the constitution of Hungary. Any one of these was as much as a wise prince would have undertaken at any one time. Quod vult, valde vult, sed non diu vult.

I send you Voltaire's legacy to the K. of Prussia, a libel which will do much more injury to Voltaire than to the king. Many of the traits in the character of the latter to which the former gives a turn satyrical and malicious, are real virtues. I should remind you that two packets have now come without bringing me a letter from you, and should scold you soundly, but that I consider it as certain evidence of your being sick. If this be so, you know you have my sincere prayers for better health. But why has no body else written to me? Is it that one is forgotten as soon as their back is turned? I have a better opinion of men. It must be either that they think that the details known to themselves are known to every body and so come to us thro' a thousand channels, or that we should set no value on them. Nothing can be more erroneous than both those opinions. We value those details, little and great, public and private, in proportion to our distance from our own country: and so far are they from getting to us through a thousand channels, that we hear no more of them or of our country here than if we were among the dead. I have never received a tittle from any [mem]ber of Congress but yourself and one letter from Dr. Williamson. The D. de Rochefoucault is kind enough to communicate to us the intelligence which he receives from Mr. St. John, and the M. de la F. what he gets from his correspondents. These have been our only sources of intelligence since the middle of December.

There are particular public papers here which collect and publish with a good deal of accuracy the facts connected with political arithmetic. In one of these I have just read the following table of the proportion between the value of gold and silver in several countries.

Germany 1. to $14\frac{11}{71}$
England 1. to $15\frac{1}{2}$
Russia 1. to 15

Spain 1. to $14\frac{3}{10}$
France 1. to $14\frac{42}{100}$
Holland 1. to $14\frac{3}{4}$
Savoy 1. to $14\frac{3}{5}$

The average is 1. to $14\frac{5}{8}$. As Congress were on this subject when I left them and I have not heard of their having finished it, I thought this worth your notice.

Since the warm weather has set in I am almost perfectly reestablished. I am able now to walk six or eight miles a day which I do very regularly. This must supply the place of the journey I had meditated into the South of France. Tho' our business does not afford constant occupation, it is of such a nature one does not know when our presence may be wanted. I need add no signature but wishing you every happiness bid you Adieu.

RC (DLC: Monroe Papers); unsigned; partly in code. Entry in SJL has in margin "Chaumont" and reads: "Jas. Monroe. Paragraph from Dr. P's letter—shall correct 4th. article in our draught in every instance—probably peace yet a while but not long. Emperor cannot be quiet—send Volt.'s life of K. of P. Will injure writer most—complaint that nobody writes to me. Our only intelligence since middle of Dec. thro D. de Rochef. and M. de la F.—proportion between Gold and Silver in these countries averages 1:14⅝ from

Gazette de France, 15. Avr. 1785. My health reinstated almost." Enclosure: Probably Voltaire's *Das Privatleben des Königs von Preussen*, 1784.

The ONE WHO SAW HIS INSTRUCTIONS may have been Dr. Edward Bancroft; see TJ to Jean Holker, 17 Apr. 1785.

[1] This and subsequent words in italics were written in code and have been decoded by the editors, employing Code No. 5.

To the Governor of Virginia

SIR   Paris, April 15th 1785.

I had the honor of informing your excellency in my letter of Feb. 3[1] that I had received and presented Mr. Alexander's bill on Laval & Wilfelsheim; that they had refused to pay it; that I had had it protested, but on their saying they would then accept, I had sent it to them again, but received no answer, when I was obliged to send off my letter. They returned it to me accepted, paiable in London, a trick by which you would have lost about eight per cent., the exchange between this place and London being now, and having been a long time, that much to the disadvantage of this country. They had written this so illegibly, and so hid the words "à Londres" in a corner of the note that it escaped me, as it did even Mr. Grand, through whom the note was returned to me; and this was never discovered till the day came when they should have paid it. They then insisted the demand should be made in London. After a course of chicanery, the detail of which would be tedious and only shew their rascality, they have agreed to pay in Paris the 19th instant. I sent to them yesterday to inform them I was to write this day on the subject of the bill, and to know whether I might rely that there would be no further difficulties. They said I might; yet, have they so totally destroyed my confidence in them that I am far from being satisfied on this subject. I had not meant to have required actual payment till Mons. Houdon should be setting out to America; but as I find them to be men who might fail me in the instant when it should be wanted, I shall draw the money out of their hands as soon as I can and lodge it with Mr. Grand. I must at the same time inform you that nothing more is settled yet with Mons. Houdon. He was taken ill immediately after the writing my letter to your Excellency, and has been a considerable part of the time in a situation quite despaired of. He is now out of danger, but not well enough to think of business. The picture of Genl. Washington is come safely to hand. I have the honour to be with due respect, Your Excellency's most obt. and most humble servt.,

THOS. JEFFERSON

MS not found; text from CVSP, IV, 24 (RC was sold by Parke-Bernet Galleries 1 Nov. 1940, item 669); printed also in Henry, *Henry*, III, 291-2, with two minor variations from the present text. In margin of SJL, opposite entry under this date, TJ wrote "Chaumont," by whom the letter was carried to America; entry in SJL reads: "Govr. of Virga. Laval & Wilfelsheim's chicanery. Promise paiment the 19th.—will place it in Grand's hands. Houdon's illness prevented further arrangements."

When TJ SENT TO THEM YESTERDAY, he probably wrote; if so, the letter has not been found.

[1] Thus in both printed texts. This is certainly an erroneous reading for 9 Feb., the date of the letter referred to here; TJ's 9's are easily mistaken for 3's.

From James Carmichael

Havre 16 April 1785

Your much Esteem'd favour of 10th. Curt. came duly to hand; an Absence of 2 days at Honfleur occasionned my delay in replying by Return of Poste.

We have at present no Ship bound to Virginia in the Port, but most likely in next month, there may be; two are allready Sail'd in last Month. As soon as one offers I shall take pleasure in informing you thereof, and be happy to be usefull to you, or any friend you may recommend. There's little doubt, but what between this and the End of May an occasion will offer here for your friend to proceed to Virginia.

As You have not given me your Directions I adress the present to You at the incomparable Doctor Franklin's in order to ensure it's coming to hand.

I remain very respectfully Your most humble & obedt. Servt.,

Js. CARMICHAEL

RC (DLC); endorsed.

From the Abbés Arnoux and Chalut

17. Apr. [1785]. Accept dinner invitation for Tuesday, 19 Apr.

RC (MHi); 2 p.; in French; addressed: "A Monsieur Monsieur Jefferson ministre plenipotentiaire des Etatsunis d'Amerique Dans son Hotel."

The two Abbés' names are often misspelled, particularly that of Abbé Arnoux, whose name is also frequently confused with that of the Abbé François Arnaud (1721-1784). They lived on the heights of Passy not far from Franklin, and also had a house in the city. "Whether they were spies of the court, or not, I know not," wrote John Adams, "but I should have no objection to such spies, for they were always my friends, always instructive and agreeable in conversation. They were upon so good terms, however, with the courtiers, that if they had seen anything in my conduct, or heard anything in my conversation that was dangerous or very exceptional, I doubt not they would have thought it their duty to give information of it. They were totally destitute of the English language; but by one means or another they found a way of making me understand them, and sometimes by calling an interpreter, and sometimes by gibbering something like French, I made them understand me" (quoted by Marie Kimball, *Jefferson: the Scene of Europe*, p. 98). Abigail Adams described the Abbé Chalut as being seventy-five years of age, and "Arnoux about fifty, a fine sprightly man, who takes great pleasure in obliging his friends" (C. F. Adams, ed., *Letters of Mrs. Adams*, Boston, 1841, I, 47). Young Abigail thought Arnoux older but no less agreeable: "The Abbé Arno, though 60 years old, is a man of much vivacity and wit, with always a great deal of pleasantry. The Abbé de Mably, who is always of our parties there, and dines with us with the other two, although he does not live with them; he is eighty years old, a man of great learning" (*Journal and Correspondence of Miss Adams*, p. 37-8). See TJ to Abigail Adams, 7 July 1785.

To William Carmichael

[*Paris, 17 Apr. 1785*. Entry in sᴊʟ reads: "Mr. Carmichael. Acknolege receipt of his of Mar. 29. and Apr. 4. Papers relative to Algrs. sent to Congress—books. Send me note of what will cost, except those which are at common prices and which may be bought—account of Virga. act for surrendering citizens committing offences in other countries. Made principally to restrain our people as to Span. settlements. Interest of both parties to keep peace, and is the wish of our government. Spn. no object in war, because we have nothing but territory which they cannot take. Their trade and their territory tempting to our people but not to our government. Wish they would authorize Ct. D'Aranda to enter into conferences so as to settle arrangement. We should then find no difficulty in going to Madr. to put last hand to it. [Sent this letter thro' Mr. Grand]." Not found.]

To Jean Holker

[*Paris, 17 Apr. 1785*. Entry in sᴊʟ reads: "Mr. Holker. Rouen. That my Copying press was shipped. Sep. 24. 1784. on board the Rotham Capt. Brookes at London, bound to Rouen addressed to me in Paris, to his care in Rouen. Acknoleged receipt of his of Mar. 29." Not found. The information in this letter was based on one from John Page of London to Dr. Edward Bancroft, dated at Leadenhall Street, 28 Feb. 1785 (MHi), reading as follows: "Mr. Jefferson's Machine was shipt on board the Rotham, Capt. Brookes for Rouen. A Receipt was given for the Case and Mr. Franklyn took it when he paid the Account. It was shipt at the time the Bill of Parcels was dated [*in TJ's hand at foot of text, marked by an asterisk*: i.e., Sep. 24. 1784], and directed to the Care of Mr. Holker." This letter seems to establish Bancroft's presence in France about the middle of April, and, since he was a British secret service agent who occasionally supplied information to Franklin, it may have been he who was the source of TJ's remark about the instructions to Dorset (TJ to Monroe, 15 Apr. 1785). See also S. F. Bemis, "British Secret Service and the French-American Alliance," *Am. Hist. Rev.*, xxix (1924), 474-95.]

From John Bondfield

Sɪʀ   Bordeaux, 19th. April 1785

I have to acknowledge the honor of your favors of 19th. Decr. and 10 Instt. I deferd replying sooner to your favor of the 19 Decr. hoping a change of weather would have admitted my forwarding the wine you Commissiond. Within this four Days the weather

[93]

is become moderate. I have in consequence forward[ed] to you four Cases containing thirty six Bottles each of our first Growth per the messagerie. I have also shipt on board the Brig fanny Capt. Smith, who will sail the 23 Inst. for Falmouth in Virginia recomended to the particular care of a Young Man who goes passenger in the said Brig to be forwarded to Mr. Eppes at his arrival four Cases of the said wine. I shall write Mr. Eppes by the said conveyance and inclose him a Bill of Loading for the same. Inclosed you have the Invoice for the said eight Cases for which I shall draw on you at my convenience.

I am much obliged to you for your information regarding Land Warrants. I propose to let mine lay dormant til occasion serves either to sell or Improve.

There are two Vessels bound to Virginia that will sail in this week. We have not any other at present loading for the American States. It is probable some will offer in the month of May. If any I shall advise you.

The merchants at this and the other Sea Ports have used their utmost exertions to obtain the repeal of the Arret de Conceil that admits foreign Nations to resort to the french Islands under limitted restrictions. The minister to this has appear[ed] deaf to the representations and it is generally thought will support the Arret as favoring the plantations become to[o] Powerful to be longer retaind under Prohibitive restrictions. The last Cargoe arrived of Tobacco from Virginia sold at 15 livres. It is a good Price and will support the Cost and charges. With respect I have the Honor to be Sir Your most Obed Hum Ser,

JOHN BONDFIELD

RC (DLC). Recorded in SJL as received 24 Apr. 1785. Enclosure missing, but in MHi there is a printed form from Bondfield & Gireaudeau to R. Durand & Cie., directing them to receive, "A la garde de Dieu et conduite de Revore de Blois," each of the four cases containing 36 bottles of wine, to be delivered to TJ within 24 days. This form contains on its face the marks given on the cases, the rate of transportation (to be paid by TJ to the carrier), and TJ's former address as "Hotel d'Orlean, rue des Augustins." On its verso is recorded the total of costs involved in the shipment, which tallies with TJ's statement in Account Book under 13 May 1785: "portage and duties on wine Bourdeaux 90—1 —3." Documents supporting these charges are also in MHi: (1) Receipt for payment of customs at Monlieu, 22 Apr. (2) Same for Ruffec, 26 Apr., endorsed by TJ on verso: "Bonfeild. 12. doz. bott. wine recd. May 8. 1785." (3) A receipt for charges paid a "Notaire Royal" at Angerville-la-Gaste, covering the entire shipment in the conveyance, including "quatre caisses pour Mr. Javerson," 7 May. (4) Receipt to TJ for duties paid, 10 May.

This sheaf of documents, representing as it did something unknown in the American colonial experience under the mercantile system and only lately cropping up in the form of retaliatory imposts among some of the states, must have impressed TJ at this particular moment when he was engaged in promoting the idea that nations were "wealthy and populous nearly in proportion to the freedom of their commerce; and . . . were it perfectly free, they would probably attain the highest points of wealth and population of which their circumstances would admit" (Commissioners to De Thulemeier, 14 Mch. 1785). An otherwise trivial shipment of wine became a matter of significance in the larger diplomatic task and in a comparative view of the French and American states when it was observed that internal duties accounted for almost as much of the total as actual transportation expenses did (the costs for the "voiture" and "Comission" amounted to only 48l. 12s. of the total of 90l. 1s. 3d.). This was an experience new to an American but long suffered by the French, and represented, as TJ must have later observed, one of the striking differences between the roots of revolution in the two nations. It is in light of such a personal experience as this mere shipment of wine, too, that one must view TJ's reply to James Monroe's letter of 12 Apr. 1785 in which he was as pleased as Monroe was fearful of the proposal to vest in Congress control over trade between the states—an opinion quite different from that he had expressed several years earlier (TJ to Monroe, 17 June 1785; TJ to John Adams, 17 Dec. 1777).

The BILL OF LOADING [*sic*] that Bondfield promised to send to Eppes also came to rest in TJ's papers (MHi) and is dated 25 Apr. 1785.

From William Carmichael

SIR   Aranjuez 19th. April 1785

Since I had the honor to address you, I received further Intelligence with respect to the Disposition of the Emperor of Marrocco. I inclosed a copy of the Letter communicated to me, the 15th. Inst. in one to his Excy. Benjamin Franklin which in case of his Absence, I directed to be opened by yourself or Mr. Adams. I have also received an accurate account of the Maritime Force of the Above mentioned Prince which I have not time to copy to send by this opportunity. In consequence of what Dr. Franklin wrote me the 22d. Ulto. I was in hopes to have received 'ere this the Joint Sentiments of the Commissioners on the Subject of our Difference with the Barbary States. I repeat *now* what I mentioned in my Letter of the 15th. Inst., my reliance in the good Offices of this Court; at the Same time I beg leave to recommend the Speedy adoption of measures, that at least may prevent Hostilities, until Congress may take such, as they may judge proper. My Situation here has become so very disagreable from the total Silence of my Constituents and other circumstances which for many years have been detrimental to my Little affairs, that unless things take a different turn, I shall be uneasy until I leave Europe forever. The Infant Dn. Gabriel espoused on the 12 Inst. by Proxy the Infanta of Portugal. This Court has ordered a Gala of three days with Illuminations to celebrate these Nuptials. I have not yet been able to procure an account of the Price of the Books you wished me to procure you. They are in general scarce, and you will be surprized at the price demanded for such as I have been able to discover. With the Proper Compliments to Messrs. Franklin & Adams I have the Honor to be with great Regard Your Most Obedt. Humble Sert.,   WM. CARMICHAEL

RC (DLC). Recorded in SJL as received 27 Apr. 1785.

From Peter Carr

HONOUR'D SIR   Williamsburg. April. 20th., 1785

I am very sorry to tell you I have lost a great deal of time since you left Virginia. It has been sometimes for the want of horses and sometimes for the want of money, so that I have made but little progress. I am at this time reading Horace and Homer, and Mr. Maury, with whom I have been about a week, thinks I may go to the University about this time, twelvemonth, if I will exert myself, and be assured Dr Sir, that I shall not loose a moment more than I can help, and shall try if I cant by the closest application make up the time I have lost. I have just began french and arithmetic with a Frenchman, whom I attend two or three times a week, and who is esteemed very clever. The good advice contained in the letter I received from you at Burling[ton] [I] still continue to observe [with the] greatest strictness. Polly [was we]ll when I heard from her last, and reads very prettily. Mama and the family were very well when I heard from them last. Mr. Madison has put Dabney with Mr. Smith at the Academy in Prince Edward. My love to Patsy. Adieu Dr Uncle and believe me to be your affectionate Nephew,   PETER CARR

RC (ViU); endorsed by TJ: "Carr Peter." The MS is mutilated at bottom of leaf; two remaining fragments provide a continuation of the text except for four or five words which have been supplied conjecturally. Recorded in SJL as received 22 July 1785, "by Mazzei."

Peter's account is to be compared with those given by Madison and Maury (Madison to TJ, 10 Apr. 1785; Maury to TJ, 20 Apr. 1785); the loss of time that Madison attributed merely to sickness and Maury vaguely described as having been caused by "several circumstances," Peter accounted for as the result of "want of horses and . . . want of money." The GOOD ADVICE CONTAINED IN THE LETTER may have been TJ's letter of 11 Dec. 1783.

From Madame de Doradour

ce mercredie; 20 avril [1785]

Mde. Doradour a l'honneur de souhaitter le bonjour à Monsieur jeffersson, de lui envoyer quelques refflections, quelles le suplie de garder dans sa poche et pour lui seul. Elle aurra l'honneur d'aller demain Matin lui demander son avis sur les questions quelle faits. Celles que Monsieur jeffersson trouverras d'absurdes Mde. Doradour le suplie de se ressouvenir quelles sont d'une femme et d'une femme françoise qui desire acquerir des qualites au desseu de celles que l'on accorde à sa nation, mais qui n'a pour elle jusquà present que le desir, et qui sens vivement l'interet dont Monsieur jeffersson l'honnore. Elle le suplie d'en agreer l'hommage de sa reconnoissance.

L'avantage que Mr. et Mde.[1] trouveront à vivre auprès de Mr. jeffersson, de profiter de sa compagnie, et [d]e suivrent ses conseilles les dessideront absollument pour la virginie, et surtout pour le cantons où habitent Mr. jeffersson, à moins que le Climat ne sy opposas. Mde.[1] desireres une habitation sur une côte; [el]le est accoutumée ainsi que ses enfants à un air très pur et elle ne se pardonneres pas de leurs faire changer de demeure [si] elle croyes que cela pus nuire à leurs santees.

[El]le est fort de l'avis de Mr. jefferson que Mr. Doradour [fa]sse pour son premier etablissement une acquisition tres [me]diocre où il y eut cependant de toute les choses necessair [à] la vie, et à portee de cette ettablissment, de quoi en faire [un] considerable. En cas que le local convint et que Mr.[1] se decidat à vendre en france pour placer en amerique, [il] emporte avec lui 15000[tt] milles franc de france. Mde.[1] pourra lui en envoyer encore 15000[tt] pourveu quelle soit avertie [s]ix mois d'avance, parce qu'il faut quelle aye le tems de faire [r]entrer ses fonts. Elle pourra même aller jusqua 20000[tt] sans [ri]en vendre, mais elle sen rapportera absollument sur cela [au]x conseils que Mr. jeffersson lui donnera, parceque Mr.[1] ne connoissant pas le pays pourres sy tromper. [Ma]is Md. espere que Mr. jeffersson voudra bien mettre [au]pprès de son ami en virginie asses d'interest pour qu'il [re]garde le nouveaux emigran comme un membre de la famille [de] Mr. jeffersson; Mr. et Md.[1] en ont les sentiments.

Mr.[2] s'en rapporteras absollument à Mr. Lewis et ne ferras rien sans son avis. Il prononceras avec plaisir le serment de fidelitee à l'Etat et jure d'avance de le tenir.

Mde. suplie Mr. jeffersson de voulloir bien aussi prier son ami de veiller à l'acquisition des neigres que Mr.[1] cera obbligée de faire, tant pour la force que pour la fidelitee.

Sy Mr. Lewis juge que Mr.[1] doit faire une acquisition et qu'il n'aye pas asses d'argeant, parcequ'il faudras qu'il en garde pour vivre, pour achetter des neigres, et faire travailler, [et] comme il est etrangers, lui vendra t'on une partie[2] a credit? Quelle interest payera t'il? De quelle maniere lui ferra t'on passer de l'argeant de france?

Il partira avec un domestique. Il voudres se mettre en pention[2] jusqua l'arrivée de Md., pour ne pas tenir de maison, n'emportant avec lui que les choses necessair pour son usage personnelle. Il est inutille sy il ne sy accoutumee pas de faire une trop grande depence. L'on[2] a dit à Mde. qu'il y avés une tres grandes diference dans les fortunes et que cela en faises pour l'agrément de la vie. Elle demande avec confiance à Mr. jeffersson sy cela pourres occasionner du desagrement à Mre. qui, accoutumée à vivre avec tout le monde, ne veut pas de distinction, mais qui seres fachée d'être humillié.

Mde. desire que Mr. parte par le pacbogue [paquebot], parce quelle espere que ces Messieurs qui s'embarque avec lui voudrons bien lui accorder leurs amitie et quelle sera bien plus tranq[uille]. L'idée de la mer l'effraye pour son mari, quelle voie partir sans elle avec regret. C'est une peur de femme, mais il faut passer quelques choses à la foiblesse de leurs sexes. Mr. debarqueres à New yorck et della [de là] ires par terre à la[2] Virginie.

Quoique Mde. soit effrayée de la mer pour Mr., elle ne pence pas de même sur tout. Elle connois la necessitee d'une bonne education, et se ferra gloir que son fils soit ellevée par des hommes sages. Elle n'a d'autres desirs que de le voir dignne des bontes de ces Messieurs, et que l'on veuille bien l'admettre au nombre des habitants de la nouvelle angleterre quelle respecte. C'est un sentiment quelle inspirera à ses enfants.

Dans l'habitation que Mr. achetteras, trouvera t'il une petite maison et les autres batiments necessair pour[2] l'agriculture? Parce que M[de.] desireres qu'il ne fit pas batir avant son arrivée.

RC (DLC); unsigned and without indication of the year; endorsed.

[1] At this point Madame de Doradour first wrote "Doradour" and then deleted it.

[2] An asterisk, probably inserted by TJ, is at this point in MS. This may have been a mark by TJ to indicate points he wished to take up in one of his letters of introduction (see under 11 May 1785).

From Francis Hopkinson

DEAR SIR   Philada. 20th. April 1785

Your Favour of the 13. Jany. last did not get to hand before the 16. Instt. I am much obliged to you for the philosophical Intelligence you gave me which I have communicated to Mr. Rittenhouse.

He is determined to watch carefully the appearances of the Star Eta of Antinous. I have written two or three Letters to you which I hope will get to hand. In one of them I enclosed a model of my further Improvement in the Manner of quilling a Harpsichord which I believe effectually completes that Business. It answers to Admiration in my Harpsichord which has been freely used since last Fall and not one Quill has failed, the Instrument remaining in perfect Touch, which is certainly a very great Acquisition.

I observe well what you say respecting your great Deficiency of American Intelligence and will chearfully supply you with two of our best Papers. I went however this Morning to Mr. Marbois and mentioned the Matter to him, and he tells me you are not aware of the monstrous Expence of Postage which he thinks you cannot get rid of for a Constancy and to such an Amount. I must think further on this Subject, or perhaps wait till I hear from you again, before I fully comply with your Orders. In the mean Time however I shall order two weekly Papers to be sent to me and shall keep them for you. We know little more of Congress here than you do in France—perhaps not so much. They are seldom or ever mentioned in the Papers and are less talked of than if they were in the West Indies Islands. They are settled at New York and according to Report are as little satisfied with their Situation there as they were in this City. They have resolved to build a fœderal City for themselves on the Banks of the Delaware either near or opposite to Trenton. Mr. Rt. Morris, Genl. Dickinson and a Mr. Brown of Rhode Island are appointed commissioners to carry this Resolution into Effect. Mr. Morris sets off for New York Tomorrow on that Business. What is called the Constitutional Party in this State are uppermost and playing the Mischief. They have published a Bill for Consideration which will probably pass next Session to demolish *the Bank*. The ostensible Reason is that it is incompatable with a free Government, but the real Reason is that Mr. Morris and the Directors of the Bank are not of the present ruling Party. They have also past a most iniquitous *ex post facto* Law to favour Mr. Holker in his Demands against Mr. Morris. It would be too long a Detail to give you a competent Idea of this Matter. Mr. Marbois has formed a kind of Coalition with Mr. Holker, and Mr. Morris and he are at Odds. This together with the Affair of Lonchamps, which Mr. Marbois has pursued with great Inveteracy have render'd Mr. Marbois very unpopular in this City. The Affair of Longchamps yet remains in Suspence before Congress.

I am very sorry Animal Magnetism is at End. I want much to

magnetise our Philosophical Society which still lies in a deep Trance. It will probably come to Life one of these Days and repay the Expectation of the World by giving a full and true Account of the wonderful Visions and prophecies it experienced during its State of Torpitude.

Mr. Rittenhouse has promised me that he will write to you and give his Letter to me to be forwarded, but not by this opportunity.

My Girls desire to be remember'd to their friend, Miss Patty. I am, dear Sir, with great Esteem Your truly affectionate & very humble Servt., FRAS HOPKINSON

The old Apology for a bad Scrawl—*Excuse Haste.*
I have not had an Opportunity of seeing Mr. Wright.

RC (DLC); addressed: "Honourable Mr. Jefferson at Paris." Recorded in SJL as received 8 July 1785.

On Robert Morris' dispute with HOLKER, there is in DLC: TJ Papers, 10: 1741-6, an 11-page account in the form of a letter from Morris to John Rucker in Paris, dated 18 June 1784, in which Morris authorized Rucker to show the account to various French merchants and bankers and concluded with this further authorization: "If Doctor Franklin, Mr. Adams, Mr. Jay, Mr. Jefferson, or Mr. Barclay hear any thing of this matter represented to my prejudice, you will please to shew this Letter to them and to any others you may think proper or necessary." Endorsements in the hands of Franklin and Jefferson and the presence of the signed document in TJ Papers show that this instruction was followed. Marbois' account of the Morris-Holker controversy may be found in his letters to Vergennes of 14 Mch., 5 Apr., and 17 Apr. 1785, in the first of which he said: "quoiqu'on doive regretter que les talens et la grande expérience de cet ex Ministre ne soient pas employés pour le service des Etats unis, nous y perdons cependant fort peu: Mr. Morris est certainement mal intentionné pour nous depuis que nous ne lui sommes plus utiles à rien, et surtout depuis que j'ay eté obligé d'appuier contre lui les interêts de Mr. Holker dans une affaire dont le resultat ne peut manquer de faire une grande breche à la fortune de l'un ou de l'autre." In the second of these letters Marbois sent a copy of the Pennsylvania LAW TO FAVOUR MR. HOLKER (all are found in Arch. Aff.

Etr., Paris, Corr. Pol., E.-U., Vol. XXIX, 102-7, 150-1, 158-60, 177-81; Tr in DLC). It was common gossip in Philadelphia that the bill had been passed "from envy of Mr. Morris and thro the secret machinations of Mr. Holker and Marbois (who are great friends upon this occasion but far otherwise in everything else). . . . Mr. Morris has behaved like himself throughout the whole. Some of his friends advised him to speak to some of the Assemblymen, but he refused, and took occasion one evening at the Fire Company to call the attention of the company to a speech he made to Mr. Pettit the head of Reeds party. 'Mr. Pettit by G.—if you pass that Bill which if you are not all D—d Rascals you cannot do I will be revenged upon you and all your party.' This intimidated him and he spoke faintly against it but not to any purpose" (Rebecca Vaughan to Catherine W. Livingston, 9 Apr. 1785; MHi: Ridley Papers). On this dispute the elder Holker assured Matthew Ridley that he was "brokenhearted on the occasion" and that he was certain his son's quarrel with Morris arose from a misunderstanding. Ridley wrote candidly to Morris and to Holker that he thought "both must have been to blame," though he assured Morris "it is in the anguish of my heart that I do, for I sincerely esteem both and should think myself one of the happiest of men could I be the Instrument of reconciliation between you" (Ridley to Morris, 10 Sep. 1784; MHi: Ridley Papers). To the one who later became his wife Ridley disclosed one ground of his anguish: "The differences between Mr. Holker and Mr. Morris have turned out very unlucky for me. Whilst they are disputing I am suffering. It is cruel hard to be the Victim to the quar- rels of others" (Ridley to Catherine W. Livingston, 1 Mch.; also 5 Sep. 1785; MHi: Ridley Papers).

From Walker Maury

DEAR SIR   Williamsbg. April 20th. 85

Your nephew Peter Carr, after a chasm of about 18 months, in the course of his education, arrived here a few days ago. Several circumstances, he tells me, have involuntarily detained him. I find him nearly *in statu quo*, as to his classics, but, full of regret at his lost time, and of mortification, that his former class-fellows shou'd have outstripped him so far as to have fallen into the University with some degree of eclat. Actuated by a regard for your anxiety for his advancement, as well as by his own apparent disposition to aid my exertions, I have taken him in the number of my private pupils—a situation somewhat more expensive, but much more advantageous for the studious youth, as they go thro many exercises with me, exclusive of those of the school in general. However, I wait Mr. Lewis's concurrence for his continuance in this situation. I have an excellent teacher of the French, and Spanish languages, in my school—a native of France, and a gentleman of science. You will therefore, be so obliging as to express your wish in respect to your nephew's learning the latter—perhaps it may be, to take it in, in the stead of the anglo-saxon.

As he has lost so much time, I fear, that no exertions, either on his, or my part, will enable him to enter the University with those advantages and acquirements, I am sure you wou'd wish, by the expiration of his 16th. year; But hope it may be accomplished by Octr. 12 month. Of this tho', the Professors, who are visitors and examiners of the school, will be the proper judges.

As I wish to establish a book shop, on an extensive plan for the supply of the Grammar School and university, I wou'd esteem it a particular favor in you, to furnish me, if you have the time to spare from more important affairs, a list of the french authors of most merit, with the prices affixed. With every good wish for the success of your embassy, and for data to give you more flattering accounts of the progress of your nephew, I am Dr. Sir, yours with much esteem,   WALKER MAURY

RC (MHi); addressed: "The Honble. Thos. Jefferson Embassador for the United States Amera. Paris"; endorsed. Entered in SJL as received 22 July 1785, "by Mazzei."

From P. Guillibaud & Cie.

MONSIEUR   Rouen le 22 avril 1785.

Nous venons de recevoir le duplicata du paquet que M. Holker actuellement a philadelphie nous a adressé et qui renfermait celui que notre Sr. Guillibaud a eu l'honneur de remettre à Votre excellence dans le voÿage qu'il vient de faire à Paris pour cette affaire. Ce duplicata nous a apporté celui qui doit renfermer un double de la commission que la cour Suprême de Pensilvanie a eu la bonté de vous adresser pour reconnaître la verité et la legitimité de notre crédite sur Samuel Wharton. Nous adressons ce paquet à Messrs. Detruissard Boisgent & compe. Ils auront l'honneur de vous le presenter, nous vous prions de leur accorder quelques moments d'audience pour avoir celui de conférer avec vous et pour nous faire passer vos ordres si vous en aviez quelques uns à nous donner.

Nous prions Votre Excellence d'avoir la bonté de lire et de prendre sérieusement en considération la copie de la lettre de M. Holker du 14. qui vous sera remise par nos dits amis. Il paraît que nous aurions tout à craindre de la mauvaise foi de notre débiteur qui ne cherche qu'à consommer le projet qu'il a eu d'abuser de notre confiance, si nous n'etions rassurés par vos lumières, par votre justice et par le travail que vous avez eu la bonté de faire pour eclairer les juges saisis de cette affaire. Il est clair qu'il n'a d'autres vues que d'en différer la décision, afin, s'il est possible qu'elle ne soit pas jugée avant le retour que M Holker se dispose à faire en france, ce qu'il est bien intéressant pour nous d'eviter.

Nous mettons notre unique confiance dans le raport que vous avez bien voulu vous charger de faire et Sommes bien persuadés que lui seul nous fera obtenir la condamnation sur Wharton: cependant, comme ce qui abonde ne Saurait nuire, nous croÿons devoir prendre l'expédition que M. Holker nous demande d'après son conseil et qu'il nous charge de prendre de notre Jurisdiction consulaire. Nous chargeons d'ailleurs nos amis de vous faire quelques observations et de vous prier d'ajouter à votre second raport, si vous le croÿez convenable, l'autorité du témoignage de M. le marquis de lafaÿette et celui de M. Leraÿ de chaumont pere. Enfin nous vous prions de prendre en sérieuse considération combien nous devons nous mettre en garde contre la mauvaise foi de notre debiteur et combien il est intéressant pour nous que cette affaire soit terminée pendant le sejour de M. Holker à l'amérique qui pourrait ne pas être encore long. Nous vous prions de nous aider de vos conseils dans la marche que nous avons à suivre et de nous donner vos ordres par l'entremise de Messrs. Detruissard Boisgent & compe.

Nous sommes avec respect Monsieur Vos très humbles & Très obeïssants serviteurs, P GUILLIBAUD ET COMP.

RC (DLC); in a clerk's hand, signed by initials.

From Jean Holker

SIR Rouen 25 Avril 1785

I Received your favor of the 17, had just been confind to my Bed. I should not have waited till this to Informe you, that I have had the satisfaction to find your objects, but it has not been without truble, as it had laine in the Depoe, amongst som hunderds of other objects since September last, and they was obliged to oppen amany Caisseis to find yours, as their was no directions on it; had you advised me at the time of its parting from London youd have Received it in Octobr., but as no one here claimed it, it was put amongst other goods, some of which has laine their as they say for amany years, and will Remaine than claimed. I wanted to have it sent under your Directions, but was Refused althoug the Directure of the farms is my friend, as he tells me nothing can part from this, unless a speshal order from the farmer Generals, or the Controulor General, unles it is for them or som Minister. So he proposed me sending it under the Direction of his Excelence Docter Franklin, with an acquie of Caution, which is don as youl see by the Conducteur of the Boat, which aquie youl be so good as to send me back, or they will force me to pay a fine of foure times the Vallue of the Duty.

They say the Batto will arrive in ten days, which youl be able to find out, by sending to the Buro, and young Mr. Franklin will attend your Servent and claime it as he has don the one I forwarded his Grandfather.

I have been obliged to pay 12 livers for the Mens truble to find it out and 4^{tt}. 1s. for Dutys, so youl be owing me on this 16^{tt}. 1s. which wee can Settle If ever I have the happeness of seeing you in Paris, and in the Mainetime beg you wont spaire me If I can be of any use, and am with Consideration your most Obediant & very humble Servant, J HOLKER

P.S. I am quit doune with the Gout Rencountre and cant fix it.

RC (MHi). Recorded in SJL as received 27 Apr. 1785.

In MHi there is a "lettre de voiture" issued to Holker on a printed form of the Messageries Royales ("Diligences par eau de Rouen a Paris") for "une Caisse ditte Contenir une presse," to be shipped on 25 Apr. 1785. There is also in MHi a statement of costs addressed to Holker from the DIRECTURE OF THE FARMS totaling 4l. 1s. for "Droits acquit . . . Corde et plomb . . . [et] homme de peine"; underneath the total of costs Holker added 12 l. Holker was also warned in the statement to cause to be returned "Lacquit a Caution Sans quoi M. Le docteur franklyn payra Le quadruples des droits."

Favi to the American Commissioners

MESSIEURS   Paris ce 26 Avril 1785

Le projet du Traité, que vous m'avés fait l'honneur de m'adresser dans le mois de Decembre dernier, et que vous avés proposé à Son Altesse Royale Msgr. L'Archiduc Grand Duc de Toscane mon Maitre etoit trop conforme à Ses principes pourqu'il ne fût pas agrée.

Ce Prince, après L'avoir pris en consideration est venu dans la determination d'y adherer, et c'est par son ordre, que j'ai L'honneur de vous comuniquer la traduction cy-jointe. Il y a quelques additions, qui ne changent rien à la Substance de la convention, mais que Les circonstances locales, et les reglements du pays, aux quels toutes Les nations sont soumises, rendent indispensables. Vous verrés, Messieurs, que Les Sujets des Etats unis de l'Amerique seront traités dans tous Les cas à Livourne comme la nation la plus favorisée, et qu'ils jouiront par consequent de tous Les avantages, qui sont accordés aux autres. Nous demandons Les mêmes conditions, et la même reciprocité pour Les Toscans. Ainsi la base de ce Traité ne sauroit etre fondée sur une egalité plus parfaite.

J'ai L'honneur d'etre avec Le plus grand respect Messieurs Votre trés humble, et trés obeissant Serviteur,   FAVI

RC (DNA: PCC, No. 86); endorsed by Humphreys with notation by TJ above endorsement: "No.5.a." Tr (same, and also in No. 116). English translation by John Pintard is in same, No. 86; another translation is printed in *Dipl. Corr., 1783-1789*, I, 578. Enclosure: Italian translation of proposed treaty with observations thereon (DNA: PCC, No. 86, p. 129-57; in Favi's hand with several alterations, one of which is in TJ's hand; endorsed by Humphreys with notation by TJ: "No.

5.b." Another Tr in same, p. 163-90; and another in PCC, No. 116). A copy of the Italian translation, in John Adams' hand, is in MHi: AMT. Letter and enclosures transmitted by Commissioners to John Jay 11 May 1785.

On the proposed ADDITIONS, QUI NE CHANGENT RIEN A LA SUBSTANCE DE LA CONVENTION, see TJ's translation of these alterations and his comments thereon following; see also Commissioners to Favi, 8 June 1785.

Notes on Alterations Proposed by Favi

[After 26 Apr. 1785]

Alterations made in our propositions to Tuscany.

'manufactures and merchandize' '*produce*, manufactures and mer- Art. 2. 3.
chandize, *without exception of any.*'

'whatsoever, *and shall be obliged to observe no other or greater* Agreed
formalities, regulations or cautions, than the most favored *Euro-*
pean nations are or shall be obliged to pay *and observe.*'

'exemptions in navigation and commerce' 'exemptions *for their* Agreed
persons and property and in navigation and commerce.'

'the most favored nation' 'the most favored *European* nation.' Here
and in Art. 4. et pass[im].

'to carry their own produce manufactures and merchandize in their [Art.] 4.
own vessels' 'to carry *any kinds* of produce, manufactures and
merchandize of *whatsoever place or growth* in their own or *in any*
other vessels.'

'where it shall be lawful for all the subjects and citizens of that Agreed
other freely to purchase' &c. No change proposed here; but we
should propose as with the K. of P. to substitute 'persons' for 'the
subjects and citizens of that other.'   bis.
    Form in which I should be for agreeing to this Article.
'More especially each party shall have a right to carry *any kinds* of
produce, manufactures and merchandize *of whatever place they be*
the growth or manufacture in their own *or any other* vessels to any
parts of the dominions of the other where it shall be lawful for all
persons freely to purchase them and thence to take the produce,
manufactures and merchandize of [the other]¹ which *all persons* [of what-
shall in like manner be free to sell them, paying in both cases ever place
such duties, charges and fees, *and observing such formalities,* or growth]¹
regulations and cautions only as are or shall be paid *or observed* by
the most favored nation. Nevertheless his royal highness and the
United states and each of them reserve to themselves the right
where any nation restrains the transportation of merchandize to
the vessels of the country of which it is the growth produce or
manufacture to establish against such nation retaliating regulations: and also the right to prohibit in their respective countries the
importation and exportation of all merchandize whatsoever when

reasons of state shall require it. In this case the subjects or citizens of the contracting parties shall not import nor export the merchandize prohibited by the other. But if one of the contracting parties permits any other nation to import or export the same merchandize, the citizens or subjects of the other shall immediately enjoy the same liberty.'

[Art.] 5.

'All merchants &c. or any part thereof for them: *provided the person so employed be thereto authorized*: nor shall they be obliged to make use of any interpreter &c. unless they chuse to make use of them. *And as to the lading and unlading their vessels and the transportation of their merchandize they shall use the public porters in places where they are or shall be established according to the regulations of the respective custom houses, and pay them the fees established by tariff, in those cases only nevertheless in which they have the right of transportation, being at liberty in all others to make use of such persons as they shall think proper without paying salaries or fees to any others.* Nor shall they be forced to unload any sort of merchandize into any other vessels, or to receive them into their own, or to wait for their being loaded longer than they please. *And generally with respect to the contents of this article each party, shall observe towards the other what shall be practised in their respective countries towards the most favoured European nation.'*

Better omit all the first and last parts of this article and let it stand as with the K. of P. respecting the unloading of vessels to wit. 'The merchants commanders of vessels or other subjects or citizens of either party shall not within the ports or jurisdiction of the other be forced to unload &c. [as above]¹—longer than they please.'

Art. 6.

Strike out this as useless or explain it
Is not this also useless?

Addition proposed by the G. D. to the end of this, viz. ['and moreover the laws of the respective countries shall be observed with respect to vessels having, or having had, on board prohibited articles,]¹ and they shall receive on board the usual guards of the custom houses, in those cases in which a similar caution is practised with the vessels of other the most favored nations of Europe. And the like cautions shall in the same manner be observed when such articles shall be unladed.'

Useless also

If any delinquent in the ports of either of the parties shall escape on board the vessels of the other, he shall, on demand, be immediately delivered to the government, and the respective Consuls, when there shall be any, shall give all possible assistance herein: and if ever delivery shall be refused, such delinquents may be freely and forcibly taken on board the vessel. The same shall be practised if any of the crew of the vessel shall commit any crime, a liberty being always reserved to do on board the same whatever may be necessary for the execution of justice.

There seems to be an omission of 'or being entered into port' [Art.] 8. 'or break bulk *they shall*[2] *send their boat ashore and yeild due* Reestablished *obedience, and give an account of themselves to the posts estab- lished for that purpose*, but they shall have liberty to depart &c.— account of their cargo: *saving what is agreed on in the 6th. article respecting prohibited articles, but they shall pay anchorage and* The preserva- *other expences and duties for*[3] *the port, and those concerning the* tion of [pro- *cautions as to health, when such are practised with the most* pose to insert these]1 *favored European nations.'*
Better as with the K. of P. 'or to pay any duties charges or fees whatsoever except those established for vessels entered into port and appropriated to the maintenance of the port itself or of other establishments for the safety and convenience of navigators, which duties charges and fees shall be the same, and shall be paid on the same footing as in the case of subjects or citizens of the coun- try where they are established.' [add]1 submitting to the precau- tions and regulations established in the health offices on the same footing also with the natives of the place.

9. 'that the whole or any part of their cargo be unladed, *the same* Art. 9. *rules shall be observed as to the paiment of dues which are ob- served in like cases with the inhabitants of the country and with the other the most favoured nations of Europe.'*

10. the word 'personal' omitted. Art. 10.
    'being subjects or citizens of the other party' 'chiunque.'
    'paying such dues only as the inhabitants of the country, *and of the nations of Europe the most favored* shall be subject to pay in like cases.'
    'And in case of the absence of the representative, *or of his attorney when no executor shall be named in the will, the courts of the country shall take* the goods into their *custody and shall keep them* until the lawful owner may take measures for receiving

them *in the same manner as is practised and prescribed by their respective laws for the succession of any other aliens whatever.'*

Propose [to] reinstate 'And where on the death &c.' 'And in the case of real estate, if in the state where it is situated there exist laws which forbid aliens to hold the property in them, the heir shall be allowed a reasonable time &c.'[4]

'guidici competenti.' reinstate 'laws and judges of the land &c.'

Art. 11.   11. 'an insult on *the reigning religion* or on the religion of others.' Our expression is simply 'an insult on the religion of others' which includes *the reigning religion*, the very expression of which is an insult on common sense, and should be excluded.

Art. 13.   'Nevertheless it shall be lawful to stop such vessels *and to make them unlade such articles in the nearest port putting them under*

Agreed *safe keeping*, and to detain them for such length of time as the captors may think necessary to prevent the inconvenience or damage &c.'

Agreed   *'and to remove all doubt respecting the merchandize and effects which shall be subject to the arrangements in this article, it is declared that they are the following, Canons, mortars &c. But these articles shall not be subject to be stayed provided they be not in greater quantity than may be necessary for the use of the ship, or of the persons in it.'*

[Art.] 14. 'the burthen' of the vessel is omitted.

Reinstated 'which passports shall be made out in good and due forms, *and in the manner and for the time which is usual with the respective nation in time of peace, on which subject such further explanations shall be entered into as occasion may render necessary* and shall be exhibited.'

[Art.] 16. 'their vessels and effects' omitted.

Disagreed 'offences committed &c. within the jurisdiction of the other' 'within the jurisdiction *and with the subjects, citizens, or inhabitants of the other.'*

[Art.] 17. 'pirates' omitted and the following addition to the clause *without any pretension whatever to salvage. But if a vessel of the one party*

Agreed *be taken by pirates or sea-rovers and retaken by a vessel of the other, one third part of the value of the vessel and cargo retaken shall be given to the recaptors.'*

[Art.] 18. 'in danger from tempests, pirates, enemies, or other accident shall take refuge' &c.

'shall come with their vessels and effects into the harbours or juris- Is this not
diction of the other *for the ordinary affairs of their commerce and* sufficiently provided for
navigation or in danger from tempests, pirates enemies or other before?
accident.'

The following addition to the clause, '*Nevertheless in every case
the vessels which shall come into the respective ports, scales or
roads shall exactly observe the laws ordinances and customs estab-* Useless
*lished with respect to the public health and for the preservation of
the neutrality and all others relative to the police, good order and
i deritti regali and generally all the laws in force in the respective
ports and states.*'

'carry freely wheresoever they please' 'wheresoever they please Art. 1[9.]
within the jurisdiction of the other.'

'without being obliged to pay any duties &c. to the officers &c.' Agreed
'without &c. to the officers &c. *other than those established for
other vessels and merchandize, and which are paid by other the
most favored nations of Europe.*'

'nor shall such prizes be arrested &c.' 'ports of the other party
except the case where the prize is charged to have been made Agreed
against the laws of neutrality existing in the country.' necess[ary]

'but may freely be carried &c. to the places expressed in their
commissions *or wheresoever they please the commanding officer of* Agreed
*the vessel making the capture being obliged to shew his commis-
sion and instructions, or to give other sufficient proofs whenever it
shall be alledged that he was not authorized to hoist the flag of
the nation under which he made the prize.*'

addition '*and the same shall take place in all those cases in which
the most Serene Grand-Duke of Tuscany [or the United states]*[1]
shall have made [or shall make][1] *like conventions with other
powers.*' d[elete] 'or the U.S.' and 'or shall make.'

20. 'on pain of being punished as a pirate' 'on pain of being Art. 20.
punished severely according to the rigor of the laws.' Our laws
could not punish in this case.

'on pain of being punished as a pirate or otherwise severely
according to the rigor of the laws.'

Instead of $\frac{1}{30}$ and $\frac{1}{10}$ for recapture, $\frac{1}{10}$ and $\frac{1}{15}$ are proposed.[5] Art. 21. 2
[If he will not give up we will][6]
'ports of each and shall be freely at the disposal of the captor [Art. 21.] 4
according to the laws usages and regulations of the state to which
the captor belongs.'

[Art.] 24. 'dungeons and prisonships' omitted.

'such individual officer or other prisoner shall forfeit so much of the benefit of this article as provides for his enlargement on parole or cantonment.' 'imedesimi perderanno il benefizio di questo articolo.' *'they shall lose the benefit of this article.'* This is too general. The benefit of the nation and of every comfort and privilege except enlargement should be reserved to him.

[Art.] 25. 'and commissaries of their own appointment *saving the usual and admissions, and on the same footing as is allowed to any other the most favored European nation.'*

[Art.] 26. 'to any other *European* nation.'

MS (DLC: TJ Papers, 12: 2152-5); entirely in TJ's hand; undated; at head of text: "Alterations made in our propositions to Tuscany." Italicized words (underscored in MS) are translations, so far as TJ was enabled to make them, of Favi's observations.

¹ Brackets in MS.
² The following deleted passage is in MS at this point: "*spedire la lancia* a term which I do not understand, but I believe it means to."
³ The insertion proposed in the margin was intended to be made at this point.
⁴ The words "And in the case of . . .

a reasonable time" were inserted in MS over the following deleted passage: "There is a technical phrase here 'veglino delle leggi &c.' which I do not understand, but the clause seems to have the same object with ours."
⁵ These two fractions were later deleted and "⅓ and ¹⁄₁₀" interlined in substitution therefor in consequence of the discovery indicated in note 6; but see Commissioners to Favi, 8 June 1785; Favi to Commissioners, 10 Nov. 1785.
⁶ The words in brackets (supplied) were later deleted and TJ wrote the following explanation above the deleted passage: "Discovered to be error of translator."

From James Madison

Dear Sir   Orange April 27. 1785.

I have received your two favors of Novr. 11 and Decr. 8. Along with the former I received the two pamphlets on animal magnetism and the last aeronautic expedition, together with the phosphoretic matches. These articles were a great treat to my curiosity. As I had left Richmd. before they were brought thither by Col. le Maire, I had no opportunity of attending myself to your wishes with regard to him; but I wrote immediately to Mr. Jones and desired him to watch over the necessities of le Maire. He wrote me for answer that the Executive tho' without regular proof of his claims were so well satisfied from circumstances of the justice of them, that they had voted him £150 for his relief till the assembly could take the whole into consideration. This information has made me easy on the subject though I have not withdrawn from the hands of Mr. Jones the provisional resource. I thank you much for your attention to my literary wants. All the purchases you have made for me, are such as I should have made for myself with the same opportunities. You will oblige me by adding to them the Dictionary in 13 vol. 4°. by Felice and others, also de Thou in French. If the utility of Moreri be not superseded by some better work I should be glad to have him too. I am afraid if I were to attempt a catalogue of my wants I should not only trouble you beyond measure, but exceed the limits which other considerations ought to prescribe to me. I cannot however abridge the commission you were so kind as to take on yourself in a former letter, of procuring me from time to time such books as may be "either old and curious or new and useful." Under this description will fall those particularised in my former letters, to wit treatises on the antient or modern fœderal republics, on the law of Nations, and the history natural and political of the New World; to which I will add such of the Greek and Roman authors where they can be got very cheap, as are worth having and are not on the common list of School classics. Other books which particularly occur, are the translation [French][1] of the Historians of the Roman Empire during its decline by ———, Paschals provincial letters—Don Ulloa in the Original—Lynnæus best edition—Ordinances Marines—Collection of Tracts in french on the Œconomics of different nations. I forget the full title. It is much referred to by Smith on the wealth of nations. I am told a Monsr. Amelot has lately published his travels into China, which if they have any merit must be very entertaining. Of Buffon I have his original work of 31 vol., 10 vol. of Supplemt. and 16 vol. on birds. I shall be glad of the continuation as it may from time to time be published. I am so pleased with the new invented lamp that I shall not grudge two guineas for one of them. I have seen a pocket compass of somewhat larger diameter than a watch and which may be carried in the same way. It has a spring for stopping the vibration of the needle when not in use. One of these would be very convenient in case of a ramble into the Western Country. In my walks for exercise or amusements, objects frequently present themselves, which it might be matter of curiosity to inspect, but which it is difficult or impossible to approach. A portable glass would consequently be a source of many little gratifications. I have fancied that such an one might be fitted into a Cane without making it too heavy. On the outside of the tube might be engraved a scale of inches &c. If such a project could be executed for a few Guineas, I should be willing to submit to the price; if not, the best substitute I suppose will be a pocket-telescope, composed of several tubes so constructed as to slide the lesser into the greater. I should feel great remorse at troubling you with so many requests, if your kind and repeated offers did not stifle it in some measure. Your proposal for my replacing here advances for me without regard to the exchange is liable to no objection except that it will probably be too unequal in my favour. I beg that you will enable me as much as you can to keep those little matters balanced.—The papers from le Grand were sent as soon as I got them to Mr. Jones with a request that he would make the use of them which you wished me to do.

Your remarks on the tax on transfers of land in a general view appear to me to be just but there were two circumstances which gave a peculiarity to the case in which our Law adopted it. One was that the tax will fall much on those who are evading their quotas of other taxes by removing to Georgia and Kentucky: the other that as such transfers are more frequent among those who do not remove, in the Western than the Eastern part of the Country, it will fall heaviest where direct taxes are least collected. With regard to the tax in general on law proceedings, it cannot perhaps be justified if tried by the strict rule which proportions the quota of every man to his ability. Time however will gradually in some measure equalize it, and if it be applied to the support of the Judiciary establishment, as was the ultimate view of the friends of the tax, it seems to square very well with the Theory of taxation.

The people of Kentucky had lately a convention which it was expected would be the mother of a separation. I am informed they proceeded no farther than to concert an address for the Legislature on some points in which they think the laws bear unequally upon them. They will be ripe for that event at least as soon as their interest calls for it. There is no danger of a concert between them and the Counties West of the Alleghany which we mean to retain. If the latter embark in a scheme for independance it will be in their own bottom. They are more disunited in every respect from Kentucky than from Virginia.

I have not learnt with certainty whether Genl. Washington will accept or decline the shares voted him by the assembly in the Companies for opening our rivers. If he does not chuse to take to himself any benefit from the donation, he has I think a fine opportunity at once of testifying his disinterested purposes, of shewing his respect for the assembly, and of rendering a service to his Country. He may accept the gift so far as to apply it to the scheme of opening the rivers, and may then appropriate the revenue which it is hereafter to produce, to some patriotic establishment. I lately dropped a hint of this sort to one of his friends and was told that such an idea had been suggested to him. The private subscriptions for Potowmac I hear amount to £10,000 Sterling. I can not discover that those for James River deserve mention, or that the undertaking is pushed with any spirit. If those who are most interested in it let slip the present opportunity, their folly will probably be severely punished by the want of such another. It is said the undertaking on the Susquehannah by Maryland goes on with great spirit and expectations. I have heard nothing of Rumsey or his boats since he went into the Northern States. If his machinery for stemming the current operates on the water alone as is given out, may it not supply the great desideratum for perfecting the Balloons?

I understand that Chase and Jennifer on the part of Maryland, Mason and Henderson on the part of Virginia have had a meeting on the proposition of Virga. for settling the navigation and jurisdiction of Potowmac below the falls, and have agreed to report to the two assemblies, the establishment of a concurrent jurisdiction on that river and Chesapeak. The most amicable spirit is said to have governed the negociation.

The Bill for a Genl. Assesst. has produced some fermentation below the Mountains and a violent one beyond them. The contest at the next Session on this question will be a warm and precarious one. The port bill will also undergo a fiery trial. I wish the Assize Courts may not partake of the danger. The elections as far as they have come to my knowledge are likely to produce a great proportion of new members. In Albemarle young Mr. Fry has turned out Mr. Carter. The late Governor Harrison I hear has been baffled in his own County, but meant to be a candidate in Surry and in case of a rebuff there to throw another die for the borough of Norfolk. I do not know how he construes the doctrine of residence. It is *surmised*[2] that the *machinations of Tyler who fears a rivailship for the chair* are *at the bottom of his difficulties. Arthur Lee is elected* in *Prince William. He is said* to have *paved the way by promises* to *overset the port bill* which is *obnoxious* to *Dumfries* and to *prevent the removal of*[3] *the assise court* from *this town to Alexandria.*

[113]

I received a letter from *the Marquis Fayette* dated on the *eve of his embarcation* which *has the following paragraph*. "*I have much confered with the general upon the Potowmac system. Many people think*[3] *the navigation of the Mississippi is not an advantage but* it *may be the excess of a very good thing viz. the opening of your rivers. I fancy it has not changed your opinion but beg you will write me on the* subject. *In the meanwhile I hope Congress will act coolly and prudently by Spain who is such a fool that allowance must be made.*" It is *unlucky that he should have left America with* such *an idea as to the Mississippi*. It may be *of the worse consequence as* it is *not wholly imaginary, the* prospect of *extending the commerce of the Atlantic states to the western waters having given birth to it*. I can not believe that *many minds are tainted with so illiberal and short sighted a policy*. I have *thought it not amiss to* write[3] *the marquis* according to the *request of his letter* and *have stated to him the motives and obligations* which must *render* the[3] *United States inflexible* on the *subject of the Mississippi, the folly of Spain in contesting it* and *our expectation from the known influence of France over Spain* and *her friendly dispositions toward us*. It is but *justice to the marquis to observe* that *in all our conversations* on *the Mississippi he expressed* with every *mark of sincerity a zeal for our claims* and *a pointed di*slike *to the national character and policy of Spain* and that if *his zeal should be found to abate* I should construe it to[4] be the effect *of a supposed* revolution *in the sentiments of America*.

This would have been of somewhat earlier date but I postponed it that I might be able to include some information relative to your Nephews. My last informed you that your eldest was then with Mr. Maury. I was so assured by Mr. Underwood from his neighbourhood, who I supposed could not be mistaken. I afterwards discovered that he was so, but could get no precise information till within a few days. One of my brothers being called into that part of the Country by business, I wrote to Mrs. Carr and got him to wait on her. The answer with which I have been favored imports that "her eldest son was taken last fall with a fever which with repeated relapses kept him extremely weak and low till about the first of Jany. from which time he was detained at home by delays in equipping him for Williamsbg. till the 1st. of April, when he set out with promises to make up his lost time; that her youngest son had also been detained at home by ill health till very lately, but that he would certainly go on to the academy as soon as a vacation on hand was over, that his time had not been entirely lost as his brother was capable of instructing him whenever his health would admit." Mr. Maury's School is said to be very flourishing. Mr. Wythe and the other gentlemen of the University have examined it from time to time and published their approbation of its management. I can not speak with the same authority as to the academy in Prince-Edward. The information which I have received has been favorable to it. In the recommendation of these Seminaries I was much governed by the probable permanency of them; nothing being more ruinous to education than the frequent interruptions and change of masters and methods incident to the private schools of this country.

Our winter has been full of vicisitudes, but on the whole far from being a severe one. The Spring has been uncommonly cold and wet, and vegetation of course very backward; till within a few days during which it has been accelerated by very uncommon heat. A pocket Thermometer which stands on the second floor and the N. W. side of the House was on the 24 inst. at 4 oClock, at 77.°, on the 25. 78., on the 26. 81½., to day 27. at 82. The weather during this period has been fair and the wind S. the atmosphere thick NW. Our Wheat in the ground is very unpromising throughout the Country. The price of that article on tide water is about 6/. Corn sells in this part of the Country at 10/. and under., below at 15/., and where the insect prevailed as high as 20/. It is said to have been raised by a demand for exportation. Tobacco is selling on Rappahannock at 32/. and Richmd. at 37/6. It is generally expected that it will at least get up to 40/. Some of our peaches are killed and most of our Cherries. Our Apples are as yet safe. I can not say how it is with the fruit in other parts of the Country. The mischief to the Cherries &c. was done on the night of the 20. when we had a severe black frost.

I can not take my leave of you without making my acknowledgments for the very friendly invitation contained in your last. If I should ever visit Europe I should wish to do it less stinted in time than your plan proposes. This crisis too would be particularly inconvenient as it would break in upon a course of reading which if I neglect now I shall probably never resume. I have some reason also to suspect that crossing the sea would be unfriendly to a singular disease of my constitution. The other part of your invitation has the strongest bias of my mind on its side, but my situation is as yet too dependant on circumstances to permit my embracing it absolutely. It gives me great satisfaction to find that you are looking forward to the moment which is to restore you to your native Country, though considerations of a public nature check my wishes that such an event may be expedited. Present my best respects to Mr. Short, and Miss Patsy, and accept of the affectionate regards of Dear Sir, Your sincere friend,

J. Madison Jr.

What has become of the subterraneous City discovered in Siberia?
Deaths. Thomson Mason
Bartholemew Dandridge
Ryland Randolph[5]
Joseph Reed of Philada.

RC (DLC: Madison Papers); at head of letter: "(No. 7)"; partly in code; date altered by overwriting from "26" to "27." Text slightly altered by Madison late in life as indicated below; there are several deletions and interlineations (chiefly having to do with phraseology) that cannot with certainty be ascribed either to composition in 1785 or to revision when Madison's letters were returned to him; one of these is indicated below. Recorded in SJL as received 22 July 1785, "by Mazzei."

I CAN NOT BELIEVE THAT MANY MINDS ARE TAINTED WITH SO ILLIBERAL AND SHORT SIGHTED A POLICY: Madison evidently did not know that Washington supported such a policy. Lafayette's letter which so alarmed its recipient was probably a mere reflection of this fact.

[1] Brackets in MS.
[2] This and subsequent words in italics were written in code and decoded interlineally by TJ; his decoding has been verified by the editors, employing Code No. 3.
[3] Madison omitted the code symbol for this word and late in life inserted it above TJ's decoding of the passage.
[4] The preceding five words appear to be in Madison's later hand; they are interlined in substitution for the words "it will." The editors believe, but cannot say certainly, that Madison originally wrote the latter and did not substitute the former until he carefully revised the text of this and other letters many years later. The various revisions indicated under note 3 clearly belong to the later date.
[5] One name below that of Randolph's is heavily obliterated. This may have been done late in life.

From John Bondfield

[*Bordeaux, 28 Apr. 1785*. Entered in SJL as received 5 May 1785. Not found.]

From John Page

My dear Jefferson   Rosewell Apl. the 28th. 1785

As it is possible that this may reach you before my other Letter of the 25th. Ulto., I think it proper in Justice to myself, to inform you that I then wrote a few Lines by a Monsr. Le croix, who afforded me the first Opportunity of acknowledging the Receipt of your kind Letter by Col. Le Maire, and of apologizing for a Long seeming Neglect. As I had but a Moment to write then, I promised to write more fully by Mr. Mazzei, but such has been my Situation, that Mazzei arrived here and is now preparing to set out to New York tomorrow, as I am also for a Journey to Richmond at the same Time, and I have not yet had it in my Power to command one half Hour to comply with my Promise. My own Affairs added to my Fathers, and Mr. Burwells demand my utmost Attention. The incessant Applications of Negros, Overseers, Duns and Sheriffs, ingross what little time my public Business, the Visits of Friends, and the Education of my Children have left me. What Time then have I to dedicate to my absent Friends? Believe me, next to the Conversation of my Friends, I enjoy the Satisfaction of writing to them, and you may be assured Jefferson, I have not a Friend whose Friendship I value more, or whose Conversation I esteem so much as yours. I must repeat what I told you in my last, that I am the more obliged to you for your Attention to me, as I am conscious that I must have appeared to you unworthy of it, for as I cannot write or at least have not written, to my Friends for a long Time past, I am utterly neglected by them all, except yourself. To add to the Interruptions I meet with in my Business and Correspondence with my Friends, the Executive sent me last Summer to Pennsylvania to assist in ascertaining the boundary between Virga. and that State by astronomical Observations which totally occupied me 3 Months. To make you some amends for sending me the Connoisance des Temps I inclose you the Result of our Observations, a few of them which added to some of Rittenhouses own, may be no unwellcome Present to the Royal Academy. I intend also to write to Rittenhouse by Mazzei, and endeavour to prevail on him to communicate to you the whole of our Observations and his own made on the Comet of last Year, as well as those on Hershalls Planet, which the English foolishly call Georgium Sidus. I was indulged by the Commissioners with the Choice of my Station. I did not hesitate to chuse that on the eastern Extremity of M. and Dixon's Line where I was to meet Rittenhouse. I had heard much of that Great Man and had conceived a very high Opinion of him from several Ingenious Letters I had the Honour to receive from him, but I must confess, that I found him greatly superior to any Idea I had of him. For I found that he not only was a great and ingenious Mechanic, and profound Astronomer and Philosopher making excellent Telescopes, Time Pieces and Sectors besides his famous orrery, useing them with wonderful Dexterity, and accuracy and runing through the most intricate and laborious Calculations with Perspicuity and Ease, but that his great and comprehensive Mind had taken a View of every Thing. His Genius had penetrated as deep into the Secrets of the moral and political World, as into those of the natural. I have seen him when closely engaged in Observations discuss a Point in Metaphysics with as much clearness as in Physics. I have been entertained with his Conversation on the Subject of our Historians, Poets, and Novel Writers; and I can assure you, that though he was engaged in making many Observations which Called for his Attention at all Hours of the Day and Night and in Calculations which would be called laborious, he found Leisure to translate a considerable Part of a German Comedy whilst I was with him. As an Astronomer I doubt when the World can produce such another for, if every Instrument and Book upon Earth which Astronomers use were destroyed, I am certain, from the Instruments which he made and the manner in which I saw him use them, that he himself without any Assistance could replace Astronomy in the present State of its Perfection. Though I write in extreme Haste and have but a few Minutes to spare, as I have several other Letters to write, and many Papers to put up before I can set out, yet I could not refrain from saying what I find has taken up much Paper, as I think too much can not be said of a Man who I find is not sufficiently known in the learned World. His Modesty has restrained him from making a Display of Talents which would really astonish the World. I found from a Conversation with Doctr. Smith that he gave Rittenhouse Credit for all the Papers in their Philosophical Transactions which were published under the Doctor's Name and which procured their Society so much Honour abroad. For Particulars respecting your Friends here I must refer you to Mazzei. As to the Proceedings of the Assembly I must refer you to him in Part, and to the Bills and a few Papers which I luckily have by me and inclose with this Letter. Mazzei can inform you of the Debates respecting a general Assessment, and of the Appearance of a Letter Writer in our Papers against that Measure. I will endeavour to procure you a Copy of the Bill for the Assessment which has been published for the Consideration of our fellow Citizens.

I have written to Col. Le Maire, and invited him to Rosewell offering him all the Services in my Power but I can hear nothing of him.

I was much pleased with the little Sketch you gave me of the State of the Dispute between the Emperor and the Dutch. As far as I have been able to judge from Accounts in News-papers that Affair must be nearly compromised by this Time. Is it true that the Emperor of Morocco had made advances to Congress which were not attended to, and of Consequence disgusted that Prince to the Misfortune of many Americans? This I hope is a british Tale, but surely it is high Time to be secured against the piratical Depredations of the Moors and Algerines. I should think a little Flattery, a few Presents, and a Prospect of our Trade with them would go a great Way to secure us the safe Navigation of the Mediterranean. I forgot that my Friend Wm. Short was with you when I wrote last. Be pleased to remember me to him most affectionately. If you should see General Chatelux present my most respectful Compliments to him and tell him that when I can have Leisure I will endeavour to shew him that I have a just Sense of the Honour he did me in his Letter to Mr. Bellini, that I was happy in being able to furnish him with any thing worthy of a Place in the Cabinet of his most Christian Majesty, who is undoubtedly intituled not only to the Gratitude and Love of every American, but may reasonably expect every Contribution of this sort which America can afford. You must know that I, finding our Society on the Decline, withdrew a Present I had promised it, and gave it to Genl. Chatelux, which he did me the Honor to say he would present to the King. It was the Amythest with a fluid contained in a Cavity in which floated a Bubble of Air, and which Dr. Bland had found on our Mountains and intended for the Royal Society of London till I reminded him that our infant Society stood more in need of it, on which he gave it to me to dispose of as I might think proper. I had promised it to the Society here, but not being very well pleased with our Curators Attention, any more than with the Diligence of our Members, I retained it in my own Hands, till I gave it to Genl. Chatelux, which was a very fortunate Circumstance, as the Curator's House was burnt, and our Museum consumed with it. I intend shortly to endeavour to revive our Society, and shall recommend you as President and McClurg as Vice President. It was unfortunate for the Society that I was appointed President for it restrained me from making the Exertions in its behalf, which I otherwise should. Had I done half I wished to do

I should have appeared proud of my Office, and too officious in calling the Members to read my own Productions. As soon as I get out of Office I shall spare no Pains to revive the Society and make it useful. I have almost reached the Bottom of my Paper, which can now scarcely contain the good Wishes which we all unite in sending to you, your Daughter, and Mr. Short, and the Assurances of that Attachment & Friendship with which my dear Jefferson I am sincerly yours,   JOHN PAGE

RC (DLC); endorsed: "Page John Apr. 28. 1785. recd. July 22. 1785." Entered in SJL as received on that date "by Mr. Mazzei." Enclosures: (1) Data resulting from astronomical observations made during the summer of 1784 as originally proposed by TJ for ascertaining the boundary between Va. and Pa., in which Page observed: "These Mensurations appear to be the first which have been made with sufficient Accuracy and of sufficient Extent to determine the Measure of a Degree of Long." (DLC) (2) The "few Papers" relating to the proceedings of the Assembly have not been identified.

THE SOCIETY HERE, of course, was the Virginia Philosophical Society that had been founded a decade earlier.

Vergennes to the American Commissioners

Versailles, 28 Apr. 1785. Has forwarded to De Castries all the papers sent to him by the Commissioners on the subject of the Barbary powers and now encloses a copy of the reply he has just received from that minister.

RC (DNA: PCC, No. 59, II); 2 p.; in French; above endorsement, in TJ's hand: "No.3.a." Tr (DNA: PCC, Nos. 86 and 116); both in Humphreys' hand. FC (Arch. Aff. Etr., Paris, Corr. Pol., E.-U., Vol. XXIX; Tr in DLC). Enclosure: Copy of De Castries to Vergennes, 24 Apr. 1785 (DNA: PCC, No. 59, II; above endorsement, "No.3. b."; copy also in each of other sources cited), in which he informed Vergennes that about three weeks earlier the Commissioners had been furnished with "instructions of the contributions and presents of the Christian Powers, and of the value and species of those which France has made them for purposes of State"; that it was up to Congress to decide whether "a good understanding with the Barbarians is worth the sacrifice"; that, of the three modes of dealing with the Barbary powers, he only thought "the last advisable," &c. (translation in *Dipl. Corr., 1783-1789*, I, 572-4). Vergennes' covering letter and enclosure were sent by Commissioners to Jay in theirs of 11 May 1785. Vergennes' letter to De Castries of 21 Apr. 1785, covering the Commissioners' letter of 28 Mch. 1785 and the various papers that Adams had left with him (see Adams to Franklin and TJ, 20 Mch. 1785) and De Castries' reply of 24 Apr. 1785 are in Arch. Aff. Etr., Paris, Corr. Pol., E.-U., Vol. XXIX, 183, 196-7; Tr in DLC.

From Jacques Le Maire

VOTRE EXELLENCE   Richemont le 30. avril 1785

Apres mêtre aquitté de vos commissions, Et avoir mis quelques ordres a mes affaires, je n'ai eu rien de plus pressé que de vous En rendre compte, En vous temoignant ma tres juste Reconnoissance pour tous les Services Essentiels que vous m'avez rendus. Je noublirai jamais que c'est a votre puissante recommendation que je dois toutes les graces dont m'a comblé le Gouvernement de Virginie representé par le tres Digne Respectable Sir Patrick Hennery. Cette honnête Magistra ma comblé de sa bienveillance, il m'a fait compter cent cinquante ponds Sitot mon arrivé pour me soutenir jusqu'a ce que mes affaires Soit totalement fini, il sinteresse vivement à moi, il a eu la bonté de donner les ordres les plus pressantes à fin de me faire avoir la patente des deux mille arpens de terres qui m'a été accordé En gratification, ce qui aura lieu dapres la decouverte que lon trouvéra, car jusqu'a ce moment on ne Sait point dans quel compté où elle sont. J'ai découvert que c'est le Col. chelby [Shelby] où le Col. Martin qui a été chargé par vôtre Exellence de plasser mon voirant [warrant] avec recommendation de me donner ce qu'il y avoit de mieux; Et certainement sous de pareilles ospices je ne puis qu'Esperer que dêtre favorablement bien traité. Aussitot que je Serai nanti de ce titre jen ferai la vente pour les remplasser dans une petite habitation dans les Environs de Richemont, où allieur dans la province de la virginie, Etant décidé a me fixer le reste de mes jours sous larbre de la liberté.

Vous trouvairai-cy inclus un mémoire qui Est fait daprès de tres juste observations, Et jose vous assurer qui c'est vrait. J'en Envoy une copie, à Monsieur Beudet homme tres riche et en credy au pres des Ministres. Il a de tres grands projets d'etablissement sur le Kentockée ou sur L'ohio; je lui Envoy un Echantillion de Soye blange fabriqué dans ces lieux occidentaux. Je prend la liberté de laddresser à vôtre Exellence, je ne doute point que vous ne Lengagiés au parti que je lui propose, et je ne le fait que dapres ce qu'il m'a prié de lui Envoyer Les détails les plus circonstenciés.

Lon m'a aussi promy que je serois admis dans la Société de l'ordre de Sincinnatus, au quatre juillet prochin; je rend compte de tout ces bien faits au Ministres de france particulierement à Monsieur le Comte de Vergenne ne voulant point laisser l'equité du votre.

Il me semble que je me suis deja trop Etendu sur mon chapitre, et qu'il Est tems de parler de ce qui vous conserne.

J'ai eu L'honneur de visitaire vôtre Respectable famille Et vos amis, qui sont En grand Nombre. J'en ai recu L'accueil le plus Satisfaisant. Le Colonel Cayry, auroit été tres charmé que vous lui Eussie Ecrit. Monsieur Et Madame Eppes ainsi que Monsieur

Hylton me charge de vous dire mille chose honnête de leur part, de même que, Monsieur le Gouverneur; j'ai remy les deux paquets Et les deux barilles deau de vie que lon a trouvé Exellente.

La charmante Demoiselle Geffersonn, Enbrasse son bon papa, du mielleur de son coeur sans oublier sa chere soeur. Elle Se porte à merveille, elle Est grace comme un petit mouton. Ses cheres Cousines, qui ce porte Egalement, on ne peut mieux ce joigne au voeux de Mademoiselle Geffersonn. Tous vos lettres et autres paquets ont été Egalement remis a leur destinations. Monsieur Madiconn, Est le Seul qui ne mait point repondu. Il n'avoit pas Sans doute reçu vôtre lettre que j'ai remy à Monsieur le president de lacademie de Welliamburg. Il Est Sur lhabitation de Monsieur son pere.

Je suis chargé de la part de Monsieur, Et Madame Eppes de vous prier de leur Envoyer des graines de toutes Especes, pour du Jardinages, Et pour des fleures a fin dorner leur jardin.

Je dois retourner incessament chez Ses aimables gens, Et chez le Colonel Skipworth je compte y faire un long séjour si mes affaires me le permettent. Je vous assure que tout a prodigieusement Enchery dans vôtre patrie, de puis que vous lavez quitté. Main deuvre, vie annimalle, tout coute au moins le double que dans la capitale de la france, qui Est la ville la plus chere; vous ne croirié pas que lon ma demandé vingt a vingt Six ponds pour Etablir une grille semblable a celle que j'ai fait faire pour vous a paris. Ce prix Exsorbitant a dégouté les personnes qui En vouloit faire faire.

Jose vous prier de me rappelle au Souvenir de Messieurs Colonel Huntsfrieds [et] Short. Je les prie dagreer les assurances du plus parfait attachement.

Il ne me reste plus que de reiterer à Votre Exellence, les Sentimens de la plus parfaite reconnoissance, Et de vous prier de maccorder la continuation de vos bontés Et de votre bienveillance que je sollicite toujours avec confiance. Je ferai toujours tout ce qui dependera de moi pour la meriter, veuille le ciel vous faire jouir de la Santé la plus parfaite. Ce sont la les voeux les plus chere à mon coeur; pénétré de ses Sentimens Je suis avec le plus profond Respect Votre Exellence, Votre tres humble Et tres obeissant Serviteur,   LE MAIRE

P.S. Monsieur Beudet demeure au paloit Royal, No. 18.

Mémoire de M. le Maire

Sans entrer dans le détail des causes morales qui ont influé sur l'accroissement prodigieux de la population, du commerce et de l'aisence des etats unis de L'Amérique, L'on parcourra rapidement les causes phisiques, qui secondant sa constitution religieuse et civile ont tant contribué à ses progrès. L'on doit convenir que si L'étendüe de ces terres, la multitude de ces port et bayes et rivieres favorisent le Commerce et les communications, la proffondeur de ces terres, leur Situation salubre et leur fertilité extraordinaire en facilitant les subsistances, les acquisition et les proprietés rendent raison de cette progression si interessante; L'on peut même assurer que ce sont ces mêmes terres communément appeller pays de derriere qui feront la base solide de la puissance future de l'Amerique Septentrionale.

Une chene de Montagnes connüe sous le nom d'Apalaches et alleghany qui, courant nord est, traverce tout le continant depuis le golfe St. Laurent jusqu'au Cap des florides, est la limitte naturelle qui Sépare ces pays de derriere de la Basse Virginie. Les costes de l'Amerique courent dans une direction presque pararelle [parrallèle] à cette chaine et à une distance d'environ 200. miles. Les terres de cette lisiere comprise entre la mer et ces Montagnes sont en général d'une qualité médiocre, et quoique dans ce moment cy elles soient infiniment plus peuplees que celles de derriere elles n'augmentent presque point en population, sur tout dans le Sud; touttes les emigrations, tant de l'Europe que de L'Amerique meme se portant dans ces Contrées plus occidentales dont on va parler.

Ces contrées sont bornées à L'est par Les Montagnes Alleghany et Apalaches comme Je l'ai dit, au Nord par Les grands Lacs qui les separent du Canada, â l'ouest par le Missisipy, et au sud par les florides, Comprenant une Espace d'environ 300 Lieües de L'Est à L'Oüest et un peu plus du Nord au Sud. Ce pays est travercé dans toutte sa largeur par une grande riviere dont les deux branches principalles, la Monongalsela et L'Alleghany, partant de deux endroits de ces Montagnes fort éloignés l'un de l'autre, viennent ce réunir sous les murs de fort pitt, y prenant le nom *d'Ohyo*, et après avoir reçu un nombre prodigieux de Rivieres vont tomber dans le Missisipy, 400. lieües au dessous de ce même fort pitt, autrefois fort *duquesne*. A l'exeption de quelques foibles Etablissements formés depuis longtems par les françois au detroit, aux Illinois et sur la riviere Wabash, toute la partie qui est au Nord de la riviere Ohio est encore la propriété des indiens qui en sont les Seuls habitants. Les differents Etats de la Confédération Americaine ont abandonné au Congrès qui represente les Etats Unis les droits particuliers qu'ils pouvoient avoir sur cette portion. Lorsque le Congrès en aura achetté quelques districts de ces mêmes indiens, L'on croit qu'il les vendra afin de pouvoir payer une portion des dettes Continantales. Mais Jusques à L'époque d'un tel achat il est impossible et défendu même par le Congrès d'y faire aucun Etablissement, et quoyque les Indiens soient dans les meilleures dispositions pour les Americains et que le traité avec l'Angleterre les ait Laissés à la mercy de ces derniers, il sera difficille de Longtems de faire des cessions pour commencer des Etablissements solides. C'est donc sur la partie Meridional seule de L'ohyo que se portent touttes les Emigrations et la seule sur Laquelle on puisse faire quelques Spéculations solides et dont on peut attendre un Succès prochain.

Cette partie de terres appartient à cinq Etats seulement, la pensil-vanie, la Virginie, les deux Carolines et la Georgie. Ces trois derniers, n'ayant rien sur La riviere Ohio même (qu'on peut considérer pour L'avenir plus ou moins eloigné comme un débouché à la mer) et étant séparés du Missisipy par les Cherokes et Les Chicasaws, les plus turbu-lants des Sauvages, n'offrent par les mêmes avantages que ceux qu'on peut trouver sur les bords de L'Ohyo. Les possessions de la pensilvanie sur cette rivière ne s'étendant qu'environ 80. miles au dessous du fort pitt et sont deja touttes peuplées et etablies. Tout L'Espace compris entre la Pensilvanie, la rivière Ohio, le Missisipy et la limitte de la Caroline Septentrional se trouve appartenir à la Virginie.* Cet Etat pour acquitter une partie de ces dettes dont il etoit plus oberé qu'aucun autre a vendu indifferament touttes ces terres à ceux qui ont voulu les achetter. Les Speculateurs, attirés par le bas prix auquel on les offroit et par leur bonnes qualité en genéral, en ont achetté sans aucun choix, et la plus part d'entreux se trouvent avec des terres d'une qualité in-férieure, et qui, par les fraix d'arpentage et les mesures posterieures de L'Etat, leur coutent bien plus cher qu'on ne s'y attendoit.

Les derrieres de la Virginie peuvent se diviser naturellement en trois portions. La plus orientale qui joint la pensilvanie s'étant [s'étend] jusqu'à la riviere connüe sous le nom de *tottery, ou bid Sandy* qui tombe dans L'Ohyo environ 400. miles en dessous du fort pitt. L'Espace compris entre le tottery et la riviere verte (Green River), qui va aussi se reunir à L'Ohyo 4. à 500. miles plus bas, forme la Seconde. La plus occidental est bornée par le Missisipy. Cet derniere est un pays absolu-ment plat asses fertile, mais entre les mains des Cherokes qui ne l'ont pas encore vendu aux Virginiens et qui se sont jusqu'à présent opposé à son Etablissement. D'ailleur il a été reservé entier pour les officiers et Soldats de L'Armée et, se trouvant par là très divisé, il a été impossible d'y faire des acquisitions à bon marché, ou en un seul corps. Le climat chaud et humide ne paroissoit pas devoir convenir à des Européens, et l'éloignement de tous Etablissements rendoit plus difficiles les com-mencements de ceux que L'on desiroit former.

La Seconde division, connüe sous le nom de Kentuckey que luy a donné une rivière qui la traverce, est le pays le plus fertile de toutte L'Amérique. Sans être aussy plat que ce pre[mier] dont je viens de parler, les colines y sont si peu elevés et leur pentes cy douce qu'il n'y a presque pas un seul acre qui ne soit labourable. Les Virginiens et les Caroliniens, attirés par de tels avantages, s'y sont jettés en foule et, quoyque les premiers habitants y soient arrivé seulement en 1776., quoyque depuis cette Epoque ils ayent eu une guerre perpetuelle contre les Sauvages et les Anglais, et que les incursions des premiers n'ayent cessé que depuis Six mois, quoyqu'ils soient separés par des deserts au

---

* La Limitte Nord de ce dernier Etat n'est pas encore déterminée mais elle frapera le Missisipy dix à vingt lieues au dessous de l'Embouchure de L'Ohyo.

moins de 300. miles de tout autre etablissement, on y compte actuellement 50000. âmes, population d'autant plus étonnante que L'éloignement des Ports de mer et la crainte des Sauvages a empeché les Europeens de s'y porter et que c'est la Virginie, qui ne contient pas 400 000.
Blancs qui a fourny presque seul tous ces Emigrants.

L'Empressement que Chacun avoit pour faire des acquisitions dans
cette partie, la concurrence qui en résultoit et qui faisoit hausser les
prix des terres déjà occupées et augmentoit beaucoup la difficulté d'en
trouver de bonnes vacantes, n'empêcherent pas plusieurs habitants d'en
acquerir sur le champ plusieurs partie assés considerable, et comme il
n'y avoit point de temps à perdre, ils en firent prendre possessions avant
même d'être sur les lieux. La haute attente qu'ils avoient connüe de la
fertilité des pays ne fut point trompée à leur arrivée. Mais en Exami-
nant attentivement ce pays, Je vis que le climat etoit le même que celuy
de la basse Virginie, qu'il y avoit beaucoup d'eaux stagnantes dont
L'écoulement etoit difficile, que même dans les endroits plus elevés et
plus sain les habitants étoient incommodés par des fievres annuelles
que les defrichements actuels avoient plutôt augmentées que de di-
minuées, que les sources d'eau courante etoient si rares que dans plusieurs endroit on etoit obligé de porter ses grains à 20. lieües pour
trouver un moulin, et qu'il n'y avoit presque point qui fut bonne à boire,§
que les terres, quoyque très riches, étoient peu propre à la culture du
froment, et ne pouvoient convenir qu'à celle du mays et surtout du
tabac, plante qui exige beaucoup de bras et qui ne peut être cultivée
icy avec avantage que par des negres. Enfin que dans la situation actuelle du pays, il n'y avoit point de débouché pour exporter le Superflu
des denrées.

Cette partie est actuellement divisé en cinq Comtés: ohyo, Monongalia, harrisson, Green briar, et Montgomery. Ces deux derniers n'ont
formé d'établissement que dans les Vallées de ces Montagnes; la population actuelle des trois premières ne passe pas trois mille Ames, on en
compte le double dans les possessions de la pensilvanie qui les joignent
et qui sont divisées en trois comtés: Westmoreland, fayette et Washington, l'on [dont] J'ai deja dit qu'elles s'étendoient 80. miles sur
L'ohyo. Les derniers Etablissements qu'on trouve en Virginie sur la
riviere Ohio etoient dans L'année 1784. dans le Comté du même nom
sur la riviere de la peche (fishing Creek), à 130. miles au dessous du
fort pitt et à 60. au dessus de la riviere petit Kanhawa. Il s'en forme
actuellement deux nouveaux, L'un composé D'anabaptistes venus des
nouvelles Jerseys et qui se placent au dessous de fishing Creek, l'autre
d'Irlandais et de Pensilvaniens qui se fixent 30 miles plus bas un peu
au dessous de L'Embouchure du petit Canhawa.

Comme touttes les terres au delà des monts alleghany sont plus
riches et plus fortes que les sables qui couvrent la plus part de celles
entre ces monts et la mer, les arbres y sont tous plus gros, plus com-
pacts et plus durables. Les plus communs de ceux que L'on trouve dans

§ C'est surtout ce qui a empeché les Européens et les pensilvaniens à s'y portés.
Un grand nombre de ces derniers, après avoir visité le pays, sont revenus dans
le leur, et les Virginiens seuls, déjà accoutumés à ces desavantages dans la Basse
Californie [sic] s'y sont plus est [et] fixés.

le pays que Je dEcrit sont le *Sicomore* remarcable par sa grosseur, Le *peuplier* presqu'aussy gros que le Sicomore mais beaucoup plus haut et plus droit; L'on en fait des Canots d'une seul pièce qui ont quelque fois jusqu'à 50. et communement 35. pieds de long; *L'erable* ordinaire et *L'erable à Sucre*, substance qui se tire de l'arbre par incision dans le printems et remplace par le gout et L'usage le Sucre dont on luy a donné le nom; *maronier d'inde; L'ormeau, le frêne, le hêtre*, celuy-cy très commun; le papayer, arbre qui croit aussy dans les Isles et qui produit un fruit de la grosseur du point [poing] assés nourrissant et sain quoyqu'un peu fade au gout; *le cerisier*, et *le noyer* de divers qualités; *L'acacia ordinaire* et *L'acacia à épine*. Tous ces Arbres se plaisent surtout dans les terres basses. L'on trouve quelquefois des Erables, des hêtres, des Noyers et des Cerisiers dans les Coteaux, mais seulement dans le Sol le plus riches. Presque touttes les autres terres ne sont couvertes que de Chênes de plusieurs Espèces, le chêne blanc qui est le plus Estimé pour faire les Enclos à cause de sa facilité à se fendre et qui ne le Sede qu'au Cedre et au chene rouge pour la Charpente, est le plus commun. Dans les terres de la Seconde qualité il est mêlé avec le chêne noir et rouge, le cedre et quelques especes de noyers. Dans celle de la 3me. il croît presque seul, exepté dans les Espaces les plus mauvais où il est mêlé de pins et de chatagnier, ces derniers exigent un sol très sec et aride, se trouvent en abondance dans les Montagnes, mais très rarement dans les terres près de L'Ohyo. Outre ces arbres il y en a deux fort abondant qui, par les avantages qu'on peut en retirer, meritent d'etre nommés separément; ce sont le Meurie et la Vigne. L'on a deja fait de foibles essays sur les vers à soyes qui ont parfaitement reussy. La Soye qu'on en a recuillie a été manufacturée par les habitants même et, quoyqu'ils n'eussent que des tisserans irlandais, ils en ont fait une espece de florence dont je me suis procuré des échantillons. A L'Egard de la Vigne, il y en a deux Especes généralement répendües dans toutte L'Amerique, L'une (fox Grape) donne un raisin blanc très gros, très desagreable au gout et dont il ne paroit pas probable qu'on puisse jamais faire aucun usage. L'autre (fall Grape) produit des raisins rouges de la grosseur d'un pois mangable, mais aigres. L'on trouve sur les isles de L'ohyo entre le fort pitt et la riviere tottery (jamais au dessous) une 3me. Espece qui n'existe nulle autre part en Amerique, qui est de la même grausseur que la 2me. et qui n'en differe que parce que son fruit est d'un gout sucré et très agréable. Soit comme quelques personnes le pretendent, que ces raisins proviennent de vignes plantés autres fois par les françois près du fort Duquesne (à present fort pitt, ou pitsburg) lorsqu'ils en etoient les Matres [Maîtres] et qu'ils jettèrent dans L'Ohyo lorsqu'ils evacuerent le pays en 1759; soit que le Climat, le Sol et surtout L'exposition ayent Seules ameliorés les raisins de la 2me. Espece, il n'en résulte pas moins de ce fait existant que la culture de la vigne ne peut manquer de reussir dans cette partie.

Les animaux Sauvages qui peuplent ces forets sont le *Bison* ou Beuf bossu, improprement appellé bufle par les habitants. Son gout est absolument le même que le boeuf domestique, ils marchent en troupe, on est parvenu à en apprivoiser quelques uns, mais on n'a pas encore essayé de les employer au travail.

L'elan de Virginie, ayant le Corps, Le cou, la teste de celuy d'Europe et de L'orignal du Canada, mais le bois du Cerf. On ne le trouve que dans ces Climats temperées d'Amerique et nulle part en Europe. Son gout est Exquis. Le Chevreuil très abondant et parfaitement semblable à celuy d'Europe. L'ours et le Loup, diminutif de celuy d'europe, les derniers n'attaquent que les moutons, L'autre attaque quelquefois le chasseur Lorsqu'il est blessé. Il en est de même de la panthere connüe, je crois, sous le nom de *Janquart de pensilvanie* qui est grisse, haute de deux pieds et Longue de quatre, non compris la queüe. Le Renard noir et rouge, le Blaireau et le Castor. L'on y trouve aussi des pigeons, des canards, des oyes, et surtout des poulles d'inde, fort grosses et d'un goût Exquis.

Les Reptiles dangereux sont, comme dans le reste de la Virginie, les Serpent à Sonnettes et le Serpent cuivré; ils sont assés commun dans les Montagnes, plus rare dans [la] basse Virginie, et dans le Kentuckey, mais nulle part en aussy grand nombre que dans la partie dont je parle. Les remedes sont aisés et actuellement connüe de tout le monde, les accident n'ont presque jamais de Suittes facheuses. Dans un Séjour de cinq mois dans les bois, J'ai été blessé par un de ces Serpens et je continuay mon chemin après le pensement sans autres inconvenient depuis. Les seuls insectes incomodes sont une grosse mouche qui s'attache aux quadrupedes, et une sorte de tique qui ne se trouve que dans les buissons et qui disparoit dès qu'on défriche. Mais il n'y a ni cousins, n'y Maringoins, n'y aucun de ces insectent [insectes] qui incomodent presque tous les habitants de l'Amerique dans les endroits bas et situées près des Eaux.

A L'égard des productions et des animaux domestiques qu'on a transporté d'Europe, ils ont tous réussy. Le pommier et le pêcher sont les arbres fruitiers que les habitants cultivent le plus, ils font du cidre et de L'eau de vie de pêche. Le Boeuf et le cochon surtout y sont multiplié en plus grande porportion que le Mouton, parce que les habitants ne font pas autant de cas de ce dernier que des autres. Le lait, le beure, les vollailles y sont exellentes. Le froment y rend 30. à 35. boisseaux l'acre,† le Mays de 45 à 50., les autres plantes en proportions; à mesure que les défrichements augmentent et que le bétail se multiplie, on supplée par les engrais à la richesse des terres vierges. Mais ce n'est qu'après 20. à 30. ans qu'on est obligé d'avoir recours à cette ressource, et si les habitants mieux dirigés faisoient succéder une culture à l'autre, laissoient subsister un plus grand nombre d'arbres dans leur defrichements et connoissoient en un mot les premiers principes de l'agriculture, L'on ne s'appercevroient jamais du moindre appauvrissement. C'est ce qui est arrivé dans les Cantons de la pensilvanie et du Mariland habités par les Allemands et qui, quoyque defrichés depuis 80. ans, rendent toujours la même quantité de froment.

Tout ce pays composé des cinq Comtés, *Ohio, Monongalia, harisson, Green Bryar* et *Montgomery* est à peu près de la même Nature. Il est composée par une infinité de ruisseaux qui vont se réunir dans dif-

† L'acre contient 4900. yard qui fait 14700. pieds Anglais, le yard N'est que de trois pieds.

ferentes rivieres lesquelles tombent dans L'Ohyo. Les terres qui joignent
ces ruisseaux et rivieres sont de petites pleines [plaines] surmontées par
des Colines dont la rapidités depend de la largeur des bas-fonds qui les
dominent. Près des embouchures des ruisseaux où les plaines sont plus
larges, les hauteurs sont presque à pic et leurs Sommets est très étroit.
A mesure que L'on remonte les ruisseaux, les pleines se retroissent
[rétrécissent], la pente des Colines devient plus douce et L'on retrouve
à leur Sommet de nouvelles plaines. Les terres basses sont comme partout les plus riches et on les garde pour faire des prairies et pour planter
le Mays nécessaire à La nouriture du betail et de la Vollaille. Les
coteaux dont la pente est la plus douce sont consacrés à la culture du
froment et des autres grains, les plus rapides dont quelques uns seroient
à peine labourables sont réservés pour les bois qu'il est nécessaire de
laisser subsister, tant pour le feu, les enclos et la charpente que pour
L'Exportation, et ils fournissent du paturage au bétail pendant toutte
la belle Saison qui commence à la my mars et fini à la my desembre.
L'on compte que dans les bonnes terres il y a un quart ou un cinquieme
de ces terres basses ou de première qualité; environ un tiers des terres
de la 3me. qualité qu'on ne défriche point, et le reste des terres dans
la 2me. qualité egalement propres à la culture des grains, du chamvre,
des arbres fruitiers et de touttes les plantes qui n'exigent pas la terre
la plus riche comme le Mays et le tabac.

L'Ohyo qui arrose tout ce pays est une riviere qui a environ 400.
verges de larges, depuis le fort pitt jusqu'à l'embouchure du petit
Kanhawa; elle s'élargit ensuite et a un mile de largeur, bien au dessus
de sa jonction avec le Missisipy, depuis le fort pitt jusqu'au fort Weeling qui est à cent miles au dessous. La navigation est difficile dans les
grandes secheresses de l'Eté. L'on peut compter environ deux mois
chaque années pendant Lequel on ne peut se servir dans cet Espace
que de Canots ou petits bateaux depuis Weeling jusqu'à la Nouvelle
Orleans. La navigation n'est interompue que par une chute, ou plus
tot des rapides, qui sont environ à Sept cent miles au dessous du fort
pitt. On est obligé en Eté de decharger les bateaux à cette chute où est
batie une petitte Ville connüe sous le nom de Camwhell's town, ou
Louisville. Dans le printems et L'automne, L'ohyo et touttes les autres
rivieres grossissent prodigieusement, surtout dans la premiere Saison
où elle S'elevent de 20. à 25. pieds, en Sorte qu'un batiment de 500
tonneaux pourroit alors desendent [descendre] du fort pitt jusqu'à la
Mer. Mais pendant presque toutte L'année des bateaux plats portant
de 10. à 20. tonneaux desendent L'Ohyo. Ils peuvent même partir de
jies ferry sur la riviere cheat, huit miles au dessous de sa junction avec
la Monongahela et plus de 100 miles par eau au dessus du fort pitt.

L'Alleghany est navigable par des bateaux de la même grandeur
pendant une distance encore plus Considerable, le Kanwha environ 30.
miles et 50. miles plus haut avec des canots, Le grand Kanhawa beaucoup plus. Touttes ces rivieres sont remplies de poissons. Les plus communs sont la perche, le Brochet, le Barbot (ou Cat fish) qui pèse jusquà
80. livres, ainsy nommé à cause de ces moustaches, et le poisson bufle,
le meilleur de tous, dont le poid n'exede pas vienq livres et qui tire son
nom d'une bosse qu'il a sur le dos.

Le Commerce de ce pays consiste en farine que L'on envoye à Kentuckey et quelques fois à la Nouvelle Orleans, en bétail, pelleterie et Ginzang. Ces trois derniers Articles sont Exportés à philadelphie, à Baltimore, A Lexandrie et dans les autres Ports de la Virginie. Le Commerce de pelleteries étoit déchu pendant la guerre, mais on espere que le traité avec les Sauvages va lui faire reprendre vigeur; celuy du betail et du gainzang est celui qui a le plus soutenu les habitants depuis trois ans; ce dernier paroit devenir plus Considerable, si les Marchands plus eclairés refusoient de prendre tout le gainzang qui est ceuilly avant L'autonne. Faute d'avoir pris cette precation [précaution] le prix de cette racine a baissé dans les Marchés Europeens où on L'exportoit, mais malgré cela Son Abondance, et consequament le bas prix auquel on pouvoit l'acquerir, ont empeché qu'on ne fit aucune perte sur cet article. Les habitants et les premiers Acheteurs en ont fait des proffits très honnestes. La plante qui ne coute à l'habitant d'autre peine que de L'arracher S'achetoit sur les lieux de 20. à 30. Sols Argent de france la livres et se vendoit dans les ports de mer de 45 à 70. En Angleterre, son prix a été de 4. à 12. Shellings Sterlins. Cependant il ne faut considérer cet objet ainsy que celuy de la pelleterie que comme Secondaire, le premier parce que il n'y a qu'un seul marché de Consommation dans tout L'univers, le Second parce que, Exepté ce que les habitants tuent eux-mêmes et qui n'est pas la 10ème partie de ce que les Sauvages fournissent, il faut le payer avec des Marchandises qui ne sont point le produit du pays, pas même de L'Amerique. Ainsy s'est purement un objet de spéculation de commerce qui n'a nul rapport avec l'agriculture du pays, dont les habitants s'occupent principalement à present, et non des objets de secondaire qui ne sont que des ressources addisionelles et precaire. Ce sont dans les produits de L'industrie du cultivateur que l'on doit regarder comme la basse [base] la plus solide du Commerce de ce pays, la faciliter d'elever et transporter le betail rendant actuellement cet objet preferables aux grains. Cependant les habitants ont jusques à present toujours trouvé à se defaire avantageusement de leur superflu de cette denrée. Le froment s'y vend de 60. à 70. sous le boisseau pesent [pesant] 60. livres, la meilleur farine 7. à 8. livres le quintal. La grande quantité de ruisseaux a fait multiplier le nombre des moulins. Pendant la guerre ils envoyoient leur farine à la Nouvelle Orleans où ils etoient receus à bras ouverts. Depuis la paix les emigrations prodigieuses à Kentuckey ont obligé les habitants de cette derniere partie avoir recours à ceux dont je cite pour leur Subsistance, mais la fertilité des terres de Kentuckey et le gout que les Virginiens ont pour le Mays ne permettent pas de douter qu'ils ne soient dans peu d'années en etat de se passer de ces secours. Cependant on pourra toujours leur envoyer un peu de farine de promiere qualité et quelques bois de charpente et construction dont ils ont en bien moindre quantité que plus haut sur L'Ohyo.

Si la nouvelle Orleans appartenoit à une Nation moins Jalouse que L'Espagne, ou que cette puissance altera un peu ses principes rigides de Commerce, L'on verroit cette place devenir bientôt L'entrepot de touttes les farines, de tous les mats et bois de construction qu'il seroit si facile d'y envoyer et ses habitants y gagneroit autant que ceux de

L'Ohyo. Mais il est à craindre que les Espagnols, ne s'attachant à la Lettre du Traité, ne mettent tous les obstacles en leur pouvoir à la navigation des Americains sur le Missisipy. L'on sait qu'en 1763, par le traité entre la France et L'Angleterre, le Missisipy fut pris comme la limite entre les deux Puissances à Lexption [l'exception] de La Nouvelle Orleans elle-même qui, quoyque baty sur le rivage oriental du fleuve, fut laissé avec son distric aux françois, mais il fut stipulé en même temps que la Navigation du Missisipy dans toutte son étendue seroit libre aux deux Nations, les Ameriquains autant qu'anglais jouissent de ce privilege, et il leur fut confirmé par le traité de 1783. avec l'Angleterre. Par les preliminaires de ce traité signé en Xbre. 1782. les limites des Etats Unis et de la floride, alors appartenant aux Anglais, furent fixés au 31eme degré de latitude, ce qui laissoit aux Americains le poste nommé le baton rouge, L'endroit le plus haut où Les Vaisseaux puissent remonter le Missisipy. Mais l'Espagne, voulant absolument mettre une barriere suffisante entre le Mexique et les Etats Unis, ne se contenta pas de la cession que L'Angleterre lui faisoit de la floride suivant les limites reglées avec les Americains, mais elle obligea les uns et les autres à reculer ces limites jusqu'au 32eme. degré, ce qui fut enfin agreé par le traité diffinitif; par là, sans rien oter aux Americains de leurs droits à la Navigation du Missisipy, on leur enleva presque tous les avantages qu'ils pouvoient en retirer, puisqu'ils ne peuvent plus recevoir par ce fleuve aucun Vaisseaux un peu considerables. Il est vrai qu'ils pourroit batir des petits Navires sur L'Ohyo et sur le Missisipy et du moins exporter par eux leurs productions. C'est bien là leur projets et il ne tardera pas à s'executer, mais en attendant on empêche leurs bateaux plats (qui ne peuvent aller en Mer) de ren [rien] debarquer sur les terres Espagnolles, et on a comme de coutume Confisqué la farine, emprisonné, et même dernierement fait disparaitre quelques uns des contrevenants. L'on sent aisement combien cette Jalousie, ces procedés et la Conduitte plus que reservé que L'Espagne a toujours tennüe avec les Americains ont du aigrir ces derniers. Ils disent, et c'est un cri general, qu'il est contre l'ordre naturel des choses qu'un pays immence dont toutes les eaux et par consequent tous les débouchés vont aboutir à un seul point soit, non seulement privé de la possession de ce port unique, mais qu'on refuse encore à ses habitants la permission d'y aller faire les echanges qui leur sont necessaires. Ils disent que le meilleur moyen que peut prendre L'Espagne pour retarder les revolutions qu'elle craint dans ces Colonies n'est pas de ce faire des ennemis de ceux qui peuvent si aisement les secourir. Ils pretendent au contraire que ce n'est qu'en leur donnant presque tous les avantages que pourroit leur procurer la possession de la Nouvelle Orleans qu'on les empêchera de faire des voeux, ou des efforts à la premiere occasion pour hâter cette revolution. Ils disent hautement que si les Espagnolles continuent à les regarder comme des voisins dangereux et même comme des ennemis, ils ne doivent pas être surpris si les Americains s'accoutument à les voir du même oeil, et qu'aussitôt que la population des pays de derriere le permetera on tachera de s'assurer par la force de ces avantages, que la Seine [scène] politique devroit engager l'Espagne à accorder de bonne grace. On ne s'étonnera pas de ces discours malgré leur foiblesse actuelle, quand on considerera combien L'Espagne doit apprehender tout mouvement dans cette partie, qui aura lieu un peut plustôt ou un peut plustart et dont on parle comme d'un evenement naturel. Le seul obstacle qui pourroit encore retarder cette revolution est L'opposition que Leur nouvel Allié pourroit y mettre, et ils font des voeux bien sinceres pour que la desunion se mettent entre les deux branches de la Maison de Bourbon, ou que du moins, et cecy ne leur paroit pas improbable, la France vit avec indifference ces changements inevitables, du moins dans la Suitte des temps.‡

Cependant, comme L'on ignore si ces raisons feront quelqu'impressions sur L'Espagne, que L'Epoque où l'on seroit assés fort pour ce passer de son approbation paroit eloignée, au moins de 15 à 20. ans, et qu'en attendant on sera à Sa mercy dans toutes Les tentatives que L'on fera pour S'ouvrir un débouché de ce Coté-là. L'on a cherché à S'en procurer quelqu'autre.

Le General Wasington, toujours animé par des vues patriotiques, et que d'ailleur ses possessions dans les derrieres de la Virginie doivent exiter plus qu'un autre à L'encouragement d'un projet aussy utile, s'est rendu sur les lieux en 7bre. 1784., a examiné avec des gens de l'Art jusqu'à quel poient [point] les divers rivieres etoient navigables, qu'els etoient les endroits où il seroit le plus convenable d'ouvrir ou de perfectioner les routes à travers les Montagnes, qu'elles etoient les branches navigables des rivieres qui tombent dans L'Atlantique qui s'approchassent le plus des branches Navigables de L'Ohyo. Et comme ce projet a été examiné avec attention, et d'après ces resultats et L'opinion des Commissaires nommés par les Etats de Virginie et de Mariland pour examiner murement ce projet, on a été convaincu que de touttes les rivieres de L'Atlantique celle qui s'approche le plus des branches Navigables de L'Ohyo etoit le poutoumack, n'y ayant que 30 à 40. miles au plus depuis L'og'stown où [c]ette riviere cesse d'etre navigable jusqu'à Jeesferry sur la riviere Cheat dont j'ai parlé cy dessus. Il est vray que la navigation du poutoumack est interompüe par quelques chûtes ou endroits rapides, dont la plus considerables est à 12. miles au dessus d'Alexandrie et à cinq au dessus de Gearge town où les Vaisseaux peuvent remonter. Les chûtes ont été Examinées avec le plus grand Soin et l'on a vu qu'il etoit non seulement praticable, mais même peu difficile à les rendre Navigables. En consequence une Compagnie par Action s'est formée sous la protection des gouvernements de Virginie et du Mariland et on luy a accordé le privilege de lever de certains droits (qu'on a irrevocablement fixés d'avance) sur les bateaux qui passeroient dans la Suitte sur le poutoumack à condition qu'ils enleveroient les obstacles qui en obstruent la navigation. Cette Compagnie consiste en

‡ Si l'on jette un coup d'oeil sur la Carte, on verra qu'il n'y a point de pays dont la Situation locale soit aussy singuliere à cet egard que celle des derrieres de L'Amerique. La chaine des alleghany qui est si près de la Mer empeche touttes les eaux qui preinnent leur sources au delà de s'y jetter, il ne tombe presque [que] des ruisseaux dans les lacs du Canada qui s'écoulent à Quebec, et dans cette partie du Golfe du Mexique situé entre le Cap des florides et le Missisipy, touttes les grandes Rivieres vont se jetter dans L'Ohyo, dans le Missisipy, tout ce [se] reunit à L'Embouchure de ce dernier.

600. Actions de 433. piastres fortes chacune. L'Etat de Mariland a souscrit luy même pour 50. Actions, celuy de Virginie pour 100. Actions dont il a donné 50. au General Wasington. Le reste de la Souscription s'est remplie avec la rapidité qu'y donnent L'interet personnel, L'exemple et L'enthousiasme.

Ce projet va être entrepris et ne demande qu'une Couple d'années pour être Achevé. On conçoit combien cela va donner de valeur à touttes les terres qui avoisineront ou qui pourront se servir de ce debouché pour le transport de leurs denrées. On ne peut calculer à quel point le prix peut monter, mais seulement la connoissance du projet a fait doubler le teaux de tout ce qui pouvoit [être] à portée d'en proffiter.

RC (DLC); endorsed by TJ: "Le Maire Apr. 30. 1785. recd. Aug. 22. 1785." Recorded in SJL under date of receipt. Enclosure: (1) "Un Echantillon de Soye Blange" (missing). (2) Memoir on Kentucky, of which a copy was enclosed in Le Maire's letter to Vergennes of 30 Apr. 1785 (both in Arch. Aff. Etr., Paris, Corr. Pol., E.-U., XXIX, 207-12; Tr in DLC). In the text above, a few of Le Maire's slips and omissions have been silently corrected and more clarified by corrections within square brackets; the footnotes, here keyed to the text by symbols, are in the original designated by the letters A-E, though there is no note B.

To Vergennes Le Maire not only described the courtesies and favors extended by SIR PATRICK HENNERY and others in Virginia, but also explained how he had come to write the account of Kentucky: "La guerre m'ayant fait faire un Sejour de plus de six ans dans presque tous les cantons qui dependent de cette nouvelle Puissance, mayant mis a porté de le connoitre parfaitement, et beaucoup mieux sans doute que bien d'autres personnes, je vous joint ici un Memoire sur les terres du Kentokée, fait d'après mes propres observations, consernant les resources des Etats-Unis de l'Amérique, dont je vous ferai le detail si vous me lordonné"

(same). It is obvious that many of Le Maire's observations were his own (and certainly expressed in his own phonetic spelling), but doubtless he had consulted many Virginians and perhaps had seen Filson's *Kentucke* (1784) before setting down his own comments. Apparently unpublished, based in large part on personal observation, and belonging to the earliest accounts of Kentucky, Le Maire's memoir is worthy of publication also as a reflection of the close attention paid to that region by the French ministry because of its impact upon the Mississippi question and, in consequence, upon Spanish, French, and American relations (see communications from Dargés and Otto to Vergennes, 1785-1786, on Kentucky — "cette terre promise" — in same, XXX-XXXI). Le Maire, indeed, had informed Patrick Henry that it was "Jefferson, and the Count de Vergennes, who persuaded me to come over"; it is possible, therefore, that the account of Kentucky had been written at Vergennes' instigation (Le Maire to Henry, 16. Jan. 1786, Vi). Le Maire did not mention MONSIEUR BEUDET in his letter to Vergennes, but the minister can scarcely have been ignorant of his TRES GRANDS PROJETS, particularly if they were the same as those described by TJ in his letter to Monroe of 11 Nov. 1784.

To William Short

Apr. 30. 1785.

Another packet is arrived which sailed from N. York the 22d. of March. As yet we have only a few letters which come through the post office. We have reason to expect there is a passenger from New York and that he may have letters for us. We know that Mr.

Adams is appointed minister to the court of London, and a Colo.
Smith his Secretary of legation. The newspapers tell us that Rhode
island has passed the Impost, and the resolutions for investing
Congress 25 years with a power to regulate commerce, and that
N. York has laid 10 per cent on all British goods, and double
duties on British vessels and portage.—The Marqs. and Marqse.
Fayette, Mr. Adams's family, a Ct. and Countess Doradour who
are going to settle in America, are to dine with me on Thursday.
This is the day after that on which you have flattered us with your
return. We therefore hope you will be of the company. Colo.
Humphries is ill. He was taken two days ago with symptoms which
threatened a plurisy. These are now removed, and he remains only
with a fever which however does not remit. Ct. de Doradour and
young Mr. Adams go in the next packet. W[illiamos] probably will
not go. Adieu.

RC (ViW); unsigned; at head of letter: "Th:J to W. Short"; endorsed in part:
"recd. at St. Germain." Not recorded in SJL.

From Madame de Doradour

Paris, 1 May 1785. She and her husband accept TJ's invitation for
Thursday next.

RC (MHi); 1 p.; dated only: "ce Dimanche Matin." This is one of a group of
five notes from Madame de Doradour which are undated and accompanied by three
leaves bearing addresses to TJ.

To William Short

DEAR SIR   Paris May 2. 1785.

By your servant I inclose you a bill of the Caisse d'escomte for
two hundred livres. We have received this day some public letters
from America. These contain a permission to Doctr. Franklin to
return, and a substitution of myself in his place. There is no appointment of a Secretary of legation, but I suppose it out of doubt
that Colo. H. will be annexed to this legation. Smith is fixed in that
of Mr. Adams to London. W. F. seems to be dropped. While you
know with certainty that any appointment left to me would be at
your command, and that in this I should be actuated by a sentiment of that duty which requires every one to place in office those
who are most worthy of them, I must at the same time say I have
no reason to expect any appointment will be put to my disposal.

It is not easy indeed as yet to know what will be the system of Congress. Mercer is married to Miss Sprigg. Monroe I am afraid is dead, for three packets have now come without bringing me a line from him or concerning him. We shall be all happy to see you on the 4th. and hope you will make some stay if you still propose to return. Colo. H. is got well. Mr. Adams junr. goes the 10th. for N. York, and Monsr. de Doradour with him for Virginia. I am with much affection Your friend & servt.,   TH: JEFFERSON

RC (ViW); endorsed in part: "recd. at St. Germain." Not recorded in SJL. Enclosure not found.

To William Carmichael

[*Paris, 3 May 1785*. Entry in SJL reads: "Wm. Carmichael. Receipt his of Apr. 19. Rh. isld. passed impost imperfectly.—N.Y. double duties on British bottoms—not passed impost. Georga. brought in bill for impost—Moultrie Govr. S.C. Reed of Pensva. dead—Indian purchase said to be to meridian of falls of Ohio but I doubt it. Mr. A. minister at Lond. Smith Secretary of legation—Dr. F. leave to return, myself his successor. Propose full correspondence. Will send cypher— as to Barbary states we wrote Congress in Nov. and expect their answer. Better keep things as they are without committing us as to complexion of our proceedings. He shall be informed as soon as we know.—bought Herrera." Not found.]

De Thulemeier to the American Commissioners

MESSIEURS   à la Haye le 3. Mai 1785.

Les ordres du Roi que je viens de recevoir, me mettent à même de Vous fournir, Messieurs, les éclaircissemens que Vous m'avez demandés par la lettre dont Vous m'avez honoré en date du 14. de Mars de l'année courrante. Sa Majesté veut bien agréer l'Article 19. tel qu'il a été minuté en dernier lieu: "que les vaisseaux armés de l'une des deux Nations pourront entrer avec les prises faites sur leurs ennemis dans les ports de l'autre, en ressortir librement, ou les y vendre."

Elle se flatte que les Etats-Unis de l'Amérique apprécieront cette condescendance, et y reconnoîtront le desir de Sa Majesté de Leur donner des preuves de Son Amitié, d'autant plus qu'Elle ne fait point équiper des vaisseaux en course, et que Ses Sujets ne sont par conséquent pas dans le cas de faire des prises sur mer.

Le Roi se prête également à laisser subsister la clause ajoutée à l'Article 19, "que tout vaisseau qui aura fait des prises sur les Sujets de Sa Majesté Très Chrêtienne, ne sauroit trouver un asile dans les ports ou havres des Etats-Unis."

Sa Majesté consent aussi que l'Article 4. du Traité soit minuté ainsi que Messieurs les Plénipotentiaires Américains me l'ont proposé par la lettre ci-dessus mentionnée, hormis qu'on rétablira les mots de *Sujets* et *Citoyens* qui se trouvoient dans le Contre-Projet, au lieu de *personnes* ou de *tous et un chacun*, et qu'on omettra le passage: "que le présent Article ne dérogera point aux loix de la Ville de Königsberg, qui défendent le commerce entre Etrangers dans l'enceinte de sa jurisdiction"; le droit d'étape de la Ville de Königsberg n'ayant été allégué que comme un exemple pour servir d'éclaircissement, et pour faire sentir la nécessité de la clause générale des Articles 2. et 3. "se soumettant néanmoins aux loix et usages y établis," &ca.

Je me félicite de pouvoir regarder la négociation que j'ai eu l'avantage de traiter avec Vous, Messieurs, à peu près comme terminée. Les Etats-Unis de l'Amérique envisageront certainement l'empressement avec lequel le Roi a souscrit aux différentes altérations du Projet du Traité de Commerce, comme un nouveau motif de protéger et favoriser le négoce et les liaisons que les Sujets de Sa Majesté formeront avec les Citoyens de la République. Il ne me reste que de Vous proposer, Messieurs, s'il ne conviendroit point de faire mettre au net le Traité même, afin que muni de notre Signature, en conformité des pleinpouvoirs qui se trouvent entre nos mains, il puisse être échangé avec les formes usitées.

J'ai l'honneur d'être avec la considération la plus distinguée, Messieurs, Votre Très humble et Très obéissant Serviteur,

DE THULEMEIER

RC (DNA: PCC, No. 86); in a clerk's hand, with final phrase of complimentary close and signature in De Thulemeier's hand; endorsed by David Humphreys. Tr (DNA: PCC, No. 116); in Humphreys' hand. The letter was sent by Commissioners to Jay with theirs of 11 May 1785.

From Eliza House Trist

On board the Ship Matilda, Balize Mississippi
May the 4th. 1785

I embark'd on board a Spanish Ship bound for the Havanah, sixteen days ago and have been detained at this place by contrary

winds thirteen days. There are several Vessels by us likwise waiting for a fair wind. I have just heard that one of them is bound for
france. So favorable an oppertunity induces me to take up my pen
to address a few lines to you, notwithstanding my situation is not
the most agreeable for such an undertaking. I am envelop'd with
noise and confusion. Above they are preparing to weigh anchor
and my fellow Passengers being in number four, 2 Spaniards and
2 french gentlemen, and but one that can speak any english. Their
loquacity and mirth are incessant, but they are very polite and
attentive to us and our accomodations are good or else it wou'd
be intolarable. I have undertaken this voyage without any certainty
that I shall get a Passage from the Havanah to Philad. but if no
immediate oppertunity shou'd offer I must go via the cape. I had
taken my passage in a vessel which was to have saild the later end
of March for Jamaica. I exerted my self to settle my affairs by that
time and came down to Orleans in expectation of embarking
directly, when to my great mortification I found the vessel wou'd
not be ready in four or five weeks. I staid at the House of an english
or rather an American lady who was very polite and kind to me
as indeed are every one that I have had any acquaintance with since
I have been in the country. But my encumberence's of stock for
my voyage, baggage &c. made my situation irksome to me because
I was certain I put the family to inconvenience. Hearing of this
vessel I eagerly imbraced it. How I shall succeed in the undertaking God only knows. My trust in him is my support. There
being no trade between the United States and this Country it seems
allmost impossible to get from here. I found so many difficulties
attending it that I some times was allmost ready to relinquish the
attempt. I have no fault to find with the country or climate or
inhabitants under any other government, tho it has been the source
of much sorrow to me. But a Paradise wou'd not tempt me to be
seperated any longer from My Dear Mother and child, since I am
deprived of what cou'd only make me amends for the loss of their
society.

I did my self the pleasure to write you some time ago acknowledging the receipt of a letter from you dated at Philad. and returning you my sincere acknowledgements for your goodness towards
me, the remembrance of which will never be eras'd from my heart.
May you my worthy friend ever experience that felicity which your
benevolent mind is intitled to. May health and prosperity attend
you, and your children live to call you blessed. Poly joines me in

affectionate love to Patsy who I suppose by this time is quite a french woman.

How long *ere* you expect to finish your Embassy? Shall I ever rank among my other pleasures on my return to my native country that of seeing you again? I am afeard that they mean to keep you there in the room of Doct. Franklin—and I am not so great a patriot as formerly for I wou'd prefer seeing you among your friends in domestick life than serving an ungrateful Publick. Believe me to be with unfeign'd Respect your much obliged friend, E TRIST

RC (MHi); endorsed. Recorded in SJL as received 23 July 1785.

From William Carmichael

SIR   Aranjuez, 5th. April [i.e., May] 1785

I received on the 30th. Ulto. the Letter which you did me the honor to address me the 17th. ditto. I have purchased such books contained in your catalogue as I judged not too dear. The Moment I am furnished with an account of the price of others which are rarely to be met with I will immediately forward it to you. I Shall make the proper use of the Intelligence you are pleased to give me and only wait an opportunity to do it without affectation. I have heard nothing from Barbary since My last by a Cabinet courier from hence. The Infanta set out for Portugal the 27th. The Princess married to the Infant Dn. Gabriel is expected the 22d. of this month. Mr. Gardoqui charged with Instructions from this Court to treat with Congress was still at the Havanna the Last of Feby. I Informed His Excy. B. Franklin of the Nature of that Gentleman's Mission. But I do not recollect that I sent him a copy of a Letter which I received from the Ct. de Florida Blanca on this Subject. I therefore inclose it for your satisfaction. You will see, that this Court finding that after Mr. Jay left this Country no measures had been taken by Congress to accelerate the Treaty determined to send Mr. Gardoqui for this purpose. His appointment was fixed early in the month of Septr. Had Congress thought proper to communicate to me Their resolution of appointing Commissioners to treat with Spain in Europe I might perhaps easily have decided the Ministry to have sent the abovementioned Gentleman merely as Chargé D'Affaires; But not knowing until too late their intentions and these by a private Letter, I could only mention, which I did, the purpose of the new Commission. On the 12th. of October I forwarded to Congress a copy of the Letter I now send you. Mr. Gardoqui's delay in arriving in America, has given great pain to the Ct. de Florida Blanca who I am persuaded is sincerely disposed to terminate a treaty which may remove the causes of present Jealousies. The Ct. de Galvez, Governor of the Havanna and Luisiana will be consulted, I beleive with respect to the Limits: This and other *Circumstances* which I cannot mention *here* may have contributed to decide this Court to treat on the Spot. The Maritime Force of the Emperor of Morocco is every way Contemptible. I have sent to Congress the relation I received of it. Should the United States be disposed to treat with these Pirates in a respectable manner, that is by accompanying their envoys with an Armed Force, It will be necessary to take previous measures to Assure places of retreat for their Vessels. This Country and the States of Italy I presume would not be displeased to see an armed Force of the States in the Mediterannean. But as that armed Force by its activity would become a Protection in some measure to their Commerce, I should think that measures might be taken to engage them to contribute to its permanency in that Sea. I know not what may be the powers you are invested with for treating with the Nations in question, but permit me to Observe that it will not be difficult to sound their Intentions or rather dispositions *eventually*. With respectful Compliments to Their Excellencies B. F. & J. A. I have the honor to be Your Most Obedt. Humble Sert.,

Wm. Carmichael

P.S. Motives of Delicacy induce me to request you not to show to the Ct. de Aranda the inclosed paper, unless you should find that he has received a copy of it.

RC (DLC); endorsed. Entry in SJL reads: "received, W. Carmichael's. Aranjuez Apr. 5. 1785 should have been May 5." Enclosure: A copy of the letter from Floridablanca to Carmichael, 7 Oct. 1784 (Tr in DLC, in Spanish, and in Carmichael's hand; an English translation is printed in *Dipl. Corr., 1783-1789*, III, 289-90).

Carmichael was more certain than he appears to be in this letter that the CT. DE GALVEZ . . . WILL BE CONSULTED. For, in his letter to Congress of 12 Oct. 1784 transmitting a copy of Floridablanca's letter stating the nature of Gardoqui's mission (that, though only a chargé d'affaires, he was given plenipotentiary rank and full power to treat), Carmichael also sent a copy of a letter from Floridablanca to Galvez which he had "had the good fortune to see" and whose acquisition he regarded "as fortunate, because it contradicts assertions made to me by the Minister of the Indies, his nephew the Governor of Havana, and Mr. Gardoqui, as if the proposal of the navigation of the Mississippi in favor of the United States was inadmissible on the part of Spain, which, on no consideration, would enter into negotiation on this subject" (*Dipl. Corr., 1783-1789*, III, 287-8). The letter from Floridablanca to Galvez of 2 Oct. 1784 had stated that Gardoqui was authorized to confer with Galvez on the subject of the regulation of boundaries with the United States and the navigation of the Mississippi, since these were "the most important subjects of which he will have to treat" (same, III, 289). In his letter to Congress covering this secretly acquired letter (which Floridablanca doubtless made available) Carmichael added: "As it is of the utmost importance for the future services which I may render them, that an account of this letter, having fallen into my hands, should not become known to this Court, I hope I shall be pardoned in recommending the greatest secrecy" (same, III, 288). These were undoubtedly the CIRCUMSTANCES WHICH I CANNOT MENTION HERE, but it is very likely that both Floridablanca and Carmichael were more concerned over the access to this information by the court of France than by America. On 8 Feb. 1785 Vergennes had written Marbois: "Je prévois, M. que le Mississipi sera une pomme de discorde entre l'Espagne et les américains; ceux cy voudront se prévaloir de leur traité avec l'Angleterre pour avoir une navigation libre sur ce fleuve, et la Cour de Madrid la

leur refusera par ce que celle de Londres lui a donné ce qui ne lui appartenoit pas. Dans cet etat des choses, si les deux parties veulent conserver la paix, elles doivent aviser à des termes moyens: celui que l'Espagne propose, savoir l'etablissement d'un port franc à la Nouvelle-Orleans, me paroit on ne peut pas plus raisonnable, et les Américains sont à peu près sans intérêt comme sans titre pour s'y refuser. Au surplus, M., je dois vous recommander beaucoup de circonspection dans toutes les affaires qui concerneront l'Espagne, et d'attendre pour agir pour Elle des instructions de ma part, à moins de circonstances extraordinaires qui ne sauroient être prévües" (Arch. Aff. Etr., Paris, Corr. Pol., E.-U., Vol. XXIX, 43-4; Tr in DLC). For all his perspicacity, Vergennes probably did not foresee that the Americans, when hard-driven for justifying arguments, would fall back upon the doctrines of natural law and apply them to the navigation of the Mississippi as they had to the right of revolution.

From Martha Jefferson Carr

[*6 May 1785.* Recorded in SJL as received 22 July 1785 "by Mr. Mazzei." Not found.]

From Madame de Doradour

[8 May 1785]
ce Dimanche a cinq heure du soir

Md. Doradour envoi savoir des nouvelles de Monsieur jeffersson. Elle aurra celui de le voir Demain matin chez lui; elle a etee deux jours de suite a hauteuille; le depart de Mr. Doradour est fixé a jeudi prochain; elle a le coeur gros de se separer de son mari; sa seule consollation est l'interest que Monsieur jeffersson lui a promis de mettre a ses recomandations en amerique; sy Md. Doradour n'avés pas craint de le deranger elle aurres été ches lui ce soir, car elle se promene sur le boullevar Du temple; elle a l'honneur d'assurer Monsieur jeffersson de son attachement.

RC (MHi). The present note is one of a group of five from Madame de Doradour which are undated and accompanied by three leaves bearing addresses to TJ.

From C. W. F. Dumas

The Hague, 10 May 1785. Mr. Koopman, a young man of Utrecht, has consulted him about settling as a planter in Georgia or South Carolina; Dumas has promised in turn to consult TJ on the matter and requests TJ's advice and an early reply to the questions enclosed. Sends compliments on TJ's appointment to succeed Franklin and asks TJ's address.

RC (DLC); 1 p.; in French; at head of text: "à Son Excellence Mr. Jepherson, Min. Pl. des Et. Un." FC (Dumas Letter Book, Rijksarchief, The Hague; Photostats in DLC); lacks postscript of RC. Recorded in SJL as received 17 May 1785. Enclosure not found.

American Commissioners to John Jay

SIR   Paris May 11th. 1785

Our last letter to you was dated April 13. 1785. and went by the packet of that month from l'Orient. Since that date the letter No. 1.a. directed to Dr. Franklin enclosing those marked No. 1.b and c. and also the paper No. 2. have come to hand. These relate to supplies furnished by Mr. Harrison to the crew of the ship Betsy taken by the Emperor of Morocco, on which subject Congress will be pleased to make known their pleasure to Mr. Harrison or Mr. Carmichael; they relate further to the general affairs of the Barbary States. A letter from the Marshal de Castries forwarded to us by the Count de Vergennes, marked No. 3.a.b. will shew the opinion of that Minister on the best method of conducting a treaty with those States. As we are as yet uninstructed from what sources to call for the monies necessary for conducting and concluding treaties with them, and no step can be taken but with cash in hand, we await orders on this subject, and in the mean time wish to keep matters with the Emperor of Morocco suspended in their present state. The attention of Congress will have been called to this circumstance by our letter of Novr. 11 and several letters subsequent to that date.

As it is always well to know the dispositions of our neighbours, we enclose the letter No. 4. from a refugee of Louisiana to Doctr. Franklin. It contains moreover a proposition for the consideration of Congress.

No. 5.a. and b. are a counterproject, with a letter covering it, from the Chargé des Affaires for Tuscany at this court. As some of the alterations of our draught which the counterproject proposes required explanations these have been desired and obtained in verbal conferences with Mr. Favi. In consequence of these we shall immediately communicate to him in writing our dispositions on the several parts of it.

The letter No. 6. from the Baron de Thulemeier received the 9th. instant contains the decisions of the King of Prussia on our last propositions. We shall close with him on the ground established in the several papers which have passed between us, and take immediate measures for putting the last hand to this treaty.

We have the honor to be With great respect Sir Your most obedient & Most humble Servants,

JOHN ADAMS
B. FRANKLIN
TH: JEFFERSON

RC (DNA: PCC, No. 86); in Humphreys' hand, signed by Adams, Franklin, and TJ. FC (DNA: PCC, No. 116); also in Humphreys' hand. Enclosures: Nos. 1a. through 1c.: William Carmichael to Franklin, 15 Apr. 1785 and its enclosures. No. 2: An account of presents made to the Dey of Algiers, enclosed in Carmichael to TJ, 4 Apr. 1785. Nos. 3a. and 3b.: Vergennes to the American Commissioners, 28 Apr. 1785 and its enclosure. No. 4: S. Hilaire de Génévaux to Franklin, 14 Apr. 1785 (Tr and translation in DNA: PCC, No. 86). Nos. 5a. and 5b.: Favi to the Commissioners, 26 Apr. 1785 and its enclosure. No. 6: De Thulemeier to the American Commissioners, 3 May 1785.

From Madame de Doradour

[11? May 1785]

Mde. Doradour cera comblée D'avoir l'honneur de voir Monsieur jeffersson. Elle voudres pouvoir l'aller chercher pour lui eviter cette promenade; elle l'assure de sa reconnoissance.

RC (MHi). Date is conjectured on the ground that TJ may have informed Madame de Doradour that he would bring to her the packet of letters written on 11 May that he expected to entrust to her husband. This is one of a group of five notes from Madame Doradour which are undated and accompanied by three leaves bearing addresses to TJ.

To Francis Eppes

[Paris, 11 May 1785. Entry in SJL reads: "F. Eppes. Receipt of his and Mrs. E's of Oct. 13. and 14. My appointment will keep me somewhat longer. I must have Polly. As would not have her at sea but between 1st. of Apr. and Sep. this will allow time for decision—is there any woman in Virga. could be hired to come. I sometimes think to send one. Pray his advice and Mrs. E's.—his wine shipped for Falmth.

Apr. 13. Mine good. Peace. Compliments to [those at] Hors du monde."
Opposite entry in sɪʟ is the notation: "by Mr. Adams. May packet."
Not found.⟧

To Elbridge Gerry

Dear Sir   Paris, May 11, 1785.

Your favour of February 25th came to hand on the 26th of
April. I am not a little at a loss to devise how it has happened that
mine of November 11th, which I sent by colonel Le Mair, and who
I know arrived at New-York the 15th of January, should have been
so long kept from your hands as till the 25th February. I am much
afraid that many letters sent by the same hand have experienced
the same delay, and among these a public letter from the commissioners to congress, which we do not yet know that they have ever
received, any more than the subsequent ones sent regularly by
every packet since. We are told that this government will in the
course of the ensuing months remove their packets to Havre, which
will facilitate the conveyance through the posts to the packets, but
most of all will enable us to forward packages too heavy for the
post. That port is more convenient too for our trade while at peace
with England. The marquis de Lafayette, whose zeal for America
is great, expressed to me a desire of endeavouring to obtain it as a
free port, and asked my opinion. I knew that it would be disagreeable to the government that free ports, round which is drawn a
wall of separation from the country in which they are, from which
commodities are not permitted to be sold to the interior country,
and which in fact are restrained to the sole office of an entrepot,
were of little value to us, because our merchants will never find it
answer their account to unship their produce merely to ship it
again for another market. They must always know beforehand
where they can sell, and carry directly thither. I therefore recommended to the marquis not to attempt it, that by asking small
favours we should weaken our pretensions to great ones, and that
I wished him to reserve his efforts and influence for the great objects of our mission. I think he will do it, as nothing seems to be
nearer his heart than the serving America. As yet nothing has
been opened here; the times did not admit it. The arrêt on the West
India commerce last winter raised a furious tempest against the
minister. It has been with difficulty that he could keep the ground
which that had gained. The storm is not yet over, but its force is

so far spent that I think there is little danger of the merchants forcing him to retract: but whether more can be got is a desperate question; it shall be tried when circumstances are ripe for it. The marquis has showed his attention to us in another instance, as you will see by a contract for the supply of whale oil, which Mr. Adams carries over. There were circumstances in this which were not as precise as could have been wished, but as it will rest with our merchants to accept or to refuse the contract, I thought it worth concluding; on which question the marquis was so good as to consult Mr. Adams, sen. and myself. I have great reason to be grateful to my friends in congress for the partialities so often shown me in their European appointments. I will endeavour honestly to deserve them, and shall be supremely rewarded if I can give them content. Mr. Adams sets out in a few days for London: on him we shall rest the desperate task of negotiation with that court. Perhaps the just resentment lately excited in America by their conduct and the probability of our acting as a nation by retaliating measures may induce them to lend a listening ear to equal propositions. I have much feared that their measures and their temper would lead towards hostilities. As yet we ought not to think of war with a powerful nation: there are, to be sure, measures which would force it on us. Under the possibility of this event, we were anxious to obtain a right of selling prizes in war in the Prussian ports, and the cession of this point by the king may in that case have the most important consequences. Great Britain has but two resources for naval stores, America and Russia. The first of these ceases to be open to her in case of a war with us, and we can in a great measure intercept her supplies from Russia, possessing protection and a free sale in the Prussian ports. It will employ a respectable part of her naval force to protect her supplies from that quarter. Much could have been done against her in this way in the last war, had we possessed this privilege. We are glad also to close this treaty on account of the respect paid to whatever the king of Prussia does. Of all the powers not holding American territory, a connexion with him will give us the most credit.

I think it probable that the peace will be kept in Europe, at least between the emperour and Dutch. This country has just lost a great statesman in the duke de Choiseul. Though out of the administration, he was universally esteemed, and always supposed to be in the way of entering into it again. He died two days ago.

I pray you to write to me as often as you can find time. I will be punctual in returning it. Besides the public transactions of America, the objects of the different parts of congress, their workings and counterworkings, what you refuse to do as well as what you do will be most interesting to me. A dry reading of the journals does not give that intimate knowledge of their dispositions, which may enable one to act to their wishes in cases unprovided for. This will be delivered you by young Mr. Adams. His being the son of your particular friend renders unnecessary from me those commendations of him which I could with truth enter into. I congratulate your country on their prospect in this young man. I pray you to believe me with much sincerity, Your affectionate friend and servant,

TH: JEFFERSON

MS not found; text from James T. Austin, *The Life of Elbridge Gerry*, Boston, 1828, I, 486-90. Entry in SJL reads: "Elbridge Gherry. Receipt of his of Feb. 25. Packets go to Havre next month. M. Fay[ette]'s proposition to get it made free port. My objections. His zeal. Arret on W. India commerce. Ferment not subsiding. Marquis bargain for whale oil. My appointment. Mr. Ad[ams] goes in a few days to Engld. Perhaps American resentment may open their ears. Importance of article in Prussian treaty for selling our prizes in their ports. Peace. Death of Choiseul. Write me history of Congressional proceedings. Young Adams." In margin opposite entry in SJL is the notation: "by Mr. Adams. May packet."

THE ARRÊT . . . RAISED A FURIOUS TEMPEST AGAINST THE MINISTER: The protest of the Chamber of Commerce of Picardy of 25 Jan. 1785 was typical. It declared that "L'Arrêt du Conseil du 30 Aoust dernier qui ouvre différents Ports d'Entrepots dans les Isles françoises de l'Amérique avec la faculté d'y admettre les Batimens Etrangers, porte le Coup le plus funeste à la prosperité de la Nation. . . . En conséquence la Chambre du Commerce de Picardie ose espérer de la Sagesse comme de la Justice de Sa Majesté, qu'elle gainera retirer cette Loy aussi nuisible aux Revenus de l'Etat, qu'Onéreuse et destructive du Commerce de la Monarchie" (Arch. Aff. Etr., Paris, Corr. Pol., E.-U., XXIX, 32-8; Tr in DLC; a copy of the Arrêt of 30 Aug. 1784 is among TJ's books in DLC, Sowerby, No. 2293). The CONTRACT FOR THE SUPPLY OF THE WHALE OIL, dated 7 May 1785, and signed by Tourtille de Sangrain,

is in DLC: TJ Papers, 51: 8740-4. For an account of this contract, which Lafayette negotiated in order to promote the sale of whale oil for street illumination in Paris and other cities of France, see Gottschalk, *Lafayette*, *1783-89*, p. 165-6 text and references cited there. The original of Lafayette's letter to Adams, 8 May 1785, reporting the consummation of the agreement, is also in DLC: TJ Papers, 12: 2068, and reads in part as follows: "If you think the Bargain is good, your son might propose the proposition to our New England friends, and take charge of the Samples of oil that will be Ready to Morrow—in which Case, I would propose His Meeting Mr. Jefferson Where a man of the police will attend at Whatever Hour in the morning you please to Appoint. When you send Back the papers, I will show them to Mr. Jefferson and Know from Him if it is Convenient we should wait upon Him, your son, the police Man and myself about ten in the Morning." Though the final terms of the contract were agreed upon at TJ's house (Gottschalk, same, p. 166), the negotiations had been begun by Lafayette with Adams: "I am indeed no stranger to the Marquis's exertions in the affair of the Oil, and it may not be improper to mention to you the particulars of the Rise and Progress of them. One day at dinner I believe at his House or mine, he addressed himself to me, and said, he had been treated with so much affection and respect at Boston and its Neighborhood that he wished it was in his Power to do some service to that part of America. I said it would be easy to put him in a Way to do a very valuable service. He said I had but to mention any Thing in his Power and it should be done. I replied that we wanted to know 1. with what sort of Oil the *Riverberes* of Paris and other Cities were illuminated. 2. what was the Price of that Oil. 3. whether it was the Growth and Manufacture of France or of Foreign countries. 4. whether it were paid for in Cash or French produce or Manufactures. 5. who had the Care of the Lamps Oil and Illumination, whether the court or the City. 6. what Duties were now payable on the Importation of Foreign Fish Oil. 7. whether those Duties would be taken off and lastly whether any plan could be contrived to introduce into the *reverbers* of France, the White Sperma Coeti oil of New England? He said he was very much obliged to me and I should hear further from him. He was as good as his Word and soon informed me that Monsieur Tourtille de Sangrain had a Contract for Illuminating thirty Cities for fifteen years. That he had seen him and concerted a plan, that he had obtained of Monsieur de Calonne his promise to take off the Duties for a Trial, and without any more details he obtained of Mr. de Sangrain the Proposals and samples sent to America by my son. In an affair of such Consequence, and in so critical a moment it is to be wished that some voluntary association of private Gentlemen, or even the Legislature of the state had agreed to the proposals at a Venture. Perhaps however the method taken is a better one" (Adams to Nathaniel Barrett, 2 Dec. 1785, MHi: AMT; see also Adams to TJ, 2 Dec. 1785).

To George Gilmer

[*Paris, 11 May 1785*. Entry in SJL reads: "Dr. Gilmer. Recommending Doradour. My appointment not keep me long. Ill health. That I send for Polly. Patsy well. Peace." Opposite entry in SJL is the notation: "delivered Monsr. Doradour. May. 11." Not found.]

To Samuel Hardy

[*Paris, 11 May 1785*. Entry in SJL reads: "Saml. Hardy esq. Recommend Adams, Doradour. What become of Monroe? Mercer married and you? Peace. Emperor inquiet. No propositions to this court occupied with Dutch quarrel and great ferment about arrêt as to W.I. trade. Perhaps American measures may produce change in dispositions of Engld. Write me history proceedings of Congress. Send letters by passengers. Barbary affair puzzling. Lamb. Well to be at peace with Spain. My appointment. Thanks for it." Opposite entry in SJL is the notation: "by Mr. Adams. May packet." Not found.]

To John Jay

SIR   Paris May 11. 1785.

I was honoured on the 2d. instant with the receipt of your favor of Mar. 15. inclosing the resolution of Congress of the 10th. of the same month appointing me their Minister plenipotentiary at this court; and also of your second letter of Mar. 22. covering the commission and letter of credence for that appointment. I beg permission through you, Sir, to testify to Congress my gratitude for this new mark of their favor, and my assurances of endeavoring to merit it by a faithful attention to the discharge of the duties annexed to it. Fervent zeal is all which I can be sure of carrying into their service, and where I fail thro a want of those powers which nature and circumstances deny me, I shall rely on their indulgence, and much also on the candour with which your goodness will present my proceedings to their eye. The kind terms in which you are pleased to notify this honor to me require my sincere thanks. I beg you to accept them, and to be assured of the perfect esteem with which I have the honor to be Sir your most obedient and most humble servt., TH: JEFFERSON

RC (DNA: PCC, No. 87, I). With RC is fragment of wrapper bearing the following notation: "Letters from Mr. Jefferson at Paris from 11 May 1785 to 31. December 1786 inclusive and from 5 February 1788 to 23 November 1789. inclusive." Dft (DLC: TJ Papers); has numerous deletions and insertions, but differs from RC in phraseology only. Tr (DNA: PCC, No. 107). Entry in SJL reads: "Mr. Jay. thanks to Congress for appointment"; opposite the entry is the notation: "by Mr. Adams. May packet." Entry in SJPL reads: "Jay John. Receipt of my commission as Minister Plenipotentiary."

To John Jay

SIR   Paris May 11. 1785.

As it frequently happens that we cannot meet with passengers going hence to the packet to whom we may commit our letters, and it may be often necessary to write to you on subjects improper for the inspection of this government to which the letters by post are subject, I have made out a cypher which I now inclose and deliver to young Mr. Adams who will have the honor of delivering you this. The plate and impression have been made under my own eye, with circumstances of such caution as may give you the most perfect confidence in it. I have the honor to be with great esteem Sir your most obedient & most humble servt., TH: JEFFERSON

RC (DNA: PCC, No. 87, I). Tr (DNA: PCC, No. 107, I). Entry in SJL reads: "[Mr. Jay] inclosing cypher"; opposite the entry is the notation: "by Mr. Adams. May packet." Enclosure: The code that TJ caused to be engraved has not been found among the collections of the Library of Congress or the National Archives; it may be among the Jay Papers. In his Account Book for 25 May 1785 TJ wrote: "paid engraver of my cyphers. 48f." See TJ to Madison and to Monroe, this date.

To Nicholas Lewis

[Paris, 11 May—3 June 1785. Entry in SJL reads: "N. Lewis. Recommending Doradour. My appointment. Not keep long. Have porticos covered with shed roof. Take care of stuff sawed. Key to send me annually his cash account—send two cones of Cedar of Lebanon. Anthony to plant them in a nursery. Anthony to write me a full state of his proceedings since I left home. Send some trifles to Mrs. L. Peace. Plough to go without horses &c. P.S. Doradour cannot take in the clock, silk &c. Will send them in June packet to N.Y. by Williamos who will forward to Richmd. to J. Buch[anan]." Opposite entry is the notation: "delivered Monsr. Doradour. May 11." A later entry in SJL under 3 June 1785 reads: "Added a P.S. to my letter of May 11. to N. Lewis. That Doradour would hire place at first till Madame comes over which will not be [until?] next summer. That instead of carrying cash I advise him to lodge it with Grand. Williamos will carry the things in Aug. packet." Not found.]

To James Madison

DEAR SIR   Paris May 11. 1785.

Your favor of Jan. 9. came to my hands on the 13th. of April. The very full and satisfactory detail of the proceedings of assembly which it contained, gave me the highest pleasure. The value of these communications cannot be calculated at a shorter distance than the breadth of the Atlantic. Having lately made a cypher on a more convenient plan than the one we have used, I now transmit it to you by a Monsr. Doradour who goes to settle in Virginia. His family will follow him next year. Should he have occasion of your patronage I beg leave to solicit it for him. They yesterday finished printing my notes. I had 200 copies printed, but do not put them out of my own hands, except two or three copies here, and two which I shall send to America, to yourself and Colo. Monroe, if they can be ready this evening as promised. In this case you will receive one by Monsr. Doradour. I beg you to peruse it carefully because I ask your advice on it and ask nobody's else. I wish to put it into the hands of the young men at the college, as well on account of the political as physical parts. But there are sentiments on some subjects which I apprehend might be displeasing to the country perhaps to the assembly or to some who lead it. I do not wish to be exposed to their censure, nor do I know how far their influence, if exerted, might effect a misapplication of law to such a publication were it made. Communicate it then in confidence to those whose judgments and information you would pay respect to: and if you think it will give no offence I will send a copy to each of the students of W.M.C. and some others to my friends and to your disposal. Otherwise I shall only send over a very few copies to particular friends in confidence and burn the rest. Answer me soon and without reserve. Do not view me as an author, and attached to what he has written. I am neither. They were at first intended only for Marbois. When I had enlarged them, I thought first of giving copies to three or four friends. I have since supposed they might set our young students into a useful train of thought and in no event do I propose to admit them to go to the public at large. A variety of accidents have postponed my writing to you till I have no further time to continue my letter. The next packet will sail from Havre. I will then send your books and write more fully. But answer me immediately on the preceding subject. I am with much affection Dr. Sir Your friend and servt.,   TH: JEFFERSON

RC (DLC: Madison Papers); endorsed. Entry in SJL reads: "Jas. Madison. Receipt of his of Jan. 9. Thanks for detail. Recommend Doradour—send cypher. Will send him copy of my notes if ready by the evening. Only send one other copy to Amer. viz to Monroe. Ask his advice. I want to send to each of students at W.M.C. but apprehend will give offence. Next packet goes from Havre. Will then send his books and write more fully." Opposite the entry is the notation: "delivered Monsr. Doradour. May 11." Enclosure: Code

No. 9 to be substituted for Code No. 3. THEY YESTERDAY FINISHED PRINTING MY NOTES: The first "private" edition of *Notes on the State of Virginia*, which will be printed in the topical series in this edition. See (in illustrations) presentation inscription in Richard Price's copy of the *Notes*; Marbois' Queries concerning Virginia (Vol. 4: 166-7); see also Alice H. Lerch, "Who Was the Printer of Jefferson's *Notes*," *Bookmen's Holiday, Notes and Studies Written in Tribute to Harry Miller Lydenberg*, New York Public Library, 1943.

To James Maury

[[*Paris, 11 May 1785*. Entry in SJL reads: "James Maury. Recommending Doradour." Opposite entry is the notation: "delivered Monsr. Doradour. May 11." Not found.]

To James Monroe

DEAR SIR   Paris May 11. 1785.

This will be delivered you by young Mr. Adams whom I beg leave to introduce to your acquaintance and recommend as worthy of your friendship. He possesses abilities, learning, application, and the best of dispositions. Considering his age too you will find him more improved by travel than could have been expected. A Monsr. Doradour also goes in the packet to New York, and from thence proceeds to Virginia, and particularly to that neighborhood which is mine, and I hope will be yours, where he proposes to settle. He will at first purchase a small settlement only, to receive and lodge Madme. de Doradour and their family till they can have time to look about them, and decide on their principal acquisition. She will follow him, probably, the next year, if by that time she can complete the business of selling their property and remitting it to America. They were introduced to me, a few days ago only, by a friend of mine here, and he departing immediately for America and she returning to Auvergne, their residence, 300 miles from Paris, give me little opportunity of knowing them personally. However the commendations of them from the gentleman who is their and my friend, are sufficient to interest me in their success, and to pray of you whatever counsels and civilities his situation may require.

I have not received a line from you since that of Dec. 14. since which I have written to you by every packet. My letters have been dated *Nov. 11. Dec. 10. Jan. 14. Feb. 6. Mar. 18.* and *Apr. 15.* all of which are yet unanswered. I continue however to pester you, being thoroughly satisfied there is some substantial cause of my not hearing from you. I shall endeavor to complete a cypher to accompany this letter by young Mr. Adams.

Matters in Europe are subsiding into quiet. The Emperor and Dutch will probably make friends. Yet it does not seem as if the fevered head of that prince would long leave his neighbors in quiet. Under pretence of running a line between him and the Turks he wants to take off a large district of territory. The Bavarian exchange seems to be hushed. He found too determined an opposition to that. The establishment of a ninth electorate and election of his nephew as king of the Romans will furnish him something to be busy about. No change of disposition begins yet to shew itself in England. The probability of the impost, the concurrence of all the states in the resolutions of Apr. 1784., the measures for making Congress the head of our Confederacy in commerce as well as in war, will probably begin to make them see a possibility of our acting as a nation. The spirit which has appeared in our legislatures and newspapers lately will, I think, dispose them to lend a more favorable ear, and form a favourable groundwork for Mr. Adams to take his stand on. His going to London will at any rate produce

[149]

a decision of some sort.—We hear nothing from Spain but that they do us friendly turns with other nations.—The Marocco business distresses us extremely. Tho' none of us are disposed to join in encouraging their depredations by laying the other hemisphere also at their feet, yet if we had the money at our command we should proceed on that tract, because it seems to have been the intention of Congress in their last resolutions as to these people which are in our hands. A Mr. Jarvis who is here gave us reason to hope Congress were sending a Mr. Lamb as Consul to treat with these states. It is the only practicable method as it is equally impossible for us to go to them, and ineligible to invite them to come to us. You will find that the M. de Castries is also of this sentiment, who seems to have taken pains to misunderstand a passage in our letter to [the Ct. de Vergennes][1] in order to shew a misplaced peice of pride. Almost every mediterranean power (except France) is now at war with the Barbary states. She cannot take the dishonourable part of joining them, and there seems lately to be a misunderstanding between the English and Algerines. Indeed I know not what to do, nor can I say what it would be wise in Congress to do, unless I better knew whether the good will of our citizens would concur to support a war with those Barbarians.

Since writing so far I have received the appointment of Congress to succeed Dr. Franklin here. I give them my sincere thanks for this mark of their favour. I wish I were as able to render services which would justify their choice as I am zealous to do it. I am sure I shall often do wrong, and tho it will be a good excuse for me that my intentions were good, it will be but a barren consolation to my country.

What measures have you taken for establishing yourself near Monticello? Nothing in this world will keep me long from that spot of ultimate repose for me. I keep my eye on yourself and Short for society and do not despair of Madison. I am with much sincerity Dr. Sir your affectionate friend & servt.,

TH: JEFFERSON

RC (DLC: Monroe Papers); endorsed. Entry in SJL reads: "James Monroe. Recommend J. Adams. Doradour. No letters from him. Peace. Emperor inquiet. Spirit lately appearing in America will help Mr. Ad. in treaty. Nothing from Spain. Marocco business puzzling. Jarvis sais Lamb is coming. Received appointment—what measures has he taken for settling near Monti- cello." Opposite entry is the notation: "by Mr. Adams. May packet." Enclosure: Code No. 9.

[1] The name is supplied conjecturally, almost all of it having been carefully erased. The reference is certainly to the Commissioners' letter to Vergennes of 28 Mch. 1785.

To John Walker

[*Paris, 11 May 1785*. Entry in SJL reads: "J. Walker. Do. [recommending Doradour]. My appointment for 3. years. Probably longer than I may stay. Ill health. Patsy well and well fixed. Peace. Engld. not treat. Compliments to Mrs. W., Kinl[och] and Dr. W.—write to me, or Mrs. W. write." Opposite entry is the notation: "delivered Monsr. Doradour. May 11." Not found.]

To Edward Burd

[*Paris, 12 May 1785*. Entry in SJL reads: "Edwd. Burd prothonotary supreme court Pennsylva. Inclosing commission and depositions in Guillebaut et al. v. Wharton." Opposite the entry is the notation: "by Mr. Adams." Not found. The enclosures were doubtless the same (with the addition of the certification by Siot de St. Pol of 26 Mch.) as those enclosed in TJ to Holker, 24 Mch. 1785. See also TJ to Holker, 20 May 1785.]

From Madame de Doradour

[12 May 1785]

ce jeudi a dix heure

Vous serés bien etonné Monsieur de ce que Mr. Doradour ne part pas avec Mr. Adams, mais la voëture ne peut porter qu'une malle, et mon mari ne peut pas s'en aller sans effets. Il est dezollee de ce contre tems, mais il est impossible dy parer; il partira par le paquebot de juin; j'ai renvoyée le cabriollet à Mr. Adams.

Mr. De la fayette ne m'a pas envoyée de lettre; avés vous eu la bonté de lui en parler hier au soir? Donnes-moi, Monsieur De vos nouvelles et recevés l'assurance de mon attachement.

RC (MHi). Date has been assigned from internal evidence. The present note is one of a group of five from Madame de Doradour which are undated and accompanied by three leaves bearing addresses to TJ.

To the Governor of Virginia

SIR   Paris May 12. 1785.

I have the honor to inform you that at length Messrs. Laval & Wilfelsheim have paid the bill of exchange remitted. It will enable me to furnish Monsr. Houdon for his voiage to Virginia when he shall be sufficiently reestablished in his health to undertake it. Dr Franklin proposing to return either the next month or the month following, I think it probable that Houdon will accompany him.

I have the honour to be with due respect your Excellency's most obedt. & most humble servt.,   TH: JEFFERSON

RC (Vi); addressed: "His Excellency the Governor of Virginia"; endorsed in part: "Mr. Jeffersons Lr. recd August 85 acknowledging payment of Mr. Alexrs. bill." Entry in SJL reads: "Governor of Virginia. Laval & Wilfelsheim have paid. Will enable me to furnish Houdon for journey. Probably he will accompany Dr. Fr. who returns the next month or month following." Opposite the entry is the notation: "by Mr. Adams."

To Philip Mazzei

⟦*Paris, 12 May 1785.* Entry in SJL reads: "P. Mazzei. Receipt of his of Dec. 1. Peace. Likely to form rational connection with Tuscany, but barren unless Tuscans carry on in own bottoms. Barbary states. Query if ask peace with sword or money. Ill health. Begin now to go out. My appointment. Send for Polly next spring. Patsy well. Mr. Short also, and at St. Germ.'s. Mr. Ad. goes to Lond. His son to America. Doradour. Mably dead. Favi and myself intimate. Write me political news." Opposite entry is the notation: "by Mr. Adams." Not found. For Mazzei's letter of "Dec. 1." see Mazzei to TJ, 6 Dec. 1784.⟧

From John Polson

SIR   Paris 13th. May 1785

I have the honor to inclose you two Copies of my Case with relation to my Lands in the State of Virginia, and as I am a Native of Great Britain, and not been on any part of the Continent of America during the last war, Excepting for about Seven months on the Mosquito Shore and Spanish main, I flatter myself that through your good offices in representing my Case that my Property will be restored to me.

Such was my Reliance on the Justice and Equity of your State, and on the Justice of my own Claim, that I would not give in an Account of these Lands as a loss Sustained by the War with America, to the British Commissarys Appointed by Parliament to take an Account of the losses sustained by British Subjects.

I have the honor to be with great respect Sir your most Hum Servt.,   JNO. POLSON

RC (MHi). Enclosures not found, but see TJ to Joseph Jones and Adam Stephen, 19 June 1785.

American Commissioners to Dorset

My Lord Duke   Passy near Paris May 16th. 1785

We received in due time the letter which your Grace did us the honour to write us on the 26th. day of March last, and have delayed the acknowledgment of it in expectation of the arrival of the packets, by which we hoped for further Instructions from Congress.

We have now the honor to inform your Grace that Congress on the 24th. day of Feby. last, appointed a Minister Plenipotentiary to reside at the court of His Britannic Majesty, who proposes to proceed to London in the course of two or three weeks, which makes a more particular answer to your letter unnecessary. With great respect We have the honor to be Your Grace's Most obedient and Most humble Servants,

JOHN ADAMS

B. FRANKLIN

T. JEFFERSON

FC (DNA: PCC, No. 116); in David Humphreys' hand; at head of letter: "Answer to the Duke of Dorset's letter to the Ministers dated March 26. 1785." A copy was sent as enclosure No. 3 in the letter from the Commissioners to John Jay of 18 June 1785.

On 7 Apr. 1785, Dorset wrote Carmarthen that he had had no answer from the American Commissioners, adding: "it is however certain that the States of America are daily strengthening the hands of Congress with respect to Commercial regulations, and with the power already delegated to the Messr. Adams, Franklin and Jefferson, they may be consider'd as fully authorized to treat, notwithstanding any appearance of want of subordination to Congress on the part of the States in other matters." Again on 28 Apr.: "The American ministers are much offended at the question I put to them in consequence of your letter to me; they don't *mean* to answer it. I think we need not be in a hurry to form any commercial treaty with America, Adams strongly suspects we are playing that game." On 2 June 1785 Dorset sent a copy of the above letter to Carmarthen "which by mistake was omitted to be sent to your Lordship sooner" (Public Record Office, London, Foreign Office Records, 27/16 France).

From Richard Henry Lee

Sir   New York May 16th. 1785.

I thank you for your obliging congratulation on my appointment to the Chair of Congress, and I do with particular pleasure return my congratulation on your sole appointment as Minister of the United States to so eminently respectable a Court as that of his most Christian Majesty. My ill state of health, added to the business and the ceremonies of my Office, has hitherto prevented me from paying my respects to you, which certainly would have been the case if the former of these circumstances had not principally prevented me. Altho' my health is now better, yet I am very far from being well. I can judge how anxious you must be for minute information of public proceedings in the United States, and of such other matters as your letter imports a desire to be acquainted with. But unfortunately all letters are inspected, and thus the impertinent eye of curiosity may be gratified with such communications as were intended only for you, and which wicked selfishness may make a bad use of. This imposes great restraint, which will remain until Congress shall establish a system of Packets and Couriers of their own. How detestable is this dishonorable mode of obtaining intelligence. The virtue of Lord Falkland, when Secretary of State, would never suffer him to obtain information by such nefarious means. The appointment of Mr. Adams to the Court of London will probably draw out quickly the sense of Great Britain upon the points in dispute with them. And the Authority given by Congress to treat with the Piratical States will, I hope, accommodate all differences with them, and give future security to our Commerce with the South of Europe. I am much obliged to you for the pamphlet. I think it is greatly to be regretted, that the avaricious, monopolizing Spirit of Commerce and Commercial Men, should be suffered to interrupt that diffusion of benefits, and communication between the human species in different parts of the world, which would probably take place if trade were put upon more liberal principles and less shackled than it is. The first attempt made by these States for the trade of the East Indies was from this City. A Ship has gone to, and returned from Canton in fourteen months with a valuable Cargo, and met with the most friendly treatment from the Chinese. Other Vessels are gone and soon expected back. The great Object with the United States now is to dispose speedily of the western lands for the discharge of public debt, and a way for this is opened by treaties already made, and making with the Indians. Coinage, requisition, and Post Office are also objects of great moment and subjects of discussion. Effectual measures are taking by the Assemblies of Virginia and Maryland and by the former alone for opening the navigation between the Potomac and James Rivers with the western waters. Laws with suspending clauses have passed in Virginia for establishing a single Port on each river and for circuit Courts. A general assessment for religion is also a subject of much discussion with us. Mr. Patrick Henry is our Governor, and Col. Harrison has lost his Election in his own County of James City. Great and general efforts have been made to get into the Legislature during the late Elections and I hear that there are many changes. It remains uncertain whether Congress will adjourn or not this year but as I value extreemly your Correspondence Your letters for me may always be safely enclosed to the Virginia Delegates in Congress, so that whether Congress or the Committee of States should be setting, your letters will reach me safely. Be so good as to thank Mr. Short for his letter to me and inform him that I will reply by the next Packet. I heartily wish you health and happiness and I am with the truest esteem and regard, Sir, Your Most Obedient and very humble Servant,   RICHARD HENRY LEE

P.S. I know that your goodness will excuse my having used an amanuensis, when you know that this cold climate has so afflicted my hand and head as to make writing painful.   R. H. L.

RC (DLC); in a clerk's hand, with signature and postscript in the hand of Lee; endorsed: "Lee Richd. Henry. recd. July 10." Recorded in SJL under date of receipt.

From St. John de Crèvecoeur

SIR   New York 18th. May 1785

I am much obliged to you for your Good and Kind Letter. I never knew before of your having been Sick. Happy am I to hear from Yourself, that you are a Great deal better. Your idea of having the Statuary to come over himself, was the only Infallible one. I am waiting for the arrival of the April Packet with Impatience. It will be une Epoque dans les Arts that so renowned a Statuary Shou'd Cross the Seas himself to take the Bust of so renowned a Man. I am much obliged to you for the directions you sent to Virginia. They have Proved of no avail. I have Received nothing. I wrote myself to richmond Last Fall. I have had no answer; that is both a loss and a disappointment. Luckily my Good Friend the vice consul of Carolina sent me an assortment Wherein I found the Magnolia Grandyflora and Do. umbrella. I have obtained a Congé of 6 Months and so Expect to have the Pleasure of seeing you in Novre. I am much obliged to you for your Care in correcting errors in the Cultivator's Letters. I lost so Many Manuscripts whilst I was confined, that 'tis no Wonder Errors in Fact shou'd have made their way in my Poor composition—for I am no author. I lost My Sketches of Maryland and so on Southerly and Perhaps it is for the best. Cou'd not you help me to Them in case of a Second Edition. Pardon the thought. It is not Vanity that Inspires it, but a desire that the Second Edition might be more usefull and more correct than the first. As I was saying I am no author mais Seulement un Ecriveur, which my Singular destiny has Led from the *actual* Cultivation of my Fields to be a Consul, and from sketching what I saw and Felt, for a Friend, to be an author. I am but a scrib[bler] after all, but if the Europeans Can form a better Idea of the united States than before I am satisfyed; for altho' a French Consul I am a Citizen of one of these States and a considerable Freeholder. If you had Some Anecdotes to communicate me I'd willingly Inrich with them the Second reappearence of these 2 Vol: and shou'd Put your name To them. I have Collected materials Enough for a 3d. Vol: which Wou'd be really Instructif if it was thought Proper by the conoisseurs. God Preserve Your health you are now in a fine Climat. Receive I beg the Tokens of the Esteem and the Respect with which I have the Honor to be Sir Your Very Humble Sert.,   St. John

RC (DLC). Recorded in sjl as received 7 July 1785.

From Madame de Doradour

[18 May 1785]
ce Mercredie a huit heure

Mde. Doradour a l'honneur de souhaitter le bonjour à Monsieur jeffersson; elle est obligée de sortir ce matin et ce soir elle iras a hauteuil; elle suplie Monsieur jeffersson de voulloir bien se ressouvenir qu'il a eu la bonté de promettre qu'il parleres a Mr. grand. Sy il menés aujourd'hui Mademoiselle sa fille faire ses adieux à Md. adams, elle seres enchantee d'y trouver Monsieur jeffersson et de le convaincre de son attachement.

RC (MHi); date has been assigned from internal evidence. The present note is one of a group of five from Madame Doradour which are undated and accompanied by three leaves bearing addresses to TJ.

On this same day Adams wrote to C. W. F. Dumas: "We propose to leave Auteuil for London, on Fryday the 20. but we shall not travel very fast. My son left us the 12, and will sail from L'Orient probably on the same day that we shall depart from Auteuil. . . . Mr. Jefferson had yesterday his Audience of the King and presented his Credentials as Minister Plenipotentiary to his Majesty. Mr. Jefferson lives in the Cul-de-sac Tete bout pres les Boulevards. Dr. Franklin is packing up his Effects and proposes to embark next Month" (Adams to Dumas, 18 May 1785, PHi).

From John Adams

Dear Sir   Auteuil May. 19. 1785

Messieurs Wilhem and Jan Willink, Nicholas and Jacob Vanstaphorst and De la Lande and Fynje of Amsterdam, have lodged
in the Hands of Messrs. Van den Yvers Bankers in Paris one
Thousand Pounds Sterling for the Purpose of paying for certain
Medals and Swords which Coll. Humphreys has orders to cause
to be made for the United States. This is therefore to authorize
and to request you to draw upon Messrs. Van den Yvers in favour
of Coll. Humphreys, for Cash to pay for those Medals and Swords
as they shall be made, not to exceed however the said sum of one
Thousand Pounds Sterling.

With great esteem I have the Honour to be, dear Sir, your
affectionate Colleague and most obedient Servant, John Adams

RC (DLC); at foot of text: "His Excellency Thomas Jefferson Esqr. Minister
Plenipotentiary from the United States of America to the Court of Versailles."
In DLC: TJ Papers, 12: 2079 there is the following memorandum in TJ's hand:
"Nov. 16. 1785. drew for 6500 livres in favor Colo. Humphreys for 10. swords."

To De Blome

à Paris ce 19. Mai 1785.
Cul de sac Tetebout

Monsr. Jefferson a l'honneur de vous faire part qu'il a eu le
17me. de ce mois ses premieres audiences du Roi, de la reine, et
de la famille royale en qualité de Ministre plenipotentiaire des
etats unis d'Amerique près sa Majesté.

FC (DLC); addressed: "A Monsr.
Monsr. le Baron de Blome." Not recorded in sjl. Similar formal notices
were doubtless addressed to all members of the diplomatic corps in Paris
(see note to following letter; also
Adams to TJ, 27 May 1785 concerning
the differences between the two courts
in this matter of etiquette).

On 14 May, presumably in a personal interview, TJ communicated to
Vergennes the news of his appointment
as minister and on the 17th delivered
his "letter of credence to the king at a
private audience and went through the
other ceremonies usual on such occasions" (TJ to Jay, 17 June 1785).
Unlike Adams, who of course had valid

reasons for giving a particular account
of his accreditation at the court of St.
James, TJ did not amplify his statement to Jay (see Marie Kimball, *Jefferson: Scene of Europe*, p. 34-8).
Tradition has attributed to this interview a famous remark of TJ's, but its
origin was not so dramatic, though it
was, like many traditions, based on
truth. TJ himself gave rise to the tradition in his letter to Dr. William Smith
of 19 Feb. 1791: "The succession to
Dr. Franklin at the court of France
was an excellent school of humility. On
being presented to ⟨individuals⟩ any
one as the Minister of America, the
common-place question, used in such
cases, was 'c'est vous, Monsieur, qui

remplacez le Docteur Franklin?' . . . I generally answered, 'no one can replace him, Sir; I am only his successor.' " This letter was quoted by Smith in his *Eulogium on Benjamin Franklin . . . Delivered March 1, 1791 . . . before* *the American Philosophical Society* (Philadelphia, 1792), and from that time on the tradition gained currency, at times the king and at other times Vergennes being designated as TJ's interlocutor.

From the Ambassador of Venice at the Court of Versailles

[ca. 19 May 1785]

L'Ambassadeur de Venise a l'honneur de faire ses compliments de felicitation à Monsieur Jefferson sur les Audiences qu'il a eu le 17. de ce mois du Roi, de la Reine, et de la Famille Royale en qualité de Ministre Plenipotentiaire des Etats-Units d'Amérique près Sa Majesté.

RC (DLC); undated; addressed: "A Monsieur Monsieur Jefferson Ministre Plenipotentiaire des Etats-Unis d'Amérique Cul de Sac Tetebout En son Hotel"; endorsed: "Visits of ceremony returned." On 19, 20, and 21 May TJ received numerous formal notes of congratulation similar to the present one from the various members of the diplomatic corps, varying in phraseology but unvarying in substance. These congratulatory notes are to be found in DLC: TJ Papers, 12: 2080, 2082, 2083, 2086, 2087, 2089, 2091, 2092, 2094, 2096, 2099, 2100, 2101, 2103, and 2105.

To John Bondfield

[*Paris, 20 May 1785.* Entry in sjl reads: "Jno. Bonfield. Receipt of his of Apr. 19. and 25. and of wine in good order. Will answer his bill. Wine good." TJ must have erred either in the present entry or in that of 5 May in which he recorded the receipt of "Bondfeild's Bordeaux Apr. 28. 1785," for if there had been two letters he doubtless would have acknowledged them in the present; at any rate, neither a letter dated the 25th or 28th nor the present acknowledgement has been found.]

To C. W. F. Dumas

SIR   Paris May 20. 1785.

I am honored with your favor of the 10th. inst. and am sorry it is not in my power to answer any one of the questions proposed in the papers inclosed to me. They relate altogether to the lands and culture of South Carolina, which are so totally different from those of Virginia that I am unable to give any information on the subject. The staples of S. Carolina are rice and indigo; those of Virginia tobacco, and wheat. Nor have I ever been in S. Carolina. At present there is nobody in Paris from that state or I would have taken pleasure in procuring answers to the questions. I re-inclose the papers.

I thank you for your congratulations on my appointment to this court. I shall be happy to have the advantage of your correspondence, as the public service will be best promoted by a free communication among it's servants. I have found the speediest channel of conveiance to be the post, but the Couriers of the Dutch Ambassador the safest. I have taken an hotel on the Cul-de-sac Tetebout près de la comedie Italienne, to which you will be so good as to direct your letters. I have hitherto directed my letters to you generally at the Hague, and beleive it has sufficed. If a more special direction be necessary I will ask the favor of you to advise me of it. Mr. Adams departs for London this day. I have the honour to be with much respect Sir your most obedt. humble servt.,

TH: JEFFERSON

RC (MHi: Guild Coll.). Entry in SJL reads: "C. W. F. Dumas. Receipt of his of May. 10. Unable to answer questions as to S. Carola. therefore re-inclose them. No body here from that state. Thanks for his congratulations. Wish his correspondence. Give him my address and ask his." Enclosure not found; see Dumas to TJ, 10 May 1785. On 12 May Dumas wrote to Adams, asking him to inform TJ that, not knowing his local address, he had written him with no further address than his name and rank and that he could claim the letter at the post office if it did not reach him (it was actually sent under cover to Ferdinand Grand). This must have referred to Dumas' letter of 10 May (Dumas to Adams, 12 May 1785; MHi: AMT).

To Jean Holker

[*Paris, 20 May 1785*. Entry in SJL reads: "J. Holker. Receipt of his of Apr. 25. and of the copying press. Will send the 16ᵗʰ—1 by Williamos or answer his order. Inclose the Acquit à caution (which la Motte had delivered me). Dr. F's caisse not come. He writes to Mr. Holker. I sent by young Mr. Adams duplicates in Guillebaut v. Wharton." Not found.]

From John Adams

MY DEAR SIR   Montreuil sur mer May 22. 1785

We left Auteuil the 20th. afternoon and have made easy Journeys. Indeed We could not have done otherwise, because the Post-horses were engaged, by the unusual Number of Travellers, in such Numbers that We have been sometimes obliged to wait. The Country is an heap of Ashes. Grass is scarcely to be seen and all sorts of Grain is short, thin, pale and feeble while the Flax is quite dead. You see indeed more green Things than in some of our sharp Drouths in America, but as the Heat of this Clymate is not sufficient to destroy vegetation so effectually as with us, it is not enough neither to produce so rapid a Revivication of the Universe, upon the Return of Rains, so that their Prospects are more melancholly than ours upon such Occasions. I pity this People from my soul. There is at this Moment as little appearance of a change of Weather as ever.

Tomorrow we shall reach Calais, but I cannot calculate how long it will take us to cross the Channel. I allow two days from Dover to London as I am determined to be in a hurry about nothing from the Beginning to the End of this Adventure. It is best to give myself as well as others time to think.

The Ladies join in respects to you and Mr. Humphreys and Mr. Williamos, the Marquis and his Lady and all other Friends. Be so good as to inform me, if you learn any Thing of the sailing of the Packet, and of the Health of my Boy. I thank you kindly for your Book. It is our Meditation all the Day long. I cannot now say much about it, but I think it will do its Author and his Country great Honour. The Passages upon Slavery, are worth Diamonds. They will have more effect than Volumes written by mere Philosophers. The Ladies say you should have mentioned West and Copeley at least among your American Genius's, because they think them the greatest Painters of the Age. Madam[e says] I have not expressed her sentiments politely enough. It should run thus: The Ladies desire that in the next Edition you would insert West and Copeley &c.

The melancholly Face of Nature, added to the dull political Prospect before us, on the other side of the Channell, coming upon the Back of our natural Regretts at parting with our Son and our fine Summer Situation at Auteuil, and all our Friends in and about Paris, make the Journey rather triste, but we have passed through scenes bien plus triste encore. Adieu.　　　　J. ADAMS

RC (NNP); addressed: "A son Excellence Monsieur Jefferson Ministre Plenipotentiaire des Etats Unis de L'Amerique, a la Cour de France, Cul-de-Sac Tetebout Paris"; endorsed. Recorded in SJL as received 25 May 1785.

From John Adams

DEAR SIR   Dessin's Calais May 23. 1785. Monday.

We are just arrived, covered with Dust, and we have hired our Boat, to go over tomorrow at ten. No green Peas, no Sallad, no Vegetables to be had upon the Road, and the Sky is still as clear dry and cold as ever. The Flocks of Sheep and herds of Cattle, through the Country, stalk about the Fields like Droves of Walking Skeletons. The Sheep are pastured chiefly I think in the plowed grounds, upon the Fibres as I suppose of the Roots of Grass turn'd up by the Plow.

From a motive of Humanity I wish that our Country may have plentifull Rains, and our Husbandmen Industry, that they may supply the Wants of their Suffering Fellow Creatures in Europe. You see I have nothing so mean as a selfish or even a patriotic wish in all this. But from the same regard to Europe and her worthy Colonists in the West Indies, I hope that these rainless, heatless Heavens will convince them that it is abundantly for their good that we should bring and carry freely, our Flour, Wheat, Corn, Rice, Flesh, and Fish for their Soulagement. Yours affectionately,

J. ADAMS

The Ladies Compliments of course.

RC (DLC); endorsed.

To Giovanni Fabbroni

[*Paris, 23 May 1785.* Entry in SJL reads: "Febroni. Accompanying a copy of Notes on Virginia." Not found.]

From Alexander Learmonth

Paris, 23 May 1785. Since he is not acquainted with TJ, though had once long ago in Norfolk, Va. been in his company, introduces himself as a gentleman from Charleston, S.C.; appeals to TJ, because "from the amiable Character You bear in life, by that You are well knowing to be a Gentleman, of Noble principalls, and whoes goodness of heart leads You to Simpithise, I feell, for a misfortunate country-man." Had been a prosperous merchant and respected resident of the island of Saint Eustatia, but upon its capture by Admiral Rodney, he, his wife, and six children were left destitute. After the treaty of peace, they moved back to Charleston, and he left for London where, with other Saint Eustatia merchants, he began litigation against Rodney; after long-drawn out proceedings, he lost the suit and was required to pay costs. Then went to Dunkirk to seek help from a friend who he found had already left for Bordeaux, and Learmonth now must follow in order to embark on the friend's vessel for Charleston; there he will make a new start. Is forced by his many misfortunes and present penury reluctantly to ask TJ's help for the journey to Bordeaux, for his "[ne]edy Sircomstances, and Distresd Situation, Oblidges me to walk all the way," and would be forever indebted to TJ for his kindness. Has been referred to TJ by Benjamin Franklin for a passport to Bordeaux and must leave the next morning. Encloses a note from Franklin's clerk to TJ and will await his reply.

RC (DLC); 6 p.; endorsed: "Learmonth Alexr. May. 23. 1785. Gave him passport for 2. months and 36. livres"; Masonic symbols drawn at foot of text by Learmonth. Enclosure and passport not found.

From the Abbés Arnoux and Chalut

24 May 1785. Accept TJ's invitation.

RC (MHi); 2 p.; in French; addressed.

From Jean Holker

MONSIEUR   Rouen ce 24. May 1785.

Je viens de recevoir ce matin une Lettre de M. Lair DeLamotte de La part de M. Le Docteur Francklin, qui me marque que Son Excelence a eté surprise de ne pas trouver dans la Caisse qui renfermoit Votre presse des Livres qu'il avoit demandés et qu'il comptoit recevoir par la meme voye. Comme vous etes à portée de le voir je vous prie de l'engager d'ecrire à Londre, afin de s'assurer par quel navire et à qu'elle adresse l'Expedition en a esté faite, car sans cette connoissance, il n'est guere possible de le découvrir dans un dépôt aussi nombreux que celui de notre Douane.

J'ai reçû lacquit a caution qui etoit dans Votre Lettre Et lai fait décharger au Bureau.

J'ai fait part à M. Guillibaud de l'Expedition que vous avés faite au sujet de Laffaire de M. Wharton. Recevés en je vous prie tous mes remerciments et me croyés, avec un inviolable attachement Monsieur Votre tres Humble et tres obeissant Serviteur,

J HOLKER

PS Ne vous donnés pas la peine de chercher d'occasion pour me faire passer les 16^{tt}. 1s. de mes debours. Nous terminerons ceci à la premiere entrevue. Je vous observe que je ne suis point *negociant* et quand vous aurés occasion de m'écrire vous voudrés bien Le faire sous le titre du Chevalier Holker, où d'Inspecteur General des Manufactures du Royaume.

RC (MHi). Recorded in SJL as received 25 May 1785.

From Louis Guillaume Otto

SIR   Versailles May 24th. 1785.

I have had the honor to wait upon your Excellency on Sunday last, but your indisposition did not permit me to see you. Col. Humphreys has probably acquainted you that I have received Orders to sail next month to America and that I should be extreemely happy to carry Your Excellency's Dispatches to Congress or to execute any private Orders You will be pleased to honor me with. I shall be at Paris in the Beginning of next month and probably leave the City towards the tenth. Permit me to assure you that I shall look upon it as a particular favour to receive your Commands during my residence at Newyorck and to have it in my power to convince you of the respectful attachments, with which I have the honor to be Sir, your Excellency's Most humble and very obedient Servant,   OTTO

RC (MHi); endorsed. Recorded in SJL as received 25 May 1785.

To John Adams

DEAR SIR   Paris May 25. 1785.

Your letter of the 22d. from Montreuil sur mer is put into my hands this moment, and having received information of your son, and two American gentlemen being to set out for London tomorrow morning, I seize a moment to inform you that he had arrived well at l'Orient and was well on the 20th. when the packet was still detained by contrary winds. Mr. Barclay, who is arrived, had also seen him. Be so good as to inform the ladies that Mrs. Hayes is arrived. I have not yet seen her, but am this moment going to perform that duty. I fear the ladies have had a more triste journey than we had calculated on. The poverty of the country and distress of the drought would of course produce this effect. I am the more convinced of this as you say they have found amusement in my notes. They presented themselves to their notice under fortunate circumstances. I am happy if you find any thing in them worthy your approbation. But my country will probably estimate them differently. A foreknowlege of this has retarded my communicating them to my friends two years. But enough of them. The departure of your family has left me in the dumps. My afternoons hang heavily on me. I go sometimes to Passy and Mont Parnasse. When they are gone too I shall be ready for the dark and narrow house of Ossian. We attended the Queen's entrance yesterday, but lost the sight of her. You can calculate, and without many figures, the extent of this mortification to me. To render it more complete I had placed myself and my daughter in my carriage very finely before the Palais Bourbon to see the illuminations of the Garde meubles which are to cost the king of Spain two or three thousand guineas. But they sent a parcel of souldiers to drive us all away. We submitted without making battle; I carried my daughter to the Abbaye and came home to bed myself. I have now given you all the news of Paris as far as I know it and after recommending myself to the friendly recollection of the ladies I conclude with assurances of the esteem with which I have the honour to be dear Sir Your affectionate friend & servt., TH: JEFFERSON

P.S. Send me your address au plutot.

RC (MHi: AMT); endorsed in part: "ansd. June 7. 1785." Entry in SJL reads: "Mr. Adams. Answer to his of May 22. His son safe arrived at l'Orient. Queen's entry yesterday. (By Chew and Chamberlayne)."

From Vergennes

Versailles le 25 May 1785.

J'ai l'honneur de vous envoyer, Monsieur, une Ordonnance que le Roi a rendue en dernier lieu, pour rappeller et renouveller les défenses du Port d'armes, des épaulettes et cocardes, aux chasseurs, heiduques, Négres et à tous autres domestiques, gens de livrée et personnes sans état; Sa Majesté m'a ordonné, Monsieur, de vous faire part de cette nouvelle ordonnance, qui ne fait que confirmer les dispositions des précédentes sur cette matiere, et de vous engager à tenir la main à ce qu'elle soit observée par les domestiques et gens de livrée de votre Maison. Je vous prie aussi, Monsieur, de vouloir bien la participer aux personnes de votre Nation qui sont actuellement à Paris où qui pourront y venir, afin qu'elles soient averties de l'Obligation de se conformer aux dispositions du nouveau Réglement.

J'ai l'honneur d'être trés parfaitement, Monsieur, Votre trés humble et trés Obéissant Serviteur,   DE VERGENNES

RC (DLC); in a clerk's hand, signed by Vergennes; endorsed in part: "ordonnance against servants armed." Enclosure (missing): Copy of ordinance of 6 May 1785 (*Recueil Général des Anciennes Lois Françaises*, Paris, 1827, p. 49, No. 2069).

American Commissioners to De Thulemeier

SIR   Passy May 26st. 1785

We received the letter you did us the honour of writing to us the 3d. inst. and are happy to find that all points of the proposed Treaty being thro the King's goodness and condescension now agreed, nothing remains but to transcribe it fairly and to sign and exchange the copies according to our powers and the usual forms. But the signature of at least two of our number being necessary, and Mr. Adams being called away by his mission to the court of Great Britain, and another of us rendered unable by age and a painful malady to perform a land journey, there is a difficulty in meeting with your Excellency for the purpose, either at any intermediate place, or at that of your residence, (which in respect to the King we might otherwise willingly do). We therefore propose it for your consideration, whether, tho' not usual, the Act would not be equally valid, if, in case it should not suit you to come to Paris (where however we should be glad to see you) we were to sign separately the instruments, dating our respective signatures with time and place, and exchanging them by some confidential person who might deliver to you that which shall be signed by us, to be there signed and kept by you, and receive that signed by you, which we can afterwards sign here. We request your opinion and determination, and are with great respect, Sir Your Excellency's Most obed. & most hble. Servants,   B. FRANKLIN
                                                T. JEFFERSON

P.S. We have the honour to enclose a copy of the treaty as we understand it to be settled: and to propose that the blank in the last article for its continuance shall be filled up with the number "*ten*."

FC (DNA: PCC, No. 116); in David Humphreys' hand; at head of text: "Answer to the letter of the Baron de Thulemeier dated a la Haye 3 Mai

1785." Tr (DNA: PCC, No. 86); also in Humphreys' hand. Copy of covering letter was sent by the Commissioners to Jay as enclosure No. 1 in their letter of 18 June 1785.

To Louis Guillaume Otto

[*Paris, 26 May 1785.* Entry in SJL reads: "Mr. Otto. Receipt of his of May 24. Congratulations on appointment. Consider him as collegue. What will be my line of conduct—recommend Doradour." Not found.]

From John Adams

Dear Sir   London May 27. 1785

I arrived yesterday and have made my visit to day, and been very politely received by the Marquis, but of this more hereafter. This is devoted to a smaller subject.

Upon Enquiry I find that I cannot be exempted from paying duties upon my Wines, because no foreign Minister is, except for a less quantity than I have of the best qualities in my Cellar at the Hague, so that I must stop all that I have in France if I can. To pay six or Eight Shillings Sterling a Bottle upon the Small Wines I packed at Auteuil would be folly. I must beg you then if possible to stop it all except one Case of Madeira and Frontenac together. Let me beg you too to write to Mr. Garvey and stop the order for five hundred Bottles of Bourdeaux. All my other Things may be sent on to me, as proposed.

Coll. Smith has Letters for you, but waits a private Hand. He Sends his Respects to you and Coll. Humphreys. If my Things are gone and cannot be stopped I must pay the Impost, heavy as it is. I am sorry to give you this Trouble but I beg you to take the Wine, at any Price you please. Let your own Maitre D'Hotel judge, or accept it as a present or sell it at Vendue, i.e. let Petit dispose of it as he will, give you an Account of proceeds and give me credit, and then order me to pay Stockdale or any Body here for you to the amount.

My Esteem, & Regards as due. Yours affectionately

JOHN ADAMS

RC (DLC). Recorded in SJL as received 31 May 1785. Enclosed in TJ to Anthony Garvey, 2 June 1785.

From John Adams

DEAR SIR   Bath Hotel London May 27. 1785

I found that either the Duke of Dorsetts Letter to the Premier had produced an order at Dover or that his Graces Letter to the Custom House Office had as good an effect, for I was allowed to pass without Molestation, and indeed received Marks of particular Respect.

We arrived yesterday 26. in the afternoon, and as Fortune would have it Coll. Smith arrived the Night before 25. We soon met. I wrote a Card to the Marquis of Carmarthen, at Nine at Night, acquainting his Lordship of my Arrival and desiring an Hour to wait on him. This Morning I had an Answer, that his Lordship would be glad to see me at one at his House, or at four at his office, as I chose. I replyed that I would have the Honour to wait on him at one.

Coll. Smith went with me, we were admitted in an Instant, and politely received. I laid before him my Commission, and left him a Copy. Coll. Smith did the same with his. I consulted his Lordship about the Ettiquette of my Letter of Credence, and he gave me the same Answers as the Comte de Vergennes gave you. His Lordship then said that on Wednesday next after the Levee, I should be presented to his Majesty in his Closett, and there deliver my Letter of Credence, and that on the next Levee Day Coll. Smith would be presented. This he said was according to the usage.

I have since seen the Dutch Minister, who enquired of every particular step by step, and then said that I was received precisely upon the same Footing with all the other Ministers. I learned from the Dutch Minister too another Particular which gave me Pleasure, vizt that the usage here is directly contrary to that in Holland and France. Here the new Minister receives the first Visit, from all the foreign Ministers, whereas in France and Holland the new Minister makes the first Visit to all the foreign Ministers and notifies formally to them his Reception. This saves me from an Embarrassment, and we shall now see who will and who will not. We shall see what will be done by Imperial Ministers, &c. With the most cordial Esteem I have the Honour to be, Sir, your most obedient and most humble Servant,   JOHN ADAMS

RC (DLC). FC (MHi: AMT); in the hand of W. S. Smith. Recorded in SJL as received 31 May 1785.

From Samuel Amory

SIR   London 27th. May 1785

Mr. Alexr. Moore having sail'd for America before the receipt of your Letter to him address'd to my Care; I am fearfull the want of that very kind introduction you favor'd him with to your Friends in Virgina. will be of great detriment to him.

I intend forwarding your Letter, and at the Same time again to solicit your friendship in his Behalf, by a request of your writing again to those Friends in America, in case of the miscarriage or loss of your former Letter. The very great marks of esteem and regard with which you have treated Mr. Moore, induc'd me to take the Liberty of writing you, as I hear it is uncertain whether you come to England. If the latter had been the case I shou'd have done myself the pleasure of personally waiting on you.

I have the Honor to be, Sr, Yr. most obed. Servt.,

SAM. AMORY

RC (MHi); endorsed. The letter from TJ to Moore was probably that of 19 Mch. 1785.

From Barré

EXCELLENCE   [L'Orient] Ce 28 may 1785.

Monsieur Thevenard Chef d'Escadre et Commandant de la Marine en ce port, Désirant avoir une copie du portrait du Général Waginston, dont vous possédez L'original, Je me suis chargé de vous prier de vouloir bien lui envoyer, persuadé que Votre Excellence, se ferait un plaisir de satisfaire mon Général à ce Sujet. Comme il possede déja celui de Monsieur Franklin, cela perpétuera la mémoire des Grands Hommes sortis de L'Amérique, en attendant que vous vouliés lui Donner Le vôtre pour Couronner L'oeuvre et finir La Collection.

Je suis avec Respect De votre Excellence Le très humble et très obéissant Serviteur,   BARRÉ

P.S. Monsieur Thévenard Désireroit que le Tableau fut de Deux pieds cinq Pouces et demi de hauteur, sur dix huit de Largeur, et Remets à votre choix celui du peintre.

RC (DLC); endorsed.

From Samuel House

Philadelphia, 28 May 1785. Though TJ probably has little time for "so trifling a correspondence," House is urged by his mother to write him, as one of the foremost of her "Chosen friends." They were all pleased to hear of his arrival in France; House's mother is well but misses the gentlemanly conduct of the members of Congress who boarded with her.

They have received several letters from Mrs. Trist; she is in good health, and by a vessel just arrived they learn that she left New Orleans on 18 Apr. for Havana, en route to Philadelphia. This letter accompanies one from her to TJ.

Business lags here. House manages to sell goods which he buys on short credit to country stores and can get unlimited credit, but "buying goods from Merchants here does not Establish a person. If I Could get Credit in Europe, I could do amazing well and sell a great many Goods." Foreign merchants bringing cargoes to Philadelphia are at a disadvantage, for in the city they bring no profit when "Every Man who has Cash goes to Vendue were he buys goods for little or nothing"; it is only through customers in the country that goods command a profit. Since many fabrics in demand in America come at lower prices from France, he hopes TJ might induce manufacturers there to ship their goods to him to be sold on commission or "to give Credit for a few thousand Livers." Though House has a "Correspondent in Amsterdam who ship me Goods on Credit," another in France would establish him; assures TJ he will "act with the greatest honor and Integrity and merit your Recommendation."

He hopes the Commissioners intend action against the Barbary pirates: "They are a great hurt to our Trade insomuch that no American Bottom can procure a freight in Europe. The diffirence of Insurance is such that every Merchant Orders their Goods Shipd in British Bottoms." Sends his good wishes, and those of his mother and Browse, to TJ and Patsy.

RC (MHi); 4 p.; endorsed. Recorded in SJL as received 22 July 1785 "by Mr. Mazzei." Enclosure: Mrs. Trist to TJ, 25 Dec. 1784.

From Louis Guillaume Otto

SIR   Versailles May 28th. 1785.

I received only this moment the Notes on the State of Virginia together with the congratulation and invitation Your Excellency have honoured me with the 23d. of this month. This delay will I hope sufficiently apologise for my having not sooner acknowledged the favor you have done me.

According to your desire I shall be very careful not to trust your work to any person, who might make an improper use of it, and tho' I conceive that the public would be very much gratified with the interesting particulars contained in it, Your Excellency's determination on this point is a Law, which I shall never attempt to infringe.

A part of these learned Notes I had already perused in America; but I see that they have been considerably enlarged and I expect a great deal of instruction from them. I wish most sincerely that the present situation of every State in the Union would be illustrated in the same manner and I am confident that our notions about America would be highly improved by it.

Tho I have the honor to be particularly acquainted with many respectable Characters of your Country I am persuaded that a few Words of recommendation from your Excellency to some of your Friends in Congress would be highly favourable to the success of the business I am to be entrusted with.

I hope to be at Paris next Week and to take your Excellency's Orders before my Departure to L'Orient. It is needless to assure you that you can not trust your Commands to any person more anxious than I am, to convince you of the respectful and inviolable attachment with which I have the honor to be Sir Your Excellency's Most obedient and very humble Servant,   OTTO

P.S. Permit me to add my best compliments to Col. Humphreys.

RC (DLC). TJ's letter of 23 May has not been found; it was probably written to accompany a copy of *Notes on Virginia* and in consequence of Otto's visit of the previous day when he was prevented from seeing TJ because of the latter's illness (see Otto to TJ, 24 May 1785).

John Adams to Franklin and Jefferson

GENTLEMEN   Bath Hotel May 29. 1785. Westminster

Our Secretary of State for foreign affairs, in a Letter of 13. Ap. informs me, that he wrote Us a Letter by Capt. Lamb dated 11. March, inclosing a Variety of Papers respecting the Treaties we are directed to negotiate and conclude with the Barbary Powers.

Inclosed is a Copy of a Resolution of Congress of 14. February 1785, inclosed to me, in the Secretary's Letter. I know nothing of Capt. Lambs Arrival or of the Dispatches by him.

On the 26. I communicated to Lord Carmarthen my Credentials, and left him Copies, as we have done upon former occasions in France, and am to have my Audience of the King in his Closet as the Secretary of State informs me, next Wednesday. I have the Honour to be, very respectfully, Gentlemen, your most obedient and most humble Servant, JOHN ADAMS

RC (DNA: PCC, No. 84); endorsed by David Humphreys. Enclosure (Tr of principal part of resolution of 14 Feb. 1785 in Adams' hand, attested by him, also in PCC, No. 84): See Jay to Commissioners, 11 Mch. 1785.

From John Jay

[*New York, 30 May 1785*. Recorded in SJL as received 2 Nov. 1785 by "Dr. Rogers." Not found.]

From Nathanael Greene

[*Charleston, S.C., 1 June 1785*. Recorded in SJL as received 3 Sep. 1785. Not found.]

From Louis Guillaume Otto

SIR   Paris June 1st. 1785.

I was honoured yesterday with Your Excellency's Letter of the 26th. of last month and I am extremely flattered by the Confidence you seem to place in my zeal for your Country. I can assure you that after my own Nation there is none in the World to whom I am more Sincerely attached than to the American, and the small influence my Correspondance may have upon the determination of Government will be entirely directed towards the Benefit of both nations. There has indeed never been an alliance more natural and better calculated for mutual advantages than that which so happily subsists between France and America. As to me in particular, it will be extremely favorable to my transactions in America to be honoured with the esteem and confidence of a Minister who represents amongst us the United States with so much dignity and ability. The proposal of a Correspondence with Your Excellency I therefore most heartily embrace and I hope that experience will convince you that your conjectures on my personal dispositions have been well founded.

I have not been so happy as to see M. le Comte de Doradour, but the small services I shall be able to render him, he may entirely dispose of. I am glad to have his Company on my passage to

America and I beg your Excellency to assure him of all the good offices I shall have in my power.

Mr. de Couteulx informs me just now that the packet is to sail *from L'Orient* on the first of July. I intend to set off from Paris towards the 15th. and flatter myself to be favoured with your orders before my Departure.

With great respect and gratitude I have the honor to be Sir Your Excellency's Most obedient and very humble Servant,

OTTO

RC (DLC).

To John Adams

DEAR SIR   Paris June 2. 1785.

Your favours of May 23. and the two of May 27. came safely to hand, the first being open. That of the 22d. from Montreuil sur mer had been received and answered on the 25th.

The day before the receipt of the letters of the 27th. we had had your cases brought to the barrier of Paris in order to get the proper officer to go that far to plumb them. From there they were put on board the boat for Rouen and their portage paid. In the instant of receiving your letter I sent Petit off to try to stop them if not gone. The boat was just departing and they declared it impossible to reland them: and that could it be done, a new passport from the C. de Vergennes would be necessary for the part not landed. I now forward your letter to Mr. Garvey, countermanding your order of the wine from him, and praying him to retain all the cases of wine now sent except that which has the Madeira and Frontignac, till he shall receive your orders. These therefore you will be so good as to send him as soon as convenient. I was very sorry we could not stop the wine. It would have suited me perfectly to have taken it either at the prices it cost you, if known to Petit, or if not known, then at such prices as he and Marc should have estimated it at: and this would have saved you trouble. I inclose you Petit's note of disbursements which I immediately repaid him. You will know the exchange between London and Paris, which is considerably in favor of the former. Make the allowance for that and either retain the money in your own hands or put it into Stockdale's as most convenient. Can you take the trouble of ordering me the two best of the London papers (that is to say one of each party) and by any channel which will save me postage and the search of government?

The inclosed letter to Miss Adams is from a young gentleman of her acquaintance who has a very sincere and high affection for her. When you transferred to her the commission of Secretary, I well hoped the pleasure of her being the intermediate of our communications: but I did not flatter myself with the further one of becoming the confident between herself and persons of the foregoing description. The following paragraphs are for her eye only. Be so good therefore as to deliver over the letter to her. The cypher I suppose to be in her custody.

By[1] *a dutch Courier which went yesterday we sent an answer to Baron Thulemyer. It contained what we had agreed on when you were here.* That is to say *we closed and expressing our doubts that it might not suit him to come here, we propose[d] that every one should sign separately puting the date and place of his Signature. We mean to sign here, send it by some confidential Person to you and that he shall carry it on to the Baron, deliver it to him and receive in exchange the copy signd by him.*

Our answer to Tuscany is copying. It is *precisely what we had agreed when you were with us.*[2]

Be so good as to present my highest esteem to the ladies and to be assured of the sincerity with which I am Dear Sir Your friend & servt.,

TH: JEFFERSON

P.S. *My visits have been all returned save by the Portuguese [ambassador] who I imagine has [neglect]ed [others?].*[3]

RC (MHi: AMT); endorsed in part by Adams: "ansd. July 16. 1785"; partly in code; accompanied by a separate leaf bearing young Abigail Adams' decoding of two of the coded paragraphs. Entry in SJL reads: "Mr. Adams. His wine and other things gone to Rouen. My letter to Garvey. Paid for him 173ᵗ 8s. allowing exchange. Keep it in own hands and pay it to Stockdale. Send me 2 best Lond. papers (out and in) clear of postage and search. Inclose letter to Miss Adams from her brother. Explain our answer and proposition to Thulemeyer. Our answer to Tuscany now copying. Both are what we had agreed on with him. Acknolege receipt of his of May 23. and the two of 27. P.S. My visits all returned except by Portugal." Enclosures: Petit's "note of disbursements" and John Quincy Adams' letter to his sister, Abigail Adams, have not been identified. In his Account Book for 2 June 1785 TJ recorded that he had "repaid Petit for portage &c. of Mr. Adams's things 173f 8."

[1] This and subsequent words in italics are written in code. The text of this and the following paragraph is taken from Abigail Adams' decoding which accompanies RC.

[2] The text of Abigail Adams' decoding ends at this point.

[3] No copy of the code employed in the Adams-TJ correspondence of this period having been found, the editors have made a partial reconstruction of it from those letters (including the present) which are accompanied by the recipient's decoding of coded passages and have designated this missing code as Code No. 8. The text presented in the postscript is supplied in large part from the editors' partial reconstruction of Code No. 8, and is confirmed in part from the entry in SJL. The bracketed words in the postscript are conjectured;

they are supported, perhaps, by TJ's low opinion of De Souza, the Portuguese ambassador—a few months later he referred to him as a "torpid uninformed machine" (TJ to Adams, 27 Nov. 1785).

From Chastellux

à Marly le 2 juin 1785

J'ai recu, Monsieur, avec la plus vive reconnoissance le precieux present que vous m'avés envoyé, et malgré la cruelle situation où je me suis trouvé alors, gardant une de mes amies les plus intimes, qui etoit attaquée d'une fievre continue avec redoublemens, j'ai eu la satisfaction de lire la plus grande partie de votre ouvrage. Tous les motifs se trouvent réunis pour rendre cette lecture bien interressante pour moi. Mon attachement pour l'auteur, celui que je conserverai toujours pour le pais qu'il a décrit et la quantité de connoissances piquantes et utiles qui résultent de ses observations; j'ajouterai encore la plaisir que j'ai eu à me rappeller nos entretiens de *Monticello*. Tout concourt, Monsieur, à donner le plus grand prix à mes yeux, à un ouvrage qui en aura pour tous ceux qui le liront. Je regrette seulement que vous en ayes limité le nombre, en ne voulant pas rendre vos observations publiques. J'espere du moins que vous ne trouverés pas mauvais que j'en donne quelques extraits au journal de physique. Je me propose pendant que je ferai mes inspections d'employer mes heures de loisir à faire ces extraits, et je vous prie, instament, Monsieur, de me donner votre agrément pour cela.

Deux jours après avoir recu l'exemplaire que vous avés eu la bonté de m'adresser, on m'a apporté de Paris un paquet à l'adresse de M. de Buffon qui avoit eté remis[1] chés moi. Comme j'ai crû reconnoitre la forme du paquet et l'écriture de l'adresse, j'ai imaginé, Monsieur, que c'etoit un exemplaire de votre ouvrage que vous me chargiés de lui faire passer. Comme il est parti pour Montbar, je me propose d'envoyer ce paquet à Mr. d'Aubenton pour qu'il le lui fasse parvenir par la première occasion. J'ai lû l'article où vous avés combattu notre grand naturaliste: certainement, il ne pourra s'éttonner que votre opinion soit differente de la sienne et il aprouvera egalement et les raisons dont vous vous appuyés et la maniere honnete et philosophique dont vous les avancés. J'avois lu dans les *noticias americanas* l'article dont vous avés fait mention et je ne vous dissimule pas qu'il m'avoit frappé. L'auteur ajoute une chose qui m'avoit fait encore plus d'impression, c'est que les motifs venant d'une négresse et d'un espagnol, ont plus de force et d'industrie que ceux qui naissent d'une indienne et d'un espagnol. Mr. Robertson dans son histoire de l'amerique paroit avoir suivi l'opinion de M. de Buffon et de M. d'Ulloa. Quant à moi, sans prétendre decider la question, je me contenterois d'affirmer que dans l'état de civilisation et de societé, les differences que le climat ou le sol peuvent apporter dans les espèces sont si legeres rélativement aux causes morales qu'on peut les regarder comme des infiniments petits et les negliger absolument. Le *cæteris paribus* ne se trouve que parmi les brutes. Tandis que les nuances données par la nature restent les mêmes, les causes morales vont toujours croissant de sorte qu'il y a un terme et les premieres sont presque réduites à zero. Je ne doute pas que l'amerique n'ait dejà produit et ne produise en tout genre plus de grands hommes, proportion gardée, que les autres parties du monde et cependant les observations physiques pourront encore etre justes. Mais c'est un objet dont il me sera bien plus agréable de m'entretenir avec vous de vive voix que par écrit. J'ai bien peu joui, Monsieur, de votre sejour à Paris sur lequel j'avois fondé de grandes esperances, mais j'ai eté bien malheureux depuis huit mois, malheureux par un sentiment plus connu dans le pais que vous avés quitté que dans celui que vous habités maintenant. L'amitié et les allarmes qu'elle cause ne sont pas la maladie regnante des monarchies, des cours et des capitales, mais vous aves dejà dit que tout [subit] des exceptions. Il n'en est point cependant aux sentimens d'estime, de considération et d'attachement que je vous ai voués.

LE MIS DE CHASTELLUX

RC (MoSHi); endorsed. Recorded in SJL as received 3 June 1785. The entire letter was interlineally transcribed by TJ, apparently in an effort to read Chastellux' difficult hand.

[1] TJ interpreted this word as "reçu." In six other instances (in addition to variant spellings) he erred in transcribing Chastellux' words. He also omitted some sixteen words which he evidently could not decipher.

To Anthony Garvey

[*Paris, 2 June 1785*. Entry in SJL reads: "Mr. Garvey. Rouen. Inclosing Mr. Adams's letter informing him 15. caisses and trunks, and a coach box had gone on to his address. Praying him to stop all the caisses of wine except the one with Madeira and Frontignac, and not to send the 500. bottles. I will answer his draughts for expences." Not found. Enclosure: Adams to TJ, 27 May 1785 (first letter).]

From John Adams

SIR   Bath Hotel Westminster June 3. 1785

I have now the Honour to inform you, that having shewn my Commission to the Right Honourable the Marquis of Carmarthen, and left an authenticated Copy together with a Copy of my Letter of Credence to the King according to the usage, I had the Honour on the first of this Month to be introduced by his Lordship to his Majesty, in his Closet with all the Ceremonies and Formalities, practised on such occasions, with other foreign Ministers, where I delivered to his Majesty, my Letter of Credence from the United States of America, as their Minister Plenipotentiary to the Court of Great Britain. The Mission was treated by his Majesty with all the Respect, and the Person with all the Kindness, which could have been expected or reasonably desired, and with much more, I confess, than was in fact expected by me.

Coll. Smith, has also shewn his Commission as Secretary of Legation, to the Secretary of State and left an authenticated Copy, and is to be presented to the King on the next Levee Day. The Time is not yet fixed for my Introduction to the Queen, but having received an Invitation to dine with the Secretary of State, on Saturday the fourth of this Month, being the Anniversary of his Majestys Birth, I must go to Court again on that Day.

With great Respect, I have the Honour to be, Sir your most obedient and most humble servant,   JOHN ADAMS

RC (DLC). Recorded in SJL as received 14 June 1785. FC (MHi: AMT); in W. S. Smith's hand, headed "(Circular)" and bearing at foot of text: "His Excellency Thomas Jefferson Esqr. Min. Plenipo. . . . To Messrs. Franklin and Jefferson Ministers Plenipo., for treaties of Commerce. Mr. Carmichael Charge des affairs at Madrid. Mr. Dumas at the Hague." RC of the same letter (variant only in form of salutation and complimentary close) as addressed to Franklin and TJ (DNA: PCC, No. 84); also in Smith's hand; signed by Adams.

To Barré

SIR   Paris June 3. 1785.

I am this moment favored with your letter of the 28th. of May. I have two pictures of Genl. Washington: the one a whole length by Peale taken at the beginning of the war; the other a half length taken by Wright the last year. The first is better coloured, more softly painted, more flattering, but less like. The last is dryer,

however, but more like. The painter has seised the gravest lineaments of the General's face, so that tho' it is a faithful likeness at
certain times, it is an unfavourable one. It shews him as he was
in the moments of his gravest difficulties. Monsr. de Thevenard
is very welcome to have either of them copied. If he chuses the
former it may be done immediately; if the latter it may be two
months before it can be permitted, because Wright, before he
would draw it for me, exacted a promise that it should not be
copied till his mother in London should have time to procure and
sell the first prints to be taken from it. Any order which Monsr.
de Thevenard shall think proper to give on this subject shall be
complied with as far as rests on me. I am with much esteem Sir
Your most obedient humble servt.,   TH: JEFFERSON

PrC (DCL). This appears to be the first extant letter of which TJ retained a press copy. The entry in SJL reads merely: "June 3. Barré s.c. (see copy)." From this point on in SJL TJ rarely summarized letters as he had been in the habit of doing; a line is drawn across the middle of the page in SJL immediately above the entry for the present letter (and the preceding entry for receipt of Chastellux' letter of 2 June), probably to designate the beginning of the use of the copying press.

From Anthony Garvey

SIR   Rouen the 5 June 1785.

I received your Excellency's letter of the 2d. Inst. I shall take
care of the Effects that you have addressed to me, and forward them
agreable to orders on board the first vessel that sails for London
after their reception, except the Cases of Wine, which I shall keep
here for Mr. Adams' further orders; the one containing Madeira
and Frontignac shall be sent. Be so good as to let me know how
many Cases of Wine there are, and what particular mark or numbers the one containing Madeira and Frontignac bears, that no
mistake may happen. If you cannot give me these informations I
shall have them opened here, this in order to prevent mistakes.

I shall be always happy to be favored with your and Friends
Commands in this City, and request you will imploy me on every
occasion that I can be of use; being with the greatest respect &
truth Your Excellency's most Hume. & obedient Servant,

ANTHY. GARVEY

RC (MHi); endorsed. Recorded in SJL as received 6 June 1785.

From James Jarvis

[*Amsterdam, 5 June 1785*. Recorded in SJL as received 10 June 1785. Not found, but see TJ to Carmichael, 22 June 1785.]

From Abigail Adams, with Enclosure

London Bath Hotel Westminster

DEAR SIR   June 6. 1785

Mr. Adams has already written you that we arrived in London upon the 27 of May. We journey'd slowly and sometimes silently. I think I have somewhere met with the observation that nobody ever leaves paris but with a degree of tristeness. I own I was loth to leave my garden because I did not expect to find its place supplied. I was still more loth on account of the increasing pleasure, and intimacy which a longer acquaintance with a respected Friend promised, to leave behind me the only person with whom my Companion could associate with perfect freedom, and unreserve: and whose place he had no reason to expect supplied in the Land to which he is destinied.

At leaving Auteuil our domesticks surrounded our Carriage and in tears took leave of us, which gave us that painfull kind of pleasure, which arises from a consciousness, that the good will of our dependants is not misplaced.

My little Bird I was obliged, after taking it into the Carriage to resign to my parisian chamber maid, or the poor thing would have fluttered itself to Death. I mourned its loss, but its place was happily supplied by a present of two others which were given me on board the Dover pacquet, by a young Gentleman whom we had received on Board with us, and who being excessively sick I admitted into the cabin, in gratitude for which he insisted upon my accepting a pair of his Birds. As they had been used to travelling I brought them here in safety, for which they hourly repay me by their melodious notes. When we arrived we went to our old Lodgings at the Adelphia, but could not be received as it was full, and almost every other hotel in the city. From thence we came to the Bath Hotel where we at present are, and where Mr. Storer had partly engaged Lodgings for us, tho he thought we should have objections upon account of the Noise, and the constant assemblage of carriages round it, but it was no time for choice, as the sitting

[178]

of parliament, the Birth Day of the King, and the celebration of Handles Musick had drawn together such a Number of people as allready to increase the price of Lodgings near double. We did not however hesitate at keeping them, tho the four rooms which we occupy costs a third more than our House and Garden Stables &c. did at Auteuil. I had lived so quietly in that calm retreat, that the Noise and bustle of this proud city almost turnd my Brain for the first two or three Days. The figure which this city makes in respect to Equipages is vastly superiour to Paris, and gives one the Idea of superiour wealth and grandeur. I have seen few carriages in paris and no horses superiour to what are used here for Hackneys. My time has been much taken up since my arrival in looking out for a House. I could find many which would suit in all respects but the price, but none realy fit to occupy under 240 £. 250. besides the taxes, which are serious matters here. At last I found one in Grovenor Square which we have engaged.

Mr. Adams has written you an account of his reception at Court, which has been as gracious and as agreeable as the reception given to the Ministers of any other foreign powers. Tomorrow he is to be presented to the Queen.

Mr. Smith appears to be a modest worthy man, if I may judge from so short an acquaintance. I think we shall have much pleasure in our connection with him. All the Foreign Ministers and the Secretaries of Embassies have made their visits here, as well as some English Earls and Lords. Nothing as yet has discovered any acrimony. Whilst the Coals are cover'd the blaize will not burst, but the first wind which blows them into action will I expect envelop all in flames. If the actors pass the ordeal without being burnt they may be considerd in future of the Asbestos kind. Whilst I am writing the papers of this day are handed me. From the publick Advertiser I extract the following. "Yesterday morning a messenger was sent from Mr. Pitt to Mr. Adams the American plenipotentiary with notice to suspend for the present their intended interview" (absolutely false). From the same paper:

"An Ambassador from America! Good heavens what a sound! The Gazette surely never announced any thing so extraordinary before, nor once on a day so little expected. This will be such a phœnomenon in the Corps Diplomatique that tis hard to say which can excite indignation most, the insolence of those who appoint the Character, or the meanness of those who receive it. Such a thing could never have happened in any former Administration, not even that of Lord North. It was reserved like some other Humiliating circumstances to take place

> Sub Jove, sed Jove nondum
> Barbato ————.”

From the morning post and daily advertiser it is said that “Mr. Adams the Minister plenipotentiary from America is extremly desirious of visiting Lord North whom he Regards as one of the best Friends the Americans ever had.” Thus you see sir the begining squibs.

I went last week to hear the musick in Westminster Abbey. The Messiah was performd. It was sublime beyond description. I most sincerely wisht for your presence as your favorite passion would have received the highest gratification. I should have sometimes fancied myself amongst a higher order of Beings; if it had not been for a very troublesome female, who was unfortunately seated behind me; and whose volubility not all the powers of Musick could still.

I thank you sir for the information respecting my son from whom we received Letters. He desires to be remembered to you, to Col. Humphries and to Mr. Williamos. My Daughter also joins in the same request. We present our Love to Miss Jefferson and compliments to Mr. Short. I suppose Madam de la Fayette is gone from paris. If she is not, be so good sir as to present my respects to her. I design writing her very soon. I have to apoligize for thus freely scribling to you. I will not deny that there may be a little vanity in the hope of being honourd with a line from you. Having heard you upon some occasions express a desire to hear from your Friends, even the Minutia respecting their Situation, I have ventured to class myself in that number and to subscribe myself, Sir, your Friend and Humble Servant,   A. ADAMS

ENCLOSURE

The publick Advertiser—

“Yesterday Lord George Gordon had the Honour of a long conference with his Excellency John Adams (honest John Adams), the Ambassador of America, at the hotel of Mons. de Lynden Envoye extrordinaire de Leur Hautes puissances.”

This is true, and I suppose inserted by his Lordship who is as wild and as enthusiastic as when he headed the mob. His Lordship came here but not finding Mr. Adams at home was determind to see him, and accordingly followed him to the Dutch Ministers. The conversation was curious, and pretty much in the Stile of Mrs. Wright with whom his Lordship has frequent conferences.

An other paragraph from the same paper—"Amongst the various personages who drew the attention of the drawing-room on Saturday last, Mr. Adams, minister plenipotentiary from the States of America was not the least noticed. From this gentleman the Eye of Majesty and the Court glanced on Lord ———; to whose united Labours this Country stands indebted for the loss of a large territory and a divided and interrupted Commerce."

RC (DLC). Recorded in SJL as received 14 June 1785. The enclosure, also in Abigail Adams' hand, is in DLC: TJ Papers, 14: 2409, being separated from the letter itself and filed with that from her to TJ of 21 Aug. 1785. Despite this, there can scarcely be any doubt that the additional squibs were added on a separate leaf and enclosed with this letter, perhaps because the newspaper containing them arrived after the letter had been completed; for TJ's endorsement ("Mrs. Adams") is on the verso of the leaf containing the text here regarded as an enclosure, and there is also on the verso TJ's list of topics to be discussed in his reply of 21 June 1785 to the present letter. This notation reads:

> "Sanois
> Nightingale
> Pilatre
> Houserent
> Wealth of Lond.
> Squib."

Of these, all save the fourth and last are crossed off. It is to be noted also that this letter, though dated 6 June, was not completed until 8 June and perhaps even later; Mrs. Adams' remark that her husband would "Tomorrow . . . be presented to the Queen" could only have been written on 8 June, since Adams was presented to Queen Charlotte on Thursday, 9 June (Adams to TJ, 7 June 1785). Mrs. Adams erred in thinking they had ARRIVED IN LONDON UPON THE 27 OF MAY; it was on that day that Adams wrote TJ of their arrival in the afternoon of the preceding day. MRS. WRIGHT was Patience Lovell Wright, mother of Joseph Wright the artist, who was outspoken, vigorous, somewhat eccentric, probably a spy in the American cause, and yet greatly in vogue in London during the Revolution as a modeler in wax of such personages as the king and queen, Lord Chatham, Benjamin Franklin, Thomas Penn, and others. She began to write curious letters to John Adams as soon as he arrived in England. Mrs. Adams was impressed by her waxworks, but to her sister, Mrs. Richard Cranch, she wrote of Mrs. Wright: "Her person and countenance resemble an old maiden in your neighbourhood, Nelly Penniman, except that one is neat, the other the queen of sluts, and her tongue runs like Unity Badlam's" (25 July 1784; C. F. Adams, ed., *Letters of Mrs. Adams*, Boston, 1841, II, 33). Mrs. Adams' regret at leaving the RESPECTED FRIEND was genuine; on the eve of their departure from Auteuil she wrote to her sister: "I shall really regret to leave Mr. Jefferson: he is one of the choice ones of the earth" (8 May 1785; same, II, 94).

From Jean François Briet

MONSEIGNEUR   L'Orient le 6 Juin 1785.

Je prends la Liberté de récommander à Son Excellençe, une affaire qui Regarde sa Nation. J'ai achetté pour Compte de Mr. Peter Dischong à philadelphie, une partie de 854. pièces Nankins qui fûrent saisis dans les magazins du Sr. LeChene en cette ville, par les Emploïés de la Ferme générale, parcequ'ils supposaient qu'on voulait les faire Entrer par fraude dans le Royaume. Son Excellence verra par la Lettre que J'adresse aujourdhui au Mr.

Le Contrôleur Général, dont Copie cy-Jointe, L'Injustice et L'horreur de cette Saisie dans une ville franche. Comme Je ne rembourserai pas à mon ami de philadelphie sa Remise qu'il m'a faite à Compte des dits Nankins, avant de les avoir et d'être Indemnisé de la perte que Mr. Dischong éprouve dans cette occasion, vu le Retard affreux et la Diminution sur cet article à l'arrivée des Vaisseaux de Chine, non seulement en Amérique mais encore en Europe, Je Supplie Son Excellence, de faire ensorte que la demande que Je fais à Mgr. DeCalonne me soit accordée le plus promptement possible. Car chaque Jour de Retard porte un plus grand préjudice. Pour cet Effet elle voudra bien Exposer à Mgr. DeCalonne le Ridicule de cette Saisie et le Risque qu'il y aurait si les Américains ne se trouvaient plus en Sureté avec leurs Marchandises dans leurs Magazins de cette ville, où la ferme n'à aucun droit de Saisie et aucune raison vallable à alléguer pour garder cette Marchandise qu'elle à Enlevé de force des dits Mag[azins quoique] Les C[omm]is du Sr. LeChene, propriétaire de la Maison où elle était et où La ferme n'à nul droit d'Inquisition, lui eussent déclaré en son absence ne savoir à qui ces Nankins pouvaient appartenir, et L'Exposé des Emploïés de la ferme qu'ils sont plombés avec de vieux Plombs est des plus absurdes, en ce que l'on se soucie peu ici dans L'Orient que les plombs soient neufs ou vieux, et que la Marchandise soit plombée ou non. D'ailleurs ces Nankins sont peut-être venus tels d'Ostende, et Je ne devais pas considérer les plombs, mais la bonté de la Marchandise que mon Commettant me recommandait.

J'ose Espérer que Son Excellence daignera prendre serieusement à Coeur cette affaire pour la terminer le plus promptement possible. Toute la Nation américaine souffrirait d'une pareille Vexation, et elle est de la plus grande Importance. D'ans l'attente d'une réponse favorable, Je suis avec un profond respect, Monseigneur, De Son Excellence, Votre très humble et très Obéïssant Serviteur,

JN. FOIS. BRIET

RC (DLC); endorsed: "Briet, negociant à l'Orient for Pet. Duschong. Philadelphia." TJ's entry in SJL of 10 June, which reads: "received Briet's. of l'Orient June 5," is probably an error for the present letter. Enclosure: Briet to Calonne, 6 June 1785 (Tr in DLC; at head of text: "Copie de la Lettre Ecrite à Mr. De Calonne Controleur Gal. du 6 Juin 1785"), to which was attached an attested copy "d'une lettre ecrite de Monsieur Pierre Dischong de Philadelphie en Datte du 14 feby. 1785 à Mr. Briet a L'Orient"; see TJ to Briet, 11 June; Briet to TJ, 15 and 20 June, 1785.

To Anthony Garvey

⟦*Paris, 6 June 1785*. Entry in sjl reads: "Received Mr. Garvey's June 5. and answered it same day. 8 caisses of wine." Not found.⟧

From John Adams

Dear Sir   Bath Hotel Westminster June 7. 1785.

I have received yours of 25. May, and thank you for the News of my Son, and for the News of Paris. I wished to have seen the Queens Entrance into Paris, but I saw the Queen of England on Saturday, the Kings Birth day, in all her Glory. It is paying very dear to be a King or Queen to pass One such a day in a year. To be obliged to enter into Conversation with four or five hundred, or four or five Thousand People of both Sexes, in one day and to find Small Talk enough for the Purpose, adapted to the Taste and Character of every one, is a Task which would be out of all Proportion to my Forces of Mind or Body. The K and Q. speak to every Body. I stood next to the Spanish Minister, with whom his Majesty conversed in good French, for half or Quarter of an Hour, and I did not loose any Part of the discourse, and he said several, clever Things enough. One was Je suis convaincu que le plus grand Ennemy du Bien, est le mieux. You would have applied it as I did, to the Croud of Gentlemen present who had advised his Majesty, to renounce the Bien for the Mieux in America, and I believe he too had that Instance in his mind. Thursday I must be presented to the Queen, who I hope will say as many pretty Things to me, as the K. did.

You would die of ennui here, for these Ceremonies are more numerous and continue much longer here than at Versailles.

I find I shall be accablé with Business and Ceremony together, and I miss my fine walks and pure Air at Auteuil. The Smoke and Damp of this City is ominous to me. London boasts of its Trottoir, but there is a space between it and the Houses through which all the Air from Kitchens, Cellars, Stables and Servants Appartements ascends into the Street and pours directly on the Passenger on Foot. Such Whiffs and puffs assault you every few Steps as are enough to breed the Plague if they do not Suffocate you on the Spot.

For Mercy Sake stop all my Wine but the Bourdeaux and Madeira, and Frontenac. And stop my order to Rouen for 500

Additional Bottles. I shall be ruined, for each Minister is not permitted to import more than 5 or 600 Bottles which will not more than cover what I have at the Hague which is very rich wine and my Madeira Frontenac and Bourdeaux at Auteuil. Petit will do the Business.

Regards to Coll. Humphreys and Mr. Williamos. Adieu.

JOHN ADAMS

RC (DLC); endorsed. Recorded in SJL as received 14 June.

To Chastellux

DEAR SIR   Paris June 7, 1785

I have been honoured with the receipt of your letter of the 2d. instant, and am to thank you, as I do sincerely for the partiality with which you receive the copy of the Notes on my country. As I can answer for the facts therein reported on my own observation, and have admitted none on the report of others which were not supported by evidence sufficient to command my own assent, I am not afraid that you should make any extracts you please for the Journal de physique which come within their plan of publication. The strictures on slavery and on the constitution of Virginia are not of that kind, and they are the parts which I do not wish to have made public, at least till I know whether their publication would do most harm or good. It is possible that in my own country these strictures might produce an irritation which would indispose the people towards the two great objects I have in view, that is the emancipation of their slaves, and the settlement of their constitution on a firmer and more permanent basis. If I learn from thence, that they will not produce that effect, I have printed and reserved just copies enough to be able to give one to every young man at the College. It is to them I look, to the rising generation, and not to the one now in power for these great reformations. The other copy delivered at your hotel was for Monsr. de Buffon. I meant to ask the favour of you to have it sent to him, as I was ignorant how to do it. I have one also for Monsr. Daubenton: but being utterly unknown to him I cannot take the liberty of presenting it till I can do it through some common acquaintance.

I will beg leave to say here a few words on the general question of the degeneracy of animals in America. 1. As to the degeneracy of the man of Europe transplanted to America, it is no part of

[184]

Monsr. de Buffon's system. He goes indeed within one step of it, but he stops there. The Abbé Raynal alone has taken that step. Your knowlege of America enables you to judge this question, to say whether the lower class of people in America, are less informed and less susceptible of information than the lower class in Europe: and whether those in America who have received such an education as that country can give, are less improved by it than Europeans of the same degree of education. 2. As to the Aboriginal man of America, I know of no respectable evidence on which the opinion of his inferiority of genius has been founded but that of Don Ulloa. As to Robertson, he never was in America, he relates nothing on his own knowlege, he is a compiler only of the relations of others, and a mere translator of the opinions of Monsr. de Buffon. I should as soon therefore add the translators of Robertson to the witnesses of this fact, as himself. Paw, the beginner of this charge, was a compiler from the works of others; and of the most unlucky description; for he seems to have read the writings of travellers only to collect and republish their lies. It is really remarkeable that in three volumes 12mo. of small print it is scarcely possible to find one truth, and yet that the author should be able to produce authority for every fact he states, as he says he can. Don Ulloa's testimony is of the most respectable. He wrote of what he saw. But he saw the Indian of South America only, and that after he had passed through ten generations of slavery. It is very unfair, from this sample, to judge of the natural genius of this race of men: and after supposing that Don Ulloa had not sufficiently calculated the allowance which should be made for this circumstance, we do him no injury in considering the picture he draws of the present Indians of S. America as no picture of what their ancestors were 300 years ago. It is in N. America we are to seek their original character: and I am safe in affirming that the proofs of genius given by the Indians of N. America, place them on a level with Whites in the same uncultivated state. The North of Europe furnishes subjects enough for comparison with them, and for a proof of their equality. I have seen some thousands myself, and conversed much with them, and have found in them a male, sound understanding. I have had much information from men who had lived among them, and whose veracity and good sense were so far known to me as to establish a reliance on their information. They have all agreed in bearing witness in favour of the genius of this people. As to their bodily strength, their manners rendering it disgraceful to labour, those muscles employed in labour will be weaker with them than with the European labourer: but those which are exerted in the chase and those faculties which are employed in the tracing an enemy or a wild beast, in contriving ambuscades for him, and in carrying them through their execution, are much stronger than with us, because they are more exercised. I beleive the Indian then to be in body and mind equal to the whiteman. I have supposed the blackman, in his present state, might not be so. But it would be hazardous to affirm that, equally cultivated for a few generations, he would not become so. 3. As to the inferiority of the other animals of America, without more facts I can add nothing to what I have said in my Notes. As to the theory of Monsr. de Buffon that heat is friendly and moisture adverse to the production of large animals, I am lately furnished with a fact by Doctr. Franklin which proves the air of London and of Paris to be more humid than that of Philadelphia, and so creates a suspicion that the opinion of the superior humidity of America may perhaps have been too hastily adopted. And supposing that fact admitted, I think the physical reasonings urged to shew that in a moist country animals must be small, and that in a hot one they must be large, are not built on the basis of experiment. These questions however cannot be decided ultimately at this day. More facts must be collected, and more time flow off, before the world will be ripe for decision. In the mean time doubt is wisdom.

I have been fully sensible of the anxieties of your situation, and that your attentions were wholly consecrated, where alone they were wholly due, to the succour of friendship and worth. However much I prize your society I wait with patience the moment when I can have it without taking what is due to another. In the mean time I am solaced with the hope of possessing your friendship, and that it is not ungrateful to you to receive assurances of that with which I have the honour to be Dear Sir Your most obedient and most humble servt.,   TH: JEFFERSON

PrC (DLC); at foot of first page: "Genl. Chastellux." Entry in SJL reads: "[June] 8. Genl. Chastellux. See copy this date"; but it is clear that TJ had originally written "7" and then altered it to "8." Entry in SJPL for 7 June reads: "Chastellux, Marquis. My Notes. Buffon's theory of degeneration."

From C. W. F. Dumas

MONSIEUR   Paris 7e. Juin 1785.

Honoré de la vôtre du 20 May, j'ai fait part à Mr. Koopman de ce qui le regarde, et que je ne puis rien de plus à son service, que de le munir, quand il partira, d'une Lettre de recommandation auprès du Gouvernement de l'Etat où il jugera à propos de s'établir.

Mon nom à la Haie est assez connu, surtout au Bureau de la Poste, pour que mes Lettres me soient rendues exactement, quand il n'y auroit d'autre direction.

Votre Excellence aura la bonté de vouloir bien acheminer les Incluses, après avoir arrêté avec une oublie le cachet volant de celle du Genl. Washington, que je laisse ouverte, pour que vous puissiez, Monsieur, la lire auparavant.

J'en aurois ajouté une pour le Congrès, s'il y avoit quelque chose de décidé quant à la paix ou à la guerre. Il se passe à ce sujet des choses interessantes en Allemagne, qui se développeront, dit-on, ce mois-ci.

J'ai l'honneur d'être avec un très-grand respect, De Votre Excellence le très-humble et très-obéissant Serviteur,   C W F DUMAS

RC (DLC); at head of text: "à Son Excellence Mr. Jepherson." Enclosures: Dumas to Washington, 26 May 1785, telling of the Marquis de Verac's gift to him of the bust of Washington (FC in Dumas Letter Book, Rijksarchief, The Hague; Photostats in DLC; with a French translation); the other enclosures have not been identified.

American Commissioners to Favi, with Observations on Treaty Project

SIR   Passy June 8th. 1785

We have the honour of transmitting herewith our sentiments on the counter-draught of the treaty proposed to be established between His Royal Highness the Grand Duke of Tuscany and the United States of America; you will therein perceive that we accede to most of the changes proposed by the counter-draught. Some of them we wish to modify, and on others we offer reasons which we hope will be satisfactory to your court. It is with great pleasure that we meet their dispositions to promote by this establishment the friendship and happiness of the two nations. We have the

honour to be With very high respect & esteem Sir Your most obt. & Most humble Servts.,   B. FRANKLIN
T. JEFFERSON

ENCLOSURE

Observations on the alterations proposed on the part of His Royal Highness the Grand Duke of Tuscany in the articles of treaty offered by the Commissioners of the United States of America.[1]

We agree that the 2nd. and 3d. articles shall stand with the changes proposed as follows.

Art. 2. The subjects of His Royal Highness may frequent all the coasts and countries of the United States of America and reside and trade therein in all sorts of produce, manufactures and merchandize, *without exception of any*, and shall pay within the said U.S. no other or greater duties, charges, or fees whatsoever, *and shall be obliged to observe no other or stricter formalities, regulations, or cautions* than the most favoured *European* nations are or shall be obliged to pay *and observe*: and they shall enjoy all the rights, privileges and exemptions *for their persons and property* and in navigation and commerce which the most favoured *European* nation does or shall enjoy.

Art. 3. In like manner the Citizens of the U.S. of America may frequent the coasts and countries of His Royal Highness the Grand Duke of Tuscany and reside and trade therein in all sorts of produce, manufactures and merchandize, *without exception of any*, and shall pay in the dominions of His said Royal Highness no other or greater duties, charges and fees whatsoever, *and shall be obliged to observe no other or stricter formalities, regulations, or cautions* than the most favoured European nations are or shall be obliged to pay *and observe*: and they shall enjoy all the rights, privileges, and exemptions *for their persons and property* and in navigation and commerce which the most favoured *European* nation does or shall enjoy.

Art. 4. We accede to the alterations proposed for the 4th. article. But we wish then to add two modifications to that article which seem equally necessary and proper for both parties. 1. That each party reserve a power to prohibit absolutely within their own territories the exportation or importation of any particular commodity when necessity or reasons of state require it. As for instance the exportation of grain when a famine prevails or is apprehended: or the importation of any particular manufacture which either party wishes to encourage at home by excluding what would come from abroad. It is only necessary in these cases to provide that the moment such exportation or importation is allowed to any persons at all, it shall be permitted to the other party also. The 2. modification is that where any nation restrains the transportation of commodities to the vessels of the state of which they are the produce, each party shall have a right to establish against that nation retaliating restraints. We therefore propose that the 4th. article with the alterations offered on the other part, and the modifications abovementioned shall stand in this form.[2]

Art. 4. More especially each party shall have a right to carry *any kinds* of produce, manufactures and merchandize *of whatever place they be the growth or manufacture* in their own *or any other* vessels to any parts of the dominions of the other, where it shall be lawful for *all persons* freely to purchase them, and thence to take produce, manufactures and merchandize *of whatever place or growth* which *all persons* shall in like manner be free to sell them, paying in both cases such duties, charges and fees, *and observing such formalities, regulations and cautions only* as are or shall be paid *or observed* by the most favoured European nation. *Nevertheless His Royal Highness and the United States and each of them reserve to themselves the right, where any nation restrains the transportation of merchandize to the vessels of the country of which it is the growth produce or manufacture to establish against such nation retaliating regulations. And also the right to prohibit in their respective countries the importation and exportation of all merchandize whatsoever when reasons of state shall require* it. *In this case the subjects or citizens of the contracting parties shall not import nor export the merchandize prohibited by the other. But whenever*[3] *one of the contracting parties permits any other nation or its own citizens or subjects*[4] *to import or export the same merchandize, the citizens or subjects of the other shall immediately enjoy the same liberty.*

Art. 5. This article had in view to authorize the merchants on each side to employ 1. what persons they please, and 2. what vessels they please, in the transaction of their business, lading and unlading their ships. The Tuscan regulations of commerce having rendered it necessary as to the first object to add a proviso *"that the person so employed be thereunto authorized"* and again *"that they should use the public porters in places where they are or shall be established"* it is apprehended that these restrictions of the first branch of the article are so broad as to leave very little for it to operate on, while at the same time it might in some cases produce embarrassment and contradictory[5] constructions. It is therefore proposed to omit altogether what relates to the persons to be employed, and retain only what relates to the vessels: so that this article may[6] stand thus.

Art. 5. The merchants commanders of vessels or other subjects or citizens of either party shall not, within the ports or jurisdiction of the other be forced to unload any sort of merchandize into any other vessels, or to receive them into their own, or to wait for their being loaded longer than they please.

Art. 6. The additions proposed to this article are 1. that the laws as to prohibited merchandize shall be observed by the vessels of each party: 2. that they shall receive on board the usual custom house guards: and 3. that vessels in harbour shall not be asylums for delinquents. It is supposed that these effects flow from the laws of every state; and as there is no stipulation proposed in this treaty which would suspend the force of these laws, it is submitted whether it be necessary to stipulate their observance; and whether the referring the obligation of these laws to a false basis, that of national convention, when the true basis of their obligation is the authority of the legislature within its own territories, might not weaken the energy of the laws in some other possible cases, and in the end produce more doubt than these stipulations would remove. Nevertheless the American Commissioners not objecting to the effect of the additions, but only supposing they will take place without express stipulation, are ready to acquiesce in them if it will be more satisfactory to the other party. But if thought indifferent by them, we propose that the 6th. Art. shall remain as originally formed.

Art. 8. We agree to the 8th. Art. in the following form, which it is apprehended will include the additions proposed.[7]

Art. 8. The vessels of the subjects or citizens of either party coming on any coast belonging to the other, but not willing to enter into port or being entered into port, and not willing to unload their cargoes or break bulk, shall put out and send their boat to the proper place, and shall give due account of themselves: but they shall then have liberty to depart and to pursue their voyage without molestation, and without being obliged to pay any duties, charges or fees whatsoever, *except those established for vessels entered into port and appropriated to the maintenance of the port itself, or of other establishments for the safety and convenience of navigators and excepting also the charges of the visits of the health officer, which duties, charges and fees shall be the same and shall be paid on the same footing as in the case of subjects or citizens of the country where they are established:*

Art. 9. We agree to the alterations proposed in this article, the latter clause of which will stand, with the alterations, in these words: "And if the operations of repair shall require that the whole or any part of their cargo be unladed, *the same rules shall be observed as to the paiment of dues which are observed in like cases with the inhabitants of the country, and with the other the most favoured nations of Europe.*"

Art. 10. One of the alterations proposes that a subject or citizen of either party dying in the country of the other, and leaving no person on the spot to take care of his goods, *the courts of the country* shall take them into their custody and keep them &c. but by the laws of our states the courts do not take into their own custody the goods of persons dying,[8] but appoint trusty persons to do it, and make those persons accountable to the owners. Therefore we proposed that in such cases, the goods should be taken care of in the same way as those of natives are in the like case, leaving the particular mode to the laws of the country. We still suppose this will be best for both parties and therefore propose the tenth article, with the alterations to which we accede, in the following form.

Art. 10. The citizens or subjects of each party shall have power to dispose of their personal goods within the jurisdiction of the other by testament, donation or otherwise: and their representatives, *whosoever they be*, shall succeed to their said personal goods whether by testament or ab intestato; and may take possession thereof either by themselves or by others acting for them and dispose of the same at their will, paying such dues only as the inhabitants of the country *and of the nations of Europe the most favoured* shall be subject to pay in like cases. And in case of the absence of the *executor, attorney and other* representatives, such care shall be taken of the said goods and for so long a time as would by the laws of the Country[9] be taken of the goods of a native in like case until the lawful owner may take measures for receiving them. And if question shall arise among several claimants to which of them the said goods belong, the same shall be decided finally by the laws and judges of the land wherein the said goods are. And where on the death of any person holding real estate within the territories of the one party, such real estate would by the laws of the land descend on a subject or citizen of the other were he not disqualified by alienage, such subject shall be allowed a reasonable time to sell the same and to withdraw the proceeds without molestation.

Art. 13. We agree to the alterations proposed in the 13th. article, and that it shall stand thus:

Art. 13. And in the same case of one of the contracting parties being engaged in war with any other power, to prevent all the difficulties and misunderstandings that usually arise respecting the merchandize heretofore called contraband, such as arms ammunition and military stores of every kind, no such articles carried in the vessels or by the subjects or citizens of one of the parties to the enemies of the other shall be deemed contraband so as to induce confiscation or condemnation and a loss of property to individuals. Nevertheless it shall be lawful to stop such vessels *and to make them unlade such articles in the nearest port putting them under safekeeping*, and to detain them for such length of time as the captors may think necessary to prevent the inconvenience or damage that might ensue from their proceeding, paying however a reasonable compensation for the loss such arrest shall occasion to the proprietors: and it shall further be allowed to use in the service of the captors the whole or any part of the military stores so detained, paying the owners the full value of the same, to be ascertained by the current price at the place of its destination. *And to remove all doubt respecting the merchandize and effects which shall be subject to the arrangements in this article, it is declared that they are the following, Canons, mortars &c. but these articles shall not be subject to be stayed, provided they be not in greater quantity than may be necessary for the use of the ship, or of the persons in it.*

Art. 14. We agree to the alteration proposed in the 14th. article, and that the clause "shall be provided" &c. shall stand thus "shall be provided with sea-letters or passports which shall express the name the property and burthen of the vessel, as also the name and dwelling of the master, which passports shall be made out in good and due forms, *and in the manner and for the time which is usual with the respective nation in time of peace, on which subject such further explanations shall be entered into as occasion may render necessary; and shall be exhibited whensoever required &c.*" to the end of the clause as proposed in the original draught.

Art. 16. The 16th. Article, among other things, proposes that no other than the ordinary legal procedure shall be used against subjects or citizens of the one party committing offences within the jurisdiction of the other: it has been proposed to add "*and with the subjects, citizens or inhabitants of the other.*" If the effect of this addition is rightly understood, it would be contrary to our wish in such cases as these. A Tuscan commits an offence against an Englishman, both of them being transiently in a port of America. This article would not prohibit an extraordinary procedure contrary to the common course of law against the Tuscan. It is submitted therefore whether it is not better to extend to our people the benefits of the ordinary course of procedure in every case of offence committed by one of them within the jurisdiction of the other, whether the party offended be an inhabitant or not. This is what was proposed by the article as it stands in the original draught.[10]

Art. 17. We agree to the alterations proposed to the 17th. article, and that it shall stand thus.

Art. 17. If any vessel or effects of the neutral power be taken by an enemy of the other, and retaken by that other, they shall be brought into some port of one of the parties and delivered into the custody of the officers of that port in order to be restored entire to the true proprietor as soon as due proof shall be made concerning the property thereof, without any pretensions whatever to salvage. But if a vessel of the one party be taken by pirates or sea rovers and retaken by a vessel of the other, one third part of the value of the vessel and cargo retaken shall be given to the recaptors.

Art. 18. Two additions are proposed in the 18th. article. 1. to insert among the causes of refuge in each others ports, that *for the ordinary affairs of their commerce and navigation.* But as the 2d. and 3d. articles relate solely to cases of commerce, and give every privilege and still more in all such cases, it is submitted whether the insertion here proposed is necessary or can give any additional advantage to our merchants and sailors; and if it cannot, then whether it is not better omitted, as two articles relating to the subject but differently expressed may sometimes produce confusion. The 2. addition is of these words: "*nevertheless in every case the vessels which shall come into the respective ports, scales, or roads shall exactly observe the laws &c.*" We beg leave to refer to our observations on the 6th. article as containing our sentiments on this addition also. We propose therefore that this 18th. article shall retain its original form.

Art. 19. The 19th. Article had provided that the armed vessels of either party might carry their prizes freely wheresoever they please:

the words *"within the jurisdiction of the other"* are proposed to be added, to which there could be no objection but that they produce an implication that they may not be carried *out of their jurisdiction* when once they shall have entered into it.

We agree to all the other alterations of this article, only proposing that the last shall be in these words *"and the same shall take place in all those cases in which the most serene Grand Duke of Tuscany has made like conventions with other powers."* It is just that preceding obligations should prevail against the present treaty, but that the present should prevail against those which shall be subsequent. The Article with its alterations will stand thus.

Art. 19. The vessels of war public and private of both parties shall carry freely wheresoever they please the vessels and effects taken from their enemies without being obliged to pay to officers of admiralty, of the customs or any others, any duties charges or fees, *other than those established for other vessels and merchandize, and which are paid by other the most favoured nations of Europe*: nor shall such prizes be arrested, searched or put under legal process when they come to and enter the ports of the other party, *except the case where the prize is charged to have been made against the laws of neutrality existing in the country*: but may freely be carried out again at any time by the captors to the places expressed in their commissions, *or wheresoever they please, the commanding officer of the vessel making the capture being obliged to shew his commission and instructions*, or to give other sufficient proofs whenever it shall be alledged that he was not authorized to hoist the flag of the nation under which he made the prize. But no vessel which shall have made prizes on the subjects of his most Christian Majesty the King of France shall have a right of asylum in the ports or havens of the U.S. and if any such be forced therein by tempest or dangers of the sea they shall be obliged to depart as soon as possible, according to the tenor of the treaties existing between his said most Christian Majesty and the United States. *And the same shall take place in all those cases in which the most serene Grand Duke of Tuscany has made like conventions with other powers.*

Art. 20. Our laws do not assume cognisance of acts done neither within their jurisdiction, nor by their citizens. Therefore a subject of Tuscany, committing hostilities on us, at sea, under the flag of another power, would not be liable to their sentence. But a stipulation by his Sovereign that he should be liable, would give that authority. It would be necessary however to say in what predicament he should stand liable. That of a pirate seems most analogous to his proceedings. We propose therefore to retain that word in order to adapt the article to our laws, while those proposed on the other part may be also retained to adapt it to the laws of Tuscany: and that the article shall stand thus:

Art. 20. No citizen or subject of either of the contracting parties shall take from any power with which the other may be at war any commission or letter of marque for arming any vessel to act as a privateer against the other, on pain of being punished as a pirate or otherwise severely according to the rigor of the laws.

Art. 21. §4. We agree that the 4th. section of the 21st. article shall stand as proposed, thus. 4thly. The vessels of war public and private of the two parties shall be reciprocally admitted with their prizes into the respective ports of each: *and shall be freely at the disposal of the captor, according to the laws, usages, and regulations of the state to which the captor belongs.*

Art. 24. The 24th. Article proposed that officers breaking their parole, and privates escaping from their cantonment should lose so much of the benefit of the article as provides for their enlargement on parole or in cantonment. It is proposed on the other part that *they shall lose the benefit of this article*; that is to say the whole benefit of it. But it would seem to be a rigour neither laudable nor useful, to deprive them of their wholesome and plentiful ration, and all other the benefits of this article, for a breach of the limits of their confinement. We would therefore repeat our wish that they should thereupon be subject only to close confinement, as originally proposed, and of course that this article should remain in its first form.

Art. 25. We agree that the 25. article shall be as proposed, thus
Art. 25. The two contracting parties grant to each other the liberty of having each in the ports of the other, consuls, vice consuls, agents and commissaries of their own appointment, *observing the usual forms of notification and admission and on the same footing as is or shall be allowed to any other the most favoured European nation.*

We agree also that the first part of the 26th. Art. shall stand thus.
Art. 26. If either party shall hereafter grant to any other *European* nation &c.

The articles on which no observations have been made, that is to say the 1st. 7th. 11th. 12th. 15th. 22nd. 23d. and 27th. to remain in the form originally proposed.

FC (DNA: PCC, No. 116); in David Humphreys' hand; at foot of letter: "M. Favi Charge des Affaires of Tuscany." Dft (DLC); in TJ's hand; endorsed by Humphreys. Tr (DNA: PCC, No. 86); also in Humphreys' hand. Enclosure: FC (DNA: PCC, No. 116; in Humphreys' hand); Dft (DLC; in TJ's hand, with several notations and additions in red ink in Franklin's hand); and Tr (DNA: PCC, No. 86; also in Humphreys' hand). A copy of the covering letter and its enclosure were sent with the Commissioners' letter to Jay of 18 June 1785. In addition to the textual variations between Dft and Tr of the Commissioners' observations, there are several minor differences or clerical errors not noted here. For a preliminary form of TJ's draft of the observations, see his notes on alterations proposed by Favi under 26 Apr. 1785. The contents of the present enclosure were agreed to by Adams, Franklin, and TJ before Adams left Auteuil for London on 20 May.

[1] This caption was inserted in Dft by TJ above the following deleted passage: "Many of the articles in the original Draught being returned without objections or any alterations proposed, it is presumed that they are to stand as originally proposed. We shall therefore note here [. . . such] articles only as are proposed to be changed."
[2] This sentence in Dft is interlined in substitution for the following, which TJ deleted: "The second modification is that each party shall reserve a power

of excluding from the right of transportation to or from their country the vessels of any power which shall exclude the vessels of such party from carrying productions foreign to their own country. Great Britain does this by her navigation act. A power of retaliating on her therefore, or on any other power which should adopt a similar policy, should be reserved by every nation."

³ This word was interlined in Dft by Franklin to replace TJ's "if."

⁴ This and the preceding five words were interlined in Dft by Franklin.

⁵ Dft and Tr read: "contrary."

⁶ This word was substituted in Dft by Franklin for TJ's "shall."

⁷ In Dft Franklin made the following comment which was later deleted: "One is omitted, *dovranno spedire la lancia,* &c. Perhaps not necessary, tho' usual and respectful for Strangers entring a Port to give an Account of themselves, and in some Cases it may be useful."

⁸ The words "by the laws . . . persons dying," were inserted by TJ in Dft in substitution for the following: "with us the courts never take the goods of persons dying into their own custody."

⁹ This and the preceding five words were interlined in Dft by Franklin.

¹⁰ Franklin inserted at this point in Dft the following comment which was later struck out: "Might it not be well to separate the Parts of the 16th. Article, and make of them two distinct Articles?"

From Ralph Izard, with Reports on the Trade of South Carolina

DEAR SIR   The Elms 10th. June 1785.

I have lately received your favour of 29th. Jany. and at the same time 4 Volumes of the Bibliotheque Physico Œconomique for which I am much obliged to you. As soon as I received your Letter of 22d. May 1784, I laid the contents of it before our Chamber of Commerce, and desired their sentiments on the points you mentioned. Enclosed is a copy of their Report, which has already been transmitted to you. I send you likewise enclosed a Copy of a paper which contains the sentiments of Mr. Hall, the Collector of the Customs, a very well informed Merchant in Charleston on the same subject. Another Copy of this paper I enclosed you in my Letter of last January, which I hope got safe to your hands. It will give me great pleasure to learn that those papers were received time enough to be of service to you in your negociations. The backwardness which you mention of Great Britain toward America is very astonishing. It seems to be a continuation of the same bad Policy which has already brought them into so much trouble, and which I think will bring them into more. If they were simply to check the extensive credit hitherto given, and limit their exports to this Country within moderate bounds, they would act wisely. But she is grasping at too much when she aims at the entire monopoly of the carrying Trade. This has occasioned much ill will toward her in several parts of this Continent particularly in New England. It is said that Great Britain has encouraged the piratical States to attack our Vessels. If this could be proved, I should prefer a War against her, rather than against Algiers. But it is a melancholy fact that we are not in a condition to go to War, with anybody. You are of opinion that we should go to War with the Barbarians rather than become Tributary to them. The latter is certainly disgraceful; but how shall we avoid it without falling into greater evils? The Revenues of America, under the present management do not appear to be adequate to the discharge of the public Debt. Where then shall we find resourses to carry on War? A War too without a prospect of Prizes to encourage Adventurers. The injury that was done to the commerce of Great Britain during the late War, was not effected by the Continental Frigates, but by Privateers and very few of those would be fitted out against Tripoli, Tunis, and Algiers.—The Emperor's proceedings must before this time be manifested respecting Holland. The navigation of the Scheldt is certainly an important object. But if there should be a War, I think there must be deeper designs than the Scheldt. That matter is of no consequence to Russia. Holland may be deserted by some of her Allies who wish to see the Stadt Holder Sovereign of that Country. The dismemberment of Poland has happened in our day, and I think it probable that there may be an entire partition of that Country on the death of Poniatowski. There are many other arrangements which Ambition, and Policy may dictate, and the War with Holland may be the Mask under which the execution of them may be effected. For a valuable consideration the Czarina, and the King of Prussia may even consent to make the Empire hereditary in the House of Austria. These things are at a distance from us, and we can think of them, and hear of their being executed without much emotion. But our own affairs trouble me a good deal. We owe a large sum of money, and we are not taking proper measures to pay it. This is neither consistent with our Intent, nor our Honour. Our Governments tend too much to Democracy. A Handicraftsman thinks an Apprenticeship necessary to make him acquainted with his business. But our Back Countrymen are of opinion that a Politician may be born such as well as a Poet. I live as much as possible in the Country, and shall continue a Member of the Legislature as long as my Constituents think that I can render them service. In no other situation will I ever be engaged in public business. My Farm is getting into tolerable order. I find the cultivation of Lucerne very troublesome; but I am determined to persist though on a smaller scale than I at first intended. I have two Acres transplanted in excellent order. The plants stand in squares, at thirty Inches from each other, which leaves just room enough in the intervals for the Hoe Plough to pass in both directions. Green food in Winter is what we want; in Summer we have plenty of it. Lucerne does not afford this; but I am told by some Books of Husbandry that Burnet will, and therefore I shall make some experiments with that Plant, as well as with Tares, and Rape. If you can give me any new information on this subject, I shall be obliged to you for it. I shall send you one of our News Papers as you desire, and likewise the Acts after every Session; the Journals are never printed. My eldest Daughter was married last month to Mr. Manigault, a very worthy young Gentleman in my neighbourhood. I have had a Son born since my arrival in this State, and he is just recovered from inoculation. Mrs. Izard and my Daughters desire their Compliments to you and Miss Jefferson. From what I have heard of the Abbey of Panthemont, I think her improvement will be to your satisfaction.

I am with great regard Dear Sir Your most obt. hble Servt.,

RA. IZARD

RC (DLC). Entry in SJL of receipt of the letter on 18 Sep. 1785 incorrectly dates it "1784." Izard's LETTER OF LAST JANUARY to TJ has not been found.

ENCLOSURE I

Charleston Chamber of Commerce

The Committee appointed to Report on Mr. Jefferson's Letter Delivered in the following report, which was agreed to, and the President was requested to furnish the Vice president with a Copy to be delivered to Ralph Izard Esqr.

The Committee to whom was referred a Letter from the Honorable Thomas Jefferson Esqr. requesting information relative to the products, Exports, Imports and other Commercial Matters therein Contained, Having taken the same into due Consideration, and obtained such information as they were able to procure (all the Books of the Custom House being carried away by the British) beg leave to offer the following Report to the Chamber of Commerce.

That on an Average for Several years previous to the Late Warr with Great Britain, they find the Annual Products of this State were nearly as follows—

Rice	130,000 Tierces
Indico	500,000 lbs.
Naval Stores	15,000 Barrels
Tobacco	3,000 Hogsheads
Deer Skins	1,500 Ditto

Beef & pork	5,000 Barrels
Indian Corn & pease	20,000 Bushels
Hogshead & pipe Staves	800,000
Sawed & Square Lumber	2,000,000 feet
Cypress Shingles	3,000,000

That in the year 1771 They find the Crop of Rice then made Amounted to 130,500 Tierces Were Shipped from hence as follows—

To Great Britain & for Foreign Markets	73,235½
Portugal	14,439
Spain	1,760
Italy	222
British West India Islands	30,304
Foreign	975½
Ports on the Continent	9,564
	130,500

Your Committee are of Opinion that the Annual Products of this State will in a very few Years, be as great as Ever, and that the Article of Tobacco in particular will farr Exceed the Quantity ever made.

By the prohibition lately laid on our Rice to Portugal, and the British proclamation preventing the Transportation of our produce to their Islands (Except in British Bottoms) as well as the opening many Markets for our produce, which were heretofore Restrained Your Committee are of Opinion that the Exports of this Country may Vary, and that they probably will be Shipped to the Several Ports, and in the following Proportions

130,000 Tierces Rice
- 40,000 Tierces to Great Britain
- 20,000 To Different Ports in France Spain & the Meditera[nean]
- 50,000 To Holland, Flanders, the Baltic Hambro and Breme[n]
- 20,000 To the Continent and West Indies

500,000 lbs. Indico
- 250,000 To Great Britain
- 150,000 To Holland, Flanders, the Baltic, Hambro and Bremen
- 10,000 To the Continent
- 90,000 To the different Ports in France and the Mediteranian

3,000 Hhds. Tobacco
- 1000 To Great Britain
- 1000 To Holland, Flanders, the Baltic, Hambro and Bremen
- 1000 To Different Ports in France

15,000 Barrels Naval Stores
- 10,000 Barrels to Great Britain
- 2,000 To France Spain and the Mediteranian
- 3,000 To this Continent and the West Indies

[198]

| 1000 Hhds. | 600 Hogsheads to Great Britain |
| Deer Skins | 400 To France, Holland, Flanders, Hambro and Bremen |

Corn, Peas, Beef and Pork, as well as Lumber of all Sorts (Except a Small part of the Staves) were chiefly Shipped to the West Indies, which is now prohibited to the British Islands, Except in British Bottoms—very Little of said Articles being Shipped to the other Islands, or at most not above one fifth Part of the Lumber.

The Returns generally made for the Exports from this State are as follows—

Dry Goods from Europe
Wines from France, Spain and Portugal
Negroes from the Coast of Africa
Rum, Sugar } From the West Indies
Molasses and Coffee

But your Committee are of opinion that the Exports of this State, will be regulated by the Imports from Each Country.
The Freights from this Port are as follows
To Great Britain for Rice and Naval Stores 50/ to 60/ ℔ Ton
Holland and other European Ports for Ditto 55/ to 65/ ℔ Ton
To all European ports for Indico, half penny to ¾ths ℔ pound

Do.   Do. for Tobacco, 30/ to 35/ ℔ Hhd.
Do.   Do. for Deer Skins 25/ to 30/ ℔ Do.
        for Ditto in the Hair ¾ths. to 1d. ℔ pound

Your Committee observe that as they are unacquainted with the Burthens, which may be Imposed on our Trade by Foreign Powers, They Cannot point out their Remedies. Yet they must Report that the prohibitions laid [on] our Rice to Portugal, and being restrained from Shipping in our own Bottoms to the British West Indies, are the Greatest Disadvantages, and Burthens, under which our Trade at present Labours.

Extract from the Journals
15th. October 1784
SAML. LEGARÉ
Secretary

MS (DLC); in Legaré's hand.

ENCLOSURE II

Custom House Charleston S. Carolina 31st. Decr. 1784

To form a general Idea of the Trade of South Carolina it is necessary to have a retrospect of what that Trade was before the Revolution, from which view a conclusion may be drawn of what it may be again, when the Country comes to be fully peopled. During the course of the War upwards of 20,000 Negroes were carried away by the British or died of the Small pox, Camp Fevers &ca. within their Lines, which Number must be again supplied before the produce of this Country will be equal to what it was formerly. The present Year more than 4000 Negroes have been imported from Africa and upwards of 1000 returned from St. Augustine and brought back by those who had adhered to the British and have been permitted by Law to return here.

A General View of the Trade may be known by the Account annexed of the Imports and Exports for 7 Years from 1757 to 1763, and although the Two Years where it appears the Imports exceed the Exports, owing to the very large import of Negroes in those two Years, yet the advantages resulting to the Country is evident by the acquisition of so many Labourers by whom the Trade was increased, and their Value remaining in the Country which their Labour soon enabled their possessors to pay for.

Whilst South Carolina was a British province, the Trade was of coürse restrained, and the principal part of its produce was shipped to Great Britain and its dependancies, except about 20,000 Barrels Rice which used to be shipped annually to Portugal, which Rice paid a Subsidy to Great Britain, by Bond given there for permission to carry Rice to the Southward of Cape Finisterre. This Trade is now at an end by a Prohibition from the Court of Portugal but may possibly be again renewed if that prohibition is taken off, or in case of the failure of the Crops at Maranham from whence they import their Rice.

The greatest part of the Crop of Rice (which has in some Years amounted to 155.000 Barrels) was shipped to Great Britain. What was consumed there, which was a small proportion, paid a Duty of $6/4\frac{12}{20}$ths now raised to 7/4. The rest being landed shifted and screened at some port in the British Channel, was reshipped to Holland, Hamburgh, Bremen, France, or wherever a Market offered, leaving to Great Britain (exclusive of the Profits of Commission, unlading &ca.) a subsidy of about 8d. Sterling pr. C.

Indico, Tobacco, Deer skins and Naval Stores were all shipped to Great Britain; Lumber Shingles Provisions and Live Stock were confined to the British Islands unless a Duty was paid here to ship Rice to the Foreign West Indies or Madeira, which was seldom done.

The Imports formerly were from Great Britain and the British Islands, except Wines from Madeira Teneriffe &ca. laden with a heavy Duty payable to Great Britain.

The Trade of America being now open to the World, it must take a longer time than two Years experience to ascertain the demand from the different parts of it for the produce of South Carolina but in order to throw some Light thereon I shall subjoin the exports to the several places they were shipped to in those Years, at same time remarking that a conclusion cannot be drawn therefrom of what will be in the course of a few Years—France in particular having as yet had little or no Trade with this State, and where no doubt a Market will be found for Rice, Tobacco, Naval Stores, Staves and perhaps some Indico. At present the Low Countries take the greatest part of the Crop of Rice either direct or through Great Britain, also some Tobacco and Indigo, but the largest proportion of the Indico, Tobacco, Deer skins and Naval Stores have been shipped for Great Britain in payment of the very large supplies of Goods imported from thence and for Negroes supplyed by them, no other Nation having yet sent any here. An Account is annexed of the Quantity of Articles exported from this State (of the Growth and produce thereof,) during the Course of 1783 and

1784, every one of which will in all human probability be increasing annually as the Country becomes more settled and from the Importation of Negroes, particularly the Staple Articles Rice and Indigo. Tobacco, Lumber, Naval Stores &ca. will likewise increase in the Quantity exported until North Carolina becomes rich enough to be their own Importers. At present a very considerable part of their supplies of Goods are sent them from hence for which they pay in Tobacco, Lumber and Naval Stores, which Trade if properly managed will be advantageous to this State, but it must in time take another Channel. Gensing, Reeds, Hemp, Hides, Leather and several other Articles will likewise increase in the Quantities exported.

The Imports into South Carolina since the Revolution have been chiefly from Great Britain. The United Netherlands, Hamburgh and Sweden have had several Ships here, but from their not being acquainted with the Trade have imported such Articles as are not saleable; Time and experience will teach them the proper Goods for this Country. France has hitherto carried on very little Trade with this State but that Nation I am convinced will in a short time from their Agents here soon enter largely and to advantage in it, as they have many Articles of Manufactures that will suit this Climate, as will also their Wines, Brandy &ca. But until other Nations can give as extensive a credit as the British they will have the advantage from that credit of a very large proportion of the Import Trade.

Spain and Portugal have sent and will no doubt continue to supply Salt, Wine, Fruit &ca. The Foreign and British West Indies supply their produce nd take such Articles as they want in return; such as provisions, Lumber, Shingles and Staves.

No Nation being restrained from trading here, the Carrying Trade depends wholly upon such as chuse to become Adventurers. The Northern and Middle States of America have supplied Ships to a very considerable Tonnage, nearly one half since the evacuation by the British. Great Britain and Holland have been the next, several Swedes and Danes have been here and a few French, Spanish and Portugueze Vessels. There are at present but few ships belonging to this State, but from the goodness of the Timber when Workmen come amongst us that branch will increase. All Vessels arriving here pay one shilling Sterling Pr. Ton, which is their whole Port expences, except Pilotage, no fees being taken by any Custom House Officers.

The Duties upon the different Articles imported, The Duty Law fully explains; than which there is no other restriction on the Trade of this State, there being no Duty whatever upon any Article exported.

The British restrictions upon the West India Trade, has been so much the subject of writing and conversation, it will be needless for me to enter into it.

From the foregoing it will be found that no greater burden is laid on Foreign Shipping than what is paid by Americans, therefore it ought to be expected that no heavier Tax should be laid on ours by other Nations than what their own Subjects pay. The Duties are also equal except a few Articles of British, which seems to express a resentment more than an Idea of any Advantage to the Revenue.

GEO: ABBOTT HALL
Collr.

Exports from Charleston in the State of South Carolina from Jany. 1783 to Novr. 1783 being the produce of the Year 1782.

To what Places Shipped	Rice Barrs.	Rice ½ bbls.	Casks Indico	Hhds. Tobacco	Bunds. & Hhds. Skins	Barrs. of Pitch	Barrs. of Tar	Barrs. of Turp.	Feet of Lumber	No. of Shingles	No. of Staves	Buss. of Corn	Sides of Leather & Hides
To Great Britain	8783	967	804	194	61	121	187	708	3200		8400		
To France	884	18		33									
To Amsterdam	2200	259		3									
To Rotterdam	907	21		2									
To Bremen	850	27		3									
To Bruges	320	77		5									
To Hamburgh	400			8	1				2700				
To The United States of America	2228	158	2	33	39	229	81	128	5000				
To The French West Indies	2126	86	5	278		97	76	55	165,600	75,600			
To The British West Indies	2415	159	16	35		17	151	25	74,300	130,100	2500	5990	1400
To Dutch, Danish &ca. do.	1827	323		49		101	45	20	1,300	10,000	2000	3340	
To Havana	54											100	
To Madeira	166	34											
	23,160	2129	827	643	101	565	540	936	252,100	215,700	12,900	76301	1400

NB. The Tonnage Duty not having been collected this Year, the number of Tons cannot be ascertained with Exactness, the Vessels cleared in the foregoing Period are as under—

19 Ships
1 Snow
71 Briggs
73 Sloops
139 Schooners

1 Error for 9530.

Exports from Charleston in the State of South Carolina from 14th: Novr. 1783 being the produce of the Year 1783.

To what Places shipped	Rice Barrs.	Rice half barrs.	Casks Indico	Hhds. Tobacco	Hhds. & Bales Skins	Barrels of Pitch	Barrels of Tarr	Barrels of Turp.	Feet of Lumber	Shingles	Staves	Bus. of Corn	Leather Hides	Leather Sides	Tons Hemp	Casks of Gensing	Casks of Flax Seed	Reeds
The United States of America	3589	338	156	339	3	833	157	623			52700		887		3			11000
Great Britain	25417	3089	1756	1427	608	2811	1528	5921			130235			2703		8	151	136750
Amsterdam	12215	1161	99	40	2	88	190	220			10600					9		
Rotterdam	364	35	5		1	112	185	228										
Scheidam	425	88																
Middleburgh	179	159		5														
Gottenburgh	614	226	8	61	1						650							
Hamburgh	1648	146	4	175		70		249			10,000							
Bremen	2808	56	2	8				4										
Altona	391																	
Ostend	368				4													
Bruges	200			125							2000							
Nantz	1815	152	8	14														
Bourdeaux	1278						180											
Cadiz	1080	99				400					4700							
Gibraltar	448	83									4100							
Corke	85		7	18	4	104					5000							
Teneriffe	308						19				49,000							
Madeira					3						20000							
Fyat	150	24	7								3000							
British West India Islands	2555	247		124		399	165	178	407,100	503450	48650	13380						
French do.	2583	140		140		25	35	28	253,200	314500	23000							
Dutch Danish &c. do.	402	59		198		10	30		44900	264800	9300	400						
50.961 Tons	58922	6102	2052	2674	626	4852	2489	7451	705,200	1,081,750²	372,935	13780	887	2703	3	17	1718³	147,750

2 Error for 1,082,750.
3 Error for 151.

General Amount of Imports and Exports at Charleston, So. Carolina from 1757 to 1763 inclusive as pr. Account taken from the Custom House Books & shewing the Ballance gained by excess of the Exports, with the acquisition of Negroe Slaves.

	Yearly Amount of Imports			Yearly Amount of Exports			Imports exceed the Exports			Exports exceed the Imports			Value of Negroes annually imported	Amount gained annually		
1757	1,762,975	15		2,054,372	13	2[4]				291,396	18	3	279,104	570,500	18	3
1758	2,215,497	5		1,900,125	13	7	315,371	11	5				623,476	308,104	8	7
1759	1,828,659	2		1,969,706	2	7				141,047	2	7	352,016	493,063	2	7
1760	2,335,490	15		1,856,091	11	8	479,399	3	4				733,040	253,640	16	8
1761	2,000,700	15		2,051,542	1	6				50,841	6	6	294,588	345,429	6	6
1762	1,635,591	1		1,814,675	1					179,084	1		140,924	320,008	1	8
1763	1,919,620	10		2,424,333	18	8				504,713	8	8	225,792	730,505	8	8
	13,698,535			14,070,847	2	3	794,770	14	9	1,167,082	17		2,648,940	3,021,252	2	3

The valuation of the several Commodities is taken from a Medium of 7 Years last past.

[4] Error for 3.

MS (DLC); in Hall's hand.

To Jean François Briet

SIR   Paris June 11. 1785.

I received yesterday your favour of the 6th. instant with the papers inclosed. I shall with pleasure use such endeavors as might be proper from me to procure redress of the injury which is said to have been done to Mr. Peter Dischong: but before I take any measure I must beg the favor of you to inform me whether Mr. Dischong is a subject of France, a citizen of Holland or of the United States of America, and to furnish me with the best proof you can as to the state to which he belongs, this being necessary to shew the ground on which I am to make application.

I am Sir Your very humble Servt.,   TH: JEFFERSON

PrC (DLC); endorsed: "Briet sent by post."

Favi to the American Commissioners

MESSIEURS   Paris ce 11. Juin 1785.

J'ai reçu avec la lettre, que vous m'avés fait L'honneur de m'ecrire Le 8 de ce mois Les observations qu'elle renfermoit sur Les changements, que la Cour de Toscane a fait à quelques articles du Traité, que vous Lui avés proposé.

Je Les Lui ferai passer incessamment, et aurai L'honneur de vous informer en son tems de la reponse que j'en recevrai, presumant qu'elle sera pour La Conclusion de cette Convention, qui ne peut etre qu'utile aux deux pays.

Je suis avec Le plus grand respect, Messieurs Votre très humble, et très obeissant Serviteur,   FAVI

RC (DNA: PCC, No. 86); endorsed by Humphreys and TJ. Tr (DNA: PCC, No. 86); in Humphreys' hand, with an English translation. Another Tr (DNA: PCC, No. 116); also in Humphreys' hand. Sent by Franklin and TJ as enclosure No. 2c. in theirs to Jay of 18 June 1785.

From Nathanael Greene

DEAR SIR   Charleston June 11th. 1785.

This letter will be handed you by my friend Mr. John McQueen whose principal errand to Paris is to form a contract for live oak on which I wrote you some time since. I beg leave to recommend him to your good offices on the business which he comes but I hope the matter may be so managed that our propositions may not interfere with each other.

Mr. McQueen can give you full history of the politicks of this country. We are in anxious expectation to have the ultimate determination of the emperor Joseph and the Court of France respecting the Dutch war.

I have the honor to be with great respect Your Excellencys most ob. hble ser.,   NATH. GREENE

Tr (CSmH). Entry in SJL of receipt on 14 Jan. 1786 of a letter from Greene dated "June 1 . . . by Mr. McQueen" probably refers to the present letter, since the letter of 1 June (missing) was recorded as having been received on 3 Sep. 1785. The letter that Greene wrote "some time since" may have been that of 1 June 1785.

From Madame de Doradour

a clermont en auvergnne ce 14 juin [1785]

Je suis arrivée, Monsieur, depuis deux jours, ecrasée de fatigue, et fort incomodée par la challeur. Le regret d'avoir quitee paris contribue, dit ont, beaucoup à me faire souffrir. Nous autres femmes de france aimont la capital, j'y etee attachée, Monsieur, par l'avantage que j'avois de cultiver vos bontés. J'espere que vous daignneres les continuer à mon mari en le recomandant de nouveaux aux personnes de votre connoissance lorsque vous ecrires en amérique. J'irai vous en solliciter cet otonne [automne], contant aller passer à cet epoque quelques tems à paris.

Permettes, Monsieur, que je vous suplie d'embrasser pour moi Melle. votre fille; je desirerois qu'elle ne m'oublia pas et qu'elle voullue bien avoir un peu d'amitié pour moi.

Milles compliments, je vous prie, à tous vos Messieurs. Recevés, Monsieur, l'assurance de l'attachement sincere avec lequel j'ai l'honneur d'être Votre tres humble et tres obeissante servante,

DUBOURG DORADOUR

Je vous prie, Monsieur, de voulloir bien metre l'adresse de la lettre ci jointe pour mon mari.

RC (DLC). Enclosure not found.

From Neil Jamieson

SIR   New york 14th. June 1785.

A parcle of Philad. News Papers came to hand some days ago to forward for you. I have sent those of this City till todays date.

I hope they will get safe to hand. I wrote you and Colo. Humphreys, which I presume you receved. If I can render any acceptable services here you will be pleased to Command Sir your obd. Hbe. Serv.,

NIEL JAMIESON

RC (MHi); endorsed. Recorded in SJL as received 22 July 1785 "by Mr. Mazzei."

From John Jay

[*New York, 14 June 1785.* Recorded in SJL as received 22 July 1785 "by Mr. Mazzei." Not found.]

From Jean François Briet

MONSEIGNEUR   L'Orient le 15 Juin 1785.

J'ai reçû la Lettre que Son Excellençe, m'à fait l'honneur de m'adresser le 11 Courant par laquelle Je vois avec beaucoup de plaisir qu'elle daigne s'intéresser à la saisie des 3 Ballots Nankins appartenant à Mr. Peter Dischong à philadelphie, et que préalablement avant de s'expliquer avec Mgr. Le Contrôleur général, il fallait que Son Excellence sache de quel pays Mr. Peter Dischong est natif. Je ne peux sur ce point l'assurer positivement. J'ai fait sa Connaissance sur la Recommandation d'un de ses amis aujourd-hui à Nantes et qui est de Neuwied en allemagne, et Je suppose que mon dit Sr. Dischong qui est allemand et Etabli depuis fort longtems à philadelphie, est du même pays. J'aurai l'honneur d'instruire plus positivement, Son Excellence, à cet égard par ma prochaine.

Je suis avec Respect, De Son Excellence, Son très humble et très Obeissant Serviteur,   JN. FOIS. BRIET

RC (DLC).

To James Buchanan and William Hay

[*Paris, 15 June 1785.* Recorded in SJL with notation "see copy." Not found. A notation in SJL opposite entries for letters of 17 June reads: "letters of 14. 16. 17. and 19. went by Mr. Otto"; since, however, TJ records under 14 June 1785 only letters received, "14." must apply to those listed as written 15 June. On the matter dealt with in the present letter, see TJ to Buchanan and Hay, 13 Aug. 1785, and Buchanan and Hay to TJ, 18 Oct. 1785.]

Franklin and Jefferson to John Adams

SIR   Passy June 15, 1785.

Among the instructions given to the Ministers of the United States for treating with foreign powers, was one of the 11th. of May 1784. relative to an individual of the name of John Baptist Pecquet. It contains an acknowlegement on the part of Congress of his merits and sufferings by friendly services rendered to great numbers of American seamen carried prisoners into Lisbon, and refers to us the delivering him these acknowlegements in honourable terms and the making him such gratification as may indemnify his losses and properly reward his zeal. This person is now in Paris and asks whatever return is intended for him. Being in immediate want of money he has been furnished with ten guineas. He expressed desires of some appointment either for himself or son at Lisbon, but has been told that none such are in our gift, and that nothing more could be done for him in that line than to mention to Congress that his services will merit their recollection, if they should make any appointment there analogous to his talents. He sais his expences in the relief of our prisoners have been upwards of fifty Moidores. Supposing that, as he is poor, a pecuniary gratification will be most useful to him, we propose in addition to what he has received, to give him a hundred and fifty guineas or perhaps 4000. livres, and to write a joint letter to him expressing the sense Congress entertain of his services. We pray you to give us your sentiments on this subject by return of the first post, as he is waiting here, and we wish the aid of your [coun]sels therein. We are to acknowlege the receipt of your letter of June 3. 1785 informing us of your reception at the court of London.

PrC (DLC); in TJ's hand, lacking complimentary close and signatures. Recorded in SJL under this date; a notation opposite the entries for letters of 17 June reads: "letters of 14. 16. 17. and 19. went by Mr. Otto." Since, however, TJ recorded under 14 June only letters received, "14." must actually apply to those listed as written 15 June. Entry in SJPL reads: "Adams John. Pecquet's case."

In DLC: TJ Papers, 53: 9018-9, endorsed by TJ and obviously written from Lisbon, there is a 3-page memorial from Pecquet, without date or addressee but clearly submitted to the American minister to France, declaring that Pecquet, "Agent interprete de la Nation

francaise à Lisbonne, a l'honneur d'exposer à Votre Excellence qu'il a été assez heureux pour rendre, depuis le commencement de la rupture entre les Etats unis de L'Amérique et l'Angleterre, des Services essentiels aux différens matelots américains, que les hazards de la Guerre ont amenés dans ce Port, principalement avant que la France se fut déclaré en faveur de l'Amérique, et bien avant que le Congrès eut dans cette Ville une personne [Arnold H. Dohrman] pour pourvoir a leurs besoins." This activity, the memorial asserts, was carried on from 1775 until the time Pecquet learned that Dohrman was appointed agent at Lisbon by Congress (21 June 1780;

JCC, XVII, 541). It exposed him to danger and expense and caused him to be ordered to leave Portugal for having violated her neutrality. This order was revoked, however, and Pecquet entered with renewed vigor on the task of aiding American prisoners. He concluded: "La liberté même qu'il eut de le faire peu de tems après au nom de la France, en ecartant tous les risques et dangers, ne fit que redoubler son ardeur, son attachement et son zèle pour les Américains." This memorial, together with certificates from the French and Spanish ambassadors to Portugal and the French vice consulgeneral, evidently was transmitted to Vergennes and by him to the American minister. The document in DLC: TJ Papers is catalogued as having been addressed to TJ and bears on its face, in a later hand, the date "1789." It seems clear from the foregoing, however, that this must be a copy of the memorial that Franklin received through Vergennes and transmitted to Congress in his letter of 13 Sep. 1783 (Wharton, *Dipl. Corr. Amer. Rev.*, VI, 698), on the basis of which Congress included among the INSTRUCTIONS GIVEN TO THE MINISTERS OF THE UNITED STATES . . . ONE relating to Pecquet (see Vol. 6: 400).

From John Jay

DEAR SIR   Office for foreign Affairs 15th. June 1785

I have had the Honor of receiving the joint Letters from Mr. Adams, Dr. Franklin and yourself with their several Enclosures of December [15] 1784, and 9th. February, 18th. March and 13th. April 1785.

At present I am not charged with communicating to you any Instructions of Congress on the Subjects of them, tho it is probable they may give Occasion to some.

I have now the Honor of transmitting to you herewith enclosed, a Letter from Congress to his Most Christian Majesty; and for your Satisfaction I also enclose a Copy of it. Permit me to hint that as the United States have a Minister Plenipotentiary residing at the Court of Versailles, it is natural for them to expect one from thence.

I have directed a Packet of the latest Newspapers to be prepared and sent with this, from which you will be enabled to acquire a Knowledge of the most material public Occurrences in Detail.

Our commercial People grow uneasy and dissatisfied with Restrictions on our foreign Trade, and particularly with british Dominions. This Uneasiness promotes the System of perfecting our Union and strengthening the fœderal Government. There is Reason to hope that the Legislatures in the ensuing winter Sessions will direct much of their Attention to these important Objects.

I have the Honor to be &ca.,   JOHN JAY

FC (DNA: PCC, No. 121). Recorded in SJL as received 22 July 1785 "by Mr. Mazzei." Enclosure: President of Congress to Louis XVI, 14 June 1785 (text printed in JCC, XXVIII, 458).

From David Ramsay

New York June 15th. 1785

Presuming on a slight acquaintance with your Excellency in the year 1782 or 1783 in Philada. by the introduction of our common friend Mr. Madison I take the liberty to inclose a part of a work which is now in the press written by myself and entitled the "History of the revolution of South Carolina from a British Province to an Independent State." It originated when I was in confinement in Augustine in the year 1781 and has employed my leisure hours ever since. I am printing it at my own risque and expence and have already advanced above fourteen hundred dollars for it. When completed it will consist of two volumes and will contain over and above the civil police of South Carolina the whole of the Military operations in Georgia and both Carolinas and also the reduction of Lord Cornwallis in Virginia. The importance of the subject and of the contents of the second volume is great, and may perhaps excite the public attention. Your Excellency knows the infant state of literature in the United States and the risque a person runs who undertakes a work of this kind without subscription. I have from principles of delicacy perhaps excessive avoided this; but it is no part of my plan to lose by my publication. It has cost me a considerable sum of money and a great deal of labor. What I wish upon this occasion is to concert with your Excellency the best plan of introducing it into France. M. De Marbois the Consul General has seen a great part of it and approves it and had it not been for an accident a copy of what is printed would have gone from him to General Chattelleaux with a recommendation that he should have it translated and published in France.

I would thank you for your candid advice on the subject. Would it be best to send over a number of copies in English and if so to whose care should I address them? Or would it not be more advisable to contract with a printer and translator and have a French edition of it. The French nation will have no reason to dislike it as it contains many things to their credit and much to the dishonor of the British on the score of their plunderings and cruelties in South Carolina, all of which are circumstantially related. If you think that a translation of it would be well received I would be obliged to you for engaging on my part with a printer and a Translator so as to give us all an interest in the profits of the sale on equitable conditions. The work will be finished in this country by the middle of August. It will contain about 700 pages octavo and will be in two volumes. If it should be translated it might very well be comprised in one volume and several local matters omitted as uninteresting to foreigners. I send you by this conveyance all of it that is printed and the successive packets shall take the remainder as fast as it comes out. The printer does about forty pages a week. The importance of the materials of my work, the circumstance of its being the first of its kind together with the prepossession the public will have for an history of the late revolution written by a member of Congress will introduce it notwithstanding its imperfections under favorable circumstances to the public. It has occurred to me that a pirated European edition might not only defraud me of my just rights but also involve me in considerable expence as that could be afforded much lower than an American copy. I therefore propose to be aforehand with them, and if any advantage is to be made of the work in Europe I think myself entitled to it preferably to a piratical printer.

I submit the whole matter to Your Excellency. If you think any advantage would arise from a French edition I will be obliged to you to set forward the work so as that it may appear soon after the American edition which would perhaps check piratical adventurers. If you think it would not answer I shall be contented. At all events whatsoever engagements you make on my behalf shall be faithfully executed by me and you shall receive my most grateful acknowledgements. I am sorry for the trouble I propose to your Excellency but hope you will forgive it as I could not with propriety apply to any other person. I am again in Congress for this year and shall receive any answer with which you may honor this letter in the city of New York. With the most exalted sentiments of esteem for your public and private character I have the honor to be your Excellencys most obedient servant,

DAVID RAMSAY

RC (DLC); endorsed. Recorded in SJL as received 22 July 1785 "by Mr. Mazzei."

To John Banister

DEAR SIR   Paris June 16. 1785.

I received your favors of Feb. 8. and 9. by your son, and am happy to be able to assure you that his health is perfectly reestablished. On this subject however I suppose his own letter which accompanies this will give you more particular details. We were not able to decide what would be the best place for him to go to. He left this four days ago proposing to go to Lisle 4 leagues from Avignon and make some stay during which he could inform himself what would be his best position. Of this, as soon as known, you shall be informed. I gave him a plan of reading as well adapted to his views as I was able, and have endeavored to convince him he cannot oblige me more than by putting it in my power to be useful to him. I think the sum you propose is as much as he can spend usefully, if the purchase of books be made an additional article: but should any unexpected circumstances call for more I will take the liberty of advising him and informing you. His dispositions seem so perfectly good and regular that I think there is no danger of his even wishing to go beyond what is proper. I shall be happy on his account if I can be of service to him: I am very much so on your account as it enables me to repair the insult I was guilty of to you in supposing an impostor to be your son. I shall endeavor to convince you that that error flowed from a warm desire to oblige you. But after pardoning me this, I have a right to insist that you never propose again the reimbursing that money. The admitting this would place me too nearly on a level with the principal plunderer himself. It would be saddling you with my follies. Be so good as to present me affectionately to Mrs. Bannister. During the little time I was at Portsmouth I went to Titchfeild to see my old acquaintance [Mrs.] Thomson, but she was too much indisposed to be seen, and was not informed who it was asked to see her till I was gone. I was to cross the channel that evening. Everything seems quiet here at present, so that I have nothing interesting to communicate. I am with very great esteem Dr. Sir Your friend & servt.,   TH: JEFFERSON

PrC (DLC). Recorded in sjl under date of 15 June 1785 and as sent "by Mr. Otto."

To the Governor of Virginia, with Enclosure

SIR   Paris June 16. 1785

I had the honor of receiving the day before yesterday the resolution of council of Mar. 10. and your letter of Mar. 30. and shall with great pleasure unite my endeavours with those of the M. de la

Fayette and Mr. Barclay for the purpose of procuring the arms desired. Nothing can be more wise than this determination to arm our people as it is impossible to say when our neighbors may think proper to give them exercise. I suppose that the establishing a manufacture of arms to go hand in hand with the purchase of them from hence is at present opposed by good reasons. This alone would make us independant for an article essential to our preservation; and workmen could probably be either got here, or drawn from England to be embarked hence.

In a letter of Jan. 12. to Govr. Harrison I informed him of the necessity that the statuary should see Genl. Washington, that we should accordingly send him over unless the Executive disapproved of it, in which case I prayed to receive their pleasure. Mr. Houdon being now re-established in his health, and no countermand received, I hope this measure met the approbation of the Executive: Mr. Houdon will therefore go over with Dr. Franklin some time in the next month.

I have the honour of inclosing you the substance of propositions which have been made from London to the Farmers general of this country to furnish them with the tobaccoes of Virginia and Maryland, which propositions were procured for me by the M. de la Fayette. I take the liberty of troubling you with them on a supposition that it may be possible to have this article furnished from those two states to this country immediately without it's passing through the entrepot of London, and the returns for it being made of course in London merchandize. 20,000 hhds. of tobo. a year delivered here in exchange for the produce and manufactures of this country, many of which are as good, some better, and most of them cheaper than in England, would establish a rivalship for our commerce which would have happy effects in all the three countries. Whether this end will be best effected by giving out these propositions to our merchants, and exciting them to become candidates with the farmers general for this contract or by any other means, your Excellency will best judge on the spot.

I have the honor to be with sentiments of due respect Your Excellency's Most obedt. and most humble servt.,

Th: Jefferson

P.S. I have written on the last subject to the Governor of Maryland also.

ENCLOSURE

June 16. 1785.[1]

Sir Robert Herries of London proposes to the Farmers general of France to furnish them with 40000 hhds. of tobo. on the following terms.

One half shall be delivered in the present year, and the remaining half the next year, in such ports of France as shall be required.

The qualities shall be, one half *Virginia ordinary*, one eighth *Virginia superior*, and three eighths *Maryland ordinary*.

The price of the first 20,000 hhds. shall be 10. pr. Ct. less than the current prices at the three principal markets of Europe, viz. London, Amsterdam, and Hamburgh. These current prices shall be certified monthly by sworn brokers of each place, they shall be reduced to the money of France according to the exchange of the day, and an average formed which shall be the price for all the tobacco delivered in that month. But freight, insurance and commission are not to be deemed included in this price.

There shall be a deduction of 15. pr. C. for tare, *allowance* and es[*comptes.*]

For the remaining 20,000 hhds., delivered in such ports of France as shall be required, the prices shall be 40. livres for the Virginia superior, 38. livres for the Virginia ordinary, and 35. livres for the Maryland, for every quintal, *poids de Marc*, deducting 15. pr. C. for tare, *allowances and escomptes* and all charges included except Commission.

On accepting these propositions the Farmers general shall permit Sr. R. H. to draw on them for the amount of 10,000 hhds., which 10,000 hhds. shall be delivered by him one third in 2. months, another in 4. months, and another in 6. months. And every subsequent parcel of 10,000 hhds. shall be drawn for and delivered in the same way.

If the agents of the farmers general should have already engaged so much that the above quantity may not be wanting, the Farmers general may decline so much of what should be last delivered, giving 6. months notice.

RC (Vi); endorsed. PrC (DLC). Recorded in SJL as sent "by Mr. Otto"; entry in SJPL under this date reads: "Gov. Virga. Arms. Genl. Washington's statue. Farmers genl. do. Sr. Robt. Herries & Farmers genl." Enclosure (PrC in MHi); in TJ's hand. The full text of Herries' proposal is in Arch. Aff. Etr., Paris, Corr. Pol., E.-U., XXIX; Tr in DLC.

[1] The date, of course, is that of TJ's summary; Herries' proposal was dated 12 Apr. 1785.

From Patrick Henry

DEAR SIR   Council Chamber Richmond June 16. 1785

The inclosed resolution will inform you of the change which has taken place respecting the Bust formerly voted to the Marquis de la Fayette. I have to entreat that you will take the trouble to

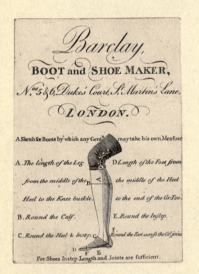
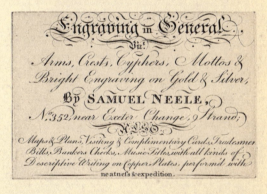

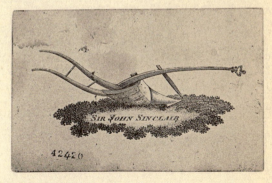

Calling cards and trade cards used and received by Jefferson
in France and England. (See p. xxvii.)

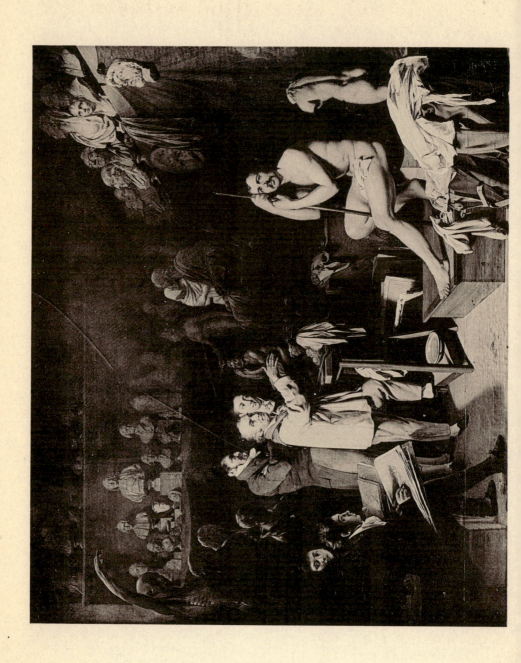

settle with Mr. Barclay the several Matters necessary to give Effect to the views of the Assembly in that particular.

With the highest regard I am Dr. Sir Your most obed. Servt.,

P. H.

FC (Vi). Recorded in SJL as received 21 Aug. 1785. Enclosure: Resolution of General Assembly of 1 Dec. 1784 (see TJ to Prévôt des Marchands et Echevins, 27 Sep. 1786).

From James Monroe

DEAR SIR   New York June 16[th.] 1785.

By Colo. Smith secretary to the London Legation I wrote you in April last very fully upon our transactions previous to that date. I also inclos'd you the Journals that were then printed with the copy of a report upon the first paragraph of the 9th. of the articles of Confideration proposing a change in it and the absolute investment of the U.S. with the controul of commerce. I now inclose you a copy of the journals as well those sent by Colo. Smith as those since printed, likewise an ordinance for surveying and disposing of the lands beyond the Ohio. Unfortunately I have not been able to command my cypher from Virga. so that your communications in the last and preceding letters, have been hid from my view. I left it with Mr. Jones who hath placd it among his papers but where he knows not. He promises to search again on his return home which will be shortly. I hope to receive the one by young Mr. Adams which will terminate the difficulty. The report upon the 9th. article hath not been taken up. The importance of the subject and the deep and radical change it will create in the bond of the union, together with the conviction that something must be done, seems to create an aversion or rather a fear of acting on it. If the report should ultimately be adopted it will certainly form the most permanent and powerful principle in the confideration. At present the alliance is little more than an offensive and defensive one, and if the right to raise troops at pleasure is denied, merely a defensive one. The political œconomy of each State is intirely within its own direction and to carry into effect its regulations with other powers to attain any substantial ends to the State they[1] must apply as well to the States of the union as other powers, and such a course as this will produce very mischievous effects. On the other hand the effect of this report would be to put the commercial œconomy of every state intirely under the hands of the Union. The measures

[215]

necessary to obtain the carrying trade, to incourage domestic by a tax on foreign industry, or any other ends which in the changes of things become necessary will depend intirely on the union. In short you will perceive that this will give the union an authority upon the States respectively which will last with it and hold it together in its present form longer than any principle it now contains will effect. I think the expedience in a great degree of the measure turns on one point (especially to the southern States) whether the obtainment of the carrying trade and the extention of our national resources is an object. And this depends entirely upon the prospect of our connection with other powers; if like the empire of China we were seperated and perfectly independent of them it might perhaps be unnecessary: but even in that event a question arises which may be of consequence, "whether the giving our own citizens a share in the carrying trade will not otherwise be advantageous to them than as it obtains the particular object which the regulations necessary to effect it have in view; whether it will not in effect increase the value of land, the number of inhabitants, the proportion of circulating medium, and be the foundation upon which all those regulations which are necessary to turn what is call'd 'the balance of trade' in our favor, must be form'd." A preference to our own citizens is the foundation of the carrying trade and upon it I suspect will depend all these consequences. Yet an opinion seems to be entertain'd by the late commercial writers and particularly a Mr. Smith on the wealth of nations that the doctrine of the balance of trade is a chimera in pursuit of which G. B. hath expos'd herself to great injury. If it should be found that the carrying trade was only useful as it added to the national strength, and it of no great consequence, I should suspect that the apprehensions already entertain'd and which will no doubt form great embarrassment to the passage of this or any such measure, should have great weight—"that the pursuit of this object will put it in the power of those States more immediately interested in it, to carry the regulations further than the attainment of it may make necessary, so as to give them advantages that will be almost exclusive and operate essentially to our prejudice: so as to lessen the price of our produce, discourage its cultivation and throw the monopoly in the purchase principally in their favor." Whether this under the report will probably be the case or possibly is doubtful: the regulation of the fishery is as much under our controul, even without the bounds of the State, as the tobo. of Virga., and all the states have produce, so that I am inclin'd to hope that the productions of the south, though disproportionate to that of the East, would not induce, more especially as the revenue accrues to the States and not the Union, any unequal restrictions. The subject [is] of great magnitude and I very earnestly wish to hear from you on it before it obtains its fate and this I am persuaded may be the case especially if the letter by Colo. Smith obtain'd a ready conveyance. I inform'd you in my letter by Mr. Smith that a Committee was appointed to revise the instructions subsisting to our Commissioners authoriz'd to form commercial treaties and report what alterations if any were necessary. This Committee hath reported and repeal'd the two first articles. I think it will be adopted. As I have no cypher I cannot risque anything upon this head further than to observe that the letter I allude to will serve to give you some idea of the alteration. It is prefac'd with reasoning upon the propriety of the alteration, upon which it is form'd and of course if the reasoning is illy founded the superstructure falls to the ground. I hope the whole will either be adopted or negativ'd for it will, if adopted, enable our ministers to investigate the truth of the positions and represent them to us, which their situation enables them to effect. There seems in Congress an earnest disposition to wind up our affairs as they respect foreign nations, exclude their interests totally from our councils, and preserving our faith with the utmost punctuality with those to whom it is plighted make such regulations as will effectually promote our interests. Information and a knowledge in what it consists are the only points in which they are defective. I have never seen a body of men collected in which there was less party for there is not the shadow of it here; I think there will be no adjournment and I sincerely wish there may not be for I fear it will not be easy to collect men from the States with more upright intentions. That you may have in view whatever is in agitation respecting the western country, to judge of the system if there is one, I enclose you the copy of a report now before Congress which comprehends whatever is propos'd to be done respecting it for the present. Upon the report of the Indian Commissioners the matter will again be taken up and then it will be determin'd what authority Congress will exercise over the people who may settle within the bounds of either of the new Sta[tes] previous to the establishment of a temporary government, whether they will leave them to themselves or appoint majistrates over them. I think the enclos'd report will be adopted: it hath been several times before Congress and each time there were 8. states; tomorrow it is believ'd there will be 9. The plan of a requisition is before Congress. The States have fail'd essentially during the last year in making their payments. Virga. hath paid I believe more than all the rest. The present plan is the pressure of the requisition of 8,000,000 as was that of the last year. The amount necessary for the current year about 3,000,-000—1. for the interest upon the foreign debt and expences of government and 2. the domestic debt. For the latter purpose facilities are propos'd to be admitted. I must confess I doubt the propriety of pressing old requisitions and think it would be better to ascertain what had been paid by the several States upon that requisition, and upon the apportionment under it, what claims those paying most had on the others, and then begin anew making also a new apportionment; this would be more simple and better understood. I am also rather doubtful of the propriety of doing anything whatever in the domestic debt. Several of the States, Pena. in particular hath appropriated her money to her own citizens only. From her and the other States, taking the same course, we shall have no support. It appears then better to recommend it to the States to take on themselves the debts of the U.S. to their citizens respectively, let them be paid by State operations and then after liquidating the whole, and the quota of each is ascertain'd, of the proportion of expences of the late war, let the balance which either shall have advanc'd beyond its proportion be paid it by the union. This is a new idea nor do I know that I shall suggest it further, but perhaps may hereafter more especially if it shall appear founded in justice and expedience. During the recess of Congress last year No. Carolina made a cession of territory to the U.S. authorizing her Delegates to make the deed. Before Congress conven'd she repeal'd it. Lately a motion was made and a report upon it accepting the cession supposing the acceptance conclusive on the State. I was surpris'd to find it had so many advocates there being six States in favor of it. I suspected it would have again been taken up but was agreeably disappointed. The act gave Congress a year to accept it in and uses the term "at the end of it provided it shall not be accepted within that term it shall revert to the State." Yet I would not conceive it obligatory on the State untill accepted by the U.S. and of course untill that event within the controul of the State. The people within the said territory had seperated themselves from the State and declar'd themselves an independent state under the name of Franklin; their agent was also here at the time upon that subject. He received no countenance whatever, and all that was done relative to it was to renew the recommendation to the State to make a 2d. cession. It is in contemplation to send a committee to No. Carolina and Georgia upon the subject of western land and of finance to press their attention to those subjects. But of this as well as of the other objects to which commerce may be turnd I will write you more fully in my next. The great points which will be before the Union as well in those lines as that of commerce will perhaps have taken their ultimate direction here in a few months or in the course of the year and then the several legislatures will be the theatre of investigation. Committees of Congress may perhaps expedite their passage. I should not have wrote thus freely without the cover of a cypher but from the confidence I repose in Mr. Mazzai. He will deliver it to you personally. He hath been here about a fortnight and sails today in the packet. I have been much concern'd for an accident which happen'd to him here. While with us one evening his room was forc'd open and his trunk with papers and money taken out. He recover'd every thing except about 40. guineas. As my colleagues write Mr. Short I must beg his excuse for the present. I hope he is well. I am with great respect & esteem yr. affec: friend & servt., JAS. MONROE

RC (DLC); endorsed. Recorded in SJL as received 22 July 1785, "by Mr. Mazzei." Enclosures: (1) *Journal of the United States in Congress Assembled*, 1785 (JCC, XXIX, 931, No. 510). (2) *An Ordinance for Ascertaining the Mode of Disposing of Lands in the Western Territory*, as adopted 20 May 1785 (see above, under 30 Apr. 1784). Despite the fact that Monroe must have sent a copy of the ordinance as adopted, of which 500 copies were run off on 26 May (JCC, XXIX, 923, No. 478) and that the present letter was received by TJ on 22 July, TJ wrote to Adams on 28 July 1785 that Congress had "passed an ordinance for selling their lands" but added: "I have not received it." If this statement is correct, then Monroe must either have failed to enclose the report as stated or else it was not actually an enclosure but was given by Monroe to Mazzei to hand to TJ and Mazzei failed to do so before the letter to Adams was written; the former seems more probable. (3) This cannot be conclusively identified, but it was almost certainly the report of 14 Mch. 1785 proposing a plan for the government of the Kaskaskia and

Illinois settlements in advance of any general plan for the establishment of governments in the Western territory (JCC, XXIX, 918, No. 458). On 15 June the Indian commissioners were given an instruction on this matter, but even this tentative step was rescinded on 29 June 1785 and the question was left in suspension (see Burnett, *Letters of Members*, VIII, No. 156, note 5).

THE COMMITTEE HATH REPORTED AND REPEAL'D THE TWO FIRST ARTICLES: Monroe did not reveal in this or other letters that the committee's chairman was Monroe himself and it was he who drafted the report. It seems clear that in this effort he was influenced by Jay's attitude toward the instructions of 7 May 1784 and toward the project of a commercial treaty that the Commissioners had submitted to Congress on 10 Nov. 1784 (JCC, CCVIII, 229; Monroe to TJ, 12 Apr. 1785). Jay had reported on the treaty on 17 May 1785 that "in his Opinion, a System for regulating the Trade of the United States should be formed and adopted, before they enter into further Treaties of Commerce. It appearing to him more wise, that such Treaties should be accommodated to their System, than that their System should be accommodated to such Treaties" (JCC, XXVIII, 367). On this premise Jay based detailed criticisms of the treaty and particularly of the most-favored-nation principle. Monroe's report paralleled this criticism of the so-called Plan of 1784 by raising doubt as to "Whether the U.S. were possess'd of sufficient powers to form commercial treaties so as that their engagements should be binding on the Union," from which it was concluded that, lacking such powers "to give what indulgence, or lay what restraints they please, upon the intercourse of other powers with these States all propositions on their part, found in the principles of reciprocity, will be ineffectual" (JCC, XXVIII, 419). The report recommended that the first two articles of the instructions of 7 May 1784 be repealed, and in substitution therefor proposed that a distinction be made between those European powers having possessions in the West Indies and those lacking them, whereby, abandoning the most-favored-nation

principle, the idea of making treaties with the latter would be given up as embarrassing to the primary object of gaining access to the West Indies (2 June 1785: JCC, XXVIII, 418-22; Monroe to TJ, 15 Aug. 1785). This view of the treaty powers of Congress was at variance with that set forth by TJ in his to Monroe of 17 June and to Adams of 7 July; see also TJ to Gerry, TJ to Jay, 11 Oct. 1785. THE LAST AND PRECEDING LETTERS, HAVE BEEN HID FROM MY VIEW: These were TJ's letters to Monroe of 6 Feb., 18 Mch., and 15 Apr. 1785. THE ONE BY YOUNG MR. ADAMS was the code that TJ intended to enclose in his to Monroe of 11 May 1785 (see TJ to Monroe, 18 Mch. 1785).

[1] This awkward sentence may be somewhat clarified by the knowledge that the pronoun "they" was interlined by Monroe in substitution for the words "its regulations," which he deleted in a commendable but not wholly successful effort to improve the phraseology.

From Benjamin Rush

Philadelphia, 16 June 1785. Introduces Samuel Fox, a descendant of "one of the most respectable Quaker families in Pennsylvania."

RC (NNP); 1 p. Recorded in SJL as received 1 Nov. 1785, "by Saml. Fox."

To the Governor of Maryland

SIR   Paris June 16. 1785

I have the honour of inclosing to your Excellency some propositions which have been made from London to the Farmers general to furnish them with the tobaccoes of Maryland and Virginia. For this paper I am indebted to the zeal of the M. de la Fayette. I take the liberty of troubling you with it on a supposition that it may be possible to have this article furnished from those states to this country immediately without it's passing through the entrepot of London, and the returns for it being made of course in London merchandize. Twenty thousand hhds. of tobo. a year delivered here in exchange for the produce and manufactures of this country, many of which are as good and cheaper than in England, would establish a rivalship for our commerce which would have happy effects in both countries. Whether this end will be best effected by giving out these propositions to our merchants and exciting them to become candidates with the farmers general for this contract or by any other means, your Excellency can best judge. I shall mention this matter also to the governor of Virginia. The other paper which accompanies the one before mentioned is too miserable to need notice. I will take measures here for apprising them of it's errors.

I have the honor to be with sentiments of the highest respect & esteem Your excellency's Most obedt. & most humble servt.,

TH: JEFFERSON

PrC (DLC). Tr (DLC); in an unidentified hand and without signature. Recorded in SJL as sent "by Mr. Otto"; entry in SJPL under this date reads: "Govr. of Maryld. Farmers Genl." Enclosures: Propositions of Sir Robert Herries (see enclosure to TJ's letter to Gov. Henry, this date). The "other paper" has not been identified. William Smallwood was governor of Maryland.

From Louis Alexandre, with Enclosure

MONSIEUR   Bayonne ce 17: Juin 1785

Le motif d'Etre utile à ma Patrie, et à la Vôtre, guidé encore par une honnête ambition d'augmenter ma fortune, qui me suffit déja pour paroitre avec agrément dans le monde, m'engage à prendre la liberté de vous écrire, heureux si vous voulez bien m'écouter, et m'honnorer de votre Réponse.

Le nombre des Connoissances que j'ai dans tout le Continent de l'amérique, et les avantages qu'offroient la franchise du Port entre le commerce des Etats unis, et le nôtre, m'a engagé, Monsieur, de solliciter l'adresse des navires de mes amis. J'ai déja joui des offres que je leur ai faites, puis qu'ils m'en ont Consigné trois, chargés de tabac Virginie, et mariland, Ris, et autres d'enrées de leur productions, pour en recevoir des nôtres; J'ai fait proposer suivant l'usage, quelques Jours aprez leur arrivée, ces cargaisons à Messrs. les fermiers Généraux à un prix, que j'ai cru convenable relativement à leur qualité; ils m'ont fait répondre, qu'ils ne pouvoient entrer en prix, sans qu'au préalable je ne me rapprochasse des leurs. J'ai du depuis modéré mes demandes, en fixant le virgie., a 48^{tt}. le: [premier?] et 45^{tt}. le beau Mariland. Jugez, Monsieur, si j'avois lieu d'attendre qu'ils eussent donné des ordres à leur Receveur, soit pour les prendre à ces derniers prix, ou du moins à une petite refaction? Point du tout, ils ont gardé pendant quelques courriers un profond silence, et enfin, ils ont répondu les mêmes môts qu'ils avoient déjà fait; je vous proteste, Monsieur, que cette conduite n'engagera pas mes amis, à répéter leurs envois, et jugez du déplaisir qu'ils auront de jouir si peu de la franchise de nôtre Port, où ils peuvent débiter infiniment mieux leur marchandize qu'à L'orient ou ailleurs, tant en tabac, morue, huille de Poisson, Ris, Péletrie &ca. et rápporter avec eux de l'eau de vie, des vins, du lainage, et soyries, de la première main.

Pardon, Monsieur, si j'abuse trop de votre Complaisance par un narré mercantil. L'agrandissement de notre Commerce reciproque m'a engagé d'y entrer, non Seulement avec vous, qui cherchez sans doute à favoriser votre Patrie mais encore avec Monsr. DeVergennes, à qui j'ai déja eu l'honneur de faire mes représentations, et m'ayant fait celui de me répondre, que Monsr. le Controleur Général pouvoit Seul faire le choix, et l'application des moyens à encourager les expéditions de tabacs, en donnant à la ferme les ordres nécessaires à ce Sujet. Je prends ce Jour la liberté de lui écrire, et d'ont je vous deman[de] l'agrément de vous remettre la Copie pour éviter des répétitions peu nécessaires.

Votre intercession à mes justes demandes, Monsieur, ne peuvent qu'en augmenter le poids; je vous serai infinim[ent] obligé de vouloir [bien] en solliciter vivement le Succèce, et soyez assuré sur ma reconnoissance particulière, et Sur le profond Respect avec lequel J'ai lhonneur d'Etre Monsieur Votre trez humble et trez obéissant Serviteur,

Par Procuration de mon Pere D'Alexandre,
Louis Alexandre

ENCLOSURE

Alexandre to Calonne

Monseigneur [17 June 1785]

La franchise de notre Port que nôtre bon Roy à bien voulu nous accorder, pour l'acroisement de la ville de Bayonne, présente des grands avantages à son Commerce Maritime, avec la Confiance que Votre Grandeur voudra bien le favoriser de votre Protection, lorsqu'il se présentera des inconvenients susceptibles de votre attention, et qu'on ne scauroit vaincre Monseigr. Sans ce préalable, je suis dans ce moment forcé de vous demander respectueusemt: la permition de mettre sous vos Yeux ceux que j'éprouve moi même.

J'ai depuis deux mois recu successivement trois navires des Etats unis chargés de tabac, Ris, et autres objets; mes amis du Continent me font espérer une Continuation d'affaires, si le Succès de la premiere répond a leur Souhaits; vous n'ignorez pas Monseigr. que l'objet le plus

conséquent de l'amerique anglaise est en tabac feuille virginie et mariland, et dont la Consomation la plus considérable est subordonée aux
achapts que fait la ferme Générale; cette compagnie n'ayant point encore
un prix fixe à Bayonne, je lui ai fait offrir mes tabacs a un prix raison-
able et relativement à leur qualité; ne devois-je pas me flater qu'elle
auroit donné des ordres pour les prendre aux pris proportionnés à leur
valeur, et même préférablemt. à tout autre Port de France, afin d'encourager les Américains a cimenter cette branche et par ce moyen les
attirer dans notre Port y traffiquer, et rapporter avec eux des denrées de
nos productions.

Le profond silence qu'a gardè la ferme sur mes offres et les sollicitations répétées de mes amis du continent, pour la Célérité de leurs
retours, m'ont forcé malgré moi de faire les avances que j'aurois évité
Monseig. si messrs. les fermiers Générx. avoient voulu fixer leur prix,
comme dans les Ports de L'Orient et Bordx., où l'instant de l'arrivée
de tabacs s'ils sont proposés a la Compage. sont acceptés par leur
Commisre. [Commissaire] suivant lappreciation que méritent leur
qualités; pourquoi celui de Bayonne aura-t-il des pouvoirs plus res-
serrés, lorsqu'au contraire ils devroient l'Etre moins qu'ailleurs,

Je dois encore vous observer Monseig; qu'il est probable d'aprez les
nouvelles que je recois chaque jour du Continent que je recois d'autres
navres [navires] a mon adresse, et si le defaut de vente Existe je ne
scaurai continuer de faire les retours crainte de me trouver surchargé
par trop d'avances qui ne scauroit convenir ni à mon honneur dont je
suis jaloux de conserver, ni a mes Intérêts de sorte que se voyant rebutés
ainsi ils s'eloigneront de notre Port et Yront porter leur produits chez
l'Etranger, en voici une preuve incontestable.

Un des trois navres. qui me sont consignés, et d'ont le proprietaire est
a Bord, ennuyé de rester sans débiter sa marchze. [marchandise],
projete d'aller la vendre à Londres, ou dans tout autre Port ou la ferme
achepte le tabac, ce qui Seroit non seulement bien fâcheux pour moi
Monseigr., mais encore pour notre Port, qui détruiroit totalement les
espérances d'un avenir heureux, qu'on avoit lieu d'attendre par un Commerce Suivi entre les américains et nous; il seroit fâcheux dis-je de voir
passer chez les Etrangers, un bien qui se présente dans notre Port, un
bien que nous avons si fort désiré, et que nous avons sans pouvoir en
Jouir.

L'Espoir que j'ai sur la bienveillance que vous accordès aux sujets
de notre Auguste Monarque, et le bien Général que vous desirez à
l'Etat, en faisant fleurir la ville de Bayonne dans sa franchise, me
rassurent qu'il vous plaira ordonner Monseigr., que la ferme générale
forme un Etablissement dans cette ville comme elle a à *Toneins*, et
prendre les tabacs qui nous viendront des Etats unis, c'est-a-dire, a des
prix proportionés toujours à leur valeur, pour éviter par ce moyen de
rebuter langlo americain a répéter leurs envoyes, priver nos francais
d'employer les d'enrées de nos Crus, et soustraire l'exposant dune
Commission ligitimement due.

Voules vous me permettre encore Monseigr: une dernière représenta-
tion nécessaire, pour rendre le succès de la nouvelle Angleterre moins
douteux; il arrive souvent que les circonstances exigent des ventes

publiques avec un simple huissier, et nous ne scaurions prendre ce parti, quoique par fois plus convenable aux Intérêts de mes amis, par le droit de 4 d. par livre que le Controleur des actes du Domaine exige; j'ai lieu d'Espérer que le Roy, ayant accordé la franchise Générale, a la ville de Baye. [Bayonne] ne voudroit pas gréver les produits des marchzes. americaines par un droit bien plus haut, que celui qu'ils auroient payé dans les Douanes avant la franchise du Port; comptant sur vos bontés il vous plaira ordonner, que ce droit de 4 d. par ^{it}. ne sera point percu sur les ventes publiques, qu'on pourroient faire sur les marchzes. venant des Etats unis, qui en seront exemptes ainsi que sur tout autre usage, et Coutume de la ville de Bayonne.

L'amour pour ma Patrie, et pour le Commerce que je fais depuis 50 ans dans cette ville, m'encourage dans les Remontrances que j'ai l'honneur de vous faire, heureux si elles sont accueillies favorablement, et si je puis en espérer le Succèce; Soyez assuré d'avance Monseigneur, que je ne Cesserai jamais de faire des voeux, pour la prosperité et la Conservation de votre Grandeur. Monseigneur, le plus Soumis et le plus Respecteux Serv,   Signé D'Alexandre

RC (DLC); endorsed. Enclosure (Tr in DLC): Undated, but evidently written the same day as Alexandre's letter to TJ, according to the reference therein. Both letter and enclosure were sent to TJ under cover of P. & V. French & Nephew to TJ, 21 June 1785.

From John Banister, Jr.

Lyons June 17th. 1785

I take a pleasure which I cannot well express in embraceing the opportunity which, by your desire, is afforded me of writing you and shall think myself extreemly happy if my letters compensate for the trouble you will have in reading them. Yesterday evening I arrived here after a Journey which for want of sleep has proved a very fatigueing one and tomorrow I shall depart for Avignion, as I find myself very unwell and wish as soon as possible to fix myself. The inclosed letter to my Father I take the liberty to trouble you with and shall take it as a favor if you will send it by the first opportunity which offers as its arrival is of some consequence to me. Should there be any thing of instruction or advice which may occur to you as necessary or useful to me it will be the greatest favor you can possibly confer on me to communicate it, as instruction is at present my principal object. Immediately on my arrival at Avignion I shall do myself the pleasure to write you again. My head is so disordered at present that I scarcely know what I am about. I am Sir respectfully your Humble Servt.,

JNO. BANISTER Junr.

RC (MHi); endorsed. Enclosure not found.

From David S. Franks

DEAR SIR   Paris 17th. June 1785

A disappointment in my expectations of remittances from America has brought me into great distress; My time I find will be lost in waiting untill affairs are settled with the Algiereens &c. I wish therefore to return as soon as possible. This cannot be effected untill my debts are paid. If you will kindly assist me in doing it, I will immediately on my arrival at Philadelphia transmit you the Money you may advance for me or pay it to any one there you may order. It is in confidence of your goodness that I am induced to apply to you, fully conscious that on, or shortly after my arrival at Philadelphia, I shall be able to repay you and shall allways acknowledge the obligation with gratitude. I am Dear Sir with much respect, Your very humble Servt.,   DAVD. S. FRANKS

RC (DLC); endorsed.

To David S. Franks

DEAR SIR   Paris June 17. 1785.

Your letter of this day distresses me not a little as it finds me utterly unable to give you the assistance needed. My outfit here, for the articles of furniture, clothes and carriage only has cost me fifteen hundred guineas. No allowance of this kind being made I have been obliged to run in debt for it. The uneasiness which this has given me for some time past has preyed on my spirits night and day. And indeed my situation is not a little delicate. The laws not giving remedy against me, the first creditor whom I can neither pay nor prevail to wait, carries his complaint to the king immediately, and exposes me of necessity to censure and recall. These circumstances have not only reduced me to a rigid œconomy, but render it impossible for me either to advance money or further hazard my credit. I am fully sensible that this information may be distressing to you, and this increases the pain with which I communicate it. I am unhappily in a condition to feel much for your difficulties without a power to lessen them. Nothing would have been more pleasing to me than the exercise of such a power, as I am with real esteem Dr. Sir Your most obedt. humble servt.,
TH: JEFFERSON

PrC (DLC). Not recorded in SJL. TJ's Account Book shows that on 2 Sep. 1785 he "lent Colo. Franks 200f."

To John Jay

Paris June 17. 1785.

I had the honour of addressing you on the 11th. of the last month by young Mr. Adams who sailed in the packet of that month. That of the present is likely to be retarded to the first of July if not longer.

On the 14th. of May I communicated to the Count de Vergennes my appointment as minister plenipotentiary to this court and on the 17th. delivered my letter of credence to the king at a private audience and went through the other ceremonies usual on such occasions.

We have reason to expect that Europe will enjoy peace another year. The negociations between the Emperor and United Netherlands have been spun out to an unexpected length, but there seems little doubt but they will end in peace. Whether the exchange projected between the Emperor and Elector of Bavaria, or the pretensions of the former in his line of demarcation with the Ottoman porte will produce war is yet incertain. If either of them does, this country will probably take part in it, to prevent a dangerous accession of power to the house of Austria. The zeal with which they have appeared to negotiate a peace between Holland and the empire seems to prove that they do not apprehend being engaged in war against the emperor for any other power; because if they had such an apprehension they would not wish to deprive themselves of the assistance of the Dutch: and their opinion on this subject is better evidence than the details we get from the newspapers, and must weigh against the affected delays of the Porte as to the line of demarcation, the change in their ministry, their preparations for war, and other symptoms of like aspect. This question is not altogether uninteresting to us. Should this country be involved in a continental war while diffrences are existing between us and Great Britain, the latter might carry less moderation into the negociations for settling them.

I send you herewith the gazettes of Leyden and that of France for the last two months. The latter because it is the best in this country, the former as being the best in Europe. The Courier de l'Europe you will get genuine from London. As reprinted here it is of less worth. Should your knowlege of the newspapers of this country lead you to wish for any other I shall take the greatest pleasure in adding it to the regular transmissions of the two others which I shall make you in future.

I have the honour to be with the highest esteem & respect Sir Your most obedt. and most humble servt.,   TH: JEFFERSON

RC (DNA: PCC, No. 87); endorsed. PrC (DLC). Tr (DNA: PCC, No. 107). Recorded in SJL as sent "by Mr. Otto"; entry in SJPL under this date reads: "Jay John.—My presentment to King. State of Europe. Gazettes." Enclosures not found.

To James Milligan

SIR   Paris June 17. 1785

I have been honored with your letter of Apr. 15. inclosing certificates for Genls. Duportail, and Laumoy and Col. Gouvion. I have delivered the 1st., and shall deliver the two last as soon as the gentlemen return to town from which they are absent at this time. I inclose you the original certificates which had been lodged with Dr. Franklin, according to your desire & have the honor to be &c.,   TH: J.

FC (ViWC); in TJ's hand; at foot of letter: "Jas. Milligan Comptroller of the Treasury. sent by Mr. Otto." Enclosures: U.S. Treasury certificates (see Milligan to TJ, 15 Apr. 1785).

To James Monroe

DEAR SIR   Paris, June 17. 1785.

I received three days ago your favor of Apr. 12. You therein speak of a former letter to me, but it has not come to hand, nor any other of later date than the 14th. of December. My last to you was of the 11th. of May by Mr. Adams who went in the packet of that month. These conveiances are now becoming deranged. We have had expectations of their coming to Havre which would infinitely facilitate the communication between Paris and Congress: but their deliberations on the subject seem to be taking another turn. They complain of the expence, and that their commerce with us is too small to justify it. They therefore talk of sending a packet every six weeks only. The present one therefore, which should have sailed about this time, will not sail till the 1st. of July. However the whole matter is as yet undecided. I have hopes that when Mr. St. John arrives from N. York he will get them replaced on their monthly system. By the bye what is the meaning of a very angry resolution of Congress on his subject? I have it not by me and therefore cannot cite it by date, but you will remember it, and will oblige me by explaining it's foundation. This will be handed you by Mr. Otto who comes to America as Chargé des affaires in the room of Mr. Marbois promoted to the Intendancy of Hispaniola, which office is next to that of Governor. He becomes the head of the civil as the Governor is of the military department. I am much pleased with Otto's appointment. He is good humoured, affectionate to America, will see things in a friendly light when they admit of it, in a rational one always, and will not pique himself on writing every trifling circumstance of irritation to his court. I wish you to be acquainted with him, as a friendly intercourse between individuals who do business together produces a mutual spirit of accomodation useful to both parties. It is very much our interest to keep up the affection of this country for us, which is considerable. A court has no affections. But those of the people whom they govern influence their decisions even in the most arbitrary governments.— The negociations between the Emperor and Dutch are spun out to an amazing length. At present there is no apprehension but that they will terminate in peace. This court seems to press it with ardour, and the Dutch are averse, considering the terms cruel and unjust, as they evidently are. The present delays therefore are imputed to their coldness and to their forms. In the mean time the Turk is delaying the demarcation of limits between him and the emperor, is making the most vigourous preparations for war, and has composed his ministry of warlike characters deemed personally hostile to the emperor. Thus time seems to be spinning out both by the Dutch and Turks, and time is wanting for France. Every year's delay is a great thing to her. It is not impossible therefore but that she may secretly encourage the delays of the Dutch, and hasten the preparations of the Porte, while she is recovering vigour herself also, in order to be able to present such a combination to the emperor as may dictate to him to be quiet. But the designs of these courts are unsearcheable. It is our interest to pray that this country may have no continental war till our peace with England is perfectly settled. The merchants of this country continue as loud and furious as ever against the Arret of August 1784, permitting our commerce with their islands to a certain degree. Many of them have actually abandoned their trade. The ministry are disposed to be firm, but there is a point at which they will give way. That is if the clamours should become such as to endanger their places. It is evident that nothing can be done by us, at this time, if we may hope it hereafter. I like your removal to N. York, and hope Congress will continue there and never execute the idea of building their federal town. Before it could be finished a change of members in Congress, or the admission of new states would remove them somewhere else. It is evident that when a sufficient number of the Western states come in, they will remove it to George town. In the mean time it is our interest that it should remain where it is, and give no new pretensions to any other place. I am also much pleased with the proposition to the states to invest Congress with the regulation of their trade, reserving it's revenue to the states. I think it a happy idea, removing the only objection which could have been justly made to the proposition. The time too is the present, before the admission of the Western states. I am very differently affected towards the new plan of opening our land office by dividing the lands among the states and selling them at vendue. It separates still more the interest of the states which ought to be made joint in every possible instance in order to cultivate the idea of our being one nation, and to multiply the instances in which the people shall look up to Congress as their head. And when the states get their portions they will either fool them away, or make a job of it to serve individuals. Proofs of both of these practices have been furnished, and by either of them that invaluable fund is lost which ought to pay our public debt. To sell them at vendue, is to give them to the bidders of the day, be they many or few. It is ripping up the hen which lays golden eggs. If sold in lots at a fixed price as first proposed, the best lots will be sold first. As these become occupied it gives a value to the interjacent ones, and raises them, tho' of inferior quality, to the price of the first. I send you by Mr. Otto a copy of my book. Be so good as to apologize to Mr. Thomson for my not sending him one by this conveiance. I could not burthen Mr. Otto with more on so long a road as that from here to l'Orient. I will send him one by a Mr. Williamos who will go ere long. I have taken measures to prevent it's publication. My reason is that I fear the terms in which I speak of slavery and of our constitution may produce an irritation which will revolt the minds of our countrymen against reformation in these two articles, and thus do more harm than good. I have asked of Mr. Madison to sound this matter as far as he can, and if he thinks it will not produce that effect, I have then copies enough printed to give one to each of the young men at the college, and to my friends in the country. *I*[1] *am sorry* to see a possibility of *Arthur Lee's being put into the Treasury. He* has no *talents* for the *office* and what *he has* will be *employed* in *rummaging old accounts* to *involve* you in *eternal war with Morris* and *he* will in a short time *introduce* such *dissentions* into the *Commission* as to *break it up*. If *he goes* on the *other appointment to Kaskaskia he will produce a revolt* of that *settlement from* the *United States*. *I thank you* for *your attention* to *my outfit for* the *articles* of *household furniture, clothes* and a *carriage. I have already paid twenty eight thousand livres* and *have* still *more to pay*. For the *greatest part* of *this I* have *been obliged* to *anticipate my salary* from which *however I* shall never be *able to repay* it. *I find* that by a *rigid economy bordering* however on *meanness I* can *save* perhaps *five hundred livres a month* in the *summer* at least. The *residue* goes for *expences* so much of *course* and of *necessity that I* cannot *avoid* them *without abandoning all respect* to *my public character. Yet I* will *pray you* to *touch* this *string* which *I know* to be a *tender one* with *Congress* with the *utmost delicacy. I* had *rather* be *ruined* in *my fortune than* in their *esteem*. If they *allow me half* a *year's salary* as an *outfit I* can get *thro my debts in time. If they raise* the *salary* to what *it was* or *even pay our house rent* and *taxes I* can *live* with *more decency. I trust* that *Mr. Adams's house* at the *Hague* and *Doctor Franklin's* at *Passy* the *rent* of which has been always *paid* will *give just expectations* of the *same allowance* to *me. Mr. Jay* however did not *charge it but he lived economically* and *laid up money*. I will take the liberty of hazarding to you some thoughts on the policy of entering into treaties with the European nations, and the nature of them. I am not wedded to these ideas, and therefore shall relinquish them chearfully when Congress shall adopt others, and zealously endeavor to carry theirs into effect. First as to the policy of making treaties. Congress, by the Confederation have no original and inherent power over the commerce of the states. But by the 9th. article they are authorised to enter into treaties of commerce. The moment these treaties are concluded the jurisdiction of Congress over the commerce of the states springs into existence, and that of the particular states is superseded so far as the articles of the treaty may have taken up the subject. There are two restrictions only on the exercise of the powers of treaty by Congress. 1st. That they shall not by such treaty restrain the legislatures of the state from imposing such duties on foreigners as their own people are subjected to: 2dly. nor from prohibiting the exportation or importation of any particular species of goods. Leaving these two points free, Congress may by treaty establish any system of commerce they please. But, as I before observed, it is by treaty alone they can do it. Tho' they may exercise their other powers by resolution or ordinance, those over commerce can only be exercised by forming a treaty and this probably by an accidental wording of our confederation. If therefore it is better for the states that Congress should regulate their commerce, it is proper that they should form treaties with all nations with whom we may possibly trade. You see that my primary object in the formation of treaties is to take the commerce of the states out of the hands of the states, and to place it under the superintendance of Congress, so far as the imperfect provisions of our constitution will admit, and until the states shall by new compact make them more perfect. I would say then to every nation on earth, *by treaty*,[2] your people shall trade freely with us, and ours with you, paying no more than the most favoured nation, in order to put an end to the right of individual states acting by fits and starts to interrupt our commerce or to embroil us with any nation. As to the terms of these treaties, the question becomes more difficult. I will mention three different plans. 1. That no duties shall be laid by either party on the productions of the other. 2. That each may be permitted to equalize their duties to those laid by the other. 3. That each shall pay in the ports of the other such duties only as the most favoured nations pay. 1. Were the nations of Europe as free and unembarrassed of established system as we are, I do verily beleive they would concur with us in the first plan. But it is impossible. These establishments are fixed upon them, they are interwoven with the body of their laws and the organisation of their government, and they make a great part of their revenue; they cannot then get rid of them. 2. The plan of equal imposts presents difficulties insurmountable. For how are the equal imposts to be effected? Is it by laying in the ports of A an equal percent on the goods of B. with that which B has laid in his ports on the goods of A? But how are we to find what is that percent? For this is not the usual form of imposts. They generally pay by the ton, by the measure, by the weight, and not by the value. Besides if A. sends a million's worth of goods to B. and takes back but the half of that, and each pays the same percent, it is evident that A. pays the double of what he recovers in the same way with B. This would be our case with Spain. Shall we endeavour to effect equality then by saying A may levy so much on the sum of B's importations into his ports, as B does on the sum of A's importations into the ports of B? But how find out that sum? Will either party lay open their customhouse books candidly to evince this sum? Does either keep their books so exactly as to trouble to do it? This proposition was started in Congress when our instructions were formed, as you may remember, and the impossibility of executing it occasioned it to be disapproved. Besides who should have a right of deciding when the imposts were equal. A. would say to B. my imposts do not raise so much as yours; I raise them therefore. B. would then say you have made them greater than mine, I will raise mine, and thus a kind of auction would be carried on between them, and a mutual irritation, which would end in any thing sooner than equality, and right. 3. I confess then to you that I see no alternative left but that which Congress adopted, of each party placing the other on the footing of the most favoured nation. If the nations of Europe from their actual establishments are not at liberty to say to America that she shall trade in their ports duty free, they may say she may trade there paying no higher duties than the most favoured nation and this is valuable in many of these countries where a very great difference is made between different nations. There is no difficulty in the execution of this contract, because there is not a merchant who does not know, or may not know, the duty paid by every nation on every article. This stipulation leaves each party at liberty to regulate their own commerce by general rules; while it secures the other from partial and oppressive discriminations. The difficulty which arises in our case is, with the nations having American territory. Access to the West Indies is indispensably necessary to us. Yet how to gain it when it is the established system of these nations to exclude all foreigners from their colonies. The only chance seems to be this. Our commerce to the mother countries is valuable to them. We must endeavor then to make this the price of an admission into their West Indies, and to those who refuse the admission we must refuse our commerce or load theirs by odious discriminations in our ports. We have this circumstance in our favor too that what one grants us in their islands the others will not find it worth their while to refuse. The misfortune is that with this country we gave this price for their aid in the war, and we have now nothing more to offer. She being withdrawn from the competition leaves Gr. Britain much more at liberty to hold out against us. This is the difficult part of the business of treaty, and I own it does not hold out the most flattering prospect.—I wish you would consider this subject and write me your thoughts on it. Mr. Gherry wrote me on the same subject. Will you give me leave to impose on you the trouble of communicating this to him? It is long, and will save me much labour in copying. I hope he will be so indulgent as to consider it as an answer to that part of his letter, and will give me his further thoughts on it.

Shall I send you so much of the Encyclopedie as is already published or reserve it here till you come? It is about 40. vols., which probably is about half the work. Give yourself no uneasiness about the money. Perhaps I may find it convenient to ask you to pay trifles occasionally for me in America. I sincerely wish you may find it convenient to come here. The pleasure of the trip will be less than you expect but the utility greater. It will make you adore your own country, it's soil, it's climate, it's equality, liberty, laws, people and manners. My god! How little do my countrymen know what precious blessings they are in possession of, and which no other people on earth enjoy. I confess I had no idea of it myself. While we shall see multiplied instances of Europeans going to live in America, I will venture to say no man now living will ever see an instance of an American removing to settle in Europe and continuing there. Come then and see the proofs of this, and on your return add your testimony to that of every thinking American, in order to satisfy our countrymen how much it is their interest to preserve uninfected by contagion those peculiarities in their government and manners to which they are indebted for these blessings. Adieu my dear friend. Present me affectionately to your collegues. If any of them think me worth writing to, they may be assured that in the epistolary account I will keep the debit side against them. Once more Adieu.

June 19.

Since writing the above we receive the following account. Monsr. Pilatre de Rosieres, who has been waiting some months at Boulogne for a fair wind to cross the channel, at length took his ascent with a companion. The wind changed after a while and brought him back on the French coast. Being at a height of about 6000 feet, some accident happened to his baloon of inflammable air, it burst, they fell from that height, and were crushed to atoms. There was a Montgolfier combined with the balloon of inflammable air. It is suspected the heat of the Montgolfier rarified too much the inflammable air of the other and occasioned it to burst. The Montgolfier came down in good order.

RC (James Monroe Law Office, Fredericksburg, Va., 1950); unsigned; partly in code. PrC (DLC). Recorded in SJL as sent "by Mr. Otto"; entry in SJPL under this date reads: "Monroe James. Packets. Otto. State of Europe. W. Ind. Commerce. Federal city—land office. Notes on Virga. Dr. Lee. Outfit.

Treaties with Europe. Baloon."

¹ This and the following words in italics, unless otherwise noted, were written in code and have been decoded by the editors using Code No. 9.

² These two words are underscored in RC.

From Du Portail

17 June 1785. Acknowledges papers sent by TJ.

RC (ViWC); 1 p.; endorsed by TJ: "This was the certificate inclosed to me for him by Mr. Millegan."

De Thulemeier to the American Commissioners

MESSIEURS   à la Haye le 17. Juin 1785.

J'ai reçu la lettre dont Vous m'avez honoré, Messieurs, en date du 26 de Mai, le 4 du mois courrant. Mes premiers soins ont été consacrés à faire soigner la traduction françoise du Traité annexe en langue angloise, et de la faire passer à ma Cour. Le Roi apprendra certainement avec beaucoup de satisfaction que la négociation qui a été confiée à nos soins communs, est avancée au point qu'il n'est plus question que de faire transcrire le Traité même dans la forme requise. Si Vous l'agréez, Messieurs, l'échange que Vous me proposez de faire par une personne de confiance, vu l'éloignement de Votre domicile actuel, de celui de Monsieur Adams, et du mien, pourroit avoir lieu à la Haye par Monsieur Dumas, Chargé d'Affaires des Etats-Unis d'Amérique. C'est dans ce sens que je me suis expliqué aujourd'hui envers le Roi, et j'ai de plus informé Sa Majesté, que Vous projettiez, Messieurs, de fixer la durée du Traité préalablement au terme de dix années. Je me promets pour Votre Patrie et pour la mienne des avantages solides de ces nouvelles liaisons de commerce établies sur la base de réciprocité et d'une parfaite égalité. J'aurois desiré que les circonstances dans lesquelles je me trouve, m'eussent permis de me rapprocher de Vous, et de Vous assurer de bouche des sentimens de la haute considération avec laquelle je ne cesserai jamais d'être, Messieurs, Vôtre très humble et très obéissant Serviteur,

DE THULEMEIER

RC (DNA: PCC, No. 86); in a clerk's hand; signed by De Thulemeier.

American Commissioners to John Jay

SIR   Passy June 18th. 1785

In our last to you of May 11. we had the honour of inclosing among other papers a letter from Baron Thulemeier, drawing to a close our negociation with the court of Berlin. We have now that of forwarding our answer marked No. 1.

No. 2.a. contains our observations on the counterdraught from the court of Tuscany, No. 2.b. the letter inclosing them, and No. 2.c. Mr. Favi's answer acknowledging their receipt.

Mr. Adams's appointment to the court of London rendering it more convenient, more speedy and probably more effectual that that negociation should be conducted on the spot, we wrote to the Duke of Dorset a letter of which No. 3. is a copy in answer to one received from him and transmitted to you in April.

Since Mr. Adams's departure we have been favoured by him with information which he received from you that a Mr. Lambe had been charged with letters and instructions for us on the subject of the treaties with the States of Barbary. He sent us at the same time the copy of a resolution of Congress on the subject. As yet we have heard nothing more of Mr. Lambe, but hope his arrival hourly that we may take decisive measures for establishing an amity with those powers.

Mr. John Baptist Pecquet, who was the subject of an instruction to us of May. 11. 1784. is now in Paris, and has applied for such acknowledgements of his services as may be thought proper. He seemed to desire most some appointment at Lisbon either for himself or his son. We informed him none such were in our gift and that all we could do in that line would be to mention him to Congress as worthy of their recollection, if they should make any appointment there analogous to his talents. We have written to Mr. Adams proposing to give to Mr. Pecquet, in addition to ten guineas which he has received for present supply, 150 guineas or perhaps 4000 livres as a compensation for his expences and good dispositions. His expences on our prisoners had been about 50 Moidores.

Our first letter to Congress was of the 11 of Novr. and was sent by a Colonel Lemaire. Having lately received proofs that he omitted to deliver private letters with which he was charged, tho' he saw in New York the persons to whom they were addressed, we begin to fear he was capable of omitting to deliver also that to the President of Congress. We are equally incertain whether our subsequent letters may have got to hand. To relieve our anxieties on this subject we will pray you to be so good as to inform us which of them may have been received. Their dates have been Novr. 11. 1784. Decr. 15. 1784. and [9] Febry. 1785 addressed to the President of Congress, and March 18. April 13. and May 11. addressed to yourself.

We have the honour to be With the highest esteem & regard Sir Your Most obedient & Most humble Servants,

B. FRANKLIN
TH: JEFFERSON

RC (DNA: PCC, No. 86); in David Humphreys' hand, signed by Franklin and TJ. PrC of Dft (DLC); in TJ's hand; with minor variations from RC. FC (DNA: PCC, No. 116); in Humphreys' hand; at head of letter: "7th. Report to Congress, addressed to Mr. Jay, Secretary for foreign Affairs." Entry in SJPL under this date reads: "do. [John Jay] joint with Dr. F. Treaties with Prussia. Tuscany. Engld. Barbary. Pecquet." Enclosures: No. 1:

Commissioners to De Thulemeier, 26 May 1785. Nos. 2a. and 2b.: Commissioners to Favi, 8 June 1785, and its enclosure. No. 2c.: Favi to Commissioners, 11 June 1785. No. 3: Commissioners to Dorset, 16 May 1785.

In his letter to TJ of 15 June 1785, Jay acknowledged receipt of all of the letters listed in the final paragraph save those of 11 Nov. 1784 and, of course, 11 May 1785.

To Joseph Jones

DEAR SIR   Paris June 19. 1785.

I take the liberty of inclosing to you a state of the case of one Polson, and of begging your enquiries and information whether the lands therein mentioned have been escheated and sold, and if they have what would be the proper method of application to obtain a compensation for them.

The negociations between Holland and the emperor are slow, but will probably end in peace. It is believed the emperor will not at present push the Bavarian exchange. The Porte delays the demarcation of limits with him, and is making vigorous preparations for war. But neither will this latter be permitted to produce a war if France can prevent it, because wherever the emperor is seeking to enlarge his dominions France will present to him the point of a bayonet. But she wishes extremely for repose and has need of it. She is the wealthiest but worst governed country on earth; and her finances utterly unprepared for war. We have need to pray for her repose, and that she may not be engaged in a continental war while our matters with Gr. Britain are so unsettled and so little like being settled.

An accident has happened here which will probably damp the ardour with which aerial navigation has been pursued. Monsr. Pilatre de Rosiere had been attending many months at Boulogne a fair wind to cross the channel in a baloon which was compounded of one of inflammable air and another called a Montgolfier with rarefied air only. He at length thought the wind fair and with a companion ascended. After proceeding in a proper direction about two leagues the wind changed and brought them again over the French coast. Being at the height of about 6000 feet some accident, unknown, burst the balloon of inflammable air and the Montgolfier being unequal alone to sustain their weight they precipitated from that height to the earth and were crushed to atoms. Though navigation by water is attended with frequent accidents, and in it's infancy must have been attended with more, yet these are now so familiar that we think little of them, while that which has signalised the two first martyrs to the aeronautical art will probably deter very many from the experiments they would have been disposed to make. Will you give me leave to hope the pleasure of hearing from you sometimes. The details from my own country of the proceedings of the legislative, executive and judiciary bodies, and even those which respect individuals only are the most pleasing treat we can receive at this distance, and the most useful also. I will promise in return whatever may be interesting to you here. I am with very perfect esteem Sir Your friend & servt.,

Th: Jefferson

PrC (DLC). Recorded in sjl as sent "by Mr. Otto." Enclosure not found, but see John Polson to TJ, 13 May 1785 and TJ to Adam Stephen, this date.

To Adam Stephen

Sir   Paris June 19. 1785.

A Mr. John Polson lately came over from England to see whether I could give him any information as to some lands he owned in Virginia. The inclosed paper contains a state of his case. Finding your name in it, I take the liberty on his behalf of asking the favour of you to inform me as far as you shall be able, whether these lands have been escheated, where they lie, and what is their present situation. A line addressed to me and forwarded by post to New York will come safely by the French packet.

The negotiations between Holland and the emperor are slow, but will probably end in peace. It is beleived the emperor will not at present push the Bavarian exchange. The Porte delays the demarcation of limits with him, and is making vigorous preparations for war. But neither will this latter produce a war if France can prevent it, because if it does she must meet the emperor in it.

I am with very great respect Sir your most obedt. & most humble servt.,   TH: JEFFERSON

PrC (ViWC). Recorded in SJL as carried "by Mr. Otto." Enclosure not found, but see John Polson to TJ, 13 May 1785 and TJ to Joseph Jones, this date.

John Adams to Franklin and Jefferson

GENTLEMEN   Bath Hotel Westminster June 20. 1785.

Let me request of you, to turn your Attention as soon as possible to the Subject of a Treaty of Commerce between the United States of America and Great Britain, and transmit to me, a Project that you would advise me to propose in the first Instance. For my own Part I like the Plan agreed on with Prussia so well, that I must request you to send me a Copy of it, and with such Changes as you may advise me to adopt I should be for proposing that. With great Respect &c.

FC (MHi: AMT); at foot of text: "Their Excellencies Benjamin Franklin Esq. and Thomas Jefferson Esq." RC (DNA: PCC, No. 84); in W. S. Smith's hand; unsigned; endorsed by David Humphreys; body of text in code, with interlineal decoding begun by TJ; accompanied by another leaf bearing TJ's decoding of the entire letter. Code No. 8 was employed by Adams.

John Adams to Franklin and Jefferson

Westminster, London, 20 June 1785. Acknowledges their letter of 15 June; agrees "entirely . . . in sentiment respecting Gratification to be given to Mr. John Baptist Pecquet and the Letter to be written to him."

RC (DNA: PCC, No. 84, v); 1 p.; at foot of letter: "Their Excellencies Messrs. Franklin & Jefferson." FC (MHi: AMT); in Adams' hand.

From Jean François Briet

L'Orient le 20 Juin 1785.

J'ai eu l'honneur d'écrire à Son Excellençe le 15 Court. relativement à Mr. Peter Dischong, et elle apprendra directement de Nantes par mon ami à qui j'ai écris le même jour, de quel païs il est natif. Mais comme j'apprends aujourd'hui que Mgr. de Calonne vient d'ordonner la restitution de la Marchandise suivant et Conformément à l'ordonnançe qu'avait rendu Mr. L'Intendant de la provinçe, mais sans Dédomagement, Je Supplie Son Excellence, Si elle daigne me Continuer Sa bienveillançe, de vouloir bien faire quelques représentations à Mgr. Le Contrôleur genéral, afin de me faire obtenir pour Mr. Dischong une indemnité Justement acquise pour la perte qu'il éprouve, non Seulement par le retard de trois mois, mais encore par la diminution de la Marchdise. qui a Couté. 6.ᵗᵗ. 10s., tandis qu'on ne trouverait aujourdhuy d'acheteurs au dessus de 4.ᵗᵗ. 10s. à 4.ᵗᵗ. 15s. Dans cette attente, Je suis avec Respect, de Son Exçellençe, Son très humble et Très Obéïssant Serviteur,   JN. FOIS. BRIET

RC (DLC).

To Abigail Adams

DEAR MADAM   Paris June 21. 1785

I have received duly the honor of your letter, and am now to return you thanks for your condescension in having taken the first step for settling a correspondence which I so much desired; for I now consider it as *settled* and proceed accordingly. I have always found it best to remove obstacles first. I will do so therefore in the present case by telling you that I consider your boasts of the splendour of your city and of it's superb hackney coaches as a flout, and declaring that I would not give the polite, self-denying, feeling, hospitable, goodhumoured people of this country and their amability in every point of view, (tho' it must be confessed our streets are somewhat dirty, and our fiacres rather indifferent) for ten such races of rich, proud, hectoring, swearing, squibbing, carnivorous animals as those among whom you are; and that I do love this *people* with all my heart, and think that with a better religion and a better form of government and their present governors their condition and country would be most enviable. I pray you to observe that I have used the term *people* and that this is a noun of the masculine as well as feminine gender. I must add too that we are about reforming our fiacres, and that I expect soon an Ordonance that all their drivers shall wear breeches unless any difficulty should arise whether this is a subject for the police or for the general legislation of the country, to take care of. We have lately had an incident of some consequence, as it shews a spirit of treason, and audaciousness which was hardly thought to exist in this country. Some eight or ten years ago a Chevalier ————— was sent on a message of state to the princess of ————— of ————— of (before I proceed an inch further I must confess my profound stupidity; for tho' I have heard this story told fifty times in all it's circumstances, I declare I am unable to recollect the name of the ambassador, the name of the princess, and the nation he was sent to; I must therefore proceed to tell you the naked story, shorn of all those precious circumstances) some chevalier or other was sent on some business or other to some princess or other. Not succeeding in his negociation, he wrote on his return the following song.

Ennivré du brillant poste
Que j'occupe récemment,
Dans une chaise de poste
Je me campe fierement:
Et je vais en ambassade
Au nom de mon souverain
Dire que je suis malade,
Et que lui se porte bien.

Avec une joue enflée
Je debarque tout honteux:
La princesse boursoufflée,
Au lieu d'une, en avoit deux;
Et son altesse sauvage
Sans doute a trouvé mauvais
Que j'eusse sur mon visage
La moitié de ses attraits.

Princesse, le roi mon maitre
M'a pris pour Ambassadeur;
Je viens vous faire connoitre
Quelle est pour vous son ardeur.
Quand vous seriez sous le
    chaume,
Il donneroit, m'a-t-il dit,
La moitié de son royaume
Pour celle de votre lit.

La princesse à son pupitre
Compose un remerciment:
Elle me donne une epitre
Que j'emporte lestement,
Et je m'en vais dans la rue
Fort satisfait d'ajouter
A l'honneur de l'avoir vue
Le plaisir de la quitter.

This song run through all companies and was known to every body. A book was afterwards printed, with a regular license, called 'Les quatres saisons litteraires' which being a collection of little things, contained this also, and all the world bought it or might buy it if they would, the government taking no notice of it. It being the office of the Journal de Paris to give an account and criticism of new publications, this book came in turn to be criticised by the redacteur, and he happened to select and print in his journal this song as a specimen of what the collection contained.

He was seised in his bed that night and has been never since heard of. Our excellent journal de Paris then is suppressed and this bold traitor has been in jail now three weeks, and for ought any body knows will end his days there. Thus you see, madam, the value of energy in government; our feeble republic would in such a case have probably been wrapt in the flames of war and desolation for want of a power lodged in a single hand to punish summarily those who write songs. The fate of poor Pilatre de Rosiere will have reached you before this does, and with more certainty than we yet know it. This will damp for a while the ardor of the Phaetons of our race who are endeavoring to learn us the way to heaven on wings of our own. I took a trip yesterday to Sannois and commenced an acquaintance with the old Countess d'Hocquetout. I received much pleasure from it and hope it has opened a door of admission for me to the circle of literati with which she is environed. I heard there the Nightingale in all it's perfection: and I do not hesitate to pronounce that in America it would be deemed a bird of the third rank only, our mockingbird, and fox-coloured thrush being unquestionably superior to it. The squibs against Mr. Adams are such as I expected from the polished, mild tempered, truth speaking people he is sent to. It would be ill policy to attempt to answer or refute them. But counter-squibs I think would be good policy. Be pleased to tell him that as I had before ordered his Madeira and Frontignac to be forwarded, and had asked his orders to Mr. Garvey as to the residue, which I doubt not he has given, I was afraid to send another order about the Bourdeaux lest it should produce confusion. In stating my accounts with the United states, I am at a loss whether to charge house rent or not. It has always been allowed to Dr. Franklin. Does Mr. Adams mean to charge this for Auteuil and London? Because if he does, I certainly will, being convinced by experience that my expences here will otherwise exceed my allowance. I ask this information of you, Madam, because I think you know better than Mr. Adams what may be necessary and right for him to do in occasions of this class. I will beg the favor of you to present my respects to Miss Adams. I have no secrets to communicate to her in cypher at this moment, what I write to Mr. Adams being mere commonplace stuff, not meriting a communication to the Secretary. I have the honour to be with the most perfect esteem Dr. Madam Your most obedient & most humble servt.,   TH: JEFFERSON

RC (MHi: AMT). PrC (DLC); lacks the year in date-line. Letter not   sent until early July; see TJ to Abigail Adams, 7 July 1785. See also Abigail

Adams to TJ, 6 June 1785, for TJ's outline of topics discussed in present letter.

On 31 May 1785 the *Journal de Paris* reviewed the first of four parts of *Les Quatres Saisons Littéraires*. The verses quoted by TJ are printed in full in that issue, and are prefaced by the following remarks: "Le Cahier qui paroît aujourd'hui est intitulé: *le Printems*. Il y a beaucoup de vieilles poésies. Une des meilleures Pièces est une Chanson attribuée a M. le Chevalier De * *, et intitulée: *l'Ambassade*. Elle court depuis sept ou huit ans au moins dans les Sociétés: mais elle n'étoit pas encore imprimée. Ceux qui ne la connoissent pas nous sauront gré de la rapporter ici. Air: *De la Fanfare de S. Cloud*." TJ's inability to RECOLLECT THE NAME OF THE AMBASSADOR and other circumstances was obviously feigned. The ambassador was the Chevalier de Boufflers; the princess was Princess Christine of Saxony, sister of Joseph II of Austria; and the BOLD TRAITOR was seized on the demand of the Count de Lusace, brother of Princess Christine. The *Journal de Paris* was suspended from 4 June to 27 June 1785 and M. de Corancez, the principal owner, issued a complaint at the end of June in which he referred to "cette malheureuse chanson, faite il y a plus de vingt ans, et que tout le monde sait par cœur. On ne peut nier que ce ne soit une grande sottise d'imprimer dans une feuille qu'on envoie à toute la famille royale des vers où l'on s'est permis de tourner en ridicule la tante de Sa Majesté: mais il n'est pas moins certain que ce n'est que par pure ignorance qu'on a commis une pareille faute; que la chanson est assez ancienne pour qu'on ait pu en oublier le véritable sujet, et qu'apres tout le rédacteur de l'article n'a fait que citer des couplets qu'on avait imprimés impunément avant lui dans un livre publié et vendu depuis deux mois, avec privilége et approbation" (Maurice Tourneux, *Correspond-*

ance Littéraire, Philosophique et Critique par Grimm, Diderot, &c., Paris, 1880, XIV, p. 162-4). THE OLD COUNTESS D'HOCQUETOUT was, of course, the Countess d'Houdetot, who lived at "her country seat at Sannois, some ten miles from Paris. Here she lived amicably with her husband and her lover, St. Lambert, the poet and philosopher, and held court. Her *salon* was rivaled in importance only by those of the well-known Madame Helvétius, the widow of the philosopher and the adored of Franklin, and of Madame Necker, wife of the financier and statesman, whom Jefferson admired. Here he met her brilliant daughter, Madame de Staël, with whom he exchanged letters on European affairs" (Marie Kimball, *Jefferson: The Scene of Europe*, p. 101). At this time the "old Countess" was fifty-five years of age. IN STATING MY ACCOUNTS WITH THE PUBLIC, I AM AT A LOSS: Franklin himself was not always certain what constituted a public or private charge. On the day before this letter was written, he had supplied TJ with a complete statement of his own accounts as minister. In DLC: Franklin Papers there is a triplicate copy of these accounts, dated at Paris, 20 June 1785, signed by Thomas Barclay and endorsed (perhaps much later) by TJ: "Doctr. Franklin's account as settled by Mr. Barclay and furnished by him to me for my government in my own accounts with the US." With this is a letter from Franklin to Barclay of 19 June 1785 which concludes with the following: "If for want of knowing precisely the Intention of Congress, what Expences should be deem'd Public and what not public, I have charg'd any Articles to the Public which should be defray'd by me, their Banker has my order as soon as the Pleasure of Congress shall be made known to him, to rectify the Error by transferring the Amount to my private Account, and discharging by so much that of the Public."

From F. W. Bleibtrear

MONSEIGNEUR   Nantes le 21. Juin 1785.

Mr. Briet à L'Orient m'a fait part de la Saisie de 3. Bales Nankin qu'il avait achetté d'ordre et pour Compte de Mr. Peter

Dischong de Philadelphie. Il m'a aussi communiqué la Lettre dont Son Exçellençe l'avait honnoré en date du 11. de çe Mois par laquelle Elle desire de savoir de quelle Nation était Mr. Peter Dischong.

Comme ç'est par ma recommandation que le dit Sieur Briet est lié d'affaires avec mon intime Ami et Parent Mr. Dischong, je m'interesse particulièrement à tout çe qui le régarde et m'empresse de Satisfaire directement à la Demande que Son Exçellence a faite à Mr. Briet.

Mr. Peter Dischong, çet honnet et bon Citoyen de Philadelphie, où il est établie depuis une vingtaine d'années et qui y jouit de la meilleure réputation, est né à Dierdorff petite ville à 4. Lieües de Neuwïed en Allemagne.

Il serait vraiment affreux si le Commerce de la Nation des Etats unies serait chéné et interrompu à un tel point, de se laisser saisir leurs Marchandises par capriçe des Employés dans le Centre de la Ville Franche de L'Orient.

La Satisfaction la plus complette de çette Injustiçe ne peut étre refusée dès que Son Exçellençe l'Exige. Elle me permettra que je Lui Temoigne d'avançe toute ma reconnaisançe au nom de Mr. Peter Dischong, et j'aurai soin de lui en faire part. En attendant je suis avec Réspect de Son Exçellençe très humble et très obeïssant Serviteur,   F. W. BLEIBTREAR

RC (DLC).

From Katherine Sprowle Douglas

London, 21 June 1785. She had sent to TJ by Dr. John Wither-spoon, when he was there, a memorial and copies of the correspondence between the Committee of Safety and Andrew Sprowle of Gosport, Virginia, "your *once* worthyly Esteemd freind . . . , who you *well* know fell a martyar to Tyranny and oppression." Not having heard from TJ and, learning he is in Paris, she encloses other copies. Asks if he advises that she and her son go to Virginia to claim their property, which is still undisposed of by the state; she and her six fatherless children will turn to the "Justice and Clemency, of the Assembly of Virginia." She hopes for a reply through John Adams.

RC (ViWC); 2 p.; upper left corner and edge of MS are torn away. The enclosure has not been found, but it was doubtless similar to, if not a copy of, the "Petition and Memorial of Kath. Douglas, late widow of the deceased Andrew Sproule Esqr. of Gosport in Virginia, to His Excellency Benjamin Harrison Governor there" (Vi; see below).

Andrew Sprowle, a Virginia merchant, had signed the non-importation associations of 1770 and 1774, but was later accused of having dealings with

Lord Dunmore. A letter from Sprowle to Peter Paterson was published in Purdie's *Va. Gaz.* for 29 Dec. 1775 as proof of his "strict adherence to the association," in which he is quoted as saying that "I would have no fear in bringing in a vessel with osnabrugs, Irish linens, and other sortable goods; would be protected by man of war . . . some forces, and ships of war, daily looked for from Britain. God send them soon. While the soldiers *remains* at Gosport, I am safe." And in the *Va. Gaz.* (D & H) for 15 June 1776 there appeared the following: "We learn from Gloucester . . . that his [Lord Dunmore's] old friend Andrew Sprowle is dead." But Katherine Sprowle Douglas in her memorial declared that in the fall of 1775 Dunmore with his entire retinue appeared at her husband's house and that he, "being aged and infirm, was easily terrify'd by their threats, and forced not only to lay open his Stores, Cellars &c to their Ravenous and Rapacious pleasure; but to go on board the fleet then in Elizabeth River, together with your Petitioner and the rest of his family, after they had devoured great part of his property by living and Rioting for five months solely at his expence"; and that Sprowle, "wore out with age and infirmity, and repining bitterly at his misfortune, in being in the power of such an unmercifull Tyrant, broke his heart and departed this life, uttering the most bitter execrations, against the said Dunmore and his associates" (MS in Vi, dated at London 28 Nov. 1783, and signed "Kath Sprowle, Now Douglas").

From P. & V. French & Nephew

SIR   Bordeaux 21. June 1785.

Though we have not as yet the honor of being known to you, and before we Could write to our most particular friend Wm. Carmichael Esqr. at Madrid, with whom we are in Constant Correspondence, the Connexions of our houses both in this City and at Baÿonne transacting the principal part of the Trade with the different States of America, hurry and oblige us to address freely to your Excellency without any reccommendation, having at this Juncture Several American vessels Consigned to us, and to Sollicit your immediate application to Monsieur de Calonne, the Controlleur General, to oblige the Farmers General to put the Tobacco Trade on a proper Footing in Every respect at Bayonne. The whole matter is fully Explained to your Excellency in the inclosed Petitions addressed to you by Mr. D'Alexandre the manager of our house at Baÿonne.

We Entreat your reply soon and address your answers to us in this City, which will very much oblige Sir, Your respectfull and Devoted H'ble Sts.,   P. & V. FRENCH AND NEPHEW

Mr. Thoms. Barclay the Consul General can give you Every Information respecting our house as he is now at Paris.

RC (DLC). Enclosures: Louis Alexandre to TJ, 17 June 1785, and its enclosure.

To Charles Thomson

Dear Sir   Paris June 21. 1785

Your favour of Mar. 6. is come duly to hand. You therein acknowlege the receipt of mine of Nov. 11. At that time you could not have received my last of Feb. 8. At present there is so little new in politicks, literature, or the arts that I write rather to prove to you my desire of nourishing your correspondence, than of being able to give you any thing interesting at this time. The political world is almost lulled to sleep by the lethargic state of the Dutch negociation, which will probably end in peace. Nor does this court profess to apprehend that the emperor will involve this hemisphere in war by his schemes on Bavaria and Turkey. The arts instead of advancing have lately received a check, which will probably render stationary for a while that branch of them which had promised to elevate us to the skies. Pilatre de Roziere, who had first ventured into that region has fallen a sacrifice to it. In an attempt to pass from Boulogne over to England, a change in the wind having brought him back on the coast of France, some accident happened to his baloon of inflammable air which occasioned it to burst, and that of rarefied air combined with it being then unequal to the weight, they fell to the earth from a height which the first reports made 6000 f. but later ones have reduced to 1600 feet. Pilatre de Roziere was dead when a peasant, distant 100 yards only run to him. But Romain his companion lived about 10. minutes, but speechless and without his senses. In literature nothing new: for I do not consider as having added any thing to that feild my own Notes of which I have had a few copies printed. I will send you a copy by the first safe conveyance. Having troubled Mr. Otto with one for Colo. Monro, I could not charge him with one for you. Pray ask the favor of Colo. Monroe in page 5. line 17. to strike out the words 'above the mouth of Appamattox,' which makes nonsense of the passage, and I forgot to correct it before I had inclosed and sent off the copy to him. I am desirous of preventing the reprinting this, should any book merchant think it worth it, till I hear from my friends whether the terms in which I have spoken of slavery and of the constitution of our state will not, by producing an irritation, retard that reformation which I wish instead of promoting it. Dr. Franklin proposes to sail for America about the 1st. or 2d. week of July. He does not yet know however by what conveiance he can go. Unable to travel by land he must descend the Seine in a boat to Havre. He has sent to England to get some vessel bound for Philadelphia to touch at Havre for him, but he receives information that this cannot be done. He has been on the lookout ever since he received his permission to return, but as yet no possible means of getting a passage has offered, and I fear it is very incertain when any will offer.

I am with very great esteem Dr. Sir Your friend & servt.,

Th: Jefferson

P.S. I send you another peice of Mesmerism which I suspect will not make so great a sensation as the first.

RC (DLC: Charles Thomson Papers). PrC (DLC: TJ Papers); lacks postscript. Entry in SJPL reads: "Thomson Chas. Europn. politics. Baloon. Notes. Dr. Franklin." The other "peice of Mesmerism" that TJ promised to send (and probably enclosed in the present letter) has not been identified, but it may have been *Supplément aux Observations de M. Bergasse, ou Règlemens des sociétés de l'harmonie universelle (rédigés par Mesmer), adoptés par la Société de l'harmonie de France dans l'assemblée générale tenue à Paris, le 12 mai 1785.*

To John Adams

Dear Sir   Paris June 22. 1785.

My last to you was of the 2d. inst. since which I have received yours of the 3d. and 7th. I informed you in mine of the substance of our letter to Baron Thulemeyer. Last night came to hand his acknolegement of the receipt of it. He accedes to the method proposed for signing, and has forwarded our dispatch to the king. I inclose you a copy of our letter to Mr. Jay to go by the packet of this month. It contains a state of our proceedings since the preceding letter which you had signed with us. This contains nothing but what you had concurred with us in, and as Dr. Franklin expects to go early in July for America, it is probable that the future letters must be written by you and myself. I shall therefore take care that you be furnished with copies of every thing which comes to hand on the joint business.

What is become of this Mr. Lambe? I am uneasy at the delay of that business, since we know the ultimate decision of Congress. Dr. Franklin having a copy of the Corps Diplomatique has promised to prepare a draught of a treaty to be offered to the Barbary states; as soon as he has done so we will send it to you for your corrections. We think it will be best to have it in readiness against

[246]

Th. Jefferson begs Doct.' Price's acceptance of a copy
of these Notes. the circumstances under which they
were written, with the talents of the writer, will account
for their errors & defects. the original was sent to Mons.
de Marbois in Decemb. 1781. being asked for a copy by a
friend who wished to possess some of the details they
contain, he revised them in the subsequent winter.
the vices however of their original composition were
such as forbid material amendment. he now has a
few copies printed with a design of offering them to
some of his friends, and to some other estimable cha-
-racters beyond that line. a copy is presented to Doct.'
Price as a testimony of the respect which the writer
bears him. unwilling to expose them to the public
eye, he asks the favor of Doct.' Price to put them into
the hands of no person on whose care & fidelity he
cannot rely to guard them against publication.

Jefferson's presentation inscription in the copy of the *Notes on
the State of Virginia* sent to Richard Price. (See p. xxviii.)

The Grille de Chaillot in 1779, the site of Jefferson's residence
in Paris from 1785 to 1789. (See p. xxviii.)

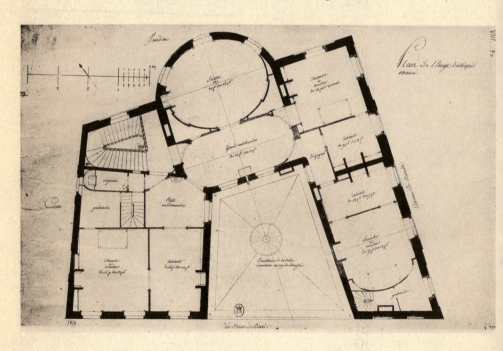

Plan of the second floor of the Hôtel de Langeac, Jefferson's residence
situated at the Grille de Chaillot. (See p. xxviii.)

the arrival of Mr. Lambe on the supposition that he may be addressed to the joint ministers for instructions.

I asked the favour of you in my last to chuse two of the best London papers for me, one for each party. The D. of Dorset has given me leave to have them put under his address, and sent to the office from which his despatches come. (I think he called it Cleveland office, or Cleveland row¹ or by some such name: however I suppose it can easily be known there.) Will Mr. Stockdale undertake to have these papers sent regularly, or is this out of the line of his business? Pray order me also any really good pamphlets which come out from time to time, which he will charge to me. I have the honour to be with sentiments of real respect and affection Dr. Sir Your most obedient and most humble servt.,

TH: JEFFERSON

RC (MHi: AMT); endorsed in part: "Gazettes." PrC (DLC); lacks second page bearing complimentary close and signature. Entry in SJPL under this date reads: "Adams John. Treaty with Prussia. Barbary. Papers, pamphlets."

Enclosure: Copy of Commissioners to Jay, 18 June 1785.

¹ This word interlined in RC in substitution for "lane," deleted; the correction was not made in PrC.

To William Carmichael

SIR   Paris June 22d. 1785.

Your letter of April 4. came to my hands on the 16th. of that month and was acknowleged by mine of May 3. That which you did me the honour to write me on the 5th. of April never came to hand till the 19th. of May, upwards of a month after the one of the day before. I have hopes of sending the present¹ by a Mr. Jarvis who went from hence to Holland some time ago. About this date I suppose him to be at Brussels and that from thence he will inform me whether in his way to Madrid he will pass by this place. If he does, this shall be accompanied by a cypher for our future use, if he does not I must still await a safe opportunity. Mr. Jarvis is a citizen of the United states from New York, a gentleman of intelligence, in the mercantile line, from whom you will be able to get considerable information of American affairs. I think he left America in January. He informed us that Congress were about to appoint a Mr. Lambe of Connecticut their Consul to Marocco and to send him to their ministers commissioned to treat with the Barbary powers for instructions. Since that Mr. Jay inclosed to Mr. Adams in London, a resolution of Congress decid-

[247]

ing definitively on amicable treaties with the Barbary states in the usual way, and informing him that he had sent a letter and instructions to us by a Mr. Lambe. Tho' it is near three weeks since we received a communication of this from Mr. Adams, yet we hear nothing further of Mr. Lambe. Our powers of treating with the Barbary states are full, but in the amount of the expence we are limited. I believe you may safely assure them that they will soon receive propositions from us, if you find such an assurance necessary to keep them quiet. Turning at this instant to your letter dated Apr. 5. and considering it attentively I am persuaded it must have been written on the 5th. of May: of this little mistake I ought to have been sooner sensible. Our latest letters from America are of the middle of April and are extremely barren of news. Congress had not yet proposed a time for their recess, tho' it was thought a recess would take place. Mr. Morris had retired and the treasury was actually administered by Commissioners. Their land office was not yet opened. The settlements at Kaskaskia within the territory ceded to them by Virginia had prayed the establishment of a regular government and they were about sending a Commissioner to them. General Knox was appointed their Secretary of the War office. These I think are the only facts we have learnt which are worth communicating to you. The inhabitants of Canada have sent a sensible petition to their king praying the establishment of an assembly, the benefits of the habeas corpus laws and other privileges of British subjects. The establishment of an assembly is denied, but most of their other desires granted. We are now in hourly expectation of the arrival of the packet which should have sailed from New York in May. Perhaps that may bring us matter which may furnish the subject of a more interesting letter. In the mean time I have the honour to be with the highest respect Sir Your most obedient and most humble servt., TH: JEFFERSON

July 14. 1785. I have thus long waited day after day hoping to hear from Mr. Jarvis that I might send a cypher with this: but now give up the hope. No news yet of Mr. Lambe. The packet is arrived but brings no intelligence, except that it is doubtful whether Congress will adjourn this summer. The assembly of Pennsylvania propose to suppress their bank on principles of policy.

PrC (DLC). Entry for postscript in SJL under 14 July 1785 reads in part: "by Mr. Grand."

¹ Thus in TJR, I, 241-2, but the PrC is faded and the word may even be "poem"; Carmichael had requested a copy of Humphreys' poem in his letter to Franklin [or TJ] of 15 Apr. 1785. If the correct reading is "present," as seems probable, the nature or intent of the gift has not been ascertained.

To William Stephens Smith

SIR   Paris June 22. 1785.

I have been honoured with your letter of May 28. inclosing those you had been so kind as to bring for me from America, as I had before been with a note informing me that such letters were in your possession. We had hoped you might have taken your passage in the French packet which might have given us the pleasure of seeing you here. Your arrival however in London was so well timed with respect to that of Mr. Adams that our regrets must give place to the general object of your mission which appears in event to have been better consulted by you than by our wishes. I congratulate you sincerely on your appointment and safe arrival. I wish you may find your situation agreeable. You will have one disagreeable circumstance the less than we have here, that of speaking the language of the country you are in. No one can know the value of this advantage till he has experienced the want of it. The external manners of the people too are more like those of your own countrymen, tho' I doubt whether in benignity of disposition we do not find a greater resemblance here. The public papers tell us of a conference between Mr. Adams and Mr. Pitt. I am anxious to hear what passes on our business, tho' I have little doubt what it will be. During the late war I had an infallible rule for deciding what that nation would do on every occasion. It was, to consider what they ought to do, and to take the reverse of that as what they would assuredly do, and I can say with truth that I was never deceived. It remains to see whether the present administration is under the influence of the same fatality. I shall with great pleasure receive your letters from time to time if you will be so good as to honour me with them, and will make you such returns as our information here will enable us, and am with great respect Sir Your most obedt. humble servt.,   TH: JEFFERSON

RC (Rosenbach Co., Philadelphia, 1951). PrC (DLC).

Smith's letter of 28 May 1785 has not been found, but the NOTE informing TJ that the letters were in his possession was doubtless that from Adams to TJ, 27 May 1785. Smith had arrived in London the day before

Adams did, but he had been traveling in leisurely fashion from Falmouth for ten days and reporting his adventures at considerable length to his old commander, Baron Steuben (Smith to Steuben, 16-18 May 1785; NHi: Steuben Papers). When he finally arrived at London at six in the evening of 25 May, he reported to Steuben that he "put up at the Royal Hotel in Pall Mall near the Palace at St. James, thinking it best to strike at the highest Peg at once. Very fortunately Mr. Adams and his Lady and Daughter arrived on the 26th. I waited on them immediately and was much pleased with the reception I met with and could very plainly discover that they had taken the pains to make some enquiry after me for they knew me perfectly and those who gave the account must have been pretty well acquainted and have dealt candidly. They have continued to be very attentive and polite and I have a great prospect of passing my time pleasantly with them" (Smith to Steuben, 15 June 1785; same). Adams had indeed been concerned about his new secretary, particularly because of Smith's membership in the Cincinnati, on which their views were poles apart. "When Virtue is lost Ambition succeeds," Adams had written Gerry in April. "Then indeed Ribbons and Garters become necessary; but never till then. . . . I don't wonder at a Marquis de la Fayette or a Baron Steuben. They were born and bred to such Decorations and the taste for them" (Adams to Gerry, 25 Apr. 1785). Smith, a few days after meeting Adams, revealed his contrary opinion of the Society of the Cincinnati when he reported to Steuben: "I met Colo. Robinson of the Pennsylvania Line at the theatre with the Medal of the Cincinnati in his button Hole ridiculously sporting with a Cyprean Nymph. If Gentlemen are above attending to their personal character some little attention should be paid to the Character of a Society who may honour them with their Badge" (Smith to Steuben, 15 June 1785; NHi: Steuben Papers). But the entire Adams family was immediately won over by the charm and good qualities of the future husband of young Abigail, and he by theirs. For TJ's high opinion of Smith, see his letter to Abigail Adams, 20 Nov. 1785.

From John Bondfield

SIR   Bordeaux 25 June 1785

I receivd in due Course the honor of your favor of the 20th. May. I have this day given my draft on you favor of M. Parmentier for £590.8 amount of my advances to which request you will give due honor.

A Ship from Alexandria in Virginia arived at this port the 20th. Inst. By the papers up to the 6th. may it appears the back Country is settling very fast. The Crops in Virginia are Reported very promising which is not the case in this province. The dry Season has totally destroy'd all the Corn, pease, Oats, Rye, white Beans and like small vegitables. Wheat to the Southward has a good appearance but to the north of this River every where short of its usual quantity. I have wrote to Virginia for two Cargoes of Indian Corn and white homily [hominy?] beans. If they arrive in good order will come to a good market. A few days past I was in Company with an Inhabitant of Consiquince of Louisiana. The conversation led to the present differences arising on the free Navigation of the Missisipi. He had been examined by Mons.

D'Aranda at paris. Being unknown to him, he spoke as he thought from the sentiments that appeard to govern the present Spanish System, which is built that Spain having during the War Conquered the ports possest by the English on the Banks of that River England had no right to Cede what she no longer possest. We expect a ship from that port every day. If any thing Interesting shall advise you. With Respect I have the Honor to be Sir Your very hble. Serv.,   JOHN BONDFIELD

RC (DLC); endorsed. The draft in favor of Parmentier, dated 25 June 1785, is in DLC.

From William Carmichael, with Enclosures

SIR   Madrid 27th. June 1785

I received on the 15th. May the Letter you did me the honor to address me the third of that month and should sooner have replied to it, had I not expected to avail myself of a private conveyance from hence, by which I might write with greater security, than I can do by the Post. It is with the greatest satisfaction that I find you are disposed to cultivate an intercourse, which for the reasons you mention, cannot but contribute to the advantage of the public Service, while it will afford the highest pleasure to myself. It has been long my surprise that Congress hath not instructed those they employ abroad on this head: For this purpose a common cypher should be sent to each of their Ministers and Chargé Des Affaires. The actual situation of affairs is such, that I am persuaded Mr. Adams might profit where he is by a knowledge of what passes here and I vice versa. Mr. Jays Letter gives me no general Intelligence. It contains instructions only in what manner to represent to his Christian Majesty the sentiments of Congress on receiving information from me of the nature of Mr. Gardoqui's mission. That Gentleman was still at the Havanna the 3d. of May. I inclose you the answer I received to a Letter I wrote the Minister of State on this occasion. No. 1 is the copy of that answer. The Sentiments of this Court to cultivate a good understanding between the two Countries seem to continue. No. 2 furnishes a new proof of his Christian Majesty's good will. Since receiving that communication a Letter of which No. 3 is a copy has reached me. It perhaps may not be improper to give a copy of it to Mr. Barclay. I have sent one to Mr. Harrison at Cadiz. No. 4 is a copy of another Letter to me from Barbary. It appears not to have been written by the emperors order, Because it doth not bear the Mark which he generally affixes to his Secretaries Letters. The Author is probably one of those who wish to come in for a share of the presents which they suppose must be made whenever a treaty is concluded. I answer these Correspondents in General terms but not *officially*.

The new Establishments of the Bank and Philippine Company in part occupy the Attention of this Cabinet. Projects for Canals and improvements of all kinds in all parts of the Spanish part of the Peninsula are the favorite Objects of the Minister, Projects which do honor to his Patriotism, even should circumstances prevent their being compleatly Executed. A war would put an end at once to these Patriotic Plans, and however successful its issue might be, it cannot be supposed, that the advantages derived from it, would compensate for the irreparable loss that for a long series of years, this Country would feel from the check given to its manufactures, commerce and agriculture, which severally may make rapid advances should the same Spirit of improvement continue. As you are in the center of Politics, it may appear presumption in me to dwell in the Slightest manner on the Subject of the present intrigues Jealousies and Alarms which appear to agitate Europe; I cannot however forbear informing you that a few days ago the Chargé Des Affaires of the Emperor presented by order of his Court to the Ct. de Florida Blanca a memorial containing, as I am told, severe Strictures on the conduct of the King of Prussia, who is accused in this peice of endeavours to excite jealousies among the Princes of the Empire and other Powers to the disadvantage of the Emperor. My Information comes from a quarter intimately connected with the Court of Vienna and since from others. As it appears from the nature of this peice that it must have been sent to the other Courts of Europe, I shall for particular reasons be glad to be Advised of the time it was received at Versailles. A Small Armament is preparing at Cadiz supposed for Carthagena in America. It consists of one vessel of the Line one frigate and 3 transports on Board of which one regiment and 4 or 500 recruits are to be embarked. It is imagined that the Disputes between this court and that of G.B on the Mosquito shore is the cause of it. Other causes might be assigned. The two nations may bully, but not fight in their present circumstances for such an object. At Least the British Minister here holds a pacific Language and I am further told that Del Campo at London advances somewhat in his negotiations for a commercial Treaty. This to me is doubtful for I know not how a treaty on this point can coincide with the pretentions of G.B and the apparent System of this Court. An article in this System is levelled against the N. foundland Fisheries. Altho the Squadron destined to cruize on the Algerine Coast is ready for Sea as is confidently reported here, there are some who maintain that a peace or Truce is likely to be concluded between this Country and those Pirates. I am of this opinion. It is the interest of this Country and the Ct. de F. B. is too good a Patriot not to pursue steadily what he beleives to be its Interests. He may be sometimes mistaken and who is not? In case the abovementioned Peace or Truce should take place, These Pirates will have the more Leisure to Infest our Commerce which I think will inevitably be the case and therefore Speedy measures ought to be taken to prevent hostilities on their part. As I expect to send off shortly as many of the Books as I have been able to procure agreable to your directions, it will be proper for you to Obtain orders to the officers of the Custom house on the Frontier to let them pass without inspection. The trunk containing them will be addressed to you in your Ministerial Capacity and forwarded to Paris by a Correspondent of mine at Bayonne who will advise you of the Time of its being sent to the Capital. It will be a great satisfaction to me to have the means of giving you without reserve my sentiments on every Subject that may be in the Slightest measure productive of public utility or of personal Satisfaction to you. You will please to inform Mr. Barclay that I have received his Letter with an enclosure of an Ancient Date and that as soon as the hurry of visits and attendance at Court and of feasts and entertainments given on occasion of the Double Marriages will permit me, I shall answer the one and the other in a manner that will be as satisfactory as the nature of the contents will permit me. The heats of Summer here have already burdened me with bile which lowers my Spirits and almost incapacitates me from Business. With compliments to all who do me the honor to remember me I beg you to beleive me with great Respect Your Excellencys Obliged & Obedt. Hble. Sert.,   WM. CARMICHAEL

ENCLOSURE I

Louis Goublot to Carmichael

MONSEIGNEUR   À Salé le 20 may 1785

J'espère qu'à l'époque présente votre Excellence aura reçu la lettre que j'eus l'honneur de lui adresser en datte du 8 avril passé, et je me réfere à son contenu.

Je me flatte, Monseigneur que vous ne désapprouverez point la Liberté que je prends de vous écrire nouvellement pour vous participer que parmi les Frégates Corsaires de Sa Majesté l'Empereur de Maroc, l'une se trouve actuellement à Lisbonne, deux à Gibraltar et cinq ou Six à Larache.

Du nombre de ces derniéres, deux viennent d'être destinées pour l'Ambassade que le Monarque Africain envoie à Constantinople, l'une desquelles est Commandée par le même Arraez Capitaine nommé Akhmet Turki qui prit l'infortuné Capitaine James Ervin. Le Surplus des frégates qui resteront à Larache sortiront cet été été pour croiser.

De ce que je viens d'exposer, je ne veux point inférer que l'Empereur de Maroc donne de nouveaux ordres de commettre des hostilités contre les batimens Américains, mais ce que je puis dire avec assurance, c'est que, soit que ce Souverain ne prescrive pas à Ses Marins une ordonnance exacte, ou soit que ceux ci, lorsqu'ils sont en mer, s'émancipent à faire des prises sans y être ordonnés, il y a toujours à craindre pour les batimens Américains jusqu'à ce que le Congres fasse parler directement à l'Empereur de Maroc.

Comme je suppose, Monseigneur, que vous aurez fait passer à son tems des Avis, tant à Marseille que dans d'autres ports de la Méditerranée, où il peut se trouver des Batimens Américains, pour que Leurs Capitaines naviguent avec précaution, je crois devoir vous représenter que si un Capitaine Marchand Américain étoit instruit de la Manoeuvre que les Corsaires Maroccains observent dans un Combat, de la confusion qui regne dans leur commandement sans subordination, de l'épouvante qui les saisit lorsqu'ils voient couler le Sang d'un des leurs, du manque de munitions et de vivres où ils se trouvent fort souvent, de la disproportion de leurs boulets rélativement au Calibre des Canons &c. &c. le dit Capitaine Américain, avec six canons seulement, des munitions, et tout au plus vingt hommes d'équipage, non seulement, ne se laissera pas prendre par un Corsaire Marroccain, mais il l'obligera encore à fuir. Un Corsaire de ce pays-ci ne prendra jamais qu'un batiment marchand non armé, et l'on ne doit point croire en Europe que la Marine de Maroc soit comparable à celle d'Alger, ni en discipline, ni en bravoure: voila ce que j'ose avancer avec certitude.

Je ne sais si votre Excellence recevra avec plaisir ces avis, qui seront plus ou moins importans selon les instructions que l'on jugera à propos de donner aux Capitaines Américains concernant leur navigation dans ces mers-ci, ou selon le retard qu'il peut encore y avoir avant que l'empereur de Maroc recoive des lettres du Congres. Quoiqu'il en soit, je desire tres fort que ma lettre puisse sortir heureusement de Barbarie et parvenir en toute sureté à votre Excellence, qui n'ignorera pas à quoi je m'expose en lui faisant passer de tels avis, qui demandent tout le secret possible; mais l'affection dont je me sens porté pour la nouvelle République, et le Respectueux amour dont je suis pénétré pour les Augustes Membres qui la composent me font mépriser tous les dangers et les périls pour lui témoigner combien je desire de lui être utile et d'être employé à son Service.

J'ai l'honneur d'être avec le plus profond Respect, Monseigneur, De votre Excellence Le tres humble et tres obéissant Serviteur

LOUIS GOUBLOT

ENCLOSURE II

Alcaid Driss to Carmichael

SON EXCELLENCE   Maroc le 24 avril 1785.

Votre honorable en date 6 fevrier dernier me fut remise le 20 de ce mois d'Avril: j'eus l'honneur de la communiquer et interpreter le lendemain à S. M. I. mon maitre qui se montroit fort content, disant que ce n'étoit que l'amour de la paix qui l'avoit fait agir, et qu'il seroit charmé de contracter de telle façon avec la nouvelle illustre Republique qu'elle n'aura qu'à s'applaudir de tout ce que sa ditte Mté. veut faire en sa faveur; de façon Cépendant qu'il vient une personne qualifiée expressément de la part du Congrès pour traiter des interets mutuels pour le Bonheur reciproque, et qu'un Consul reside dans les Etats de Sa Mté. I. suivant la Coutume de toutes les Puissances Européennes.

S. M. I. mon Maitre n'est pas moins que l'illustre Congrès, pénétré de sentiments dignes de la nouvelle République, il prend tout en consideration, ce fut en Consequence d'icelle et de mes instances que S. M. fit rentrer les cinq frégates en croisière contre les batimens Américains, immediatement apres la prise du Capitaine Ervin, qu'en outre il avoit publiquement déclaré qu'il n'avoit point la guerre avec la nouvelle République et que le dit Capitaine avec son Équipage n'etoient point esclaves, mais des êtres Libres dans ses Etats et ils se trouvent fort bien a Mogador. Je n'attende qu'un moment favorable pour demander a S. M. I. mon maitre la permission de les renvoyer a Cadiz

Joignez a ce préliminaire amical les dispositions favorables de S. M. I. mon maitre, et votre Excellence verra que j'ai fait tout ce que j'ai pu en faveur de l'illustre Congrès vis à vis un Monarque aussi despotique que l'est l'Empereur de Maroc, et cela dans un temps ou il n'y avoit absolument personne qui osoit s'entremettre en faveur de cette respectable Republique de L'Amérique du Nord.

Je desire vivement que le tres illustre Congrès ne tarde pas a terminer une affaire, dont je me ferai un honneur eternel d'y avoir contribué, et si les circonstances demandoient un delai pour l'année prochaine, il faudroit au moins une lettre du Congres, munie de son Seaux par laquelle il annonceroit la ditte Ambassade, et qu'il chargeroit quelqu'un ad interim aupres de Sa Majté. imple. mon maitre: munie de tels pouvoire j'oserois me flatter d'arreter le ressentiment que S. M. imperiale mon maitre pourroit concevoir par un delai au quel il ne s'attende point, ainsique les feux soudaines que les Capitaines de Corsaires marocquins ne cessent de fomenter, afin d'obtenir la permission de reprendre leur croisiere pour L'année Lunaire prochaine, c'est a dire dans cinq mois d'ici.

Votre Excellence n'ignore pas, qu'a la cour de maroc, comme a tout autre cour, il s'y trouvent des Personnes qui cherchent à traverser les Bonnes offices, qu'un être qui pense bien y emploit, souvent il faut les détourner par une générosité qui ne convient pas à chaqun, Graces au Destin, j'ai Su mannier les affaires de façon que j'en ai été quitte pour quelques petits presents. Je vous prie enfin d'être persuadé que je n'omettrai rien pour entretenir la bienveillance de S. M. I. mon maitre a l'égard des circonstances actuelles. Assurez en le tres illustre Congrès et croyez moi en particulier avec respectueuse estime, De votre Excellence, Le tres humble et tres obeisst. Serviteur

ALCAID DRISS
Secr. de S. M. I. de Maroc.

RC (DLC). Recorded in SJL as received 23 July 1785. Enclosures (all in DLC: TJ Papers, Nos. 1-2 in Spanish and Nos. 3-4 in French, the first two having their enclosure numbers in TJ's hand and the last two in Carmichael's): No. 1: Floridablanca to Carmichael, 14 May 1785, acklowledging his of 7 May and expressing the king's pleasure over the news that Congress would welcome a Spanish agent with "the mission of promoting harmony between His Majesty and the States" and also expressing the king's concern over Gardoqui's delayed arrival in America. No. 2: Floridablanca to Carmichael, 16 May 1785, pertaining to the "American brig (*Bergantin*) which was seized by the Moroccan Corsairs" and informing him of the repairs on her undertaken "as the result of representations made by the Spanish Consul in behalf of the Americans," a procedure which had met with the king's approval. No. 3: Louis Goblot to Carmichael, 20 May 1785, printed above, as Enclosure I. No. 4: Alcaid Driss to Carmichael, 24 Apr. 1785, printed above as Enclosure II.

From the Abbés Arnoux and Chalut

Paris mardi 28. juin [1785]

Les abbés de Chalut et Arnoux ont l'honneur de faire leurs compliments à Monsieur jefferson et de Le prier de la part de M. de Chalut de Lui faire L'honneur d'aller diner chez lui à St. Cloud jeudi prochain 30 juin. M. de Chalut fait la meme priere à M. Le Colonel humphries et à M. Williasmos il espere qu'ils voudront bien être de la partie.

Les deux abbés iront diner à St. Cloud ce jour là, ils attendront les trois Messieurs à la place vendome jusqu'à midi, pour partir de là avec eux. On dine à deux heures à St. Cloud.

RC (MHi). TJ's reply has not been found, but see note to TJ to Short, 28 June 1785.

From Barré

EXCELLENCE   L'orient ce 28 Juillet [i.e., Juin] 1785.

Mr. Thévenard me charge de vous remercier de votre bonté et vous prie de vouloir bien Lui faire copier celui des portraits que vous jugerés le plus ressemblant: il préfere celui qui à été fait depuis la Guerre; à l'égard de l'attente il se réglera à ce sujet sur votre volonté, persuadé que vous voudrés bien ne pas l'oublier, lors que vous en aurés le loisir. Il désire aussi que vous vouliés Le faire copier par un bon maitre. Il y mettra le prix que vous jugeres à propos se réposant à cet égard absolument sur tout ce que vous ferés pour Lui. Permettés, Excellence, que j'ay l'honneur de vous assurer de mon profond Respect et de celui dans lequel je serai toute ma vie. Les bontés dont vous m'avés honnorés pendant mon Séjour à Paris, me feront Ressouvenir de celles dont tous les américains honnorent ceux de ma nation, trop heureux si je puis conserver les votres dans tous les tems.

J'ai L'honneur dêtre avec Respéct Excellence Votre tres humble et tres Obeissant Serviteur,   BARRÉ

P.S.R. Je prend la Liberté d'assurer MM. Humphreis et Schort, de mes Respects.

RC (DLC); at foot of text "Mr. Barré, offr. de marine hotel de Mr. Thevenard Commandant de la marine à l'orient"; endorsed. Entry in SJL reads: "Received Barré's. l'Orient *July* for June 28."

To William Short

DEAR SIR   Paris June 28. 1785.

I must beg a thousand pardons for not having sooner answered your kind enquiries after Patsy's health. I was yesterday out the whole day, therefore scribble a line just as I am setting out to Versailles this morning. Her indisposition was slight, occasioned by a cold. The cold still remains, but the headach, and slight fever have left her. If we make an appointment to meet you at all it will be for Sunday, because on Monday I expect some friends to dine with me, and it may be convenient for you to come with us the day before. I have received orders from Virginia to furnish plans for the public buildings, and am now occupied on that. Should we not write to you to meet us on Sunday, you may as well come on that day as it is only one day sooner than you had intended. I am with much esteem Dr. Sir Your friend & Servt.,

TH: JEFFERSON

RC (ViW); endorsed. Not recorded in SJL.

From the fact that Martha was ill and TJ seemed in doubt whether he could make an appointment at all except possibly on Sunday, 3 July, it is probable that he had declined the invitation of the Abbés Arnoux and Chalut to dine at St. Cloud on Thursday the 30th, an invitation which had included Short (see the Abbés Arnoux and Chalut to TJ, 28 June 1785). Presumably Short's ENQUIRIES AFTER PATSY'S HEALTH were by letter; if so, it has not been found. Monday, of course, was the Fourth of July and TJ had invited SOME FRIENDS to dine in honor of the occasion. Among these friends was Lafayette: "By the blessed fourth day of July, I found myself Magnetized to Mr. Jefferson's table, where we chearfully Began our tenth Year of independance" (Lafayette to John Adams, Sarreguemines, 13 July 1785; MHi: AMT).

From John Polson

Paris, 1 July 1785. Expects to pass a few months at Pont Sur Seine, but will return to Paris before going to England. If TJ should have any thing to communicate on subject of his lands in Virginia, write "to the Care of Monsr. Cuming Chevalier de Saint Louis Pont Sur Seine."

RC (MHi); 2 p.; endorsed.

From Richard Price

DEAR SIR   Newington: Green July 2d. 1785

This letter will probably be deliver'd to you by *Dr. D'Ivernois*, lately a citizen of Geneva, and the author of an interesting work lately publish'd and entitled *An Historical and Political view of the constitution and Revolutions of Geneva in the 18th. century*. He wishes to be introduced to you; and I doubt not but the respectableness of his character and abilities and the active part he has taken in defending the liberties of a republic once happy but now ruined, will recommend him to your notice and esteem. His habits and principles carry his views to America; and should he remove thither he will make a very valuable addition to the number of virtuous and enlighten'd citizens in the united States.

Accept my best thanks for the account of Virginia which you were so good as to Send me by Mr. Adams. This has been, indeed, a most acceptable present to me, and you may depend on my performing the condition upon which you have honoured me with it. I have read it with Singular pleasure and a warm admiration of your Sentiments and character. How happy would the united States be were all of them under the direction of Such wisdom and liberality as yours?—But this is not the case. I have lately been discouraged by an account which I have received from Mr. Laurens in South-Carolina. Mr. *Grimkey* the Speaker of the House of Representatives, and Mr. *Izard* have agree'd in reprobating my pamphlet on the American Revolution because it recommends measures for preventing too great an inequality of property and for gradually abolishing the Negro trade and Slavery; these being measures which (as the former says in a letter to Mr. Laurens) will never find encouragement in that State: and it appears that Mr. *Grimkey* thought himself almost affronted by having the pamphlet presented to him by Mr. Laurens. Should Such a disposition prevail in the other United States, I shall have reason to fear that I have made myself ridiculous by Speaking of the American Revolution in the manner I have done; it will appear that the people who have been Struggling so earnestly to save *themselves* from Slavery are very ready to enslave *others*; the friends of liberty and humanity in Europe will be mortify'd, and an event which had raised their hopes will prove only an introduction to a new Scene of aristocratic tyranny and human debasement.

I am very happy in the acquaintance of Mr. Adams and Coll. Smith. I wish them Success in their mission, but I have reason to fear that this country is still under a cloud with respect to America which threatens it with farther calamities. With the greatest respect I am, Sir, Your very obedt: and humble Servt.,

RICH: PRICE

Should Dr. Franklin be still at Paris deliver to him my best remembrances.

RC (DLC); endorsed. Recorded in SJL as received 22 July 1785.

DR. D'IVERNOIS was François D'Ivernois, 1757-1842, who later corresponded with TJ about his plan of transporting to America the College of Geneva, founded by John Calvin in 1559 (see D'Ivernois to TJ, 23 Sep. 1794; Otto Karmin, *Sir Francis D'Ivernois*, Geneva, 1920).

To Samuel Hardy, James Madison, and James Monroe

[*Paris, 4 July 1785*. Entry in SJL reads: "Madison, Monroe & Hardy. Letters of recommendation for W. T. Franklin." None of these letters has been found; but see TJ to Monroe, 5 July 1785.]

To Katherine Sprowle Douglas

MADAM   Paris July 5. 1785.

Your letter of the 21st. of June has come safely to hand. That which you had done me the honour of writing before has not yet been received. Having gone by Dr. Witherspoon to America, which I had left before his return to it, the delay is easily accounted for.

I wish you may be rightly informed that the property of Mr. Sprowle is yet unsold. It was advertized for sale so long ago as to found a presumption that the sale has taken place. In any event you may go safely to Virginia. It is in the London newspapers only that exist those mobs and riots which are fabricated to deter strangers from going to America. Your person will be sacredly safe, and free from insult. You can best judge from the character and qualities of your son whether he may be an useful coadjutor to you there. I suppose him to have taken side with the British before our declaration of independance; and if this was the case, I respect the candour of the measure, tho I do not it's wisdom. A right to take the side which every man's conscience approves in a civil contest is too precious a right and too favourable to the preservation of liberty not to be protected by all it's well informed friends. The assembly of Virginia have given sanction to this right in several of their laws, discriminating honourably those who took side against us before the declaration of independance, from those who remained among us and strove to injure us by their treacheries. I sincerely wish that you and every other to whom this distinction applies favourably, may find in the assembly of Virginia the good effects of that justice and generosity which have dictated to them this discrimination. It is a sentiment which will gain strength in their breasts in proportion as they can forget the savage cruelties committed on them, and will I hope in the end induce them to restore the property itself wherever it is unsold, and the price received for it where it has been actually sold. I am Madam Your very humble servt.,   TH: JEFFERSON

PrC (DLC). Entry in sjpl reads: "Sprowle Mrs. Confiscation." The letter sent by Dr. Witherspoon has not been found.

From Giovanni Fabbroni

Florence, 5 July 1785. Fabbroni was no less pleased than surprised by the receipt of TJ's most courteous letter from Paris [of 23 May]. "You are, then, in Europe, O Sir, and, in the midst of the weighty duties of your splendid office, you deign still to remember me. I am infinitely flattered by this circumstance. . . . Your new Republic could not have found a better person than you to handle its affairs in one of the most enlightened courts in Europe; I can say this without fear of being suspected of flattery, because I have heard from too many quarters how great your talents, how great your heart. Thus I am convinced in advance that America could not have a better historian than it has found in you. The modest apology which you make for your work only increases the value of the same, and I earnestly desire its arrival in order to enjoy the reading of it and then to present it to my Sovereign." He is certain that TJ's *Notes on Virginia* must fall into Bacon's class of books that are to be chewed and digested, "because it was dictated by experience, by a perfect knowledge of the place and of the causes no less than by philosophy and humanity." His friend Favi is the dearest person in the world to him, next to his wife and brother, and TJ must have found him worthy of friendship. TJ reopens "an old wound never healed by reawakening in me the idea of your fair country. The thought I once cherished, of settling in that happy clime where man still breathes a true and perfect liberty, has never been abandoned by me." He would like to make some return for TJ's valued gift, but as aid to the Director of the Royal Museum and as Secretary of the Royal Academy of Agriculture, he has not been able to bring to completion any work worthy of publication. While in London and Paris he published a "few youthful things one of which is a little volume containing some *Réflections sur l'Agriculture*, the other a dissertation on arsenic, and a few comments on Cronstedt's Mineralogy. These are by now out-of-date and worthless affairs of which I no longer have any copies. If literature concerning the explanation of ancient things attracts you, I can have the honor of sending you two little works by my brother, if you will be good enough to inform me how to address them to you." Wishes to know how TJ sent the *Notes on Virginia*, in order that he might make inquiry about it.

RC (MHi); 4 p.; in Italian; endorsed. Recorded in SJL as received 22 July 1785.

To James Monroe

DEAR SIR   Paris July 5. 1785.

I wrote you by Mr. Adams May. 11. and by Mr. Otto June 17. The latter acknoleged the receipt of yours of Apr. 12. which is the only one come to hand of later date than Dec. 14. Little new has occurred since my last. Peace seems to shew herself under a more decided form. The emperor is now on a journey to Italy, and the two Dutch plenipotentiaries are set out for Vienna there to make an apology for their state having dared to fire a gun in defence of their invaded rights. This is insisted on as a preliminary condition. The emperor seems to prefer the glory of terror to that of justice, and to satisfy this tinsel passion plants a dagger in the heart of every Dutchman which no time will extract. I enquired lately of a gentleman who lived long at Constantinople in a public character and enjoyed the confidence of that government insomuch as to become well acquainted with it's spirit and it's powers, what he thought might be the issue of the present affairs between the emperor and porte. He thinks the latter will not push matters to a war, and that if they do they must fail under it. They have lost their warlike spirit, and their troops cannot be induced to adopt the European arms.—We have no news yet of Mr. Lambe. Of course our Barbary proceedings are still at a stand. *This*[1] will be *handed you by Mr. Franklin. He* has a separate *letter* of *introduction* to *you. I* have *never been with him enough* to *unravel his character* with certainty. *It seems* to be *good* in the *main. I see sometimes* an *attempt* to *keep himself unpenetrated* which perhaps is the *effect* of the *cause*[2]—*lessons* of *his grandfather. His understanding* is *good enough* for *common uses* but not *great enough* for *uncommon* ones. However *you* will have *better opportunities* of *knowing him.* The *doctor* is *extremely wounded by* the *inattention* of *congress* to his *applications* for *him. He expected* something to be *done* as a *reward for his own services. He* will *preserve* a *determind silence* on this *subject* in *future.* Adieu. Your's affectionately.

P.S. Europe fixes an attentive eye on *your reception of Doctr. Franklin. He* is infinitely *esteemed. Do* not *neglect* any *marks* of *your approbation* which *you think just* or *proper.* It will *honour you* here.

RC (James Monroe Law Office, Fredericksburg, Va., 1947); unsigned; endorsed; partly in code. PrC (DLC). Recorded in SJL as sent "by W. T. Franklin"; entry in SJPL under this date reads: "Monroe Jas. Europe."

[1] This and subsequent words in italics are written in code and in part were decoded interlineally by Monroe, who experienced some difficulty in the process. The text presented here is a decoding by the editors, employing Code No. 9.

[2] The decoding here makes sense, follows that given by Burnett, *Letters of Members*, VIII, No. 315, note 3, and could be accepted without question were it not for one puzzling fact. The symbol for "cause" in Code No. 9 is "534," and in the present instance it occurs at the end of a line, bearing underneath each of the last two figures a mark resembling a cedilla. Such marks are employed in two other instances in the code passages of this letter and require the decoder to delete the last two letters of the word for which the number stands. This, if done in the present instance, would of course make a nonsense reading ("cau") which could be explained only on the ground that TJ had intended to encode the phrase "cautionary lessons" (or some equivalent), but failed to complete the encoding of the first word in the phrase. It is also possible that TJ intended this but, after making the marks for subtraction, saw that the word "cause" made sense as it was and allowed it to stand, but failed to erase the marks. The editors have assumed, but without full confidence, that the latter is the correct explanation.

To Francis Hopkinson

DEAR SIR   Paris July 6. 1785.

My last to you was of the 13. of January. About ten days after that date I received yours of Nov. 18. and about three weeks ago that of Mar. 28. came to hand. Soon after the receipt of the first I published your proposition for improving the quilling of the harpsichord. I inclose you a copy of the advertisement. One applica-

tion only was made, and that was unsuccessful. I do not despair yet
of availing you of it as soon as I can get acquainted with some of
the principal musicians. But that probably will not be till the
beginning of winter as all the beau monde leave Paris in the summer, during which the musical entertainments of a private nature
are suspended. I communicated to Doctr. Franklin your idea of
Mesmerising the harpsichord. He has not tried it, probably because
his affairs have been long packed and packing. As I do not play
on that instrument I cannot try it myself. The Doctor carries with
him a pretty little instrument. It is the sticcado, with glass bars
instead of wooden ones, and with keys applied to it. It's principal
defect is the want of extent, having but three octaves. I wish you
would exercise your ingenuity to give it an upper and a lower
octave, by finding out other substances which will yeild tones in
those parts of the scale, bearing a proper affinity to those of glass
bars. The middle octave of this is very sweet. Have you any person
on Dr. Franklin's departure to attend to the receiving and forwarding your volumes of Encyclopedie as they come out? If you have
not, be pleased to lay your commands on me. Do not be anxious
about remitting the prices as it would be a convenience to me to
have some little fund in Philadelphia to answer little purposes.
I wrote you for newspapers from thence, and shall hope to begin
soon to receive them. The dearth of American information places
us as to our own country in the silence of the grave. I also petitioned you to know whether I am yet at liberty to permit a copy
to be taken of Genl. Washington's picture. Because till I am I
cannot trust it in the hands of a painter to be finished. Another
petition was for a copy of your battle of the kegs.—Having slipped
the opportunity of sending copies of my Notes for yourself, and
Mr. Rittenhouse when Dr. Franklin's baggage went, I am doubtful whether he can take them with him. If he can you shall receive
them by him; if not, then by the first good opportunity. I am
obliged to pray that they may not be permitted to get into the
hands of the public till I know whether they will promote or retard
certain reformations in my own country. I have written to Mr.
Madison to inform me on that head. No news. A tolerable certainty
of peace leaves us without that unfortunate species of intelligence
which war furnishes. My daughter is well. I inclose a letter[1] to
Mrs. Hopkinson, which she wrote four months ago, and has lain
by me till I should write to you. Justice to her obliges me to take
this censure on myself. I take the liberty of using your cover also

for her letter to Miss Hetty Rittenhouse. Present my most friendly respects to Mrs. Hopkinson (both of that name) to Mr. Rittenhouse and family, and accept assurances of the esteem with which I am Dr. Sir Your friend & servt.,   TH: JEFFERSON

July 8.

P.S. Since writing the above, yours of Apr. 20. is put into my hands. I will pray you to send the newspapers (trimming off the margins) as the postage is not an object of so much value with me as the knowing something of what is passing in my own country. Whenever I find an opportunity of sending you a copy of my Notes I shall send also the Bibliotheque physique to you. It is a collection of all the improvements in the arts which have been made for some time past. Let me add another commission to those above given you, that is to present mine and my daughter's affectionate remembrance to Mrs. House and to Mrs. Trist if she be returned. From the latter I shall hope for letters as soon as she returns. I would write to her but for the incertainty where she is.

RC (Independence Hall, Philadelphia, 1945); mutilated; the missing words (about thirty) have been supplied from PrC in DLC. Enclosures: Copy of TJ's advertisement of Hopkinson's method for improving the quilling of the harpsichord, printed above under Feb. 1785; Martha Jefferson's letters to "Mrs. Hopkinson" and to "Miss Hetty Rittenhouse" have not been found.

TJ evidently erred in referring to a letter OF MAR. 28 from Hopkinson; he must have meant that of 20 Mch. 1785 which was the letter that included the IDEA OF MESMERISING THE HARPSICHORD.

1 At this point in PrC TJ inserted: "from my daughter."

To Abigail Adams

DEAR MADAM   Paris July 7. 1785.

I had the honour of writing you on the 21st. of June, but the letter being full of treason has waited a private conveiance. Since that date there has been received for you at Auteuil a cask of about 60. gallons of wine. I would have examined it's quality and have ventured to decide on it's disposal, but it is in a cask within a cask, and therefore cannot be got at but by operations which would muddy it and disguise it's quality. As you probably know what it is, what it cost, &c. be so good as to give me your orders on the subject and they shall be complied with.

Since my last I can add another chapter to the history of the redacteur of the Journal de Paris. After the paper had been discontinued about three weeks, it appeared again, but announcing in the first sentence a changement de domicile of the redacteur, the English of which is that the redaction of the paper had been taken from the imprisoned culprit, and given to another. Whether the imprisonment of the former has been made to cease, or what will be the last chapter of his history I cannot tell. I love energy in government dearly. It is evident it was become necessary on this occasion, and that a very daring spirit has lately appeared in this country. For notwithstanding the several examples lately made of suppressing the London papers, suppressing the Leyden gazette, imprisoning Beaumarchais, and imprisoning the redacteur of the journal, the author of the Mercure of the last week has had the presumption, speaking of the German newspapers, to say 'car les journaux de ce pays-la ne sont pas forcés de s'en tenir à juger des hemistiches, ou à annoncer des programes academiques.' Probably he is now suffering in a jail the just punishments of his insolent sneer on this mild government, tho' as yet we do not know the fact.

The settlement of the affairs of the Abbé Mably is likely to detain his friends Arnoud and Chalut in Paris the greatest part of the summer. It is a fortunate circumstance for me, as I have much society with them. What mischeif is this which is brewing anew between Faneuil hall and the nation of God-dem-mees? Will that focus of sedition be never extinguished? I apprehend the fire will take thro' all the states and involve us again in the displeasure of our mother country.

I have the honour to be with the most perfect esteem Madam Your most obedt. & most humble servt.,   TH: JEFFERSON

RC (MHi: AMT). PrC (DLC).

The JOURNAL DE PARIS, suspended from 4 June to 27 June, continued to be printed during the period of suspension. The issue of 26 June announced that subscriptions were received at "rue de Grenelle S. Honoré, la 3e porte cochère à gauche après la rue du Péli-can." Under the heading "Changement de Domicile," the issue of 27 June announced: "Le Bureau du Journal de Paris est actuellement, rue Plâtrière, No. 11, vis-a-vis l'Hotel des Postes." The paper continued to be printed by Quilleau, No. 3 rue de Fouarre.

To John Adams

DEAR SIR   Paris July 7. 1785.

This will accompany a joint letter inclosing the draught of a treaty, and my private letter of June 22,[1] which has waited so long for a private conveiance. We daily expect from the Baron Thulemeyer the French column for our treaty with his sovereign. In the mean while two copies are preparing with the English column which Doctr. Franklin wishes to sign before his departure, which will be within four or five days. The French, when received, will be inserted in the blank column of each copy. As the measure of signing at separate times and places is new, we think it necessary to omit no other circumstance of ceremony which can be observed. That of sending it by a person of confidence and invested with a character relative to the object, who shall attest our signature here, yours in London and Baron Thulemeyer's at the Hague, and who shall make the actual exchanges, we think will contribute to supply the departure from the usual form in other instances. For this reason we have agreed to send Mr. Short on this business, to make him a Secretary pro hac vice, and to join Mr. Dumas for the operations of exchange &c. As Dr. Franklin will have left us before Mr. Short's mission will commence, and I have never been concerned in the ceremonials of a treaty, I will thank you for your immediate information as to the papers he should be furnished with from hence. He will repair first to you in London, thence to the Hague, and so return to Paris.—What is become of Mr. Lambe? Supposing he was to call on the Commissioners for instructions, and thinking it best these should be in readiness, Dr. Franklin undertook to consult well the Barbary treaties with other nations, and to prepare a sketch which we should have sent for your correction. He tells me he has consulted those treaties, and made references to the articles proper for us, which however he shall not have time to put into form, but will leave them with me to reduce. As soon as I see them you shall hear from me.—A late conversation with an English gentleman here makes me beleive, what I did not believe before, that his nation think seriously that Congress have no power to form a treaty of commerce. As the explanations of this matter which you and I may separately give may be handed to their minister, it would be well that they should agree. For this reason, as well as for the hope of your shewing me wherein I am wrong, and confirming me where I am right, I will give you my creed on the subject. It is contained in these few principles. By the Confederation Congress have no power given them in the first instance over the commerce of the states. But they have a power given them of entering into treaties of commerce, and these treaties may cover the whole feild of commerce, with two restrictions only. 1. That the states may impose equal duties on foreigners as natives, and 2. that they may prohibit the exportation or importation of any species of goods whatsoever. When they shall have entered into such treaty the superintendance of it results to them, all the operations of commerce which are protected by it's stipulations, come under their jurisdiction, and the power of the states to thwart them by their separate acts ceases. If Great Britain asks then why she should enter into treaty with us, why not carry on her commerce without treaty? I answer, because till a treaty is made no Consul of hers can be received (his functions being called into existence by a convention only, and the states having abandoned the right of separate agreements and treaties) no protection to her commerce can be given by Congress, no cover to it from those checks and discouragements with which the states will oppress it, acting separately and by fits and starts. That they will act so till a treaty is made, Great Britain has had several proofs, and I am convinced those proofs will become general. It is then to put her commerce with us on systematical ground, and under safe cover, that it behoves Great Britain to enter into treaty. And I own to you that my wish to enter into treaties with the other powers of Europe arises more from a desire of bringing all our commerce under the jurisdiction of Congress, than from any other views. Because, according to my idea, the commerce of the United states with those countries not under treaty with us, is under the jurisdiction of each state separately, but that of the countries which have treated with us is under the jurisdiction of Congress, with the two fundamental restraints only, which I have before noted.—I shall be happy to receive your corrections of these ideas as I have found in the course of our joint services that I think right when I think with you. I am with sincere affection Dear Sir Your friend & servt.,   TH: JEFFERSON

P.S. Monsr. Houdon has agreed to go to America to take the figure of General Washington. In case of his death between his departure from Paris and his return to it we may lose 20,000 livres. I ask the favour of you to enquire what it will cost to ensure that sum, on his life, in London, and to give me as early an answer as possible that I may order the insurance if I think the terms easy enough. He is I beleive between 30 and 35 years of age, healthy enough, and will be absent about 6 months.

RC (MHi: AMT). PrC (DLC). Entry in SJL under 5 July reads: "Adams J. Prussian treaty. Barbary. British. Houdon." The joint letter accompanying this was, of course, that from Franklin and TJ to Adams, 8 July 1785.

The MEASURE OF SIGNING AT SEPARATE TIMES AND PLACES was highly unusual, as Hunter Miller has pointed out, but the proposal was not first made in the Commissioners' letter to De Thulemeier of 26 May 1785 as he assumed (Hunter Miller, ed., *Treaties* and *Other International Acts of the United States*, II, 183). Rather, the idea was advanced by De Thulemeier himself. On 11 May Adams informed both Dumas and De Thulemeier that his appointment at London and TJ's at Versailles did not mean a cessation of the powers of the Commissioners, and to the latter he added: "I know of no objection against signing the Treaty as you Propose, by yourself at the Hague, by me in London and Mr. Franklin and Mr. Jefferson at Paris. We may communicate by the Courriers of their High Mightinesses to London or by our own or by Private Hand" (Adams to Dumas and to De Thulemeier, 11 May, and to Dumas, 18 May 1785; MHi: AMT). Franklin signed before the treaty assumed its final form —the term of years during which the treaty was to be effective had not been agreed upon when Franklin departed from Passy and the French text, which developed some differences, had not been entered in parallel columns with the English text. On 3 May 1785 De Thulemeier wrote Adams of the satisfaction he had received in putting the final touches to a work that the two of them had begun, and added: "Il s'agit actuellement que vous aves la

bonté de faire mettre au net un exemplaire du traité dont nous sommes convenus. J'en ferai autant de mon coté" (MHi: AMT). The French text was transmitted to TJ on 19 July, received by him on the 24th of that month, and "copied into the two instruments which Doctr. Franklin had signed" (De Thulemeier to TJ, 19 July 1785; TJ to Adams, 28 July 1785). De Thulemeier had also suggested to Adams that Dumas be employed FOR THE OPERATIONS OF EXCHANGE, and to this Adams replied: "I have received the Honor of your Letter, and am happy to learn that all Points are agreed between us, and hope soon to receive either from you, sir, or from my colleagues at Paris the fair Draught of the Treaty between the King of Prussia and the United States of America for Signature. I agree with Pleasure to your Proposition of making the Exchange by Mr. Dumas, and presume that Dr. Franklin and Mr. Jefferson will equally approve of it" (De Thulemeier to Adams, 17 June and 19 July 1785; Adams to De Thulemeier, 16 July 1785; MHi: AMT).

[1] RC has "22," changed from "23," possibly by Adams; PrC reads, "23."

From Laumoy

MONSIEUR   pithiviers le 7 juillet 1785.

Je viens de recevoir une lettre de Mr. de Gouvion, qui me mande que les nouveaux Certificats, que nous attendions, des Sommes qui nous sont dues par les Etats unis, sont actuellement entre vos mains. Comme Je ne puis pas aller à Paris dans ce moment-ci, oserois-je vous prier de vouloir bien m'envoyer celui qui me concerne, par la poste, à *pithiviers en Gatinois*, où je demeure.

Comme Mr. de Gouvion me mande aussi, qu'il y a encor quelqu'erreur dans les derniers comptes d'après lesquels ces nouveaux certificats ont été faits, je vous serois infiniment obligé de vouloir bien, me mander le nom d'un des Messieurs, *of the treasury Board at Newyork*, afin que je puisse m'adresser à eux, leur faire observer l'erreur, et la faire corriger s'il est possible.

J'ai l'honneur d'être avec Respect Monsieur, Votre très humble et très obéîssant Serviteur,   LAUMOY
                                                    Lt. Colel. d'Infanterie.

RC (ViWC); endorsed: "Genl. Laumoy." On the subject of the CERTIFICATS, see Milligan to TJ, 15 Apr. 1785, and TJ to Milligan, 17 June 1785.

To Charles Williamos

SIR   Paris July 7. 1785.

The inclosed letter will inform you how much reason I have to be dissatisfied with the liberty you have taken with my name. Did the humiliating light in which you have represented me concern me as an individual only, I should be disposed to neglect it, and to spare myself the pain of the present letter. But in my present situation my conduct and character is interesting to the nation whose servant I am. I have no right therefore to neglect this transaction. The man upon whom the pecuniary injury falls has applied to me for a certificate that you were not authorized by me in what you did, of which he means to avail himself with the Police. I have desired him to apply to you, with an assurance that if he did not obtain immediate satisfaction, I would give him the certificate desired. To remove the foundation of such an abuse hereafter I must pray a discontinuance of all further intercourse between us. I find this the more necessary as an opinion has got abroad, I know not how, that you are invested with some public character from the United States. It is not proper that their reputation should be staked on the conduct of any person with whom they have not really entrusted it. I have, as was my duty, contradicted this opinion, on every proper occasion, by assuring those who had entertained it that you had not received this mark of confidence from our new republic, and that you could not as yet be a citizen of it, as you had visited it only for two or three months since the peace, and were still as I had understood an officer on half pay in the British service, a condition inconsistent with the abjuration of allegiance to any foreign power which is necessary on becoming an American citizen. I rely on your concurrence in setting the public opinion to rights on this subject; and if I have been misinformed as to the circumstance of your being still on British pay I shall be glad to be set to rights myself. I am Sir Your humble servt.,   TH: JEFFERSON

PrC (DLC). The "inclosed letter" has not been found, but it was probably from Lonpry, a tailor.

Williamos' indebtedness to Lonpry, a tailor, was evidently the immediate occasion for TJ's cold dismissal of one who had enjoyed his friendship in 1784-1785, but it is also apparent that his anger, which seldom reached such intensity, is itself a measure of the intimacy and trust that TJ believed Williamos had violated in other respects as well. Because of this and because of the mystery—not to say confusion as to identity—that has surrounded Williamos, the shadowy figure who provoked this unusual letter demands attention. "Mr. Williamos," wrote Abigail Adams, who was charmed by him and who seldom failed to report character accurately, ". . . is a Swiss by birth, a very clever, sensible, obliging man, who is a very great intimate of Mr. Jefferson's, which alone would be sufficient to recommend him" (8 Mch. 1785; C. F. Adams, ed., *Letters of Mrs. Adams*, Boston, 1848, p. 238). Shortly before leaving Auteuil Mrs. Adams again wrote: "I have returned from Mr. Jefferson's. When I got there, I found a pretty large company. . . . Mr. Williamos, of course, as he always dines with Mr. Jefferson" (7 May 1785; same, p. 240). TJ had seen something of Williamos in Boston in 1784 (see entries for TJ to Crèvecoeur and to Williamos, 1 July 1784; House to TJ, 10 Aug. 1784). Williamos came to Paris in the autumn of that year bearing a letter from Horatio Gates, who thought that he had "a great deal of Information" and that his "Observations and Talents, entitle him to be heard with attention" (Gates to TJ, 16 Aug. 1784). During the ensuing months Williamos became an intimate of TJ's household. Indeed, the references to him in TJ's Account Book seem more numerous than those to Humphreys and Short. These entries confirm the observant comment of Abigail Adams and reflect the warm friendship and mutual confidence that existed between the two men. Among them the following may be noted—5 Dec. 1784: "Pd Mr. Williamos . . . 1327f" for "things bought for A. S. Jefferson" and for TJ's children; 16 Dec. 1784: "Recd of Mr. Wiliamos in part for Adams's bill sold Couteux 300f"; 20 Dec. 1784: "Repaid Mr. Williamos for sundries for Patsy 24f18"; 30 Dec. 1784: "Pd Mr. Williamos for etrennes for Patsy 78f"; 1 Mch. 1785: "borrowed of Mr. Williamos 6f"; 2 Mch. 1785: "lent Williamos 12f"; 18 Mch. 1785: "lent Mr. Williamos 48f"; 15 Apr. 1785: "Pd Mr. Williamos for 12 lb. bougies 27f." The final entry is dated 8 Nov. 1785: "gave Mayer for support of Williamos 120f" (see Mazzei to TJ, 26 Oct. 1785). Shortly after this TJ reported to Abigail Adams that Williamos had died about ten days

earlier (TJ to Abigail Adams, 20 Nov. 1785). He merely reported the fact, and though others mentioned Williamos in their letters after the break, TJ never did in a way to reveal his feelings (Crèvecoeur to TJ, 15 and 30 Aug. 1785; TJ to Banister, 16 Aug. 1785; Abigail Adams to TJ, 25 Oct. 1785). But even after his unhappy days were ended, Williamos unwittingly injured TJ; at his death a copy of *Notes on Virginia*, presumably given to him by TJ, "got into the hands of a bookseller, who was about publishing a very abominable translation . . . when the Abbé Morellet heard of it, and diverted him from it by undertaking to translate it for him" (TJ to Bancroft, 26 Feb. 1786; TJ to Madison, 8 Feb. 1786).

Charles Williamos was commissioned a lieutenant of the 80th. Regiment of Light Armed Foot in America on 29 Dec. 1757; the name is given as Willyamoz. On 22 Mch., 3 May, and 6 May 1760 Charles Williamos was paid "on account for recruiting the Regiment," and as "Acting Paymaster to the said Regiment on account . . . from 24 Febr. to 24 April" (Public Record Office, London, Army lists, Index 5448; Deputy-paymasters' Accounts, America). His facility in the French language, his military service in America, his experiences as a deputy of Sir William Johnson, Superintendent of Indian Affairs for the Northern Department, enabled Williamos to develop an understanding of Indian and colonial affairs to which the Duke of Manchester attested in 1766 by recommending to Lord Dartmouth that he be retained in British service (NYHS, *Colls.*, 1922: *Letters and Papers of Cadwallader Colden*, VI, 158, 169, 209; *Calendar of Sir William Johnson Manuscripts*, Albany, 1909, p. 123, 166-8, 206, 213, 267, 285; Hist. MSS. Com., *Fourteenth Report*, Appendix, Part x, London, 1895: *The Manuscripts of the Earl of Dartmouth*, II, 37). In July of 1766 Williamos visited the Southern colonies, where he reported to Dartmouth on affairs in Virginia, advocated the establishment of a bank to remedy the scarcity of money there, and urged that the culture of silk, vines, and olive trees be encouraged in Carolina and Georgia. Both Williamos and TJ happened to be in Williamsburg in July, 1766, and it is possible that their friendship dated from that time, since a young British officer enjoying the notice of Dartmouth would inevitably have been drawn into the circle of which the governor was the center and of which TJ was a member (Williamos to Dartmouth, 3 July 1766, Williamsburg; same, Part x, II, 45). From 1768 to 1772 Williamos served as collector of customs in Jamaica; in the latter year he applied for appointment as naval officer of New York on the ground that service in Jamaica had been "detrimental to health and fortune" (Williamos to Dartmouth, 28 Sep. 1772; same, Part x, II, 97, 527). In the next few years he sought various colonial posts and drew up land and fiscal proposals which recommended the establishment of offices whose encumbents would need qualifications remarkably similar to those possessed by Williamos himself. In 1773 he submitted to Dartmouth the idea "of establishing an office of Inspector General of the sales and grants of land, of the Receiver General's accounts and of the Surveyor General's offices in North America," and declared that this was an office which "he would endeavour to discharge with satisfaction" (4 June 1773; same, Part x, II, 153). A few months later he addressed to Dartmouth a plan to establish "an office for inspecting the sale of lands in North America," and argued in support of it that the "Spirit of emigration to North America being now so prevailing in Europe the Immense tracts of land which the Crown possesses in that Continent are of course of the greatest importance, and therefore every step ought to be taken to regulate every thing relative to them." Williamos, of course, expressed a desire for this office, but, he added, "should such an office appear inadmissible [he] offers himself as a candidate to succeed Mr. Shuckburgh as secretary to the Indian affairs under Sir William Johnson" (18 Nov. 1773; same, Part x, II, 181). In 1774 he applied for the office of surveyor-general of New York, and the next year, in connection with Lord North's conciliatory resolutions, he suggested that "a Bill . . . be brought in immediately to appoint a temporary commission to go to America to meet their assemblies separately, and explain to them these resolutions which are liable otherwise to be grossly misrepresented and perverted." He further suggested the measures to be taken by such a commission in order to "remove the prejudices the Americans now labour under." Again Williamos doubtless had himself in mind as one of the commissioners (no date; same, Part x, II, p. 431).

As he explained in his letter to TJ of 8 July 1785, Williamos passed the years of the Revolution in England without performing military service because "it did not suit my principles." But, as one whose loyalties seem to have been determined somewhat by his perennial and none-too-successful applications for office before the Revolution, Williamos can scarcely be regarded as having become a neutral as a matter of principle. Also, he continued through the Revolution to correspond with an American loyalist who urged the sending of troops and ships to quell the Southern colonies and to rout the "rebellious scoundrels in this Province" (John Wetherhead to Williamos, New York, 5 July 1775; same, Part x, II, p. 327; Williamos to Wetherhead, London, 1 July 1778, PPAP: Franklin Papers). Late in 1783 Williamos wrote to Franklin from Paris, requesting passports for America and stating that he intended to set out in two days; he also listed, at about the same time, the tracts of land owned by him in America and asked Franklin's advice about proceedings that he should begin concerning them (Williamos to Franklin, 16 Dec. 1783; PPAP: Franklin Papers, XXX, LVI). It was probably at this time that Williamos gave to Franklin a document concerning the western territory which Franklin forwarded to Congress as from a "Captain Williams, formerly in the British Service, and employed upon the Lakes" (Franklin to Mifflin, 25 Dec. 1783; Franklin, *Writings*, ed. Smyth, IX, 135). This paper was referred on 5 Mch. 1784 to a committee of which TJ was chairman, but there is no evidence that any report was ever submitted as a result nor has the document itself been found (DNA: PCC, No. 186, p. 151). Williamos evidently did not clear up the matter of his American lands satisfactorily, for early in 1785 Wetherhead, in London, wrote to William Franklin concerning Williamos' debt to him and at the same time gave him instructions as to collecting it. These instructions, Wetherhead's letter, and a draft on Williamos were enclosed by Franklin in a letter to an unidentified person suggesting that Williamos would no doubt settle the account in order to prevent Benjamin Franklin from becoming acquainted with his conduct towards Wetherhead (Wetherhead to William Franklin, 2 Feb. 1785, with instructions; PPAP: Franklin Papers; William Franklin to ———, 10 Feb. 1785; same). From this time until August of 1785 Williamos evidently intended to return to America, but pressure from Wetherhead for an overdue debt, threatened disclosure to Franklin, and, later, ill health, combined to prevent him from ever making the voyage.

But it was the newly-appointed chargé d'affaires, Louis Guillaume Otto, who furnished what may be the best explanation for TJ's uncharacteristically harsh dismissal of Williamos. While waiting to take passage for America, Otto occupied his time at L'Orient by inquiring among the merchants concerning the state of American trade. He found that the merchants there and at Nantes and Bordeaux had been so discouraged by repeated losses and by "peut être trop peu de bonne foi de la part des Americains" that they had resolved not to sell to them except for cash account, a condition that would be almost impossible for them to meet on account of the scarcity of specie in America. Most of the Americans who had established houses at L'Orient, he added, had failed "et le nom Americain est devenu partout un signal de crainte et de mefiance." There was also anxiety among the merchants lest the packet boats should be changed from L'Orient to Le Havre, and Otto reported that "M. Thevenard Commandant de cette place m'a dit que quoique les paquebots lui donnent beaucoup d'embarras, il desire infiniment pour le bien public que leur destination ne soit changée, qu'il etoit dans l'ordre des choses que ces batimens abordent dans l'endroit où les Americains ont le plus de liaisons et que les retards de la navigation de la manche seroient un grand obstacle à la promptitude des nouvelles d'Amerique." He went on to say that an American merchant of probity who was attached to France and whom he had known for four years had just confided to him "qu'il soupçonnoit M. Williamos d'être un des principaux partisans du deplacement des paquebots et qu'il se mefioit en general des intentions secrettes de ce par-

ticulier qui paroit avoir toute la confiance de M. Jefferson. 'M. Williamos, m'a-t-il dit, est un de ces hommes qui ont le talent d'adopter les moeurs et les principes de tous les pays où ils se trouvent. Genevois de naissance, il est Anglois à Londres, Americain à Newyorck et françois à Paris. Cependant on doit le croire plutôt Anglois parcequ'il a non seulement servi dans les troupes Britanniques, mais qu'il a été longtems Directeur des Douanes de la Jamaïque, et que ce n'est qu'a la paix qu'il est venu en Amerique afficher l'enthousiasme de la liberté et se concilier par ses declarations contre l'Angleterre l'amitié des personnes les plus considerables des differens Etats. Il n'a pas eu moins de succès à Paris à captiver les ministres Americains et à devenir le Depositaire de leurs secrets. Je ne sais s'il est reellement dans les interêts de l'Angleterre, mais il a assés d'esprit et de connoissance du coeur humain pour mener avec succès les intrigues les plus compliquées et je desire infiniment qu'on se mette en garde contre ses conseils.'—Je ne puis dire, Monseigneur, jusqu'à quel point ces soupçons sont fondés et s'ils ne sont point le resultat d'une haine personnelle. Je connois M. Williamos comme un homme de beaucoup d'instruction et de talens sans avoir jamais eu lieu de le croire opposé à nos interêts; mais il est de mon devoir de Vous informer de tout ce qui me revient sur le caractere des personnes qui ont quelqu'influence dans les affaires de l'Amerique et il me semble que M. Williamos en a beaucoup auprès de M. Jefferson. Je sais qu'il aime à se meler de nos affaires; il m'en a donné encore avant mon depart de Paris une preuve très forte en me montrant un memoire qu'il se proposoit de faire remettre à M. le Mal. de Castries pour lui demontrer la necessité d'etablir un Vice Consul dans le Connecticut et pour solliciter cette place en faveur d'un françois de sa connoissance. Il est grand partisan du Commerce libre des Antilles et de la navigation du Mississipi et à l'entendre la france et l'Espagne sont essentiellement interessés a se laisser depouiller par les Americains" (Otto to Vergennes, 30 June 1785; Arch. Aff. Etr., Corr. Pol., E.-U., xxx; Tr in DLC).

Everything that the unidentified American merchant reported to Otto and all that he himself asserted on the basis of personal knowledge has the ring of truth when compared with Williamos' known history as a place-hunter. Since TJ's abrupt ending of his relationship with Williamos came only one week after Otto's letter to Vergennes, the conclusion is almost inescapable that, indirectly or directly, the astute French minister made its contents known to TJ or hinted to him that there were strong grounds for believing he had admitted a British spy to his confidence. TJ was habituated to debt himself, and throughout life he suffered patiently the importunations of friends, acquaintances, and even strangers without exploding in white anger. But to admit a British agent into his utmost confidence, or even to be thought by the highest of French officials to lie under suspicion of having done so, was something else. The supposition that this was the case is the best explanation for the total severance of relations with Williamos. But, as always, TJ did not allow an imposition or even a supposed betrayal of confidence to triumph over humane feelings. The perennial office-seeker was at last at the end of his resources, and when Williamos' need became evident a few weeks later, TJ sent money to him indirectly and in a manner to keep its recipient from squandering it or from knowing whence it came (Mazzei to TJ, 26 Oct. 1785). THE CIRCUMSTANCE OF YOUR BEING STILL ON BRITISH PAY: Williamos had continued to draw half-pay. The last recorded payment was for six months ending 24 Dec. 1784; the Paymaster General's Accounts for 1785 and 1786 are missing (Public Record Office, London, PMG, 4/35). His name continued on the army list until 1799, probably because no official notice of death was received.

Franklin and Jefferson to Adams, with Proposed Treaty with Great Britain

SIR   Passy July 8. 1785.

We duly received your letter of the 20th. of June and now in consequence thereof send you a draught of a treaty which we should be willing to have proposed to the court of London. We have taken for our ground work the original draught proposed to Denmark, making such alterations and additions only as had occurred in the course of our negociations with Prussia and Tuscany and which we thought were for the better. These you will find in the 4th. 9th. 13th. and 25th. articles, and are such as met your approbation when we were considering those treaties. Nevertheless we shall be happy to concur with you in any thing better which you may wish to propose either in the original draught or the amendments. Particularly we wish it were possible to convince the British court that it might be for their interest to continue their former bounties on the productions of our country on account of their quality, and of the nature of the returns, which have always been in manufactures and not in money.

We have the honour to be with sentiments of the highest respect Sir Your most obedt. & most humble servts.

Draught of a treaty of Amity and Commerce between his Britannic majesty and the United states of America

The parties being willing &c. [as in the draught proposed to Denmark in every part, except in the following passages.]

Art. 4.[1] More especially each party shall have a right to carry any kinds of produce manufactures and merchandize of whatever place they be the growth or manufacture in their own or any other vessels to any parts of the Dominions of the other where it shall be lawful for all persons freely to purchase them, and thence to take the produce manufactures and merchandize of whatever place or growth, which all persons shall in like manner be free to sell them, paying in both cases such duties charges and fees only as are or shall be paid by the most favoured nation. Nevertheless each party reserves to itself the right where any nation restrains the transportation of merchandize to the vessels of the country of which it is the growth or manufacture to establish against such nation retaliating regulations: and also the right to prohibit in their respective countries the exportation or importation of any species of goods or commodities whatsoever, when reasons of state shall require it. In this case the subjects or citizens of either of the contracting parties shall not import nor export the merchandize prohibited by the other. But if one of the contracting parties permits any person of their own or any other nation to import or export the same merchandize the citizens or subjects of the other shall immediately enjoy the same liberty.

Art. 9. Add to the end of the article 'the antient and barbarous right to wrecks of the sea shall be entirely abolished, with respect to the subjects or citizens of the two contracting parties.'[2]

Art. 13.[3] The passage 'Nevertheless &c.' to run as follows. 'Nevertheless it shall be lawful to stop such vessels, and to make them unlade such articles in the nearest port, putting them under safekeeping; or to detain them for such length of time as the Captors may think necessary to prevent the inconvenience or damage that might ensue from their proceeding; paying however a reasonable compensation for the loss such arrest shall occasion to the proprietors: or it shall be allowed to use in the service of the captors the whole or any part of the military stores so detained, paying the owners the full value of the same to be ascertained by the current price at the place of it's destination. But in the case of a vessel so stopped for articles heretofore deemed contraband, if the master will deliver out the goods supposed to be of contraband nature, he shall be admitted to do it, and the vessel shall not in that case be carried into any port, nor further detained, but shall be allowed to proceed on her voiage. Nor shall any such articles be subject to be taken or delayed in any case if they be not in greater quantity than may be necessary for the use of the ship, or of the persons in it.'

Art. 22. Between 'places' and 'whose' insert 'and in general all others.'

Art. 24. For 'necessaries' substitute 'comforts.'

Art. 25. Add to the clause 'but if any such Consuls shall exercise commerce, they shall be submitted to the same laws and usages to which the private individuals of their nation are submitted in the same place.'

Dft (DLC); in TJ's hand. Enclosure (Dft in DLC in TJ's hand); undated, with marginal instructions to the copy-ist in French in Humphreys' hand. PrC (DLC). The full text of this proposed treaty is to be found copied into Adams' letter-book (MHi: AMT) immediately following his letter to TJ of 18 Aug. 1785, which acknowledges TJ's of 6 Aug. "with the Notes and Project in-closed"—i.e., Franklin's notes and TJ's projet of a treaty with the Barbary states.

1 In margin: "Inserez."
2 In margin: "ajoutez a la fin."
3 In margin: "pour Art.13."

From Charles Williamos

Sir   Paris 8th. July 1785

Astonished and Surprised as I must be at the contents of your Excellencies unexpected letter, my indignation at the atrocious falshoods which have too Successfully been attempted by the lowest and most infernal Malice, is the Juster from the weight of so unexpected a stroke—good God Sir is it possible? That con-vinced by your own experiences of the constant blunders and mis-aprehensions to say no worse, of the people of this country, you should so readily admitt as truth, things destitute of every proof or even appearance of probability. For such give me leave to assure you, is the whole of that as ridiculous as infamous tale invented by the Taylor, had he only produced what I may have written to him on the subject, you would have found my positive expressions that you *had not*, *never had*, any Conection in my affairs, and by one moment's recollection it would Strike you as a plain truth, that not having had a draught *from you* it was *impossible* to shew it.—I am not by any means "the first honest man of property" who has been a little in arrear by unexpected disappointments, but untill I can realise some of that property, how can any threats, persecutions, or certificates enable me to furnish money at a mo-ment's warning especially when every unjust and unfair Method is put in use to cut me off from every resource.—Yet if Longpry or others never meet with more *pecuniary Injuries* than at my hands they may rest very secure, for I defy him, and all mankind, to say that any one ever lost one single farthing by me, or is likely to do it, for I have means thank God and principles which do not make it even a Chance.

Determined to bear every thing, however unjust and Cruel with equal patience, I shall not expatiate on the other matter, any further than to beg leave to assure you that *No State*, or Individual in them, has ever been in danger of suffering, much less of *having their reputation at Stake by My Conduct*. No Sir I defy the utmost malice to point out the smallest Injury willfully done by me, directly or Indirectly, to bodies at large or Individually. Far very far from it, and what ever *may* have got a broad will prove on fair investigation to have as little foundation *from me*, as other ridiculous tales. Why then I beseech? admit of such cruel prejudices on so vague a ground. I must either be guilty or not. In the first case Comon humanity as well as strict Justice require full, very full proof. Let it then be brought forwards. I defy the dark base assassins. Let them if they dare, come forwards. I shall meet them with that consciousness which is ever the surest defence of a true honest heart, who ever made doing every good in his power, the basis of his Conduct. Think then Sir how deeply I must feel the base attempts which have too well succeeded, and towards whom, yes towards whom, let my whole conduct, every action, every word, every look of mine since I had the honor of some Intimacy with you, be brought forth. They can only evince the highest respect, esteem, and veneration, as well as the warmest wishes to merit your good opinion and friendship by every endeavour in my power. Could I then, even suspect what I so unjustly experience now, because of my having your Interest so warmly at heart, run counter other people's.

I do not know how far I may be right or wrong in point of half pay. The best authorities in England, as well as the received practice of other European Powers, have determined it to be only a reward or indemnification to reduced officers for past services, which lays them under no kind of restraint whatever, Nor Supposes the least obligation to render any further Service or to hold allegiance. General Lee and Several others with whom I have Served kept it during the last war. I have not understood besides that it was made an objection to any American Citizen. Mine was hard very hard earned, and at the breaking out of this war, I had youth, activity, interest and money enough to have got any Comission I pleased, but it did not suit my principles which my whole conduct have proved. Yet I did not think it incumbent on me to give up what I looked upon to be my undefeasable right, any more than the lands I hold on the same ground. However Sir should it ever become a *determined question* I shall not hesitate to abide by it, let it be what it will.

It is peculiarly hard on me to meet at this critical moment with the affront I do but conscious of my Innocence, let the consequences be what they will, I shall bear them with fortitude and as truth ever comes to light sooner or later the day is not far off perhaps, which will confound the utmost efforts of baseness and convince you, that you never had or can know any one more truly and disinteressedly attached to you than Sir Your Excellency's Most humble Servant, C: WILLIAMOS

RC (DLC); endorsed. See note to TJ to Williamos, 7 July 1785.

Castries to the American Commissioners

Versailles le [9?] Juillet 1785

Mr. Jones, Messieurs, demande que les parts qui reviennent aux sujets des Etats unis, dans les prises faites par l'Escadre qu'il a commandée, lui soient délivrées. J'ai cru devoir exiger de cet officier la garantie d'un sujet du Roi; mais il represente qu'il est autorisé à recevoir par un acte spécial du Congrés auquel il a deja fourni caution. Je vous prie de me faire connoitre officielement le caractére dont Mr. Jones est revêtu; afin que je puisse prendre les ordres du Roi sur l'objet de sa demande.

J'ai l'honneur de vous envoyer les pieces que Mr. Jones a produites, et J'ai celui d'etre avec la consideration la plus distinguée Messieurs, votre trés humble et trés obeïssant Serviteur,

LE MAL. DE CASTRIES

RC (DLC); in a clerk's hand, signed by Castries; without indication of the day of the month, which has been supplied from internal evidence and John Paul Jones' letter to Castries of 10 July 1785 (Dipl. Corr., 1783-1789, III, 679), enclosing TJ's reply of 10 July 1785; at head of text: "Invalide et prise" and "on les prie de faire con- noitre le caractère dont Mr. Jones est revêtu"; at foot of text: "À Msrs. Adams et Gefersson Ministres pleni- potentiaires des Etats unis." The letter, of course, should have been addressed only to TJ, who answered it. Cas- tries failed to enclose the "pieces que Mr. Jones a produites" (see TJ's reply of 10 July, below).

From Philip Mazzei

L'Orient, 9 July 1785. He sailed from New York 17 June and arrived in L'Orient this day. "I have with me so many bundles of letters and other papers for you as to cost you perhaps 30 louis, were the whole to be sent by post. Mr. Short could perhaps have his for 60 or 70 francs. I cannot get to Paris before the 21st or 22nd of this month; nonetheless I esteem it proper to bring all of it myself, since I do not know which are of greatest urgency." TJ will have time to reply to these by the next packet, since it will not sail during July. Asks TJ to write him at Versailles *poste restante* and to let him know if he may have a room "in the *hotel* where you are staying." Encloses a letter to be given by TJ or Short to the post, since because of its urgency it is "not a matter to be entrusted to a servant." Will pass through Nantes and stop there three or four days. "If you see the Marquis de Lafayette you may tell him that I have letters for him too and the rattlesnake."

RC (DLC); 1 p.; in Italian. Enclosure has not been identified. Mazzei's message to Lafayette makes it appear that "the rattlesnake" may be the nickname of a person; what he evidently intended to say was that he had letters and a rattlesnake for Lafayette.

To Castries

SIR   Paris July 10. 1785.

I am honoured with your Excellency's letter on the prize money for which Mr. Jones applies. The papers intended to have been therein inclosed, not having been actually inclosed, I am unable to say any thing on their subject. But I find that Congress on the first day of November 1783. recommended Capt. Jones to their Minister here, as Agent, to sollicit, under his direction, paiment to the officers and crews for the prizes taken in Europe under his command; requiring him previously to give to their Superintendant of finance good security for paying to him whatever he should receive, to be by him distributed to those entitled. In consequence of this Capt. Jones gave the security required as is certified by the Superintendant of finance on the 6th. of November 1783. and received from Doctor Franklin on the 17th. of December 1783. due authority, as Agent, to sollicit the said paiments.

From these documents I consider Capt. Jones as Agent for the citizens of the United States interested in the prizes taken in Europe under his command, and that he is properly authorized to receive the money due to them, having given good security to transmit it to the Treasury office of the United States, whence it will be distributed under the care of Congress to the officers and crews originally intitled, or to their representatives.

I have the honour to be with sentiments of the highest respect Your Excellency's most obedient and most humble servant,

TH: JEFFERSON

PrC (DLC). Tr (DNA: PCC, No. 87, I); in TJ's hand; at head of text: "Copy of a letter from Th: Jefferson to the Mareschal de Castries in answer to one received from him, desiring to know how far Capt. Jones was authorised to receive the prize-money due to the crew of the Alliance." Tr (DNA: PCC, No. 107, I). The letter was enclosed in John Paul Jones to Castries (FC in DLC: John Paul Jones Papers, undated; printed under 10 July 1785 in *Dipl. Corr., 1783-1789*, III, 679); a copy was later sent to Jay with TJ's letter of 30 Aug. 1785.

Jones had transmitted to Castries, on 1 Feb. 1784, copies of Congress' resolution of 1 Nov. 1783 and of Franklin's authorization of 17 Dec. 1783, together with a statement of the force, in guns and men, in the squadron under his command; in his letter, he pointed out that "It is the custom . . . to multiply the number of the crew by the sum of the calibre of the cannon mounted on board each ship. The product gives the intrinsic force, in proportion to which the share of the prize-money arising to each ship is determined." On the basis of this formula, he claimed the proportion due to the officers and crews of the *Bon Homme Richard* and the *Alliance*, to be divided among them "by the American Superintendent of Finance, agreeable to the rules of the American navy" (*Dipl. Corr., 1783-1789*, III, 664-6; in DLC: TJ Papers, 9: 1542 there are copies in TJ's hand of Robert Morris' certificate of 6 Nov. 1783 and of Franklin's authorization of 17 Dec. 1783).

To Laumoy

[*Paris, 10 July 1785.* Entry in SJL reads: "Genl. Laumoy. Inclosing his certificate. By post." Not found, but see Laumoy to TJ, 7 July 1785.]

To George Washington

DEAR SIR   Paris July 10. 1785.

Mr. Houdon would much sooner have had the honour of attending you but for a spell of sickness which long gave us to despair of his recovery and from which he is but recently recovered. He comes now for the purpose of lending the aid of his art to transmit you to posterity. He is without rivalship in it, being employed from all parts of Europe in whatever is capital. He has had a difficulty to withdraw himself from an order of the Empress of Russia, a difficulty however which arose from a desire to shew her respect, but which never gave him a moment's hesitation about his present voyage which he considers as promising the brightest chapter of his history. I have spoke of him as an Artist only; but I can assure you also that, as a man, he is disinterested, generous, candid, and panting after glory: in every circumstance meriting your good opinion. He will have need to see you much while he shall have the honour of being with you, which you can the more freely admit as his eminence and merit gives him admission into genteel societies here. He will need an interpreter. I supposed you could procure some person from Alexandria who might be agreeable to yourself to perform this office. He brings with him a subordinate workman or two, who of course will associate with their own class only.

On receiving the favour of your letter of Feb. 25. I communicated the plan for clearing the Patowmac, with the act of assembly, and an explanation of it's probable advantages, to Mr. Grand, whose acquaintance and connection with the monied men here enabled him best to try it's success. He has done so, but to no end. I inclose you his letter. I am pleased to hear in the mean time that the subscriptions were likely to be filled up at home. This is infinitely better, and will render the proceedings of the companies much more harmonious. I place an immense importance to my own country on this channel of connection with the new Western states. I shall continue uneasy till I know that Virginia has assumed her ultimate boundary to the Westward. The late example of the state of Franklin separated from N. Carolina increases my anxieties for Virginia.

The confidence you are so good as to place in me on the subject of the interest lately given you by Virginia in the Patowmac company is very flattering to me. But it is distressing also, inasmuch as, to deserve it, it obliges me to give my whole opinion. My wishes to see you made perfectly easy by receiving those just returns of gratitude from our country, to which you are entitled, would induce me to be contented with saying, what is a certain truth, that the world would be pleased with seeing them heaped on you, and would consider your receiving them as no derogation from your reputation. But I must own that the declining them will add to that reputation, as it will shew that your motives have been pure and without any alloy. This testimony however is not wanting either to those who know you or who do not. I must therefore repeat that I think the receiving them will not in the least lessen the respect of the world if from any circumstances they would be convenient to you. The candour of my communication will find it's justification I know with you.

A tolerable certainty of peace leaves little interesting in the way of intelligence. Holland and the emperor will be quiet. If any thing is brewing it is between the latter and the Porte. Nothing in prospect as yet from England. We shall bring them however to decision now that Mr. Adams is received there.—I wish much to hear that the canal thro the Dismal is resumed. I have the honour to be with the most perfect esteem & respect Dr. Sir Your most obedient & most humble servt., TH: JEFFERSON

RC (DLC: Washington Papers); endorsed. PrC (DLC: TJ Papers); lacking complimentary close and signature. Entry in sjpl reads: "Washington Genl. Houdon. Potomak. Western boundary. Gift to him." The enclosed letter from Grand was probably addressed to TJ, but no copy of it has been found.

To John Adams

DEAR SIR   Paris July 11. 1785.

Doctr. Franklin sets out this morning for Havre from whence he is to cross over to Cowes there to be taken on board Capt. Truxen's ship bound from London to Philadelphia. The Doctor's baggage will be contained in 150. or 200 boxes &c. We doubt that the laws of England will not permit these things to be removed from one vessel into another; and it must be[1] attended with great difficulty, delay and expence should he be obliged to enter them regularly merely to pass them from one vessel to another. Will you be so good as to interest yourself (if it be necessary) to obtain a passport for these things or other letters which may protect them in the transfer from one vessel to another. The Doctor being extremely engaged in the moment of departure I informed him that Mr. Harrison was setting out for London today and that I would by him sollicit your interference in this matter. You will judge best whether the orders had better be delivered to capt. Truxent or sent to Cowes. I rather think the last best, as they would put it in his power to land and store them and to discharge the vessel which carries them. Whatever is done should be speedily done. I am with sincere esteem Dr. Sir Your friend & servt.,

TH: JEFFERSON

RC (MHi: AMT); addressed; endorsed in part: "relative to Dr. Franklins Baggage." Entry in sjl for 10 July, which reads: "Mr. Adams to get protection for Dr. Franklin's baggage. By Mr. Harrison," refers, despite its date, to the present letter.

[1] Preceding four words are not certain. TJ first wrote: "tho' the [. . .] attended," &c. and then altered this by erasure and overwriting to read as above.

To Barré

SIR   Paris July 11. 1785.

I have this moment received your letter of the 28th. of June and will have the copy of Genl. Washington's picture taken for Mr. Thevenot as soon as I receive an answer to my letter from

America. I have reason to expect it by the first or second packet. I have no hesitation in pronouncing Wright's drawing to be a better likeness of the General than Peale's. I thank you for your friendly dispositions as well to myself as my country. I think it of great importance to both nations that the present cordial harmony should be cultivated. Late occurrences in America prove it to be strong there, and I have no reason to doubt it here.

I am with great respect Sir Your most obedient humble servt.,

TH: JEFFERSON

PrC (DLC). The ANSWER TO MY LETTER FROM AMERICA that TJ expected was one from Hopkinson to him in answer to his of 13 Jan. 1785; see also TJ to Hopkinson, 6 July 1785.

From Benjamin Franklin

Passy July 11. 85.

Mr. Franklin presents his respectful Compliments to Mr. Jefferson, and requests he would be so good as to ask either of the Imperial and Sardinian Ambassadors the Favour of forwarding the enclos'd Letters, of which they will make no Difficulty. Mr. F. also recommends Dr. Ingenhauss to Mr. Jefferson, as a proper Correspondent in case he should have any thing to insinuate to that Court. Dr. F's best Wishes attend Mr. Jefferson.

RC (DLC); endorsed by TJ: "Ingenhausz. Monsr. Ingenhausz medecin de la cour &c. &c. à Vienne." Enclosures not identified. On 11 June 1785 Jan Ingenhousz wrote to Franklin asking that he be recommended to Franklin's successor (PPAP).

From Benjamin Franklin

Passy 11 July 1785.

Dr. Franklin requests Mr. Jefferson to do what he thinks is proper on the subject of the Letter inclosed, and afterwards to make answer to the writer.

RC (DLC); in William Temple Franklin's hand. Enclosure not identified.

To the Governor of Virginia

SIR   Paris July 11. [1785]

Mr. Houdon's long and desperate illness has retarded till now his departure for Virginia. We had hoped from our first conversations with him that it would be easy to make our terms, and that the cost of the statue and expence of sending him would be but about a thousand guineas. But when we came to settle this precisely, he thought himself obliged to ask vastly more. Insomuch that at one moment we thought our treaty at an end, but unwilling to commit such a work to an inferior hand, we made him an ultimate proposition on our part. He was as much mortified at the prospect of not being the executor of such a work, as we were not to have it done by such a hand. He therefore acceded to our terms, tho' we are satisfied he will be a considerable loser. We were led to insist on them because in a former letter to the Governor I had given the hope we entertained of bringing the whole within 1000 guineas. The terms are 25,000 livres or 1000 English guineas (the English guinea being worth 25. livres) for the statue and pedestal. Besides this we pay his expences going and returning, which we expect will be between four and five thousand livres: and if he dies in the voiage we pay his family 10,000 livres. This latter proposition was disagreeable to us. But he has a father, mother and sisters who have no resource but in his labour: and he is himself one of the best men in the world. He therefore made it a sine quo non, without which all would have been off. We have reconciled it to ourselves by determining to get insurance on his life made in London, which we expect can be done for 5. per cent, so that it becomes an additional sum of 500 livres. I have written to Mr. Adams to know for what per cent the insurance can be had. I inclose you, for a more particular detail, a copy of the agreement. Dr. Franklin being on his departure did not become a party to the instrument, tho it has been concluded with his approbation. He was disposed to give 250 guineas more, which would have split the difference between the actual terms and Mr. Houdon's demand. I wish the state, at the conclusion of the work may agree to give him this much more, because I am persuaded he will be a loser, which I am sure their generosity would not wish. But I have not given him the smallest expectation of it, chusing the proposition should come from the state which will be more honourable. You will perceive by the agreement that I pay him immediately 8333⅓ livres, which is to be employed in getting the marble in Italy, it's transportation &c. The package and transportation of his stucco to make the moulds will be about 500 livres. I shall furnish him with money for his expences in France and I have authorised Dr. Franklin when he arrives in Philadelphia to draw

on me for money for his other expences going, staying and returning. These draughts will have been made probably and will be
on their way to me before you receive this, and with the paiments
made here will amount to about 5000 livres more than the amount
of the bill remitted me. Another third, of 8333⅓ livres will become
due at the end of the ensuing year. Dr. Franklin leaves Passy this
morning. As he travels in a litter, Mr. Houdon will follow him
some days hence and will embark with him for Philadelphia.
I am in hopes he need not stay in America more than a month.

I have the honour to be with due respect your Excellency's most
obedient & most humble servt.,　　　　　TH: JEFFERSON

RC (Vi). PrC (DLC). Recorded in
SJL as sent by Houdon; entry in SJPL
reads: "Govr. Virga. Houdon. Dr. Fr.
leaves Passy this morning." The enclosed copy of the agreement with
Houdon has not been found, but it was
executed on 8 July 1785; on 8 Sep.
1796 Houdon wrote Gov. Robert
Brooke: "The 8. July 1785 it was
agreed between his excellency Mr. Jefferson in the Virginia's State's name
and me that I should executed in marble the statute [sic] of Mr. Washington,
for the price of 25,000ℓt french money,
to be paid in three times" (DLC: TJ
Papers).
The FORMER LETTER TO THE GOVER-
NOR was TJ's of 12 Jan. 1785. In addition to this letter Houdon was supposed
to have conveyed to America the following: TJ to the Virginia delegates in
Congress, to R. H. Lee, to John Jay, and
to James Monroe, 12 July; to Charles
Thomson, 14 July; to George Washington and to Ezra Stiles, 17 July 1785.
But these letters were placed in Houdon's trunks which arrived at Havre
after he had departed, and in consequence did not come to America until
about Mch. 1786. On 14 Sep. 1785 Houdon wrote: "Je Crois que les premiers
Lettres que m'a remis Mons. Jefferson
sont dans mes Malles restés au havre
mais les derniers sont avec nous" (Extract of letter from Houdon to Grand,
Philadelphia, 14 Sep. 1785; DLC: TJ
Papers).

To John Jay

SIR　　　　　　　　　　　　　　Paris July 12. 1785.

My last letter to you was dated the 17th. of June. The present
serves to cover some papers put into my hands by Capt. Paul
Jones. They respect an antient matter which is shortly this. While
Capt. Jones was hovering on the coast of England in the year
1779. a British pilot, John Jackson by name, came on board him
supposing him to be British. Capt. Jones found it convenient to
detain him as a pilot and in the action with the Serapis, which
ensued, this man lost his arm. It is thought that this gives him
a just claim to the same allowance with others who have met with
the like misfortune in the service of the United states. Congress
alone being competent to this application, it is my duty to present
the case to their consideration, which I beg leave to do through
you.

Dr. Franklin will be able to give you so perfect a state of all transactions relative to his particular office in France, as well as to the subjects included in our general commission, that it is unnecessary for me to enter on them. His departure, with the separate situation of Mr. Adams and myself will render it difficult to communicate to you the future proceedings of the commission, as regularly as they have been heretofore. We shall do it however with all the punctuality practicable, either separately or jointly as circumstances may require and admit.

I have the honour to be with sentiments of the highest respect Sir Your most obedient & most humble servt.,

TH: JEFFERSON

RC (DNA: PCC, No. 87). PrC (DLC). Tr (DNA: PCC, No. 107). Recorded in SJL as sent "by Houdon"; entry in SJPL under this date reads: "P. Jones and Jackson's case. Dr. Fr." Enclosures: (1) John Paul Jones to Franklin, 23 Sep. 1784, declaring that "Humanity and justice require that I should earnestly recommend that unfortunate man John Jackson for a Reward for the important service he performed and the great loss and suffering he sustained. I thought and still think he merited half Pay as a Pilot in the Service of the United States" (DNA: PCC, Nos. 87 and 107; printed in *Dipl. Corr., 1783-1789*, I, 621-2, under date of 1785). (2) An enclosure in the foregoing—Jackson to Franklin, 16 Oct. 1780, stating that, following the action of 22 Sep. 1779, Jones gave Jackson "a Hundred Ducats, and at the same time Promisd him, that he should be paid by the American Embassador at the Court of France—Half pay of a Pilot the remainder of his life to commence from the 22nd day of Septr. 1779," and asking that this be done "agreeable to Mr. Paul Jones' writing as he is rendered incapable of geting Bread for his poor family" (same, I, 622; copies in DNA: PCC, Nos. 87 and 107). (3) Jones' certification of Jackson's claim, 15 Nov. 1779, a copy of which was also enclosed in Jones to Franklin, 23 Sep. 1784, stating the facts as above, save that half-pay for life was to begin from the date of the certificate (*Dipl. Corr., 1783-1789*, I, 423-4; copies in DNA: PCC, Nos. 87 and 107).

Shortly after TJ transmitted the above papers to Jay, James Blunt wrote to Franklin that Jackson had "waited for some time the Arrival of the American Ambassador at this Court [London], to whom he has shown his Claim, but been referred by him to Mr. Jefferson at Paris"; this letter and its enclosed certified copy of Jones's promise of half-pay, dated 15 Nov. 1779, were not transmitted by Franklin until three years later when he wrote Jay: "In arranging some old Papers I lately found the enclos'd Letter from Mr. Blunt, inclosing Copy of a Certificate of Comme. Jones in favour of John Jackson. I ought, (tho' so long delay'd) to send some Answer. Can you inform me, whether any thing has been done for Jackson in consequence of the Commodore's Promise?" (Franklin to Jay, Philadelphia, 27 June 1788; DNA: PCC, No. 82, III; its enclosures are in same). Jay had transmitted TJ's letter to Congress on 20 Sep. 1785 and a committee reported in favor of granting half-pay to Jackson in accordance with Jones' promise (JCC, XXIX, 733, 778); and, shortly before Franklin found the "old Papers," TJ wrote the Secretary at War again enclosing the pertinent documents (TJ to Knox, 6 Feb. 1788). Again Congress took under advisement the report of 1785, at that time listed under "Reports Old, Obsolete, or Negative," but no action was taken (JCC, XXXIV, 127, 134, 622). See also Garvey to TJ, 1 Feb. 1788.

To Richard Henry Lee

Dr. Sir   Paris July 12. 1785.

I was honoured two days ago with yours of May 16. and thank you for the intelligence it contained, much of which was new to me. It was the only letter I received by this packet except one from Mr. Hopkinson on philosophical subjects. I generally write about a dozen by every packet, and receive sometimes one, sometimes two, and sometimes ne'er a one. You are right in supposing all letters opened which come either thro' the French or English channel, unless trusted to a passenger. Yours had been evidently opened, and I think I never received one through the post office which had not been. It is generally discoverable by the smoakiness of the wax and faintness of the re-impression. Once they sent me a letter open, having forgotten to re-seal it. I should be happy to hear that Congress thought of establishing packets of their own between N. York and Havre. To send a packet from each port once in two months, the business might possibly be done by two packets, as will be seen by the following scheme, wherein we will call the two packets A. and B.

Jan. A sails from New York. B. from Havre		
Feb.		
Mar. B.	New York	A. Havre
Apr.		
May A.	New York	B. Havre
June		
July B.	New York	A. Havre
Aug.		
Sep. A.	New York	B. Havre
Oct.		
Nov. B.	New York	A. Havre
Dec.		

I am persuaded this government would gladly arrange this matter with us, and send their packets in the intermediate months, as they are tired of expence. We should then have a safe conveiance every two months, and one for common matters every two months. A courier would pass between this and Havre in twenty four hours. Could not the surplus of the Post office revenue be applied to this? This establishment would look like the commencement of a little navy, the only kind of force we ought to possess. You mention that Congress is on the subject of requisition. No subject is more interesting to the honour of the states. It is an opinion which prevails much in Europe that our government wants authority to draw money from the states, and that the states want faith to pay their debts. I shall wish much to hear how far the requisitions on the states are productive of actual cash. Mr. Grand informed me the other day that the Commissioners were dissatisfied with his having paid to this country but 200,000 livres of the 400,000 for which Mr. Adams drew on Holland, reserving the residue to replace his advances and furnish current expences. They observed that these last objects might have been effected by the residue of the money in Holland which was lying dead. Mr. Grand's observation to me was that Mr. Adams did not like to draw for these purposes, that he himself had no authority, and that the Commissioners had not accompanied their complaints with any draught on that fund, so that the debt still remains unpaid while the money is lying dead in Holland. He did not desire me to mention this circumstance, but should you see the Commissioners it might not be amiss to communicate it to them, that they may take any measures they please, if they think it proper to do any thing in it. I am anxious to hear what is done with the states of Vermont and Franklin. I think that the former is the only innovation on the system of Apr. 23. 1784. which ought ever possibly to be admitted. If Congress are not firm on that head, our several states will crumble to atoms by the spirit of establishing every little canton into a separate state. I hope Virginia will concur in that plan as to her territory South of the Ohio and not leave to the Western country to withdraw themselves by force and become our worst enemies instead of our best friends. Europe is likely to be quiet. The departure of the Dutch deputies for Vienna, is a proof that matters are arranged between the Emperor and Dutch. The Turks shew a disposition to rally against the pursuits of the Emperor: but if this country can preserve the peace she will do it. She is not ready for war, and yet could not see peaceably any new accession of power to him. A lover of humanity would wish to see that charming country from which the Turks exclude science and freedom, in any hands rather than theirs, and in those of the native Greeks rather than any others. The recovery of their antient language would not be desperate, could they recover their antient liberty. But those who wish to remove the Turks, wish to put themselves in their places. This would be exchanging one set of Barbarians for another only. I am sorry to hear your health is not yet established. I was in hopes a change of climate would have effected it. Perhaps the summer of N. York may have produced that good effect.

This will be handed you by Monsr. Houdon. The letter which I give him to our delegation will apprise you of his character and mission, as well as of the object he would propose with Congress. I will here only add my request to you personally to render him such civilities as may be convenient, and to avail him of those opportunities which are in your power of making him acquainted with the members of Congress and of disposing them in his favour. He will well merit their notice. I am with great esteem Dear Sir your most obedt. humble servt.,   TH: JEFFERSON

PrC (DLC); at foot of first page: "President of Congress. private"; endorsed. Recorded in SJL as sent by Houdon (but see note to TJ to Governor of Virginia, 11 July 1785);

entry in SJPL reads: "Presdt. of Congr. Private. Packets, post offices. Money affairs. New states. Vermont. Franklin. Turkey. Grew [Grand]. Houdon."

To James Monroe

DEAR SIR   Paris July 12. 1785.

I wrote you fully on the 5th. and gave also to young Mr. Franklin a letter of introduction to you dated the 4th. Besides these I have addressed this day a letter to our delegation in Congress on the subject of Mr. Houdon. That will apprise you fully of his merit and objects. I have now only to add in a particular letter to yourself my prayers to give him personally all those aids and counsels of which a stranger stands in need, and especially a stranger who cannot speak a word of English. He is an excellent character, eminent in his art which is one of the most respectable in Europe. If you can make him acquainted with members of Congress who will be disposed to gratify his desire of making the General's equestrian statue, you will have the merit of aiding to put that matter into the best hands into which it can possibly be put. I am with much esteem Dr. Sir Your affectionate friend & servt.,   TH: JEFFERSON

RC (The Rosenbach Company, New York City, 1946); endorsed. Entry in SJL reads: "Jas. Monroe. Letter of recommendation for Houdon" (see note to TJ to Governor of Virginia, 11 July 1785).

To the Virginia Delegates in Congress

GENTLEMEN   Paris July 12. 1785.

In consequence of the orders of the Legislative and Executive bodies of Virginia, I have engaged Monsr. Houdon to make the Statue of Genl. Washington. For this purpose it is necessary for him to see the General. He therefore goes with Doctr. Franklin, and will have the honor of delivering you this himself. As his journey is at the expence of the state according to our contract, I will pray you to favor him with your patronage and counsels, and to protect him as much as possible from those impositions to which strangers are but too much exposed. I have advised him to proceed in the stages to the General's. I have also agreed, if he can see Generals Greene and Gates, whose busts he has a desire to make, that he may make a moderate deviation for this purpose, after he is done with General Washington.

But the most important object with him is to be employed to make General Washington's equestrian statue for Congress. Nothing but the expectation of this could have engaged him to have undertaken this voiage, as the pedestrian statue for Virginia will not make it worth the business he loses by absenting himself. I was therefore obliged to assure him of my recommendations for this greater work. Having acted in this for the state, you will I hope think yourselves in some measure bound to patronize and urge his being employed by Congress. I would not have done this myself, nor asked you to do it, did I not see that it would be better for Congress to put this business into his hands, than into those of any other person living, for these reasons: 1. He is without rivalship the first statuary of this age; as a proof of which he receives orders from every other country for things intended to be capital. 2. He will have seen General Washington, have taken his measures in every part, and of course whatever he does of him will have the merit of being original, from which other workmen can only furnish copies. 3. He is in possession of the house, the furnaces, and all the apparatus provided for making the statue of Louis XV. If any other workman is employed, this will all be to be provided anew and of course to be added to the price of the statue, for no man can ever expect to make two equestrian statues. The addition which this would be to the price will much exceed the expectation of any person who has not seen that apparatus. In truth it is immense. As to the price of the work it will be much greater than Congress is aware of, probably. I have enquired some-what into this circumstance, and find the prices of those made for two centuries past have been from 120,000 guineas down to 16,000 guineas, according to the size. And as far as I have seen, the smaller they are, the more agreeable. The smallest yet made is infinitely above the size of the life, and they all appear outrée and monstrous. That of Louis XV is probably the best in the world, and it is the smallest here. Yet it is impossible to find a point of view from which it does not appear a monster, unless you go so far as to lose sight of the features and finer lineaments of the face and body. A statue is not made, like a mountain, to be seen at a great distance. To perceive those minuter circumstances which constitute it's beauty you must be near it, and, in that case, it should be so little above the size of the life, as to appear actually of that size from your point of view. I should not therefore fear to propose that the one intended by Congress should be consider-ably smaller than any of those to be seen here; as I think it will be more beautiful, and also cheaper. I have troubled you with these observations as they have been suggested to me from an actual sight of works in this kind, and supposed they might assist you in making up your minds on this subject. In making a contract with Monsr. Houdon it would not be proper to advance money, but as his disbursements and labour advance. As it is a work of many years, this will render the expence insensible. The pedestrian statue of marble is to take three years, the equestrian of course much more. Therefore the sooner it is begun the better. I have the honour to be with the highest respect Gentlemen your most obedient & most humble servt.,   TH: JEFFERSON

RC (Musée de la Coopération Franco-Américaine, Blérancourt, Aisne, France, 1949); endorsed. PrC (DLC); lacks complimentary close and signature, which in RC were carried over to third page; part of first page torn away. Re-corded in SJL as sent by Houdon. Entry in SJL reads: "Virginia delegation in Congress. See copy by Houdon" (but see note to TJ to Governor of Virginia, 11 July 1785).

To Louis Alexandre

Paris, 13 July 1785. The text of this letter is identical with TJ's letter to P. & V. French & Nephew of this date, q.v.

PrC (MHi); 1 p.; at foot of letter: "Lewis Alexander." Entry for this letter in SJL follows that for "French & Nephew" and reads: "L. Alexander. Verbatim the same. By post."

To Jean François Briet

Sir   Paris July 13. 1785.

I am glad to hear that the council have ordered restitution of the merchandize seized in l'Orient contrary to the freedom of the place. When a court of justice has taken cognisance of a complaint and have given restitution of the principal subject, if it refuses some of the accessories, we are to presume that some circumstances of evidence appeared to them, unknown to us, and which rendered it's refusal just and proper. As in the present case if any circumstances in the conduct of the owner, or relative to the merchandize itself gave probable grounds of suspicion that they were not entitled to the freedom of the port, damages for the detention might be properly denied. Respect for the integrity of courts of justice and especially of so high a one as that of the king's council obliges us to presume that circumstances arose which justified this part of their order. It is only in cases where justice is palpably denied that one nation, or it's ministers, are authorized to complain of the courts of another. I hope you will see therefore that an application from me as to the damages for detention would be improper.

I have the honour to be Sir Your most obedient humble servt.,

TH: JEFFERSON

PrC (DLC). Entry in SJPL reads: "Briet. His case." See Briet to TJ, 20 June 1785.

To B. Contée

[*Paris, 13 July 1785.* Entry in SJL reads: "B. Contee. Bayonne. See copy. By post (copy lost or mislaid)." Neither the copy that TJ "lost or mislaid" nor the RC has been found; see Contée's letter of 18 July 1785.]

To P. & V. French & Nephew

Gentlemen   Paris July 13. 1785.

I had the honour of your letter of June 21. inclosing one from Mr. Alexander of June 17. and a copy of his application to Monsr. de Calonnes. I am very sensible that no trade can be on a more desperate footing than that of tobacco in this country; and that our merchants must abandon the French markets if they are not permitted[1] to sell the productions they bring on such terms as will enable them to purchase reasonable returns in the manufactures of France. I know but one remedy to the evil; that of allowing a free vent: and I should be very happy in being instrumental to the obtaining this. But while the purchase of tobacco is monopolized by a company, and they pay for that monopoly a heavy price to the government, they doubtless are at liberty to fix such places and terms of purchase as may enable them to make good their engagements with government. I see no more reason for obliging them to give a greater price for tobacco than they think they can afford than to do the same between two individuals treating for a horse, a house, or any thing else. Could this be effected by applications to the minister, it would only be a palliative which would retard the ultimate cure which every friend to this country as well as to America should wish for and aim at.

I have the honour to be Gentlemen Your most obedient humble servt.,
TH: JEFFERSON

PrC (DLC). Entry in SJPL reads: "French & nephew. Monopoly of tobacco."

YOUR LETTER OF JUNE 21: This sentence appears both in PrC of the present letter and in that to Alexandre of this date. It refers only to the letter of French & Nephew of 21 June, of course, but the appearance of the sentence in the PrC of both letters and the identity of the copies in all respects show that both were made from the same prototype. In view of this (and the fact that the SJL entry for the letter to Alexander states that it was a ver-batim copy of that to French & Nephew), it is clear that TJ must have made three PrC from the RC of the letter to French & Nephew—one on which the present text is based, one retained as a file copy of the letter to Alexandre, and one actually sent to Alexandre. Perhaps the last was altered in salutation, opening sentence, and complimentary close to make it suitable to its use.

[1] This word interlined in substitution for "enabled," deleted.

From John Jay

DR. SIR   Office for foreign Affairs 13th July 1785

Since mine to you of the 15th. June last which mentioned the Receipt of such of your Letters as had then come to Hand, I have not been favored with any from you. Those Letters were immediately laid before Congress, and are still under their Consideration. Whether any and what further Resolutions or Instructions will result from their Deliberations is as yet uncertain and therefore lest their Sentiments and mine should clash I forbear saying anything officially on the Subject for the present.

The Convention respecting Consuls, or rather a Copy of it sent by Doctr. Franklin has also been received and laid before Congress. They have taken it into Consideration but have as yet come to no Resolutions.

We have Intelligence (which though not entirely authentic is believed by many) that the British are enticing our People to settle Lands within our Lines under their Government and Protection by gratuitous Supplies of Provisions, Implements of Husbandry &ca. The truth of this Report will soon be ascertained. I wish it may prove groundless; if true, the Evacuation of the frontier Posts is not to be expected, and another War is to be looked and prepared for.

We suppose but have not heard that Mr. Adams is in London. We are anxious to receive Letters from him, and to learn with certainty the Intentions of that Court with Respect to those Posts and other interesting Subjects.

Mr. Gardoqui has at length arrived. He is charged with the Affairs of Spain, with plenipotentiary Powers.

Congress appointed Governor Livingston to succeed Mr. Adams at the Hague, but he declining it they have since elected Governor Rutledge, whose Answer cannot be expected for some time yet.

I have the Honor to be &ca.,   JOHN JAY

FC (DNA: PCC, No. 121). Recorded in SJL as received 21 Aug. 1785.

From David Ramsay

SIR   New York July 13th. 1785

By the French packet which sailed on the fifteenth of June I did my self the honour to inclose to your care 184 pages of the history of the revolution of South Carolina with propositions relative to a translation of it into the French language. I now do myself the honor to inclose to you all that is now printed, which is to page 328.

M. De Marbois the Consul General of France has done me the honor to enclose a copy of it to Count Chatelleaux to interest him in the translation if it should be thought advisable. I therefore request that any thing which may be done in the matter may be done in concert with that Gentleman. From the infant state of literature in America I shall probably lose money by my publication in the United States. Unless nine hundred copies sell at four dollars a piece I shall not be reimbursed for the expences of the impression. I therefore wish that whatsoever may be done in Europe may be done in such a manner as will interest me in the profits as well as the bookseller and the Translator and Printer. The second volume will be much more interesting than the first as it will contain the campaigns of 1780 and 1781 in the Southern States inclusive of Lord Cornwallis's surrender. If a translation should not be thought advisable I am contentd, if it should I hold myself entitled to a share of the profits. Whatsoever you do I beg may be done in concert with M. De Marbois' correspondent.

I have shewn the whole manuscript to M. De Marbois who thinks it will bear a translation. I add that whatsoever you may do in the matter will be not only approved but received as a favor conferred on your most obedient most humble Servt.,

DAVID RAMSAY

RC (DLC); endorsed: "Ramsay. Dr. July 13. 1785 recd. Aug. 22. 1785 2d. lre. on subject of his work."

From John Bondfield

[*Bordeaux, after 14 July 1785.*] Sends TJ a copy of a letter received by the last post from Toulon, which indicates that the Algerines' activities are "influenced by other than their private piratical passion"; he will also advise Gov. Hancock.

Tr (DNA: PCC, No. 87, 1); 2 p.; in David Humphreys' hand; undated; at foot of letter: "No. 9." The text of Tr follows immediately after that of the letter transmitted—Soulange to the directors of commerce of Guienne Province, 14 July 1785, advising that Algiers had armed 8 vessels to cruise from Cape St. Vincent to the Azores against the Americans (in French, with an English translation). Tr (DNA: PCC, No. 107, 1). A similar letter, except for one additional paragraph in the covering letter, was sent by Bondfield to Thomas Barclay (DNA: PCC, No. 91, 1). A copy was also sent by TJ to John Jay as enclosure No. 9 to his second letter of 14 Aug. 1785. See also John Paul Jones to TJ, 31 July 1785.

To Anthony Garvey

SIR   Paris July 14. 1785.

Your kind offers of service have encouraged me to trouble you with an enquiry whether a pair of Norman horses can be readily bought at or near Rouen, black, four feet eight or nine inches high French measure, between five and six years old, geldings, handsome, and ready broke to the carriage, and what such a pair would probably cost there? Your information on this subject will be obliging. Before this reaches you I am in hopes Doctr. Franklin will have arrived at Rouen. I shall be anxious to hear how the motion of the litter has agreed with him, and how he stands the journey. Whenever you see Mr. Holker will you have the goodness to present to him my respects?

I have the honour to be with much regard Sir Your most obedient humble servt., TH: JEFFERSON

PrC (MHi). Not recorded in SJL.

To Jan Ingenhousz

[*Paris, 14 July 1785*. Entry in SJL reads: "Monsr. Ingenhausz medecin de la cour &c. &c. à Vienne. Inclosing Dr. Franklin's letter. Count Merci." Not found.]

To Charles Thomson

DEAR SIR   Paris July 14. 1785.

By Mr. Houdon I send you a copy of my notes. I also send 100 copies of the paper I left with you on our coinage. Printing is so cheap here (they cost me but a guinea) that I thought it worth while to print as many copies as would enable you to put one into the hands of every member of Congress when they should enter on the subject, and to do the same at any succeeding session when they should resume it, as I do not expect it will be taken up and finished at the same session, in which case there might be a great change of members. It will not be necessary for you to say they come from me. They may as well be supposed to be printed on the spot and of course in the ordinary way, which will be their presumption if nothing be said about it. Mr. Houdon comes to take the likeness in plaister of General Washington. He is the first statuary of the age. His eminence, his worth, and his errand will recommend him to your notice. I am Dr. Sir Your friend & servt.,

TH: JEFFERSON

RC (DLC: Thomson Papers, II); endorsed: "Mr. Jefferson's letters 21 June & 14 July 1785 answered Novr. 2. 1785." Entry in SJL reads: "Chas. Thomson. By Houdon with a copy of my Notes and 100 copies of those on coinage."

For an account of TJ's separately printed Notes on Coinage, see Document IV printed above at end of Apr. 1784. The decision to adopt the dollar as the money unit and to apply decimal reckoning to the money system was made by Congress only a few days before this letter was written (6 July 1785; JCC, XXIX, 499-500). The copy of *Notes on Virginia* sent to Thomson in Houdon's care is in CSmH.

From James Monroe

DEAR SIR   New York July 15. 1785.

By Mr. and Mrs. Macauly Graham I have the pleasure to transmit this. They intend immediately for the south of France and as from yours in March I had reason to suspect you intended thither I have suggested to them the probability of their meeting you in that quarter. This lady is the author of the history under her name. She hath been on a visit to Mount Vernon, hath been well receiv'd by Genl. Washington and returns to Europe under the most favorable impressions of him. If you should not be in the south of France as Mr. Graham intends visiting Paris I have thought proper to inclose you by him the journals publish'd since the departure of Mr. Mazzai. The report respecting the treaty with the western indians hath been adopted, except in the change of the place at which it will be held, being the mouth of the Big Miami or the falls of the Ohio, instead of Post Vincent, and the article respecting the people of the Kaskaskias and neighboring villages, which altho' first adopted was afterwards repeald, from an apprehension it would create too great an expence. The report proposing a change in the first paragraph of the 9th. of the articles of confederation hath been before Congress in a committee of the whole for two days past. The house are to take it up again on Monday in the same manner. It hath been fully discuss'd and in my opinion the reasons in favor of it are conclusive. The opposition however is respectable in point of numbers as well as talents, in one or two instances. From our State you will readily conjecture the sentiments of one, Hardy is for it, Grayson doubtful but I think rather in favor of it. Some gentlemen have inveterate prejudices against all attempts to increase the powers of Congress, others see the necessity but fear the consequences. It is propos'd by the latter and former classes that Congress form and recommend a navigation act to the states, to continue in form for a limited time. What will or will not be done ultimately in this business is incertain. The report upon the instructions hath been before Congress, and is referr'd to the consideration of some day next week. It will most probably be adopted. I have it in contemplation after a few weeks to sit out for the Ohio to attend the treaty above mention'd. This will complete my tour thro' the western country. I hope you have recoverd your health. Short also is I hope in good health and Miss Patsy. I am sorry to request you to inform Mr. Mazzai that I have heard nothing from those he left in pursuit of the money he lost. I fear it hath not been found. I am with great respect and esteem yr. friend & servant,   JAS. MONROE

P.S. Don diego de Gardoqui hath been presented to Congress. He produc'd a letter from the King with full powers to treat upon the subjects arising between us, yet his stile is Encargado de negotios. We have had some difficulty in regulating the etiquette respecting him, whether to consider him as a minister or Encargado de Negotios, or chargé des affaires, and to avoid giving offence we have us'd the terms us'd by his master. We hope it will have the desir'd effect. A letter from the King with full powers I should suppose constituted the minister be the term or stile what it may.

RC (DLC); endorsed. Recorded in SJL as received 11 Jan. 1786.

From John Adams

DEAR SIR   Grosvenor Square Westminster, the Corner of Duke and Brook Streets July 16th. 1785

I have been so perplexed with Ceremonials, Visits, Removals and eternal applications from Beggars of one Species and another, besides the real Business of my Department, that I find I have not answered your favour of the second of June, which I received in Season. I have received from Mr. Garvey all but my wine and have written him to day to forward that and will run the risque of it, as I believe I shall easily obtain an order to receive it without paying duties. Petits Note of Expences which you paid, you either omitted to send me or I have lost it in the Confusion of a Removal, so that I must trouble you to send it again.[1]

As to News Papers, I should advise you to apply to the Comte de Vergennes or Mr. Rayneval or Mr. Gennet the Premier Commis of the Bureau des Interpretes, who, I presume will readily order your Gazettes to come with their own, through the same Channel, free of Expence for Postage. The father of the present Mr. Gennet was so good as to oblige me in this way in the year 1780.

I wrote to you and Dr. Franklin on the 20th. of June, requesting you to send me a Project of a Treaty of Commerce with this Court, and proposed that agreed on with Prussia as the Model. Let me beg your answer to this as soon as possible.

The Doctor is to embark at Spithead or the Isle of White, on board of Captain Truckston as he tells me.

The proceedings at Boston make a Sensation here. Yours most affectionately,   JOHN ADAMS

RC (DLC); in W. S. Smith's hand, signed by Adams. FC (MHi: AMT); in Adams' hand, with several minor variations in phraseology. Recorded in SJL as received 24 July 1785.

1 At this point in RC, TJ made a note of the amount: "173 f. 8."

From Plowden Garvey

Rouen, 16 July 1785. Acknowledges TJ's letter of 14 July, which in the absence of Anthony Garvey he communicated to "our Common Worthy Friend Mr. Holker." They are all anxious to be of help concerning the horses TJ wants and will continue to search, but Holker thinks "you could procure them easier, better and cheaper in Paris than here, as there are frequently people who wish to part with theirs. Another thing the Coach Horses here are much larger than those you want, a pair of which would cost 17 to 1800." They also suggest that TJ would "do well on your side to enquire on the spot, particularly at the Houses of whom the holders may die." Garvey reports that "Doctr. Franklin arrived yesterday in good health, and supported the Fatigue much better than his age could have made him expect."

RC (MHi); 1 p.

To Ezra Stiles

SIR   Paris July 17. 1785.

I have long deferred doing myself the honour of writing to you, wishing for an opportunity to accompany my letter with a copy of the Bibliotheque Physico-œconomique, a book published here lately in four small volumes, and which gives an account of all the improvements in the arts which have been made for some years past. I flatter myself you will find in it many things agreeable and useful. I accompany it with the volumes of the Connoissance des tems for the years 1781. 1784. 1785. 1786. 1787. But why, you will ask, do I send you old almanachs, which are proverbially useless? Because in these publications have appeared from time to time some of the most precious things in astronomy. I have searched out those particular volumes which might be valuable to you on this account. That of 1781. contains de la Caille's catalogue of fixed stars reduced to the commencement of that year, and a table of the Aberrations and Nutations of the principal stars. 1784 contains the same catalogue with the Nebuleuses of Messier. 1785 contains the famous catalogue of Flamsteed with the positions of the stars reduced to the beginning of the year 1784. and which supersedes the use of that immense book. 1786 gives you Euler's Lunar tables corrected; and 1787 the tables for the planet Herschel. The two last needed not an apology, as not being within the description of old almanachs. It is fixed on grounds which scarcely admit a doubt that the planet Herschel was seen by Mayer in the year 1756. and was considered by him as one of the Zodiacal stars, and as such arranged in his catalogue, being the 964th. which he describes. This 964th. of Mayer has been since missing, and the calculations for the planet Herschel shew that it should have been at the time of Mayer's observation where he places his 964th. star. The volume of 1787. gives you Mayer's Catalogue of the Zodiacal stars. The researches of the Natural philosophers of Europe seem mostly in the field of chemistry, and here principally on the subjects of air and fire. The analysis of these two subjects presents to us very new ideas. When speaking of the Bibliotheque physico-œconomique, I should have observed that since it's publication a man in this city has invented a method of moving a vessel on the water by a machine worked within the vessel. I went to see it. He did not know himself the principle of his own invention. It is a screw with a very broad thin worm, or rather it is a thin plate with it's edge applied spirally round an axis. This being turned operates on the air as a screw does, and may be literally said to screw the vessel along: the thinness of the medium and it's want of resistance occasions a loss of much of the force. The screw I think would be more effectual if placed below the surface of the water. I very much suspect that a countryman of ours, Mr. Bushnel of Connecticut is entitled to the merit of a prior discovery of this use of the screw. I remember to have heard of his submarine navigation during the war, and from what Colo. Humphreys now tells me I conjecture that the screw was the power he used. He joined to this a machine for exploding under water at a given moment. If it were not too great a liberty for a stranger to take I would ask from him a narration of his actual experiments, with or without a communication of his principle as he should chuse. If he thought proper to communicate it I would engage never to disclose it unless I could find an opportunity of doing it for his benefit. I thank you for your information as to the great bones found on the Hudson's river. I suspect that these must have been of the same animal with those found on the Ohio: and if so, they could not have belonged to any human figure, because they are accompanied with tusks of the size, form and substance of those of the elephant. I have seen of the ivory, which was very good. The animal itself must have been much larger than an elephant. Mrs. Adams gives me an account of a flower found in Connecticut which vegetates when suspended in the air. She brought one to Europe. What can be this flower? It would be a curious present to this continent.

The accomodation likely to take place between the Dutch and the Emperor leaves us without that unfortunate resource for news which wars give us. The Emperor has certainly had in view the Bavarian exchange of which you have heard: but so formidable an opposition presented itself, that he has thought proper to disavow it. The Turks shew a disposition to go to war with him. But if this country can prevail on them to remain in peace they will do so. It has been thought that the two Imperial courts have a plan of expelling the Turks from Europe. It is really a pity so charming a country should remain in the hands of a people whose religion forbids the admission of science and the arts among them. We should wish success to the object of the two empires if they meant to leave the country in possession of the Greek inhabitants. We might then expect once more to see the language of Homer and Demosthenes a living language. For I am persuaded the modern greek would easily get back to it's classical models. But this is not intended. They only propose to put the Greeks under other masters: to substitute one set of Barbarians for another.

Colo. Humphreys having satisfied you that all attempts would be fruitless here to obtain money or other advantages for your college I need add nothing on that head. It is a method of supporting colleges of which they have no idea, tho' they practise it for the support of their lazy monkish institutions.

I have the honour to be with the highest respect and esteem Sir Your most obedient & most humble servt.,   Th: Jefferson

RC (MHi); endorsed: "Recd. Oct 7 1785. Ansd. Ansd. again May 8 1786." PrC (DLC); at foot of first page: "Dr. Styles." Entry in SJL reads: "Dr. Ezra Stiles with Bibliotheque Physico-oeconomique. Connoissance des tems. See Copy. By Houdon"; entry in SJPL reads: "Styles Ezra. Books. Herschel. Chemistry. Screw vessel. Bushnel. Giants. Turkey. Modern Greeks." In his diary for 18 Oct. 1785 Stiles wrote: "Recd. sundry Letters. I lately recd one from Govr. Jefferson Ambassador dated Paris in which he informs me he has sent me Connoisance de Temps 4 v.8vo. and Bibliotheque Œconomique et Philosophique 4 v.12. also that a Parisian has made a new Invention to sail a

Vessel by a spiral Sail on an Axis which screws the vessel along" (MS in CtY).

On David Bushnell's PRIOR DISCOVERY, see TJ to Hugh Williamson, 6 Feb. 1785, note; TJ to Washington, 17 July 1785; Washington to TJ, 26 Sep. 1785.

To George Washington

SIR   Paris July 17. 1785.

Permit me to add, what I forgot in my former letter, a request to you to be so kind as to communicate to me what you can recollect of Bushnel's experiments in submarine navigation during the late war, and whether you think his method capable of being used succesfully for the destruction of vessels of war. It's not having been actually used for this purpose by us, who were so peculiarly in want of such an agent seems to prove it did not promise success. I am with the highest esteem Sir Your most obedt. & most humble servt.,   TH: JEFFERSON

RC (Mr. Justin G. Turner, Hollywood, California, 1952). PrC (DLC). Recorded in SJL as sent by Houdon; entry in SJPL reads: "Washington Genl. Bushnel's submarine."

For David Humphreys' account of BUSHNEL'S EXPERIMENTS (he may have been an eyewitness of the attempt on the British fleet in New York Harbor), see F. L. Humphreys, *Life and Times of David Humphreys*, I, 73-4. Humphreys probably related a similar account to TJ.

From John Adams

DEAR SIR   Grosvenor Square July 18th. 1785

Your Favours of June 22d. and July 7 and 11th. are before me. The delay of Mr. Lamb's arrival is unfortunate, but I think with you that the sooner a project of Treaties is prepared the better, and I will give the earliest attention to it whenever you shall send it. I shall go this morning to Stockdale, to talk with him about sending you the News Papers, and Pamphlets through the Channell of Cleveland Row, i.e. Lord Carmarthens office.

I agree with pleasure to the appointment made by the Doctor and you of Mr. Short, to carry the treaty through London to the Hague, and in joining Mr. Dumas with him in making the Exchange. A Letter to him and another to Mr. Dumas signed by you and me, as the Doctor is gone, would be sufficient Authority: But I shall have no objection of giving each of them a more formal Commission under our Hands and seals, to be our Secretaries specially *pro hac Vice*. He must carry our original Commission to shew to the Baron De Thulemeyer and a Copy of it attested by Colo. Humphries to deliver him, and Mr. Dumas and he should see the Prussian Commission and receive an attested Copy of that. I do not think of any other Papers necessary.[1]

I have given to Lord Carmarthen long ago, an Explanation of the power of Congress to form Treaties of Commerce, exactly conformable to that which you gave the English Gentleman, but I did not extend it to the Case of Consuls. He asked me no questions concerning Consuls, and I did not think it proper for me to say any thing on that subject, not having any Instructions. But I am not easy on that head. Mr. Temple talks of going out in three or four weeks, but I am very apprehensive he will meet with the difficulties you foresee.

I will enquire about insuring 20,000 Livres on the Life of Mr. Houdon. I have written to Mr. Frazier, the Under Secretary of State in Lord Carmarthens office, concerning Dr. Franklins Baggage, have stated the Circumstances as you State them to me, and have solicited the necessary Facilities. I hope for a favourable answer. Truxtun is to depart from hence on Thursday, and I will let him know the answer I may have.

I[2] *don't like the symptoms. Galloway, Deane, Chalmers, Watson are too much in favor. The Lottery for the Tories, although perhaps in Part inevitable, has been introduced with such pompous demonstrations of affection and approbation as are neither wise, nor honest. There is too much attention to the Navy, and there is another step, which allarms my apprehensions. Hanover is joining Prussia against the Views of the two Imperial Courts at least in Bavaria.* Keep this as secret as the grave, but search it to the botom[3] where you are. *Does this indicate a Doubt Whether our Business with De Thulemeyer* may be delayed? Does it indicate a design in the *British Cabinet,*[4] *to be Neutral* in order to be more *at Leisure to deal with us? Can it be a Secret Understanding between St. James's and Versailles?*[5] The *disigns* of *ruining, if they can our carrying Trade, and annihilating all our Navigation, and Seamen is too apparent.* Yours sincerely,   JOHN ADAMS

RC (DLC); in W. S. Smith's hand, signed by Adams; partly in code; accompanied by a separate leaf bearing TJ's decoding. FC (MHi: AMT). Recorded in SJL as received 24 July 1785.

[1] The following passage in FC was deleted by Adams: "But, from some Intelligence I am not without fear, that this Business may be delayed."

[2] This and subsequent words in italics are written in code in RC and were decoded by TJ on a separate leaf, employing Code No. 8. The text presented here is taken from FC, where the paragraph is preceded by a note in Adams'

hand which reads: "The Rest to be in
Cypher and kept Secret."
³ FC has the following not in RC:
"among the foreign Ministers."

⁴ TJ's reading: "court."
⁵ TJ's reading for the preceding four
words: "England and France."

From B. Contée

Bayonne, 18 July 1785. He had written on 28 June, stating that he was offered by Moracin (receiver of the Farmers-General at Bayonne) only 35 livres per quintal for 450 hogsheads of tobacco landed there, though he had previously been led to expect a higher price than that of 44 livres already refused. Since such a breach of faith is detrimental to sound commercial relations, he had urged that the matter be taken up at Versailles, and now asks advice. Maryland tobacco sells there at 40 or 41 livres and has been purchased by Moracin, though it arrived after Contée's shipment and long after he had contracted to deliver it.

RC (DLC); 2 p.; at foot of letter: "The Honble. Benjamin Franklin Esqr. in his absence the Honble. the Minister of the united States of America, at the Court of Versailles; endorsed by TJ. Recorded in SJL as received 1 Aug. 1785.

To Benjamin Franklin

SIR   Paris July 18. 1785.

I heard with much pleasure yesterday of your safe arrival at Rouen, and that you had not been much fatigued with the journey. This gives me hopes that you will find less difficulty in the rest of the voiage. On my parting with you at Passy I went to the Duke of Dorset's. He was not at home. I asked an hour the next day and waited on him. He promised to write the necessary letters to England to protect your baggage. Independantly of this I wrote to Mr. Adams by Mr. Harrison who left this the day before you. I hope therefore that between the two agents you will meet with no difficulty at Cowes. We have nothing new since your departure worth your notice. A Monsr. Duplessis called here to desire me to have copied for you a long memoire on some animals (I think) of South America. I knew neither the person nor subject, nor how far it might be interesting to you, and as it appeared to contain many sheets of paper, and I had no secretary, I declined copying it myself. If it is any thing you wish to see and will drop me a line I will have it copied. Be pleased to make my compliments to your grandsons and be assured of the esteem with which I have the honour to be Sir Your most obedt. humble servt.,

TH: JEFFERSON

RC (PU); addressed: "A son Ex-
cellence Monsr. Franklin ministre pleni-
potre. des Etats unis chez Monsr.
Limousin à Havre"; wax seal affixed.
Entry in sjl reads: "Dr. Franklin.
Measures taken to protect his baggage.
Duplessy's memoire. By Houdon."

The NECESSARY LETTERS were effective. On 25 July Franklin noted in his
journal: "Mr. Williams brought a letter from Mr. Nepean, secretary to Lord
Townshend, addressed to Mr. Vaughan,
expressing that orders would be sent
to the custom-house at Cowes not to
trouble our baggage, &c. It is still here
on board the packet that brought it
over" (*Writings*, ed. Smyth, x, p. 470).

From Samuel Henley

Rendlesham, near Melton & Ipswich in Suffolk

MY DEAR SIR   July 18. 1785.

I was much mortified to find that you had been in England some time before I knew it, and was gone from hence at the instant I was projecting a journey to pay my respects to you.

Give me leave to congratulate you on your being appointed Ambassador to the Court of France; a circumstance no less honour-able to your Country than Yourself. I shall be happy to know that Mrs. Jefferson and your family are well, and should rejoice beyond measure to see you. The Gentleman who will deliver this letter is a friend of mine, and a fellow of Benet College in the University of Cambridge. You will find him an amiable man, and capable of gratifying your curiosity in a thousand particulars. If you could spare the time to inform me of any of our old friends across the Atlantic, the state of the College at Williamsburgh, the fate of my books, &c. he will take the charge of what you might be disposed to communicate. Should there be anything in England you could wish to know from me, I should be happy to satisfy your inquiries.

Different as our situations are from what they on[ce] were, I shall ever look back with sincere pleasure on the friendship with which you honoured me and shall always be proud to subscribe myself, most sincerely Your's,   S. HENLEY

RC (MHi); addressed: "The Honourable Thos. Jefferson Ambassador
from the United States of America to
the Court of France"; endorsed. Recorded in sjl as received 1 Aug. 1785.

Henley had not received TJ's letter of
3 Mch. 1785 at the time the present
letter was written; see TJ to Henley,
14 Oct. 1785.

From Jean Holker

MONSIEUR   Rouen ce 18. Juillet 1785.

Jai eu la satisfaction pendant deux jours de posseder ici notre Vénérable ami Le Docteur franklin. Il a suporté le voyage d'une maniere surprenante. Il est réparti hier pour Le havre, je l'ai accompagné pendant trois Lieues, j'espere qu'il arrivera dans ce port de mer en bonne Santé.

Pendant son sejour ici on à visité et parcouru avec son fils les divers Bureaux de la Douanne, mais inutilement, la Caisse de Livres que vous et le Docteur franklin reclamés ne s'y est pas trouvée. J'ai fait venir avec son Registre le Courtier anglois qui a fait faire La Decharge du Navire du Capt. Brooks et nous nous sommes convaincus qu'il n'est arrivé par ce Navire que La seule Caisse qui contenoit Votre presse. M. franklin doit ecrire à Londres pour être informé de la raison de cette négligence, etant constant que Votre Caisse de Livres n'a point eté expediée.

Le Courtier m'a demandé 9.ᵗᵗ pour Les frais de votre Caisse qui a esté retirée de la Douanne, vous en avés c'y joint la quitance. Cest un malheur, que Votre correspondant à Londres n'ait donné avis à personne ici, cela auroit évité bien des frais et de l'embarras.

Je suis avec une respectueuse consideration Monsieur Votre tres humble & tres obeissant Serviteur, 	J HOLKER

RC (MHi). Franklin traveled from Passy to Havre in a royal litter. "I found that the motion of the litter," he wrote in his journal, "lent me by the Duke of Coigny, did not much incommode me. It was one of the queen's, carried by two very large mules, the muleteer riding another." At Rouen Franklin and his party stopped with Holker: "We got to Rouen about five; were most affectionately received by Mr. and Mrs. Holker. A great company of genteel people at supper, which was our dinner. . . . We lodge all at Mr. Holker's. . . . July 17th. Set out early. Mr. Holker accompanied us some miles, when we took an affectionate leave of each other" (Smyth, ed., *Writings*, x, 464-7; for an account of Franklin's departure from Passy and journey to Havre, see Van Doren, *Franklin*, p. 724-5).

From De Thulemeier

MONSIEUR 	à la Haye le 19e Juillet 1785.

Le Roi a parfaitement approuvé le Projet du Traité de Commerce et d'Amitié avec les Etats Unis de l'Amérique, tel qu'il a été le résultat de nos soins communs, et tel qu'il s'est trouvé consigné à la suite de la dernière lettre dont Vous m'avez honoré en date du 26 Mai de l'année courante. Sa Majesté agrée de plus que d'après Votre proposition, Monsieur, et celle de Messieurs Vos Collégues la durée préalable du dit Traité soit fixée à dix années, et c'est en conséquence de mes instructions que dans l'Article 27, le terme mentionné a été exprimé. Elle m'ordonne de procéder actuellement à la signature requise avec Messieurs les Ministres des Etats de l'Amérique Unie, et de diriger sous Leur bon plaisir l'introduction en conformité de celle qui a été usitée dans le Traité de Commerce conclu avec le Roi de Suède. La copie ci-jointe du Traité que je me propose de munir de ma signature en conformité de mes pleinpouvoirs, remplit ces différens objets et il ne me reste uniquement qu'à Vous rappeler, Monsieur, la proposition que j'ai pris la liberté de Vous faire par ma lettre datée du 17. de Juin passé, d'autoriser Mr. le Chargé d'affaires Dumas à la Haye de procéder avec moi à l'échange usité. Le Roi n'attend que l'envoi de l'exemplaire auquel Messieurs les Plénipotentiaires Américains auront apposé leur Signature, pour faire expédier Sa Ratification de la manière usitée.

J'ai l'honneur d'être avec la considération la plus distinguée, Monsieur, Votre très humble et très obéissant Serviteur,

DE THULEMEIER

P.S. Oserois-je me flatter, Monsieur, que Vous Vous chargeriez de faire passer en Amérique la lettre ci jointe pour Mr. le Général de Steuben; elle m'a été envoiée par une de ses parentes.

RC (DNA: PCC, No. 86); in a clerk's hand, signed by De Thulemeier, endorsed. Tr (DNA: PCC, No. 87, I); in Humphreys' hand, with a translation by John Pintard. Tr (DNA: PCC, No. 116); in Humphreys' hand; at head of letter: "A letter from Baron de Thulemeier. enclosing a french translation of the Treaty with Prussia as agreed on both parts." Tr (MHi: AMT); lacks complimentary close, signature, and postscript. Tr (DLC: PCC, No. 107, I); with an English translation. A copy of the covering letter was sent by TJ to John Jay as enclosure No. 1 in his second letter of 14 Aug. 1785. Enclosures: (1) An unidentified letter to Steuben. (2) Text of the treaty in French as agreed upon and as completed in the particulars described in the present letter (DNA: PCC, No. 116).

From William Temple Franklin

DEAR SIR   Havre, 20th. July 1785.

I know you will learn with Pleasure that my Grandfather has been able to effect his Journey hither without any addition to his usual Sufferings; and that he is in good Health and Spirits. He does not now forsee any Difficulty in getting to America. The Bargain with Capt. Truxton is terminated, and he is to be at Cowes by the 1st. August. We wait here only for the Arrival of part of our Baggage, which comes by Water from Rouen, and which we expect in a Day or two. We shall then probably freight a small Vessel to carry us to the Isle of Wight. But whether our Baggage arrives here or no, we shall certainly leave this by the

26th. Mr. Hudon therefore should not delay his Departure, if he means to accompany us.

During our short Stay at Rouen, I made all possible Inquiry concerning the Box of Papers missing which contained your Books, and went myself to the Custom House and examined every Case lying there, and even open'd some that I suspected might be it, but all to no purpose. I now begin to think that the Captain never deliver'd it, as I could find no trace of it or the Books. I shall therefore write immediately to Mr. Woodmason, requesting him to recover the Case of the Captain, or the Value thereof, if the Delivery of the same at the Custom House at Rouen cannot be proved. In packing up my Papers at Passy, I found the Captains Receipt for the *two* Cases, and had it with me at Rouen, where I believe I left it with Mr. Holker, as I cannot find it at present. It is on a small Fragment of Paper, and by no means so particular as I could wish. I did not attend to this at the time, relying entirely on Mr. Woodmason's experience in Business of such a nature. If I remember right, the Ships Name was the *Holham* and the Captains *Brookes*. If Mr. Woodmason does not however replace your Books, I shall consider myself as bound to do it; and I hereby desire Mr. Grand to procure them for you on my Account.

Permit me, my dear Sir, before I conclude to make you my most thankful Acknowledgements for the several Marks of Friendship you have been pleased to confer on me during our short Acquaintance; and particularly for the favorable Opinion you are pleased to entertain and give of me to your Friends, in the Introductory Letters you have honor'd me with. Believe me I am extreamly sensible of all your Kindness, and that it will ever be my Ambition to merit your Esteem, which alone can entitle me to a continuation of the Favors you have already confer'd on Dear Sir, Your most affectionate & grateful humble Servant,

W. T. FRANKLIN

My Grandfather desires me to present you his most affectionate Respects and joins me in best Wishes for your Health and Happiness.

P.S. Mr. Hudon is just arrived.

RC (DLC); endorsed.
The INTRODUCTORY LETTERS were those by TJ to Hardy, Madison, and Monroe, 4 July 1785; see also TJ to Monroe, 5 July 1785.

From Benjamin Franklin

SIR   Havre, July 21. 1785.

I have just received your Favour of the 18th. I thank you for
the Steps you took with the Duke of Dorset, and with Mr. Adams;
and hope they will prove effectual. I arrived here extreamly well,
not at all hurt or fatigued by the Carriage I us'd, which I found
generally very gentle. I embark this Evening for Cowes with Mr.
Houdon. I have seen that M. du Plessis twice. He appears a Man
of some Intelligence, born and bred in the East Indies. I know not
what his Manuscript is; but if on looking it over you should think
it of sufficient Importance, I wish you would put it into the Hands
of Mr: Lamotte my late Clerk, who will transcribe it for me. My
best Wishes attend you, being with sincere Esteem, Sir, Your
most obedient & most humble Servant,   B. FRANKLIN

Messrs. Bache and Franklin are very sensible of Mr. Jefferson's
kind Remembrances, and present him their most affectionate
Respects.

RC (DLC); in Franklin's hand, except for the postscript, which is in the hand
of William Temple Franklin; endorsed.

From De Pio

ce Jeudy [21 July 1785]

Mr. de Pio, Chargé d'Affaires du Roy de Naples, ayant oublié
quelqu'article de la conversation qu'il a eu avec Monsieur Jefferson Mardy à Versailles au sujet des denrées de l'Amerique Septentrionale, qu'on pourraient importer en Europe, et particulierement
dans les Ports des Siciles; il prie Mr. Jefferson de vouloir bien lui
dire, si outre les *Tabacs*, et les *Poissons salés* il y en a d'autres.

Mr. de Pio demande bien pardon de la liberté qu'il prend, n'osant
pas de venir l'importuner personnellement, et il a l'honneur de lui
faire ses trés humbles complimens.

RC (MHi); without date; endorsed: "Naples, Chargé des affaires." Date assigned from internal evidence; TJ's entry in Account Book under 19 July [i.e.,
Tuesday] 1785, reads: "paid chair hire at Versailles 1f4." See reply, following.

To De Pio

Monsr. Jefferson a l'honneur de souhaiter le bonjour à Monsr. de Pio. Les denrées que les Etats Unis d'Amerique exportent *en quantité* sont le riz, l'indigo, le goudron, le tabac, le blé, le chanvre, la potasse, les poissons salés, et les bois de construction. Les marchandises que les habitants des Etats unis prendront en echange seront les vins, les eaux de vie, l'huile, les fruits secs et confits, les soies, les manufactures de toute espece, et surtout les fabriques de laine, de coton, de lin, de fer et des autres metaux. On ne verra point, ou que tres peu, de batimens Americains dans la Mediterranée jusques à ce que nous aurons fait des arrangemens avec les barbaresques, mais, cela fait, nous y commercerons beaucoup, comme nous avons toujours fait avant la revolution sous pavillon Anglois.

PrC (MoSHi); endorsed: "Pio, Chevalr. de."

From Francis Hopkinson

MY DEAR SIR   Philada. July 23d. 1785

In Obedience to your Request I some Time since forwarded a Packet of our News papers to Mr. Jameison at New York to be transmitted to you. You will herewith receive a second Exportation. You will see by them that the present object of popular attention is the investing Congress with more executive Power, and giving a Check to the Importation of British Manufactures.

We are daily looking for the Arrival of Dr. Franklin amongst us, but as there is no certain Account of his having actually embarked, the matter may be considered as somewhat uncertain.

I have not heard from you a long Time. From your last I have given up all Expectation of deriving any Benefit from my new Method of quilling the Harpsichord further than the 30 Guineas allowed by Mr. Broadwood in the Price of my new Harpsichord, the Satisfaction I have in finding on fair Experiment that it answers the Purpose intended, and the Honour of the Invention. Since that however I have discovered another Method of quilling that Instrument upon principles entirely new, which I think still preferable—In as much as the Tone produced is much more full and round, and at the same Time perfectly sweet and free from that Jingle for which the best Harpsichords have been censured. It increases the Tone to at least double the force or Magnitude without any Diminution of Sweetness or any concomitant Imperfection that I can discover. I will shortly send you a Model of my Discovery. At present I cannot do it.

Mr. Rittenhouse has been in the West Country all Summer engaged in running the Lines of this State and not yet returned.

I have no News, and if I had, have not Time for Communication.

My Mother is well and desires her affectionate Regards to Miss Patsey. Adieu. Your's sincerely, F: HOPKINSON

RC (MHi); endorsed. Recorded in SJL as received 18 Sep. 1785.

From John Adams

DEAR SIR   Grosvenor Square July 24th. 1785

I have a Letter from the Baron De Thulemeier of the 19th. and a Copy of his Letter to you of the same date. I hope now in a few Day's to take Mr. Short by the hand in Grosvenor Square and to put my hand to the treaty. I think no time should be lost. We will join Mr. Dumas with Mr. Short in the Exchange if you please.

I applyed as you desired, and obtained the interposition of the Lords Commissioners of the treasury, and the Commissioners of the Customs for the transhipping of Dr. Franklin's Baggage. We have heared of the Doctor's arrival at Rouen, but no further.

The[1] Britons[2] Alliens Duty is a very burthensome Thing, and they may carry it hereafter as far upon Tobacco, Rice Indigo and twenty other Things, as they do now upon oil. To obviate this, I think of substituting the words "natural born Citizens of the United States," and "natural born subjects of Great Britain," instead of "the most favoured Nation." You remember We first proposed to offer this to all Nations, but upon my objecting that the English would make their ships French or Sweedish or Dutch &c. to avail themselves of it, without agreeing to it, on their Part, we altered it to the footing of "Gentis Amicissimae." But if the English will now agree to it, we shall secure ourselves against many odious Duties, and no ill Consequence can arise. It is true the French Dutch Sweeds and Prussians[3] will of Course claim the Advantage, but as they must in return allow Us the same Advantage, so much the better. Let me know if any Objection occurs to you.

[310]

There is a Bill before Parliament to prevent smuggling Tobacco, in which the restrictions are very rigorous, but cannot be effected.[4] Two thirds of the Tobacco consumed in this Kingdom, I am told is Smuggled. How can it be otherwise, when the impost is five times the original Value of the Commodity. If one Pound in five escapes nothing is lost. If two in five, a great profit is made. The Duty is 16d. pr. pound and tobacco sells for three pence. Yet all applications for lowering the Duty are rejected.[5] Yours most affectionately,

JOHN ADAMS

RC (DLC); in W. S. Smith's hand, signed by Adams; partly in code, with a separate leaf bearing TJ's decoding. FC (MHi: AMT). Recorded in SJL as received 30 July 1785.

On this same day Adams acknowledged receipt of A LETTER FROM THE BARON DE THULEMEIER and also a copy of De Thulemeier's letter "to my Colleague Mr. Jefferson" of 19 July. "It is with great Pleasure I learn," he wrote, "that the Articles of the Treaty between his Prussian Majesty and the United States are all agreed on to mutual Satisfaction, and I hope in a very few days to have the Honor of putting my Hand to it here. Mr. Short will bring it from Paris signed and sealed by Mr. Jefferson, and will carry it from hence to you signed and sealed by me. Mr. Dumas will be joined with Mr. Short in making the Exchange with you. Mr. Short is a very respectable Gentleman of Virginia, a late Member of their Council, and an intimate Friend of Mr. Jefferson.—Will you give me leave, sir, to inquire what are the Imposts upon our Tobacco in the Prussian Ports, and whether there is or may be any large Consumption of that Commodity in Prussia? The Principal Difficulty we have in Trade is to make Remittances, and we cannot trade to any large Amount with any Nation that cannot or will not receive the Produce of our Lands or Seas. Indigo is another Article which I wish to know, if it finds a Market in Prussia,

and Oil, especially Sperma Coeti oil and candles. With what kind of oil are your Cities illuminated in the Night? The Sperma Coeti oil gives the purest Flame and the clearest Light that is known. A Lamp in a City, lighted up with this Oil, at six oClock in the Evening will burn bright, until Nine the next Morning, whereas the Oil that is now used in the Lamps of London do not feed a flame longer than Eleven or Twelve oClock, the Consequence of which is that the Rogues take advantage of the Darkness after Midnight to commit Robberies and Burglaries without Number and even many Murthers, and many People had rather Suffer all these Crimes, or even introduce a military Police, than inlighten their Streets with American Sperma Coeti oil. If Prussia and Germany would have more wisdom it would greatly promote Trade between them and America" (Adams to De Thulemeier, 24 July 1785; MHi: AMT).

[1] This paragraph is written in code and was decoded by TJ on a separate sheet, employing Code No. 8. The text presented here is that of FC, where the paragraph has the words "in Cypher" at its head.

[2] TJ decoded this word as "British."

[3] TJ decoded this as "Sweden and Prussia."

[4] FC reads: "effectual."

[5] FC reads: "resisted."

From Nicolas & Jacob van Staphorst

Amsterdam 25 July 1785

Having never before had the Honor to address Your Excellency, We now embrace the Opportunity that is offered to us by Mr.

Daniel Parker a well known American Gentleman; Who informs us that having with some other People Supplied the American Army with several Necessaries and Money for the Pay of the Troops; They have liquidated their Accounts with Congress, And are credited on the Books of the Continental Treasury for a considerable Amount. That those Funds bearing an Interest of Six ₩ Cent ₩ Annum are of the same Nature in point of Security, And consequently of equal Solidity as the foreign Loans, but by reason of the present Scarcity of Money in America not saleable. Therefore He and his Partners in this Business seem desirous to raise Money in this Country upon their Stock; Which certainly would not be practicable at this Moment, American Credit as well Public as Private being at a very low Ebb, but for the late Failure of De la Lande and Fynje, Who are largely interested in Shipments to America, As in case we could have satisfactory Information about the said Funds. We would persuade the Concerned to barter their demands against the Estate of De la Lande and Fynje with Shares in a Loan on that security; Which would be very desirable for all Parties and likewise save a considerable Sum of Money belonging to the United States. For those Reasons We wish to have every possible Information about the Nature of those Funds, And whether it is apparent that Mr. Daniel Parker may be able to command an Amount of One or Two Hundred Thousand Pounds Sterling of them.

We presume your Excellency to possess the best Information on this Subject to be obtained in Europe; And therefore request you to furnish us every Eclaircissement in your Power; Which we do not doubt you will effect without delay; especially when we assure you it may tend to the Benefit of the United States, Whose Interest we are obligated to promote all in our Power. We have the Honor to be most respectfully Your Excellency's Most Obed. & very hble. Servs.,   NICS. & JACOB VAN STAPHORST

RC (DLC); in a clerk's hand, with the signature of the firm; endorsed. Entry in SJL for 29 July 1785, which reads "received Staphorst's Amsterdam July 26," undoubtedly refers to this letter of 25 July.

American Commissioners to C. W. F. Dumas

SIR   [27 July 1785]

A treaty of Amity and Commerce between the United states of America and his majesty the king of Prussia having been arranged by us with the baron de Thulemeier his majesty's envoy extraordinary at the Hague specially empowered for this purpose, and it being inconsistent with our other duties to repair to that place ourselves for the purpose of executing and exchanging[1] the instruments of treaty, we have delivered the same duly executed on our part to the bearer hereof William Short esquire, to be by him carried with other necessary papers to the Hague. When arrived there, we ask and authorize you to manage[2] in conjunction with him the execution and exchange of the instruments of treaty according to the instructions which he receives from us and will communicate to you. Your former attention to the interests of the United states, and readiness to promote them, give us an assurance that you will not withold them on the present occasion.

We have the honor to be with very great respect Sir Your most obedient & most humble servants.

Dft (DLC); in TJ's hand, undated and unsigned. RC (Dr. Frederick M. Dearborn, N.Y., 1951); text in amanuensis' hand; signed by Adams and TJ; direction and date in Adams' hand: "Mr. C. W. F. Dumas at the Hague. London August 5. 1785." Tr (DNA: PCC, No. 87, I); in Humphreys' hand, undated; at foot of text: "No. 4." (this is the copy transmitted as enclosure No. 4 in TJ to Jay, 14 Aug. 1785, second letter). Tr (MHi: AMT); in Short's hand, undated; attested by Humphreys, "Paris July 28th. 1785."

FC (DNA: PCC, No. 116); in Humphreys' hand, undated; indicates at foot of text that Adams signed at London and TJ at Paris. Tr (DNA: PCC, No. 107, I); in clerk's hand. Recorded in SJL under date of 27 July 1785; entry in SJPL for that date reads: "Dumas do. [Exchange Prussian treaty. Instructions]."

[1] The words "copies of" are deleted in Dft at this point.
[2] This word interlined in Dft in substitution for "proceed," deleted.

American Commissioners to William Short

SIR   [27 July 1785]

A Treaty of Amity and Commerce between the United States of America and his majesty the K. of P. having been arranged with the Baron de Thulemeyer his Majesty's envoy extraordinary at the Hague specially empowered[1] for this purpose and it being inconsistent with our other duties to repair to that place ourselves for the purpose of executing and exchanging the instruments of[2] treaty, we hereby appoint you special secretary for that purpose.

You receive from Colo. Humphries, Secretary of our legation the original of our full powers, and a copy of the same attested by him, the full powers heretofore communicated to us by the Baron de Thulemeier, and the two instruments of treaty arranged between us, each in two columns, the one in English and the other in

French, equally originals.[3] From us you receive a letter to Charles Dumas esq.   for the United States at the Hague, associating him with you in the objects of your mission.

You will proceed immediately to the Hague, and being arrived there will deliver the letter to Mr. Dumas and proceed conjunctly with him in the residue of your business which is to be executed there.

The original of our full powers is to be exhibited to the plenipotentiary of his Majesty the King of Prussia[4] and the attested copy is to be left with him, you taking back the original. You will in like manner ask an exhibition of the original of his full powers, and also a copy duly attested: you will compare the copy with the original, and being satisfied of its exactness you will attest it,[5] return the original and keep the copy. That you may be under no doubt whether the full powers exhibited to you be sufficient or not, you receive from Colo. Humphries those which the Baron de Thulemeier heretofore sent to us. If those which shall be exhibited agree with these in form or substance, they will be sufficient.

The full powers being approved on each side and exchanged, you will obtain the signature and seal of the Prussian plenipotentiary to the two instruments of treaty with which you are charged, and yourself and Mr. Dumas will attest the same. One of these original instruments will remain in the hands of the Prussian plenipotentiary, the other you will retain.

You will ask that the ratification of his Majesty the King of Prussia be made known to us as soon as it shall have taken place, giving an assurance on our Part that that of Congress shall also be communicated so soon as it shall have taken place. When both Ratifications shall be known measures may be concerted for exchanging them. You will confer with the said plenipotentiary on the expediency of keeping this treaty uncommunicated to the public until the exchange of ratifications, and agree accordingly.

You will then return to Paris, and redeliver to the Secretary of our legation our original full powers, the copies of those of Prussia beforementioned, and the original instrument of the Treaty which you shall have retained.

Dft (DLC); in TJ's hand, undated and unsigned; with numerous deletions and interlineations, some of which are noted below. RC (DLC: Short Papers); in Short's hand; signed by Adams and TJ; with date and direction in Adams' hand: "London, August 5. 1785. William Short Esqr." Tr (MHi: AMT); in Short's hand; attested by Humphreys, "Paris July 28th. 1785." FC (DNA: PCC, No. 116; in Humphreys' hand, without date or names of signers; at head of text: "Instructions respecting the exchange of the Instruments of the said Treaty." Tr (DNA: PCC, No. 87, I); in Humphreys' hand; at foot of text: "No. 3." (this is the copy transmitted as enclosure No. 3 in TJ to Jay, 14 Aug. 1785, second letter). Tr (DNA: PCC, No. 107, I). Recorded in SJL under 27 July 1785; entry in SJPL for that date reads: "Short Wm. Exchange Prussian treaty. Instructions."

For an explanation of TJ's reason for not adding direction giving Dumas' title in preceding letter and after Dumas' name in this letter, see TJ to Adams, 28 July 1785; strangely, Adams did not bother to fill the blank in RC of the present letter.

1 This word interlined in Dft in place of "authorised," deleted.

2 Preceding three words interlined in Dft in place of "copies of the," deleted.

3 The passage "the full powers heretofore . . . equally originals" is interlined in Dft after the words "attested by him."

4 At this point the Dft read originally: ". . . to the Baron de Thulemeier or such other plenipotentiary as his majesty the king shall have appointed"; the passage was then altered by deletion and overwriting to read as above.

5 The two preceding words were added by Adams both to the RC and to the Tr retained by him (MHi: AMT).

To Vergennes

SIR   Paris July 27. 1785.

I have the honor now to inclose to your Excellency a copy of the letter from Congress to the king which I delivered yesterday. This copy was sent to me by Mr. Jay the Secretary of Congress for Foreign affairs.

I also accompany it with a copy of the letter of Credence which I had the honour of delivering to the King, not having furnished you with a copy on that occasion.

I am with sentiments of the most profound respect Your Excellency's most obedient and most humble servant,

TH: JEFFERSON

RC (Arch. Aff. Etr., Paris, Corr. Pol., E.-U., XXX). Endorsed: "M. DeR [M. de Rayneval] Lettre ci jointe de Creance pour M. Jefferson." PrC (DLC). Entry in SJPL reads: "Vergennes. Letter of credence." Enclosures:

Copy of Congress to Louis XVI, 14 June 1785 (text printed in JCC, XXVIII, 458); copy of Congress to Louis XVI, 10 Mch. 1785 (see Jay to TJ, 22 Mch. 1785).

To John Adams, with Enclosure

DEAR SIR   Paris July 28. 1785.

Your favors of July 16. and 18. came to hand the same day on which I had received Baron Thulemeier's inclosing the ultimate draught for the treaty. As this draught, which was in French, was to be copied into the two instruments which Doctr. Franklin had signed, it is finished this day only. Mr. Short sets out immediately.

I have put into his hands a letter of instructions how to conduct himself, which I have signed, leaving a space above for your signature. The two treaties I have signed at the left hand, Dr. Franklin having informed me that the signatures are read backwards. Besides the instructions to Mr. Short I signed also a letter to Mr. Dumas associating him with Mr. Short. These two letters I made out as near as I could to your ideas expressed in your letter of the 18th. If any thing more be necessary, be so good as to make a separate instruction for them signed by yourself, to which I will accede. I have not directed Mr. Dumas's letter. I have heretofore directed to him as 'Agent for the U.S. at the Hague' that being the description under which the journals of Congress speak of him. In his last letter to me is this paragraph. 'Mon nom à la Haie est assez connu, surtout au bureau de la poste, pour que mes lettres me soient rendus exactement, quand il n'y auroit d'autre direction.' From this I conclude that the address I have used is not agreeable, and perhaps may be wrong. Will you be so good as to address the letter to him and to inform me how to address him hereafter? Mr. Short carries also the other papers necessary. His equipment for his journey requiring expences which cannot come into the account of ordinary expences, such as clothes &c. what allowance should be made him? I have supposed somewhere between a guinea a day and 1000 dollars a year which I beleive is the salary of a private secretary. This I mean as over and above his travelling expences. Be so good as to say, and I will give him an order on his return. The danger of robbery has induced me to furnish him with only money enough to carry him to London. You will be so good as to procure him enough to carry him to the Hague and back to Paris.

The Confederation of the K. of Prussia with some members of the Germanic body for the preservation of their constitution, is I think beyond a doubt. The Emperor has certainly complained of it in formal communications at several courts. By what can be collected from diplomatic conversation here I also conclude it tolerably certain that the Elector of Hanover has been invited to accede to the confederation and has done or is doing it. You will have better circumstances however, on the spot, to form a just judgment. Our matters with the first of these powers being now in conclusion, I wish it was so with the elector of Hanover. I conclude from the general expressions on your letter that little may be expected. Mr. Short furnishing so safe a conveyance that the trouble of the cypher may be dispensed with, I will thank you for such details of what has passed as may not be too troublesome to you.

The difficulties of getting books into Paris delayed for some time my receipt of the Corps diplomatique left by Dr. Franklin. Since that we have been engaged with expediting Mr. Short. A huge packet also brought by Mr. Mazzei has added to the causes which have as yet prevented me from examining Dr. Franklin's notes on the Barbary treaty. It shall be one of my first occupations. Still the possibility is too obvious that we may run counter to the instructions of Congress of which Mr. Lambe is said to be the bearer. There is a great impatience in America for these treaties. I am much distressed between this impatience, and the known will of Congress on the one hand, and the incertainty of the details committed to this tardy servant.

The D. of Dorset sets out for London tomorrow. He says he shall be absent two months. Some whisper that he will not return and that Ld. Carmarthen wishes to come here. I am sorry to lose so honest a man as the Duke. I take the liberty to ask an answer about the insurance of Houdon's life.

Congress is not likely to adjourn this summer. They have passed an ordinance for selling their lands. I have not received it.

What would you think of the inclosed Draught to be proposed to the courts of London and Versailles? I would add Madrid and Lisbon, but that they are still more desperate than the others. I know it goes beyond our powers; and beyond the powers of Congress too. But it is so evidently for the good of all the states that I should not be afraid to risk myself on it if you are of the same opinion. Consider it if you please and give me your thoughts on it by Mr. Short: but I do not communicate it to him nor any other mortal living but yourself.

Be pleased to present me in the most friendly terms to the ladies and believe me to be with great esteem Dear Sir Your friend & servant, TH: JEFFERSON

You say nothing in your letter about your wine at Auteuil. I think I sent you Petit's bill for I do not find it among my papers. It's amount was 173^{tt} 8s.

ENCLOSURE

The parties, being desirous of promoting as much as possible the happiness of their citizens and subjects respectively and mutually, believing that a free and friendly intercourse between them will contribute much to this end, and that this intercourse cannot be established on a better footing than that of a mutual adoption by each of the citizens or subjects of the other, insomuch that while those of the one shall be travelling or sojourning with the other, they shall be considered to every intent and purpose as members of the nation where they are, entitled to all the protections, rights and advantages of it's native members, have, on mature deliberation, covenanted with each other, that the intercourse between all the subjects and citizens of the two parties shall be free and unrestrained: that those of either party while in places within the jurisdiction or possession of the other, shall be entitled to the same protection, the same privileges, immunities, capacities, advantages and rights of every possible species or description, which the subjects or citizens natives of the same place shall at the same time be entitled to:

And that property in places within the jurisdiction or possession of either belonging to a citizen or subject of the other, or which would belong to him were he a native of the place where it is, shall belong to such citizen or subject as if he were a native, and shall be at his disposal by deed or will, or by other his act with or without writing, or, in case of his death without will, shall pass to his representatives designated by the laws of the land where such property is as if he were a native citizen or subject of the same country; and in all cases shall be covered with the same protections, privileges and exemptions, and shall give the same advantages, rights, and capacities to the owner, as if he were a native citizen or subject of the place where it is: insomuch that no distinction between the two nations shall be known to the laws of either as to persons within their jurisdiction citizens or subjects of the other, or property within their jurisdiction belonging to subjects or citizens of the other, or which would belong to them if they were natives.

And lest an attempt to enumerate and describe these rights more particularly might give rise to inferences that none are meant to be communicated but those which such enumeration or description might perfectly comprehend, the parties will not attempt such description, but chuse to rest this covenant for it's greatest effect on the general terms before used, which are to be understood at all times, in all places, and in every possible case as meant to be extended to every right of a native citizen or subject which any subject or citizen of the other may at any time or place think proper to claim.

The following cases only are meant to be excepted out of these general stipulations.

1. Laws made, or hereafter to be made for restraining public offices to native citizens or subjects shall exclude the citizens or subjects of the other from a capacity to hold them, so long as the subjects or citizens of all other nations are likewise excluded.

2. Ambassadors, ministers, or other persons who by the usages of nations are exempt from the jurisdiction of the laws of the country where they are shall retain that exemption: and the Consuls of either party with the other shall enjoy the protection and privileges of the law of nations. But if any such Ambassador, Minister, Consul or other person exercises or is interested in commerce within the territories of

the party with whom his functions lay, neither his person nor property shall have the protection or privileges of the law of nations, but shall be submitted to the same laws as those of the natives of the place where he is.

3. The subjects or citizens of either party in the territories of the other shall be free in the exercise of their religion, shall not be required to conform in word or deed to any other, not suffer any molestation on account of religion, unless it be for a real insult on that of any other person.

And as the interests and happiness of the subjects and citizens of the two parties will be further promoted by the establishment of a free commerce between them, it is moreover agreed that it shall be lawful for the subjects or citizens of either party freely to transport in their own or any other bottoms any merchandize of the produce or manufacture of either party from any part of the territories of either party into any part of the territories of the other paying on the exportation or importation not more than   per cent on the value of the said merchandize at the place where it is exported or imported by way of duties, imposts, fees, taxes on alienation, or in any other form whatever.

And to solace as much as possible the condition of humanity in it's worst situations, particularly to mitigate the calamities with which it is afflicted in times of war, and to remove some of the inducements to enter into war, the following stipulations are provided in the several cases: 1. where one of the parties only shall be at war; 2. where both shall be at war against a common enemy; or 3. where there shall be a war between the two parties. [Then add the articles from the general draught from Art. 13. inclusive to the end, except the 25th.]¹

RC (MHi: AMT); endorsed in part: "4. Augt. recd." and in part "ansd. Aug. 4."; lacks postscript, and, in view of the fact that postscript appears on PrC, TJ must have written it on a separate slip or on the address leaf; the former is more likely, since it is on p. 3 of PrC. PrC (DLC); fragment, including only the last two pages of the letter. Recorded in SJL as sent by Short; entry in SJPL reads: "Adams John. Instructions to Short. Engld. Mazzei. Lambe. Barbary. Dorset. Caermarthen. Project of treaty Engld. and France." Enclosure: MS (DLC: TJ Papers, 17: 2970; undated and without caption; in TJ's hand); PrC (MHi: AMT).

The remarkable document printed above as an enclosure is not associated with the text of the letter either in MHi: AMT or in DLC: TJ Papers. Being also undated and without a caption or other external evidence that it was actually sent to Adams, it can nevertheless be certainly identified as the proposal that was BEYOND OUR POWERS; AND BEYOND THE POWERS OF CONGRESS TOO and that was, moreover,

so daring a venture that TJ was unwilling to tell Short about it or to COMMUNICATE IT TO . . . ANY OTHER MORTAL LIVING BUT Adams. No other draft of a treaty fits the case. This document was doubtless intended to supplant the existing "general form" of a treaty, at least with respect to England and France (see above, under 10 Nov. 1784), and it could not have been written before the arrival of TJ's copying press, since TJ retained the DRAUGHT—actually a fair copy of some earlier composition draft—and sent Adams a press copy of it (see TJ to Barré, 3 June 1785, note). Evidently this far-reaching proposal has escaped publication until now. The idea itself, at least in elementary form, had been advanced at an early meeting of the Commissioners. Presumably TJ himself had made the initial proposal. Adams must not have done so, since, by his own admission, he had opposed it at that time (Adams to TJ, 24 July 1785; but see Adams to TJ, 31 July 1785, especially note 3). Franklin, aged, infirm, and bent on returning to America, would not have been likely to advance so revolutionary a proposition under these circumstances when he had failed to do so in his treaty negotiations before 1784. When, late in June, Adams requested Franklin and TJ to prepare a projet of a treaty to be proposed to Great Britain, the one they drew up and forwarded was only a revision of the earlier "general form" of a treaty and was, like that, based on the most-favored-nation principle (Franklin and TJ to Adams, 8 July 1785). It is significant, too, that, immediately after Franklin had departed, TJ not only brought forth the present elaboration of the idea but Adams himself, in a letter that crossed this one in the mails, recurred to it (Adams to TJ, 24 July 1785). Adams seems to have referred to the subject in noncommittal terms in his reply to the present letter, and perhaps did not elaborate because, as Short reported to TJ, "he thought it unnecessary [to write] and communicated to me, as he said, what he wished you to know" (Short to TJ, 23 Aug. 1785; Adams to TJ, 4 Aug. 1785). We can only conjecture what it was Adams wished TJ to know. Perhaps he cautioned against making the proposal to Great Britain because of the existing state of feeling between the two countries. More probably, he may have advised against any proposal of the sort, since TJ's extension of the idea was much more revolutionary than the original plan which was merely that of placing aliens and natives on an equal footing commercially. He may have suggested that TJ put out a feeler toward France. Whatever his advice, TJ did open the subject with Vergennes: "Both

nations," he wrote, "perhaps may come into the opinion that their friendship and their interest may be better cemented by approaching the condition of their citizens reciprocally to that of *natives*, as a better ground of intercourse than that of *the most favoured nation*" (TJ to Vergennes, 20 Nov. 1785).

As late as June 17, when he wrote Monroe, TJ revealed himself to be very conscious of the limitations imposed upon the treaty power by the reserved powers of the states and to be willing to abide by those limitations. Yet, little over a month later, he had drafted this projet of a treaty that, as he well knew, would clearly have contravened the Commissioners' powers and also the powers of the Confederation. Indeed, if successfully carried out, it would have altered the very nature of the union and of the society of nations.

It is puzzling that TJ says he had not received Congress' ORDINANCE FOR SELLING THEIR LANDS, for it was enclosed in Monroe to TJ, 16 June 1785, which was received on 22 July in the HUGE PACKET . . . BROUGHT BY MR. MAZZEI; also, TJ's letter to Hogendorp, 29 July 1785, shows that he had received the ordinance. The other letters received in Mazzei's packet were those from Mrs. Trist, 25 Dec. 1784; the Rev. James Madison, 10 Apr.; Peter Carr, 20 Apr.; Maury, 20 Apr.; Madison, 27 Apr.; Page, 28 Apr.; Mrs. Carr, 6 May; House, 28 May; Jay, 14 and 15 June; Jamieson, 14 June; and Ramsay, 15 June 1785.

1 Opening bracket in MS but closing bracket supplied.

From William Carmichael

SIR   Madrid 28th. July 1785

I received on the 26th. Inst. your Letter dated the 22d. June and 14th. July. On the 27th. and Ulto. I had the honor to write you. On the 25th. inst. I received a Letter from his Excellency the Ct. de Florida Blanca of which I inclose you a copy, as a thorough knowledge of the Situation of our Affairs in Barbary may be useful to you in the business you have to transact with these Powers. You will easily judge that I could return no other Answer to the Offer of mediation made by his Catholic Majesty, than that I should transmit a copy of the Ministers Letter immediately to Congress. The Conduct of this court in the whole process of this business has been highly frank and Liberal and I should be happy to have an oppertunity of expressing to the Ct. de Florida Blanca the Sentiments of Mr. Adams and yourself thereon. I also inclose you a copy of a Letter which I received from Mr. Harrison and of another from a Correspondent in Barbary, to which I join a list of the Presents made to the Emperor of Morrocco by the Dutch in the year 1784. You will please to communicate to Mr. Adams these papers. In the 26th. Inst. I received a Letter from him Dated the 3d. of June, which I answer this night referring him to you for Information. About a fortnight ago the Russian Minister presented a memorial to this Court couched in much the Same terms as that from the Emperor mentioned in my Letter of the 27th. June. It appears that the Idea of the exchange proposed by the Latter to the Elector of Bavaria and by the former to the Duke of Deux Pons is relinquished for the moment. It is said the negotiation with the Algerines meets with Obstacles, and circumstances seem to confirm this report. My health has been and is so bad that it has not been in my power to go abroad for near a week. I have no letters from Congress, but have now before me American papers of the 21st. May sent me from the Secretary of States Office. They announce the arrival of Mr. Gardoqui at Philadelphia the 20th. and there are official Letters from him the 22d. of May. He is very much pleased with his reception. If you should find a proper occasion to send me a cypher, might it not be useful to give Mr. Adams a copy of the same? I inclose you a Letter for Dn. Gomez Friero de Andrade a portuguese nobleman of distinction which Letter contains one of Introduction for you and another for the Marquis de la Fayette. I intreat your Civilities to this young gentleman. He was one of those who accompanied the Infanta Donna Maria Victoria married to the Infant Dn. Gabriel. His Address will be discovered at the Portuguese Ambassadors. I recollect nothing at present that can excuse my troubling you with a longer Letter. If any thing occurs worth your Observation I shall not fail to advise you.

I have the honor to be with the highest Respect Your Excys. Most Obedt. & Most Hble. Sert.,   WM. CARMICHAEL

RC (DLC). Recorded in SJL as received 10 Aug. 1785. Enclosures: (1) Floridablanca to Carmichael, 24 July 1785 (two Tr in DLC, two in MHi: AMT, one in DNA: PCC, No. 87, I, and one in DNA: PCC, No. 107, I—

all are in Spanish and accompanied by an English translation; an undated translation is printed in *Dipl. Corr., 1783-1789*, I, 634-5), informing him that, on application of the Spanish minister to Morocco, ten American prisoners and their vessel had been freed and that Morocco had made an overture of peace with the United States through the mediation of Spain. (2) Carmichael to Floridablanca, 25 July 1785 (Tr in DLC and another in MHi: AMT), acknowledging the foregoing, assuring him it "is with the highest satisfaction . . . that I shall immediately transmit to Congress this additional proof of His Majesty's friendly and beneficent regard to the Interests of the United States in order that they may . . . avail themselves of a mediation from which they cannot but expect advantageous consequences," and hinting that, though he had always expected to return to America when he left Spain, this offer of good offices, together with Floridablanca's continued friendship, would induce him to remain and carry out whatever instructions Congress might give. (3) Richard Harrison to Carmichael, 19 July 1785 (Tr in DNA: PCC, No. 87, I; in Humphreys' hand, without indication of addressee or writer, and at foot of text: "No. 5."; Tr in DNA: PCC, No. 107, erroneously identified as a letter from Carmichael to TJ and so printed in *Dipl. Corr., 1783-1789*, I, 632-3), informing him that the captain and crew of the brig *Betsy* had arrived at Cadiz the day before from Morocco, that they had already "cost me a good deal of money, and must cost me more before they can be shipped off, which will be as soon as possible," that he was of opinion that the public was justly liable for these charges, but "since the Commissioners are off a different opinion we must see what can

be done at home," that he had that morning waited on the Spanish minister to Morocco "to return him thanks in the best Spanish I could muster," and that he was alarmed on account of the Algerines. (4) The letter "from a Correspondent in Barbary" probably was that from Louis Goublot to Carmichael, 25 June 1785 (Tr in DNA: PCC, No. 88, II; No. 87, I; and No. 107, I; and in MHi: AMT—all in French and all save that in MHi have an English translation; Tr in DNA: PCC, No. 88, II, is designated "No. 3" at head of text; a translation is printed in *Dipl. Corr., 1783-1789*, I, 633-4), informing him that, in consequence of what he had hinted at in his of 10 June, the prisoners had been released to the Spanish minister in Morocco, and explaining that one of the motives of the emperor may have been the expectation that this act of generosity would cause the Americans more earnestly to "seek his friendship, in a manner that will be beneficial to him." (5) A list of presents given by the States General to the emperor of Morocco in 1784 (Tr in DNA: PCC, No. 87, I, and No. 107, I; both in French, with an English translation; a translation is printed in *Dipl. Corr., 1783-1789*, I, 635-7). (6) Carmichael to TJ and to Lafayette introducing Don Gomez (not found; but see TJ to Carmichael, 18 Aug. 1785). Copies of the first, third, fourth, and fifth enclosures were sent by TJ to Jay in his second letter of 14 Aug. 1785.

On 18 Aug. Carmichael wrote to Adams: "This court *appears* sincerely disposed to cultivate a good understanding with the United States. Ere this letter will reach you Mr. Jefferson will have communicated to you copies of my last despatches to him, on which I hope to have your excellency's opinion" (MHi: AMT).

To John Stockdale

SIR   Paris July 28. 1785.

I shall have occasion for books and pamphlets sometimes to be sent here and sometimes to America, which will render a correspondent in London in your way convenient. Mr. Adams has been kind enough to promise to direct such pamphlets and new publications to be sent me as he shall suppose will be agreeable. The price of these or of any thing else which I may order for myself shall be remitted you from time to time or paid to your own draught on sight. For the present I will ask the favour of you to have the underwritten books packed in a very tight box directed to James Madison president of the college in Williamsburg Virginia, and to furnish me with the cost, noting whether you will draw on me for the money or prefer my remitting it to you. I must further desire you to find some opportunity of sending the box by some vessel bound from London to James or York river in Virginia. I am Sir Your very humble servt.,　　　　　Th: Jefferson

Herodotus Gr. Lat. 9. vols. 12mo.
Thucydides Gr. Lat. 8 vols. 12mo.
Xenophontis Hellenica Gr. Lat 4. v. 12mo.
Xenophontis Cyri expeditio Gr. Lat. 4. 12mo.
Xenophontis Memorabilia Gr. 12mo.
Ciceronis opera 20. vols. 16s.
　The above of the Glasgow editions by Foulis.
Martin's philosophical grammar.
Martin's philosophia Britannica. 3. v. 8vo.
　to be bound tolerably neat and lettered.

PrC (DLC).

To De Thulemeier

Sir　　　　　　　　　　　　　　　Paris July 28 1785.

I was honoured with the receipt of your letter on the 24th. instant, together with the French draught of the treaty proposed, as it ultimately meets his majesty's approbation. Doctor Franklin our collegue having assisted us thro' the progress of this business we were desirous he also should join in the execution. Duplicate instruments were therefore prepared, each divided into two columns, in one of which we entered the English form as it had been settled between us, leaving the other blank to receive the French which we expected from you. In this state the Doctor, before his departure, put his signature and seal to the two instruments. We have since put into the blank column the French form received from you verbatim. As we thought that such instruments should not be trusted out of confidential hands, and the bearer hereof, William Short esquire, heretofore a member of the council of state in Virginia, happened to be in Paris, and willing to give us his assistance herein, they are delivered into his hands with other necessary papers, according to an arrangement previously made between Mr. Adams, Doctr. Franklin and myself. He will proceed to London to obtain Mr. Adams's signature, and thence to the Hague where we have, according to your desire, associated Mr. Dumas with him to concur with you in the final execution. It is with singular pleasure I see this connection formed by my country with a sovereign whose character gives a lustre to all the transactions of which he makes part.[1]

Give me leave to recommend Mr. Short to your notice. His talents and merit are such as to have placed him, young as he is, in the Supreme executive council of Virginia, an office which he relinquished to visit Europe. The letter to Baron Steuben shall be taken care of. I have the honour to be with sentiments of the highest respect Sir Your most obedient and most humble servant,

TH: JEFFERSON

PrC (DLC); endorsed: "Prussia. Barn. Thulemeier Minister at the Hague." FC (DNA: PCC, No. 116); in Humphreys' hand; without indication of the day of the month and lacking final paragraph, except for complimentary close; printed in *Dipl. Corr., 1783-1789*, I, 597. A Tr similar to FC is in DNA: PCC, No. 87, I; Tr also in DNA: PCC, No. 107, I. Entry in SJPL reads: "Thulemeyer Baron do. [Exchange Prussian treaty. Instructions]." A copy was sent by TJ to Jay in his second letter of 14 Aug. 1785.

[1] All of the copies described above, save PrC and, of course, the missing RC, end at this point.

To G. K. van Hogendorp

DEAR SIR   Paris July 29. 1785.

By an American gentleman who went to the Hague about a month ago I sent you a copy of my Notes on Virginia. Having since that received some copies of the revisal of our laws, of which you had desired one, I now send it to you. I congratulate you sincerely on the prospect of your country's being freed from the prospect of war, which however just, is always expensive and calamitous and sometimes unsuccesful.

Congress having made a very considerable purchase of lands from the Indians have established a land office and settled the mode of selling the lands. Their plan is judicious. I suspect some inconveniences in some parts of it, but if such should be found actually, they will amend them. They receive in paiment their own certificates at par with actual money. We have a proof the last year that the failure of the states to bring money into the treasury has proceeded, not from any unwillingness, but from the distresses of their situation. Heretofore Massachusets and Pensylvania had brought in the most money and Virginia was among the least. The last year Virginia has paid in more than all the rest together. The reason is that she is at liberty to avail herself of her natural resources and has free markets for them. Whereas the others, which, while they were sure of a sale for their commodities, brought money into the treasury, now that that sale is by circumstances rendered more precarious, they bring in but little. The impost is not yet granted. Rhode island and New York hold off. Congress have it in contemplation to propose to the states that the direction of all their commerce shall be committed to Congress, reserving to the states respectively the revenue which shall be laid on it. The operations of our good friends the English are calculated as precisely to bring the states into this measure as if we directed them ourselves, and as they were thro the whole war to produce that union which was so necessary for us. I doubt whether Congress will adjourn this summer. Should you be at the Hague I will beg leave to make known to you the bearer hereof Mr. William Short. He is of Virginia, has come to stay some time with me at Paris, being among my most particular friends. Tho' young his talents and merit are such as to have placed him in the Council of state of Virginia, an office which he relinquished to make a visit to Europe. I have the honour to be with very high esteem Dear Sir Your most obedient & most humble servt.,

TH: JEFFERSON

RC (Rijksarchief, The Hague). PrC (DLC). Enclosure: Copy of the *Report of the Committee of Revisors Appointed by the General Assembly of Virginia in MDCCLXXVI* (Richmond, Nov. 1784). Entry in SJPL reads: "Hogen-dorp. Notes. Revised Code. American affairs. Short."

The AMERICAN GENTLEMAN was James Jarvis (see TJ to Carmichael, 22 June 1785).

To Jean Holker

SIR   Paris July 29.

I am to acknowledge the honour of your letter of the 18th. I had before that received Mr. Plowden Garvey's of the 16th. in which he informed me you had been so kind as to express your willingness to assist me in the purchase of a pair of horses such as I had described to him. He observed to me that the horses to be bought at Rouen were considerably larger than what I desired (4 feet 8. or 9 inches high) and much dearer than I had expected. I find on further enquiry that the height I mentioned would be too little, and that they should be five feet high. I think from the enquiries I have made that such are sometimes to be bought here for 1000 or 1200 livres: but it is accidental and requires attendance at the sales *après decés*. I shall be on the look out; but should any such be offered for sale within your knowlege at or about those prices I will thank you to purchase them. Should I purchase myself I will take the liberty of writing instantly to you to prevent a double supply. I am chagrined at not having replaced by Mr. Franklin the little sums you had advanced for me. This is rendering my commissions doubly burthensome to you. I will try to be more thoughtful when another occasion offers. I have not heard from Dr. Franklin since the day he was to embark at Havre. I am anxious to know how he bears every step he takes. I have the honour to be with great respect Sir Your most obedient humble servant, TH: JEFFERSON

PrC (MHi).

From John Paul Jones

SIR   L'Orient July 29th. 1785.

I have been with Mr. Clouet, the ordonnateur here, to whom the Marechal de Castries sent Orders the 15th. of this Month to pay into my hands the Money arising to the subjects of the United States from the Prizes taken by the Squadron I commanded in Europe. I find that a French Merchant, Mr. Puchilberg of this place, who opposed Dr. Franklin and did all in his power to promote the Revolt that took place in the Alliance, has produced a Letter of Attorney, which he obtained from the officers and Men of that Frigate when their Minds were unsettled, authorizing him to Recieve their Share in the Prizes. And, notwithstanding the orders of the Marechal of the 15th., I find there is a disposition here to pay the Money to Mr. Puchilberg in preference to me.

When I undertook the difficult and disagreeable Business of settling for the Prize-Money with the Marechal de Castries, I thought it necessary, to prevent any reflection on my conduct, to give security for two hundred thousand Dollars to remit the Money I recovered to the Treasury of the United States, to be from thence divided among the persons concerned. Not to mention the great expence I have been at, and the loss of two Years of my time since the Peace to obtain a settlement, I may be permitted to say that Mr. Puchilberg was at no expence and never took any effectual steps to obtain a settlement of the Prize-Money; and it would have been very difficult, if not impossible, for him to have obtained any satisfaction for the Concerned; because no other Man but myself (except Dr. Franklin who would not Act) could have explained at Versailles the nature and circumstances of my connection with that Court. And I may add, that Mr. Puchilberg will not, and cannot, if he had the best intentions, do justice to the Subjects of America. He has given no security to do them Justice. He has no authentic Roll of the Crew of the Alliance, which can only be had in America; and he is unacquainted with the manner of classing the Officers and Men in the division of Prize-Money by the Laws of the American Flag.

What I request of you therefore is, to write to the Court to obtain an explicit Order from the Marechal de Castries to Mr. Clouet to pay into my hands the whole Mass of the Prize-Money that appears due to the Alliance, and also the Share of the Bon-Homme-Richard (after deducting the proportion due to the French Volunteers who were embarked on board that Ship as Marines).

As my situation here is exceedingly disagreeable; because, 'till this new difficulty is removed I cannot receive any Part of the Money that appears due; I shall hope to be relieved from my embarrassment as soon as possible by a Letter from you.

They have objected here, that the Captain of the Alliance was born in France. But he had abjured the Church of Rome and been naturalized in America (as his Officers reported to me) before he took command of the Alliance, and his Crew were all the Subjects of the United States.

I am sorry to give you this trouble, but I am convinced that the Business would have continued in suspense for a long time if I had not come here myself.

I am, with great esteem and respect, Sir, Your most obedient & most humble Servant, J PAUL JONES

NB. Mr. Clouet has Written to Court by this Post, therefore it will be necessary to make your application immediately. Mr. Barcley can give you the Character of Mr. Puchilberg.

RC (CtY); endorsed. Recorded in SJL as received 2 Aug. 1785. Copy enclosed in TJ to Castries, 3 Aug. 1785.

From William Bingham

Sir   Hague July 30th. 1785

Intending to remain some Time at Beuvelles on my Return from Spa, I shall pay my Respects to the french Minister at that Court, and shall be much indebted to you for a Letter of Introduction to him, which you will please to address under Cover to me, to the Care of Monsieur J. C. de Bay at Beuvelles.

I hope you will excuse the Trouble I shall occasion you, and that you will be assured of my entertaining a proper Sense of this Act of Civility.

Your Intelligence from America I imagine is too regular, to admit of any Prospect of Communications on my Part, not being anticipated, by Similar advices.

My last Letters mention, that the Inhabitants of the trading Towns of America, are entering into very Spirited (and in some places, violent) Measures, to operate the Exclusion of British Factors and British Shipping and that many of the Legislatures, in Compliance with Memorials from their Constituents, were about vesting in Congress, such Powers as were deemed necessary for the regulation of foreign Trade.

That the Distresses of the Country were very great, arising from the immense Importations from Europe, and the relatively small value of the American Exports.

Mr. Jay writes me, in June, that "the Frontier Posts still had British Garrisons, and that Congress was very impatient to hear, why they were not evacuated; that federal Ideas were daily gaining Ground, which would probably influence the States to extend the Powers of Congress, and thereby enable them to resent European Restrictions; that a Rage for emigrating to the Western Country prevailed, and that the seeds of a great People were daily planting beyond the Mountains."

I have the Honor to be with Respect & Esteem Sir Your obed. hble. Serv.,   Wm. Bingham

RC (DLC); endorsed.

The letter from MR. JAY and that from Bingham which it acknowledged were letters whose unrevealed passages would have interested, but not surprised, TJ. On 16 Oct. 1784 Bingham wrote from Paris: "The British seem to recede every day more and more from the paths to reconciliation. A certain nation, to whom we are indebted for political favours, will endeavour to cherish this disposition, as she is sure to benefit by such growing feuds and divisions. From the observations I have made since my arrival here, I can discover the necessity of a very complying conduct on the part of those Americans who have public business to transact with this court. . . . No one is better acquainted than you are with the system of *this court*, and no one is more jealous of their country's honour, in essential points. You may well imagine, then, that your appointment was *not regarded with satisfaction*, nor will the congratulations that you will receive on it from certain persons be *sincere*." To this allusion, which Jay well under-stood, he replied on 31 May 1785, in the letter that Bingham quoted from here: "Your observations in France, respecting a certain event, coincide exactly with what I expected on that subject" (William Jay, ed., *Life of John Jay*, II, 165-6).

From B. Contée

⟦*Bayonne, 30 July 1785.* Recorded in SJL as received 6 Aug. Not found.⟧

From Katherine Sprowle Douglas

SIR   London, July 30th. 1785

I was Honor'd with your obliging favor of the 5th. the Contents of which truely Animates me! The enlivning Hopes of Restitution of that property I am Conscious we have not in your Just Discrimination forfeited. Mr. Sproule never took any active or Sinester Part against the American Interest. On the Contra He was their most sincere freind which the Copies of the Letters I troubled you with will evince, and the Sacrefice of His Life, a melancholy Confirmation! My poor Infatuated Son had neither merite, nor Demerite att His unthinking time of Life! Under Sixteen He had a Comission Cram'd down His Throat by the Lawless Govr. Dunmore. The fatal Night before the Mad attempt of the great Bridge, Totaly unknown to Mr. Sproule or me, He was thank God taken prisoner, kept for two years upon Parole which I flatter myself he did no Discreditt to till He was Exchanged. When he came here He was offer'd a Company of Foot by Lord George Germain which he Nobly Refus'd, and said He had one fatal Night Carried arms against the Americans but never woud again. He was also Sollicited by Dunmore to go with him when He went in 1781 on His more than Quixot scheme of Retaking Possession of the govrment of Virginia, which he refus'd and went to Scotland where he has since Lived frugaly and Peacably Longing for the Now Happy æra of being again united with the American States to Rejoin them. As for myself, I shall leave to the Virginians to witness to the Resolute Part I acted, tho sorrounded by the Fleet and army Headed by the mad, Blood Thirsty Governor who att Last sent me Here as an Enemy to the *British* Goverment.

I never doubted being Honord with an appartment in the Tower as the reward of my Demerites. When an old freind of mine Procur'd me a Pension of £150 ℘ annum for the support of my seven smal Children, he manfully struck me off the List as a Traitor to my Country. How they and I have struggled on since Heaven only knows as we have never yet been able to Touch a farthing of the scaterd Remains of Mr. Sproule's mangled fortune. But now I flatter myself the Justice and Clemency of the States will *Restore* the Price of the Lands sold which [by] the Inclosd Advertisment from the april Virginia News paper youll see your Conjectures were *well* founded. I therefore worthy Sir Intreat your Influence with the assembly you once so wisely Govern'd for that urgently wishd for Retribution. If you think my Personal Presence in Virginia woud in *any* measure Facilatate that desirable End I am willing and ready to Enconter every Danger which past the meridian of Life may be Judg'd *Terribble* By the weak Timid Deffenceless Sex: But where Justice to, and the Interest of my Dear *Helpless* Children is Concern'd I will Brave *all* Difficulties By again Returning to a place *ever* Rever'd as the Land of Promise to Sir your most obedt. Sert.,   K. SPROULE

If you honor me with answer throu the medium of Mr. Adams, I will esteem as a Particular favor.

RC (DLC). Recorded in SJL as received 7 Aug. 1785. Enclosure: Notice of commissioners for sale of land in Gosport, Va., 1 Apr. 1785 (Tr in ViWC), reading in part as follows: ". . . Gosport is situated on the Southern Branch of Elizabeth River, near to Norfolk and contiguous to the thriving Town of Portsmouth, to which it is annex'd by Law as part of the said Town, and will be laid off in Lotts, with Convenient streets. . . . The goodness of the Harbour, and the depth of Water close to the shore, which will admit the largest Merchant Ships to load, and where Ships of the Line have frequently hove down, renders this place superior to any in the State, for building large ships, and erecting Wharffs, and is deemed equal in situation with any in Virginia for commercial purposes, it is more convenient than Norfolk to the North Carolina Trade and has an easy communication with the Waters of Chesapeak Bay, with the advantage of a safer Harbour and deeper Water, and the Canal prepared to unite the Waters of North Carolina with the Chesapeak will greatly enhance the Value of these Lands. About 300 Lotts will be laid off, thirty of which will be prime Water Lotts, the whole forming an agreeable and convenient Situation for a Considerable Commercial Town."

To Nicolas & Jacob van Staphorst

GENTLEMEN   Paris July 30. 1785.

I received yesterday your favor of the 25th. Supposing that the funds which are the object of your enquiry are those which constitute what we call our *Domestic* debt, it is my opinion that they are absolutely secure: I have no doubt at all but that they will be paid with their interest at six percent. But I cannot say that they are as secure and solid as the funds which constitute our *foreign* debt: because no man in America ever entertained a doubt but that our foreign debt is to be paid fully; but some people in America have seriously contended that the certificates and other evidences of our domestic debt ought to be redeemed only at what they have cost the holder; for I must observe to you that these certificates of Domestic debt having as yet no provision for the payment either of principal or interest, and the original holders being mostly needy, they have been sold at a very great discount. When I left America (July 1784) they sold in different states at from 15/ to 2/6 in the pound, and any amount of them might then have been purchased. Hence some thought that full justice would be done if the public paid the purchasers of them what they actually paid for them, and interest on that. But this is very far from being a general opinion; a very great majority being firmly decided that they shall be paid fully. Were I the holder of any of them, I should not have the least fear of their full paiment. There is also a difference between different species of certificates, some of them being receivable in taxes, others having the benefit of particular assurances &c. Again some of these certificates are for paper money debts. A deception here must be guarded against. Congress ordered all such to be resettled by the depreciation tables, and a new certificate to be given in exchange for them expressing their value in real money. Yet all have not yet been resettled. In short this is a science in which few in America are expert, and no person in a foreign country can be so. Foreigners should therefore be sure that they are well advised before they meddle with them, or they may suffer. If you will reflect with what degree of success persons actually in America could speculate in the European funds which rise and fall daily, you may judge how far those in Europe may do it in the American funds, which are more variable from a variety of causes.

I am not at all acquainted with Mr. Daniel Parker, but as having once seen him in Philadelphia. He is of Massachusets (I beleive) and I am of Virginia. His circumstances are utterly unknown to me. I think there are few men in America, if there is a single one, who could command a hundred thousand pounds sterling's worth of these notes, at their real value. In their nominal amount this might be done perhaps with 25,000£ sterling, if the market price of them be as low as when I left America. I am with very great respect Gentlemen Your most obedient humble servt.,

Tн: Jefferson

PrC (DLC); at foot of letter: "Messrs. Nichs. & Jacob van Staphorst. Amsterdam." Entry in SJPL under this date reads: "V. Staphorsts. American funds. Dan. Parker." RC was evidently dated 31 July; see van Staphorst to TJ, 19 Sep. 1785.

To John Adams

DEAR SIR   Paris July 31. 1785.

I was honoured yesterday with yours of the 24th. instant. When the *1st.*¹ *article* of *our instructions* of May 7. 1784. was *under debate in Congress*, it was *proposed* that *neither party* should make *the other pay* in *their ports greater duties than* they *paid* in the *ports* of the *other.* One *objection* to this was *it's impracticability*,² another *that it* would *put it* out *of our power to lay* such *duties* on *alien importation* as might *encourage importation* by *natives. Some members* much *attached* to *English policy* thought such a *distinction* should actually be *established. Some* thought the *power* to do it should be *reserved* in *case any* peculiar circumstances should *call for it,* tho under the present or *perhaps any* probable *circumstances they* did not *think* it would be *good policy* ever to *exercise* it. The *footing gentis amicissimi* was therefore *adopted* as you see in the *instruction.*³ As far as my enquiries enable me to judge *France and Holland* make no *distinction of duties between Aliens and natives. I* also rather believe that the *other states of Europe* make *none, England* excepted, to whom this *policy,* as that of her *navigation act, seems peculiar.* The question then *is, Should* we *disarm ourselves* of the *power to* make this *distinction against all nations* in order to *purchase an exemption* from the *Alien duties* in *England* only; for if we *put her importations* on the *footing of native,* all other *nations with whom we treat will* have a *right to claim the same. I* think we *should, because against other nations* who make no *distinction* in their *ports between us* and their *own subjects,* we ought *not to* make a *distinction in ours.* And *if the English* will *agree* in *like manner to* make none, we *should with equal reason abandon* the *right* as against *them. I* think all the *world would gain* by *setting commerce* at perfect *liberty. I* remember that when we were *digesting* the *general form* of *our treaty* this *proposition* to *put foreigners* and *natives on the same* *footing* was *considered*: and we were *all three* (*Dr. F.*) as *well as you* and *myself* in *favor of it. We* finally however *did not admit* it partly from the *objection* you *mention, but* more *still* on account of *our instructions.* But tho' the *English proclamation* had *appeared* in *America* at the time of *framing these instructions* I think it's *effect*⁴ as to *alien duties* had *not yet been experienced* and therefore was *not attended* to. *If it* had been *noted* in the *debate I am* sure that the *annihilation of our whale*⁵ *trade* would have been *thought too great a price to pay* for the *reservation of* a *barren power* which a *majority of the members* did not propose *ever to exercise tho* they were willing to *retain it. Stipulating equal rights* for *foreigners and natives we* obtain more in *foreign ports than* our *instructions required,* and *we* only *part*⁶ with, in⁷ *our own ports,* a *power* of which *sound policy* would *probably* for *ever forbid* the *exercise.* Add to this that *our treaty will be* for a very *short term,* and *if any* evil be *experienced under it,* a *reformation will soon* be in *our power. I am therefore* for *putting* this among *our original propositions* to the *court of London. If* it should *prove* an *insuperable obstacle with them, or if* it should *stand* in the way of *a greater advantage, we* can *but abandon* it in the *course* of the *negociation.*

In my copy of the cypher, on the Alphabetical side, numbers are wanting from 'Denmark' to 'disc' inclusive, and from 'gone' to 'governor' inclusive. I suppose them to have been omitted in copying. Will you be so good as to send them to me from yours by the first safe conveyance? Compliments to the ladies and to Colo. Smith from Dr. Sir Your friend & servant, TH: JEFFERSON

Dft (DLC); lacks complimentary close, here supplied from RC. RC (MHi: AMT); partly in code, with interlineal decoding in W. S. Smith's hand. Tr (MHi: AMT); contains text of the entire letter as decoded; labelled at head of text "(Translation)"; endorsed. PrC (DLC). Entry in SJPL reads: "Adams John. In cypher. Principles of the project."

¹ This and subsequent words in italics are underscored in Dft, written in code in RC, and decoded interlineally by Smith, employing Code No. 8.
² RC and Tr read: "impracticableness."
³ The following passage is deleted in Dft: "I do not recollect whether your proposition, to put foreigners on the footing of natives, was made at all, but the object which excluded the other proposition would oppose this also. I am of opinion the effect of Alien duties in England was not at that moment known or attended to. From the enquiries which I have made I think that."
⁴ Thus in RC, but incorrectly copied into Tr as "offset."
⁵ Dft reads "whale"; the code number employed (301) represents "al"; and Smith decoded the word as "whale"; but Tr errs in giving the reading as "whole." All previous editions read "whole": TJR, I, 263-5; HAW, I, 370-2; Ford, IV, 79-82; L & B, V, 46-9; Burnett, *Letters of Members*, VII, No. 591, note 3.
⁶ RC and Tr supply no decoding for this word, because of TJ's error in encoding it in RC, which he corrected in margin of PrC from "1672" to "1072."
⁷ Tr reads for this and the preceding word: "within."

From John Paul Jones

Sir   L'Orient July 31st. 1785.

I had the honor to write you the 29th. of this Month, praying you to address the Court, to prevent Mr. Puchilberg, a French Merchant here, from receiving the Prize-money due to the Subjects of the United-States who served on board the Squadron I commanded in Europe. I have done my Duty, and with great trouble and expence, both of time and money, obtained a settlement in their favor from Government. But, if Mr. Puchilberg (who has taken no trouble, and been at no expence to obtain a settlement) should receive the Money, the greatest part of it will never reach America, nor find it's way into the Pockets of the Captors: were Mr. Puchilberg the honestest Man in the World, he cannot, at this distance from America and being ignorant of the Laws of the American Flag, do justice to the concerned. Besides, a preference is due to the application of one Government to another for what regards the Interest of it's Subjects, especially where it is clear that every caution has been observed for obtaining Justice to each individual.

The enclosed Copy of a Letter, which has just now been communicated to me, from Monsieur de Soulanges à M. M. les Juges Consuls—dated at Toulon the 14th. of this Month, announcing that the Algerians have declared War against the United States, is of too serious a nature not to be sent immediately to you.

This event may, I believe, surprize some of our fellow Citizens; but, for my part, I am rather surprized that it did not take place sooner. It will produce a good effect, if it unites the People of America in measures consistent with their national honor and interest, and rouses them from that illjudged security which the intoxication of Success has produced since the Revolution.

My best wishes will always attend that Land of Freedom, and my Pride will be always gratifyed when such measures are adopted as will make us respected as a great People who deserve to be Free.

I am, Sir, with great esteem and respect your most obedient & most humble Servt.,   J. Paul Jones

Tr (DNA: PCC, No. 87, I); in Jones' hand; at head of letter: "*Copy*"; at foot of letter: "His Excellency Thos. Jefferson Esqr. Minister Plenipotentiary of the United States at the Court of France." Tr (DNA: PCC, No. 107, I). Enclosure: Soulanges' letter, addressed to the judges and consuls at Nantes, informing them of the Algerines' declaration of war against Americans, and requesting that they advise American captains of this fact, is printed in Sherburne, *Life of John Paul Jones*, p. 267; see also Bondfield to TJ, 14 July 1785.

From John Banister, Jr.

[Avignon] August 1st. 1785

Upwards of a month has now elapsed since I had the pleasure to address you from Lyons during which time my residence has been chiefly at this place. The society in which I find myself here is so agreeable as to determine my stay during the winter. Through the means of the Marquis La Fayette I have become acquainted with several of the most agreeable families here and such as perfectly accord with my situation being by no means in the expensive line. Two days ago I received letters from my father. The latest dated the twenty second of May mentions that the New England States have interdicted all British ships and British goods from entering their ports hoping thereby to put them in a more liberal way of thinking with respect to the carrying trade, which from their present policy they seem inclined to engross. Wheather this will be productive of advantages to them time *only* can determine, and we are left *only* the liberty of conjecturing on the event. It appears to me however that one of the great ends of the late contest viz: an extention of commerce, will be sooner brought about by that than any other means. At present the merchandise of almost all Europe passes through the hands of British merchants before it finds its entrance into our ports, and as often as the person of its proprietor changes so often does it experience an accumulation of price, which load, heavy as it is necessarily finds a resting place on the sholders of the consumer. As soon as the commerce through the channel of Great Britain is impeeded it will necessarily find its way by some other means and we shall be supplied with the productions of the Southern as well as the northern parts of Europe from the sources from whence they spring; without incuring the expence of loading and unloading ships unnecessarily; and of paying a commission to British merchants to transact that business for us which with the same ease we might do ourselves. I have been led into these reflections by comparing the prices of the productions of this country here, and in America, and I am surprised that the infatuation prevails whereby we are supplyed with silks and various other articles of commerce from Great Britain which we might have as good and infinitely cheaper from here. Since my stay here I have made but one excurtion into the country, can consequently convey but a very imperfect idea of it. From its general appearance however I should suppose that about one half

[335]

of it might claim a right to fertility, the other with a great deal of labor is made to produce vines, olives, &c.

The consequence of this poverty of soil is that grain is dear here, bearing a price rather higher than at Paris. All the other necessaries of life abound. I find the climate much cooler than I could have expected owing to the North and north west winds which generally prevail and which some times are extreemly inconvenient. It is some time since I wrote Mr. Williamos and I fear the letter may not have been received as I was not certain with regard to the address. In giving my thanks and compliments for his great attentions to me, you will oblige me highly, also Colo. Humphrys and Mr. Short. If there is a possibility of my being in any degree serviceable to you here nothing would please me more than to receive your commands. I am sir yours most respectfuly,

JNO. BANISTER Junr.

RC (DLC); without indication of addressee. Entry in sjl for its receipt on 11 Aug. 1785 has the following note: "should have been Avignon."

From the Marquis and Marquise De Spinola

Paris, 1 Aug. 1785. Dinner invitation to TJ for Wednesday, 10 Aug.

RC (MHi); 2 p.; in French; addressed: "A Monsieur Monsieur de Jefferson Ministre Plenipre. des Etats Unis de l'Amerique Cul de Sac Tetebout à Paris."

From Stael de Holstein

Paris, 1 Aug. 1785. Dinner invitation to TJ for 7 Aug.

Printed invitation from "L'Ambassadeur de Suede," with blanks filled in (MHi); 2 p.; dated: "Lundi 1e. Aoust"; addressed "A Monsieur Monsieur de Jefferson" and, in pencil in an unknown hand, "the tetebou."

From John Cooper

Bristol, Eng. 2 Aug. 1785. Encloses a letter from James Monroe; he would have delivered it in person, but will not be in Paris before October or November; hopes to see TJ at that time.

RC (DLC); 1 p. Recorded in sjl as received 23 Sep. "by W. Short." Enclosure: James Monroe to TJ, 6 Apr. 1785.

From C. W. F. Dumas

MONSIEUR   Lahaie 2e. Août 1785

Persuadé que Votre Excellence sera bien aise de connoître le contenu de l'incluse, je la lui adresse ouverte, avec priere de vouloir bien, après l'avoir lue, la cacheter et l'expédier par le Paquebot qui partira ce mois de L'Orient. Je regrette de ne pouvoir y entrer dans les mêmes détails que dans mes Dépeches qui vont directement de ce pays. Mais j'ai dû promettre de ne point les exposer par la poste, et nommément par cette voie ici; et il faut être fidele à la parole donnée. J'espere que bientôt les raisons d'une telle circonspection cesseront. J'ai l'honneur d'être avec grand respect De Votre Excellence le très humble et très-obeissant Serviteur,

                                                C W F DUMAS

RC (DLC); at head of letter: "A. S. E. Mr. Jepherson M. P." Recorded in SJL as received 6 Aug. 1785. Enclosure: Probably Dumas' letter to the president of Congress, 2 Aug. 1785, enclosing several papers relative to negotiations between Austria and The Netherlands (Dumas Letter Book, Rijksarchief, The Hague; Photostat in DLC).

To Castries

SIR   Paris Aug. 3. 1785

The inclosed copy of a letter from Capt. John Paul Jones on the subject on which your Excellency did me the honour to write me on the   day of July will inform you that there is still occasion to be troublesome to you. A Mr. Puchelberg, a merchant of l'Orient, who seems to have kept himself unknown till money was to be received, now presents powers to receive it, signed by the American officers and crews: and this produces a hesitation in the person to whom your order was directed. Congress however having substituted Capt. Jones as Agent to sollicit and receive this money, he having given them security to forward it, when received, to their treasury, to be thence distributed to the claimants, and having at a considerable expence of time, trouble and money attended it to a conclusion, are circumstances of weight, against which Mr. Puchelberg seems to have nothing to oppose but a nomination by individuals of the crew, under which he has declined to act, and permitted the business to be done by another, without contradiction from him. Against him too it is urged that he fomented the sedition which took place among them, that he obtained this nomination from them while their minds were under ferment, and that he has given no security for the faithful paiment of the money to those entitled to it. I will add to these one other circumstance which appears to render it impossible that he should execute this trust. It is now several years since the right to this money arose. The persons in whom it originally vested were probably from different states in America. Many of them must be now dead, and their rights passed on to their representatives. But who are their representatives? The laws of some states prefer one degree of relations; those of others prefer others, there being no uniformity among the states on this point. Mr. Puchelberg therefore should know which of the parties are dead; in what order the laws of their respective states call their relations to the succession, and, in every case, which of those orders are actually in existence and entitled to the share of the deceased. With the Atlantic ocean between the principals and their substitute, your Excellency will perceive what an inexhaustible source of difficulties, of chicanery, and of delay, this might furnish to a person who should find an interest in keeping this money as long as possible in his own hands. Whereas if it be lodged in the treasury of Congress, they, by an easy reference to the tribunals of the different states, can have every one's portion immediately rendered, to himself if living, and, if dead, to such of his relations as the laws of his particular state prefer, and as shall be found actually living. I the rather urge this course, as I foresee that it will relieve your Excellency from numberless appeals which these people will be continually making from the decisions of Mr. Puchilberg, appeals likely to perpetuate that trouble of which you have already had too much, and to which I am sorry to be obliged to add by asking a peremptory order for the execution of what you were before pleased to decide on this subject.

I have the honor to be &c.   TH: J.

Tr (DNA: PCC, No. 87, I); in TJ's hand; at head of text: "a second letter to the Marechal de Castries." PrC of RC (DLC); portions of MS faded. Tr (DNA: PCC, No. 107, I). Entry in SJPL reads: "Castries. Puchilberg." A copy was sent to John Jay with TJ's letter of 30 Aug. 1785. Enclosure: Copy of John Paul Jones to TJ, 29 July 1785.

To John Paul Jones

SIR   Paris Aug. 3. 1785.

I received yesterday your favour of the 29'th, and have written on the subject of it to the Mareshall de Castries this morning. You shall have an answer as soon as I receive one. Will you be so good as to make an enquiry into all the circumstances relative to Peyrouse's expedition which seem to ascertain his destination. Particularly what number of men and of what conditions and vocations had he on board? What animals, their species and number? What trees, plants or seeds? What utensils? What merchandize or other necessaries? This enquiry should be made with as little appearance of interest in it as possible. Should you not be able to get satisfactory information without going to Brest, and it be convenient for you to go there, I will have the expences, this shall occasion you, paid. Commit all the circumstances to writing, and bring them when you come yourself, or send them by a safe hand. I am with much respect Sir Your most obedt. humble servt.,

TH: JEFFERSON

PrC (DLC). Tr (DNA: PCC, No. 87, I); in Short's hand, with a note at head of text ("To Capt. J. P. Jones") and signature in TJ's hand. Tr (DNA: PCC, No. 107, I). Entry in SJPL reads: "Jones John Paul. Peyrouse." A copy was enclosed in TJ to John Jay, 6 Oct. 1785.

The objects of Lapérouse's EXPEDITION, equipped and sponsored by Louis XVI, were stated in directions from the king dated 26 June 1785; it was on 1 Aug. 1785 that the *Boussole* and *Astrolabe* set forth from Brest on their voyage of geographical and scientific discovery (See *Voyage de La Pérouse autour du Monde*, Paris, 1797, 4 vols.; and Gilbert Chinard, ed., *Le Voyage de Lapérouse sur les Côtes de l'Alaska et de la Californie*, Baltimore, 1937).

From Pierrard

MONSIEUR   Fénétrange, en Lorraine allemande, le 3e. août 1785.

Il y a déja plus d'une an, que j'ai eû l'honneur d'écrire à M. franklin, prédécesseur de Votre Excellence, pour avoir des nouvelles de l'existence des Nommés Jean philippe et Laurent Pierson; Anne Marie, Marguerite, et Sara Pierson, leurs Soeurs; originaires de ce pays-ci, et établis depuis longtemps dans la province de Pensylvanie. Les deux premiers s'étoient fixés à Nockomixon dans le Comté de Bucks: Marguerite Pierson avoit épousé un Nommé Jean Schmitt; et Sara Pierson Dietrich Welcker; qui résidoient à Schippach, et Parkyoeman [Perkiomen], dans le Comté de philadelphie. Il y a ici un procès, pour la décision duquel il seroit très intéressant d'être légalement informé Si ces personnes Sont encore actuellement en vie, ou S'ils ont laissé des Enfants ou petits Enfants, qui les représentent: ne sachant mieux m'adresser qu'à Votre Excellence pour acquérir les Eclaircissements, dont on a besoin, je prens la liberté Monsieur, de Vous Supplier de vouloir bien contribuer à me les procurer, en écrivant à ce Sujet dans le pays. Je prie aussi Votre Excellence de m'honorer d'une réponse, pour me faire Savoir si Elle aura la bonté de S'intéresser à ce que je lui demande; et pour quel temps à peu près je pourrai recevoir les instructions désirées.

J'ai l'honneur d'être avec la considération la plus distinguée, Monsieur, Votre très humble et très obèissant serviteur,

PIERRARD
avocat en parlement

RC (MHi); endorsed. Recorded in SJL as received 7 Aug. 1785. Pierrard's letter to FRANKLIN, dated 28 July 1784, is in PPAP: Franklin Papers, XXXII, 66.

From John Adams

MY DEAR SIR   Grosvenor Square Augt. 4. 1785.

Yesterday our Friend Mr. Short arrived. Mr. Dumas had never any Commission from Congress, and therefore can have no Title under the United States. He never had any other Authorization than a Letter from Dr. Franklin and another from the Committee of Secret Correspondence, in the year 1775. I wish he had a regular Commission. I direct my Letters to Monsieur C. W. F. Dumas a la Haye, only. I should advise you to allow Mr. Short a Guinea a day except Sundays, which will amount to something near your Ideas.

Houdons Life may be insured for five Per Cent, two for the Life and three for the Voyage. I mentioned it at Table with several Merchants; they all agreed that it would not be done for less. But Dr. Price, who was present undertook to enquire and inform me. His answer is, that it may be done at an office in Hackney for five Per Cent. He cannot yet say for less, but will endeavour to reduce it a little. You may write to the Doctor to get it done, and he will reduce it, if possible. I will let you know by Mr. Short, how far I have ventured in conformity to the Propositions you inclose, knowing your sentiments before, but I think we had better wait sometime before we propose them any where else.

Mr. Samuel Watson a Citizen of the U. States, and settled at Charlestown S.C. as a Merchant, sailed from thence about two years ago, for the Havannah, and has not been heard of since, till lately a Gentleman from the Havannah has reported that a Mr. Watson from Charlestown was taken in the Bay of Mexico and carried into Carthagena, from thence sent to the Castle of St. Juan, de Ullua la Vera Cruz and afterwards sent to Trascala, where it is supposed he is at present. His Father and numerous Relations are very anxious for his Fate, and earnestly beg that you would interest yourself with the Comte D'Aranda and Mr. Charmichael for his Release, but if that cannot be had in full that you would endeavour to procure his removal to old Spain, that his Friends may hear from him, and gain Intelligence respecting the Property he may have left in Carolina. I have written to Charmichael, and intend to speak to Don Del Campo.

Pray send me the Arrêt against English Manufactures and every other new Arrêt, which may any Way affect the United States. It is confidently given out here that our Vessells are not admitted into the French W. Indies. Has there been any new Arret, since that of August 1784? Can you discover the Cause, of the great Ballance of Exchange in favour of England, from France, Spain, Holland, &c. as well as America? And whether this Appearance of Prosperity will continue?[1] I think that at the Peace, the British Merchants sent their Factors abroad with immense quantities of their Manufactures, the whole Stock they had on hand. These Factors have sold as they could, and bought Remittances especially Bills of Exchange as they could, i.e. very dear, so that the loss on the Exchange is that of the British Merchant, and consequently that this appearance is not so much in favour of England. Spain I expect will follow the Example of France in prohibiting Brit. Manufactures, at least if Del Campo does not make a commercial Treaty with Woodward who is appointed to treat with him. But the Diplomaticks are of opinion nothing will be done with him, nor with Crawford. The two Years expire in January. If Crawford is likely to do any Thing be so good as to let me know it.

The words "Ship and Sailor," still turn the Heads of this People. They grudge to every other People, a single ship and a single seaman. The Consequence of this Envy, in the End, will be the loss of all their own. They seem at present to dread American Ships and Seamen more than any other. Their Jealousy of our Navigation is so strong, that it is odds if it does not stimulate them to hazard their own Revenue.

I am, my dear Sir, with Sincere Esteem your Friend,

JOHN ADAMS

RC (DLC). FC (MHi: AMT); in W. S. Smith's hand. Recorded in SJL as received 9 Aug. 1785.

Adams' letter to Carmichael about WATSON is dated 29 July 1785 and is in MHi: AMT. On Short's arrival in London, Adams recorded in his letter-book under 5 Aug. 1785 (MHi: AMT, p. 107-24) the French and English texts of the treaty with Prussia set in parallel columns. He had advised De Thulemeier of Short's mission, and De Thule-

meier assured him that "M. Short . . . sera acceuilli avec toute la distinction qu'il peut exiger de ma part, d'autant plus qu'étant porteur du Traité de Commerce que j'ai eu l'avantage de negocier avec Vous, votre ami et celui de M. Jefferson" (Adams to De Thulemeier, 24 July 1785; De Thulemeier to Adams, 5 Aug. 1785; MHi: AMT).

[1] This question is not in FC.

From James Currie

DR SIR   Richmond Augt. 5th. 1785

Your favor of Novr. the 11th. 84. by Coll. Le Maire came safe to hand, with the 2 Pamphletts on the Animal Magnetism, and the one giving an account of the then last Aerial Voyage of Mssrs. Roberts, for both of which I thank you kindly, as an instance that I had the honor to be remembred by you, at so great a distance. I would have given a great deal to have seen their ascension, with the mingled emotions of the Spectators. With regard to the Encyclopedie my being rather a Novice in the French language, makes it a matter of more indifference to me than it would Otherwise be if I could read the language easily. If you think proper I should have it you may (if you please) subscribe for me. The Politicks of the Emperor and the Mynheers seem to have been very Ambiguous and after all, I fancy no blows. The Dutch must pay the piper. By the bye old Alberti died and was interrd last night here. He was one of a Band of musick to whom I have subscribed tho never heard them, at all; they surpass in execution, hardly the Jews Harp and Banjer performers. I tendered your friendly respects and remembrances to the families of Ampthill and Tuckahoe. The Partridges &c. &c. mentioned in your letter by Le Maire have never arrived here, tho it would have been an agreeable task for Coll: Cary to have seen their multiplying, here. Joseph Mayo of Powtan [Powhatan] died on his passage from Lisbon to Boston, has enriched some of his relations by his Legacies and has astonished some of our acquaintances by his will giving liberty to all his Slaves, their number from 150 to 170. I believe its report has caused 2 or 3 combats between Slaves and their Owners, now struggling for the liberty to which they conceive themselves entitled. The Legislature's attention I imagine will be taken up with it next Session. We have had a Meeting of the Episcopal Clergy and laymen from every county to modify their mode of Worship &c. &c. They have monopolised all the former Glebes and their appendages. The other Sectarists complain heavily of the preference given them, have wrote severe things against them in the publick papers and intend a petition to next assembly to abrogate the law of the last in their faver and all the Consequences it invoked. How it will End I don't know but there is to be a Convention in Philadelphia soon up[on] this business. Our Delegates both Laymen and clergy, I have forgot. Jno. Page [of] Rosesell is one I believe. E. R. Jr., Attorney General was no blank in their meetings here. I believe he has studied [the] true Gospel, for both this and the World of Spirits.

The Js. River Company of which I have the honor to be one, are to meet here the 20th. current to incorporate themselves, as more than one half the money necessary for the purpose is Subscribed, which entitles us to meet and Elect our President &c. &c. The Potomack members are before hand with us, however. I hope we'll do something now (if ever). The State has 100 shares, Genl. W. 100, D. Ross 50. I took 40. 200 Drs. is a share and every share till 10 has a Vote. When above 10, every 5 shares has only 1 Vote. The Capitol ground is now Marked out here and astonishing to me, indeed is the place fixed upon for it. Œconomy has made the directors (who are A. Cary, E. Randolph, Wm. Hay, Jaq. Ambler, Robt. Goode, Js. Buchn., Richd. Adams and Turner Southall Esqrs.) fix the publick buildings all under one roof. They have marked out the ground which is now digging. The first Brick to be laid on Wednesday next, with a Medal &c. &c. —honors[1]—they have brought it to the point of the hill above my house with a deep Ravine or gulley on each side. By the time the Portico and Steps &c. &c. are finished, it leaves no room for a Street, unless it is to serpentine along the bottom beginning below my house and going up by the Spring called the governors. By receding 100 feet backward, they would have had a spacious field on each side, with room for Capitol Yard and Spacious Avenues on every hand for pleasure or use. I wish you had been here, and one of the directors. It has appeared to the Gentlemen in a different light than to every other person without exception that has viewed the ground. In the 100 feet there is a rise of between 7 and 8 feet, and a great many Bricks and other Expences to the publick would have been saved. As they have consulted you about the plan of the building I wish to God you would offer your advice as to its site if you please. It may not come too late. Self Interest the prime mover of human actions has something I confess to say in my sollicitations to you, on this head. I have almost finished a Brick house on the main Street below my own house in expectation of its being continued and the hill cut down to allow an easy access to the Capitol up the face of the hill from my house there. But cutting down the hill here now will answer no purpose as there is no Street to pass by the Capitol leading up the Country except the serpentine along the bottom [. . .] described.—enough of this. I dare say I have tired you but as your Opinion has influence I thot proper to Mention it to you. Perhaps you may have time Enough to Animadvert before it is too late. The Opinion I think that every foreigner will form is Obvious, in regard to the Choice made of this ground, when there was enough left of publick property to admit of the easiest and pleasantest prospects and access to it on all hands by its being moved 100 feet back. What I have said on this head, I don't wish mentioned as coming from me. But I have related facts, you may depend. As I am much hurried at present I have room only to add your letter of Jany. inclosing Mr. Shorts I perused with attention and consulted Our friend Mr. Ross on that head, who with me intended to have executed your and Mr. Shorts orders in the best manner we could and have apprised you of it. But your favor by the Feby. packet put a stop to it Effectually and I have thought no more of it since. Mr. D. Ross had parted with his lotts to Mr. Greenhough. However we could have got others. Not the Square of Turpins as he had likewise Sold the Square you mention'd. Lotts have rise[n] to an enormous price on Shocoe Hill and the number of its respectable inhabitants are not a few for such a plaice as Richmond; the Governor, the attorney General, the Treasurer, Register, Mr. Pendleton, Mr. Marshall town Recorder; Mr. Blair, Mr. Pennock, Mr. Alexr. Donald, Mr. Dixon, Mr. Matthews and a long list more, some of them very respectable, make up the number. Tobacco has bore a high price, 42/6 once, now fallen to 30/ ℔ C. It is supposed it will soon rise again. We have had a Bugg which has destroyed a great deal of the wheat and now preying upon the Corn. Some will hardly make

bread to eat, when the Effects of this Bugg and the dry weather
we have lately had are taken into the account. I dont know whether
I told you before, Peyton Randolph of Wilton, the Hble. Batt.
Dandridge and Old Coll. Lewis Burwell are among the number
of the dead. Coll. Brent who married Miss Ambler died in about
2 Months after consummation, it has been said, an imprudent use
of cold Liquor after having taken an antimone. Vomit accelerated
his flight. Dr. McLurg, Miles Selden and Genl. Wood are of the
Council; Wm. Nelson Jr. Esqr. has retired from that board to
practise law, having got Mr. Tazwell['s] business, who was appointed by the Executive in room of the H. B. Dandridge, one of
the former judges of the General Court. I don't think of anything
else at present you would wish to know. All the family at Eppinton
are well and all your other friends and connexions here. Col. Randolph of Tuckahoe who has just left me desires his best respects
to you, and hopes and wishes you soon to revisit your native Clime
if agreeable to yourself. D. Ross and McLurg both told me they
intended writing you soon. Since a dangerous illness about to
attack me when I did myself the honor to write you by the Marquis
Fayette and which had well nigh put an end to me, since my
recovery from it have been tolerably well and in much bustle and
confusion having engaged in Several buildings which are Exorbi-
tantly expensive and slow in their progress owing to sundry causes,
of which you may easily guess. Till they are Compleated I am
rivetted here. Should I change this Climate for Europe, I shall
surely Enquire you out. If there is any thing you think would be
instructive and usefull to me circumstanced as I am here in the
book way I'll thank you to send them to me. We have got a circulating Library here in its Infancy. Our first Importation has ar-
ri[ved] but I have not yet seen any of the books. I hope it will be
usefull. It has cost me 6 Guineas already and they want more. We
have likewise got an Organ in our Church, and Old Selden is dead
and given way, for the Revd. John Buchanan, our present incumbent. This Vulgar miscellany I am afraid will disgust you, but
I gave you the things here mentioned just as they Occurred. The
Kentuckians are for separate goverment instantly. Next assembly
are to hear their petition. George Muter is their present Chief
Judge and Harry Innis their Attorney General, the Indians or their
Associates having dispatched Walker Daniel, their former attorney
general. I know nothing what Congress are doing.
Would mention it, I most [sincerely?] sympathise with you in

your loss of your youngest daughter and am much pained at a paragraph in your last wherein you mention the Sun of your happiness having been clouded over, never again to brighten, and in one fatal moment all the Schemes of your life have been shifted from before you, and that afflictions and ill health have conspired to fix the depression of your mind. Forbid it Heaven. I hope the cloud is dispelled and that your Sun has again beamed upon you in its fullest lustre. Should my most Sanguine hopes and wishes be dissapointed in this, if there is any thing upon Earth in my power to alleviate or remove any difficulty or load from you, be assured you may Confide in me and always command me and my best Services. I now come to beg your pardon and hope youll have the lenity to forgive my not having answered your polite and very friendly letters of the different dates before mentioned. Your honors in future which, I hope will be regular, shall be punctually attended to and answered. No letter from any friend upon earth gives me so much pleasure as one from Mr. Jefferson, whose former politeness and friendship to me will never be Effac'd from my mind. Please tender my most respectfull Regards to Miss Jefferson and Mr. Short (if with you). I intend to write him a few lines by this opportunity. In expectation of being often honored by a letter from you I subscribe myself with the greatest truth & the most profound Respect, Dr. Sir, Your Most Obedt. and H Servt.,

JAMES CURRIE

RC (DLC) addressed and endorsed. Recorded in SJL as received 18 Sep. 1785.

The will of JOSEPH MAYO of Henrico county was drawn on 27 May 1780 and was probated 10 Oct. 1785. It contained the following paragraph: "It is my most earnest request that the gentlemen who shall be named and appointed executors . . . petition the general assembly for leave to set free all and every one of the slaves of which I may die possessed, on account of their services to me whilst alive, and I intreat my said executors to leave nothing undone which may be requisite for obtaining the manumission of the said slaves." Under an Act passed Oct. 1787 Paul Carrington, Miles Selden, and Joseph Carrington were appointed trustees to carry Mayo's intentions "into effect, under such limitations and restrictions, as will guard the rights of all persons having claims upon the estate of the said Mayo either as creditors or legatees

under his will." This emancipation, however, was made subject to "the direction and control of the high court of chancery." That court was authorized and required to make all orders and decrees in the premises as should seem "just and reasonable, for carrying the said bequest into full effect, having regard to the payment of all debts due by the said Joseph Mayo, and the legacies devised by him, if any such devisees there be, which ought in the opinion of the court be complied with." The Act also declared that an creditor or legatee could, before the high court of chancery rendered its final decree, institute any suit in law or equity for the recovery of a debt or legacy (Hening, XII, 611-13). The paragraph in TJ's LAST was in that of 5 Feb. 1785, which is missing. A FEW LINES to Mr. Short: Currie's letter to Short of this date is in DLC: Short Papers.

[1] It is possible that Currie, whose

handwriting is as erratic as his spelling and punctuation, and even more difficult, intended this word to be "horrors." But "honors" not only seems the more likely, but also, as here written, closely resembles the same word further on in the letter.

To John Adams, with Draft of Treaty Proposed for Barbary States

DEAR SIR   Paris Aug. 6. 1785.

I now inclose you a draught of a treaty for the Barbary states, together with the notes Dr. Franklin left me. I have retained a presscopy of this draught, so that by referring to any article, line and word in it you can propose amendments and send them by the post without any body's being able to make much of the main subject. I shall be glad to receive any alterations you may think necessary as soon as convenient, that this matter may be in readiness. I inclose also a letter containing intelligence from Algiers. I know not how far it is to be relied on. My anxiety is extreme indeed as to these treaties. What are we to do? We know that Congress have decided ultimately to treat. We know how far they will go. But unfortunately we know also that a particular person has been charged with instructions for us, these five months who neither comes nor writes to us. What are we to do? It is my opinion that if Mr. Lambe does not come in either of the packets (English or French) now expected, we ought to proceed. I therefore propose to you this term, as the end of our expectations of him, and that if he does not come we send some other person. Dr. Bancroft or Capt. Jones occur to me as the fittest. If we consider the present object only, I think the former would be most proper: but if we look forward to the very probable event of war with those pirates, an important object would be obtained by Capt. Jones's becoming acquainted with their ports, force, tactics &c. Let me know your opinion on this. I have never mentioned it to either, but I suppose either might be induced to go. Present me affectionately to the ladies & Colo. Smith & be assured of the sincerity with which I am Dr. Sir Your friend & servt.,   TH: JEFFERSON

ENCLOSURE

Draught of a Treaty of Amity and Commerce between the United states of America and
For the purpose of establishing peace, friendship and commerce

between the United states of America and their citizens on the one part
and

and his subjects on the other, the parties have established the following
articles.

G.D.1.   1. There shall be a firm, inviolable and universal peace and sincere
friendship between the United states of America and their citizens on
the one part and

and his subjects on the other part, without exception
of persons or places.

D.M.1610.16.   2. His majesty agrees to release all citizens of the United states now
in captivity within his dominions, and to restore all property which
has been taken by any of his subjects from citizens of the United states.

D.M.1683.8.   3. No vessel of his majesty shall make captures or cruize within
E.A.1686.8. sight of the coasts of the United states.

G.D.20.   4. No citizen or subject of either party shall take from any power
D.M.1683.7. with whom the other may be at war any commission or letter of
F.A.1684.15. marque for arming any vessel to act as a privateer against the other
on pain of being punished as a pirate.

G.D.12.   5. If one of the parties should be engaged in war with any other
D.M.1683.3.19. power, the free intercourse and commerce of the subjects or citizens
F.A.1684.12. of the party remaining neuter with the belligerent powers shall not be
interrupted. On the contrary in that case as in full peace the vessels
of the neutral party may navigate freely to and from the ports and on
the coasts of the belligerent parties, free vessels making free goods,
insomuch that all things shall be adjudged free which shall be on board
any vessel belonging to the neutral party although such things belong
to an enemy of the other: and the same freedom shall be extended to
persons who shall be on board a free vessel, although they should be
enemies to the other party, unless they be souldiers in actual service

Prussn. of such enemy. In like manner all persons subjects or citizens of either
decln. of party, and all property belonging to subjects or citizens of either party
Apr. found on board a vessel of the enemy of the other shall be free from
30. 1781. capture and detention.

G.D.14.   6. In the same case where one of the parties is engaged in war with
D.M.1610.2. any other power that the vessels of the neutral party may be readily
F.M.1682.3. and certainly known it is agreed that they shall be provided with sea
letters or passports which shall express the name, the property and
burthen of the vessel, as also the name and dwelling of the master,
which passports shall be made out in good and due forms (to be settled
by conventions between the parties whenever occasion shall require)
shall be renewed as often as the vessel shall return into port, and shall
be exhibited whensoever required as well in the open sea as in port.
But if the said vessel be under convoy of one or more vessels of war
belonging to the neutral party, the simple declaration of the officer
commanding the convoy that the said vessel belongs to the party of
which he is shall be considered as establishing the fact and shall
relieve both parties from the trouble of further examination.

G.D.15.   7. And to prevent entirely all disorder and violence in such cases it is
D.M.1610.3. stipulated that when the vessels of the neutral party, sailing without
D.M.1683.4. convoy, shall be met by any vessel of war public or private of the other

party, such vessel of war shall not approach within cannon shot of the said neutral vessel nor send more than two or three men in their boat on board the same to examine her sea letters or passports.

8. All persons belonging to any vessel of war public or private who shall molest or injure in any manner whatever the people, vessels, or effects of the other party, shall be responsible in their persons and property for damages and interest, sufficient security for which shall be given by all commanders of private armed vessels before they are commissioned. G.D.15. F.M.1682.18.

9. All citizens of the United states taken by any of the powers of Barbary or their subjects and brought into any of the ports or dominions of the emperor of Marocco shall be immediately set at liberty by the emperor: and all vessels and merchandize belonging to citizens of the United states, and taken by any of the said powers or their subjects and brought into any of the ports or dominions of his Majesty shall in like manner be caused by his majesty to be delivered up by the captors without being carried out of port, and shall be faithfully restored to the said citizens owning them. F.M.1682.6. D.M.1610.4.

10. If the citizens or subjects of either party, in danger from tempests, pirates, enemies or other accident, or needing repairs, or supplies of water, food or other necessaries, shall take refuge with their vessels or effects within the harbours or jurisdiction of the other, or if the armed vessels public or private of either party, shall take such refuge for any the same causes, they shall be received, protected and treated with humanity and kindness, and shall be permitted to furnish themselves at reasonable prices with all refreshments, provisions and other things necessary for their sustenance, health and accomodation and for the repair of their vessels. G.D.18. D.M.1610.8.12. D.M.1683.6. F.A.1684.13.

11. When any vessel of either party shall be wrecked, foundered, or otherwise damaged on the coasts or within the dominions of the other, their respective subjects or citizens shall receive, as well for themselves as for their vessels and effects the same assistance which would be due to the inhabitants of the country where the damage happens, and shall pay the same charges and dues only as the said inhabitants would be subject to pay in a like case: and if the operations of repair shall require that the whole or any part of their cargo be unladed, they shall pay no duties, charges or fees on the part which they shall relade and carry away. G.D.9. D.M.1610.12. D.M.1683.6. F.A.1684.13.

12. The vessels of the subjects or citizens of either party coming on any coast belonging to the other but not willing to enter into port, or being entered into port and not willing to unload their cargoes or break bulk, shall have liberty to depart and to pursue their voiage without molestation and without being obliged to pay any duties charges or fees whatsoever or to render any account of their cargo. G.D.8.

13. Each party shall endeavor by all the means in their power to protect and defend all vessels and other effects belonging to the citizens or subjects of the other, and the persons of the citizens and subjects of the other, which shall be within the extent of their jurisdiction by sea or land, and shall use all their efforts to liberate such persons and to recover and cause to be restored to the right owners their vessels and G.D.7.

effects which shall be taken within the extent of their said jurisdiction.

F.M.1682.5.　　14. Whenever the vessels of either party in any port of the other shall be about to depart, all hostile vessels in the same port or it's vicinities shall be detained by the party within whose jurisdiction they are until such vessel shall have had a reasonable time to escape.

E.A.1686.11.　　15. No vessels of war of the United states within the ports of his
D.M.1683.11. majesty shall be searched under pretence of their having on board fugitive slaves, or under any other pretence whatever, nor shall any person be required to pay for any such slaves, nor to redeliver them if any such should really have taken asylum therein.

F.A.1684.27.　　16. The vessels of war of either party coming to anchor in a port of the other shall be saluted by the forts or batteries with as many guns as a vessel of the same size of any other nation, which vessel shall return the salute, gun for gun.

G.D.2.3.　　17. The subjects and citizens of either party may frequent the coasts and countries of the other, and reside and trade there in all sorts of produce, manufactures and merchandize, the purchase and sale of which shall be free to all persons of every description [unembarrassed by monopoly],[1] paying no greater duties than the [natives of the country or the] most favoured nation pay; and they shall enjoy all the rights privileges and exemptions in navigation and commerce which [native subjects or citizens, or] the subjects of the most favored nation
D.M.1610.1. enjoy. They shall also be free to pass and repass with their merchandize within the territories of the other without being obliged to obtain passports.

G.D.5.　　18. All merchants, commanders of vessels and other subjects and
D.M.1683.14. citizens of each party shall have free liberty in all places within the dominion or jurisdiction of the other to manage their own business themselves, or to employ whomsoever they please to manage the whole or any part thereof for them: and shall not be obliged to make use of any interpreter broker or other person whatsoever, nor to pay them any salary or fees unless they chuse to make use of them. Moreover, they shall not be obliged in loading or unloading their vessels to make use of those workmen which may be appointed by public authority for that purpose, but it shall be entirely free for them to load or unload them by themselves, or to make use of such persons in loading or unloading them as they shall think fit, without paying any fees or salary to any other whomsoever: neither shall they be forced to unload any
F.A.1684.16. sort of merchandize into any other vessels, or to receive them into their own or to wait for their being loaded longer than they please.

D.M.1683.14.　　19. No merchant or other citizen or subject of either party within the territories of the other shall be obliged to buy or sell any merchandize or thing against his will, and shall be free to buy and sell whatever he may think[2] proper.

G.D.6.　　20. That the vessels of either party loading within the ports or jurisdiction of the other may not be uselessly harrassed or detained, it is agreed that all examinations of goods required by the laws shall be made before they are laden on board the vessel, and that there shall be no examination after, nor shall the vessel be searched at any time unless articles shall have been laden therein clandestinely and illegally, in which case the person by whose order they were carried on board, or who carried them without order, shall be liable to the laws of the land in which he is. But no other person shall be molested, nor shall any other goods nor the vessel be seised or detained for that cause.

21. The subjects or citizens of either party, their vessels and effects shall not be liable to any embargo seisure or detention on the part of the other for any military expedition or other public or private purpose whatsoever. And in all cases of seizure, detention or arrest for debts contracted by any citizen or subject of the one party within the jurisdiction of the other, the same shall be made and prosecuted by order and authority of law only and according to the regular course of proceeding usual in such cases. F.D.16. D.M.1610.7.

22. If any difference either civil or criminal arise between two citizens of the United States within the territories of his majesty neither shall be bound to answer or appear before the judiciary institutions of the country nor to obey any officer or process thereof, but it shall be decided by the Consul for the United states, who shall have full authority in every such case civil and criminal to proceed according to the instructions he shall have received from Congress. But if the power of the country shall be necessary to aid him in the arrest, detention or punishment of one of the parties, he shall receive such aid. D.M.1683.15. E.A.1686.15.

23. If any citizen of the United states within the territories of his majesty, assault, strike, wound, or kill a subject of his majesty or any other person under his protection (other than a fellow-citizen which case is herein before provided for) he shall be punished in the same manner and not more rigorously than a subject who should have committed the same offence. Nor shall he be punished until the Consul of his nation shall have been called on to defend him. And if he make his escape, neither the said Consul nor any other citizen of the said United states shall be detained or molested on that account. A subject of his majesty committing a like offence within his territories on a citizen of the United states shall be punished in the same manner as if he had committed it on one of his majesty's subjects. D.M.1683.16. F.M.1682.16.

24. The citizens or subjects of the United states shall have power to dispose of their personal goods within the jurisdiction of his majesty by testament, donation or otherwise: and their representatives shall succeed to their said personal goods within the same jurisdiction by testament, or ab intestato and may take possession thereof either by themselves or by others acting for them, and dispose of the same at their will, paying such dues only as the inhabitants of the country wherein the said goods are shall be subject to pay in like cases. And in case of the absence of the representative the Consul, vice consul or agent for the United states shall take care of the said goods according to his instructions, or if there be no such Consul, vice consul or agent, then certain good and principal people of the country shall be appointed to make an inventory of them and to take care of them for the representative, so that the officers of the said country may not meddle G.D.10. D.M.1610.10. F.M.1682.14. D.M.1683.13. D.M.1610.11.

with them on pretence of escheat, forfeiture or on any other pretence whatever.

G.D.25.
D.M.1683.14.17.
F.M.1682.14.
F.A.1684.20.

25. Each party shall be at liberty to keep within any the ports of the other Consuls, viceconsuls, agents, or commissaries of their own appointment who shall be free and secure in their persons, houses, and effects, and shall not in any case be bound to answer for the debts of any citizens of their nation or others unless they shall have obliged themselves thereto by writing. Each of them shall be at liberty to chuse his own interpreters, brokers and other agents and servants, to go as often as he pleases on board any vessels in the harbours, to pass and repass in the country, to practise his own religion in his own house openly and freely and receive any other persons there to do the same, without being subject to molestation or insult by word or deed.

F.M.1682.15.
F.A.1684.21.
D.A.1683.12.

He shall enjoy an exemption from all duties for the provisions and necessaries of every kind for his house and family, shall be authorised to take depositions, authenticate contracts, deeds, wills, and other writings, give passports, and perform all other the functions of his office according to his instructions, without impediment from any, but on the contrary shall be aided therein by the power of the country when he shall ask such aid.

D.M.1683.21.
F.M.1682.17.

26. If any contravention to this treaty shall happen, the peace shall continue nevertheless: but the party injured shall demand amicable reparation, and until this shall have been denied shall not appeal to arms.

G.D.23.
F.M.1682.19.
F.A.1684.28.

27. If war should arise between the two parties, the subjects and citizens of either country, then residing or being in the other, shall be allowed to remain nine months to collect their debts and settle their affairs, and may depart freely, carrying off all their effects without molestation or hinderance.

G.D.26.

28. If either party shall hereafter grant to any other nation any particular favour in navigation or commerce, it shall immediately become common to the other party, freely where it is freely granted to such other nation, or on yeilding the compensation where such other nation does the same.

G.D.27.

29. This treaty shall be in force fifty years from the exchange of ratifications which exchange shall be within eighteen months from the date hereof, and in the mean time the several articles thereof shall be observed on both sides as if they were already ratified.

In witness whereof &c.

Note, in the marginal references G.D. stands for our General Draught, and the number following it for the article of that general draught. A. stands for Algerines. D. for Dutch. E. for English. F. for French. M. for Moors, the first number for the date and the second for the article of the treaty. Thus D.M.1683. 21. stands for the treaty between the Dutch and Moors, 1683. art. 21. All those here referred to will be found in the 5th. and 7th. vols. of the Corps Diplomatique.

1. There shall be peace.
2. Prisoners shall be released.

3. No Moorish vessels shall cruise on our coasts.
4. The citizens of neither to arm against the other under a foreign power.
5. Free vessels shall make free goods and persons, and free goods and persons not to lose freedom tho' in enemy's vessels.
6. Vessels to be provided with passports.
7. Armed vessels not to approach trading vessels.
8. Masters of armed vessels to give security.

Vessels at Sea.

9. Citizens of U.S. and their property brought by any Barbary vessel into Marocco, to be released.
10. Vessels forced by enemy, tempest or other necessity, shall be received into harbour and protected.
11. Vessels wrecked or damaged shall be protected and aided.
12. Vessels not breaking bulk to pay no duties.
13. Vessels and effects mutually protected in the harbours of each other.
14. On their departure, hostile vessels to be detained.
15. Vessels of war not be searched, asylum for fugitive slaves.
16. Vessels of war to be saluted.

Vessels in Port.

17. Free intercourse and commerce between the parties. no monopolies.
18. Individuals may transact their own business.
19. Every one free to buy and sell, but shall not be compelled to buy or sell.
20. Goods shall be examined before laden on board the vessel.
21. No embargo on vessels. persons and effects not to be seized. procedure for debts.
22. Differences between citizens of U.S. to be decided by Consul.
23. Assault between American and Moor to be punished as if both were Moors.
24. The goods of persons dying shall go to their representatives.
25. Consuls and their privileges.

Persons on Shore.

26. Contravention.
27. War.
28. Future favors to other nations to become common to these parties.
29. Duration of treaty. Ratification. In mean time, in force.

RC (MHi: AMT); endorsed in part: "ansd. 18 [Aug.] 1785." PrC (DLC). Recorded in SJL as sent "by Mr. Prentis"; entry in SJPL reads: "Adams John. Barbary." Enclosures: Draft of a treaty (MS in MHi: AMT); undated, in TJ's hand; the "retained . . . press copy" has not been found, nor have Franklin's notes been located. The "letter containing intelligence from Algiers" has not been found, though it may have been that enclosed in Jones to TJ, 31 July 1785, or Bondfield to TJ, 14 July 1785.

Although Franklin has generally been credited with writing the first draft of the treaty with the Barbary states (e.g., Van Doren, *Franklin*, p. 713), it is apparent that in the few short weeks before his departure he had time to prepare but little more than a table of references to pertinent articles in existing treaties. These notes he did not "have time to put into form," but left them for TJ to "reduce" (see TJ to Adams, 22 June, 7 July, and 28 July 1785). Whether TJ used all of the indicated articles cannot be determined in the absence of Franklin's notes, but, as in the preparation of the GENERAL DRAUGHT (see under 10 Nov. 1784), TJ made his own classification, this time grouping the articles under "Vessels at Sea," "Vessels in Port," and

"Persons on Shore." In this and in other respects the first draft was unquestionably written by TJ.

1 The three passages in square brackets (supplied) in Article 17 are those that John Adams thought should be left out (Adams to TJ, 18 Aug. 1785). He was doubtless correct in feeling that Article 17 went "farther than our Countrymen will at present be willing to go."
2 The following words deleted at this point: "shall be useful or desireable."

From John Adams

Dear Sir   Grosvenor Square Westminster Aug. 7. 1785

As to the Cask of Wine at Auteuil, it is not paid for. If you will pay for it and take it, you will oblige me. By a sample of it, which I tasted it is good Wine, and very, extreamly cheap.

I am happy to find We agree so perfectly in the Change which is made in the Project. The Dye is cast. The Proposal is made. Let them ruminate upon it.

I thought of proposing a Tariff of Duties, that We might pay no more in their Ports than they should pay in ours. But their Taxes are so essential to their Credit, that it is impossible for them to part with any of them, and We should not choose to oblige ourselves to lay on as heavy ones. We are at Liberty to do it, however, when We please.

If the English will not abolish their Aliens Duty, relatively to us, We must establish an Alien Duty in all the United States. An Alien Duty against England alone will not answer the End. She will elude it by employing Dutch, French, Sweedish, or any other ships, and by frenchifying, dutchifying, or Sweedishizing her own Ships. If the English will persevere in excluding our Ships from their West India Islands, Canada, Nova Scotia, and Newfoundland, and in demanding any Alien Duty of us in their Ports within the Realm, and in refusing to amercian built Ships the Priviledges of british built Ships, We must take an higher Ground, a Vantage Ground. We must do more than lay on Alien Duties. We must take measures by which the Increase of Shipping and Seamen will be not only encouraged, but rendered inevitable. We must adopt in all the States the Regulations which were once made in England 5. Ric. 2. c. 3., and ordain that no American Citizen, or Denizen, or alien friend or Ennemy, shall ship any Merchandise out of, or into the United States and navigated with an American Captain and three fourths American Seamen. I should be sorry to adopt a Monopoly. But, driven to the necessity of it, I would not do Business by the Halves. The French deserve it of us as much as the English; for they are as much Ennemies to our Ships and Mariners. Their Navigation Acts are not quite so severe as those of Spain, Portugal and England, as they relate to their Colonies I mean. But they are not much less so. And they discover as strong a Lust to annihilate our navigation as any body.

Or might We modify a little? Might We lay a Duty of ten per Cent on all Goods imported in any but ships built in the United States, without saying any Thing about Seamen?

If we were to prohibit all foreign Vessells from carrying on our Coasting Trade, i.e. from trading from one State to another, and from one Port to another in the same State, We should do Something, for this Commerce will be so considerable as to employ many Ships and many Seamen, of so much the more Value to us as they will be always at home and ready for the Defence of their Country. But if We should only prohibit Importations, except in our own Bottoms or in the Bottoms of the Country or Nation of whose Growth or Production the Merchandises are, We should do nothing effectual against Great Britain. She would desire nothing better than to send her Productions to our Ports in her own Bottoms and bring away ours in return.

I hope the Members of Congress and the Legislatures of the States will study the British Acts of Navigation, and make themselves Masters of their Letter and Spirit, that they may judge how far they can be adopted by us, and indeed whether they are sufficient to do Justice to our Citizens in their Commerce with Great Britain.

There is another Enquiry which I hope our Countrymen will enter upon, and that is, what Articles of our Produce will bear a Duty upon Exportation? All such Duties are paid by the Consumer, and therefore are so much clear gain. Some of our Commodities will not bear any such Duties; on the contrary, they will require Encouragement by Bounties: But I suspect that Several Articles would bear an handsome Impost.

We shall find our Commerce a complicated Machine and difficult to manage, and I fear We have not many Men, who have turned their Thoughts to it. It must be comprehended by Somebody in its System and in its detail, before it will be regulated as it should be.

With great and Sincere Esteem I am dear Sir, your most obedient,   JOHN ADAMS

The Vacancy in your alphabet may be filled from points to

points inclusive 1506. 970. 331. 504. 1186. 1268. 356. 517. 754. 1085. 269. 148. 205. 1318. 1258. 942. 712. 75. 246. 127. 609. 885. 1461. 837. 1327. and secondly, in like manner 472. 560. 820. 83.—Now give *me* leave. You make use of the number 1672.[1] It has no meaning in my Cypher. Indeed there is a vacancy from 1596 to 1700 inclusive. When you have filled them up as you proposed I should thank you for a Copy by the first safe Conveyance &c.[2]

RC (DLC); in Adams' hand, with an additional page bearing postscript in W. S. Smith's hand. FC (MHi: AMT); also in Smith's hand; lacks postscript of RC. Entry in SJL of its receipt on 16 Aug. 1785 reads: "Received J. Adams's. Aug. 7. by post. It had been evidently opened, and came 4. days later than W. Short's of same date."

[1] This figure in RC is keyed by asterisk to a note in TJ's hand, which reads: "error for 1072. part."

[2] This paragraph, in Smith's hand in RC, is not in FC.

To Wilson Miles Cary

[*Paris, 7 Aug. 1785.* Entry in SJL reads: "W. M. Cary. By Dr. O'Connor." Not found.]

To Richard Price

SIR   Paris Aug. 7. 1785.

Your favor of July 2. came duly to hand. The concern you therein express as to the effect of your pamphlet in America, induces me to trouble you with some observations on that subject. From my acquaintance with that country I think I am able to judge with some degree of certainty of the manner in which it will have been received. Southward of the Chesapeak it will find but few readers concurring with it in sentiment on the subject of slavery. From the mouth to the head of the Chesapeak, the bulk of the people will approve it in theory, and it will find a respectable minority ready to adopt it in practice, a minority which for weight and worth of character preponderates against the greater number, who have not the courage to divest their families of a property which however keeps their consciences inquiet. Northward of the Chesapeak you may find here and there an opponent to your doctrine as you may find here and there a robber and a murderer, but in no greater number. In that part of America, there being but few slaves, they can easily disencumber themselves of them, and emancipation is put into such a train that in a few years there will be no slaves Northward of Maryland. In Maryland I do not find such a disposition to begin the redress of this enormity as in Virginia. This is the next state to which we may turn our eyes for the interesting spectacle of justice in conflict with avarice and oppression: a conflict wherein the sacred side is gaining daily recruits from the influx into office of young men grown and growing up. These have sucked in the principles of liberty as it were with their mother's milk, and it is to them I look with anxiety to turn the fate of this question. Be not therefore discouraged. What you have written will do a great deal of good: and could you still trouble yourself with our welfare, no man is more able to give aid to the labouring side. The college of William and Mary in Williamsburg, since the remodelling of it's plan, is the place where are collected together all the young men of Virginia under preparation for public life. They are there under the direction (most of them) of a Mr. Wythe one of the most virtuous of characters, and whose sentiments on the subject of slavery are unequivocal. I am satisfied if you could resolve to address an exhortation to those young men, with all that eloquence of which you are master, that it's influence on the future decision of this important question would be great, perhaps decisive. Thus you see that, so far from thinking you have cause to repent of what you have done, I wish you to do more, and wish it on an assurance of it's effect. The information I have received from America of the reception of your pamphlet in the different states agrees with the expectations I had formed.—Our country is getting into a ferment against yours, or rather have caught it from yours. God knows how this will end: but assuredly in one extreme or the other. There can be no medium between those who have loved so much. I think the decision is in your power as yet, but will not be so long. I pray you to be assured of the sincerity of the esteem & respect with which I have the honour to be Sir Your most obedt. humble servt.,

TH: JEFFERSON

P.S. I thank you for making me acquainted with Monsr. D'Ivernois.

PrC (DLC); endorsed, partly in shorthand. Tr (DLC); in a contemporary hand. PrC (DLC). Recorded in SJL as sent "by Dr. Bancroft"; entry in SJPL reads: "Price Dr. Slavery."

From William Short

                                                          London August 7th. 85

My last will have informed you of my Arrival at Boulogne. I was detained the next Day at Calais because no Packet sailed in the Evening. I by Accident heard of Comte Rochambeau being there and waited on him. He enquired in a most particular Manner after you, desired me to tell you what Pleasure he had recieved in reading your Notes, and related to a very large Company with general Marks of Approbation, the Manner in which you had treated the unphilosophical Opinion of human Degeneracy in America.

On Monday I embarked and after a tedious Passage of $12\frac{1}{2}$ hours arrived at Dover 9 o'Clock in the Evening. London strikes me on Account of its fine streets and excellent Horses and Carriages. But the Buildings and such of the Equestrian Statues as I have seen impress on the Mind an Idea of Insignificance in Comparison with those of Paris. I except here St. Pauls Church, which is immensely great, and being surrounded with Houses of Brick appears to very great Advantage.

I have been every Day to Mr. Adams's since my Arrival. I do not know whether he is writing to you as fully as you wished. I shall see to day.

Vessels are frequently arriving here from Virginia. The Price of Tobacco at this Market is frequently as low as 5 or 6 Pounds the Hhd. and yet they bring it. It is a Paradox in Trade which the Merchants themselves cannot or will not solve. You will be surprized when I tell you that Ross's Credit here is absolutely wrecked, his Debts selling at a considerable Discount and in the Hands of Trustees. This is another Paradox. I am told he could not be trusted for a Shilling and yet I think he must still be rich.

I was surprized to find that F. Skipwith had left London a few Days only before I arrived. He has been here some Months to settle some Commercial Correspondence and I am told he has succeeded very well.

There is a very careful Woman hired lately to go to Virginia with Mr. W. Lee's Children. Colo. Forrest knows her and thinks it probable that she might be also hired to return with your Daughter, although it is her present Plan to stay with Mr. Lee. It is probable she will not like Virginia as much as she supposes and will be glad to return.

I shall leave this Place in two or three Days. Accept my best Wishes Sir, and believe me as I ought to be Your's sincerely,

W SHORT

RC (ViWC).
Short's letter which informed TJ of his arrival AT BOULOGNE has not been found.

To William Bingham

[*Paris, 8 Aug. 1785*. Entry in SJL reads: "W. Bingham. Inclosing letter to Ct. d'Andlau. By post." Neither letter nor enclosure has been found.]

From James Gordon

[*Le Havre, 8 Aug. 1785*. Entry in SJL for 10 Aug. reads: "Received Jas. Gordon's. Havre. Aug. 8. proposing to carry Dr. F.'s baggage to Portsmouth in N. Hampshire." Not found.]

From David Ramsay

SIR   New York August 8th. 1785

In conformity to my promise I continue to send you my history as it comes out. The notes of the first volume though necessary to strangers are well known to Americans who have been in public Stations. I flatter myself the second volume which you will next receive will be more worthy your attention than the first. It contains the brilliant campaigns of 1780 and 1781 which were superior in materials for history to any that preceded them.

Mr. De Marbois has flattered me with an assurance that the work would be acceptable in France and that a translation of it would be desired. He transmits copies of it with a view to this to the Chevalier de Chatellux. Should an European edition and a translation be thought advisable I have taken the liberty of suggesting a few alterations and hints. I leave this matter wholly to yourself and Mr. Marbois' correspondent to determine. Perhaps you will not be so well able to decide on it till you see the whole text which I hope you will by the next packet. If there is any merit in the work it is in the chapters that are now striking off. Whatsoever you shall do in the matter shall meet my approbation.

If a translation is thought proper you shall not in any event lose by it: if it is not I shall have the pleasure of furnishing you with the reading of the first copy of my work that crossed the Atlantic. I shall be absent from Congress till the latter end of October. I have obtained the favor of Col. Monroe to transmit to you the succeeding chapters by the next packets.

I have the honor to be with the most exalted sentiments of respect & esteem your most obedient & very humble Servt.,

DAVID RAMSAY

RC (DLC); endorsed. Recorded in SJL as received 8 Dec. 1785.

Marbois did more than assure Ramsay that his work WOULD BE ACCEPTABLE IN FRANCE. He read the sheets that had been printed and also the remaining manuscript of the *History*, and on 7 June 1785 Ramsay acknowledged this assistance in part as follows: "I . . . am much obliged to you for the valuable hint you have suggested. . . . I draughted a paragraph substantially the same in sentiment with the one you did me the honor to suggest. . . . As I desire to have my work perfect I received with gratitude any intelligence, hints or suggestions that tend to improve it"; two days later Ramsay again thanked Marbois for his "remarks all of which are judicious and most of which shall be incorporated in my work. What I said respecting Commodore Gillons command was according to my best information. Truth is my object, and I will impartially examine that matter over again before it is printed. —Your second note is just come to hand and the contents of it shall be attended to and justice shall be done to Major L'Enfant. The circumstance was unknown to me or it should have been inserted" (Ramsay to Marbois, 7 and 9 June; Arch. Aff. Etr., Corr. Pol., E.-U., xxx; Tr in DLC). Marbois sent copies of Ramsay's letters to Vergennes, informing him that he had known for some time Ramsay was at work on his history and adding: "Je desirois beaucoup d'en avoir connoissance avant qu'elle fût imprimée. Mr. Ramsay est un homme de merite, est estimé pour ses principes et ses talents, quoiqu'il ne réunisse pas à beaucoup prés, tous ceux qu'on a droit d'exiger d'un historien. Il y a quelques jours qu'il m'a communiqué les premieres feuilles imprimées, et j'ai saisi cette occasion pour lui demander à voir son manuscrit avant qu'on en continuât l'impression. Je n'ai pas hesité a l'assurer d'aprés la lecture de ces premieres feuilles, que son livre seroit lu avec beaucoup d'empressement en France, et j'ai ajouté que, sans porter aucune atteinte à la verité historique, il pourroit présenter quelques faits sous un point de vue plus satisfaisant pour la nation alliée des Etats unis, soit lorsqu'il traite des évenemens politiques, soit quand il rapporte les actions militaires, aux quelles l'armée du Roi a pris part; que j'étois si sur d'avance du Succés de son histoire que j'en prendrois au moins quatrevingt exemplaires pour mes amis et pour moi. Cette ouverture a été bien reçue: Mr. Ramsay m'a confié la suite non encore imprimée du manuscrit et vous verrez par la lettre cy-jointe Monseigneur, qu'il a trés bien reçu les premieres observations que j'ai été dans le cas de lui addresser aprés cette lecture et qu'il me promet de recevoir egalement bien les subsequentes. Mr. Ramsay est fort attaché à son pays et il aime la France. . . . Son livre sera certainement lu avec empressement dans les Etats unis, il tend à corriger le penchant qui entraine les Americains vers l'Angleterre, à les rapprocher de nous, et de la sorte à retablir plus d'egalité dans leurs affections. Il s'agit d'un des événemens les plus glorieux pour notre nation et les plus propres à embellir son histoire. . . . Si vous croyez devoir reconnoitre sa condescendance, vous pourriez lui accorder quelque faveur indirecte en faisant faire une partie des avances de la traduction et de l'impression de son histoire. Au reste je me suis abstenu de toucher ce point avec lui, et j'aurai également soin que personne ne se doute de la confiance qu'il me marque; elle nuiroit infailliblement à l'opinion qu'on doit avoir de l'independance de ses principes" (Marbois to Vergennes, 10 June 1785; same, XXX). Marbois again wrote that he had seen all of Ramsay's work, that he had offered upwards of a hundred changes in the manuscript, that Ramsay had adopted nearly all of his suggestions, and that the history "excitera surement beaucoup de mecontentement en Angleterre"; the letter from Ramsay that Marbois enclosed, however, only stated that he had "incorporated nine or ten" of Marbois' remarks, though he added: "I beg the favor of you to continue them and to suggest any thing that occurs which ought to be altered added or suppressed" (Ramsay to Marbois, 28 June 1785; Marbois to Vergennes, 15 July 1785; same, XXX). Vergennes thought Ramsay's work "ne sauroit manquer d'etre intéressant," asked Marbois to subscribe for six copies in his name, and said that if the French translator would call on him, he would see "ce que je pourroi faire pour faciliter sa besogne" (Vergennes to Marbois, 20 Sep. 1785; same, XXX). Marbois subscribed for *eighty* copies, and Otto explained that his predecessor "a cru devoir prendre sur lui cette depense extraordinaire pour recompenser indirectement M. Ramsay de l'impartialité qu'il a mise dans les parties de son histoire qui sont relatives a la france" (Otto to Vergennes, 28 Nov. 1785; same, XXX).

To John Adams

DEAR SIR   Paris Aug. 10. 1785.

Your favor of the 4th. inst. came to hand yesterday. I now inclose you the two Arrets against the importation of foreign manufactures into this kingdom. The cause of the balance against this country in favor of England as well as it's amount is not agreed on. No doubt the rage for English manufactures must be a principal cause. The speculators in Exchange say also that those of the circumjacent countries who have a balance in their favor against France remit that balance to England from France. If so it is possible that the English may count this balance twice: that is, in summing their exports to one of those states, and their imports from it, they count the difference once in their favour: then a second time when they sum the remittances of cash they receive from France. There has been no arret relative to our commerce since that of Aug. 1784. and all the late advices from the French West Indies are that they have now in their ports always three times as many vessels as there ever were before, and that the increase is principally from our States. I have now no further fears of that arret's standing it's ground. When it shall become firm I do not think it's extension desperate. But whether the placing it on the firm basis of treaty be practicable is a very different question. As far as it is possible to judge from appearances I conjecture that Crawford will do nothing. I infer this from some things in his conversation, and from an expression of the Count de Vergennes in a conversation with me yesterday. I pressed upon him the importance of opening their ports freely to us in the moment of the oppressions of the English regulations against us and perhaps of the suspension of their commerce. He admitted it but said we had free ingress with our productions. I enumerated them to him and shewed him on what footing they were and how they might be improved. We are to have further conversations on the subject. I am afraid the voiage to Fontainebleau will interrupt them. From the enquiries I have made I find I cannot get a very small and indifferent house there for the season (that is, for a month) for less than 100. or 150 guineas. This is nearly the whole salary for the time and would leave nothing to eat. I therefore cannot accompany the court there, but I will endeavor to go occasionally there from Paris. They tell me it is the most favourable scene for business with the Count de Vergennes, because he is then more abstracted from the domestic applications. Count D'Aranda is not yet returned from the waters of Vichy. As soon as he returns I will apply to him in the case of Mr. Watson. I will pray you to insure Houdon's life from the 27th. of last month to his return to Paris. As he was to stay in America a month or two, he will probably be about 6 months absent: but the 3 per cent for the voiage being once paid I suppose they will ensure his life by the month whether his absence be longer or shorter. The sum to be insured is fifteen thousand livres tournois. If it be not necessary to pay the money immediately there is a prospect of exchange becoming more favourable. But whenever it is necessary be so good as to procure it by selling a draught on Mr. Grand which I will take care shall be honoured. Compliments to the ladies & am Dr. Sir Your friend & servt.,

TH: JEFFERSON

RC (MHi: AMT); endorsed. PrC (DLC). Recorded in SJL as sent "by Dr. Bancroft." Entry in SJPL reads: "Adams John. Arret on foreign commerce. Ours. Houdon"; the remainder of this entry, which reads "Sprowle Mrs. Her case," refers actually to TJ's letter to Katherine Sprowle Douglas of this date. Enclosures: The two decrees of 10 and 17 July 1785 intended to prohibit importation of English merchandise (Sowerby No. 2295, 2296; *Mercure de France*, 30 July 1785. *Recueil Général des Anciennes Lois Françaises*, 1785-89, Paris, 1827, p. 67).

TJ was correct in his CONJECTURE THAT CRAWFORD (George Craufurd) would do nothing. A few days before this letter was written, Dorset sent

the following despatch to Carmarthen: "In my first conversations with Mons. de Vergennes, which, during my residence here of eighteen months, have been very frequent, that minister . . . shewed no unwillingness to coincide in any measures that might be proposed for the mutual advantage of the two kingdoms, but his conduct as well as his language have of late taken a very different cast. . . . There is also another cause (in addition to the claims of the St. Eustatius merchants), of much greater weight in my opinion, to which no attention whatever seems to have been given, I mean the Treaty of Commerce between Great Britain and France. I mentioned to your Lordship at the time the extreme desire

Mons. de Vergennes expressed to me before the arrival of Mr. Craufurd that that matter might be entered upon, and he seemed indeed to promise himself that, as His Majesty had appointed a Commissioner expressly for the purpose, the business would at once be seriously introduced. But now after so many months, when a large portion of the time fixed by mutual consent for the arrangement is expired, that nothing has been done or even proposed on our part, it is not very surprising to observe a degree of ill-humour, which has already shown itself and is but too plainly manifested by the Arrêts du Conseil that are directly leveled at the commerce of England. Mr. Craufurd transmitted one to you last week, and another is expected to make its appearance in the course of a few days, whereby a duty of 30 per cent will be laid upon English goods of every kind. These Arrêts may be considered also as proofs that the balance of trade is at present much against France, and it is not improbable that the measure has been taken at this time with a design of increasing the discontents which are supposed to be already subsisting amongst our Manufacturers, on account of the arrangements with Ireland" (*Camden Society Publications*, 3rd ser., XVI; Oscar Browing, ed., "Despatches from Paris, 1784-1790," I, 63-5; see also p. 67, 77). George Craufurd had been instructed on 2 Sep. 1784 to open negotiations for the commercial treaty that had been stipulated in Article 18 of the Treaty of Paris of 1783 (*Camden Society Publications*, 3rd ser., XLIX; L. G. Wickham Legg, ed., "British Diplomatic Instructions, 1689-1789," VII, France, Pt. iv, 1745-1789, p. 315-7). In MHi there is a calling card reading "Mr. Craufurd, Commissaire de sa Majesté Britannique. Hôtel d'Orleans, Rue des Petits Augustins."

To James Gordon

[*Paris, 10 Aug. 1785.* Entry in SJL reads: "Jas. Gordon. Referring him to Limousin. By post." Not found.]

To Pierrard

SIR   Paris Aug. 10. 1785.

I received your letter of the 3d. instant. I think I cannot better serve you than by advising you to the most certain channel through which you can possibly procure the information you ask as to certain persons named in your letter. That is, to write to Mr. Otto the Chargé des affaires of your court with Congress. He will be at New-York, or Philadelphia. He is well acquainted in Pennsylvania where those persons are supposed to be, and being on the spot can renew his enquiries from time to time, send them to different quarters or to different correspondents as circumstances may require. Were I to undertake the same enquiries across the Atlantic I should be as many years in obtaining a final answer as he will be weeks, and should in fact prevent your getting information while I should be prosecuting so slow a method of obtaining it for you. I am with much respect Sir Your most obedient humble servt.,

TH: JEFFERSON

PrC (MHi).

To Katherine Sprowle Douglas

MADAM   Paris Aug. 10. 1785.

In your letter of June 21. you asked 'my opinion whether yourself or your son might venture to go to Virginia to claim your possessions there'? I had the honour of writing you on the 5th. of July that you might safely go there, that your person would be sacredly safe and free from insult. I expressed my hopes too that they would in the end adopt the just and useful measure of restoring property unsold and the price of that actually sold. In yours of July 30. you 'intreat my influence with the assembly for retribution and that if I think your personal presence in Virginia would facilitate that end you were willing and ready to go.' This seems to propose to me to take on myself the sollicitation of your cause, and that you will go if I think your personal presence will be auxiliary to my applications. I feel myself obliged to inform you frankly that it is improper for me to sollicit your case with the assembly of Virginia. The application can only go with propriety from yourself, or the minister of your court to America whenever there shall be one. If you think the sentiments expressed in my former letter will serve you, you are free to exhibit it to members individually, but I wish the letter not to be offered to the assembly as a body, or referred to in any petition or memorial to them as a body. I am with much respect Madam Your most obedient humble servant,   TH: JEFFERSON

PrC (DLC). Recorded in SJL as sent "by Dr. Bancroft"; part of the subject entry in SJPL for TJ's letter to John Adams of this date, which reads "Sprowle Mrs. Her case," is clearly an error and refers to the present letter.

From Abigail Adams

[London, 12 Aug. 1785. Record in SJL of its receipt on 23 Sep. 1785 reads: "Mrs. Adams's. Grosvenor sq. Lond. Aug. 12. by W. Short." Not found; see Abigail Adams to TJ, 21 Aug. 1785.]

From Castries

Versailles le 12. Aoust 1785.

J'ai reçu, Monsieur, avec la lettre que vous m'avés fait l'honneur de m'ecrire le 3 de ce mois, les observations de Mr. Jones sur l'insuffisance des pouvoirs dont le Sr. Puchilberg est revêtu pour toucher les parts des prises qui reviennent aux sujets des Etats unis. D'aprés votre assertion et vos propres réflexions, je ne hésiterois point à confirmer les ordres que j'ai déjà donnés de remettre à Mr. Jones tout ce qui est dû aux americains; Mais il se présente une autre difficulté: Le commissaire ordonnateur à L'Orient me marque que, quelque recherche que l'on ait faite, il n'a pas été possible de se procurer un rôlle exact des gens de l'equipage de la fregate americaine L'alliance, et que, dans la supposition, trés-probable, que des françois ayent servi sur cette fregate, il résulteroit de la remise totale des fonds faite à Mr. Jones, que les parts revenantes aux sujets du Roi seroient versées dans le trésor du congrés.

Dans cette circonstance, je présume qu'il vous paroîtra juste d'exiger de Mr. Jones une caution pour assurer le païement de ce qui pouroit revenir aux françois, dans le cas où il en auroit été embarqué sur la fregate L'alliance.

Je vous prie de me faire l'honneur de me repondre à ce sujet, et J'ai celui d'être avec un trés sincere attachement, Monsieur, votre trés humble et trés obeissant Serviteur,

LE MAL. DE CASTRIES

RC (DLC); in a clerk's hand, signed by Castries; endorsed. Tr (DNA: PCC, No. 87, I); in TJ's hand; with an English translation. PrC (DLC). Tr (DNA: PCC, No. 107, I); also with a translation. Recorded in SJL as received 16 Aug. 1785. Enclosed in TJ to John Jay, 30 Aug. 1785.

From John Stockdale

SIR   Piccadilly 12th. Augt. 1785.

I received Yours dated the 28th. of July by the bearer of this Letter. All orders that I may have the honor to receive from You shall be punctually executed. As to payment I am in no hurry but will once or twice a Year transmit a Bill which may be paid in London when Convenient. The books orderd, I shall have to procure from Scotland before I can dispatch them to America, which will be done with all convenient speed. I shall take occasion to send You such publications as are valuable by every opportunity that may offer. The Bearer brings the first parcel. I am Sir Yr. much obligd. & very Hble Servant,   JOHN STOCKDALE

RC (MHi); endorsed. Recorded in SJL as received 23 Sep. 1785 "by W. Short."

From Thomas Thompson

Dover, Eng., 12 Aug. 1785. Thompson, a wine merchant, has for some time supplied Benjamin Franklin with two London newspapers, *The Morning Chronicle* and *The London Chronicle*; these he forwarded three times a week to Mouron, proprietor of the French packets at Calais, who then relayed them to Perregaux, a banker in Paris. TJ may send for those which are unclaimed. They come to Thompson free from postage charges by order of a member of Parliament, and he will continue to supply them by the same route to TJ at the cost of only "threepence for each paper and . . . one halfpenny for putting them up, directing them," &c. Thompson's "only compensation . . . is the reading them when they arrive if time permits before they are sent over." He has ordered them to be discontinued, but if TJ wishes to receive them, he is to notify and instruct Thompson care of Mouron.

RC (MoSHi); 2 p.; endorsed; at foot of text: "His Excellency Col Jefferson &c."

To James Buchanan and William Hay

GENTLEMEN   Paris Aug. 13. 1785.

Your favor of March 20. came to hand the 14th. of June, and the next day I wrote to you acknowleging the receipt, and apprising you that between that date and the 1st. of August it would be impossible to procure and get to your hands the draughts you desired. I did hope indeed to have had them prepared before this, but it will yet be some time before they will be in readiness. I flatter myself however they will give you satisfaction when you receive them and that you will think the object will not have lost by the delay. I was a considerable time before I could find an architect whose taste had been formed on a study of the antient models of this art: the style of architecture in this capital being far from chaste. I at length heard of one, to whom I immediatley addressed myself, and who perfectly fulfills my wishes. He has studied 20 years in Rome, and has given proofs of his skill and taste by a publication of some antiquities of this country. You intimate that you should be willing to have a workman sent to you to superintend the execution of this work. Were I to send one on this errand from hence, he would consider himself as the Superintendant of the Directors themselves and probably of the Government of the state also. I will give you my ideas on this subject. The columns of the building and the external architraves of the doors and windows should be of stone. Whether these are made here, or there, you will need one good stone-cutter, and one will be enough because, under his direction, negroes who never saw a tool, will be able to prepare the work for him to finish. I will therefore send you such a one, in time to begin work in the spring. All the internal cornices and other ornaments not exposed to the weather will be much handsomer, cheaper and more durable in plaister than in wood. I will therefore employ a good workman in this way and send him to you. But he will have no employment till the house is covered, of course he need not be sent till next summer. I will take him on wages so long beforehand as that he may draw all the ornaments in detail, under the eye of the architect, which he will have to execute when he comes to you. It will be the cheapest way of getting them drawn and the most certain of putting him in possession of his precise duty. Plaister will not answer for your external cornice, and stone will be too dear. You will probably find yourselves obliged to be contented with wood. For this therefore, and for your windowsashes, doors, forms, wainscoting &c. you will need a capital housejoiner, and a capital one he ought to be, capable of directing all the circumstances in the construction of the walls which the execution of the plans will require. Such a workman cannot be got here. Nothing can be worse done than the house-joinery of Paris. Besides that his speaking the language perfectly would be essential. I think this character must be got from England. There are no workmen in wood in Europe comparable to those of England. I submit to you therefore the following proposition: to wit, I will get a correspondent in England to engage a workman of this kind. I will direct him to come here, which will cost five guineas. We will make proof of his execution. He shall also make himself, under the eye of the architect, all the drawings for the building which he is to execute himself: and if we find him sober and capable, he shall be forwarded to you. I expect that in the article of the drawings and the cheapness of passage from France you will save the expence of his coming here. But as to this workman I shall do nothing unless I receive your commands. With respect to your stone work, it may be got much cheaper here than in England. The stone of Paris is very white and beautiful, but it always remains soft, and suffers from the weather. The cliffs of the Seine from hence to Havre are all of stone. I am not yet informed whether it is all liable to the same objections. At Lyons and all along the Rhone is a stone as beautiful as that of Paris, soft when it comes out of the quarry, but very soon becoming hard in the open air, and very durable. I doubt however whether the commerce between Virginia and Marseilles would afford opportunities of conveiance sufficient. It remains to be enquired what addition to the original cost would be made by the short land carriage from Lyons to the Loire and the water transportation down that to Bourdeaux, and also whether a stone of the same quality may not be found on the Loire. In this and all other matters relative to your charge you may command my services freely.

Having heard high commendations of a plan of a prison drawn by an architect at Lyons I sent there for it. The architect furnished me with it. It is certainly the best plan I ever saw. It unites in the most perfect manner the objects of security and health, and has moreover the advantage, valuable to us, of being capable of being adjusted to any number of prisoners, small or great and admitting an execution from time to time as it may be convenient. The plan is under preparation as for 40. prisoners. Will you have any occasion for slate? It may be got very good and ready prepared at Havre, and a workman or more might be sent on easy terms. Perhaps the quarry at Tuckahoe would leave you no other want than a workman.

I shall be glad to receive your sentiments on the several matters herein mentioned, that I may know how far you approve of them, as I shall with pleasure pursue strictly whatever you desire. I have the honour to be with great respect and esteem, gentlemen, Your most obedient & most humble servant,   TH: JEFFERSON

PrC (DLC). Recorded in SJL as sent "by Fitzhugh"; entry in SJPL reads: "Buchanan & Hay. Drawings of Capitol &c."

The ARCHITECT found by TJ was Charles Clérisseau (1721-1820), who made, under TJ's direction, the plaster model for the Virginia state capitol.

From Plowden Garvey

Rouen, 13 Aug. 1785. On request of John Adams, remaining seven cases of his wine have been shipped on board the *Sophie*, Captain Knight. Bill of lading and note of charges, 96l. 16s. 6d., sent to Adams and sight draft payable to John Fred: Perregaux has been drawn on TJ.

RC (DLC). 1 p. The sight draft, signed by R. and A. Garvey per Plowden Garvey and drawn in favor of Perregaux for the amount stated, is in DLC: TJ Papers, 14: 2347.

From John Jay

Since the Date of my last to you which was the 13th. Ultimo I have been honored with your Joint Letter of the 11th. May and with two others from you of the same Date.

As yet Congress have not communicated to me any Resolutions on the Subjects of the several Letters from their Ministers which have been received and laid before them, and the Convention respecting consular Powers is still under their Consideration.

The Board of Commissioners for the Treasury is now complete, Congress having been pleased to appoint Mr. Arthur Lee to be one of them.

The Answer of Governor Rutledge who has been elected for the Hague, has not yet come to Hand.

A Requisition on the States for Supplies is preparing and it is thought will pass in the Course of the next Month. If punctually complied with, it will greatly reestablish our Credit with those, who entertain Doubts respecting it.

Our Harvest is good, and though the Productions of the Country are plenty, yet they bear a high Cash Price, so that the Complaint of the want of Money in the Country, is less well founded than a Complaint of Distrust and want of Credit between Man and Man would be. For the apprehension of paper Money alarms those who have any Thing to lend, while they who have Debts to pay are zealous Advocates for the Measure. Until that Matter is decided there will be little Credit, and I sometimes think the less the better.

The Letters I have received from Mr. Adams were written immediately after his Presentation and contain nothing of Business, so that our Suspence on certain interesting Points still continues.

I herewith enclose by Order of Congress some Papers on the Subject of our Trade with the French which it may be useful for you to know the Contents of, and also some late newspapers which tho' not very interesting may not be altogether useless. I have the honor to be &c.,   John Jay

FC (DNA: PCC, No. 121); at head of letter: "To the Honorable Thos. Jefferson Esquire." Recorded in SJL as received 18 Sep. 1785. Enclosures (DNA: PCC, No. 121): (1) Robert Morris to the President of Congress, 30 Sep. 1784, enclosing copy of Lafayette to Morris, 14 Aug. 1784; he praises Lafayette's efforts toward lifting the French restrictions on American commerce, though he is aware of "the Delicacy and perhaps Danger of asking from France the Moderation or Abolition of particular Duties, thereby establishing a Precedent for similar Requests on her Part." (2) Lafayette to Calonne, 31 Jan. 1784, expressing his appreciation of the designation of four free French ports: "it is very opportunely you have step'd in to turn the Current which carried the whole of the american commerce to England"; he urges the reduction of the "Fees of Office, of Anchorage, of the Admiralty" and reports the observations of certain American merchants, Wadsworth, Carter, and Nesbitt, on the regulations and the difficulties they might encounter. (3) Lafayette to Calonne, 10 Feb. 1784, repeating his requests for reducing the duties; he expresses his apprehensions of the "bad Consequences from the Commission given by the Farmers of Virginia Tobacco. At present it is brought from the Ukraine, and in general instead of buying that of America, the Farmers take the other at a low Price and of a very bad Quality"; American merchants have suggested too that Le Havre might also be made a free port, for "it would give a Superiority to the Manufactures of Normandy and facilitate the Vent of the Articles fabricated at Paris. Vessels loaded in England, tempted by the Commodity and the Vicinity of the Port, would call and take in some french Productions." (4) Lafayette to Calonne, 26 Feb. 1784, enclosing the opinions of American merchants on the duties in the free ports, which "are less burthensome from their Amount than from their Multiplicity; to abolish them entirely would perhaps be difficult, but they might be at first lessened and afterwards united under one Denomination, to be paid at so much for a Vessel of three Masts, so much for one of two Masts, and so on without troubling themselves about the Tonnage. . . . This method will deprive no one of their Dues for the Subdivision of the Profits can be made by those who claim them." (5) Lafayette to Calonne, 5 Mch. 1784, informing him that he has seen Chardon who foresees the need for "new and more particular Statements [of the duties]"; Lafayette urges the concluding touches to the establishment of the free ports and passes on the American merchants' suggestion that returns for the importation of flour into the French islands be made in wines, or French manufactures, which "may be joined with the excellent Idea which Mr. the Comptroller General as well as the Count d'Estaing gave me, of a moderate Duty subject to Drawback." (6) Calonne to Lafayette, 8 Mch. 1784, saying that the time to submit to the king a proposal to reduce and simplify duties in the free ports will be when Calonne receives an account of their present nature and number; "the Determination that his Majesty has just taken on my Report to suppress all Duties on the Exportation of our Brandies, is a further Proof of the Attention given to every Part of our Commerce with the United States." (7) Calonne to Lafayette, 17 May 1784, enclosing copies of the act designating the free ports; though a brief delay in its force will be necessary, he has taken precautions that no American vessels shall be denied the privileges of the free port if they sailed from America in anticipation of them; refutes certain claims made in Le Couteulx's memorial on tobacco but reports that the Farmers-General have agreed to buy tobacco only in France or America and that a warehouse will be established in L'Orient. (8) Calonne to Lafayette, 11 June 1784, enclosing a list to be sent to American merchants of the duties payable by American vessels in the free ports; when their specific recommendations and observations are received, Calonne will submit his proposals to the King. (9) Calonne to Lafayette, 16 June 1784, saying that he cannot accede to Lafayette's request for the reduction and unification of duties before the latter leaves for America: "The Duties payable by the United States belong to the Admiral to Officers of the Admiralty and to particular Cities and Noblemen. Both one and the other would be apt to lay Claims of Indemnity for the Privation or Reductions of their Duties, and you will agree that it would not be just to reduce them or even to suspend them, without hearing the Parties interested. The same may be urged against reducing the whole of the Duties to one Denomination." (10) Castries to Lafayette, 17 June 1784, saying that, though he appreciates Lafayette's reasons for his proposals, "it will be impossible for us to give that Degree of Liberty which you desire"; he can promise only a free port in each colony, the perpetuation of previous privileges, and "that the Duties will be as moderate as possible"; the "Interest of our own Commerce demands some Consideration," but he will discuss the matter with Franklin and Thomas Barclay. (11) A printed broadside dated 14 Mch. 1785 entitled "State of the Duties Payable by Vessels of the United States of America, In the Ports of Marseilles, Bayonne, L'Orient, and Dunkirk" (JCC, XXIX, 917, No. 457; Jay had previously sent a copy of this same broadside to TJ with his letter of 15 Apr. 1785).

From John Jay

DR. SIR   Office for foreign Affairs 13th. August 1785

I have received a Letter from Mr. Morris in which he requests my Attention to the Case stated in the Papers[1] herewith enclosed. There is reason to apprehend that Justice is at least unnecessarily delayed if intended. The Circumstances of the Persons interested have Claims on the Humanity and good Offices of those in whose Power it may be to promote their obtaining Justice. I therefore readily comply with their Request in laying these Papers before you. They entreat your Attention to them, and that you will direct such Enquiries to be made as may be necessary to ascertain the Reality, Nature and Extent of the Difficulties which it is said lay in their Way. With great Esteem and Regard &c.,   JOHN JAY

FC (DNA: PCC, No. 121). Recorded in SJL as received 18 Sep. "on Fortin's case." Enclosures not identified; but see Limozin to TJ, 4 Oct. 1785.

[1] This word is keyed by an asterisk to a note at foot of text, which reads: "respecting an estate left to a Mr. Fortin in France."

To John Paul Jones

SIR   Paris Aug. 13. 1785.

Supposing you may be anxious to hear from hence, tho' there should be nothing interesting to communicate, I write by Mr. Cairnes merely to inform you that I have as yet received no answer from the Marshal de Castries. I am in daily expectation of one. Should it not be received soon I shall urge it again, which I wish to avoid however if possible, because I think it better to await with patience a favourable decision than, by becoming importunate, to produce unfavourable dispositions, and perhaps a final determination of the same complexion. Should my occupations prevent my writing awhile, be assured that it will only be as long as I have nothing to communicate and that as soon as I receive any answer it shall be forwarded to you.

I am with much esteem Sir Your most obedient humble servt.,
                                            TH: JEFFERSON

PrC (DLC). Recorded in SJL as sent "by Cairnes"; entry in SJPL reads: "Jones J. Paul. His case."

To John Jay

Paris Aug. 14. 1785.

I was honoured on the 22d. Ult. with the receipt of your letter
of June 15. and delivered the letter therein inclosed from the
President of Congress to the king. I took an opportunity of asking
the Count de Vergennes whether the Chevalier Luzerne proposed
to return to America? He answered me that he did, and that he
was here, for a time only, to arrange his private affairs. Of course
this stopped my proceeding further, in compliance with the hint
in your letter. I knew that the Chevalier Luzerne still retained the
character of minister to Congress, which occasioned my premising
the question I did. But notwithstanding the answer, which indeed
was the only one the Ct. de Vergennes could give me, I believe
that it is not expected that the Chevalier will return to America:
that he is waiting an appointment here to some of their embassies,
or some other promotion, and in the meantime, as a favor, is permitted to retain his former character. Knowing the esteem borne
him in America, I did not suppose it would be wished that I
should add any thing which might occasion an injury to him; and
the rather as I presumed that at this time there did not exist the
same reason for wishing the arrival of a minister in America which
perhaps existed there at the date of your letter. Count Adhemar is
just arrived from London on account of a paralytic disease with
which he has been struck. It does not seem improbable that his
place will be supplied, and perhaps by the Chevalier de la Luzerne.
A French vessel has lately refused the salute to a British armed
vessel in the channel. The Chargé des affaires of Great Britain at
this court (their Ambassador having gone to London a few days
ago) made this the subject of a conference with the Ct. de Vergennes on tuesday last. He told me that the Count explained the
transaction as the act of the individual master of the French vessel,
not founded in any public orders. His earnestness, and his endeavors to find terms sufficiently soft to express the Count's explanation,
had no tendency to lessen any doubts I might have entertained on
this subject. I think it possible the refusal may have been by
order. Nor can I believe that Great Britain is in a condition to
resent it, if it was so. In this case we shall see it repeated by
France, and the example will then be soon followed by other
nations. The newswriters bring together this circumstance, with
the departure of the French Ambassador from London and the

English Ambassador from Paris, the manoeuvring of a French fleet just off the channel, the collecting some English vessels of war in the channel, the failure of a commercial treaty between the two countries, a severe arret here against English manufactures, as foreboding war. It is possible that the fleet of manoeuvre, the refusal of the salute, and the English fleet of observation may have a connection with one another. But I am persuaded the other facts are totally independant of these and of one another, and are accidentally brought together in point of time. Neither nation is in a condition to go to war: Great Britain indeed the least so of the two. The latter power, or rather it's monarch as elector of Hanover is lately confederated with the K. of Prussia and others of the Germanic body, evidently in opposition to the Emperor's designs on Bavaria. An alliance too between the Empress of Russia and republic of Venice seems to have had him in view, as he had meditated some exchange of territory with that republic. This desertion of the powers heretofore thought friendly to him, seems to leave no issue for his ambition but on the side of Turkey. His demarcation with that country is still unsettled. His difference with the Dutch is certainly agreed. The articles are not yet made public; perhaps not quite adjusted. Upon the whole we may count on another year's peace in Europe, and that our friends will not within that time be brought into any embarrassments which might encourage Great Britain to be difficult in settling the points still unsettled between us.

You have doubtless seen in the papers that this court was sending two vessels into the South sea, under the conduct of a Capt. Peyrouse. They give out that the object is merely for the improvement of our knowlege of the geography of that part of the globe. And certain it is that they carry men of eminence in different branches of science. Their loading however as detailed in conversations and some other circumstances appeared to me to indicate some other design: perhaps that of colonising on the Western coast of America, or perhaps only to establish one or more factories there for the fur trade. We may be little interested in either of these objects. But we are interested in another, that is, to know whether they are perfectly weaned from the desire of possessing continental colonies in America. Events might arise which would render it very desireable for Congress to be satisfied they have no such wish. If they would desire a colony on the Western side of America, I should not be quite satisfied that they would refuse one which should offer itself on the Eastern side. Capt. Paul Jones being at l'Orient, within a day's journey of Brest, where Capt. Peyrouse's vessels lay, I desired him if he could not satisfy himself at l'Orient of the nature of this equipment that he would go to Brest for that purpose: conducting himself so as to excite no suspicion that we attended at all to this expedition. His discretion can be relied on, and his expences for so short a journey will be a trifling price for satisfaction on this point. I hope therefore that my undertaking that the expences of his journey shall be reimbursed him, will not be disapproved.

A gentleman lately arrived from New York tells me he thinks it will be satisfactory to Congress to be informed of the effect produced here by the insult of Longchamps on Monsr. de Marbois. Soon after my arrival in France last summer, it was the matter of a conversation between the count de Vergennes and myself. I explained to him the effect of the judgment against Longchamps. He did not say that it was satisfactory, but neither did he say a word from which I could collect that it was not satisfactory. The conversation was not official because foreign to the character in which I then was. He has never mentioned a word on the subject to me since, and it was not for me to introduce it at any time. I have never once heard it mentioned in conversation by any person of this country, and have no reason to suppose that there remains any uneasiness on the subject. I have indeed been told that they had sent orders to make a formal demand of Longchamps from Congress, and had immediately countermanded these orders. You know whether this be true. If it be, I should suspect the first orders to have been surprised from them by some exaggeration, and that the latter was a correction of their error in the moment of further reflection. Upon the whole there certainly appears to me no reason to urge the state in which the fact happened to any violation of their laws, nor to set a precedent which might hereafter be used in cases more interesting to us than the late one.

In a late conversation with the Count de Vergennes he asked me if the condition of our finances was improving. He did not make an application of the question to the arrearages of their interest, tho' perhaps he meant that I should apply it. I told him the impost still found obstacles, and explained to him the effects which I hoped from our land office. Your letter of the 15th. of April did not come to hand till the 27th. Ult. I inclose a letter from Mr. Dumas to the President of Congress, and accompany the present with the Leyden gazettes and gazette of France from the date last sent you to the present time. I have the honour to be with high esteem Sir Your most obedient and most humble servant,

TH: JEFFERSON

RC (DNA: PCC, No. 87, 1). PrC (DLC). Tr (DNA: PCC, No. 107, 1). Recorded in SJL as sent "by Mr. Cannon"; the entry for this letter in SJPL under this date reads: "Do. Jay Luzerne. British right of salute in the channel. Europe. Peyrouse. Longchamps." Enclosure: Probably C. W. F. Dumas to the President of Congress of 2 Aug. 1785, which was enclosed in Dumas to TJ, 2 Aug. 1785.

Shortly after this letter was written, Louis G. Otto arrived in New York as chargé d'affaires in place of Marbois. "We are informed," wrote Grayson to Washington, "the Chevalier de la Luzerne is to be here shortly in quality of Minister" (Grayson to Washington, 5 Sep. 1785; Burnett, Letters of Members, VIII, No. 219). But Otto reported to Vergennes that the members of Con-

gress regarded his coming with some distress, taking it as an indication that France did not intend to send a minister to the United States. He added: "Les ennemis de M. Jefferson comptoient profiter de cette occasion pour faire rapeler ce ministre et pour ne laisser en france qu'un chargé d'affaires ou du moins pour nommer M. Jefferson Ministre à Paris et à la haye en même tems. Mais la lettre dont Vous avés bien voulu me charger pour M. Jay a pleinement levé cette difficulté puisqu'il y est dit expressement que je ne serois chargé des affaires de S.M. qu'en attendant le retour du Ministre Plenipotentiaire" (Otto to Vergennes, 30 Aug. 1785; Arch. Aff. Etr., Corr. Pol., E.-U., XXX; Tr in DLC). Otto did not specify the names of "Les ennemis de M. Jefferson."

To John Jay

SIR   Paris Aug. 14. 1785.

The letter of June 18. signed by Dr. Franklin and myself is the last addressed to you from hence on the objects of the general commission. As circumstances rendered it necessary that the signature of the Prussian treaty whenever it should be in readiness, should be made separately, the intervention of a person of confidence between the Prussian plenipotentiary and us became also requisite. His office would be to receive the duplicates of the treaty here, signed by Dr. Franklin and myself, to carry them to London to Mr. Adams and to the Hague to Baron Thulemeyer for their signature. Moreover to take hence the original of our full powers to shew to Baron Thulemeyer, and the copy of his which he had before communicated to us, to ask from him a sight of the original, to compare the copy with it and certify the latter to be true. Mr. Adams Dr. Franklin and myself therefore had concluded to engage Mr. Short (a gentleman of Virginia who lives with me at present) to transact this business and to invest him with the character of Secretary pro hâc vice, in order that his signature of the truth of the copy of Baron Thulemeyer's full powers might authenticate that copy. On the receipt of the letter No. 1. therefore from that minister Mr. Short set out hence with the necessary papers. By a letter lately received from him I expect he left London for the Hague about the 10th. inst. and that the treaty is ultimately executed by this time. In respect to the desire expressed by Baron Thulemeyer in his letter we associated Mr. Dumas with Mr. Short to assist in the exchange of signatures and other ceremonies of execution. We agreed to bear Mr. Short's expences, and have thought that a guinea a day (Sundays excluded) would be a proper compensation for his trouble and the necessary equipments for his journey which could not enter into the account of travelling expences. I hope by the first safe conveyance to be able to forward to you the original of the treaty. No. 2. is my answer to Baron Thulemeyer's letter, No. 3. our instructions to Mr. Short, and No. 4. our letter to Mr. Dumas.

Mr. Lambe's delay gives me infinite uneasiness. You will see by the inclosed papers No. 5. 6. and 7. sent me by Mr. Carmichael that the Emperor of Marocco at the instance of the Spanish court has delivered up the crew of the Betsy. No. 8. also received from Mr. Carmichael is a list of articles given the Emperor of Marocco the last year by the States General. It is believed that the Spanish negociator at Algiers has concluded a peace with that state, and has agreed to give them a million of dollars, besides a very considerable quantity of things in kind. The treaty meets with difficulties in the ratification. Perhaps the exorbitance of the price may occasion them. Rumors are spread abroad that they are pointing their preparations at us. The inclosed paper No. 9. is the only colourable evidence of this which has come to my knowlege. I have proposed to Mr. Adams that if Mr. Lambe does not come either in the French or English packet then (Aug. 6.) next expected, to send some person immediately to negotiate these treaties, on the presumption that Mr. Lambe's purpose has been changed. We shall still be at a loss for the instructions of which he is said to have been the bearer. I expect Mr. Adams's answer on this subject.

I have the honour to be with sentiments of the highest respect & esteem Sir Your most obedient & most humble servant,

TH: JEFFERSON

RC (DNA: PCC, No. 87, 1). PrC (DLC). Tr (DNA: PCC, No. 116); in David Humphreys' hand; at head of text: "N.B. Copies of the papers marked 5. 6. 7. and 8 enclosed in the subsequent report to Congress are deposited in the files containing documents relative to the affairs of the

Barbary States. 8th. Report to Congress addressed to Mr. Jay Secretary for foreign Affairs." Tr (DNA: PCC, No. 107, I). Recorded in SJL as sent "by Mr. Cannon"; entry in SJPL reads: "Jay John. Prussian treaty. Lambe. Barbary. Spain." Enclosures: No. 1: De Thulemeier to TJ, 19 July 1785.

No. 2: TJ to De Thulemeier, 28 July. Nos. 3 and 4: Adams and TJ to Short and to Dumas, both printed under 27 July to 5 Aug. Nos. 5-8: The first, third, fourth, and fifth items described as enclosures in the note to Carmichael to TJ, 28 July 1785. No. 9: John Bondfield to TJ, 14 July 1785.

From Gilles de Lavallée

Au havre le 14 août 1785

La recommandation qu'il a plu à votre Excellence de me Donner pour les etats Unis, ainsi que la promesse de Mr. Frankelin de m'obliger en tout ce qui dependra de lui, m'ont determiné à passer aux dits etats Unis. Je suis arrivé au Havre de grace avec mes machines et je peux Les passer. J'ai resté à Rouen et à Bolbec ou J'ai Vû et ai travaillé dans les fabriques de Cotton en Molton. J'ai aussi travaillé Sur les machines à filler et retordre les cottons. J'ose croire pouvoir rendre ces dites machines Sans Deffaut, je Suis en parole pour notre passage avec le Capitaine J. Pernet commandant le Navire le Vicomte de Roth que vous connoitrez par le porteur. S'il plaisoit à votre Excellence de vouloir bien faire mettre au compte du Congré le tout ou la partie qu'il vous plaira des frais de notre passage, je vous en aurai une entierre obligation. Si J'etois riche, je N'interromprois pas Votre Excellence pour si peu de chose. Je remets tout à votre Disposition Soit que vous accordiez à ma Demande, soit que Vous ne puissiez L'accorder, je n'en auray pas moins la reconnoissance et le Respect le plus parfait pour Son obligeante recommandation, ce Sont là les Sentimens de celuy qui Se dit avec Respect De Votre Excellence Monsieur Le tres humble et tres obeissant Serviteur,

GILLES DE LAVALLÉE

P.S. N'ayant pû trouver de Navire pour Richemont J'espere M'i rendre sitot mon arrivée à l'amerique. Si vous m'honnorez d'une reponse donnez-la S.V.P. au porteur.

RC (MHi); endorsed. Recorded in SJL as received 10 Sep. 1785.

TJ's RECOMMANDATION of Lavallée, a French textile manufacturer, was personal rather than official, if one may judge from his reply to the present letter (TJ to Lavallée, 11 Sep. 1785). This fact is all the more interesting in view of the general conception of TJ's attitude toward manufactures. The

RECOMMANDATION itself is not known to be extant, but its subsequent history is traceable. That history, which might have earned for Lavallée the title of "father of American manufactures" that was bestowed upon Samuel Slater, who established the first complete cotton textile manufactory at Pawtucket in 1789, came to a fruitless end along with other similar ventures in the post-war years. But this result in Lavallée's case is surprising in view of the fact that Washington and Franklin, as well as TJ, lent the great weight of their influence to his proposals. Around 1782 Lavallée had shown Franklin his plans for establishing in Philadelphia or elsewhere one or more manufactories for making textiles. Franklin seems to have encouraged him but to have advised delay until peace had been established. Late in 1784 Lavallée wrote for an interview, which was presumably given and Franklin's PROMESSE, whatever it was, obtained then (Lavallée to Franklin, 1 Nov. 1784; PPAP). TJ may even have met Lavallée at that time or have given him the recommendation or letter of introduction. Lavallée left France not long after receiving TJ's reply to the present letter. Early in 1786 he arrived at Portsmouth, N.H., with his son, a young workman skilled in weaving fine cloth, and his mechanical looms ("mes métiers mécaniques"). He reported to Benjamin Franklin that, on TJ's recommendation, Gen. Sullivan had given him a warm welcome, providing all that he needed—lodgings, food, workmen, a carpenter, a locksmith, and even such materials as silk, wool, flax, and cotton. Finding that Sullivan also had a fulling mill, power to stretch the cloth, a boiler for dyeing, a glossing press, and carding brushes, he set up two of his looms, one for ribbons capable of weaving ten pieces at a time, and the other for fine cloth three-quarters wide. The prospect seemed bright for the new textile company that Lavallée proposed, and he prophesied that in twenty years America would be able to manufacture all of her textiles (Lavallée to Franklin, 10 Jan. 1786; PPAP). But these bright hopes were soon dashed. Late in 1786 Lavallée wrote to Washington, submitting to him his plans and TJ's recommendation. Washington was interested but personally too occupied with other matters to give Lavallée "the aids he requires, or to have him upon my hands till he can be properly established," but he wrote to Gov. Edmund Randolph: "To promote industry and œconomy, and to encourage manufactures, is certainly consistent with that sound policy which ought to actuate every State. There are times, too, which call loudly for the exercise of these virtues; and the present, in my humble opinion, may be accounted a

fit one for the adoption of them in this Commonwealth.—How far the proposition which I have the honor to enclose merits Legislative encouragement, your Excellency will determine. As it came to me, you will receive it. The writer is unknown to me; of him, or his plan, I had not the smallest intimation till the papers were handed to me from the Post Office. The document in the hand writing of Mr Jefferson (with which it is accompanied) entitles the latter to consideration." Washington added that he thought Alexandria was not "so proper a situation as a more southern one for the Manufacture of Cotton," and he requested that, if Randolph should not think the matter worthy of public attention or if it should "not find encouragement from the Assembly," the letters and papers should be returned that he might "give Mr. de la Vallee an answer as soon as possible; his circumstances seeming to require one" (Washington to Randolph, 25 Dec. 1786; Writings, ed. Fitzpatrick, XXIX, 120-1). Nothing resulted from this—there is no reply from Randolph in the Washington Papers—and on 13 Mch. 1787 Lavallée washed his hands of America in the following remarks to Washington: "I did myself the honor to write to your Excellency upon the subject of Manufactures, and enclosed a Copy of a recommendation from Mr. Jefferson. You was pleased to return me an answer by which Your Excellency informed me that you had forwarded my memorial to the Legislature of Virginia to know their determination upon the matter, which you would do me the favor to send to me. I have waited until this time and have received no news respecting it; in consequence I have made an engagement with Spain, for which place I shall take my departure this day. I thank your Excellency for your attention; but no establishment of European manufacture can succeed here—America is not suitable for the business on account of the scarcity of money—the deficiency of power in the Government—the personal interest of every member—the want of the confidence of the people in their Rulers—the fluctuation of the Legislature. You have given liberty to America—she has abused it—her manners are corrupted—Craft and subtlety have taken place of good faith—labour is despised—the innocence and modesty of the females is succeeded by effrontery and impudence—the facility of obtaining a divorce has dissolved the sanctity of marriage—the early independence of children has disturbed the peace of families—your Laws have neither energy nor firmness—the disunion of the States facilitates and encourages disobedience &c. &c.—I quit America sick of its Liberty, its manners and its laws.—I respect and admire its great men, particularly your Excellency. It gives me pain to see that so much is done for a people unworthy of the benefits. My soul is pierced to see such abuse of Liberty. I am well acquainted with the Laws of the Ancients and moderns. I have travelled through Europe. I am a friend to humanity, I would sacrifice my life for it, but here, my wishes, my desires, my knowledge, my talents are superfluous, useless and even prejudicial. I depart therefore filled with respect and admiration for the great Characters and with pity for the People" (Lavallée to Washington, New York, 13 Mch. 1787; DLC: Washington Papers [English translation]). This outburst is perhaps the best evidence of the cause of failure of Lavallée's American dream. Washington endorsed the letter methodically, but made no reply. At the moment that he received it he was busy preparing to go northward to preside over the Federal Convention, whose outcome gave a greater impetus to manufactures than anything Lavallée could have anticipated.

From Jean Holker

Sir   Rouen 14 of Aug. 1785

I Received the Pleaseur of yours of the 29 past and being obliged to goe into the Contery on the account of my health, I spoeke to a friend to see If he could not meet with a pear of horseis fitting for you, came here too days agoe and find he has not been able to doe the Commision, or have I any Expectations at present. One thing is certin all horse Marchands air Harpers and maks no Scrupel of cheating their father, all which I know to my Expenceis, so woud advise you to keep a Lookeout and see If you cant fit your Self in Paris, for Really I dont beleive you can be so well served here, unless one could meet with some one out of the Contery, who has a pear of horseis to sell. This may happen, but the occasions air not Common. Our friend Docter Bancroft past to see me in the Contery, on Friday last and tould me you was well. May you allways continue so, for life without health is little worth; it woud be agreeable to me could I in any Shape be of use, and as such beg on every occasion youl Imploy me, and believe me most Sincearly with Respect Sir you Most Obed. & very humble Servant,

J Holker

RC (MHi); endorsed. Recorded in SJL as received 18 Aug. 1785.

From Neil Jamieson

New York, 14 Aug. 1785. Letter accompanies two packets from Charleston, S.C., a letter from James Currie at Richmond, and some New York newspapers; these probably will be forwarded to TJ by a passenger going in the August packet.

RC (MHi); 2 p.; endorsed. Entered in SJL as received 18 Sep. 1785, along with James Currie to TJ, 5 Aug. 1785, and Ralph Izard to TJ, 10 June 1785"; the latter was probably one of the "two packets" from Charleston, but the second has not been identified.

From Patience Wright

HONOURED SIR   London, at the wax-work, Aug. 14, 1785.

I had the pleasure to hear that my son Joseph Wright had painted the best likeness of our HERO Washington, of any painter in America; and my friends are anxious that I should make a likeness, a bust in wax, to be placed in the state-house, or some new public building that may be erected by congress. The flattering letters from gentlemen of distinguished virtues and rank, and one from that general himself, wherein he says, 'He shall think himself happy to have his bust done by Mrs. Wright, whose *uncommon talents, &c. &c.*' make me happy in the prospect of seeing him in my own country.

I most sincerely wish not only to make the likeness of Washington, but of those *five* gentlemen, who assisted at the signing the treaty of peace, that put an end to so bloody and dreadful a war. The more public the honours bestowed on such men by their country, the better. To shame the English king, I would go to any trouble and expense to add my mite in the stock of honour due to Adams, Jefferson, and others, to send to America; and I will, if it is thought proper to pay my expense of travelling to Paris, come myself and model the likeness of Mr. Jefferson; and at the same time see the picture, and if possible by this painting, which is said to be so like him, make a likeness of the General. I wish likewise to consult with you, how best we may honour our country, by holding up the likenesses of her eminent men, either in painting or wax-work. A statue in marble is already ordered, and an artist gone to Philadelphia to begin the work. This is as I wished and hoped.

MS not found; text from the extract printed in William Dunlap, *History of* *the Rise and Progress of the Arts of Design in the United States,* New York,

1834, I, 135-6. Dunlap's summary of the remainder of the letter reads: "The letter concludes by hinting the danger of sending Washington's picture to London, from the enmity of the government, and the *espionage* of the police; which she says has all the 'folly, without the abilities of the French.' She subscribes herself 'Patience Wright.'"

From St. John de Crèvecoeur

SIR   Caen 15th. Augt. 1785

Had my health Permitted me I shou'd Long since have enjoyed the Pleasure of Seeing you in Paris. But I feel that I shall not be able to Perform that Journey untill the Midle of the Fall. I have the Minister's Leave to stay here during that Time. Mr. Williamos has Informed me that the State of Your health is better than heretofore. I hope the difference of Climate will prove advantageous to you. Mr. P. Mazzei has delivered you I make no doubt Many dispatches, one in particular Wrapt up in brown Paper which Mr. Jay had Sent to my office in New York. I wish it had been in my Power to have delivered it myself. Permit me to Inquire after Miss Jefferson's state of health: She No doubt Now Speaks french Very Well. At her age Languages are Soon Learnt. I was in hopes to have Seen Mr. Houdon in America before my departure, but I have been disappointed.

I have the Honor to be with unfeigned Respect Sir Your Very Humble Servt.,   ST. JOHN

RC (DLC); at foot of letter: "His Excellency Thos. Jefferson Esqr."; endorsed in part: "recd. Aug. 20. 17[85]."

From James Monroe

DEAR SIR   New York August 15th. 1785

I have had the pleasure to receive yours by Mr. Adams with the cypher accompanying it and am happy to hear of the recovery of your health. I have only fail'd writing you by two of the packets the first of which sail'd before I had been advis'd she would, and the 2d. while I was ill of a pleurisy which I caught by walking in the rain to Congress and had like to have given me my final repose. Colo. Smith, Mr. Mazzai and Mrs. Macaulay Graham have since carried my letters to you, or rather took charge of them for that purpose. In those letters I gave you full information of the previous transactions in Congress as well as of the important business still before us. It therefore now remains to give you the progress since that time. *The¹ report proposing to invest Congress with the power to regulate commerce hath been twice before Congress in committee of the whole.* It met with no opponant except *the president.* By this I do not mean that there were no others oppos'd to it, for the contrary is the case. They however said but little or rather committed their side of the question to his care. In favor of it there were but few speakers also. *The committee came to no* [conclusion]² *but desired leave to sit again.* A second plan hath been proposd, *a navigation act digested here* and *recommended to the States.* This hath not been presented but probably will be. One would expect in a *particular quarter of the union perfect concert in this business,* yet this is not altogether the case. The 2d. plan above attended to takes its origin *with MacHenry. The Eastern people* wish something more lasting and will of course in the first instance not agree to it. They must therefore come in with that propos'd in *the report.* You will ask me why they hesitate? To be candid I believe it arises from the real magnitude of the subject, for I have the most confidential communications with them and am satisfied they act ingenuously. *They fear the consequences* may possibly result from it. The longer it is delayd the more certain is its passage thro *the several states* ultimately. Their minds will be better informd by evidences within their views of the necessity of *committing the power to Congress* for *the commerce of the union is daily declining; the merchants of this town* own I am told not more than *two ships.* I wish much to hear from you upon this subject. I expect it will be brought on again shortly, if for the purpose only of *committing it to the journals.* It may then be delay'd for sometime untill we may obtain full *information on it: the report changing the instructions for forming commercial treaties* will I believe be adopted. *It changes the principle* and puts an end to that *of the right of the most favored nation.* The policy of forming *a treaty with powers* not having *possessions in the West Indies is doubted* since from them we can obtain as much without as *with a treaty,* and such *treaties* whether upon that or any other *principle* in effecting the main object we have in view, *the opening the islands by treaty* with those who have them, may embarrass us. This is conceiv'd to be the only end which can be obtain'd upon principles of expedience to us *by treaty.* Of course that with *Sweden* &c. is unfortunate. Mr. *Adams* seems to suppose *the principal object in his mission to the court of London was the* formation³ *of a treaty;* but the contrary was certainly the case: it was merely *to conciliate*, and prevent *a variance* which seem'd to threaten at that time. He might however readily make this mistake under the present instructions. *A treaty* is not expected and I am satisfied the majority here wish all propositions on that head to cease, at least for the present, and untill *our restrictions on their commerce have effected a different disposition.* Mr. *Jay is authorised to treat with* Mr. *Gardoqui* upon *the subjects arising between the two parties. He is to lay every proposition before Congress before he enters into any engagement with him. As yet we have heard nothing from him.* The *consulate convention lately formed with France* is universally *disapproved.* It was form'd under instructions *but* in the opinion of *the secretary of foreign affairs hath been deviated from.* I have not had time to examine it attentively so cannot decide as to this fact. I shall sit out on the first of Sepr. for the Indian treaty on the Ohio and return thence thro Virga., and provided I shall be continued in Congress, to this place. I shall however attend the fœderal court for the trial of the controversy between Massachusetts and New York in Novr. so that I doubt whether I shall reach this before Decr. or Jany. next. The requisition will pass I expect this week and most of the important business remaining in a train for decision or be postponed for the winter. I have however no expectation that Congress will adjourn for the present year. I intended to have given you something of domestic news but am inform'd the mail is just closing. By this however, do not suppose that I have any thing worthy communication for the contrary is the case. I should be forc'd to look about me to find out any thing you would have patience to read. A. Lee is elected in the Board of treasury. We were under the necessity of having someone from this State and advocated his appointment. How is Miss Patsy? How is Short? How are they pleas'd with France. I must observe that *Congress* seem to expect *the court of France will send a minister here.* To visit you would give me infinite pleasure. Whether I shall be able or not depends on circumstances. If I do it will be in the spring after Congress adjourn or at least the most important business is finish'd. I send you the journals and am dear Sir yr. affectionate friend & servt.,   JAS. MONROE

RC (DLC); partly in code, with interlineal decoding by TJ.

The INSTRUCTIONS of Congress concerning the consular convention were those of 25 Jan. 1782, in pursuance of which Franklin had negotiated the convention signed by him and Vergennes on 29 July 1784 (two texts of the former are in DLC: TJ Papers, 7: 1209-10, and three of the latter in same, 11: 1780-5, 1786-91, 1792-1804). On 4 July 1785 Jay set forth an elaborate analysis of the manner in which these INSTRUCTIONS . . . HATH BEEN DEVIATED FROM, wherein he showed in parallel columns the form of convention Franklin had been authorized to negotiate and the form that had been agreed upon by him. There is scarcely room for question that the privileges and immunities granted French consuls were so extensive and so unusual as to make the result "incompatible with American sovereignty, and which had been so drafted as to emphasize the sovereign qualities of the 'Thirteen United States of North America'" rather than the United States of America (S. F. Bemis, *Diplomatic History of the United States*, 3rd edn., p. 83). A copy of the printed text of Jay's report is in DLC: TJ Papers, 13: 2215-9 (JCC, XXIX, 500-15, 924, No. 483). On 17 July 1785 Marbois sent Vergennes a summary account of most of Jay's objections and added: "Ce rapport ou Mr. Jay ne dissimule point ses dispositions à notre égard est plus considérable, mais comme il est tenu fort secret, je n'ai pu en obtenir que la partie dont je viens d'avoir l'honneur de vous rendre compte; j'aurai celui de vous faire parvenir le reste si je puis en obtenir la communication, mais on n'a pû me le promettre" (Arch. Aff. Etr., Corr. Pol., E.-U., xxx; Tr in DLC; Marbois sent the complete text of Jay's report to Vergennes on 8 Aug. 1785; same). Otto reported that Franklin, on his arrival in America, appeared "fort etonné" at the news that the convention had not been ratified. He also assured Vergennes that Franklin "trouve les objections de M. Jay si superficielles qu'il ne les croit pas même dignes de faire l'objet d'une negociation" (Otto to Vergennes, 18 and 28 Nov. 1785; same, xxx). In 1786 Jay recommended that TJ be instructed to negotiate a new convention in conformity with the original instructions, and Congress approved this suggestion (JCC, XXXI, 713-35; XXXIII, 421-7; Jay to TJ, 3 Oct. 1786; TJ to Jay, 9 Jan. 1787). Vergennes was disturbed by Jay's hostility to the convention arranged with Franklin, and

wrote Otto: "Je me suis fait rendre compte, M. des observations que doit avoir faites M. Jay sur notre convention relative aux Consuls, et j'ai jugé qu'il n'y en avoit pas une qui méritât d'être prise en considération. Quoiqu'il en soit, j'attendroi pour discuter la matiére que M. Jefferson soit autorisé à la traiter avec moi" (Vergennes to Otto, 20 Sep. 1785; Arch. Aff. Etr., Corr. Pol., E.-U., xxx; Tr in DLC). Otto at this time was reporting to Vergennes that Adams' dispatches to Congress had been unfavorable to France and were likely to have an ill effect if not countered; he added: "Ainsi, Monseigneur, le moyen le plus sûr que je connoisse de detruire ces impressions facheuses seroit que M. Jefferson fut instruit par quelque voye indirecte de ce qui se passe ici et ses relations seroient le contre-poison de celles de M. Adams.—M. Jefferson . . . est très attaché a l'alliance, il jouit ici d'une reputation excellente et meritée quoiqu'on doute de sa fermeté. S'il a connoissance de la difference des deux projets de convention il pourra peut-être s'en prévaloir envers le Congrès pour faire sentir les inconveniens du delai de la ratification et proposer que la convention soit redigée conformement au projet communiqué a M. le Chevr. De la Luzerne et ratifiée sans delai. . . . Je crois la convention une chose extrêmement desirable, mais nous serons bien plus forts en faisant agir Mr. Jefferson et en n'agissant nous mêmes ici que par nos amis" (Otto to Vergennes, 6 Sep. 1785; same, xxx; Tr in DLC). But Jay's opposition prevailed.

[1] This and subsequent words in italics are written in code and were decoded interlineally by TJ; the text presented here is a decoding by the editors, employing Code No. 9. The only significant variation from TJ's reading is noted below.

[2] This word is not in text; supplied conjecturally.

[3] TJ's reading for this word is "relation"; Burnett, *Letters of Members*, VIII, No. 186, Monroe, *Writings*, I, 103-6, and others follow TJ's error.

To Vergennes

Sir   Paris August 15. 1785.

In the conversation which I had the honor of having with your Excellency a few days ago, on the importance of placing, *at this time* the commerce between France and America on the best footing possible, among other objects of this commerce, that of tobacco was mentioned as susceptible of greater encouragement and advantage to the two nations. Always distrusting what I say in a language I speak so imperfectly, I will beg your permission to state in English the substance of what I had then the honour to observe, adding some more particular details for your consideration.

I find the consumption of tobacco in France estimated at from 15. to 30. millions of pounds. The most probable estimate however places it at 24. millions. This costing 8. sous the pound, delivered in a port of France amounts to . . . . 9,600,000. livres.
Allow 6 sous a pound, as the average cost of
 the different manufactures . . . . 7,200,000.
The revenue which the king derives from this
 is something less than . . . . .30,000,000.
             ─────────
Which would make the cost of the whole . . . .46,800,000.
But it is sold to the Consumers at an average of
 3^{lt} the pound . . . . .72,000,000.
             ─────────
There remains then for the expences of collec-
 tion . . . . .25,200,000. livres,
which is within a sixth as much as the king receives, and so gives nearly one half for collecting the other.[1]

It would be presumption in me, a stranger, to suppose my numbers perfectly accurate. I have taken them from the best and most distinterested authorities I could find. Your Excellency will know how far they are wrong: and should you find them considerably wrong, yet I am persuaded you will find, after strictly correcting them, that the collection of this branch of the revenue still absorbs too much.

My apology for making these remarks will I hope be found in my wishes to improve the commerce between the two nations, and the interest which my own country will derive from this improvement. The monopoly of the purchase of tobacco in France discourages both the French and American merchant from bringing it here, and from taking in exchange the manufactures and productions of France. It is contrary to the spirit of trade, and to the dispositions of merchants to carry a commodity to any market where but one person is allowed to buy it, and where of course that person fixes it's price, which the seller must receive, or re-export his commodity, at the loss of his voyage hither. Experience accordingly shews that they carry it to other markets, and that they take in exchange the merchandize of the place where they deliver it. I am misinformed if France has not been furnished from a neighboring nation with considerable quantities of tobacco, since the peace, and been obliged to pay there in coin what might have been paid here in manufactures, had the French and American merchants brought the tobacco originally here. I suppose too that the purchases made by the Farmers general in America, are paid for chiefly in coin, which coin is also remitted directly hence to England, and makes an important part of the balance supposed to be in favor of that nation against this. To satisfy government on this head, should the farmers general, by themselves, or by the company to whom they may commit the procuring these tobaccoes from America, require the exportation of a proportion of merchandize in exchange for them, it is an unpromising expedient. It will only commit the exports, as well as imports, between France and America to a monopoly, which being secure against rivals in the sale of the merchandize of France, are not likely to sell at such moderate prices as may encourage it's consumption there, and enable it to bear a competition with similar articles from other countries. I am persuaded this exportation of coin may be prevented, and that of commodities effected, by leaving both operations[2] to the French and American merchants, instead of the Farmers general. They will import a sufficient quantity of tobacco, if they are allowed a perfect freedom in the sale; and they will receive in paiment wines, oils, brandies, and manufactures instead of coin, forcing each other, by their competition, to bring tobaccoes of the best quality, to give to the French manufacturer the full worth of his merchandize, and to sell to the American consumer at the lowest price they can afford, thus encouraging him to use in preference the merchandize of this country.[3]

It is not necessary that this exchange should be favoured by any loss of revenue to the king. I do not mean to urge any thing which shall injure either his majesty or his people. On the contrary the measure I have the honour of proposing will increase his revenue, while it places both the seller and buyer on a better footing. It is not for me to say what system of collection may be best adapted to the organisation of this government; nor whether any useful hints may be taken from the practice of that country which has heretofore been the principal entrepot for this commodity. Their system is simple and little expensive. The importer there pays the whole duty to the king: and as this would be inconvenient for him to do before he has sold his tobacco, he is permitted on arrival to deposit it in the king's warehouse, under the locks of the king's officer. As soon as he has sold it, he goes with the purchaser to the warehouse, the money is there divided between the king and him, to each his proportion, and the purchaser takes out the tobacco. The paiment of the king's duty is thus ensured in ready money. What is the expence of it's collection I cannot say, but it certainly need not exceed 6. livres a hogshead of 1000 ℔. That government levies a higher duty on tobacco than is levied here.[4] Yet so tempting, and so valuable is the perfect liberty of sale, that the merchant carries it there, and finds his account in carrying it there.

If by a simplification of the collection of the king's duty on tobacco, the cost of that collection can be reduced even to 5. per cent, or a million and a half, instead of 25. millions, the price to the Consumer will be reduced from 3. to 2.ᵗᵗ the pound. For thus I calculate. The cost, manufacture and revenue on 24. million ℔. of tobacco being (as before stated) 46,800,000.ᵗᵗ

5. per cent on 30. millions of livres, expences of
    collection . . . . 1,500,000.
                                   —————————

gives what the Consumers would pay, being about
    2.ᵗᵗ a pound . . . . 48,300,000.
But they pay at present . . 3ᵗᵗ a pound . . . . 72,000,000.
                                   —————————

The difference is . . . . 23,700,000.

The price being thus reduced one third, would be brought within the reach of a new and numerous circle of the people, who cannot at present afford themselves this luxury. The consumption then would probably increase, and perhaps in the same, if not a greater, proportion with the reduction of the price, that is to say, from 24. to 36. millions of pounds: and the king continuing to receive 25. sous on the pound, as at present, would receive 45. instead of 30.

millions of livres, while his subjects would pay but 2. livres for an object which has heretofore cost them 3.^{tt} Or if, in event, the consumption were not to be increased, he would levy only 48. millions on his people where 72. millions are now levied, and would leave 24. millions in their pockets, either to remain there, or to be levied in some other form should the state of his revenues require it.[5] He will enable his subjects also to dispose of between 9. and 10. millions worth of their produce and manufactures, instead of sending nearly that sum annually in coin to enrich a neighboring nation.

I have heard two objections made to the suppression of this monopoly. 1. That it might increase the importation of tobacco in contraband. 2. That it would lessen the ability of the Farmers general to make occasional loans of money to the public treasury. These objections will surely be better answered by those who are better acquainted than I am, with the details and circumstances of the country. With respect to the 1st. however I may observe that contraband does not increase on lessening the temptations to it. It is now encouraged by being able to sell for 60. sous what costs but 14. leaving a gain of 46. sous. When the price shall be reduced from 60. to 40. sous, the gain will be but 26., that is to say a little more than one half of what it is at present.[6] It does not seem a natural consequence then that contraband should be increased by reducing it's gain nearly one half. As to the 2d. objection, if we suppose (for elucidation and without presuming to fix) the proportion of the farm on tobacco at one eighth of the whole mass farmed, the abilities of the Farmers general to lend will be reduced one eighth, that is, they can hereafter lend only 7. millions where heretofore they have lent 8. It is to be considered then whether this eighth (or other proportion, whatever it be)[7] is worth the annual sacrifice of 24[8] millions, or if a much smaller sacrifice to other monied men will not produce the same loans of money in the ordinary way.

While the advantages of an increase of revenue to the crown, a diminution of impost on the people, and a paiment in merchandise instead of money are conjectured as likely to result to France from a suppression of the monopoly on tobacco, we have also reason to hope some advantages on our part; and this hope alone could justify my entering into the present details.[9] I do not expect this advantage will be by an augmentation of price. The other markets of Europe have too much influence on this article to admit any sensible augmentation of price to take place. But the advantage I principally expect is an increase of consumption. This will give us a vent for so much more, and of consequence find employment for so many more cultivators of the earth: and in whatever proportion it increases this production for us, in the same proportion will it procure additional vent for the merchandize of France, and emploiment for the hands which produce it. I expect too that by bringing our merchants here they would procure a number of commodities in exchange, better in kind, and cheaper in price. It is with sincerity I add, that warm feelings are indulged in my breast by the further hope that it would bind the two nations still closer in friendship, by binding them in interest. In truth no two countries are better calculated for the exchanges of commerce. France wants rice, tobacco, potash, furs, ship-timber. We want wines, brandies,[10] oils and manufactures. There is an affection too between the two people which disposes them to favour one another. If they do not come together then to make the exchange in their own ports, it shews there is some substantial obstruction in the way. We have had the benefit of too many proofs of his majesty's friendly disposition towards the United states, and know too well his affectionate care of his own subjects, to doubt his willingness to remove these obstructions, if they can be unequivocally pointed out. It is for his wisdom to decide whether the monopoly which is the subject of this letter be deservedly classed with the principal of these. It is a great comfort to me too, that in presenting this to the mind of his Majesty, your Excellency will correct my ideas where an insufficient knowlege of facts may have led me into error; and that while the interests of the king and of his people are the first object of your attention, an additional one will be presented by those dispositions towards us[11] which have heretofore so often befriended our nation. We fervently invoke heaven to make the king's life and happiness the objects of it's peculiar care, and that he may long be relieved in the burthen of government by your wise counsels. Permit me to add the assurance of that high respect and esteem with which I have the honor to be your Excellency's most obedient & most humble servant,

TH: JEFFERSON

RC (Arch. Aff. Etr., Paris, Corr. Pol., E.-U., xxx); at head of text: "M. de R[ayneval] envoyé la traduction à M de Calonne le 31 aoust 1785. M. Jefferson. rep. le 31 aoust." PrC (DLC). Dft (DLC); actually a press-copy of a first draft, but with later alterations by TJ which render this copy a second draft. Tr (DLC); in French; in an unidentified hand, without indication of addressee or signature; with one correction in TJ's hand; enclosed in TJ to De la Boullaye, 18 July 1787, and printed by Ford, IV, 272-80, under 15 Aug. 1786. PrC of another Tr (DLC); in French; in William Short's hand. Tr (MHi); an undated fragment of four pages of continuing text; in an unidentified hand, with several corrections in TJ's hand. Tr (DNA: PCC, No. 107, I). There is also in DLC: Hamilton Papers, 14: 2142-5, an abstract of this letter prefaced with the following: "The object of Mr. Jefferson's conversation with the Ct Vergennes on the subject of tobacco is a destruction of the Monopoly of the Farmers General. . . ." and concluding with the following, which was deleted: "Defeated by Calonne who fears the loss of his Office &c. &c."; endorsed in part: "The propositions of Mr. Jefferson to abolish the Tobacco Farm." Entry in SJPL reads: "Vergennes. Tobacco trade." The texts of RC, PrC, the several Tr, and the second stage of Dft are identical, except for minor variations of punctuation and phrasing; the significant differences between these and the first stage of Dft, however, are noted below. TJ incorporated the text of this letter in his long report to Jay of 2 Jan. 1786, in which he gave an account of Vergennes' response to his overtures and of the immediate events preceding Lafayette's appeal to Calonne.

In his letter to De La Boullaye, 18 July 1787, TJ stated that he "took the materials for my calculation from the new Encyclopedie" and that he was "informed that article was written by the Abbé Baudeau, and that he was well acquainted with the subject." However, he had also taken the precaution of obtaining Thomas Barclay's advice and criticism of his estimates. Barclay "happened to be at Paris" at this time (TJ to Contée, 16 Aug. 1785) and TJ no doubt handed to him a copy of the letter. This copy, evidently, was the press-copy of the text here referred to as Dft, which TJ, after receiving it back from Barclay, then revised, employing some, though by no means all, of Barclay's suggestions. Barclay's comments (DLC: TJ Papers, 17: 3055-6) are as follows:

"The calculations are all right except that which states the price of Tobacco at $31\frac{1}{4}$ sols. It should be $31\frac{1}{5}$.—The Quantity annually Used in France seems to be about Thirty thousand hogsheads five thousand of which are supposed to be of the Growth of Holland, the Palatinate and the Ukerain. Therefore the Tobacco from America may stand at Twenty five thousand hogsheads.—The Expence of Manufacturing into Rolls or snuff Cannot I think be placed at less than 3 sols ℔ pound. That of Collecting the Duty wou'd not be any thing like the sum Mentiond in the Estimate. Four livres ℔ hogshead wou'd be sufficient which on 24000 hhds. wou'd amount to no more than 96000 livres.—An Estimate formed on these principals wou'd stand thus:

30,000,000 Pounds at 8 sols		12,000,000
Duty 1 livre ℔ pound		30,000,000
4 livres ℔ hhd. Expence of Collecting Duties		120,000
3 sols ℔ pound Expence of Manufacturing		4,500,000
		46,620,000
which is $31\frac{9}{25}$ sols ℔ Pound.		
But 30 Millions of Pounds at 50 sols ℔ pound the supposed average price amounts		75,000,000
From which Deduct		46,620,000
There remains		28,380,000 livres

clear annual gain to the Farmers, supposing that with the Encrease of the Consumption of Tobacco, they Pay an Encrease of the Duties which is a Very doubtfull point.—If His Majesty wou'd appoint persons to purchase Tobacco and Deliver it out again to the Farmers as they shou'd have occasions for it, it wou'd, Next to laying the Trade open as it ought to be, Certainly produce the Best Consequences. But if the Farmers hold the Monopoly and Make Contracts with Individuals, it is Easie to forsee that None of the People of Either France or America Can derive any advantage from the Commerce of the two Countries but those actually Employ'd in the Execution of the Contract.—I think the Estimate of 50 sols ℔ pound for Manufactured Tobacco low, and that the Difference between that sum and the actual produce of the Sale wou'd probably Defray the Expence of Manufacturing. But it is better to Err on the safe side and as the Soldiers and Sailors are supplied at a lower rate than the Public in general the price of 50 sols had better stand. The Copy of the letter is Inclosed."

On this general subject of the tobacco monopoly, see F. L. Nussbaum, "The Revolutionary Vergennes and Lafayette versus the Farmers General," *Jour. Mod. Hist.*, III (1931), p. 592-604, with Lafayette's communication to De Boullongne, president of the American Committee of the farmers-general, printed as an appendix, p. 605-13; also, by the same author, "American tobacco and French politics, 1783-1789," *Pol. Sci. Qu.*, XL (1926), p. 479-516. See also, for an excellent account, Gottschalk, *Lafayette, 1783-89*, p. 207-37. When Vergennes transmitted TJ's letter to Calonne, who was far from sympathetic, he remarked: "Elle semble demander la plus serieuse attention, et en séparant la routine pouvoir operer une amelioration dans votre Commerce et dans les revenus du Roi" (31 Aug. 1785; Arch. Aff. Etr., Corr. Pol., E.-U., XXX; Tr. in DLC). Calonne replied to Vergennes in part:

"La partie de cette lettre, qui traite des moiens d'établir dans ce moment le commerce entre la france et les Etats-Unis, sur le meilleur pied possible, contient des choses bien vues, et faites pour séduire au premier examen; mais indépendamment de ce que les calculs qui servent de bases au plan de M. de Jefferson sont absolument inéxacts, il est des considérations majeures, que ce Ministre n'a pu prévoir et qui, quand il ne se rencontrerait aucune difficulté dans l'exécution de son plan, ne permettroient pas de l'adopter. —J'aurai d'abord l'honneur de vous faire observer, Monsieur, que la Consommation en tabac, que M. de Jefferson, d'après ce qui lui a été raporté, suppose s'elever annuellement à 24. millions de livres pezant, ne monte pas à beaucoup plus de 14., déduction faite des matières de rebut.—Le produit brut de la vente du Tabac, bien loin d'être porté à 72. millions, n'a pas, pendant l'année la plus favorable des Six du bail précédant, et des trois premieres du bail actuel, atteint la proportion de 49. millions.—La guerre entre L'Angleterre et l'Amérique Septentrionale, ayant fait renchérir considérablement le prix des Tabacs, les frais d'achat ont Si fort augmenté qu'ils ont absorbé une grande partie du produit de la vente du tabac; en sorte que le prix de rigueur pour cette partie n'est entré dans les calculs du bail actuel que pour 25.600.000^{ft}; mais la baisse de ces prix devient de jour en jour plus sensible, et elle est telle, qu'il y a tout lieu d'espérer qu'avec l'augmentation de 4s. par Livre de tabac, imposée par l'Edit d'Aout 1781, la fixation du prix de ferme du tabac dans le nouveau bail pourra excéder cette Somme de plusieurs millions.—Une masse aussi considerable de produit ne pourrait être détachée du bail, sans en rendre les Conditions extrêmement difficiles à régler, et peut-être Même désavantageuses au Roi; et d'ailleurs si, en renonçant au privilege exclusif de la vente du tabac, on se bornait à le charger d'un droit à l'importation, ou ce droit seroit modique, et alors il serait impossible qu'il produisit une Somme Suffisante pour dédommager du Sacrifice qu'on auroit fait; ou si ce droit étoit dans une proportion telle qu'on crût pouvoir espérer de retrouver le niveau de ce que reproduit la ferme du tabac, cette esperance serait bientôt détruite par l'excès de la fraude, qu'on n'aurait plus de moyens d'arrêter.—Enfin, Monsieur, si le Roi, en suivant les mouvements de Sa Bienfaisance, pouvoit adoucir le régime des perceptions que les besoins de l'Etat le forcent à maintenir, il ne commenceroit certainement pas par celle qui porte sur le tabac, parce qu'elle est absolument volontaire et qu'il dépend de Ses Sujets de S'en affranchir. —Malgré ces considérations qui, à ce que j'espère, vous démontreront qu'il n'est pas possible d'adopter aucun des plans indiqués par M. de Jefferson, je n'en sens pas moins combien il est à désirer qu'on puisse resserrer davantage les Liaisons de Commerce entre nous et l'Amérique Septentrionale, et favoriser l'échange de nos productions avec celles de ce Peuple. Je Suis parvenu à écarter en partie les entraves que la ferme générale, au moien de Son droit de préférence sur l'achat des tabacs, peut mettre à l'importation de cette matière dans nos ports, par les Vaisseaux Américains, et j'aurai incessamment l'honneur de me concerter avec vous Sur les moiens de former un plan général de Commerce également utile aux deux Nations" (Calonne to Vergennes, Fontainebleau, 19 Oct. 1785; same, XXX). Lafayette entered the picture after his return to France, and on 16 Nov. 1785 wrote Vergennes asking for a copy of Calonne's reply:

"Vous avés eu la bonté, Monsieur le Comte, de me dire que MM les fermiers

Generaux avoient repondu à la lettre de M. jefferson; s'il nous etoit possible d'avoir cette Reponse, peut être M. jefferson qui connoit à fonds tout ce qui Regarde les tabacs, pourroit il servir à demontrer la fausseté de quelques Calculs. Ces messieurs sont si Redoutables, malgré leur desinteressement, qu'on ne sauroit assés multiplier les moiens de defense.—On nous a dit, Monsieur le Comte, que le Bail des fermes va se Renouveller. Si le Bruit est fondé, j'oserois proposer que le Renouvellement de celle du tabac, puisqu'il Reste encore du tems, fut seulement plus Retardé que les autres, afin de pouvoir Examiner les methodes proposées.—Je vous demande pardon de vous importuner, Monsieur le Comte,

mais j'ai voulu vous Communiquer mes deux idées, parce que vous les accueillés avec bonté" (same).

[1] This paragraph to this point in the first stage of Dft reads as follows (the figures in italics represent, however, TJ's *preliminary* alterations during revision for the second stage): "I find the consumption of tobacco in France estimated at 24. millions of pounds. This costing 8. sous a pound, delivered in a port of France, amounts to 9,600,000 livres. It is afterwards either powdered, or cut, or formed into rolls. Suppose these operations, on the average, add [2.] *6* sous a pound to the price; this raising the cost of a pound to 10. *14* sous, makes the whole amount

to	12. millions *16,800,000* of livres.
The king derives a revenue of a livre a pound, making	24. millions *30,000,000*
and of course raising the price of the whole to	36. millions.
But it is sold to the Consumers at an average of 50 sous the ℔, making ..	60. millions of livres.
There remains then for the expences of collection	24. millions, exactly as much...."

[2] The passage "To satisfy government . . . operations" was interlined in second stage of Dft after the following had been deleted: "I am persuaded this would be prevented by leaving the supply of tobaccoes."
[3] The words, "forcing each other . . . of this country," were interlined in second stage of Dft.
[4] This and the preceding sentence in the first stage of Dft read: ". . . in ready money, and the expence of it's collection probably does not exceed 5. or 6. per cent. At least we know from experience that it need not exceed that. Mr. Pitt, in the debate in parlia-

ment of the 21. of June last, observed that the duties on tobacco in that country amounted to fifteen pence sterling a pound. This is 30. sous. That government then levies 50 per cent more on every pound of tobacco than is levied here."
[5] The passage "can be reduced . . . require it" reads in the first stage of Dft: "can be reduced to 6. per cent, or about a million and a half instead of 24 millions, the price to the Consumer will be reduced from 50 sous to 31¼ sous the pound. For thus I calculate. First cost, in France of 24 millions of pounds of tobacco @ 8.

sous the pound is	9,600,000℔	
The king's duty on that quantity at a livre a pound is	24,000,000	*30,000,000*
6 per cent on 24 millions of livres, expences of collection	1,440,000	
2. *6* sous a pound for manufacturing 24. millions of pounds of tobacco ..	2,400,000	*7,200,000*
gives what the Consumers would pay for 24. millns. of pounds (to wit 31¼ sous pr. lb.)	37,440,000	
But they pay under the present regulations 50 sous a pound	60,000,000	
The difference is	22,5[6]0,000.	

The price being thus reduced nearly two fifths, would be brought within the reach of a new and numerous circle of the people who cannot at present afford themselves this luxury. The consumption then would increase in the same if not a greater proportion with the reduction of the price, that is to say to 3[8]. instead of 24. millions. And the king, continuing to receive only the same duty of a livre on the pound would receive 38 instead of 24. millions of livres, while his subjects would pay but [31¼] sous for an object which has heretofore cost them 50 sous. Or if, in event, the consumption were not to be increased, he would levy only 25½ millions on his people where 48 millions are now levied, and would leave 22½ millions to be levied in some other form should the state of his revenues require it."

6 This and the preceding sentence in the first stage of Dft read: "It is now encouraged by being able to sell for 50. sous what costs but 1[0] leaving a gain of 40. sous. When the price shall be reduced from [5]0. to 31¼ sous the gain will be but 21[¾], that is to say about half of what it is at present."

7 The phrase enclosed in parentheses (in RC) was inserted in the second stage of Dft.

8 This figure in the first stage of Dft reads: "22½."

9 The words "and this hope . . . present details" were inserted in the second stage of Dft.

10 This article was inserted in the French Tr in DLC: TJ Papers, 14: 2381 by TJ as "eaux de vie."

11 Instead of the words "and that while . . . towards us," Dft in its first stage reads: "and be under the influence of those dispositions which have. . . ."

To John Banister, Jr.

DEAR SIR   Paris Aug. 16. 1785.

I have been favoured with yours of the 1st. inst. which relieved me from a great deal of anxiety, your former letter having mentioned that you found yourself worse at Lyons, and being quite uninformed afterwards. I suppose you to be now at Avignon, by the post mark, for you omitted to date the place from whence you wrote. Be so good as to favor me with your address that I may know how to direct my future letters to you. The exclusion of British factors from Boston, and the discouragements on that commerce is in a course of adoption by the principal towns of the other states. I am pleased to see every thing which tends to bring our merchants at short hand to the place where the objects of their commerce are first produced, and to send them to Great Britain only for those which she manufactures better and cheaper than any other country. The price of tobacco in London is very low indeed. It is considerably fallen here too. In your letter you say nothing to me of your health, on which however I pray you to inform me. The two Fitzhughs, Franks, and Williamos will leave this in a few days for America. I shall write by them to your father and construe to him your silence as to your health into a proof of it's being good. I thank you kindly for your offers of service, and make the same to you with great cordiality and am with much affection Dr. Sir Your friend & servant, TH: JEFFERSON

PrC (DLC).

To B. Contée

SIR   Paris Aug. 16. 1785.

Your letter of July 18. to Dr. Franklin came to my hands the 1st. inst. As I knew mine of July 13. was then on the way to you no further answer to it was necessary. Your's of July 30. came to hand on the 6th. instant. I immediately communicated it to Mr. Barclay our Consul general who happened to be at Paris. He thought with me that if you had made no express contract with the agent of the farmers general previous to your bringing your tobacco to Bayonne, you could not oblige him to take it by the laws of this country, or probably of any country. Your first letters gave reason to believe there was no absolute contract. Your last seems to suppose one. On the whole we thought the best thing which could be done for you would be to apply to the discretion and justice of the Farmers general. Mr. Barclay drew a memorial, which he inclosed to one of that body of his acquaintance. It will yet be six days before he can get an answer. Lest you should be doubtful in the mean time whether any thing was doing for you, I thought it best to write you what is as yet done, with an assurance that I will communicate their final answer as soon as I receive it, which perhaps may be by the post of this day week. I am Sir Your very humble servant,   TH: JEFFERSON

PrC (DLC).

To John Adams

DEAR SIR   Paris Aug. 17. 1785.

I received yesterday your favor of the 7th. *This*[1] *was 4. days later than* Mr. Short's of the *same date. It had evidently been opened. We must* therefore consider *both governments as possessed of it's contents.* I write you a line at this moment merely to inform you that *Mr. Barclay is willing* to *go to treat with* the *Barbary states if we desire it* and that *this will* not *take him from any employment here.* It will *only retard his voiage to America.*

[394]

Let me know your sentiments hereon.[2] The number 1672. is an error in the alphabetical side of the cypher. Turn to the numerical side and in the 11th. column and 72d. line you will see the number it should have been and what it was meant to signify. Correct your alphabetical side accordingly if it is wrong as mine was. We are told this morning that the *Cardinal Prince* of *Rohan* is *confined* to *his chamber* under *guard* for *reflections* on the *Queen who was present herself* in *council on his examination,* the first *time she* was ever *there* and the first *instance* of so *high an Ecclesiastical character* under actual *force.* Adieu. Your friend & servt.,

TH: JEFFERSON

RC (MHi: AMT); endorsed by Adams in part: "ansd. 23. [Aug.] 1785"; partly in code, with a "Translation" of the passages in code. PrC (DLC). In DLC: TJ Papers, 27: 4640 there is in TJ's hand a draft for encoding purposes of the passage "This was 4. days later than Mr. Short's . . . Let me know your sentiments hereon." Entry in SJPL reads: "Adams John.

Barbary. Barclay."

[1] This and subsequent words in italics are written in code in RC; TJ employed Code No. 8. The text presented here is taken from the "Translation," except for one word.
[2] The "Translation" reads "here," but TJ's draft for encoding reads "hereon."

To Castries

Paris Aug. 17. 1785.

I was honoured yesterday with the receipt of your Excellency's letter of the 12th. instant. I have ever understood that the whole crew off the Alliance was of American citizens. But should there have been among them any subjects of his majesty, it is but just that the repaiment of their portions of the prize money should be secured. But Capt. Jones being already bound to pay what he shall receive into the treasury of the United States, I submit to your Excellency, whether it will be right to require him to be answerable for monies after they shall be put out of his power? And whether, as Congress have secured the receipt at their treasury it will not be shorter for them to order repaiment to any subjects of his majesty who may shew themselves justly entitled? I will immediately ask their pleasure on this subject, and sollicit such orders as that every such claimant, proving his title here, in the usual way, may receive immediate paiment of their banker here. And that no individual may, in the mean time be delayed, should any such present their proofs before the orders are received, I will undertake to direct paiment by the banker of the United

States in Paris; being assured that in so doing I shall forward those views of perfect justice which Congress will carry into the distribution of this money. Should any instances arise of paiment to be demanded here, I think they will be few, and the sums will of course be small.

I shall be happy if your Excellency shall think that the justice due to this part of the claimants is so sufficiently secured by these assurances as that it need not stand in the way of that which is due to the great mass of claimants who are already so much indebted for your attention to their interests. I will take the liberty of asking that I may be furnished by the proper officer with copies of Capt. Jones's receipts for the monies which shall be paid him, that, by transmitting them to the Treasury board of the United States, they may know the precise sums which they are to receive through his hands. I pray you to accept my acknolegements for your attention to this troublesome business, and assurances of the high respect and esteem with which I have the honor to be your Excellency's most obedient humble servant,   TH: JEFFERSON

PrC (DLC). Tr (DNA: PCC, No. 87, 1); in TJ's hand. Tr (DNA: PCC, No. 107, 1). Entry in SJPL under 15 Aug. 1785 reads "Castries. P. Jones's case." The date is in error, for TJ did not receive Castries' letter of 12 Aug.

until the 16th and his reply was written in the morning of the 17th (TJ to Jones, 17 Aug. 1785). TJ enclosed a copy of the present letter in his to Jay of 30 Aug. 1785.

To John Paul Jones

SIR   Paris Aug. 17. 1785.

Mine of the 13th. informed you that I had written to the M. de Castries on the subject of Puchelberg's interference. Yesterday I received his answer dated the 12th. In that he says that he is informed by the Ordonnateur that he has not been able to get an authentic roll of the crew of the Alliance, that, in the probable case of there having been some French subjects among them, it will be just that you should give security to repay their portions. I write to him this morning that as you have obliged yourself to transmit the money to the treasury of the U.S. it does not seem just to require you to be answerable for money which will be no longer within your power, that the repaiment of such portions will be incumbent on Congress, that I will immediately sollicit their orders to have all such claims paid by their banker here, and that should any be presented before I receive their orders I will undertake to direct the banker of the U.S. to pay them that there may be no delay. I trust that this will remove the difficulty, and that it is the last which will be offered. The ultimate answer shall be communicated the moment I receive it. Having pledged myself for the claims which may be offered before I receive the orders of Congress, it is necessary to arm myself with the proper checks. Can you give me a roll of the crew, pointing out the French subjects? If not, can you recollect personally the French subjects and name them to me, and the sums they are entitled to? If there were none such yet the roll will be material, because I have no doubt that Puchelberg will excite claims upon me either true or false. I am with much respect Sir Your most obedt. humble servt.,

TH: JEFFERSON

PrC (DLC). Recorded in SJL as sent "by Mr. Cannon"; entry in SJPL reads: "Jones J. Paul. Puchilberg."

From John Paul Jones

SIR   L'Orient, August 17th, 1785.

I am still waiting for a decision respecting the claim of M. Puchilberg. But I think it my duty to inform you that one or two of the common sailors that served on board the Alliance, when that frigate was under my orders, are now here in a merchant vessel, and, as I am this moment informed, they have been persuaded to write to M. Puchilberg, desiring that their share in the prizes may not be sent to America, but paid to them here. This I am told, has been urged as a reason to the Marechal to induce him to decide in favor of M. Puchilberg's claim. Those two men will, however, sail in a day or two for Boston, and perhaps may never return to France; besides, their objection is too trifling to be admitted, as it would greatly injure the other persons, both officers and men of that crew, who would, in all probability, never receive any part of their prize money unless they should come from America to L'Orient on purpose; which would not pay their expenses.

As the post is just going, I must defer answering the letter you did me the honor to write me on the 3d, till another opportunity. I am with great esteem, &c.

N.B. I beg you therefore to write again to the Marechal de Castries.

MS not found; text from J. H. Sherburne, *John Paul Jones*, Washington, 1825, p. 267. Recorded in SJL as received 21 Aug. 1785. Sherburne wrote that this and other documents were "kindly furnished by Mr. Jefferson, who was contemporary with Jones, was his friend and patron, and whose enlightened recollection embraces the whole series of revolutionary events" (same, p. viii).

To Thomas Thompson

SIR   Paris Aug. 17. 1785.

I am much obliged by your favor of the 12th. The method you are so kind as to propose to me of being furnished with the English papers would be perfectly pleasing to me, if they come clear of French postage also, a circumstance which you do not particularly mention in your letter. I had written about a fortnight ago to Mr. Adams to order me the two best papers which the D. of Dorset was so kind as to permit to come always by his courier. But I do not consider this channel as so certain as the post. I cannot decide any thing however till I hear from Mr. Adams what he has done. In the mean time if you will be so good as to inform me as to the circumstance of French postage, I shall be obliged to you. I am Sir your most obedient humble servt.,   TH: JEFFERSON

PrC (MoSHi); at foot of text: "Mr. Thos. Thompson. wine merchant Dover. To the care of Monsr. Mouron, Calais."

To Nathaniel Tracy

DEAR SIR   Paris Aug. 17. 1785.

A conveyance offering by a gentleman going directly to Salem, I cannot omit the opportunity of congratulating you on your safe return to your family and country which I see announced in the public papers. I wish that the sentiments of pleasure excited by this event could have been unmixed with those of a contrary nature which the fate of poor Temple occasioned—but let us turn to the living. What is become of Moore? Have you banished him from Boston with the rest of his countrymen? I thought I saw in the resolutions of Faneuil hall a hole made on purpose for him, and others as good as him, to creep through. But tell him from me he must alter, or he shall go the next time. He must become abstemious, chaste, ascetic, hard-hearted; in short he must mix all his good qualities with a little alloy from their opposite vices, to render them fit for common use. The proceedings in Boston on

[398]

the subject of British commerce have produced a sensation among the God-dem-mees, and will do us good in the other parts of Europe. It will do much more if the other states adopt them. I consider this measure like that of turning a strumpet out of doors. It is saying 'we have sinned, but we repent and amend: we begin by banishing the tempter.' But much remains to be done afterwards. Can you become rigorously frugal? Can you despise European modes, European follies and vices? &c. &c. For many such hacknied questions might be asked, all approved in theory, but neglected in practice. It is much to be wished that every discouragement should be thrown in the way of men who undertake to trade without capital; who therefore do not go to the market where commodities are to be had cheapest, but where they are to be had on the longest credit. The consumers pay for it in the end, and the debts contracted, and bankruptcies occasioned by such commercial adventurers, bring burthen and disgrace on our country. No man can have a natural right to enter on a calling by which it is at least ten to one he will ruin many better men than himself. Yet these are the actual links which hold us whether we will or no to Great Britain. There is a great reformation necessary in our manners and our commerce. This is for you to look to. Europe is likely to continue in peace. The affairs of the Emperor and Dutch are as good as made up. That of Bavaria is dropped. If any thing threatens it is the one between the Emperor and Porte. You will suppose from the papers that France and England are likely to quarrel. But they will not fight. One has but little money and the other none at all. I believe it may be true that the salute to the British flag in the channel has been refused by a French vessel. We shall soon see whether it was by order. If it was, it will not be resented, and I hope the other nations will seize the moment for throwing off this yoke of maritime bondage. The peace between Spain and Algiers was to have cost a million of dollars besides presents in kind. It is likely to be broke off, and that by the latter who think they cannot afford it.—Will you be so good as to send me your best newspaper? I will pay the cost on demand here, or find means of ordering paiment in Boston. They will come most regularly if sent to Mr. Neill Jamieson merchant of New York. Present me respectfully to Mrs. Tracy, to Mr. Jackson, Mr. Russel, and Lowell and beleive me to be with sincerity Dr. Sir your friend & servt.,   TH: JEFFERSON

PrC (DLC). Recorded in sjl as sent "by Mr. Derby."

From John Adams

DEAR SIR   Grosvenor Square August 18. 1785

I have received your Favour of the 6. Aug. with the Notes and Project inclosed.

How can we send another Person? We have not in our Full Power authority to Substitute. Will not the Emperor and the Regencies feel their Dignity offended if a Person appears without a Commission from Congress? Do you mean that he should only agree upon the Terms and transmit them to Us to be signed? If you think this Method will do, I have no objection to either of the Persons you mention—nor to Mr. Short. Dr. Bancroft is the greatest Master of the French Language. If We conclude to send either he should take an attested Copy at least of all our Commissions for Africa, and a Letter and Instructions from Us. If there is any Truth in any of the Reports of Captures by the Algerines, Lambes Vessell may be taken by them.

Whoever is sent by us should be instructed to Correspond constantly with us, and to send, by whatever conveyance he may find, whether thro' Spain France England Holland or otherwise, Copies of his Letters to us to Congress. He should be instructed farther to make dilligent Inquiry concerning the Productions of those Countries which would answer in America, and those of the United States which might find a Market in Barbary, and to transmit all such Information to Congress as well as to Us.

I have read over the Project with Care. The 17th. Article appears to be carried farther than our Countrymen will at present be willing to go. I presume the three last words of the third Line of this 17. Article must be left out; and in the fourth line, the 7. 8. 9. 10. 11. and 12. Words; and in the Sixth Line the first, second, third, fourth, and fifth words.

You have seen by this Time our Massachusetts Navigation Act, and the Reasonings and Dispositions of all the States tend the same Way at present, so that we must conform our Proceedings, as I suppose, to their Views. My Regards to Messrs. Humphreys, Mazzai, Williamos, &c. and believe me ever yours,

JOHN ADAMS

Mr. Short left us on Tuesday. Dr. Bancroft is just come in. This Letter will be delivered to you by Mr. James Smith, a Gentleman of South Carolina, a Relation of Mrs. Adams, whom I beg leave to introduce to you and recommend to your Civilities.

RC (DLC). FC (MHi: AMT); in an unidentified hand. Recorded in SJL as received 30 Aug. 1785. For the three passages in Article 17 of the projet that Adams objected to, see TJ to Adams, 6 Aug. 1785, note 1.

To William Carmichael

DEAR SIR   Paris Aug. 18. 1785.

My last to you was of June 22. with a P. S. of July 14. Yours of June 27. came to hand the 23d. of July and that of July 28. came to hand the 10th. inst. The papers enclosed in the last shall be communicated to Mr. Adams. I see with extreme satisfaction and gratitude the friendly interposition of the court of Spain with the emperor of Marocco on the subject of the brig Betsey, and I am persuaded it will produce the happiest effects in America. Those who are entrusted with the public affairs there are sufficiently sensible how essentially it is of our interest to cultivate peace with Spain, and they will be pleased to see a corresponding disposition in that court. The late good office of emancipating a number of our countrymen from slavery is peculiarly calculated to produce a sensation among our people, and to dispose them to relish and adopt the pacific and friendly views of their leaders towards Spain. We hear nothing yet of Mr. Lambe. I have therefore lately proposed to Mr. Adams if he does not come in the French or English packet of this month, that we will wait no longer. If he accedes to the proposition, you will be sure of hearing of, and perhaps of seeing some agent proceeding on that business. The immense sum said to have been proposed on the part of Spain to Algiers leaves us little hope of satisfying their avarice. It may happen then that the interests of Spain and America may call for a concert of proceedings against that state. The dispositions of the Emperor of Marocco give us better hopes there. May not the affairs of the Musquito coast, and our Western posts, produce another instance of a common interest? Indeed,[1] I meet this correspondence of interest in so many quarters, that I look with anxiety to the issue of Mr. Gardoqui's mission; hoping it will be a removal of the only difficulty at present subsisting between the two nations, or which is likely to arise.

Congress are not likely to adjourn this summer. They have purchased the Indian right of soil to about fifty millions of acres of land, between the Ohio and lakes, and expected to make another purchase of an equal quantity. They have, in consequence, passed

[401]

an ordinance for disposing of their lands, and I think a very judicious one. They propose to sell them at auction, for not less than a dollar an acre, receiving their own certificates of debt as money. I am of opinion all the certificates of our domestic debt will immediately be exchanged for land. Our foreign debt, in that case, will soon be discharged. New York and Rhode Island still refuse the impost. A general disposition is taking place to commit the whole management of our commerce to Congress. This has been much promoted by the interested policy of England, which, it was apparent, could not be counter-worked by the States separately. In the mean time, the other great towns are acceding to the proceedings of Boston for annihilating, in a great measure, their commercial connections with Great Britain. I will send the cypher by a gentleman who goes from here to Madrid about a month hence. It shall be a copy of the one I gave Mr. Adams. The letter of Don Gomez, has been delivered at the hotel of the Portuguese ambassador, who is, however, in the country. I am with much respect, Dear Sir, your most obedient humble servant,

TH: JEFFERSON

PrC (DLC); fragment, consisting of only the first page of letter; the remainder of the text is printed from TJR, I, 284-5. Entry in SJPL under this date reads: "Carmichael Wm.

Spain. Barbary. American news"; recorded in SJL as sent "by Mr. Grand."

[1] Text of PrC ends here.

To Samuel House

DEAR SIR   Paris Aug. 18. 1785.

Your favour of May 28. came to hand the 22d. Ultimo. I have spoken with some merchants of this place and endeavoured to shew them that it would be worth their while to try some commercial adventures to America, the disposal of which I would have endeavoured to procure for you. But this place carries on no distant commerce, but in their modes and other trifles: and the tales of want of faith and of bankruptcies in America, which are disseminated by the English papers, deter them from thinking of adventures in that way. I very much fear that it will be difficult to introduce a commerce with this country even in articles where it would be for the interest of both to trade together. Their mercantile characters are too easily rebuffed by difficulties. I wish I could have given you a more comfortable answer. I inclose a letter for Mrs. Trist. Should she not be returned be so good as to keep it till she does return. Present my most friendly respects to Mrs. House and be assured of the esteem with which I am Dr. Sir your most obedt. humble servt.,   TH: JEFFERSON

PrC (MHi). Recorded in SJL as sent "by Mr. Fitzhugh." Enclosure: TJ to Eliza House Trist of this date, following.

To Eliza House Trist

DEAR MADAM   Paris Aug. 18. 1785.

Your favor of Dec. 25. came to hand on the 22d. of July, and on the next day I had the pleasure of receiving that of May. 4. I was happy to find that you had taken the first step for a return to your own country, tho' I was sensible many difficult ones still remained. I hope however these are surmounted, and that this letter will find you in the bosom of your friends. Your last letter is an evidence of the excellence of your own dispositions which can be so much excited by so small a circumstance as the one noticed in it. Tho' I esteem you too much to wish you may ever need services from me or any other person, yet I wish you to be assured that in such an event no one would be more disposed to render them, nor more desirous of receiving such a proof of your good opinion as would be your applying for them. By this time I hope your mind has felt the good effects of time and occupation. They are slow physicians indeed, but they are the only ones. Their opiate influence lessens our sensibility tho their power does not extend to dry up the sources of sorrow. I thought there was a prospect the last winter of my taking a trip to England. Tho' I did not know who and where were Browse's relations in that country, yet I knew he had some so nearly connected as to claim their attention. I should have endeavored to have seen them, and disposed them to feel an interest both in you and him. Tho' the probability of my going there is very much lessened, yet it is not among impossible events. Will you be so good as to let me know what relations he has there and where they live, and if I should at any time go there I will certainly see them. Patsy is well, and is happily situated in the Convent of Panthemont the institutions of which leave me nothing to wish on that head. It is attended by the best masters. The most disagreeable circumstance is that I have too little of her company. I am endeavoring by some arrangements to alter this. My present anxiety is to get my other daughter over to me: for tho' my return is placed at a period not very distant, yet I cannot determine to leave her so long without me. But indeed the circumstances of such a passage, to such an infant, under any other care than that of a parent, are very distressing. My wishes are fixed, but my resolution is wavering.

I am much pleased with the people of this country. The roughnesses of the human mind are so thoroughly rubbed off with them that it seems as if one might glide thro' a whole life among them without a justle. Perhaps too their manners may be the best calculated for happiness to a people in their situation. But I am convinced they fall far short of effecting a happiness so temperate, so uniform and so lasting as is generally enjoyed with us. The domestic bonds here are absolutely done away. And where can their compensation be found? Perhaps they may catch some moments of transport above the level of the ordinary tranquil joy we experience, but they are separated by long intervals during which all the passions are at sea without rudder or compass. Yet fallacious as these pursuits of happiness are, they seem on the whole to furnish the most effectual abstraction from a contemplation of the hardness of their government. Indeed it is difficult to conceive how so good a people, with so good a king, so well disposed rulers in general, so genial a climate, so fertile a soil, should be rendered so ineffectual for producing human happiness by one single curse, that of a bad form of government. But it is a fact. In spite of the mildness of their governors the people are ground to powder by the vices of the form of government. Of twenty millions of people supposed to be in France I am of opinion there are nineteen millions more wretched, more accursed in every circumstance of human existence, than the most conspicuously wretched individual of the whole United states.—I beg your pardon for getting into politics. I will add only one sentiment more of that character. That is, nourish peace with their persons, but war against their manners. Every step we take towards the adoption of their manners is a step towards perfect misery.—I pray you to write to me often. Do not you turn politician too; but write me all the small news; the news about persons and not about states. Tell me who die, that I may meet these disagreeable events in detail, and not all at once when I return: who marry, who hang themselves because they cannot marry &c. &c. Present me in the most friendly terms to Mrs. House, and Browse, and be assured of the sincerity with which I am Dear Madam your affectionate friend & servant,

TH: JEFFERSON

P.S. In your letter of May 4. you speak of one between that and Dec. 25. but I have never received it. [It] is come to hand since writing the above.[1] It is dated Mar. 12.

PrC (DLC). Recorded in SJL as sent "by Mr. Fitzhugh." Enclosed in TJ to Samuel House of this date.

Mrs. Trist quoted a part of this letter in hers to Madison of 9 Feb. 1785, somewhat to Madison's apprehension, for he seems to have given her an oblique warning against revealing TJ's private comments on the French people: "His portrait of the French character is of itself a proof of the spirit with which he eyes Europe. He has never been so full to me on that subject, and I am therefore particularly obliged to you for the extract. Perhaps some of the traits in the picture, as coming from his political situation are unfit for indiscriminate communication and I shall accordingly use reserve in that respect" (Madison to Mrs. Trist, 14 Mch. 1786; RC owned by J. E. Fields, Chicago, Ill.). In this same letter Madison also wrote: "I am extremely sorry at the circumstance you mention of his being obliged notwithstanding his frugality, to intrench on his private resources. It is the more to be lamented, as it will probably circumscribe the collection of philosophical treasures which his return will import into his native country." TJ appears not to have mentioned this delicate subject in any surviving letter to Mrs. Trist, and would not likely have done so. She probably gained the information from the Fitzhughs or, less likely, from Monroe.

[1] This note was added on or after 24 Aug 1785, the date on which TJ received Mrs. Trist's letter of 12 Mch. 1785.

To Peter Carr

DEAR PETER   Paris Aug. 19. 1785.

I received by Mr. Mazzei your letter of April 20. I am much mortified to hear that you have lost so much time, and that when you arrived in Williamsburgh you were not at all advanced from what you were when you left Monticello. Time now begins to be precious to you. Every day you lose, will retard a day your entrance on that public stage whereon you may begin to be useful to yourself. However the way to repair the loss is to improve the future time. I trust that with your dispositions even the acquisition of science is a pleasing employment. I can assure you that the possession of it is what (next to an honest heart) will above all things render you dear to your friends, and give you fame and promotion in your own country. When your mind shall be well improved with science, nothing will be necessary to place you in the highest points of view but to pursue the interests of your country, the interests of your friends, and your own interests also with the purest integrity, the most chaste honour. The defect of these virtues can never be made up by all the other acquirements of body and mind. Make these then your first object. Give up money, give up fame, give up science, give the earth itself and all it contains rather than do an immoral act. And never suppose that in any possible situation or under any circumstances that it is best for you to do a dishonourable thing however slightly so it may appear to you. Whenever you are to do a thing tho' it can never be known but to yourself, ask yourself how you would act were all the world looking at you, and act accordingly. Encourage all your virtuous dispositions, and exercise them whenever an opportunity arises, being assured that they will gain strength by exercise as a limb of the body does, and that exercise will make them habitual. From the practice of the purest virtue you may be assured you will derive the most sublime comforts in every moment of life and in the moment of death. If ever you find yourself environed with difficulties and perplexing circumstances, out of which you are at a loss how to extricate yourself, do what is right, and be assured that that will extricate you the best out of the worst situations. Tho' you cannot see when you fetch one step, what will be the next, yet follow truth, justice, and plain-dealing, and never fear their leading you out of the labyrinth in the easiest manner possible. The knot which you thought a Gordian one will untie itself before you. Nothing is so mistaken as the supposition that a person is to extricate himself from a difficulty, by intrigue, by chicanery, by dissimulation, by trimming, by an untruth, by an injustice. This increases the difficulties tenfold, and those who pursue these methods, get themselves so involved at length that they can turn no way but their infamy becomes more exposed. It is of great importance to set a resolution, not to be shaken, never to tell an untruth. There is no vice so mean, so pitiful, so contemptible and he who permits himself to tell a lie once, finds it much easier to do it a second and third time, till at length it becomes habitual, he tells lies without attending to it, and truths without the world's beleiving him. This falshood of the tongue leads to that of the heart, and in time depraves all it's good dispositions.

An honest heart being the first blessing, a knowing head is the second. It is time for you now to begin to be choice in your reading, to begin to pursue a regular course in it and not to suffer yourself to be turned to the right or left by reading any thing out of that course. I have long ago digested a plan for you, suited to the circumstances in which you will be placed. This I will detail to you from time to time as you advance. For the present I advise you to begin a course of antient history, reading every thing in the original and not in translations. First read Goldsmith's history of Greece. This will give you a digested view of that feild. Then take up antient history in the detail, reading the following books in the following order. Herodotus. Thucydides. Xenophontis hellenica. Xenophontis Anabasis. Quintus Curtius. Justin. This shall form the first stage of your historical reading, and is all I need mention to you now. The next will be of Roman history. From that we will come down to Modern history. In Greek and Latin poetry, you have read or will read at school Virgil, Terence, Horace, Anacreon, Theocritus, Homer. Read also Milton's paradise lost, Ossian, Pope's works, Swift's works in order to form your style in your own language. In morality read Epictetus, Xenophontis memorabilia, Plato's Socratic dialogues, Cicero's philosophies. In order to assure a certain progress in this reading, consider what hours you have free from the school and the exercises of the school. Give about two of them every day to exercise; for health must not be sacrificed to learning. A strong body makes the mind strong. As to the species of exercise, I advise the gun. While this gives a moderate exercise to the body, it gives boldness, enterprize, and independance to the mind. Games played with the ball and others of that nature, are too violent for the body and stamp no character on the mind. Let your gun therefore be the constant companion of your walks. Never think of taking a book with you. The object of walking is to relax the mind. You should therefore not permit yourself even to think while you walk. But divert your attention by the objects surrounding you. Walking is the best possible exercise. Habituate yourself to walk very far. The Europeans value themselves on having subdued the horse to the uses of man. But I doubt whether we have not lost more than we have gained by the use of this animal. No one has occasioned so much the degeneracy of the human body. An Indian goes on foot nearly as far in a day, for a long journey, as an enfeebled white does on his horse, and he will tire the best horses. There is no habit you will value so much as that of walking far without fatigue. I would advise you to take your exercise in the afternoon. Not because it is the best time for exercise for certainly it is not: but because it is the best time to spare from your studies; and habit will soon reconcile it to health, and render it nearly as useful as if you gave to that the more precious hours of the day. A little walk of half an hour in the morning when you first rise is adviseable also. It shakes off sleep, and produces other good effects in the animal œconomy. Rise at a fixed and an early hour, and go to bed at a fixed and early hour also. Sitting up late at night is injurious to the health, and not useful to the mind.—Having ascribed proper hours to exercise, divide what remain (I mean of your vacant hours) into three portions. Give the principal to history, the other two, which should be shorter, to Philosophy and Poetry. Write me once every month or two and let me know the progress you make. Tell me in what manner you employ every hour in the day. The plan I have proposed for you is adapted to your present situation only. When that is changed, I shall propose a corresponding change of plan. I have ordered the following books to be sent to you from London to the care of Mr. Madison. Herodotus. Thucydides. Xenophon's Hellenics, Anabasis, and Memorabilia. Cicero's works. Baretti's Spanish and English dictionary. Martin's philosophical grammar and Martin's philosophia Britannica. I will send you the following from hence. Bezout's mathematics. De la Lande's astronomy. Muschenbroek's physics. Quintus Curtius. Justin, a Spanish grammar, and some Spanish books. You will observe that Martin, Bezout, De la Lande and Muschenbroek are not in the preceding plan. They are not to be opened till you go to the University. You are now I expect learning French. You must push this: because the books which will be put into your hands when you advance into Mathematics, Natural philosophy, Natural history, &c. will be mostly French, these sciences being better treated by the French than the English writers. Our future connection with Spain renders that the most necessary of the modern languages, after the French. When you become a public man you may have occasion for it, and the circumstance of your possessing that language may give you a preference over other candidates. I have nothing further to add for the present, than to husband well your time, cherish your instructors, strive to make every body your friend, & be assured that nothing will be so pleasing, as your success, to Dear Peter yours affectionately,   TH: JEFFERSON

PrC (DLC). Recorded in SJL as sent "by Mr. Fitzhugh"; entry in SJPL reads: "Carr Peter. Advice."

From John Paul Jones

SIR L'Orient August 19th. 1785

I am by this day's Post, honored with yours of the 13th Currt. which appears to have been intended to have been forwarded by Mr. Carnes. I esteem myself particularly obliged by that mark of your attention; but, as there is no mention made of my Letter to you of the 31st. Ult. I presume it has miscarryed, and it is therefore that I have now written the foregoing Copy. The 6th. of this month, finding a Ship here bound directly for Philadelphia, I sent a Copy of Monsieur de Soulanges's Letter to Mr. Jay for the information of Congress.

I had the honor to write you the 17th. to inform you that I was just then told that two of the Seamen formerly of the Alliance Frigate, who are now here in a Brig belonging to Boston, have been wrought upon by an expectation of immediately receiving their Prize-money, to desire that Mr. Puchilberg might in their Name object to sending the Prize-money of the Alliance to America. That Brig is now at Port-Louis, and will for Boston it is supposed to Morrow morning.

I am, with great esteem & respect, Sir your most obedient and most humble Servant, J PAUL JONES

RC (NN).

To Walker Maury, with a List of Books

DEAR SIR Paris Aug. 19. 1785.

I received your favor of April 20. by Mr. Mazzei on the 22d. of July. I am much obliged to you for your kind attention to my nephew. His education is one of the things about which I am most anxious. I think he posseses that kind of genius which will be solid and useful to himself and his country. When I came here I was not certain whether I might not find it better to send for him hither. But I am thoroughly cured of that Idea. Of all the errors which can possibly be committed in the education of youth, that of sending them to Europe is the most fatal. I see [clearly] that no American should come to Europe under 30 years of age: and [he who] does, will lose in science, in virtue, in health and in happiness, for which manners are a poor compensation, were we even to admit the hollow, unmeaning manners of Europe to be preferable to the simplicity and sincerity of our own country. I am well pleased with your having taken my nephew among your private pupils. I would have him lose no advantage on account of any difference in expence. His time begins now to be precious, and every moment [may] be valued in money, as it will retard or hasten the period when he may enter on the stage whereon he may begin to reap the benefit of his talents and acquirements. My intention had been that he should learn French and Italian, of the modern languages. But the latter must be given up (for the present at least) and Spanish substituted in it's place. I have ordered some books to be [sent] him from London. Among these is a Spanish Dictionary. I shall send him [so]me others from hence, among which shall be a Spanish grammar and other b[ooks] for his reading in that language. I will point out to him from time to time [the] course of reading I would wish him to pursue and take care to send him the [nece]ssary books, so far as he happens not to possess them. According to yo[ur des]ire I note hereon such French writers as I suppose might possibly come within [the pla]n you mention. I have inserted several books of American travels th[inking] they will be a useful species of reading for an American youth. In ge[neral] you may estimate 12mos. at $2\frac{1}{2}$. livres, 8vos. at 5. or 6 livres, 4tos. at [10? or] 15 livres, folios at 25 or 30 livres, remembering that what we call a [half] crown is 6. livres. Where these prices are departed from, I have note[d the actual?] cost as I have found in my own purchases. Books cost here bu[t about? t]wo thirds or three fourths of what they do in England. I must except [. . .] Greek, Latin, and English books. The latter of course are much dearer here [because they] are first bought in England. If I can be useful to you in pr[ocuring any] thing in this way I shall do it with pleasure. After running [thro the stocks?] of many booksellers, and suffering numberless cheats, I have at length [found] one who serves me very honestly, and finds whatever I want at the [best?] prices. I need not repeat to you Sir how much you will oblige me [by your] friendly counsels to my nephew, for the preservation of his morals and improvement of his mind. I am with much esteem Dear Sir Your most obedt. humble servt.,

TH: JEFFERSON

Telemaque

Histoire Romaine de Vertot. 3. v. 12mo.

Histoire Romaine. 2. v. 12 mo.   les traductions de Coussin.
   de Constantinople. 10. v. 12.mo.   These are translations of all the
   de l'empire de l'Occident. 2. v.   good latter historians of the Ro-
     12mo.   man empire, beginning with
   de l'eglise. 3. v. 12mo.   Xiphilinus, Zonaras, Zosimus
                                     &c. They are a very valuable
                                     collection costing in the whole
                                     about[1]

Histoire des Celtes de Pelloutier. 2 v. 12mo.

Histoire d'Espagne de Vertot. 6. v. 8vo.

Histoire de Portugal de Vertot. 12mo.

Histoire de France de Millot. 3. v. 12mo.

Abregé Chronologique de l'histoire d'Allemagne par Pfeffel.

Histoire des troubles des Pays bas de Grotius. fol.

Histoire de Suede de Vertot. 12mo.

Histoire de Dannemarck de Mallet. 6. v. 12mo.

Voltaire. Ses ouvrages historiques.

Elemens d'histoire generale, ancienne et moderne de l'Abbé Millot.

Histoire des deux Indes de Raynal. 10. v. 8 vo. 80 livres.

Moliere. 7. v. in 16s. 21f. i.e. 21 livres.

Racine. 3. v. 16s. 9f

Chef-d'oeuvres de P. & T. Corneille 5. v. 16s. 18f

Boileau

Mallet de l'Egypte.

Voiage literaire de la Grece. de Guys. 2. v. 12mo.

Voiages d'Adanson.

Voiages d'Hennepin. 4f

Voiages de Lahontan. 2 v. 12mo. 5f4 i.e. 5. livres 4 sous.

Charlevoix. histoire de la Nouvelle France.

Voiage de Bougainville.

Voiage de Condamine dans l'Amerique. 2. v. 8vo. 6f.

Decouvertes des Russes. de Muller. 2. v. in 1. 12mo. 4f4.

Histoire Naturelle de Buffon. 66. v. 12mo. about 8. guineas. But an
    edn. is publishing in Holland at half price.

Voiage autour du monde par Paget 3. v. in 1. 8vo. 9f.

Histoire Universelle de Puffendorf. (de l'Europe) 4. v. 12mo.

Histoire Universelle de l'Asie, l'Afrique, et l'Amerique de Martiniere.
    2. v. 12mo.

Grammaire Françoise de l'Abbé Girard. 2. v. 12mo.

Dictionnaire de l'Academie Françoise. 2. v. in 1. 4to. 30f.

Traité de morale et de bonheur. 2. v. in 1. 16s. 3f. (an excellent little
    thing)

Puffendorf. Devoirs de l'homme. 2. v. 12mo. 5f.

Beaumart. Dictionnaire d'hist. naturelle. 9.
v. 12mo.

Dictionnaire de Mineralogie. 2.
v. 12mo.

Dictionnaire de chimie. 2. v.
12mo.

Dictionnaire des arts et metiers.
2. v. [12mo.?]

} This forms a clever little encyclopedie and costs about 48f.

PrC (ViWC). Both pages of MS are worn vertically through the center; missing words have been supplied conjecturally. Recorded in SJL as sent "by Mr. Fitzhugh." Enclosure (ViWC).

TJ's conviction that sending young Americans to Europe to be educated was the most fatal OF ALL THE ERRORS was one that he formed soon after arriving in France and often and forcibly expressed. See, for example, his letter to Banister, 15 Oct. 1785. Young Abigail Adams recorded TJ's opinion on this subject: "We have a tableau of Paris [by Mercier, in six volumes]," she wrote early in 1785, "which is a description of Paris; and if it is a true picture, a most lamentable one . . . Well might Mr. Jefferson say, that no man was fit to come abroad until 35, unless he were under some person's care" (C. A. de Windt, ed., *Journal*

and Correspondence of Miss Adams, 1841, p. 48-9). But the diversions and temptations offered to youth were only part of the reason for TJ's feeling. Thomas Jefferson Randolph recalled many years after his grandfather's death the homely story TJ sometimes told of a young man, educated in Europe, who was helpless in the face of a saddle-girth broken at the buckle and who had to be told by a plain countryman that his problem could be solved by loosening the girth one or two notches from the other side. TJ employed this story to illustrate his low esteem for that "education that made men ignorant and helpless as to the common necessities of life" (Randall, *Life*, III, Appendix xxxvi).

¹ Blank in MS; TJ probably inserted the price in RC.

From John Bondfield

SIR   Bordeaux 20 Aug 1785

A Ship arrived yesterday from New Orleans. The Captain deliverd me the inclosed to you addrest.

The Spaniards appear intent to whatever may tend to encrease their population. The province of Louisiana yeilds very rich produce. The two Cargoes arrived here will amount to two Millions Livres in furrs and Indigo. Their population in Spaniards, french and English amounts to Twenty eight Thousand. Considerable Imports of Negros have been made this year. The Ideas of the Passengers, inhabitants at New Orleans, fix the boundaries of the United States at Point Coupée or 31° degres, that the entrance of the River belongs *exclusively* to Spain. We are without any interesting commercial intelligence from America. Our conections are very contracted. With due respect I have the honor to be Sir your most Obed Hum Serv,   JOHN BONDFIELD

RC (DLC); addressed; endorsed: "Bondfield Jno. Aug. 20. 1785. recd. Aug. 24." Enclosure: Probably Eliza House Trist to TJ, 12 Mch. 1785.

To Martha Jefferson Carr

[*Paris, 20 Aug. 1785*. Entry in sjl reads: "Mrs. Carr. See copy. By Mr. Fitzhugh." Not found.]

From James Madison

DEAR SIR   Orange Aug: 20th. 1785.

Yours of the 18th. of March never reached me till the 4 inst:. It came by post from N. York, which it did not leave till the 21. of July. My last was dated in April, and went by Mr. Mazzei who picked it up at N. York and promised to deliver it with his own hand.

The machinations of G.B. with regard to Commerce have produced much distress and noise in the Northern States, particularly in Boston, from whence the alarm has spread to New York and Philada. Your correspondence with Congress will no doubt have furnished you with full information on this head. I only know the general fact, and that the sufferers are every where calling for such augmentation of the power of Congress as may effect relief. How far the Southern States and Virginia in particular will join in this proposition cannot be foreseen. It is easy to foresee that the circumstances which in a confined view distinguish our situation from that of our brethren, will be laid hold of by the partizans of G.B., by those who are or affect to be jealous of Congress, and those who are interested in the present course of business, to give a wrong bias to our Councils. If any thing should reconcile Virga. to the idea of giving Congress a power over her trade, it will be that this power is likely to annoy G.B. against whom the animosities of our Citizens are still strong. They seem to have less sensibility to their commercial interests; which they very little understand, and which the mercantile class here have not the same motives if they had the same capacity to lay open to the public, as that class have in the States North of us. The price of our Staple since the peace is another cause of inattention in the planters to the dark side of our commercial affairs. Should these or any other causes prevail in frustrating the scheme of the Eastern and Middle

States of a general retaliation on G.B., I *tremble*[1] *for the event.*[2]
A *majority* of *the States* deprived of a *regular remedy for their
distresses* by *the want* of a *fœderal spirit in the minority* must *feel
the* strongest *motives to some* irregular *experiments.* The *dan[ger]*[3]
of such a crisis makes me surmise that the *policy of Great Britain*
results as much from *the hope of effecting a breach in our confederacy* as *of monopolising our trade.*

Our internal trade is taking an arrangement from which I hope
good consequences. Retail stores are spreading all over the Country, many of them carried on by native adventurers, some of them
branched out from the principal Stores at the heads of navigation.
The distribution of the business however into the importing and
the retail departments has not yet taken place. Should the port
bill be established it will I think quickly add this amendment
which indeed must in a little time follow of itself. It is the more
to be wished for as it is the only radical cure for credit to the
consumer which continues to be given to a degree which if not
checked will turn the[4] diffusive retail of merchandize into a
nusance. When the Shopkeeper buys his goods of the wholesale
merchant, he must buy at so short a credit, that he can venture to
give none at all.

You ask me to unriddle the *dissolution of the committee of the
states at annapolis.* I am not sure that I am myself possessed fully
of the causes, *different members of Congress* having *differed in
their accounts of the matter.* My conception of it is that *the abrupt
departure of* some of the *Eastern delegates*, which *destroyed the
quorum* and which *Dana* is said *to have been at the bottom of*
proceeded *partly from irritations among the committee, partly
from dislike to the place of their session* and *partly from an impatience to get home,* which prevailed over *their regard* for *their
private characters* as well as *for their public duty.*

Subsequent to the date of *mine in* which I gave my idea of *Fayette* I had further opportunities of *penetrating his character.*
Though *his foibles did* not *disappear* all the *favorable traits* presented themselves in a *stronger light.* On *closer inspection he* certainly possesses *talents which might figure in any line.* If *he is
ambitious* it is rather of the *praise* which virtue *dedicates to merit*
than *of the homage* which *fear renders to power. His disposition is*
naturally *warm and affectionate* and *his attachment to the United
States* unquestionable. Unless *I am grossly deceived* you will *find
his zeal sincere* and *useful* wherever it can be *employed* in behalf

of the United States without opposition [to] *the essential interests of France.*

The opposition to the general assessment gains ground. At the *instance of some* of *its adversaries I drew up the remonstrance* herewith inclosed. It has been *sent* thro' the *medium of confidential persons in a number of the upper county*[s] and I am told will be pretty extensively signed. The presbyterian clergy have at length espoused the idea of the opposition, being moved either by *a fear of their laity* or *a jealousy of the episcopalians.* The mutual hatred of these sects has been much inflamed by the late act incorporating the latter. *I am far from* being *sorry for it* as *a coalition between them* could *alone endanger our religious rights* and a tendency to *such an event had been suspected.* The fate of the Circuit Courts is uncertain. They are threatened with no small danger from the diversity of opinions entertained among the friends of some reform in that department. But the greatest danger is to be feared from those who mask a secret aversion to any reform under a zeal for such a one as they know will be rejected. The Potowmack Company are going on with very flattering prospects. Their subscriptions sometime ago amounted to upwards of four fifths of the whole sum. I have the pleasure also to find by an advertisement from the managers for James River that more than half the sum is subscribed for that undertaking, and that the subscribers are to meet shortly for the purpose of organizing themselves and going to work. I despair of seeing the Revisal taken up at the ensuing Session. The number of copies struck are so deficient (there being not above three for each County) and there has been such delay in distributing them (none of the Counties having received them till very lately and some probably not yet, tho' they were ready long ago) that the principal end of their being printed has been frustrated. Our fields promise very short crops both of Corn and Tobacco. The latter was much injured by the grass hopper and other insects; the former somewhat by the bug in the Southern parts of the State. But both have suffered most from dry weather which prevails at present in this part of the Country, and has generally prevailed I understand in most other parts. It seems certain that no future weather can make a great crop of either, particularly of Tobacco, so great a proportion of the hills being without plants in them, and so many more with plants which must come to nothing. Notwithstanding this prospect, its price has fallen from 36/ to 32 and 30/ on James River and 28/ on Rappahanock. The scarcity of cash is one cause. *Harrison the late governor* was *elected* in *Surry* whither *he previously removed with his family. A contest* for *the chair* will *no* doubt *ensue.* Should *he fail it he* will be *for Congress.*

I have not yet received any of the books which you have been so kind as to pick up for me, but expect their arrival daily, as you were probably soon after the date of your last apprised that I[5] was withdrawn from the nomination which led you to suspend the forwarding them. I am invited by Col: Monroe to an option of rambles this fall, one of which is into the Eastern States. I wish much to accept so favorable an opportunity of executing the plan from which I was diverted last fall; but cannot decide with certainty whether it will be practicable or not. I have in conjunction with a friend here a project of interest on the anvil which will carry me at least as far as Philada. or New York where I shall be able to take my final resolution. Adieu. Yrs. sincerely,   J M Jr.

RC (DLC: Madison Papers); endorsed; at head of text: "No. 8"; partly in code, with interlineal decoding by TJ; contains a few deletions, some of which may have been made late in life after Madison received the letter from TJ's estate. Recorded in SJL as received 16 Oct. 1785. Enclosure: Madison's memorial and remonstrance against the proposed bill for a general assessment for the support of teachers of the Christian religion; this may have been a copy of the broadside printed at Richmond (Swem, "Va. Bibliog.," No. 7479) or the broadside that George Mason caused to be printed at Alexandria at his own expense (Brant, *Madison*, II, 350).

For an excellent summary of the enduring significance of Madison's RE-MONSTRANCE, a staggering blow struck in defense of religious liberty, which at a single stroke destroyed the attempt "to establish a general assessment for the support of all Christian sects" and also had other far-reaching consequences, see Brant, *Madison*, II, 343-55, who writes: "By the time the legislature convened the flow of petitions had become a tidal wave. . . . There was not even a vote on the bill. So far-reaching were the results of this victory, not only as an immediate blow to church establishment but in its effect upon American laws and constitutions, that more than 150 years elapsed before any important attempt was made

to re-establish the system of state support for religion or religious schools." This memorial was not, evidently, the "outrageous piece against the assessment" that John Page discussed in his letter to TJ of 23 Aug. 1785, but Page's views stand in strong contrast to the eloquent and carefully reasoned argument set forth by Madison, who declared: "It is proper to take alarm at the first experiment on our liberties. We hold this prudent jealousy to be the first duty of citizens, and one of the noblest characteristicks of the late revolution. The freemen of America did not wait until usurped power had strengthened itself by exercise, and entangled the question in precedents. They saw all the consequences in the principle, and they avoided the consequences by denying the principle. We revere this lesson much too soon to forget it. Who does not see that the same authority which can establish Christianity, in exclusion of all other religions, may establish, with the same ease, any particular sect of Christians, in exclusion of all other sects? That the same authority which can force a citizen to contribute three-pence only of his property for the support of any one establishment, may force him to conform to any other establishment, in all cases whatsoever." Though this memorial was intended to defeat the proposed general assessment for the support of Christian ministers, it had the immediate positive result of opening the way for the adoption of TJ's Bill for establishing religious freedom, which was "passed by the General Assembly of Virginia after the presentment of the . . . Memorial and Remonstrance" (preface to the Act reprinted by Isaiah Thomas from the *Va. Gaz.* as an appendix to his edition of *A Memorial and Remonstrance, Presented to the General Assembly, of the State of Virginia, at their Session in 1785, in consequence of a Bill into that Assembly for the Establishment of Religion by Law*, Worcester, 1786, p. 13). The text of the memorial may be found in Madison, *Writings*, ed. Hunt, ii, 183-91, and, with other related documentary materials, in Charles F. James, *Documentary History of the Struggle for Religious Liberty in Virginia*, Lynchburg, 1900, p. 256-62. TJ promptly

sent a copy to Luzac by Mazzei for publication in the *Gazette de Leyde* (Mazzei to TJ, 26 Oct. 1785 and 6 Feb. 1786).

1 This and subsequent words in italics are written in code and were decoded interlineally by TJ; the text presented here is a decoding by the editors, employing Code No. 9.
2 Madison employed the code symbol for "genuine"; TJ corrected it to "event."
3 Madison omitted the code symbol for the second syllable; TJ's reading is "danger."
4 The words "advantage of a" are deleted at this point; this may have been done by Madison late in life.
5 The words "my name" are deleted at this point; this may have been done by Madison late in life.

To John Page

DEAR PAGE   Paris Aug. 20. 1785.

I received your friendly letter of Apr. 28. by Mr. Mazzei on the 22d. of July. That of the month before by Monsr. Le Croix is not come to hand. This correspondence is grateful to some of my warmest feelings, as the friendships of my youth are those which stick closest to me, and in which I most confide. My principal happiness is now in the retrospect of life. I thank you for your notes of your operations on the Pennsylvania boundary. I am in hopes that from yourself, Madison, Rittenhouse or Hutchings I shall receive a chart of the line as actually run. It will be a great present to me. I think Hutchings promised to send it to me. I have been much pleased to hear you had it in contemplation to endeavor to establish Rittenhouse in our college. This would be an immense acquisition and would draw youth to it from every part of the continent. You will do much more honour to our society on reviving it, if you place him at it's head and not so useless a member as I should be. I have been so long diverted from this my favourite line, and that too without acquiring an attachment to my adopted one, that I am become a mongrel, of no decided order, unowned by any, and incapable of serving any. I should feel myself out of my true place too to stand before McLurg. But why withdraw yourself? You have more zeal, more application, and more constant attention to the subjects proper to the society and can therefore serve them best.

The affair of the emperor and Dutch is settled tho' not signed. The particulars have not yet transpired. That of the Bavarian exchange is dropped, and his views on Venice defeated. The alliance of Russia with Venice to prevent his designs in that quarter, and that of the Hanoverian elector, with the K. of Prussia and other members of the Germanic body to prevent his acquisition of Bavaria leave him in a solitary situation. In truth he has lost much reputation by his late manoeuvres. He is a restless, ambitious character, aiming at every thing, persevering in nothing, taking up designs without calculating the force which will be opposed to him, and dropping them on the appearance of firm opposition. He has some just views, and much activity. The only quarter in which the peace of Europe seems at present capable of being disturbed is on that of the Porte. It is believed that the Emperor and Empress have schemes in contemplation for driving the Turks out of Europe. Were this with a view to re-establish the native Greeks in the sovereignty of their own country, I could wish them success and to see driven from that delightful country a set of Barbarians with whom an opposition to all science is an article of religion. The modern Greek is not yet so far departed from it's antient model but that we might still hope to see the language of Homer and Demosthenes flow with purity, from the lips of a free and ingenious people. But these powers have in object to divide the country between themselves. This is only to substitute one set of Barbarians for another breaking at the same time the balance among the European powers. You have been told with truth that the Emperor of Marocco has shewn a disposition to enter into treaty with us: but not truly that Congress has not attended to his advances and thereby disgusted him. It is long since they took measures to meet his advances. But some unlucky incidents have delayed their effect. His dispositions continue good. As a proof of this, he has lately released freely and cloathed well the crew of an American brig he took last winter; the only vessel ever taken from us by any of the states of Barbary. But what is the English of these good dispositions? Plainly this. He is ready to receive us into the number of his tributaries. What will be the amount of tribute remains yet to be known, but it probably will not be as small as you may have conjectured. It will surely be more than a free people ought to pay to a power owning only 4. or 5. frigates under 22. guns. He has not a port into which a larger vessel can enter. The Algerines possess fifteen or 20. frigates from that size up to 50 guns. Disinclination on their part has lately broken off a treaty between Spain and them whereon they were to have received a million of dollars besides great presents in naval stores. What sum they intend we shall pay I cannot say. Then follow Tunis and Tripoli. You will probably find the tribute to all these powers make such a proportion of the federal taxes as that every man will feel them sensibly when he pays those taxes. The question is whether their peace or war will be cheapest? But it is a question which should be addressed to our Honour as well as our Avarice? Nor does it respect us as to these pyrates only, but as to the nations of Europe. If we wish our commerce to be free and uninsulted, we must let these nations see that we have an energy which at present they disbelieve. The low opinion they entertain of our powers cannot fail to involve us soon in a naval war. I shall send you with this, if I can, and if not, then by the first good conveiance the Connoissance de tems for the years 1786. and 1787. being all as yet published. You will find in these the tables for the planet Herschel as far as the observations hitherto made admit them to be calculated. You will see also that Herschel was only the first astronomer who discovered it to be a planet, and not the first who saw it. Mayer saw it in the year 1756. and placed it in the catalogue of his Zodiacal stars, supposing it to be such. A Prussian astronomer in 1781. observed that the 964th. star of Mayer's catalogue was missing. And the calculations now prove that at the time Mayer saw his 964th. star, the planet Herschel should have been precisely in the place where he noted that star. I shall send you also a little publication here called the Bibliotheque physico-œconomique. It will communicate all the improvements and new discoveries in the arts and the sciences made in Europe for some years past. I shall be happy to hear from you often. Details political and literary and even of the small history of our country are the most pleasing presents possible. Present me affectionately to Mrs. Page, and to your family, in the members of which, tho' unknown to me I feel an interest on account of their parents. Believe me to be with warm esteem Dr. Page your sincere friend & servant,   TH: JEFFERSON

PrC (DLC). Recorded in SJL as sent "by Mr. Fitzhugh"; entry in SJPL reads: "Page John. Pensva. line. Europe. Barbary."

From Abigail Adams

DEAR SIR   London Grosvenor Square August 21 1785

The Gentleman who is so kind as to convey this to you is from Carolina, his name is Smith. He is a distant relation of mine, tho I have not the pleasure of much acquaintance with him. He has resided in England some time, and bears a good Character here. Give me leave Sir to introduce him to your notice.

Mr. Short left us last Tuesday for the Hague. I did myself the honour of writing to you by him.

I find by the last papers from New York that Mr. Rutledge is appointed minister at the Hague; in the room of Mr. Livingstone who declined the embassy. There is no mention made of a secretary.

You will probably see our Massachusetts Navigation act before this reaches you; it has Struck the hireling scriblers dumb. There has been less abuse against the Americans in the papers since the publication of it; than for a long time before.

Ireland has exerted herself, and Pharoah and his host are overthrown. The Courier of Europe will doubtless give you the debates. The July packet arrived last week, tho she left New York the seventh of July. She brought not a line of publick dispatch. A private Letter or two for Col. Smith, the contents of which we cannot know; as he is absent upon a Tour to Berlin.

I was much disapointed to find that my son had not arrived when the packet saild. As the French packet sails sometime after the English, I am not without hopes that I may hear by that, and I will thank you sir to give me the earliest intelligence if she brings any account of the May packet.

Be so good as to present my Regards to Col Humphries. Mr. Short gives us some encouragement to expect him here this Winter. My Love to Miss Jefferson, to whom also my daughter desires to be rememberd. Our good old Friends the Abbes, I would tender my Regards. If I could write French, I would have scribled a line to the Abbe Arnou.

I think Madam Helvetius must be very melancholy now Franklin as she used to call him is gone. It is said here by a Gentleman lately from Philadelphia, that they determine to elect the Doctor president upon his arrival, as Mr. Dickinsons office expires in october.

In my Letter by Mr. Short I had taken the Liberty to request you to procure for me two or 3 articles, and to convey them by

[420]

Col. Smith who talks of returning by way of Paris. But if he should not visit you, Mr. Smith when he returns will be so good as to take charge of them for me. But this I shall know in the course of a few weeks, and will take measures accordingly. I am sir with Sentiments of Esteem Your Humble Servant,

ABIGAIL ADAMS

RC (DLC). Recorded in SJL as received 30 Aug. 1785.

Mrs. Adams was impressed immediately on her arrival at Auteuil in 1784 with Madame Helvétius' familiarity in referring to Benjamin Franklin merely as Franklin, and evidently the impression lasted. "When we went into the room to dine," she had also reported to Lucy Cranch, "she was placed between the Doctor and Mr. Adams. She carried on the chief of the conversation at dinner, frequently locking her hand into the Doctor's, and sometimes spreading her arms upon the backs of both the gentlemen's chairs, then throwing her arm carelessly upon the Doctor's neck.—I should have been greatly astonished at this conduct, if the good Doctor had not told me that in this lady I should see a genuine Frenchwoman wholly free from affectation or stiffness of behaviour, and one of the best women in the world. For this I must take the Doctor's word; but I should have set her down for a very bad one, although sixty years of age, and a widow. I own I was highly disgusted, and never wish for an acquaintance with any ladies of this cast" (5 Sep. 1785, C. F. Adams, ed., *Letters of Mrs. Adams*, 1841, II, 56). Possibly John Adams' opinion of Franklin colored Mrs. Adams' view of Madame Helvétius, to whom Franklin had proposed and been refused (Van Doren, *Franklin*, p. 646-53).

To St. John de Crèvecoeur

SIR   Paris Aug. 22. 1785.

I have duly received your favor of the 15th. instant as I had before done that of May 18. but had not answered it, supposing you would be on your passage. Mr. Mazzei delivered safely the packet you mention. I should have been happy to have seen you here, but we are not to expect that pleasure it seems till the fall. The derangement of the packet boats will need your aid: and there are doubtless other circumstances here which may be improved by your presence. The loss sustained by your friend the Countess D'Hodetout in the death of her brother, has doubtless been participated by you as by all others of his and her acquaintance. I had become of that number just early enough to take a share in it which I did very sincerely. The confinement of the Cardinal de Rohan in the Bastile has doubtless reached you. The public is not yet possessed of the truth of his story, but from his character and all other circumstances I have little doubt that the final decision must be against him. My daughter is well and thanks you for your kind enquiries. I hope you found all your family and friends well. I am with great esteem Dr. Sir your most obedient humble servt.,

TH: JEFFERSON

PrC (DLC).

To the Governor of Virginia, with an Account of Expenses

SIR   Paris Aug. 22. 1785.

I was honoured yesterday with your Excellency's letter of June the 16th. inclosing the resolution of Assembly relative to the busts of the M. de la Fayette. I shall render chearfully any services I can in aid of Mr. Barclay for carrying this resolution into effect. The M. de la Fayette being to pass into Germany and Prussia it was thought proper to take the model of his bust in plaister before his departure. Monsr. Houdon was engaged to do it and did it accordingly. So far Mr. Barclay had thought himself authorized to go in consequence of orders formerly received. You will be so good as to instruct me as to the monies hereafter to be remitted to me whether I am to apply them solely to the Statue of General Washington, or to that and the Marquis's bust in common as shall be necessary. Supposing you wish to know the application of the monies remitted from time to time, I state hereon an account thereof so far as I am able at present. Before your receipt of the letter I am in hopes mine of July 11. by Monsr. Houdon will have come to your hands. In that I inclosed you a copy of the contract with him.

I have the honour to be with due respect Your Excellency's Most obedient & most humble servt.,   TH: JEFFERSON

ENCLOSURE

		livres	sous	
1785. Apr. 20.	Receivd. of Laval & Wilfelsheim on Alexander's bill	8957–11		
1785. Mar. 11.	To pd. portage of Genl. Washington's picture from l'Orient	13– 8		
Apr. 16.	To pd. for a frame to do.	51– 0		
July 18.	To pd. to Monsr. Houdon	10,000– 0		
Aug. 15.	To pd. Houdon's bill on me for expences	2,724–	6–6	

12,788–14–6

Besides the above sums paid
I expect daily a bill from London for insuring 15,000 livres on Houdon's life (I thought it best to ensure

enough to cover the expences of his voiage as well
as the sum to be given his family in case of his death.   livres
This, if at 5. pr. cent will be 750– 0–0
On his arrival in Philadelphia he is to draw on me for
money enough for his expences going, staying and
returning. We conjectured these would be about
5000 livres in the whole. But 2724ᵗᵗ–6–6 being
paid, the residue would be   2275–13–6
There is due to him for the model of the busts of M.
Fayette in plaister I imagine about 750– 0–0
The two first of these sums I expect I shall have paid
by the time this letter gets to hand, and I shall
pay the third if demanded. These added to 3831
livres 3 sous 6 den. already in advance as will be
seen above, will amount to between seven and
eight thousand livres. Houdon on his return will
also expect an advance for the two busts of the
M. de la Fayette.

RC (Vi); addressed: "His Excellency the Governor of Virginia"; endorsed.
PrC (DLC). Recorded in SJL as sent "by Mr. Fitzhugh"; entry in SJPL reads:
"Govr. of Virga. Fayette's bust." Enclosure (Vi).

From Thomas Thompson

Dover, 22 Aug. 1785. Acknowledges TJ's letter of 17 Aug. in reply
to Thompson's of 12 Aug. Benjamin Franklin's English newspapers
came free of postage via M. Mouron and M. Perregaux of Paris; the
former will continue to forward them if TJ wishes. If Adams sends
them, they should be directed to "Robert Preston Esq. M. P. at T.
Thompson's Dover." Franklin received the *Morning Chronicle* and
the *London Chronicle.* "Mrs. Williams and her sisters, the Miss Alex-
anders" arrived yesterday; they have gone to London to live, while her
husband, "Docr. Franklins nephew who lived at Nantes during the
War," sailed for America with Franklin.

RC (MoSHi); 2 p.

From John Adams

DEAR SIR   Grosvenor Square Aug. 23. 1785

Last night, I received your Favour of the 17. If both Governments are possessed of the Contents of my letter of the 7th. by
opening it in the Post Office, much good may those Contents do
them. They both know they have deserved it. I hope it will convince them of their Error, and induce them to adopt more liberal

Principles toward Us. I am for answering their Utmost Generosity with equal and indeed with greater Generosity. But I would not advise my Country to be the Bubble of her own Nobleness of Sentiment.

The Spirited Conduct of Ireland, I think will assist me, here. The News of the Reception in the Irish Parliament of the 20 Resolutions together with the Efforts in America towards a Navigation Act have raised my Hopes a good deal. But our States must mature their Plan and persevere in it, in order to effect the Work. In time, and with a Steady pursuit of our Purpose, I begin to think We shall prevail.

If Mr. Barclay will undertake the Voyage, I am for looking no farther. We cannot find a Steadier, or more prudent Man. He should look out for some Clerk or Companion who can write French and understands Italian.

When Dr. Price returns from his August Excursion to some Watering Place, I will get him to make the Insurance upon Houdons Life, on the best Terms he can. Adieu. Yours sincerely,

JOHN ADAMS

RC (DLC). FC (MHi: AMT); in Adams' hand. Recorded in SJL as received 30 Aug. 1785.

From C. W. F. Dumas

MONSIEUR   Lahaie 23 Août 1785.

En réponse aux ordres dont vous m'aves honoré, conjointément avec son Exce. Mr. Adams en date de Londres Aout 5, nous avons vaqué tout de suite à la Commission en question. Mr. Short est occupé à rendre un compte à Vos Excellences de ce qui a éte fait et de ce qui reste à faire, auquel je suis persuadé d'avance que je n'aurai rien à ajouter, que l'assurance de ma juste sensibilité à la confiance dont vous honores ma personne, mes principes, et mon zele invariable pour les intérêts des Etats-Unis; et du respect personnel avec lequel je suis, De Votre Excellence le très-humble, & très-obéissant serviteur,   C. W. F. DUMAS

P.S. Mr. Adams le fils m'ayant fait parvenir il y a quelques mois une Lettre de Mr. D. Humphrys, accompagnée d'un Article à insérer dans la Gazette françoise de Leide, l'Insertion fut faite; je le mandai à Mr. Adams le fils; et je n'aurois pas manqué, malgré une indisposition de plusieurs semaines, de répondre directement

à Mr. Humphrys, à qui Votre Excellence voudra bien me permettre de présenter ici mes complimens, si j'avois eu son adresse.

RC (DLC). FC (Dumas Letter Book, Rijksarchief, The Hague; Photostat in
DLC). Dumas wrote a similar letter to Adams, same date, but lacking the postscript (MHi: AMT).

From Elbridge Gerry and Others

DEAR SIR   New York 23d. August 1785

We have the honor of addressing this by our worthy friend, the
honorable Mr. Sayre, who was formerly Sheriff of London.

The active part, which at the commencement of the revolution,
he took in favor of America, is, we presume, too well known to you,
to require a relation: and the loss he sustained, in consequence of
his opposition to the british ministry, is not less a matter of general
information.

These considerations have induced his friends, in this quarter
to express a wish that he should be employed in some public office
under Congress, wherein he can render service to the United States,
in a manner that shall be consistent with his honor and their
interest.

It so happens, at this time, that there is no appointment of that
description, to which we can nominate him, but there is an office,
which he will probably accept, and the right of filling it, is vested
by Congress, in yourself and his Excellency Mr. Adams: we mean
the department for conducting the treaty with the Emperor of
Morocco, and the other Barbary Powers.

Should you be disposed to employ Mr. Sayre in this business:
we think his knowledge of mankind, his polite address, his commercial and political accomplishments, and above all, his sense of
honor, and integrity, cannot fail of insuring you as great a degree
of success, as the qualities of any other person you can employ in
that department.

We have the honor to be Sir with perfect respect Your very
humble Servants,   E. GERRY

                                          RUFUS KING

                                          S: HARDY

                                          JAS. MONROE

                                          WM. GRAYSON

RC (DLC); in a clerk's hand, signed   Grayson; endorsed: "Gerry Elbr." En-
by Gerry, King, Hardy, Monroe, and   try in SJL for 10 Oct. 1785 reads:

"Stephen Sayre. N.Y. Aug. 25. 1785. and delegates Mass. and Virga. N.Y. Aug. 23. (received now, I think)." Enclosed in the letter from Sayre, 25 Aug. 1785. A similar letter was written to Adams, 23 Aug.; see Adams to TJ, 2 Oct. 1785.

To John Jay

DEAR SIR   Paris Aug. 23, 1785.

I shall sometimes ask your permission to write you letters, not official but private. The present is of this kind, and is occasioned by the question proposed in yours of June 14 'Whether it would be useful to us to carry all our own productions, or none?' Were we perfectly free to decide this question, I should reason as follows. We have now lands enough to employ an infinite number of people in their cultivation. Cultivators of the earth are the most valuable citizens. They are the most vigorous, the most independant, the most virtuous, and they are tied to their country and wedded to it's liberty and interests by the most lasting bands. As long therefore as they can find emploiment in this line, I would not convert them into mariners, artisans, or any thing else. But our citizens will find emploiment in this line till their numbers, and of course their productions, become too great for the demand both internal and foreign. This is not the case as yet, and probably will not be for a considerable time. As soon as it is, the surplus of hands must be turned to something else. I should then perhaps wish to turn them to the sea in preference to manufactures, because comparing the characters of the two classes I find the former the most valuable citizens. I consider the class of artificers as the panders of vice and the instruments by which the liberties of a country are generally overturned. However we are not free to decide this question on principles of theory only. Our people are decided in the opinion that it is necessary for us to take a share in the occupation of the ocean, and their established habits induce them to require that the sea be kept open to them, and that that line of policy be pursued which will render the use of that element as great as possible to them. I think it a duty in those entrusted with the administration of their affairs to conform themselves to the decided choice of their constituents: and that therefore we should in every instance preserve an equality of right to them in the transportation of commodities, in the right of fishing, and in the other uses of the sea. But what will be the consequence? Frequent wars without a doubt.

Their property will be violated on the sea, and in foreign ports, their persons will be insulted, emprisoned &c. for pretended debts, contracts, crimes, contraband &c. &c. These insults must be resented, even if we had no feelings, yet to prevent their eternal repetition. Or in other words, our commerce on the ocean and in other countries must be paid for by frequent war. The justest dispositions possible in ourselves will not secure us against it. It would be necessary that all other nations were just also. Justice indeed on our part will save us from those wars which would have been produced by a contrary disposition. But how to prevent those produced by the wrongs of other nations? By putting ourselves in a condition to punish them. Weakness provokes insult and injury, while a condition to punish it often prevents it. This reasoning leads to the necessity of some naval force, that being the only weapo[n] with which we can reach an enemy. I think it to our interest to punis[h] the first insult: because an insult unpunished is the parent of many oth[ers]. We are not at this moment in a condition to do it, but we should put ourselv[es] into it as soon as possible. If a war with England should take place it see[ms] to me that the first thing necessary would be a resolution to abandon the carrying trade because we cannot protect it. Foreign nations must in that case be invited to bring us what we want and to take our productions in their own bottoms. This alone could prevent the loss of those productions to us and the acquisition of them to our enemy. Our seamen might be emploied in depredations on their trade. But how dreadfully we shall suffer on our coasts, if we have no force on the water, former experience has taught us. Indeed I look forward with horror to the very possible case of war with an European power, and think there is no protection against them but from the possession of some force on the sea. Our vicinity to their West India possessions and to the fisheries is a bridle which a small naval force on our part would hold in the mouths of the most powerful of these countries. I hope our land office will rid us of our debts, and that our first attention then will be to the beginning a naval force of some sort. This alone can countenance our people as carriers on the water, and I suppose them to be determined to continue such.

I wrote you two public letters on the 14th. inst. since which I have received yours of July 13. I shall always be pleased to receive from you in a private way such communications as you might not chuse to put into a public letter. I have the honor to be with very sincere esteem Dr. Sir your most obedient humble servt.,

TH: JEFFERSON

PrC (DLC); at head of letter: "Private." Recorded in sjl as sent "by Mr. Fitzhugh"; entry in sjpl reads: "Jay John. Private. Carrying trade. Navy."

From John Page

MY DEAR SIR   Rosewell Augt. the 23d. 1785.

I wrote a few Lines acknowledging the Receipt of yours by Col. Le Mair, and sent them by Monsr. Le Croix, a Merchant of Wmsburg. I then wrote more fully by Mazzei, and sent you some Account of our astronomical Observations on the Delaware with the Result of them respecting the 5° of Long. run out to the S.W. corner of Pennsylva., together with our last Acts of Assembly. I mention this as possibly Mazzei being robbed of his Money may have lost my Packet also. I hope *he* is with you before now. Since writing by him I have not had one Moments Leisure to write to a Friend. My Businesses as Executor, Planter, Tutor, &c. &c. engross my whole Time. To add to my Employments I am a Deputy to the General Convention of the Members of the american episcopal Church which is to meet next Month at Philada. I have inclosed you a Copy of the Proceedings of the Convention at Richmond. You will find we were liberal, and I think we shall reform the episcopal Church so as to make it truely respectable. Indeed this Sect was always the most liberal I ever heard of, not only with respect to religious Opinions but I think with Respect to political Matters too; at least they have shewed themselves such in America, for they took an open and decided Part in support of our late glorious Revolution, though at the Risk of, say the certain Destruction of their Estab[lish]ment and Importance. Such Disinterestedness entitles them to Respect, and the Liberality of their religious Sentiments is such, as is sufficient to make any one of a Liberal Way of thinking lament that this Sect is declining daily; whilst some others the most bigotted and illiberal are gaining ground. Fontaine has been almost starved; Andrews has quitted his Gown, he says, to avoid starving. Nothing but a general Assessment can prevent the State from being divided between immorality, and Enthusiastic Bigottry. We have endeavored 8 years in vain to support the rational Sects by voluntary Contributions. I think I

begin to see a Mischief arising out of the Dependence of the Teachers of the Christian Religion on their individual Followers, which
may not only be destructive to Morality but to Government itself.
The needy dependent Preacher not only can not boldly reprove
the vicious Practices of his Friends and Benefactors, his only Support; but he must, to keep well with them, fall into their Opinions,
and support their Views and Interests: so that instead of being
bound by the strongest Ties of Interest to discountenance Vice and
support and strengthen the Hands of Government, they may be
supporting the jarring Interests of the Enemies to all Government. Some may preach up the true Doctrine of Muncer [Münzer]
which may prove more fatal to some States in America than it did
to some in Germany; whilst others furthering the Views of the
rich, proud and aristocratical gentry, may amidst Tumult and
Anarchy offer their Services to restore Order and Stability to Government; fixing it on the Basis of a pure Aristocracy. I have said
the more on this Subject because I have just read an outrageous
Piece against the Assessment, in which your Opinion is quoted
and referred to, as authority against the Arguments for an Assessment, and because I have heard that you had altered your Opinion,
having found that the most rational Sects bear up with Difficulty
under the unequal Burthen of supporting their Teachers. As this
Letter was to have gone in the farmers-general's Ship Captn.
Carrol and that Ship has sprung a Leak, it reminds me to tell you
that I think the french commercial Interest suffers greatly here for
two Reasons. First because we have no Merchants who can load
and send Ships directly to France; and 2d. because Merchants in
France know not to whom they can with any Safety consign their
Vessels in America, or they are too confused in their Instructions.
Mr. Alexander the Agent employed in loading the Ship just mentioned, appears to have been in this Situation; for he constantly
restricted his Deputy to 2/ below the current Market Price of
Tobacco where it was worth purchasing. This occasioned a tedious
expensive Delay and no Doubt was also attended by a purchase of
a deal of bad Tobacco. The Deputy I know to be a Man of strict
Honour, and a zelous Friend of the French, and he assured me
that he could in one Month have loaded the Ship with good Tobacco
at 28/, but that the worst Inspections were pointed out to him,
and he was restricted to give 26/ when the Price was 28/, and 28/
when it was 30/, and so on till at length he found he could be of
no Service. He gave up his Employment charging nothing for his

Services. I have heard him declare he would with Pleasure load one Ship for the Farmers-general without any Fee or Reward provided he could be left to his own Discretion, as he could then shew them what fine Tobacco might be bought and on what good Terms. The Gentleman I mean is Matthew Anderson of Gloucester of whom Mr. Mazzei can give an Account. I fear I have intruded too much upon you, but can not refrain from making one Remark which I am led into by seeing in the last Gazettes an Account of Mr. Adams's Reception at St. James's. It is this, that I think it not a proper Time to Court the proud and haughty English. I wish we had deferred a little longer condescending to send an Ambassador to their Court. Can we not make Acts of Congress and of Assemblies, regulating our own Commerce, so as to have the desired Effect on the british Parliament and King at any Time, I mean so far as relate to any commercial Intercourse between the two Nations? May we not be drawn into some Treaty, which may not be the best adapted to the general Interest of the united States? Or possibly into one which may be injurious to some of our Allies? I confess I think it a Nice Point, not to injure some of our States by a commercial Treaty, nor our Allies, nor excite their Jealousy. This Sentence like most I write is involved and confused, but I believe you know what I mean. I can not copy my Letter or erase and blot any more words without appearing to a french Man or an english spye to intend an Insult. Excuse all this. I assure you I had intended to have written more at my Leasure, and sent my Letter by Captn. Carrol, but I find that he can not possibly sail this Month. I was very suddenly called upon by Mr. Le Croix (who has still the first Letter I wrote to you) for my further Commands to France; when I sat down and scribbled away. Your Friends in this Part of the World are all well, and will be happy to hear that you, your Daughter and Mr. Short are so. Present my best Wishes to them and believe me sincerely yours.

P.S. I believe no one in France except Mazzei and yourself can tell who it is makes so free with you. I have troubled you with a letter for Mazzei. Adieu.

RC (DLC); unsigned; addressed; endorsed. Recorded in SJL as received 15 Nov. "by La Croix." Enclosure: A copy of the journal of a convention of the clergy and laity of the Protestant Episcopal Church of Virginia, 18-25 May 1785 (printed in Francis L. Hawks in *Contributions to the Ec-* *clesiastical History of the United States*, New York, 1836, I, Appendix, 3-11).

The OUTRAGEOUS PIECE AGAINST THE ASSESSMENT has not been identified, but it may possibly have been the memorial of the ministers and lay representatives of the Presbyterian church held at Bethel, 13 Aug. 1785, in which some phrases from TJ's Bill for establishing religious freedom were employed or paraphrased (though not in direct quotation) and in which the memorialists petitioned the General Assembly to adopt "the bill in the revised law for establishing religious freedom" (Charles F. James, *Documentary History of the Struggle for Religious Liberty in Virginia*, Lynchburg, 1900, p. 236-40). See note to Madison to TJ, 20 Aug. 1785.

From William Short, with Enclosure

DEAR SIR   The Hague August 23d. 1785

After waiting on Mr. Dumas we went two Days ago by Appointment to the Baron de Thulemeiers. A simple Matter of Etiquette as you will see prevented the Business on which we were, from being completed. On my producing the two Originals of the Treaty and explaining the Intention of them, the Baron de Thulemeier told us he was instructed only to receive the Copy which should be sent and to exchange for it a Copy in French which he should have prepared in his Office, adding that the established Order of the Chancelerie of the King made this in some Measure necessary, the French being the only Language which was there recieved. He observed that this was nothing more than a meer-Matter of Form, and he hoped would give us no Difficulty in accepting the Exchange. We thought ourselves by no Means at Liberty to deviate from our Instructions even in Matters apparently formal, and on mentioning our Scruples, it was proposed that each of us should consult those by whom we were employed, as the safest Mode of proceeding. The Baron de Thulemeier writes to Berlin to-day and should he recieve Permission to accept and exchange the Instruments of Treaty which you offer, he will do it without farther Delay. In the same Manner if our Answers come first we are to communicate to him what we are at Liberty to do.

Lest there should be any other Cause of Delay we thought it best to communicate at the same Time the additional Part of our Instructions respecting the Ratifications &c. He desired that they might be explained to him in writing in Order that he might ask Advice on them at Berlin, adding there would be not the smallest Doubt of our agreeing that Matter. At his Request therefore I wrote him a short Letter in Answer to one which he sent me respecting the Exchange of the Instruments, and of which I have the Honor to inclose you a Copy.

That nothing might be left undone which we could do before recieving our Answers we met Yesterday Evening and exchanged the respective full-powers in the Form prescribed. We have at present therefore only to await farther Instructions from yourself or Mr. Adams, or the return of the Courier from Berlin. I hope the Determination we took of awaiting farther Orders from you before we ventured to accept an Instrument of the Treaty in French only will meet your Approbation, and I beg the Favor of you Sir to let me know as soon as shall be convenient what you wish should be done under the Circumstances I have just described.

I shall write to Mr. Adams also by the Post of this Day on this Subject. As he has not a Copy of the Treaty in French it will not be necessary to trouble him with what I am about to add. After the Baron de Thulemeier had examined one of the Instruments of the Treaty he found a Number of little Deviations which appear evidently to be the Faults only of the Copyist, although some of them tend to make a manifest Alteration in the Sense. He has furnished me with a List of them which I inclose for your Examination Sir and to recieve your Instructions thereon. On examining the other Instrument of the Treaty, I find none of those Faults in the Baron de Thulemeiers List except three which you will observe noted below his. But on reading over that Instrument, having no other to compare it with, I thought I discovered some other Faults of the Copyist also. I have given it to be examined by the Baron de Thulemeier and have not yet recieved any Information respecting it. I have been thus prolix Sir because I wish to have the Line we are to pursue, marked out with the most particular Precision not thinking that we are at Liberty to deviate in the smallest Instance. I beg you to be assured of the Sentiments of Respect with which I have the Honor to be your most obedient Servant, W. Short

ENCLOSURE

Fautes à corriger dans la Partie françoise à la grosse du Traité

Art: 4. ligne 11. avant la fin, au lieu de *dès que la raison de l'Etat l'exige*, corrigez *la raison d'Etat*.

Art: 7. ligne 4. au lieu, *de protéger et défendre*, corrigez *de protéger & de défendre*.

Art: 11. l: 9. 10. et 11. au lieu de *si ce n'est par insulte faite à la religion*a*d'autres*, corrigez *pour insulte faite à la religion*a*de l'autre*.

Art: 13. à la 2de. page l: 16. au lieu de *qui auroient été*, corrigez *qui auront été*.

et l: 5 avant la fin de l'article, au lieu de *le navire ne sera plus armé dans le port*, corrigez *amené dans le port*.

Art: 15. l: 4. au lieu de *stipules*, corrigez *stipulé*.

Art. 16. l: 3. au lieu de *l'une de parties*, corrigez *l'une des parties*.

Art. 21. §3. 1: 4. au lieu de,[b]*sans caution*, corrigez[b]*sous caution*.

§5. l: 3. au lieu de *faire de tels règlemens*, corrigez *faire tels règlemens*.[1]

Art. 23. l: 12. avant la fin, au lieu de *à facilities & répandre*, corrigez [c]*à faciliter et à répandre*.[1]

Art. 24. à la 3e. page, l: 4. d'en bas, *confondus au balancés*, corrigez *ou balancés*.

4e. page, l: 5 d'en bas, *qui auront été fixés*, corrigez *fixées*.

Notes on the other Instrument of Treaty
a) In the second Copy it is pour, but has *d'autres*.
b)   it is *sans* instead of *sous*.
c)   it is *à faciliter & répandre*.[2]

RC (DLC); endorsed: "Dumas & Short." Enclosures: (1) De Thulemeier to Short, 21 Aug. 1785 (RC in DLC: Short Papers, and Tr in Short's hand in DLC: TJ Papers and in MHi: AMT), reading as follows: "Je satisfais avec Empressement a l'Engagement que j'ai contracté avec vous, Monsieur, en Vous retraçant par ces lignes les Observations que j'ai pris la Liberté de vous communiquer a l'Occasion de l'Echange des Exemplaires du Traité de Commerce conclu entre le Roi et les Etats Unis de l'Amérique. Il n'est question que d'une simple Formalité. Les Ordres de ma Cour m'ont prescrit de transmettre a Berlin la Copie du Traité signée par Messieurs les Plenipotentiaires Americains apres l'avoir muni de ma signature, et de faire passer par contre entre vos Mains celle que j'aurais fait expedier en langue Française, et a laquelle j'aurais apposé ma Signature et mon Cachet. Vous avez eu la Complaisance, Monsieur, de m'offrir un double qui épargneroit au Secrétaire d'Ambassade du Roi la Peine de Transcrire le Traité, mais comme la Traduction Anglaise se trouve a Coté de l'original Français, et qu'on désire peut-etre chez vous, que l'Expedition de l'Exemplaire que je dois avoir l'honneur de Vous remettre se fasse dans la Chancellerie de la Mission Prussienne j'ai du Vous temoigner a cet égard un scrupule que les ordres de ma cour pourroient lever sans difficulté. C'est sur cet objet que je demanderai par la poste prochaine des Ordres précis, et Vous serés a même, Monsieur, de vous concerter egalement dans cet intervalle avec Messieurs Adams et Jefferson. Il me tarde de voir arriver le moment, ou je pourrai mettre la derniere Main a une transaction qui constatera sur un pié solide les liaisons de Commerce et d'Amitié etablies actuellement entre votre Patrie et la Mienne." (2) Short to De Thulemeier, 22 Aug. 1785 (Tr in DLC: Short Papers, in Short's hand), reading as follows: "The Observations which you did me the Honor to communicate Yesterday Evening shall be immediately transmitted to the American Ministers at London and Paris, their Answers to which it will be necessary for me to await. Considering myself obliged to follow the Instructions which I have had the Honor to receive from them, without the smallest Deviation, I take the Liberty of communicating also Sir, to you, what will be expected on their Part in Addition to what has been agreed on between us, in Order that you may confer thereon with your Court at present if you should find it necessary.—I am instructed Sir, 'to ask that the Ratification of his Majesty the King of Prussia be made known to the American Ministers as soon as it shall have taken Place, giving an Assurance on their Part that that of Congress shall also be communicated as soon as it shall have taken Place.' It is added that when both Ratifications shall be known Measures may be concerted for exchanging them. —I am also instructed Sir 'to confer with you on the Expediency of keeping the Treaty uncommunicated to the Public until the Exchange of Ratifications, and agree accordingly.'—Both Parties being equally interested Sir in the Articles I flatter myself no Difference of Opinion can arise on them, and that the final Hand will be soon put to those Bonds of Commerce and Friendship between our Countries, which must do Honor to those who have formed them." (3) List of errors in the French text of the treaty (DLC: TJ Papers; in a clerk's hand, with several additions in Short's hand); printed above. The covering letter and its enclosures were accompanied by Short's second letter to TJ of this date, following.

Short's letter TO MR. ADAMS . . . BY THE POST OF THIS DAY was identical with the present letter to TJ, save for the final paragraph, which reads: "I write to Mr. Jefferson also by this Post, and in addition to what I have troubled you with, I send him a List of Errors made by the Amanuensis in the French Copy of the Treaty, and which I do not think we are at Liberty to Change without your Orders, as in some Instances the sense is changed. I do not inclose you a List of these Errors because you have not a French Copy of the Treaty. Mr. Jefferson will probably communicate them to you" (Short to Adams, 23 Aug. 1785; MHi: AMT). In this Short was mistaken, for Adams had copied the French and English texts of the treaty in his letterbook (p. 107-24), at the bottom of the last page of which he made the following note: "Vide Errata at the beginning of the Book." The errors listed "at the beginning of the Book" are those printed above and also in a further enclosure to Short's second letter to TJ of this date. On 30 Aug. Adams wrote Short: "I hope 'er this the Baron has received orders to sign in both languages. This is a favorite point with me; but yet I would not make it a sine qua non. I would urge it with decency but give it up at last if it could not be avoided. Our treaty with France is in English and French: that with Holland is in English and Dutch and neither made any objection to it. I am sorry you did not enclose to me a list of the Errata. I have a Copy in both languages, made while you were here. I should be obliged to you for a Copy by the next post" (Adams to Short, 30 Aug. 1785; MHi: AMT). Short sent the list of errata to Adams on 5 Sep., saying: "I had been decieved in supposing that you had only a Copy of the English Part of the Treaty" (MHi; AMT).

[1] This correction may have been made on the copy that Dumas and Short gave to De Thulemeier, but it was not corrected on that copy that Short referred to as "the second Copy," which was the one retained by them and transmitted by TJ to Jay, and it is now among the Archives of the State Department (DNA: RG 11, American Original File Treaty Series No. 292). Hunter Miller, ed., *Treaties*, II, 179, reads "et repandre." The text of this treaty, both in its English and French versions, is a particularly poor specimen of engrossing; in addition to the errors detected in the "second Copy" as indicated in the enclosure in Short's second letter of 23 Aug., there were no less than six interlineations in the French text alone which either the amanuensis himself or Short had detected presumably prior to Short's departure from Paris. These slips may partly be explained on the ground that the transcription of the text between 24 and 28 July was hurried, but this cannot wholly justify the general slovenly appearance of the document, which was much less formal than the neat, official texts that TJ himself produced in his own communications to Vergennes, Castries, &c. The signature page of the instrument (the "second Copy") from DNA: RG 11 is illustrated in this volume.

[2] The text beginning with "Notes on the other Instrument . . ." is in Short's hand.

From William Short, with Enclosure

MY DEAR SIR   The Hague August 23d. 1785

The inclosed Papers consisting of a Letter I have the Honor to write you, of a Copy of one the Baron de Thulemeier has sent me, and of a List of Faults which he observes in the Copy of the Treaty I have been charged with, will fully explain the Situation of this Business. Being obliged to postpone doing any Thing farther in this Matter for eight Days at least, I shall make Use of that Interval to visit Amsterdam where it is necessary I should go, Mr. Adams Draughts being on the Banker there. I will thank you therefore to direct your Letters for me to the Care of Mr. Dumas at the Hague. He has promised me if by Chance I should not have returned to notify to me immediately their Arrival. I should have had Scrupules of writing to you on this Subject by Post, if these had not been done away, first by Mr. Adams inserting in his Letter to the Banker, the Cause of my coming, and secondly by the Baron de Thulemeier, who tells me he corresponded with you and Mr. Adams on these Subjects by Post.

I am sorry this little Stoppage to the Business has arisen, although I suppose it will be easily remedied by the Concession of the one or the other Party. I beg you to direct me to do any Thing you think proper in this Matter but to recross from Helvoetsluys to Harwich. An hundred Miles sailing oppress me more than a Journey by Land over all Europe. I cannot describe to you what I suffered in a short Passage of twenty four Hours. It makes me recollect with new Horror what I am to experience in my Return to America.

I attended to your Instructions respecting the Herald's office and canteens. You will not be at all satisfied with the former, and you will find the latter far beyond what you had expected.

Dr. Franklin's Idea of this Country, that it is a Machine, appears more and more just every Day. It seems to be really so much Territory absolutely formed by the Hands of Man. Every Place exhibits Monuments of the Power of human Industry. Make my Compliments if you please Sir to Colo. Humphries. I forgot to mention that you will not recieve a Letter from Mr. Adams by me. I was thirteen Days in London the last half of which I was detained by him. He did not write because he thought it unnecessary and communicated to me, as he said, what he wished you to know. Accept Sir Assurances of the sincerest Friendship & Affection with which I am yours, W SHORT

P.S. The moment I am about sealing this Letter the Baron de Thulemeier has brought me a List of the Faults he finds in the second Instrument of Treaty and which I inclose.

ENCLOSURE

Fautes à corriger dans le second Exemplaire

Art. 11. l. 10. au lieu de *insulte faite à la religion d'autres*, lisez *à la religion de l'autre.*
Art. 13. l. pénultième. au lieu de *toute la liberté*, lisez *toute liberté.*
Art. 21. § 1. ligne 6. au lieu de *restués*, lisez *restitués.*
     § 2. l. 2. au lieu de *repris pour un vaisseau de guerre*, *lisez par un vaisseau de guerre.*
     ib. l. 11. au lieu de *s'il a été*, lisez *s'il y a été.*
     § 3. l. 4. au lieu de *sans caution*, lisez *sous caution.*
Art. 24. p. 3, l. 5. au lieu de *fera pouvoir*, lisez *fera pourvoir.*

RC (DLC). Enclosures: (1) Short's first letter of this date to TJ, preceding, and its enclosures. (2) A list of errors in the second instrument of the treaty (DLC).

Martha Jefferson to Eliza House Trist

de l'abbey royale de Panthemont a Paris

MY DEAREST FRIEND   [after 24 Aug. 1785]

Your letter put an end to the inquietude that your silence had caused us. Be assured that I will remember you as long as I live. I am very happy in the convent and it is with reason for there wants nothing but the presence of my friends of America to render my situation worthy to be envied by the happiest. I do not say kings, for far from it. They are often more unfortunate than the lowest of their subjects. I have seen the king and the queen but at too great a distance to judge if they are like their pictures in Philadelphia. We had a lovely passage in a beautiful new ship that had only made one voyage before. There were only six passengers, all of whom papa knew, and a fine sun shine all the way, with the sea which was as calm as a river. I should have no objection at making an other voyage if I could be sure it would be as agreable as the first. We landed in England where we made a very short stay. The day we left it we set off at six a clock the evening, and arived in France at 7 the next morning. I can not say that this voyage was as agreable as the first, tho it was much shorter. It rained violently and the sea was exceedingly rough all the time, and I was allmost as sick as the first time, when I was sick two days. The cabane was not more than three feet wide and about four long. There was no other furniture than an old bench which was fast to the wall. The door by which we came in at was so little that one was obliged to enter on all four. There were two little doors at the side of the cabane was the way to our beds, which were composed of two boxxes and a couplle of blankets with out eather bed or matras, so that I was obliged to sleep in my cloathes. There being no winder in the cabane, we were obliged to stay in the dark for fear of the rains coming in if we opended the door. I fear we should have fared as badly at our arival for papa spoke very little french and me not a word, if an Irish gentleman, an entire stranger to us, who seeing our embarrassment, had not been so good as to conduct us to a house and was of great service to us. It is amazing to see how they cheat the strangers. It cost papa as much to have the bagadge brought from the shore to the house, which was about a half a square apart, as the bringing it from Philadelphia to Boston. From there we should have had a very agreable voyage to Paris, for havre de grace is built at the mouth of the seine, and we follow the river all the way thro the most beautiful country I ever saw in my life, it is a perfect garden if the singularity of our cariage had not atracted us the attention of all we met, and when ever we stopped we were surounded by the beggars. One day I counted no less than nine while we stopped to change horses. We saw a great number of chalk hills near Rouen, where we saw allso a church built by William the conqueror, and another at Ment which had as many steps to go to the top as there are days in the year. There are many pretty statues in it. The architectures is beautiful. All the winders are died glass of the most beautiful colours that form all kinds of figures. I wish you could have been with us when we arrived. I am sure you would have laughfed, for we were obliged to send imediately for the stay maker, the mantumaker, the milliner and even a shoe maker, before I could go out. I have never had the friseur but once, but I soon got rid of him and turned down my hair in spite of all they could say, and I differ it now as much as possible, for I think it allways too soon to suffer. I have seen two nuns take the veil. I'll tell you about that when I come to see you. I was placed in a convent at my arival and I leave you to judge of my situation. I did not speak a word of french, and no one here knew english but a little girl of 2 years old that could hardly speak french. There are about fifty or sixty pensioners in the house, so that speaking as much as I could with them I learnt the langauge very soon. At present I am charmed with my situation. I am afraid that you will be very much disapointed if you expect to see me perfect, for I have made very little progres. Give my love to Mrs. House, Brouse and Polly and when you will see hetty Rittenhouse scold her for me. She has never answerd any of my letters. Send my compliments to Mrs. Tamage and Mrs. Thomson, in short evry body that I know. I do not dout but that you were very much astonished at hearing that colonel floyed was maried. So was I, but as evry one has a different mind we must leave the world to itself and follow what we think wrighte. Tho you have a great deal of patience I am afraid that this scrawl will tire it. But if you knew the pleasure I take in writing to you and receiving letters from you, you would pardon me. Pray write me very long letters by evry occassion. I should be very glad to write for papa, but I am sure that he could not have an occupation which gives him more pleasure than that. How ever when he cant leave his business I will do it with pleasure. I do not know when we shall come. Pardon this letter, being so badly written for I have not the time at present. There comes in some new pensionars evry day. The classe is four rooms excedingly large for the pensionars to sleep in, and there is a fith and sixth one for them to stay in in the day and the other in which they take their lessens. We were the uniform which is crimson made like a frock laced behind with the tail like a robe de cour hoocked on muslin cufs and tuckers. The masters are all very good except that for the drawing. I end here for I am sure my letter must tire you. Papa sends his most affectionate compliments to you and Mrs. House and begs you not to forget that you are indebted a letter to him particularly on the subject of Brouses relations. Adieu my dear freind, be assured that I am and ever will be yours affectionately,   MARTHA JEFFERSON

Be so good as to let Mrs. Hopkinson know that I remember her with great gratitude and affection as well as Mrs. Rittenhouse.

RC (DLC); without date; endorsed. MS worn and faded. Tr (ViU); differs slightly from RC in phraseology.

Although Martha devoted a good part of her letter to the voyage and early days in France, it is certain that a year at least had elapsed before she set down her charming account of these events. TJ's letter to Mrs. Trist of 18 Aug. 1785 brought up the SUBJECT OF BROUSES RELATIONS in England and asked: "Will you be so good as to let me know what relations he [Browse] has there and where they live, and if I should at any time go there I will certainly see them." TJ added a postscript to this letter on 24 Aug.; Martha's reminder about the inquiry concerning Browse was, therefore, clearly written after that date. The probability is that it was written some weeks afterward, when the Fitzhugh brothers were in Paris and about to embark for America. The Fitzhughs conveyed a number of TJ's private and public letters to America (including that to Mrs. Trist of 18 Aug.) and, though they did not sail from Le Havre until 10 Nov., the latest date borne by any of the letters given them by TJ was 12

Oct. 1785. Early in 1786 Madison wrote to Mrs. Trist: "I received two letters from Mr. Jefferson at the same time yours came to hand. They came I find by the same two young gentlemen who were the bearers of his and Miss Patsy's to you" (Madison to Eliza House Trist, 14 Mch. 1786; RC owned by J. E. Fields, Chicago, Ill.). These facts make it evident that Martha's letter was written after 24 Aug. and before 13 Oct. 1785, and probably nearer the latter date than the former.

From John Paul Jones

SIR   L'Orient August 24th. 1785.

I yesterday received the Letter you did me the honor to write me the 17th. mentioning the difficulty made by the Marechal de Castries in his Letter to you of the 12th. and that you had removed that difficulty by your Answer. I am exceedingly Sensible of the favor you do me by your attention to my situation here; and it gives me great concern that it is not in my Power, at present, to send you the Roll you ask for of the Crew of the Alliance. The Rolls were, in the proper time, sent to Court, and put into the hands of Mr. de Sartine by Mr. Genet first Commis. of foreign Affairs, the Certificate of which I have among my Papers at Paris; and the Marechal de Castries might remember that I showed him and that he read that Certificate. Those Rolls, however, have been mislaid, or lost in the Bureau. Copys of them were sent, at the same time, to Dr. Franklin, who, I suppose, put them into the hands of Mr. Le Rey de Chaumont; but, since my return, I never could obtain any account of them. A third set of the Rolls I carryed with me to America, and, before I embarked in the French fleet at Boston, I put them into the hands of Mr. Secretary Livingston; and they were sealed up among the Papers of his Office when I left America.

It is, however, impossible that any legal demands should be made on you for french Subjects in consequence of your engagement to the Marechal. The Alliance was manned in America, and I never heard of any person's having served on board that Frigate who had been born in France, except the Captain, who, as I was informed, had in America abjured the Church of Rome, and been naturalized.

I have made all the inquiry I have been able here respecting the expedition you mentioned in a former Letter; but I have not obtained much satisfaction. I purpose to go to Brest. I am, with

great esteem and respect Sir your most obedient & most humble
Servt.,   J. PAUL JONES

MS not found; text is printed from Sherburne, *John Paul Jones*, p. 268-9; a
facsimile in Thomas F. Madigan, *Word Shadows of the Great*, N.Y., 1930, between p. 88-9. Recorded in SJL as received 29 Aug. 1785.

From Richard O'Bryen

SIR   Algier august the 24th. 1785

We the Subjects of the United States of America Having the
Misfortune of Being Captured off The Coast of Portugal the
24th. and 30th. of July By the Algerines, and Brought into this
port Where we have Become Slaves, and Sent To the workhouses,
Oure Sufferings is Beyond Oure Expressing or your Conception.
Hoping youre Honoure will be pleased to represent Oure Grievances
to Congress. Hoping They will Take Such Measures as to tend
to oure speedy Redemption. Hoping you will Consider oure Unfortunate Situation, and Make some provision for the Unfortunate
Sufferers, Untill we are reedeemed, Being Stript of all oure Cloaths
and nothing to Exist on But two small Cakes of Bread per day,
without any other Necessary of Life. Charles Logie Esqr. British
Counsil seeing oure distressed Situation has taken us Three Masters of Vessells out of the Work Houses and has Given Security
for us to the Day of Algiers, King of Cruelties. My Crew Certainly
will Starve if There is not Some Immediate Reliefe. It Being the
Method of all Christian powers whose Subjects falls in the Hands
of Those Savages to Make Some provision for them, untill they
are reedeemed, I should Esteem it a particular favoure If you would
be pleased to write to Mr. Logie, Consul here.

Ship Daupin, Richd. OBryen Master, Belonging to Messrs.
Mathew and Thomas Irwin & Co. Merchants of the City of Phila-
delphia Bound to Philadelphia from St. Ubes. Taken the 30th.
July, out two Days. Schoner Maria, Isiack Stevens Master, from
Boston bound to Cadis, Belonging to Messrs. Wm. Foster & Co.
Merchants in Boston. Taken the 24th. July, Out 26 days. The
Cruisers in This port are fitting out With all possible Expedition
and I Am of That Opinion They will Take Most of Oure Ships
that will come for urope. They will Cruise to The Northward of
the Western Islands and towards the British Channell.

The Sooner we Could put a stop to them the Better, they Valu-
ing the Number of prizes they take, To the Summ for the Peace.

The Spaniards Coming on terms with them, all other Uropian Nations must. I hope we shall aply Before any more does, for they Must Be at war with Some.

I am very respectfully your most obedt. and very Humble Servant & Petitioner, RICHD. OBRYEN

RC (DNA: PCC, No. 59, III); addressed: "To the Honourable Plenipotentary of The united States of America At Paris"; endorsed in an unidentified hand. Tr in DNA: PCC, No. 87, I and MHi: AMT, both in Humphreys' hand. Tr also in DNA: PCC, No. 107, I. Recorded in sjl as received 22 Sep. 1785, under cover of James Wilkie to TJ, 16 Sep. 1785. Enclosed in TJ to Adams, 24 Sep. 1785, and TJ to Jay, 11 Oct. 1785.

A similar appeal was addressed to John Adams, 27 Aug. 1785, signed by "Richard O'Bryen, Isack Stephens, Zachs. Coffin," on behalf of the 21 captives (MHi: AMT).

From William Robeson

Dunkirk, 24 Aug. 1785. Though he is unknown to TJ, he writes recommending the appointment of consuls in European ports, "to whom we might Apply for Explanation or Redress." An American who served the state of S.C. during the war and has spent much time in Europe, he has had "very Recent Proofs in Holland with my Unfortunate Countrymen Who have Neither the Language, Marintime knowledge, or Custom of the Port, Who Inocently are Involved, and Who have Smartted for the little Errors . . . as well Suffering the Insolence of Office, Under Every Species of Agravation and Exspence. . . ." Recommends John Moulston of Virginia, who was active during the Revolution and has acquired considerable property and reputation, for the post at Dunkirk, where he has lived since the war; he speaks French and is "Conversant in Commercial Matters and dayly is transacting of them." Robeson should be addressed at the "Hottel Chapeau Rou[ge] Rue du Sud."

RC (ViWC); 2 p.; endorsed in part: "recd. Aug. 28. answd. same day."

From Giovanni Fabbroni

[*Florence, 25 Aug. 1785.* Recorded in sjl as received 5 Jan. 1786. Not found.]

From James Monroe

DEAR SIR   New York August 25th. 1785.

Since my last nothing very material hath taken place here. I leave this meerly to inform you of my departure hence for the

Indian treaty on the Ohio which will be in about two hours. The *two*[1] *commercial propositions* are as they were. *Although congress will I believe not adjourn yet*, I apprehend *the business of consequence* will be postpon'd for the present, perhaps till the winter. There is but *a thin representation of the states and of course* not the *ability if the inclination to act on these subjects.* I intend to take within my view the country lying between Lake Erie and the Ohio, the Ohio and the Potowmack or Jas. river, as it may suit me to return by the northern or southern part of the State. I pass thro Lancaster and Carlisle at the latter of which posts I join Genl. Butler. The people of *Kentucky* intend I hear to petition the legislature for a *seperation.* I must confess I am one of those who doubt the policy of this measure (for I make no doubt it will be granted) either upon *state or federal principles.* My opinion is we could so model our regulations as to accomodate our *government* to their convenience, and unquestionably the more we *diminish the state the less consequence she will have in the union.* On the part of *the union* or rather *the states* upon *the Atlantic*, it is in my opinion their policy to keep a prevailing influence upon *the Ohio or to the westward.* What *unites us to them or rather they to us when the Mississippi shall be open?* Remov'd at a distance from whatever may affect us beyond the water *they will* necessarily be but little interested in whatever respects *us.* Beside they will outnumber *us* in *congress unless we* confine *their number as much as possible.* In my opinion this matter should be well investigated before any measure is hastily adopted. I direct your letters to be forwarded to me to Fredricksburg. So soon as I return to the settled country I shall advise you of it and am your affectionate friend & servant,

JAS. MONROE

RC (DLC: Monroe Papers); endorsed; partly in code, with interlineal decoding by TJ. Recorded in SJL as received 16 Oct. 1785.

[1] This and subsequent words in italics are written in code and were decoded interlineally by TJ, who corrected Monroe's errors of encoding; the text presented here is a decoding by the editors, employing Code No. 9.

From Stephen Sayre

SIR   New York 25 augt. 1785

I do myself the honor of transmitting a Letter to your Excellency, which the Delegates of Virginia and Massachusetts, voluntarily gave me, as soon as they understood that the appointment it mentions would be agreeable to me.

It is a duty I owe to their good will, to give you the earliest notice, that I am now ready to embark for Cadiz—shall immediately proceed to Madrid, where my private affairs may detain me twenty, or thirty days; unless your Excellency should express a wish to see me immediately at Paris.

If I can render Service to the public my private interest will become a secondary object. May I request your Excellency, to favour me with your resolutions, as soon as possible, under [cover] to Mr. Carmichael.

I am, with great respect & consideration your most obedient & most humble Servant,   STEPHEN SAYRE

RC (ViWC); endorsed. Recorded in SJL as received 10 Oct. 1785. Enclosure: Elbridge Gerry and others to TJ, 23 Aug. 1785.

On this same date, Sayre wrote to Adams, also enclosing a letter from the Massachusetts and Virginia delegates, "by which," he added, "I believe, those Gentlemen mean to render me particular service. If it does not come too late, I trust you will think yourself justified in uniting with Mr. Jefferson to send me on the business it mentions. My private affairs call me to Cadiz and Madrid. I shall sail in a Vessell of my own in two or three days. I inform your excellency of this,

that you may communicate your resolutions to me at Madrid where I shall remain some weeks, if not called upon: or make the utmost haste to obey your commands. Or, if you will take the trouble of writing to Mr. Jefferson, immediately on this subject, he will do me the honor of conveying your Sentiments" (Sayre to Adams, 25 Aug. 1785; MHi: AMT). For a brief account of Sayre's sometimes grandiose and always unsuccessful schemes, see Julian P. Boyd, "The Remarkable Adventures of Stephen Sayre," *Princeton Univ. Lib. Chronicle*, II [1941], p. 51-64).

From Castries

Versailles le 26. août 1785.

L'offre que vous me faites, Monsieur, par la lettre que vous m'avez fait l'honneur de m'ecrire le 17 de ce mois, applanit toutes difficultés. Puisque vous voulez bien vous engager à faire payer, par le banquier des Etats-unis à Paris, ce qui peut revenir aux françois qui auroient servi sur la fregate americaine l'Alliance, Je donne ordre au Commissaire de L'Orient de remettre à Mr. Jones la Somme totale qui revient aux batimens americains, et de m'adresser copie des reconnoissances qu'il exigera de cet officier.

J'ai l'honneur d'etre avec un parfait attachement, Monsieur, votre trés humble et trés obeïssant serviteur,   LE MAL. DE CASTRIES

RC (DLC); in a clerk's hand, signed by Castries; Tr (DNA: PCC, No. 87, I); in TJ's hand. Tr (DNA: PCC, No. 107, I); with an English transla- tion. Recorded in SJL as received 29 Aug. 1785. A copy was enclosed in TJ to John Paul Jones, 29 Aug., and in TJ to John Jay, 30 Aug. 1785.

To James Monroe

DEAR SIR   Paris Aug. 28. 1785.

I wrote you on the 5th. of July by Mr. Franklin and on the 12th. of the same month by Monsr. Houdon. Since that date yours of June 16. by Mr. Mazzei is received. Every thing looks like peace here. The settlement between the Emperor and Dutch is not yet published, but it is believed to be agreed. Nothing is done as yet between him and the Porte. He is much wounded by the Confedera- tion of several of the Germanic body at the head of which is the king of Prussia, and to which the king of England as elector of Hanover is believed to accede. The object is to preserve the con- stitution of that empire. It shews that these princes entertain seri- ous jealousies of the ambition of the emperor, and this will very much endanger the election of his nephew as king of the Romans. A late arret of this court against the admission of British manu- factures produces a great sensation in England. I wish it may pro- duce a disposition there to receive our commerce in all their do- minions on advantageous terms. *This*[1] is the *only balm* which can *heal* the *wounds* that has *recieved*. It is but *too true* that that *country furnished markets* for *three fourths* of the *exports* of the *eight northernmost states*, a *truth* not *proper* to be *spoken* of, but which should *influence our proceedings* with *them. How that negociation advances* you are probably better informed than I am. The infidelity of the post offices rendering the communication *be- tween Mr. Adams and myself difficult*, the improvement of our commerce *with France will be advanced more* by *negociations* at *Saint James's* than at *Versailles*.

The July French packet being arrived without bringing any news of Mr. Lambe, if the English one of the same month be also arrived without news of him, I expect Mr. Adams will concur with me in sending some other person to treat with the Barbary states. Mr. *Barclay* is willing to go, and I have proposed him to Mr. Adams but have not yet received his answer. The peace ex- pected between Spain and Algiers will probably not take place. It is said the former was to have given a million of dollars. Would it not be prudent to *send a minister to Portugal*? Our commerce with *that country* is very important, perhaps *more so than* with *any other* country *in Europe*. It is possible too that they might *permit our whaling vessels* to *refresh* in *Brazil or give* some other *indulgencies* in *America*. The lethargic character of *their ambassador here* gives a very *unhopeful aspect* to a *treaty* on this *ground*. I lately spoke with *him on the subject and he* has promised to interest himself in obtaining *an answer from his court*.

I have waited to see what was the pleasure of Congress as to the secretaryship of my office here; that is, to see whether they proposed to appoint a secretary of legation, or leave me to appoint a private secretary. Colo. Humphrey's occupation in the dispatches and records of the matters which relate to the general commissions does not afford him leisure to aid me in my office, were I entitled to ask that, and, in the mean time the lengthy papers which often accompany the communications between the ministers here and myself, and the other business of the office absolutely require a scribe. I shall therefore on Mr. Short's return from the Hague appoint him my private secretary till Congress shall think proper to signify their pleasure. The salary allowed Mr. Franklin in the same office was 1000 Dollars a year. I shall presume that Mr. Short may draw the same allowance from the funds of the U.S. here. As soon as I shall have made this appointment I shall give official notice of it to Mr. Jay, that Congress may, if they disapprove of it, say so.

I am much pleased with your land ordinance, and think it improved from the first in the most material circumstances. I had mistaken the object of the division of the lands among the states. I am sanguine in my expectations of lessening our debts by this fund, and have expressed my expectations to the minister and others here. I see by the public papers you have adopted the dollar as your money unit. In the arrangement of coins I had proposed, I ought to have inserted a gold coin of 5. dollars, which being within 2/ of the value of a guinea will be very convenient. The English papers so incessantly repeating their lies about the tumults, the anarchy, the bankruptcies and distresses of America, these ideas prevail very generally in Europe. At a large table where I dined the other day, a gentleman from Switzerland expressed his apprehensions for the fate of Doctr. Franklin as he said he had been informed he would be received with stones by the people who were generally dissatisfied with the revolution and incensed against all those who had assisted in bringing it about. I told him his ap-

prehensions were just, and that the people of America would probably salute Dr. Franklin with the same stones they had thrown at the
Marquis Fayette. The reception of the Doctor is an object of very
general attention, and will weigh in Europe as an evidence of the
satisfaction or dissatisfaction of America with their revolution. As
you are to be in Williamsburgh early in November, this is the last
letter I shall write you till about that time; I am with very sincere
esteem Dr. Sir Your friend & servt.,   Th: Jefferson

Be so good as to direct the inclosed so that it may get to it's
destination.

RC (ViU); endorsed; partly in code.
PrC (DLC); lacks postscript of RC.
In DLC: TJ Papers, 27: 4641 there
is an undated FC in TJ's hand of some
of the passages which he employed for
encoding purposes. Recorded in SJL
as sent "by Mr. Fitzhugh. Inclosing
letter from Mme. to Monsr. Doradour";
entry in SJPL reads: "Monroe James.
Our commerce. Barbary. Secretary.

Money unit. Eng. papers." Enclosure
(missing): Possibly Madame Doradour's letter to her husband enclosed
in hers to TJ, 14 June 1785.

1 This and subsequent words in italics are written in code and have been
decoded by the editors, employing Code
No. 9.

To William Robeson

[*Paris, 28 Aug. 1785*. Entry in SJL reads: "Wm. Robeson. Informing him power of appointing Consuls was in Congress. That in mean
time Mr. Barclay appointed. That he informs me a Mr. Coffin is agent
there and serves the U.S. well." Not found.]

From William Short

Dear Sir   Amsterdam Augst. 28th. 1785

I wrote you last from the Hague. Since that I have passed
through Leyden and Haarlem on my Way to this Place which I
find as busy and commercial as I think it can be. And yet I am told
it has declined and is declining. This gives me Concern because I
find several attributing it to an Intercourse with America and to
the Independence of the latter. How true this may be in Fact I cannot say, yet an Opinion of it prevailing, will injure in some Measure the American Character as Well as the American Commerce
here I should suppose. The Truth of the Case seems to me to be
that the great Wealth of this Country having raised the Price of
Labor, their poorer Neighbours are by that Means enabled to un-

dertake their carrying Business at a cheaper Rate and by that means affect them in a vital Part. Yet it is so much the Fashion in the commercial World at present to attribute all Misfortunes to America that they do not look farther and draw all their Reasonings from thence.

I received great Pleasure at Leyden from viewing the University, the Anatomical Apparatus, the Botanical Garden and the Cabinet of Natural History. In the Garden are several Aloes. Luckily this is the Year for one to bloom so that I had an Opportunity of seeing that which so rarely occurs. It is not yet in Perfection. Seven Years hence there are two More which are to bloom. Mr. Luzac the Editor of the Gazette is made Professor of the University. It was my Intention to have waited on him but was hurried from Leyden in Order to hear the famous Organ at Haarlem, which is only played three Times a week and at particular Hours. It is much admired by the Amateurs. The Information I had with Respect to the Hours was bad. It had ceased before I arrived. Yet the View of this exquisite Piece of Mechanism was very agreeable. I enter into no Description of it because I find Descriptions of these Things always difficult. I was still more curious to have seen the first Book that was ever printed by the famous Koster the Inventor of this valuable Art. It is kept in the Stadthouse to be shewn, but this also is only at particular Hours, so Strangers are frequently disappointed as I was, as they are so rigid there in the Observance of all their Customs that neither Civility or Hospitality can make them deviate from them. This Town values itself not a little on giving Birth [to] the Inventor of the Art of Printing, as well as the Success of the three Ships which it furnished in one of the holy Wars that broke the Chains laid across the Chanel at Damieta and let in all the Fleet. The Models of these Ships are hung up in the great Church in which stands the Organ.

I think it probable I shall return to the Hague before your Answer to my former letter will get there. If not Mr. Dumas will send me Information the first Moment of its Arrival, after which nothing shall detain me an Instant. I am very anxious to know if you have had any late News from America. You have long ago no Doubt heard of Mr. Rutledge's Appointment. The Boston Navigation Act arrived in London and was published in their Papers the Day before I left it. It will certainly produce a serious Consideration there.

I am curious to know if all my young Countrymen and Acquaintances are gone from Paris. I rather suppose they will stay there longer than I had thought when I saw them last. Bingham and his Lady left this Place Yesterday Morning for the Hague, on their way to Brussels and Paris. I beg the Favor of you to send the inclosed Letter to the petite Poste. Make my Compliments to Colo. Humphries and believe me with the most sincere Friendship & Affection Yours,

W SHORT

RC (ViWC). Recorded in SJL as recorded 2 Sep. 1785. Enclosure not identified.

By THIS TOWN Short meant, of course, Haarlem, of which Laurens Janszoon Coster or KOSTER was a native. The claim that Coster was the inventor of movable type has been discredited by modern scholars, who give to Johann Gutenberg of Mainz credit for having made the pivotal invention that opened up immense new possibilities in the art of printing.

From Henry Champion

[L'Orient, *29 Aug. 1785*. Recorded in SJL as received 2 Sep. 1785. Not found.]

To John Paul Jones

SIR   Paris Aug. 29. 1785.

I receive this moment a letter from the Marechal de Castries of which the inclosed is a copy. Having engaged to him to sollicit orders for the paiment of any parts of this money due to French subjects to be made here, and moreover engaged that in the mean time I will order paiment should any such claimants offer themselves, I pray you to furnish me with all the evidence you can as to what French subjects may be entitled to any part of the monies you will receive, and to how much each of them, and also to advise me by what means I can obtain a certain roll of all such claimants. I am Sir with great esteem Your most obedt. humble servt,

TH: JEFFERSON

PrC (DLC). Entry in SJPL reads: "Jones J. Paul. Frigate Alliance." Enclosure: Copy of De Castries to TJ, 26 Aug. 1785.

From Miles King

Hampton, Va., 29 Aug. 1785. Introduces the bearer, the Chevalier de Laserre, a French officer who served in Virginia during the Revolution. As he comes to France "to do some business with the Prime Minister" and "it is the duty of every Virginian to tender every service in their power to their great and good Allies," King recommends him to TJ's favor.

RC (DLC); 1 p.; the year, which is torn away in the dateline, has been supplied from TJ's record in SJL of its receipt on 3 June 1786.

From De Ponçins

MONSIEUR   à feur en forez ce 29e. août 1785

Vôtre excellence verra par les deux lettres que j'ay l'honeur de lui adrësser cy inclus, que j'ay proposé à m. le docteur franklin un projet, pour lever un état topografique, de tous les états unis de l'amerique, avec la notice du grain et qualité de terre de chaque canton, et le régime particulier à chaque lieu, pour y faire fleurir l'agriculture, le comerce, ou l'industrie. J'avois l'honeur aussi de lui demander, de me faire adjuger par le Congres des terres pour mon compte, ou je pûs former un établissement avantageux, un revers de fortune ocasioné par la perte d'un proces contre un corps éclesiastique, m'obligant à passer en amerique.

Les obstacles que m. le docteur franklin oposa, come un empechement à ces projets, ne subsistent plus aujourdhui, puisque le Congres, ayant traité avec les nations indienes et sauvages, est devenu propriétaire incontestable de tous les térritoires qu'on lui disputoit; et com'il s'occupe de conceder ces terres, j'ose vous prier d'employer vos bons offices pour m'en faire concéder une portion, avantageuse; mon traité d'agriculture qui va vous etre presenté, vous prouvera que je suis en ce genre un des grands opérateurs qu'il y ait eu depuis le Comencement du monde. J'ose vous prier de me faire sçavoir le prix, les conditions, et les avantages de ces concéssions. Je suis avec respect Monsieur vôtre tres humble et tres obant. serviteur,

                              LE MIS. DE PONÇINS
                         ancien officier aux gardes
                         Françoises chev. de Sr. Louis

J'ose vous prier de faire tenir la cy jointe à m. le docteur franklin.

RC (MoSHi); endorsed. TJ's entry in SJL under date of 8 Sep. 1785, which reads "received the Marq. de Poncin's. Feur en forez. Aug. 2. 1785," is probably an error for the present letter. Enclosures: "les deux lettres" that De Ponçins wrote Franklin are doubtless the following: (1) An undated letter of about 1783, expressing his desire to settle in America and asking for a grant of land from Congress (PPAP: Franklin Papers, XLI, 110); (2) Another letter of 12 Feb. 1785, similar to the present one to TJ, offering to form a company to survey all the lands in the United States and to render a complete report of their location and soil, as well as their commercial and economic possibilities (same, XXXIII, 29). The letter to Franklin mentioned in the postscript has not been found.

MON TRAITÉ D'AGRICULTURE: This was published in Lyon in 1779 under the title *Le Grand œuvre de l'agriculture ou l'art de régénérer les surfaces et les très-fonds, accompagnée de découvertes intéressantes sur l'agriculture et la guerre.* De Ponçins had sent a copy of this to Franklin with his letter of 12 Feb. 1785; Franklin gave it high commendation and said that he would place it in the public library [Library Company] of Philadelphia. This pleased De Ponçins so much that he immediately sent Franklin a copy of his work on education, and asked for an interview and for advice on investing his funds (De Ponçins to Franklin, 21 Feb. 1785; PPAP).

From St. John de Crèvecoeur

Sir   Caën 30th. Augt. 1785

I have received with great Pleasure yours of the 22d. Instant. I am Very Glad to See the State of your health is Improved, and that Miss Jefferson Grows and Prospers. I hope to have the pleasure of seeing you Some time in Octre. I shall go, I believe, with my two boys to spend some time at Sanoy with the Good Comtesse, who also has lost a dear and a beloved brother. I most Sincerely participate with her in the Severe Loss, which afflicts me Very Powerfully. Knowing all the Sensibility and Tenderness of her heart I feel the weight of her affliction. The derangement of the Packets has discourag'd me quite. I never was so surprised as when I was informed of it at L'orient. I cannot flatter myself with the hopes of seeing them reestablish'd up to their former Number. Some Evil Genius has from the beginning secretly opposed and destroyed the simple and usefull Idea I had given on that subject, and I do give it up. We have heard of the Confinement of the Cardinal. It is to be hoped that he wont be released before he has paid his debts, tho' he is too great a Sinner to Receive his due Punishment. What Monsters in Society these hughe over Grown Priests are. Happy Americans, whose Priests are men and Citizens. I have had the Pleasure of receiving Several Letters from my Excellent Friend Chs. Williamos and to my Very Great Surprise, my Two Last are without Answers. Pray do you know what is become of him? Is he return'd to New York? I am Very Anxious to know how and where he is. I am With great Respect & Esteem Sir Your Very Humble Servt.,

ST. JOHN

RC (DLC); at foot of letter: "Chès Mr. de Lisle Lieut. General du Bailliage Caën"; endorsed in part: "recd. Sep. 3."

To Francis Eppes

[30 Aug. 1785]

I must now repeat my wish to have Polly sent to me next summer. This, however, must depend on the circumstance of a good vessel sailing from Virginia in the months of April, May, June, or July. I would not have her set out sooner or later on account of the equinoxes. The vessel should have performed one voyage at least, but not be more than four or five years old. We do not attend to this circumstance till we have been to sea, but there the consequence of it is felt. I think it would be found that all the vessels which are lost are either on their first voyage or after they are five years old; at least there are few exceptions to this. With respect to the person to whose care she should be trusted, I must leave it to yourself and Mrs. Eppes altogether. Some good lady passing from America to France, or even England, would be most eligible; but a careful gentleman who would be so kind as to superintend her would do. In this case some woman who has had the small-pox must attend her. A careful negro woman, as Isabel, for instance, if she has had the small-pox, would suffice under the patronage of a gentleman. The woman need not come farther than Havre, l'Orient, Nantes, or whatever port she should land at, because I could go there for the child myself, and the person could return to Virginia directly. My anxieties on this subject could induce me to endless details, but your discretion and that of Mrs. Eppes saves me the necessity. I will only add that I would rather live a year longer without her than have her trusted to any but a good ship and a summer passage. Patsy is well. She speaks French as easily as English; while Humphries, Short, and myself are scarcely better at it than when we landed. . . .

I look with impatience to the moment when I may rejoin you. There is nothing to tempt me to stay here. Present me with the most cordial affection to Mrs. Eppes, the children, and the family at Hors-du-monde. I commit to Mrs. Eppes my kisses for dear Poll, who hangs on my mind night and day.

MS not found; text is taken from the partial printing in Randolph, *Domestic Life*, p. 105-6. Recorded in SJL under this date as sent "by Mr. Fitzhugh."

To John Jay

SIR   Paris Aug. 30. 1785.

I had the honour of writing to you on the 14th. inst. by a Mr.
Cannon of Connecticut who was to sail in the packet. Since that
date yours of July 13. is come to hand. The times for the sailing
of the packets being somewhat deranged, I avail myself of a
conveiance of the present by the Mr. Fitzhughs of Virginia who
expect to land at Philadelphia.

I inclose you a correspondence which has taken place between
the Marechal de Castries, minister of the Marine, and myself.
It is on the subject of the prize money due to the officers and
crew of the Alliance for prizes taken in Europe under the command of Capt. Jones. That officer has been here under the direction of Congress near two years solliciting the liquidation and
paiment of that money. Infinite delays had retarded the liquidation till the month of June. It was expected, when the liquidation
was announced to be completed, that the money was to be received. The M. de Castries doubted the authority of Capt. Jones
to receive it and wrote to me for information. I wrote him the
letter dated July 10. which seemed to clear away that difficulty.
Another arose. A Mr. Puchilberg presented powers to receive
the money. I wrote then the letter of Aug. 3. and received that
of the M. de Castries of Aug. 12. acknoleging he was satisfied
as to this difficulty, but announcing another, to wit, that possibly some French subjects might have been on board the Alliance, and therefore that Capt. Jones ought to give security for
the repaiment of their portions. Capt. Jones had before told me
there was not a Frenchman on board that vessel but the Captain.
I enquired of Mr. Barclay. He told me he was satisfied there was
not one. Here then was a mere possibility, a shadow of a right,
opposed to a certain, to a substantial one which existed in the
mass of the crew and which was likely to be delayed; for it
could not be expected that Capt. Jones could, in a strange country, find the security required. These difficulties I suppose to
have been conjured up, one after another by Mr. Puchilberg,
who wanted to get hold of the money. I saw but one way to cut
short these everlasting delays, which were ruining the officer
solliciting the paiment of the money, and keeping our seamen
out of what they had hardly fought for years ago. This was, to
undertake to ask an order from Congress for the paiment of any

French claimants by their banker in Paris, and in the mean time to undertake to order such paiment should any such claimant prove his title before the pleasure of Congress should be made known to me. I consulted with Mr. Barclay who seemed satisfied I might venture this undertaking, because no such claim could be presented. I therefore wrote the letter of Aug. 17. and received that of Aug. 26. finally closing this tedious business. Should what I have done not meet the approbation of Congress, I would pray their immediate sense, because it is not probable that the whole of this money will be paid so hastily, but that their orders may arrive in time to stop a sufficiency for any French claimants who may possibly exist. The following paragraph of a letter from Capt. Jones dated l'Orient Aug. 24. 1785. further satisfies me that my undertaking amounted to nothing in fact. He sais 'it is impossible that any legal demands should be made on you for French subjects in consequence of your engagements to the Marechal. The Alliance was manned in America, and I never heard of any person's having served on board that frigate who had been born in France, except the captain, who, as I was informed, had in America abjured the church of Rome, and been naturalized.' Should Congress approve of what I have done, I will then ask their resolution for the paiment, by their banker here, of any such claims as may be properly authenticated, and will moreover pray of you an authentic roll of the crew of the Alliance with the sums to be allowed to each person, on the subject of which roll Capt. Jones in the letter abovementioned says 'I carried a set of the rolls with me to America, and before I embarked in the French fleet at Boston, I put them into the hands of Mr. Secretary Livingston, and they were sealed up among the papers of his Office when I left America.' I think it possible that Mr. Puchilberg may excite claims. Should any name be offered which shall not be found on the roll, it will be a sufficient disproof of the pretention. Should it be found on the roll, it will remain to prove the identity of person, and to enquire if paiment may not have been made in America. I conjecture, from the journals of Congress of June 2. that Landais, who I believe was the captain, may be in America. As his portion of prize money may be considerable, I hope it will be settled in America, where only it can be known whether any advances may have been made him.

The person at the head of the post office here sais he proposed to Dr. Franklin a Convention to facilitate the passage of letters through their office and ours, and that he delivered a draught of the Convention proposed, that it might be sent to Congress. I think it possible he may be mistaken in this, as, on my mentioning it to Dr. Franklin, he did not recollect any such draught having been put into his hands. An answer however is expected by them. I mention it that Congress may decide whether they will make any Convention on the subject, and on what principle. The one proposed here was that for letters passing hence into America, the French postage should be collected by our post officers and paid every 6. months, and for letters coming from America here, the American postage should be collected by the post officers here, and paid to us in like manner. A second plan however presents itself; that is, to suppose the sums to be thus collected on each side will be equal, or so nearly equal that the balance will not pay the trouble of keeping accounts and the little bickerings that the settlement of accounts and demands of the balances may occasion: and therefore to make an exchange of postage. This would better secure our harmony, but I do not know that it would be agreed to here. If not, the other might then be agreed to.

I have waited hitherto, supposing that Congress might possibly appoint a Secretary to the legation here, or signify their pleasure that I should appoint a private Secretary to aid me in my office. The communications between the ministers and myself requiring often that many and long papers should be copied, and that in a shorter time than could be done by myself, were I otherwise unoccupied, other correspondencies and proceedings, of all which copies must be retained, and still more the necessity of having some confidential person, who in case of any accident to myself, might be authorised to take possession of the instructions, letters, and other papers of the office, have rendered it absolutely necessary for me to appoint a private Secretary. Colo. Humphries finds full occupation, and often more than he can do, in writing and recording the dispatches and proceedings of the General commissions. I shall therefore appoint Mr. Short, on his return from the Hague, with an express condition that the appointment shall cease whenever Congress shall think proper to make any other arrangement. He will of course expect the allowance heretofore made to the private secretaries of the ministers, which I believe has been a thousand dollars a year.

An improvement is made here in the construction of the musket which it may be interesting to Congress to know, should they at any time propose to procure any. It consists in the making every part of them so exactly alike that what belongs to any one, may be used for every other musket in the magazine. The government here has examined and approved the method, and is establishing a large manufactory for the purpose. As yet the inventor has only completed the lock of the musket on this plan. He will proceed immediately to have the barrel, stock, and their parts executed in the same way. Supposing it might be useful to the U.S., I went to the workman, he presented me the parts of 50. locks taken to peices, and arranged in compartments. I put several together myself taking peices at hazard as they came to hand, and they fitted in the most perfect manner. The advantages of this, when arms need repair, are evident. He effects it by tools of his own contrivance which at the same time abridge the work so that he thinks he shall be able to furnish the musket two livres cheaper than the common price. But it will be two or three years before he will be able to furnish any quantity. I mention it now, as it may have influence on the plan for furnishing our magazines with this arm.

Every thing in Europe remains as when I wrote you last. The peace between Spain and Algiers has the appearance of being broken off. The French packet being arrived without Mr. Lambe or any news of him, I await Mr. Adams's acceding to the proposition mentioned in my last. I send you the gazettes of Leyden and France to this date, and have the honour to be with the highest respect & esteem, Sir, Your most obedient humble servt.,

TH: JEFFERSON

RC (DNA: PCC, No. 87, I). PrC (DLC). Tr (DNA: PCC, No. 107, I). Recorded in SJL as sent "by Mr. Fitzhugh"; entry in SJPL reads: "Jay John. Prizemoney. Post office and postage. Short Secretary. Le Blanc's musket. Lambe not arrived." Enclosures: TJ to Castries, 10 July, 3 Aug., and 17 Aug.; John Paul Jones to TJ, 31 July; and Castries to TJ, 12 Aug. and 26 Aug. 1785.

Le Blanc's application of the principle of interchangeability of parts excited TJ and evidently interested the French government to the extent of establishing A LARGE MANUFACTORY FOR THE PURPOSE. Yet it "was an idea that took very limited hold in France, where it was first worked out, while in England it was solely applied to lowering the costs on the pulleys made for the navy. In America, however, it was applied to the mass production of more and more objects—clocks and watches, hardware and sewing machines—because it solved the shortage of workers" (Jeannette Mirsky and Allan Nevins, *The World of Eli Whitney*, 1952, p. 221). TJ later encouraged Whitney in the application of the principle to arms manufacture in the United States (see TJ to Monroe, 14 Nov. 1801). The projet for a postal convention TO FACILITATE THE PASSAGE OF LETTERS was submitted by Rigoley d'Ogny to Vergennes on 10 May 1785 with a covering letter in which it was suggested that the draft be sent to Marbois with a recommendation that he endeavor to have it concluded (both in Arch. Aff. Etr., Corr. Pol., E.-U., XXIX; Tr in DLC). Vergennes dispatched a copy of both D'Ogny's letter and the projet of the convention to Marbois, directing him to communicate the latter to Jay and adding: "je ne doute pas que les stipulations qui y sont énoncées ne lui paroissent d'une convenance reciproque et les plus propres a assurer le bien du service et de la correspondance entre les deux nations. Vous aurez soin, M. de faire les demarches necessaires pour determiner le Congrès a prendre cette affaire en consideration" (Vergennes to Marbois, 19 July 1785; same, XXX). Marbois referred the convention to Jay late in Nov. and Jay transmitted it to Congress on 2 Dec.; Congress, the same day, referred it back to Jay for a report thereon (JCC, XXIX, 898, note). Jay reported 29 Mch. 1786, submitting to Congress the form of convention that he thought proper for adoption (JCC, XXX, 141-4). See also D'Ogny to TJ, 6 Apr. 1787 and TJ's reply, 3 May 1787. Jay transmitted TJ's present letter, along with those of 6 and 11 Oct. 1785, to Congress on 9 Feb. 1786.

To John Banister

DEAR SIR   Paris Aug. 31. 1785.

Mr. Fitzhugh being to leave this within two or three days and proposing to attend the next session of Assembly in Richmond, I am thereby furnished with an opportunity of writing you a line, and knowing myself the anxieties of a parent for an absent child I know I cannot better gratify you than by informing you of the welfare of your son. From this place he went to Avignon, and not to Lisle as I expected when I wrote to you June 16. He was so well pleased with that situation and with the society he met with there that he determined to continue there. I received from him a letter dated the 1st. instant, in which he does not say a word to me about his health. I have written him a scolding one in return, tho' I was satisfied of his health from his silence on the subject, from the length of his letter, and from it's masculine observations and reasonings on the country he was then in, which I was satisfied could not have flowed from a valetudinary head.

All is calm here, and calm like to be, at least for this year. I am curious to see the result of the refusal by a French vessel to salute the British flag in the channel which I do not believe to have been accidental. The Boston navigation act and the apparent disposition of the other states to act in the same line and to invest Congress with powers over our commerce works well in England, and well also throughout Europe. I hope the best effects from it. Present me affectionately to Mrs. Bannister and be assured of the esteem

PrC (DLC); lacking second page which evidently consisted of complimentary close and signature. Recorded in SJL as sent "by Mr. Fitzhugh." Daniel Fitzhugh was a member of the House of Delegates from King George county in the session of Oct. 1785.

To David Ramsay

Paris Aug. 31. 1785.

I am honoured with your two letters of June 15. and July 13. and am to thank you for the sheets of your history sent therewith. I am much pleased to see a commencement of those special histories of the late revolution which must be written first before a good general one can be expected. I shall be more pleased to see the remaining parts as well executed as this which sets the example. Another published in the middle states and a third in the Eastern, will complete the materials for a general history which the U.S. should furnish. It will then remain for France to produce a history. That to be desired from Great Britain is probably as well done in the Annual register as any we may expect from them. On the receipt of your first letter I applied to a bookseller to see what could be done towards translating and printing it here. After various enquiries I found that the translation and the printing 1000. copies being deducted would leave about 40. guineas for the author to be received as the work sold. I was by no means satisfied with this price, but the book seller observed that as it would be only a translation, it would be impossible to hinder other translations from being made, which might come into competition on the sale. On the receipt of your second letter, I wrote immediately to the Marquis de Chastellux, supposing he might be at his seat at Marly. I have received no answer which makes me fear he is on his tour of inspection. I am therefore distressed what to do. For while I hope from his counsels that means of procuring a better translation and perhaps better terms too might be found, I fear on the other hand that a delay may permit some other translation to get the start and so defeat our prospects altogether. I will satisfy myself whether he is on his tour and when he will return and on that information will act for the best. It is thought that perhaps a couple of hundred English copies might be sold here. I shall take great pleasure in promoting your views here and am only mortified at the indifferent prospect which at present presents itself.

Europe enjoys a calm at this moment, and there se[ems] no reason to apprehend it's being disturbed this summer. There is a speck in the horison between the Emperor and Turk which may produce something, but that, at soonest, is for another year. I look with some interest on the result of the refusal by a French vessel to salute the British flag in the channel, which I am not yet satisfied was an accidental event.

I pray you to be assured of the respect & esteem with which I have the honour to be Sir Your most obedt. & most humble servt.,

TH: JEFFERSON

PrC (DLC). Recorded in SJL as sent "by Mr. Fitzhugh."

From Vergennes

à Versles. le 31. Aoust 1785.

J'ai reçu, Monsieur, la lettre que vous m'avez fait l'honneur de m'ecrire le 15. de ce mois; Le développement quelle renferme des idées que vous aviez bien voulu me communiquer de bouche, m'a paru très interressant, et je n'ai pas différé à la transmettre à Mr. le Controleur Général, au département de qui la matiere ressortit.

J'ai l'honneur d'être très sincèrement, Monsieur, votre très humble et très obéissant Serviteur,   DE VERGENNES

RC (DLC); in a clerk's hand, signed by Vergennes. Tr (Arch. Aff. Etr., Paris, Corr. Pol., E.-U., xxx; Tr in DLC). Recorded in SJL as received 2 Sep. 1785.

From Charles Bellini

[ca. Aug. 1785.] Persuaded that whatever office TJ should hold, he would wish to be no "other than Thomas Jefferson," Bellini does not use an honorific in addressing him, for "to pay compliments to a philosopher of your dignity, would be equal to blasphemy."

Acknowledges TJ's letter from Annapolis of 8 May 1784, which he found so comforting and encouraging at the time of his wife's illness: "just your name, written by your own hand now and then will sustain my waning philosophy." Encloses a packet of letters for Mazzei who instructed when he left America that his letters should be sent to TJ. Sends his compliments to Martha Jefferson, William Short, and the Marquis de Chastellux.

RC (DLC); 4 p.; in Italian; undated; endorsed. Recorded in SJL as received 26 Sep. 1785 without date.

The familiarity employed by Bellini in the salutations of this and other letters ("My dearest Thomas," "My most estimable friend and patron Thomas," "My dearest Thomas, most worthy friend and patron"; see translations by N. G. Nardini in WMQ, 2d ser., v [1925], 1-7) are not to be understood as indicating that Bellini stood on a more intimate footing with TJ than other friends who did not thus freely abandon the honorific. Even in young manhood TJ's closest friends (Nelson and Page, for example) addressed him as "Dear Jefferson" and he in turn saluted them by using their surnames, a practice which all seem to have abandoned with maturity (see Page to TJ, 23 Aug. 1785). The intimate salutations in Bellini's letters reflect, rather, a trait bordering on obsequiousness in his own character. TJ invariably replied to these embarrassingly familiar salutations by using his customary "Dear Sir" or "Sir." In this and other respects TJ's "manners were those of that polished school of the Colonial Government, so remarkable in its day—under no circumstances violating any of those minor conventional observances which constitute the well-bred gentleman, courteous and considerate to all persons" (T. J. Randolph to Henry S. Randall; Randall, *Life*, III, 674). The use of nicknames and Christian names in ordinary discourse and in correspondence among cultivated adults in the America of TJ's time was almost non-existent, despite the evidence to the contrary in historical novels and dramatizations of the 20th century. This evidence is of recent manufacture.

To C. W. F. Dumas and William Short

GENTLEMEN   Paris Sep. 1. 1785.

I have been duly honoured with the receipt of your separate letters of Aug. 23. and should sooner have returned an answer, but that as you had written also to Mr. Adams I thought it possible I might receive his sentiments on the subject in time for the post. Not thinking it proper to lose the occasion of the post, I have concluded to communicate to you my separate sentiments, which you will of course pay attention to only so far as they may concur with what you shall receive from Mr. Adams.

On a review of our letters to the Baron de Thulemeier I do not find that we had proposed that the treaty should be in two columns the one English and the other what he should think proper. We certainly intended to have proposed it, we had agreed together that it should be an article of system with us, and the omission of it in this instance has been accidental. My own opinion therefore is that, to avoid the appearance of urging new propositions when every thing appeared to be arranged, we should agree to consider the French column as the original if the Baron de Thulemeyer thinks himself bound to insist upon it: but if the practice of his court will admit of the execution in the two languages, each to be considered as equally original, it would be very pleasing to me, as it will accomodate it to our views, relieve us from the embarrasment of this precedent which may be urged against us on other occasions, and be more agreeable to our country where the French language is spoken by very few. This method will be also attended with the advantage that if any expression in any part of the treaty is equivocal in the one language, it's true sense will be known by the corresponding passage in the other.

The errors of the copyist in the French column you will correct

of course. I have the honour to be with very high esteem Gentlemen Your most obedient & most humble servt.,

TH: JEFFERSON

RC (DLC: Short Papers). PrC (DLC: TJ Papers). Tr (DNA: PCC, No. 86); in David Humphreys' hand. Entry in SJPL reads: "Dumas and Short. Prussian treaty." On De Thulemeier's acceptance of both texts as originals, see Short to TJ, 9 Sep. 1785.

To James Madison, with a List of Books

DEAR SIR   Paris Sep. 1. 1785.

My last to you was dated May 11. by Monsr. de Doradour.
Since that I have received yours of Jan. 22. with 6. copies of the
revisal, and that of Apr. 27. by Mr. Mazzei.

All is quiet here. The Emperor and Dutch are certainly agreed
tho' they have not published their agreement. Most of his schemes
in Germany must be postponed, if they are not prevented, by the
confederacy of many of the Germanic body at the head of which
is the K. of Prussia, and to which the Elector of Hanover is supposed to have acceded. The object of the league is to preserve the
members of the empire in their present state. I doubt whether the
jealousy entertained of this prince, and which is so fully evidenced
by this league, may not defeat the election of his nephew to be
king of the Romans, and thus produce an instance of breaking the
lineal succession. Nothing is as yet done between him and the
Turks. If any thing is produced in that quarter it will not be for
this year. The court of Madrid has obtained the delivery of the
crew of the brig Betsy taken by the Emperor of Marocco. The
Emperor had treated them kindly, new-cloathed them, and delivered them to the Spanish minister who sent them to Cadiz. This
is the only American vessel ever taken by the Barbary states. The
Emperor continues to give proofs of his desire to be in friendship
with us, or in other words, of receiving us into the number of his
tributaries. Nothing further need be feared from him. I wish the
Algerines may be as easily dealt with. I fancy the peace expected
between them and Spain is not likely to take place. I am well informed that the late proceedings in America have produced a
wonderful sensation in England in our favour. I mean the disposition which seems to be becoming general to invest Congress with
the regulation of our commerce, and in the mean time the measures
taken to defeat the avidity of the British government, grasping at

our carrying business. I can add with truth that it was not till these symptoms appeared in America that I have been able to discover the smallest token of respect towards the United states in any part of Europe. There was an enthusiasm towards us all over Europe at the moment of the peace. The torrent of lies published unremittingly in every day's London paper first made an impression and produced a coolness. The republication of these lies in most of the papers of Europe (done probably by authority of the governments to discourage emigrations) carried them home to the belief of every mind. They supposed every thing in America was anarchy, tumult, and civil war. The reception of the M. Fayette gave a check to these ideas. The late proceedings seem to be producing a decisive vibration in our favour. I think it possible that England may ply before them. It is a nation which nothing but views of interest can govern. If it produces us good there, it will here also. The defeat of the Irish propositions is also in our favor.

I have at length made up the purchase of books for you, as far as it can be done for the present. The objects which I have not yet been able to get, I shall continue to seek for. Those purchased, are packed this morning in two trunks, and you have the catalogue and prices herein inclosed. The future charges of transportation shall be carried into the next bill. The amount of the present is 1154 livres 13 sous which reckoning the French crown of 6. livres at 6/8 Virginia money is £64-3. which sum you will be so good as to keep in your hands to be used occasionally in the education of my nephews when the regular resources disappoint you. To the same use I would pray you to apply twenty five guineas which I have lent the two Mr. Fitzhughs of Marmion, and which I have desired them to repay into your hands. You will of course deduct the price of the revisals and any other articles you may have been so kind as to pay for me. Greek and Roman authors are dearer here than I believe any where in the world. No body here reads them, wherefore they are not reprinted. Don Ulloa in the original not to be found. The collection of tracts on the œconomics of different nations we cannot find; nor Amelot's travels into China. I shall send these two trunks of books to Havre there to wait a conveiance to America; for as to the fixing the packets there it is as incertain as ever. The other articles you mention shall be procured as far as they can be. Knowing that some of them would be better got in London, I commissioned Mr. Short, who was going there, to get them. He is not yet returned. They will be of such a nature as that I can get some gentleman who may be going to America to take them in his portmanteau. Le Maire being now able to stand on his own legs there will be no necessity for your advancing him the money I desired if it is not already done. I am anxious to hear from you on the subject of my Notes on Virginia. I have been obliged to give so many of them here that I fear their getting published. I have received an application from the Directors of the public buildings to procure them a plan for their Capitol. I shall send them one taken from the best morsel of antient architecture now remaining. It has obtained the approbation of fifteen or sixteen centuries, and is therefore preferable to any design which might be newly contrived. It will give more room, be more convenient and cost less than the plan they sent me. Pray encourage them to wait for it, and to execute it. It will be superior in beauty to any thing in America, and not inferior to any thing in the world. It is very simple. Have you a copying press? If you have not, you should get one. Mine (exclusive of paper which costs a guinea a ream) has cost me about 14. guineas. I would give ten times that sum that I had had it from the date of the stamp act. I hope you will be so good as to continue your communications both of the great and small kind which are equally useful to me. Be assured of the sincerity with which I am Dr. Sir Your friend & servt.,   TH: JEFFERSON

ENCLOSURE

	livres sous den
Dictionnaire de Trevoux. 5. vol. fol. @ 5f12	28– 0–0
La Conquista di Mexico. De Solis. fol. 7f10. relieure 7f	14–10
Traité de morale et de bonheur. 12mo. 2. v. in 1.	2– 8
Wicquefort de l'Ambassadeur. 2. v. 4to.	7– 4
Burlamaqui. Principes du droit Politique 4to. 3f12 relieure 2f5	5–17
Conquista de la China por el Tartaro por Palafox. 12mo.	3
Code de l'humanité de Felice. 13. v. 4to.	104– 0
13. first livraisons of the Encyclopedie 47. vols. 4to. (being 48f less than subscription)	348– 0
14th. livraison of do. 4. v. 4to.	24– 0
Peyssonel	2– 0
Bibliotheque physico-œconomique. 4. v. 12mo. 10f4. rel. 3f	13– 4
Cultivateur Americain. 2. v. 8vo. 7f17. rel. 2f10	10– 7
Mirabeau sur l'ordre des Cincinnati. 10f10. rel. 1f5 (prohibited)	11–15
Coutumes Anglo-Normands de Houard. 4. v. 4to. 40f rel. 10f	50– 0

Memoires sur l'Amerique 4. v. 4to. 24– 0

Tott sur les Turcs. 4. v. in 2. 8vo. 10f. rel. 2f10 12–10

Neckar sur l'Administration des Finances de France. 3. v.

12mo. 7f10 rel. 2f5 . . . . **9–15**

le bon-sens. 12mo. 6f rel. 15s (prohibited) 6–15

Mably. Principes de morale.

1. v. 12mo.	3ᵗ12		
etude de l'histoire 1. . .	2 10		
maniere d'ecrire			
l'histoire 1.	2 8		
constitution			
d'Amerique 1.	1 16		
sur l'histoire de		relieure de	
France. 2. v.	6	11 vols. @	
droit de l'Europe		15 s. 8f5	41– 1
3. v.	7 10		
ordres des societies . . .	2		
principes des			
negotiations	2 10		
entretiens de Phocion . .	2		
des Romains	2 10		

32 16

Wanting to complete Mably's works which I have not been

able to procure

les principes de legislation

sur les Grecs

sur la Pologne.

Chronologie des empires anciennes

de la Combe.   1. v. 8vo. 5– 0–0

de l'histoire universelle

de Hornot. . . . .   1. v. 8vo. 4f   4– 0–0

de l'histoire universelle

de Berlié . . . .   1. v. 8vo. 2f10 rel. 1f5 3–15

des empereurs Romains

par Richer . . . .   2. v. 8vo. 8f   rel. 2f10 10–10

des Juifs. . . . .   1. v. 8vo. 3f10. rel. 1f5 4–15

de l'histoire universelle

par Du Fresnoy. . . .   2. v. 8vo. 13f   rel. 2f10 15–10

de l'histoire du Nord.

par La Combe . . . . .   2. v. 8vo. 10f. rel. 2f10 12–10

de France. par Henault. 3. v. 8vo. 12f   rel. 3f15 15–15

Memoires de Voltaire. 2. v. in 1. 2f10 rel. 15s. 3– 5–0

Linnaei Philosophia Botanica. 1 v. 8vo. 7f rel. 1f5 . . . . . 8– 5

Genera plantarum   1. v. 8vo. 8f rel. 1f5 . . . . . 9– 5

Species plantarum.   4. v. 8vo. 32f rel. 5f 37– 0

Systema naturae   4. v. 8vo. 26f rel. 5f 31– 0

Clayton. Flora Virginica. 4to. 12f. rel. 2f10 14–10

D'Albon sur l'interet de plusieurs nations. 4. v. 12mo.

12f. rel. 3f 15– 0

Systeme de la nature de Diderot. 3. v. 8vo. 21f (prohibited)	21– 0	
Coussin [*sic*] histoire Romaine. ⎤		
2. v. in 1. 12mo. ⎟		
de Constantinople 8. v. in 10. ⎬ 16. vols. 12mo.	36– 0–0	
de l'empire de l'Occident 2. v. ⎟		
de l'eglise. 5. v. in 3. ⎦		
Droit de la Nature. por Wolff. 6. v. 12mo. 15f rel. 4f10 ..	19–10	
Voyage de Pagét 8vo. 3. v. in 1.	9	
Mirabeau. Ami des hommes 5. v. 12mo. ⎫	12	
Theorie de l'impot 2. v. in 1. 12mo. ⎭		
Buffon. Supplement 11. 12. Oiseaux 17. 18.		
Mineraux 1. 2. 3. 4.	24.	
Lettres de Pascal. 12mo. 2f. rel. 15s.	2–15	
Le sage à la cour et le roi voiageur (prohibited)	10–15	
Principes de legislation universelle 2. v. 8vo.	12– 0	
Ordonnances de la Marine par Valin. 2. v. 4to.	22	
Diderot sur les sourds and muets 12mo. ⎤		
3f12. sur les ⎬ 4. v. 12mo.	13– 7	
aveugles 3f. sur la nature 3f. sur la ⎟		
morale 3f15 ⎦		
Mariana's history of Spain 11. v. 12mo.	21	
2 trunks & packing paper	43– 0	

1154–13

RC (DLC: Madison Papers); endorsed at head of letter: "Recd. Feby. 24. 1786." PrC (DLC: TJ Papers). Recorded in SJL as sent "by Mr. Fitzhugh"; entry in SJPL reads: "Madison James. Europe. Barbary. England. Books. Lemaire. Notes. Capitol. P. and D. Carr." Enclosure (PrC in DLC: TJ Papers) consists of two pages with sub-total at bottom of first page and "Brought over" at top of second, omitted here.

From William Carmichael

SIR   St. Ildefonso 2d. Septr. 1785

I received on the 30th. ulto. the Letter you did me the honor to address me the 18th. and I am happy to find that your Sentiments with respect to the generous interposition of this Court in our Affair with Morrocco correspond with mine. The reception of Mr. Gardoqui by Congress and the People of America at Large coincides with the opinions contained in your Letter. I am persuaded that the Ct. de F. Blanca is too clear sighted and possessed of a manner of thinking too enlarged and too Liberal not to perceive the importance of a solid and permanent connection between the respective Countries, a connection of importance to each while Advantages which Nature seems to indicate form its basis. United with the States These will be a wall of Brass against the enterprizes of other Commercial Nations which at this Moment wish to arrogate the profits of a protected interlope Trade with the Spanish Colonies, and favoring ours as far as is consistent with the interests of the Mother Country. We can enable this Court to be Indifferent to the Politics of the Northern Nations, whose maritime force by that very Indifference will become every year less considerable. It would have been the highest pleasure to me to have had it in my power to offer to this Court the mite of our Country towards the humiliation and suppression of the Piratical Powers of Barbary. This offer would now I fear be too Late. In a day or two, the Algerien Deputies will Arrive here accompanied by a Ct. D'Espilly a Frenchman who made the first Advances towards their pacification. It would have been much more glorious for us to have paid a subsidy to Spain or to have sent an armed Force to cooperate with its Fleets and armies than to be constrained for the Security of our Commerce to submit perhaps to a tribute. Algiers hath already commenced hostilities against us. By Letters from Cadiz and by others which I have seen from Algiers I am advised that five American vessels had been captured of which two had been carried into the Latter Port and immediately advertized for Sale, Vessels, cargoes, and Crew. You see Sir the ruinous consequences of an illtimed attention to Parsimony and a misguided Jealousy of granting funds to our National Council; an evil which might have been prevented must now be remedied. Perhaps I may have an opportunity by insinuation to pave the Way for a truce. I had no instructions with respect to the differences with the Emperor of Morrocco. I know not even if my conduct in that business has met approbation; in this as in the latter I shall make efforts without compromising Congress, acting upon the principle that the welfare of the Commonwealth is the Suprema Lex. It would have been a very great Satisfaction to me to have been employed in our African Business, because I should have relied in a great measure for my success on the good offices of his Excy. the Ct. De F. B. But as I cannot without an express order of Congress or the Sanction of Mr. Adams and yourself quit my post here, My next pleasure will be to procure such recommendations and to furnish such light as may contribute to the Success of the Agent employed by the Commissioners named by Congress to treat with these Pirates. If the Person you mean to send can wear a Uniform, He will be better received by the Emperor of Morrocco and it will save him unnecessary expence in Cloathing.

I have Letters from New York dated the 16th. of July. Mr. Gardoqui is highly Pleased with his reception and this court I hope is not less satisfied. His Excy. the Ct. de Florida Blanca has authorized me to express his Majesty's satisfaction to Congress. In fact this is a critical Moment. The General Discontent Against G. B. will give a double value to the Liberality and Moderation of Spain and if Advantages which circumstances offer are seized by the Latter, Adieu to England for Ever. I would wish to be Able to explain personally many things which I dare not commit to paper without a cypher. Delicacy, supposed views of interest not personal but public, prevent me from even hinting what I know of the secret but determined views of the British Cabinet, not More hostile to us than to others. With their usual arrogance they eagerly embraced measures which their pride dictated and their folly pursued. They will open their Eyes too Late, unless the present moment is not laid hold of to seperate our commercial and consequently our Political Interests for ever. The Ministry here pursue indefatigably the great work of National Economy in their Finances and of improvements in Agriculture. But unless One Person has the Superintendance of all, the progress will not be rapid. The Death of the Infant Dn. Luis gave rise to conjectures with respect to the Manner in which his Children would be treated, as in Marrying he had renounced in some measure the Legitimate rights to which his Children might pretend hereafter. The King has Intrusted their Education to the Archbishop of Toledo primate of Spain. I have in my possession the Royal Decree to the Council of Castille and the Letter of the Ct. De F. B. to the Archbishop, but these are circumstances of so little moment to us, that Unless your Curiosity may induce you to wish to see these writings, I shall not trouble you nor my self by forwarding copies. This will be sent you by His Excy. the Ct. de Aranda and once a month by the Channel of that Ambassador you may have an opportunity of writing to me, Addressing your packetts under cover to Dn. Miguel Otamende who will have the goodness to put them into my hands. As I have few occasions of writing to Congress from hence and as these few become from the Algerine war more precarious I beg your Excellency to send copies of the papers which I have or may send you to America.

I take the Liberty of inclosing you a Letter for the Genoese Minister from the one employed here. We Lodge together, have a Table to which also the Charge D'Affaires of Saxony contributes.

The Latter also desires that I would follow a Letter for the Minister of Treves. The first I beg you to send to the Minister of Genoa, the Latter by the penny Post to the general Post office for Germany. When We can have an opportunity of Writing more freely, I shall endeavour to give you all the hints that I think, perhaps erroneously, which may contribute to the Public Service. In the mean time I have the honor to be with very great & Sincere Esteem Your Excellencys Most Obedt. & Hble. Sert.,

WM. CARMICHAEL

RC (DLC). Enclosures not identified. Carmichael wrote a brief letter to John Adams, also, on this date, omitting all references to Spanish affairs and stating that TJ has promised to give Adams "a safer manner of corresponding"; until this is done he cannot enter into details (MHi: AMT).

To Chastellux, with Enclosure

DEAR SIR   Paris Sep. 2. 1785.

You were so kind as to allow me a fortnight to read your journey through Virginia. But you should have thought of this indulgence while you were writing it, and have rendered it less interesting if you meant that your readers should have been longer engaged with it. In fact I devoured it at a single meal, and a second reading scarce allowed me sang froid enough to mark a few errors in the names of persons and places which I note on a paper herein inclosed, with an inconsiderable error or two in facts which I have also noted because I supposed you wished to state them correctly. From this general approbation however you must allow me to except about a dozen pages in the earlier part of the book which I read with a continued blush from beginning to end, as it presented me a lively picture of what I wish to be, but am not. No, my dear Sir, the thousand millionth part of what you there say, is more than I deserve. It might perhaps have passed in Europe at the time you wrote it, and the exaggeration might not have been detected. But consider that the animal is now brought there, and that every one will take his dimensions for himself. The friendly complexion of your mind has betrayed you into a partiality of which the European spectator will be divested. Respect to yourself therefore will require indispensably that you expunge the whole of those pages except your own judicious observations interspersed among them on Animal and physical subjects. With respect to my countrymen there is surely nothing which can render them uneasy,

[467]

in the observations made on them. They know that they are not perfect, and will be sensible that you have viewed them with a philanthropic eye. You say much good of them, and less ill than they are conscious may be said with truth. I have studied their character with attention. I have thought them, as you found them, aristocratical, pompous, clannish, indolent, hospitable, and I should have added, disinterested, but you say attached to their interest. This is the only trait in their character wherein our observations differ. I have always thought them so careless of their interests, so thoughtless in their expences and in all their transactions of business that I had placed it among the vices of their character, as indeed most virtues when carried beyond certain bounds degenerate into vices. I had even ascribed this to it's cause, to that warmth of their climate which unnerves and unmans both body and mind. While on this subject I will give you my idea of the characters of the several states.

In the North they are	In the South they are
cool	fiery
sober	Voluptuary
laborious	indolent
persevering	unsteady
independant	independant
jealous of their own liberties, and just to those of others	zealous for their own liberties, but trampling on those of others
interested	generous
chicaning	candid
superstitious and hypocritical in their religion	without attachment or pretentions to any religion but that of the heart.

These characteristics grow weaker and weaker by gradation from North to South and South to North, insomuch that an observing traveller, without the aid of the quadrant may always know his latitude by the character of the people among whom he finds himself. It is in Pennsylvania that the two characters seem to meet and blend and to form a people free from the extremes both of vice and virtue. Peculiar circumstances have given to New York the character which climate would have given had she been placed on the South instead of the North side of Pennsylvania. Perhaps too other circumstances may have occasioned in Virginia a transplantation of a particular vice foreign to it's climate. You could

judge of this with more impartiality than I could, and the probability is that your estimate of them is the most just. I think it for
their good that the vices of their character should be pointed out
to them that they may amend them; for a malady of either body
or mind once known is half cured.

I wish you would add to this peice your letter to Mr. Madison
on the expediency of introducing the arts into America. I found in
that a great deal of matter, very many observations, which would
be useful to the legislators of America, and to the general mass of
citizens. I read it with great pleasure and analysed it's contents
that I might fix them in my own mind. I have the honor to be with
very sincere esteem Dear Sir Your most obedient & most humble
servt.,   TH: JEFFERSON

ENCLOSURE

1. 2. 3. *Kent* should be Newkent.
   4. Button's bridge should be Bottom's bridge.
   5. 6. Bothwell   should be Boswell.
   7. montagnes de l'Ouest, should be South-west mountains. They
      are so called from their direction which is from North-East
      to South-west. All our mountains run in the same course, but
      these being the first discovered appropriated the name to
      themselves.
   8. The expression 'il avoit conquis tout le pais entre l'Appamatoc
      et le bay de Chesapeak,' gives an idea of Powhatan, perhaps
      not exactly true, and certainly defective. He was the head
      of all the tribes of Indians below the falls of the rivers from
      Susquehanna to the midlands of James and Roanoke rivers.
      What was the nature of his power over them, is not known;
      probably it was like that of the chiefs among the modern
      tribes of Indians, which we now know to consist in persua-
      sion and respectability of personal character. It would be
      more accurate also to say that 'Powhatan county takes it's
      name from the river on which it lies, now called James river,
      but formerly Powhatan from a tribe and chief of that name
      famous in the history of Virginia.' The truth is that the
      county of Powhatan was not occupied by the Powhatans, but
      was the chief habitation of the Monacans, the rivals and
      perpetual enemies of the Powhatans.
   9. The town of Pocahuntas does not send delegates to the assem-
      bly. The county, in which it is, sends delegates as all the
      other counties do.
   10. Ross should be Rolfe.
   11. Carter should be Cary.
   12. Mr. Beverley Randolph, should be Mr. Randolph.
   13. Colchester, should be, Manchester.
   14. The first Congress was at Philadelphia and not New York.

15. *du Congrés* should be *du Conseil du roi*. He was a tory.
16. Maryland was never purchased by the crown. It was always a proprietary government.
17. The government is divided into three departments, legislative, executive and judiciary. No person can hold an office in any two of them. Consequently all the members in any one department are excluded from both the other. Hence the judges and Attorney general cannot be of the legislature.

The clergy are excluded, because, if admitted into the legislature at all, the probability is that they would form it's majority. For they are dispersed through every county in the state, they have influence with the people, and great opportunities of persuading them to elect them into the legislature. This body, tho shattered, is still formidable, still forms a *corps*, and is still actuated by the *esprit de corps*. The nature of that spirit has been severely felt by mankind, and has filled the history of ten or twelve centuries with too many atrocities not to merit a proscription from meddling with government. Lawyers, holding no public office, may act in any of the departments. They accordingly constitute the ablest part both of the legislative and executive bodies.

RC (M. le Duc de Duras, Château de Chastellux, Yonne, France, 1952). PrC (DLC). Enclosure (PrC in DLC).

TJ's corrections were incorporated by Chastellux in the published version of his "Voyage dans la Haute Virginie"

(Chastellux, *Voyages*, Paris, 1786, II, 1-156), although his printer was capricious in the matter of American proper names: Bottom's bridge is printed as "Buttom's bridge," Rolfe as "Roll," &c.

From David S. Franks

[ca. 2 Sep. 1785]

I did not think I should be obliged to trouble you again Sir in my Affairs, but I am this morning informed that there is a writ taken out against me for a Note of hand which I gave at Lyons. When The Marquis de La Fayette went from this he gave me a Letter of Credit on which I could receive no money owing to a *want of form* which the Banker says must necessarily be. I have writen to the Marquis and shall have I am convinced a Satisfactory Answer in a week or Ten days. If you could spare me twenty Louis d'ores for about that time you will my dear Sir lay me under the highest obligation and save me from confinement. I am Sir with much respect Your very humble & obt. Servant,

DAVID S. FRANKS

RC (MHi); without date, but certainly written after 9 July 1785 when Lafayette departed from Paris on his tour of Germany (Gottschalk, *Lafayette, 1783-89*, p. 178-81). The tentative date of 2 Sep. has been assigned on the ground that TJ, as shown by his Account Book of that date, "lent Colo. Franks 200f," which was half the amount requested by Franks to save him from confinement. Since Franks' situation evidently was desperate, TJ must have responded immediately with the loan, perhaps on the same day, as was the case on 17 June when he had refused an earlier appeal. RC bears on its face the date "[June 1785]" but this was evidently a late 19th-century conjectural date.

From Chastellux

à Paris le 3 7bre. 1785

Vous m'avés charmé, monsieur, en me témoignant d'une maniere si aimable que la lecture de mon journal vous avoit interessé. Je vous avouerai que ce n'étoit pas sans une sorte d'inquietude que j'attendois le jugement que vous en auriés porté, car c'est à mon ouvrage qu'il faudroit appliquer ce que vous dittes de votre personne. Permettés moi de vous observer à cette occasion qu'il est à desirer que dans les affaires politiques que vous avés à traitter, vous sachiés mieux parvenir à votre but que dans celles dont votre modestie seule est l'objet. En effet on ne peut pas plus mal reussir que vous l'avés fait en voulant diminuer l'opinion que j'ai concue de vous en amerique; et vous meriteriés que pour preuve justificative de mes assertions, je fisse imprimer la lettre pleine de graces et de sentiment que vous venés de m'ecrire. Ne me disputés donc plus, monsieur, une opinion sur laquelle je m'obstine de plus en plus, et permettés moi au contraire de me prévaloir de ce que je peux prouver à mes compatriotes pour concilier leur confiance sur les objets qu'ils ne pourront pas approfondir. Mais est-il bien possible que vous ayés trouvé aussi peu de fautes à corriger dans mon manuscript? Me voila tout à fait encouragé et certainement mes deux journaux parroitront dans le cours de l'hiver, ainsi que ma lettre au docteur Madisson. Ce sera avec grand plaisir que j'absoudrai les virginiens du peché que je leur ai reproché, en les taxant d'etre attachés à leurs interets. Voiés ce qui m'avoit induit en erreur: dans tous les marchés que nos commissaires ont eu à faire avec les virginiens, ils ont trouvé plus de cupidité et moins de bonne foi que dans les provinces de l'est, mais ils n'ont pas eu affaire à des proprietaires, ou des gens qui puissent representer le caractere national. Sans doute ceux qui ont traitté avec eux etoient de ces hommes qui courent après toutes les entreprises et qui regardent comme leur patrie tous les lieux ou il y a de l'argent à gagner. Depuis que j'ai eu l'honneur de vous voir, j'ai recu le livre de

Mr. Ramsay, avec une lettre de lui et une autre de Mr. de Marbois, le tout dans un paquet contresigné *Vergennes*. Je vais employer mes premiers momens de loisir à lire cet ouvrage et j'aurai l'honneur d'en causer avec vous dès que vous serés debarrassé de vos dépeches. Si votre matinée etoit libre lundi prochain, voudriés vous aller voir les tableaux du palais royal? Je serai absolument à vos ordres et il suffira que vous me fassiés dire dans la journée de demain à quelle heure je devrois vous aller prendre chés vous.

Je desire ardemment, monsieur, me dedommager de ce que des circonstances malheureuses m'ont fait perdre depuis votre arrivée icy et je n'aurai jamais assés d'occasions de vous entretenir du sincère et inviolable attachement avec lequel j'ai l'honneur d'être, Monsieur, votre tres humble et tres obeissant serviteur,

LE MIS. DE CHASTELLUX

RC (MoSHi).

To Abigail Adams

DEAR MADAM   Paris Sep. 4. 1785.

I was honoured with your letter of Aug. 21. by Mr. Smith who arrived here on the 29th. I am sorry you did not repeat the commission you had favoured me with by Mr. Short as the present would have been an excellent opportunity of sending the articles you wished for. As Mr. Short's return may yet be delayed, will you be so good as to write me by post what articles you desired, lest I should not otherwise know in time to send them by either of the Mr. Smiths. The French packet brought me letters from Mr. Jay and Dr. Ramsay only. They were dated July 13. They do not mention the arrival of your son. Dr. Ramsay's letter was on a particular subject, and Mr. Jay's letter was official. He may have arrived therefore, tho these letters do not mention it. However as he did not sail till June, and Westernly winds prevail in the summer I think the 13th. of July was too early to expect him to have arrived. I will certainly transmit you information of his arrival the moment I know it.

We have little new and interesting here. The Queen has determined to wear none but French gauzes hereafter. How many English looms will this put down? You will have seen the affair of the Cardinal de Rohan so well detailed in the Leyden gazette that I need add nothing on that head. The Cardinal is still in the

Bastille. It is certain that the Queen has been compromitted with-out the smallest authority from her: and the probability is that the Cardinal has been duped into it by his mistress Madme. de la Motte. There results from this two consequences not to his honour, that he is a debauchee, and a booby. The Abbés are well. They have been kept in town this summer by the affairs of the Abbé Mably. I have at length procured a house in a situation much more pleasing to me than my present. It is at the grille des champs Elysees, but within the city. It suits me in every circumstance but the price, being dearer than the one I am now in. It has a clever garden to it. I will pray you to present my best respects to Miss Adams and to be assured of the respect & esteem with which I have the honour to be Dear Madam Your most obedient & most humble servt.,   TH: JEFFERSON

RC (MHi: AMT). PrC (DLC).

To John Adams

DEAR SIR   Paris Sep. 4. 1785.

On receipt of your favors of Aug. 18. and 23. I conferred with Mr. Barclay on the measures necessary to be taken to set our treaty with the pyratical states into motion through his agency. Supposing that we should begin with the emperor of Marocco, a letter to the emperor and instructions to Mr. Barclay seemed neces-sary. I have therefore sketched such outlines for these as appear to me to be proper. You will be so good, as to detract, add to, or alter them as you please, to return such as you approve under your signature, to which I will add mine. A person understanding Eng-lish, French and Italian, and at the same time meriting confidence, was not to be met with here. Colo. Franks understanding the two first languages perfectly, and a little Spanish instead of Italian, occurred to Mr. Barclay as the fittest person he could employ for a Secretary. We think his allowance (exclusive of his travelling expences and his board which will be paid by Mr. Barclay in com-mon with his own) should be between 100 and 150 guineas a year. Fix it where you please between these limits. What is said in the instructions to Mr. Barclay as to his own allowance was pro-posed by himself. My idea as to the partition of the whole sum to which we are limited (80,000 D.) was that one half of it should be kept in reserve for the Algerines. They certainly possess more

[473]

than half of the whole power of the Pyratical states. I thought then that Marocco might claim the half of the remainder, that is to say one fourth[1] of the whole. For this reason in the instructions[2] I propose 20,000 D. as the limits of the expences[2] of the Marocco treaty. Be so good as to think of it, and to make it what you please. I should be more disposed to enlarge than abridge it on account of their neighborhood to our Atlantic trade. I did not think that these papers should be trusted through the post office, and therefore, as Colo. Franks is engaged in the business, he comes with them. Passing by the diligence the whole expence will not exceed 12 or 14 guineas. I suppose we are bound to avail ourselves of the co-operation of France. I will join you therefore in any letter you think proper to write to the Count de Vergennes. Would you think it expedient to write to Mr. Carmichael to interest the interposition of the Spanish court? I will join you in any thing of this kind you will originate. In short be so good as to supply whatever you may think necessary. With respect to the money Mr. Jay's information to you was that it was to be drawn from Holland. It will rest therefore with you to avail Mr. Barclay of that fund either by your draughts, or by a letter of credit to the bankers in his favour to the necessary amount. I imagine the Dutch Consul at Marocco may be rendered an useful character in the remittances of money to Mr. Barclay while at Marocco.

You were apprised, by a letter from Mr. Short, of the delay which had arisen in the execution of the treaty with Prussia. I wrote a separate letter of which I inclose you a copy, hoping it would meet one from you and set them again into motion. I have the honour to be with the highest respect Dear Sir Your most obedient & most humble servt.,   TH: JEFFERSON

RC (MHi: AMT); endorsed. PrC (DLC). Tr (DNA: PCC, No. 86); in David Humphreys' hand, with one alteration in TJ's hand. Entry in SJPL reads: "Adams J. Barbary treaties. Barbary. Franks." Enclosures: TJ's "Heads for a letter to the Emperor of Marocco," "Heads of instructions," and "Heads of enquiry" for Thomas Barclay (see Commissioners to Barclay and Lamb, 11 Oct. 1785—Documents III [1], II, and IV, respectively, and notes there); and a copy of TJ to Dumas and Short, 1 Sep. 1785.

Barclay also sent Adams a letter, dated 5 Sep., by Franks, in accordance with TJ's desire that he "add any thing that occurs relative to the funds neces-

sary to accomplish the object"; gives his opinion that "Twenty thousand livres laid out in Trinkets may be quite sufficient for the present and that promises for the Remainder being deliver'd with the Treaty signed by yourself and Mr. Jefferson will answer all our purposes"; he will make an accounting of all money paid out; there will be three persons, himself, Franks, and a domestic; they will need four horses or mules and a light carriage, if one can be procured without delay; has written Carmichael about his arrival; supposes Adams will think it necessary to give him a credit on Amsterdam (RC, MHi: AMT).

[1] This word in Tr first read "half,"

in Humphreys' hand, but was corrected by TJ to "fourth."

2 This and the preceding two words are not in Tr.

To John Adams

DEAR SIR   Paris Sep. 4. 1785.

Mr. Mazzei, during the war was employed by the state of Virginia to procure them loans of money in Europe. He thinks that in allowing him for his expences they have allowed less than they actually were. You knew him in Paris, and knew of the journies which he made. I would thank you for the best guess you can make of what his expences may have been, according to the stile in which you observed him to live. My object is to have justice done him, if it has not been done, being assured that if the state has failed in this point, it has been from a want of evidence and that they will rectify their error if they find they have committed one. I am with the highest esteem Dr. Sir Your friend & servant,

TH: JEFFERSON

RC (MHi: AMT); endorsed in part in Adams' hand: "ansd. 11. [Sep.] 1785." PrC (DLC); endorsed by TJ.

The energetic Mazzei had already explained to Adams that his employment BY THE STATE OF VIRGINIA had resulted in his having to mortgage his effects to European creditors chiefly "to preserve my honor in case of death" and that he had "come over to give them personal satisfaction in regard to my conduct toward them." He believed that he had suffered more than others by reason of inflation, and added: "From the conversations I had with the Governor who employed me, I understood that I should be allowed 1000 Louis d'ors per annum for my expenditures. Having never received remittances from the state while in Europe, I was obliged to contract large debts, besides having sold in a hurry and consequently to a great disadvantage, two small estates I had in Tuscany. I was obliged to live in Europe in a manner becoming a public Agent, to save the credit of the state, and to facilitate the execution of the business entrusted to me; likewise to undertake many expensive journeys, to entertain and . . . to import newspapers at a considerable expense (particularly from Great Britain) for the purpose of confuting the falsities spread to our disadvantage by the Enemy" (Mazzei to Adams, 10 Aug. 1785; MHi: AMT). When Adams replied to this, Mazzei plunged into a discussion of politics and trade, praised the Massachusetts Navigation Act, agreed with Adams that Congress should have full and exclusive power to regulate trade, and said that he was then engaged in writing something that Marmontel would translate in order to refute the errors being published about America. He also asked for a copy of the preamble to the Virginia Constitution of 1776 since he was writing a sketch of events between the suspension of the old and the institution of new government. "I can get no assistance from any one of our Virginia Gentlemen in Paris," he added. "Mr. Jefferson's memory is not one of the best, and all his papers are in Virginia" (Mazzei to Adams, 5 Sep. 1785; MHi: AMT). When Adams replied to TJ's request on 11 Sep., Mazzei thanked him and sent him a copy of his essay on sumptuary laws read before the "Virginia Constitutional Society" which he had founded in 1784 because of his firm opinion "that Freedom cannot long subsist in any Country, unless the generality of the People are sensible of its blessings, and tolerably well acquainted with the principles on which alone it can be supported." He also enclosed with this an eight-page printed account of the Society with a statement of its purpose, members, and proceedings, and concluded this formidable budget of political discussion with the remark that he "would take it as a particular favor if you would with the whole power of your eloquence express to your most worthy Lady the high esteem, respect, and veneration which from your knowledge of me you can easily conceive I must entertain of her, after having been informed by our noble friend Mr. Jefferson of her charming, wonderful, and truly uncommon merit" (Mazzei to Adams, 27 Sep. 1785; MHi: AMT).

To John Adams

DEAR SIR   Paris Sep. 4. 1785.

Since writing my letter of this morning I have seen Mr. Grand and had a conversation with him on the subject of the interest due here. He is pressed on that subject. By a letter he received not long since from the Commissioners of the treasury it seems their intention that he should pay this interest out of the money in Holland, yet they omitted to give him any authority to ask for any of that money. I thought it possible they might have written to you on the subject and told him I would take the liberty of asking whether you had been desired to do any thing. It is a little unfortunate that our credit should be losing ground for default of paiment while money is understood to be lying dead, and sufficient for that purpose. The Commissioners themselves make this reflection in their letter. If you can give us any information on this subject I will thank you. I am with much esteem Dr. Sir Your friend & servt.,

TH: JEFFERSON

RC (MHi: AMT); endorsed in part: "ansd. 11. [Sep.] 1785."

On the SUBJECT OF THE INTEREST DUE HERE, Samuel Osgood and Walter Livingston, commissioners of the treasury, wrote to Ferdinand Grand on 30 Aug. 1785 enclosing Robert Morris' draft payable to them for "four hundred thousand Livres Tournois, dated 30th June 1785, and payable on the first day of November next." The commissioners directed Grand to pay this "amount into the Royal Treasury of France, on account of the Interest due on the Ten Million Loan" from Holland that was guaranteed by France (Tr in DLC: TJ Papers, 14: 2243-4). In this letter the commissioners also referred to theirs to Grand of 18 May 1785, which was the one doubtless that Grand had received NOT LONG SINCE and which notified Grand of their having made effectual arrangements for the interest that would become due on the Holland loan on 5 Nov. 1785.

From John Adams

DEAR SIR   Grosvenor Square Westminster Septr. 4. 1785

I have received three Letters of the Tenor and Date of the within. I cannot find in any Gazetteer or geographical Dictionary any Such Place as Roscoff, and I can make nothing of the Story. I hope you have more Skill in Divination.

I have no Letters from Congress, nor any Answer from the Ministry.

Pray what are the Sentiments in France upon the American Acts of Navigation? And what has been the Success of the French Whale Fishery? How many Ships have they sent out this Year? The Britons have introduced into theirs a Spirit of Gambling, by giving a Bounty of 500£ to the Ship which has the greatest Success; 400£ to the next. This will make many Adventurers and give a temporary Activity to the Business: But I rely upon it both the French and English Essays will fall through. My Reason for thinking so is, because the Business in itself is not profitable, and, excepting the four[1] Vessells which may obtain the Bounties, the others upon an Avarage will be loosers. I know that my Countrymen in the best Times, with all their frugality, with all their Skill, and with their particular manner of conducting the Business could but barely live, and the Fishery was valuable to Us, only as a Remittance. The English are Sacrificing the Bread of thousands of their best Manufacturers to the interested Schemes of a very few Individuals and to a narrow Prejudice and a little Jealousy: but I dont believe the Delusion will be durable. Time will Shew both them and the French, that it is better to buy our Oil and Candles and Fins, and pay for them in Buttons and Ribbons. If they dont discover their error, We will lay on Duties upon Buttons and Ribbons, equal to the Alien Duties, and grant them out again in Bounties to our Whalemen.

We must not, my Friend, be the Bubbles of our own Liberal Sentiments. If We cannot obtain reciprocal Liberality, We must adopt reciprocal Prohibitions, Exclusions, Monopolies, and Imposts. Our offers have been fair, more than fair. If they are rejected we must not be the Dupes.

With great Esteem, dear Sir, yours,   JOHN ADAMS

RC (DLC). FC (MHi: AMT). Recorded in SJL as received 11 Sep. 1785. Enclosure: Lister Asquith to Adams, Roscoff, 19 Aug. 1785 (RC in DLC: endorsed by TJ), the first of a long series of documents that came to TJ concerning the case of the *William and Catherine*, an American-owned vessel which claimed to have put in in distress at the Ile de Batz just off Roscoff, northeast of Brest, but which the farmers-general prosecuted on a charge of attempting an illegal entry with a cargo of tobacco. The case came immediately to the attention of Vergennes. Ségur, minister of war, wrote him that he had just received a letter from an officer commanding a detachment of thirty soldiers at Roscoff informing him that employees of the farm had seized the *William and Catherine*. Ségur also sent extracts of the officer's letter to Castries and Calonne. Shortly afterwards Castries informed Vergennes that he had received several representations on the subject (Ségur to Vergennes, 23 Aug.; Castries to Vergennes, 18 Sep. 1785; Arch. Aff. Etr., Corr. Pol., E.-U., xxx; Tr in DLC) .

For TJ's general statement of the case of the *William and Catherine*, see his letter to Vergennes, 14 Nov. 1785 and its enclosure, and TJ's report to Jay, 8 July 1786 (printed in *Dipl. Corr., 1783-1789*, I, 769-71, but with the erroneous date 8 Apr. 1786).

¹ This word is not in FC.

From Lafayette

MY DEAR SIR   Vienna September the 4th. 1785

This letter will be delivered By a private Courier of Mis. de Noailles who Has Been in My family, and who, I am sure, will take proper Care of my Dispatches. Since I Had the pleasure to see you, I have Been at the prussian Court, and the prussian Camps with which I was much pleased. And Now am at Vienna, with an intention soon to Return to Potsdam where there will Be great deal of Maneuvring. The kind Reception I met with in Every part of my journey Has given me the Means to Hear, and to speak much, on the affairs of America. I find the Misrepresentations of Great Britain Have not Been fruitless. The strength of the Union, the powers of Congress, the dispositions of the people, and the principles of trade are points upon which I Have Had Many opportunities to give the lye to false assertions of News papers, and to set to Rights the false ideas of Misinformed people. It is Useless to observe I wish the Good Measures Now in Contemplation may Be soon executed. But, in the mean while, I more than Ever wish we may, in the News papers, Counteract the Uncandid Accounts that are sometimes given.

On the first day I saw the King of prussia, He spoke with me on the present situation of American affairs. The Mquis. de Luchesiny¹ his friend paid me a visit in the after noon, wherein I introduced the subject of the treaty of Commerce between His prussian Majesty and the United States. Since which, the King Has sometimes at dinner put His questions to me, on the Resources, the Union, and the future existence of America and I do not think they would Have Been so properly Answered By the Duke of York, and Lord Cornwallis who were two of the guests. I fancy I may Have still More particular opportunities to know His opinions, and to introduce my ideas.

On the day before Yesterday I arrived at Vienna, and last morning waited on the Emperor. The Misrepresentations about America, the good Measures that Had Been, and were to Be taken, the Necessity to improve this moment, and come in early into liberal treaties, that would oppen the door to American importations in order to pay for Austrian goods, such were the points to which I directed, and some times forced the Conversation. It was a great object with Him to know if Americans would Be their own Carriers. The same day, in the Evening, prince Kaunitz their prime Minister Very willingly came in the subject of American trade which I Brought about in a private Conference. That carrying trade was again the topic. I advised Him to send Consuls, to settle partnerships in America, as no trade Could last But was Mixed and Reciprocal. I detailled out the objects of American Exportations, as I Had done to the Emperor. Why then said Prince Kaunitz don't they Make advances to us. I answered advances Had been made, and more in my opinion than were Necessary, But they Had not Been listened to in that time, and for the present that I Had Heard some thing, as if an Answer was expected from the Emperor. He said the demand Had Been an indirect one. At last I Concluded the Conversation with telling of him, that I knew nothing of particulars, but Had Heard Congress, the people, and their Ministers in Europe Express a desire to be upon a very friendly footing with the Emperor, that as a friend, I advised him to lose no time, and He knew very well no treaty Could go on without Reciprocity. I therefore thought the first Measure was to oppen the italian ports to the salt fish of America. From our Conversation I am apt to think He may order His Ambassadors to talk with you or Mr. Adams, and I wished to write You what Had past Between us, wherein I spoke as a man, who Being ignorant of particulars, Could only offer an Humble advice to His Imperial Majesty. But upon the whole I don't think you will Have a very great trade this Way.

As I think these Hints may be agreable to our friend Mr. adams, I beg you Will send the letter by a safe Hand as opportunities often offer. There is such a distance between Congress and Myself that I will leave to You to trouble them with the News of my German tour.

Adieu, My dear Sir, my Compliments to Humphreys, Mr. Short, and our other friends in Paris. Most respectfully and affectionately Yours,   LAFAYETTE

RC (DNA: PCC, No. 156). Tr (DNA: PCC, No. 87, I); in Humphreys' hand; docketed: "Referred 28th. March 1786. Mr. Jefferson's Letter of 11 Octr. 1785"; in TJ's hand, beneath docketing: "No. 11." Tr (DNA: PCC,

No. 107, 1). Tr (MHi: AMT); in Humphreys' hand; endorsed by Adams. Recorded in SJL as received 13 Sep. 1785. A copy was sent to John Jay with TJ's letter of 11 Oct. 1785.

¹ All three Tr read incorrectly:

"Tuchesiny"; the Marquis de Lucchesini, a close friend of Frederick the Great, "remembered until long afterward—and none too pleasantly—the French aristocrat's enthusiasms for the land of liberty" (Gottschalk, *Lafayette, 1783-89*, p. 184).

From Froullé

MONSIEUR   [Before 5 Sep. 1785]

Voici Laperçu à peu pres de ce que peut Couter L'Impression En Cicero gros euïl par chacque feuille Entre 30^{tt} à 33^{tt}; aussi je supose un volume de 25 feuilles tiréz à 2000 Exemplaires à 33^{tt} Dimpression formera la somme de   825^{tt}
4 Rames de Papier par feuilles feront
    100 Rames à 12^{tt} la rame   1200
la traduction à 24^{tt} la feuille   600
pour faux frais Dassemblage et paquetage   300
                                                                    ———
                                                                   2925^{tt}

En tirant à 3000 Exemplaires le 3e. mil
couteroit 27^{tt} La feuille, comprix papier et Impression.
Ainsi pour le 3e. mil   575
                                                                    ———
                                            Total   3500^{tt}

Voici ce que je presume du [prix?]. Les renseignemens que jai prix, ce que peut couter le susdit ouvrage si ne produit que 25 feuilles.

En me chargant des frais Dimpression, traduction, je payerez à Lauteur dans six mois¹ aprés L'impression . . . . 800^{tt}
    Plus 25 Exemplaires.
Si L'auteur veut acorder un ans de terme je donnere 900
Si au contraire L'auteur veut Etre de moitier, il sera charges de la traduction et de la moitier de L'impression, qui ce paye comptant. Je serez chargé de Lautre moitier de Limpression et fourniture du Papier comme aussi de Lassemblage, et à mesure que la vente sen fera, de mois en mois je remetere la moitier de ce qui sera vendu au Comptant.

RC (DLC); without date, signature, or indication of addressee; endorsed: "Ramsay ⟨*Jacob*⟩ David. Frouillé"; a few calculations in TJ's hand at foot of page. Froullé is listed in Gournay,

Tableau General du Commerce, p. 614, as "Ancienne Librairie . . . quai des Augustins."

¹ This word is in TJ's hand.

To Froullé

5me. Septembre. 1785.

J'ai vu le Marquis de Chastellux, Monsieur, et nous avons consulté sur l'affaire de l'histoire de Monsr. Reed. Il a eu la bonté de noter toutes les pièces justificatives qu'il croit qu'il seroit mieux de supprimer comme peu interessans aux etrangers. Mais comme on peut bien se tromper sur la nombre des feuilles, et que ce feroit tort ou à l'auteur ou à l'Imprimeur, nous croyons qu'il seroit plus juste et pour l'un et pour l'autre que l'auteur recevroit dans un an après l'impression trente six francs pour chaque feuille imprimée comme vous avez proposé. C'est sur le pied de 900^{tt} pour 25 feuilles. J'ai l'honneur de vous faire cette proposition-la et en l'acceptant de votre part, c'est une affaire finie et vous prendrez tout aussitot qu'il vous plaira vos arrangements pour la traduction et l'imprimerie.

TH: JEFFERSON

Dft (ViWC); without indication of addressee. Not recorded in sjl. On the verso are the following calculations in TJ's hand:
"The calculations for 2000 copies of 25 sheets each make the disbursements of the Undertaker as follows.

	tt	
to the translator for every sheet	24	600
to the Author	36	900
for paper, printing, and other charges	96	2400
		156x25=3900"

It is very likely that in referring to L'HISTOIRE DE MONSR. REED TJ purposely employed a false name in order to protect David Ramsay.

To David Hartley

DEAR SIR   Paris Sep. 5. 1785.

Your favour of Apr. 15, happened to be put into my hands at the same time with a large parcel of letters from America, which contained a variety of intelligence. It was then put where I usually place my unanswered letters, and I from time to time put off acknoleging the receipt of it till I should be able to furnish you American intelligence worth communicating. A favorable opportunity, by a courier, of writing to you occurring this morning, what has been my astonishment and chagrin on reading your letter again to find there was a case in it which required an immediate answer, but which, by the variety of matters which happened to be presented to my mind at the same time, had utterly escaped my recollection. I pray you to be assured that nothing but this slip of memory would have prevented my immediate answer, and no other circumstance would have prevented it's making such an impression on my mind as that it could not have escaped. I hope you will therefore obliterate the imputations of want of respect, which under actual appearances must have arisen in your mind, but which would refer to an untrue cause the occasion of my silence. I am not sufficiently acquainted with the proceedings of the New York assembly to say with certainty in what predicament the lands of Mr. Upton may stand. But on conferring with Colo. Humphries, who being from the neighboring state was more in the way of knowing what passed in New York, he thinks that the descriptions in their confiscation laws were such as not to include a case of this nature. The first thing to be done by Mr. Upton is to state his case to some intelligent lawyer of the country, that he may know with certainty whether they be confiscated, or not; and if not confiscated, to know what measures are necessary for completing and securing his grant. But if confiscated, there is then no other tribunal of redress but their general assembly. If he is unacquainted there, I would advise him to apply to Colo. Hamilton (who was Aid to Genl. Washington) and is now very eminent at the bar, and much to be relied on. Your letter in his favor to Mr. Jay will also procure him the benefit of his counsel.

With respect to America I will rather give you a general view of it's situation, than merely relate recent events. The impost is still unpassed by the two states of New York and Rhodeisland; for the manner in which the latter has passed it does not appear to me to answer the principal object, of establishing a fund, which, by being subject to Congress alone, may give such credit to the certificates of public debt as will make them negotiable. This matter then is still suspended.

Congress have lately purchased the Indian right to nearly the whole of the land lying in the new state bounded by lake Erie, Pennsylvania and the Ohio. The Northwestern corner alone is reserved to the Delawares and Wiandots. I expect a purchase is also concluded with other tribes for a considerable proportion of the state next to this on the North side of the Ohio. They have passed an ordinance establishing a land office, considerably improved I think on the plan of which I had the honour of giving you a copy. The lands are to be offered for sale to the highest bidder. For this purpose portions of them are to be proposed in each state, that each may have the means of purchase carried equally to their doors, and that the purchasers may be a proper mixture of the citizens from all the different states. But such lots as cannot be sold for a dollar an acre are not to be parted with. They will receive as money the certificates of public debt. I flatter myself that this arrangement will very soon absorb the whole of these certificates, and thus rid us of our domestic debt, which is four fifths of our whole debt. Our foreign debt will be then a bagatelle.

I think it probable that Vermont will be made independant, as I am told the state of New York is likely to agree to it. Le Maine will probably in time be also permitted to separate from Massachusetts. As yet they only begin to think of it. Whenever the people of Kentuckey shall have agreed among themselves, my friends write me word that Virginia will consent to their separation. They will constitute the new state on the South side of Ohio, joining Virginia. North-Carolina, by an act of their assembly, ceded to Congress all their lands Westward of the Alleghaney. The people inhabiting that territory thereon declared themselves independant, called their state by the name of Franklin, and sollicited Congress to be received into the Union. But before Congress met, N. Carolina (for what reasons I could never learn) resumed their cession. The people however persist; Congress recommend to the state to desist from their opposition, and I have no doubt they will do it. It will therefore result from the act of Congress laying off the Western country into new states, that these states will come into the union in the manner therein provided, and without any disputes as to their boundaries.

I am told that some hostile transaction by our people at the Natchez against the Spaniards has taken place. If it be fact Congress will certainly not protect them, but leave them to be chastised by the Spaniards, saving the right to the territory. A Spanish minister being now with Congress and both parties interested in keeping the peace I think, if such an event has happened, it will be easily arranged.

I told you when here of the propositions made by Congress to the states to be authorized to make certain regulations in their commerce; and that from the disposition to strengthen the hands of Congress, which was then growing fast, I thought they would consent to it. Most of them did so, and I suppose all of them would have done it, if they have not actually done it, but that events proved a much more extensive power would be requisite. Congress have therefore desired to be invested with the whole regulation of their trade and forever: and to prevent all temptations to abuse and all fears of it, they propose that whatever monies shall be levied on the commerce either for the purpose of revenue or by way of forfeitures or penalty, shall go directly into the coffers of the state wherein it is levied without being touched by Congress. From the present temper of the states and the conviction which your country has carried home to their minds that there is no other method of defeating the greedy attempts of other countries to trade with them on unequal terms, I think they will add an article for this purpose to their confederation. But the present powers of Congress over the commerce of the states under the Confederation seems not at all understood by your ministry. They say that body has no power to enter into a treaty of commerce; why then make one? This is a mistake. By the 6th. art. of the confederation the states renounce individually all power to make any treaty of whatever nature with a foreign nation. By the 9th. article they give the power of making treaties wholly to congress, with two reservations only. 1. That no treaty of commerce shall be made which shall restrain the legislatures from making foreigners pay the same imposts with their own people: nor 2. from prohibiting the exportation or importation of any species of merchandize which they might think proper. Were any treaty to be made which should violate either of these two reservations, it would be so far void. In the treaties therefore made with France, Holland &c. this has been cautiously avoided.[1] But are these treaties of no advantage to those nations? Besides the advantages expressly given by them, there results another of great value. The commerce of those nations with the U.S. is thereby under the protection of the Congress, and no particular state, acting by fits and starts, can harrass the trade of France, Holland &c. by such measures as several of them have practised against England by loading her merchandize with partial imposts, refusing admittance to them altogether, excluding her merchants &c. &c. For you will observe that tho by the 2d. reservation beforementioned they can prohibit the importation of any *species* of merchandize, as for instance tho' they may prohibit the importation of wines in general, yet they cannot prohibit that of *French* wines in particular. Another advantage is that the nations having treaties with Congress can and do provide in such treaties for the admission of their Consuls, a kind of officer very necessary for the regulation and protection of commerce. You know that a Consul is the creature of a treaty. No nation, without an agreement, can place an officer in another country with any powers or jurisdiction whatever. But as the states have renounced the separate power of making treaties with foreign nations, they cannot separately receive a Consul: and as Congress have by the Confederation no immediate jurisdiction over commerce, as they have only[2] a power of bringing that jurisdiction into existence by entering into a treaty; till such treaty be entered into Congress themselves cannot receive a Consul. Till a treaty then there exists no power in any part of our government, federal or particular, to admit a Consul among us: and if it be true as the papers say that you have lately sent one over, he cannot be admitted by any power in existence to an exercise of any function. Nothing less than a new article to be agreed to by all the states would enable Congress or the particular states to receive him. You must not be surprised then if he be not received.

I think I have by this time tired you with American politics and will therefore only add assurances of the sincere regard & esteem with which I have the honour to be Dr. Sir your most obedient humble servt.,   TH: JEFFERSON

PrC (DLC). Entry in SJPL reads: "Hartley David. American affairs. New states. England. Commerce."

The NEW STATE BOUNDED BY LAKE ERIE, &c. is indicated on the Jefferson-Hartley map as state number 8, and the STATE NEXT TO THIS as number 7 (see Vol. 6: 593). THE PLAN of a land office that TJ had given to Hartley was a copy of the broadside printing of TJ's report of 30 Apr. 1784 (Vol. 7: 140-8).

[1] TJ erred by putting a question mark at the end of this sentence.
[2] TJ deleted the following at this point: "an indirect."

Lease for the Hôtel de Langeac

[5 Sep. 1785]

Par devant Les Conseillers du Roy, Notaires au Chatelet de Paris, Soussignés

Fut Present

Haut et Puissant Seigneur Auguste Louis Joseph fidele Amand de Lespinasse Langeac, Chevalier Comte de Langeac, Colonel d'Infanterie, Chevalier de l'ordre Royal et militaire de St. Louis, le Gouverneur pour le Roy des villes de Guerande, Le Croisic et St. Nazaire En Bretagne, de Celle de Rüe en Picardie, et en Survivance de Celle du Puy en Velay, et ancien Capitaine des gardes de la porte de Monsieur, frère du Roy, Seigneur du Comté d'Arlet et autres Lieux, demeurant à Paris en son hotel à la grille de Chaillot, paroisse St. Philippe du Roule,

Lequel a fait Bail et donné à loyer pour trois années entières et consecutives qui commenceront à compter du Jour auquel ledit Seigneur Comte de Langeac Rendra l'hotel cy après vuide et en état d'etre occupé et en Remettra les Clefs,[1] et à compter de l'expiration desdites trois années pour tout le tems qu'il plaira au preneur cy après nommé, sans aucune augmentation au prix du loyer cy après convenu, jusqu'à concurrence de Neuf années, en avertissant Seulement le bailleur Six mois d'avance, à sa sortie de l'hotel Cy après; sans que la Faculté de donner congé appartienne respectivement audit Sieur Bailleur qui y renonce De condition expresse et essentielle du présent Bail et à ledit Sieur Bailleur promis faire jouir

À Son Excellence Thomas Jefferson, Ministre plenipotentiaire des etats unis d'amérique à la Cour de France, demeurant à Paris, Cul de sac Taitbout, paroisse St. Eustache, à Ce présent et acceptant preneur audit titre de loyer pour le dit tems et de la manière Cy devant Convenue

Un Hotel, Jardin et dependances Situés à la Grille de Chaillot et faisant l'encoignure de la Rue Neuve de Berry, appartenant audit Sieur Bailleur qui l'occupe actuellement, ainsi que le dit Hotel et dépendances se poursuivent et comportent, et dont il n'a été fait plus ample description à la Requisition dudit Sieur preneur qui a declaré les connaitre parfaitement pour les avoir vus et Visités.

Pour par ledit Sieur Preneur jouir dudit Hotel et de ses dependances audit titre de loyer pendant ledit tems et de la maniere cydevant convenue.

Le présent Bail est fait à la Charge par ledit Sieur preneur qui le promet et s'y oblige, de garnir lesdits Hotel et dépendances, et les tenir garnis pendant la durée du présent Bail de Meubles et effets Suffisant pour sûreté des loyers, l'entretenir et rendre en fin du présent Bail[2] en bon etat de toutes reparations locatives et conformes à l'etat double qui sera incessamment fait à frais communs desdits Hotel et dependances, de souffrir les grosses réparations qui pourroient survenir pendant la durée du présent Bail, de Payer la taxe des pauvres, et d'acquitter toutes[3] les charges de Ville et de police, de ne pouvoir ceder et transporter son droit au présent Bail que du Consentement exprès et par ecrit dudit Sieur Bailleur auquel la grosse des présentes sera fournie aux frais dudit Sieur Preneur, toutes lesquelles charges, Clauses et Conditions seront executées, sans aucune diminution du prix Cy après Stipulé et sans aucuns dommages et Interêts ni recours quelconques.

Et En outre moyennant la Somme de Trois Mille Cinq Cents livres de loyer annuel que ledit Sieur Preneur s'oblige à Payer audit Sieur Bailleur en sa demeure à Paris ou au porteur, de la grosse des présentes, aux quatre termes de l'an ordinaires et accoutumés, dont le premier echerra et se fera pour portion de tems[4] au premier Janvier mil Sept cent quatre vingt six; Le Second Trois mois après et ensuite continuer de terme en terme jusqu'à l'expiration desdites trois années, et ensuite tant qu'il plaira audit Sieur preneur de conserver le dit Hotel et dépendances jusqu'à concurrence desdites neuf années.

Ledit Sieur Bailleur s'oblige à vuider ledit Hotel avant le premier octobre[5] prochain et à le livrer audit Sieur preneur en etat d'etre occupé.

Il s'oblige à tenir ledit Sieur Preneur Clos et couvert suivant l'Usage, il s'oblige aussi dans le cas où il viendrait à vendre ledit Hotel et dependances à charger l'acquereur de l'execution du présent Bail.

Enfin il renonce au droit des bourgeois de Paris, propriétaires de maisons en cette ville, lequel droit consiste à ne pouvoir par le propriétaire expulser le locataire pour occuper en personne.

Ledit Sieur Preneur s'oblige à payer audit Sieur Bailleur, aussitôt qu'il sera en jouissance dudit Hotel et dependances, la Somme de Mil Sept cent cinquante livres pour six mois d'avance du loyer, à imputer sur les six derniers mois[6] de jouissance, et ce payement ne derangera pas l'ordre de ceux cy devant fixés.

Et Pour l'execution des présentes les parties ont elu domicile en leurs demeures susdites aux quels lieux Nonobstant, Promettant obligeant Renonçant

Fait et Passé à Paris en la demeure susdite des Chacune des parties l'an mil Sept cent quatre vingt cinq le Cinquieme jour de Septembre, Et ont Signé ces présentes où Dix mots sont rayés comme nuls.[7]

LE CTE. DE LESPINASSE LANGEAC

TH: JEFFERSON   PERIER

DULION

[30 Mch. 1789]

Et le trente mars mil sept cent quatre vingt neuf sont comparus par devant les conseillers du Roy notaires au Chatelet de Paris

Soussignés, Ledit Seigneur Comte de Langeac, nommé qualiffié au Bail dont La minutte est cy contre,[8] demeurant actuellement à Paris rue Cassette, paroisse St. Sulpice, et Ladite Excellence Thomas Jefferson, nommé qualiffié audit Bail, demeurant à Paris rue Neuve de Berry, paroisse St. Phillippe du Roule.

Lequel Sieur Jefferson a dit que ne pouvant continuer à occuper sa maison à luy louée par le Bail dont la Minutte est Cy contre,[8] à Raison de trois mille Cinq Cens Livres de loyer Par année, il a Donné congé au Seigneur Comte de Langeac pour le premier avril prochain, conformement au droit qu'il avoit aux termes dudit Bail; que Cependant il a proposé audit Seigneur Comte de Langeac de Continuer Le Bail aux memes Conditions, sauf toutes fois La reduction du prix à la Somme de trois mille Livres.

Et par ledit Seigneur Comte de Langeac a été dit que desirant conserver Ledit Sieur Jefferson pour locataire dudit Hotel, il acceptoit La proposition faitte par ce dernier et consentoit que le prix dudit Bail fut fixé à la somme de trois Mille Livres par année au lieu de trois mille Cinq cent livres, somme portée audit Bail.

En consequence Lesdites Parties ont par Ces presentes Prorogé pour trois années entieres et consecutives qui commenceront Le premier avril prochain, la durée du Bail Cy Contre aux memes charges et conditions que celles y portées, et à raison seulement de la Somme de trois mille Livres de Loyer par chaque année au lieu de celle de trois mille Cinq Cent Livres, à laquelle etoit fixé par ledit Bail le loyer dudit Hotel.

En consequence Son Excellence Monsieur Jefferson promet et s'oblige de nouveau Executer et accomplir les Charges, clauses et conditions portées audit Bail, et payer La dite somme de trois mille Livres de loyer audit Seigneur Comte de Langeac en sa demeure ou au porteur aux quatre termes de l'an ordinaires et accoutumés dont le premier echeoira et se fera le premier juillet prochain et le second le premier octobre suivant et ainsy continuer de terme en terme jusqu'en fin desdites trois années.

Au moyen des présentes lesdites Parties consentent respectivement la nullité du Congé qui avoit ete donné par ledit Sieur Jefferson audit Seigneur Comte de Langeac, lequel Congé sera regardé comme non avenu.

Et pour L'execution des presentes Les Parties Elisant domicile à Paris En leur demeure susdite auxquels Lieux nonobstant promettant, obligeant, Renonçant. Fait et Passé à Paris En La

[488]

demeure desdites Parties Lesdits jour et an que dessus et ont Signé ces presentes où deux mots sont Rayes comme nuls.[9]

TH: JEFFERSON

LE CTE. DE LESPINASSE LANGEAC   LEFEBURE

MS (Archives Nationales, Paris; Minutier Central [des Notaires de la Seine], fonds XCVII); at head of text: "5 7bre. 1785 Bail de maison M. Le Cte. de Langeac a S. E. M. Jefferson"; signed by De Langeac, TJ, Perier, and Dulion, with several marginal insertions initialled by TJ, and with the initials of the other three; in the margin of the third and fourth pages is the text of the modification to the agreement dated 30 Mch. 1789, signed by De Langeac, TJ, Lefebure, and Peron. Tr (DLC: Short Papers); signed by Perier and Dulion; followed by the clause added 30 Mch. 1789, signed by Lefebure and Denis. The editors are indebted to M. Jacques Monicat, curator at the Archives Nationales, for verifying the signatures of the notaries.

The original of the lease (*minute*) is that deposited among the notarial archives in the Archives Nationales and made available to H. C. Rice, Jr., April 1950, through the courtesy of Maître Paillat, notary, successor to Perier and Lefebure. The certified copy (*expédition*) in the Short papers was furnished to TJ by the notary, Louis François Perier; another, presumably was furnished to De Langeac. The actual signing took place on 8 Sep., according to an entry in TJ's Account Book, and TJ moved into the Hôtel de Langeac on 17 Oct. 1785. The modification of the lease, executed before the notary J. B. Lefebure de Saint Maur, effected a reduction in the rental from 3500 to 3000 livres. This, however, was only the price stipulated in the official lease; the actual total as fixed by the present document and by private agreement be-

tween TJ and De Langeac on 5 Sep. 1785, was 7500 livres. This explains the fact that the amounts recorded in TJ's Account Book exceed the amount called for in the official lease by 4000 livres annually; e.g., on 3 Oct. 1785 TJ "paid le Comte de Langeac the last 6. months house rent 3750^{lt}" and thereafter paid in quarterly installments 1875 livres. By the prorogation of the lease of 30 Mch. 1789 the additional annual rental was reduced from 4000 to 3000 livres, thereby reducing the total from 7500 to 6000 livres (see following document).

[1] The passage "Jour auquel . . . les Clefs" was added in the margin in place of "premier   mil Sept cent quatre Vingt cinq," deleted.
[2] The passage "de Meubles et effets . . . du présent Bail" is not in Tr.
[3] The passage "d'acquitter toutes les charges" is not in Tr.
[4] The preceding four words are written in margin of MS.
[5] This word written in margin in place of "Janvier," deleted.
[6] Preceding ten words are not in Tr.
[7] Instead of the words "ces présentes . . . comme nuls," Tr reads: "la Minute des présentes demeurée a M. Perier L'un des notaires soussignés."
[8] Instead of preceding five words, Tr reads: "l'expédition précède."
[9] Instead of the words "ces présentes . . . comme nuls," Tr reads: "la Minute des présentes demeurée à Me. Lefebure de St. Maur Notaire, ladite Minute tant en marge et celle du Bail dont l'expédition est des autres parts."

Private Agreement for Lease of the Hôtel de Langeac

[5 Sep. 1785]

Entre les soussignés
Haut et Puissant Seigneur Auguste-Louis-Joseph-Fidel-Amand De Lespinasse Langeac, Chevalier Comte de Langeac, Colonel

d'Infanterie, Chevalier de l'Ordre royal et Militaire de St. Louis, Gouverneur pour le Roi des Villes de Guerande, Le Croisic et St. Nazaire en Bretagne, de celle de Ruë en Picardie, et en Survivance de celle du Puy en Vélay, et ancien Capitaine des Gardes de la porte de Monsieur, frère du Roi, Seigneur du Comté d'Arlet de d'autres Lieux, d'une part

Et Son Excellence Thomas Jefferson, Ministre plénipotentiaire des Etats Unis d'Amérique à la Cour de France, d'autre part

A été dit, convenu et arrêté ce qui suit

Ils declarent que si, par le bail fait à sa dite Excellence, devant Me. Périer et son confrère, Notaires à Paris, ce jourd'hui, des Hôtel, Jardin et dépendances appartenant audit Seigneur, Comte de Langeac, à la grille de Chaillot, le prix annuel du loyer n'a été porté qu'à Trois mille cinq cents Livres, cette Fixation n'a été déterminée que par des motifs particuliers qui ne doivent aucunement nuire aux conventions primitives arrêtées entr'eux, et qui subsistent Toujours, et que le prix réel dudit Loyer a été convenu entr'eux et demeuré Irrévocablement fixé par ces présentes à

Sept mille cinq cents livres,

au lieu des Trois mille cinq cents Livres stipulées au Bail auquel ils dérogent expressément à cet égard seulement, et qu'ils Confirment pour le surplus des Clauses et Conditions y insérées.

En conséquence sadite Excellence s'oblige de payer à M. le Comte de Langeac par forme de Supplément et addition au prix dudit bail Quatre Mille livres aux mêmes époques et de la même maniere que doivent être payées les Trois Mille cinq Cents livres stipulées audit bail; Ce qui composera Un loyer total de Sept Mille cinq cents livres par année; [desquelles Quatre mille livres elle s'oblige de payer aussitôt son entrée en Jouissance à M. Le Comte de Langeac, Deux mille livres pour raison des six mois qu'elle doit payer d'avance aux termes du bail susdatté, à imputer sur les six derniers mois de sa Jouissance; en sorte que lesdites deux mille livres réunies aux Dix Sept cent cinquante livres qu'elle payera Conformément audit bail, formeront une Somme totale de trois mille Sept cent cinquante livres.][1]

De sa part, Monsieur le Comte de Langeac consent que sadite Excellence, même après l'Expiration des Neuf années, pendant lesquelles Il lui est loisible de Jouir desdits hôtel et dépendances, aux Termes du bail susdaté, continuë d'en Jouir à titre de tacite reconduction, tant qu'Elle le Jugera à propos, sur le pied de Sept mille Cinq cents livres par année, qui seront payées aux Epoques et de la manière que les Loyers précédents l'auront été, et en accomplissant au surplus par elle toutes les autres Charges, Clauses et Conditions stipulées audit bail qui demeurera dans toute sa force Et Vertu comme s'il n'était pas expiré, et que M. le Comte de Langeac s'oblige même de renouveller à toutes requisitions.

Fait double à Paris le Cinq Septembre, Mil sept cent quatre vingt cinq

> approuvé l'ecriture cy dessus et des autres parts
> Le Ct. de Lespinasse Langeac
> approuvé l'ecriture cy-dessus et des autres parts[2]
> TH: JEFFERSON

[30 Mch. 1789]

Entre les soussignés

Mondit Seigneur Comte de Langeac

et Son Excellence Thomas Jefferson, tous deux nommés et qualiffiés au Sous Seing privé cidessus et des autres parts, a été dit, Convenu et arreté ce qui suit.

Savoir, que par acte passé devant Me. Lefebure de St. Maur et son Confrere, notaires à Paris, ce Jourdhuy, dont la minutte est en Suitte du bail enoncé au Sous seing privé ci dessus et des autres parts, ils ont prorogé volontairement la durée Dudit bail pour trois années qui Commenceront le premier avril prochain aux memes Conditions, mais que le prix dudit bail a été moderé à la somme de Trois mille Livres de Loyer par année au lieu de celle de trois mille Cinq Cent Livres, à quoi le loyer etait fixé par ledit premier bail.

Mais ils declarent que cette fixation à la somme de Trois Mille Livres n'a été determinée que par des motifs particuliers, et que le prix réel dudit loyer a été Convenu entr'eux et demeure irrevocablement fixé par ces présentes à la somme de Six Mille Livres, au lieu de trois mille livres Stipulées à ladite prorogation dudit bail à laquelle ils derogent expressement à cet egard seulement, et qu'ils confirment pour le surplus des clauses et Conditions y insérées, Se reportant pour le Surplus aux clauses et Conditions portées au Sous Seing privé des autres parts, et renouvelant par ces présentes Les obligations qu'ils ont Contractées l'un envers l'autre, tant par cedit sous seing privé que par ledit bail.

Fait double à Paris, Le trente mars mil sept Cent quatre vingt neuf.

Approuvé l'ecriture cy dessus et des autres parts

> LE CTE. DE LESPINASSE LANGEAC

MS (DLC: Short Papers); in a clerk's hand, approved and signed by De Langeac and TJ; with a marginal insertion signed by both; followed by the text of a modification to the agreement dated 30 Mch. 1789 which was approved and signed by De Langeac and endorsed by TJ: "Monsr. de Langeac. bail sous seing privée."

In DLC: TJ Papers, 232: 42075 there is an undated memorandum reading as follows: "Count de Langeac has 1150 toises of ground for which he paid 5. Louis the toise=5750."

¹ The text enclosed in square brackets (supplied) is written in margin.
² This approval in TJ's hand.

From John Paul Jones

SIR   L'Orient, September 5th, 1785.

I am just returned here from Brest, where I have passed several days. I have received your letter of the 29th. ult. with the copy of that written to you by the Marechal de Castries, the 26th, and I have reason to expect in consequence, that my affairs here will be finished as soon as the formalities of the bureau will permit. I shall obtain a roll of the Alliance, conformable to the pretensions of Puchilberg; which though perhaps not quite exact, may however answer all your purposes. I really do not believe that ever any claims will be made on you; for I never heard that any French subject had served on board that frigate except the captain, and I commanded the Alliance in person seven months. I am, Sir, &c.

N.B. I take the liberty to enclose a letter for M. Ledyard. It contains a small bill. If he is not at Paris, I request you to keep the letter till I come.

MS not found; text from Sherburne, *John Paul Jones*, p. 269. Recorded in SJL as received 10 Sep. 1785. The enclosed letter and bill for John Ledyard have not been identified.

From Lister Asquith

SIR   [ca. 6 Sep. 1785]

As an unfortunate affair has happened to us and being subjects to Baltimore in Maryland, has taken the Liberty to implore your protection and assistance as far as lies in your power.

Being bound from Baltimore to Liverpool with Flour and Tobacco and finding in Virginia that Tobacco would answer our Markets Better in Liverpool, discharged part of our Flour and one Hdd. of Tobacco in Hampton Roads, it not being very good, and before we got our Cargo ready was drove out to Sea by a Heavy gale of wind and drove off the Coast. Our sails being not in condition to stand the Coast, was obliged to bear away for Liverpool without any clearance but that one we had from Baltimore. We made the Lands End of England but could not fetch it. We then bore away for Scilly and came to an Anchor, but blowing so very hard was obliged to get up our Anchors and put to Sea to save our lives. We made the Land of France but did not know what Part it was and having not over 10 Gallons of Water, 4 or 5 lb. of Bread, and 2 or 3 lb. of Candles and no Fire Wood and our sails not being fit to trust to any longer, we took a Pilot, that carried into Pondus-vall. But finding a Captain of a Vessel there that informed us that as we was sharp we should not be able to lie there, we went out immediately and next morning the Pilot brought us to an Anchor in Isle de Bass roads. We went on Shore to Roscoff and Protested at the Admiralty office and reported in the Custom House.[1] The Custom House Officers then came on board and brought her into the Pier where they discharged her and let her lye dry at low Water by which part of her Plank is started from the Timbers and I believe one of her upper Timbers in the Waist is broke. They have confined us on board not having above one half the Pier to Walk and Centinels over us. Hope you will do your utmost for us as we are in a Strange p[lace] and are not accquainted with their Laws and not one of us ever have been in these Parts before. Yours &c.

The above is the Substance of 2 Letters to Dr. Franklin and 1 to Mr. Jefferson and the part below part of the other Letters to Mr. Barclay but as I had not time to take Coppys of every letter cannot answer for every word being the same as the Letters wrote.

On the 18th. we were sent with the Tobacco to Landivisiau where they stored the Tobacco and next day sent us to close confinement in St. Pauls de Leon Prison and having wrote to Mr. Jefferson one Letter and one to the Prime Minister of the Court of France by Capt. Antony De Ville on the 23rd. and left us that night and having heard from Mr. Barclay on the 24th. we wrote to Capt. De Ville if he was at Paris if not it was to be directed to Mr. Barclay and on the 26th. hearing nothing of De Ville wrote to Mr. Barclay that we expected he had run off with the Money we advanced him, and, having been told of some of the Captain

Generals Pleas for seizing us, answered them in the Letter to Capt. De Ville on the 24th, as he himself saw several Circumstances of the Affairs on board. And in that Letter to Mr. Barclay on the 26th. likewise mentioned that we suspected by not hearing from Mr. Barclay that our letters were intercepted. The Suppositions answered in the Letters that were sent were as follows.

The Steelyards that were on board belonged to the Vessel when she was bought as She was at that time a Bay Trader and consequently required such things.

The Candles he mentions were part of a Box of Candles that were put in an under Locker and being broke by several things giving way by the working of the Vessel so that not one part was one Inch long and consequently fit for nothing but greasing the Masts and was therefore put in the grease Cask.

The Blanket that had Tobacco in was put there to save the Tobacco from being damaged as the rest had been in bags which were cut up to repair the Sails &c., the Hogshead being broke in Baltimore to fill up Stowage and when He took the loose Tobbacco out found some of it dammage[d] for all our Care of it.

I have since heard that he says there were shells on the Ballast stones (as if there were not shells in America as well as here) and the fish in them (and if he considered that when he was shewed the Births our Paple lay in where they were wet over head and one was obliged to heave his bed over board) he need not have wondered at it if the Fish had been alive considering What a bad passage we had being almost always under reeft Sails.

The chief of his Suspicions I hear is this, that of our being in Ponduwall, but he takes good care not to mention that we were in great distress and not fit to stand the Seas or that we had Kings officers on board the whole time we lay there or that the Capt. mentioned in Line the 2nd. in the 2nd. Page gave his Affidavit that we put nothing out or took anything in. But he says nothing of that in his Protest or that several Captains viewed the sails and condem'd them fit for nothing at all.[2]

On the 4th. Inst., not hearing from Capt. De Ville or any letters from Mr. Barclay, suspected strongly he had run away and sent a Man to Morlaix with 2 Letters for Mr. Barclay, one to Paris and the other to L'Orient, as we suspected all our Letters put into this Post are intercepted as Mr. Barclays we expect are to us. And the man was informed from good authority that that Capt. De

Ville was there on Saturday (when he was to have been at Paris having set off on Tuesday night) so we are almost certain he has destroyed our letters and is concerned with the Officers in doing what injury he can. The under wrote is a Coppy almost word for word of the Letters to Mr. Barclay dated the 4th.

Mr. Barclay

Sir

Having wrote several Letters 2 to Dr. Franklin on the 10th. and 12th. Ult. and receiving no answer, sent Capt. De Ville express to paris on the 23rd. with one Letter to Mr. Jefferson and one to the Prime Minister of France,[3] and next day received our first letter from Mr. Barclay but no date to it, and the same day wrote to Capt. De Ville (an account of it with answers to some of the Captain Generals pleas) at the Hotel de Belle or, he being not there, to Mr. Barclay. And never receiving any Answer from you since the one dated 22nd. or Capt. De Ville since he left me makes me certain he is not gone himself or forwarded our Letters but destroy'd them, and that it has been a complicated piece of Villiany amongst the Officers here and that he was concerned with them to get what Cash we had about us and the Vessel and Cargo into their hands and Confine us and intercept all Letters from us or to you from us, as I advanced him 20 Guineas to bear his Expences. And I think Appearances look very like it as the Capt. General wanted us to give him all the Cash we had about us and to sign their papers, but not understanding french we allways declined it and now as they cannot prove any thing against us are determined to stop the Vessel and Confine us and do us all the injury they can in regard of Loss of Markets, demurage, and hindring our Business in England which is very urgent and requires us there and keeping us in Close Confinem[ent] in prison, only allowing 3 sols perday as if we were Criminals, tho' he gave us his word we should have 9 Sols ℈ Day. A few days ago we had a Coppy of part of the articles of the Treaty of Alliance between America and the Crown of France which grants us the Liberty in the 19th. Article of coming into any port of France in Distress (as the Officers confess we were) without any detention whatever when we are ready for Sea. And not being able to form any thing against us but what their Suppositions are and them they cannot prove, want to put us to the utmost trouble they can, thinking that we have neither money or Friends and being in a Strange Country (themselves being moneyed men) we should not be able to stand a Suit in Law against them. In my last I answered all their Suppositions that I hear they have against us but not understanding french cannot answer every thing, only what I am told but I believe half of it is False, as I cannot trust any thing he says by the following Affair. Having summonsed him to deliver up the Vessel and Cargo by a Kings Summonser or stand by all expences and damages that might accrue by our False imprisonment, demurage &c. he refused without we could give securety for the Vessel Cargo and 6000 Livres fine which is 1000 ₩ Man which he was sensible we could not as we were in a strange Country and debared from going to Paris. When I offer'd to give 1000 Livres Cash securety for my appearance again, but he would not and a few Days since I was inform'd that he reports he offered us our Vessel and Cargo but we refused to accept them (but he never mentioned any such thing to us). And several other circumstances of his Behaviour convinces me there is no reliance on any thing he says and that it is a scheme amongst themselves to get the Vessel condemned and keep us confined where we cannot Plead for ourselves and be imposed upon in the most bareface'd manner when we cannot help ourselves. Beg you will answer this by return of Post and let me know how many Letters you have received as I expect you never received only the 2 to Dr. Franklin and we shall never be able to express our thankfulness and always remain Yours &c.

The Letter I wrote on the 5th. was as near to this as I can remember not having time to take a Copy.
Mr. Barclay
Sir

Having sent 2 Letters to Morlaix yesterday for fear of their being intercepted, having wrote 6 to Dr. Franklin, Mr. Jefferson and yourself, and never have received by [but] 2 Answers from you one no date the other dated 22nd. makes me certain my letters to you are all intercepted and yours to me the same. The man I sent to Morlaix with the Last letters is return'd and give me an account that Capt. De Ville was there on Saturday very much in Liquour and making very free with Cash and said he was going to Brest (when as he set off on Tuesday the 23rd. at night he was to have been in Paris on Saturday) which confirms my suspicions that my Letters to you are destroyed and I believe he is concern'd with the Officers to injure us all they can and condemn the Vessel without us having any Account in I believe that they keep you in the dark putting you off with Frivolous excuses till the Vessel is condemned and us fined 1000 Livres ℔ man and close confined in some goal where we shall never hear from you or you from us. And after she is condemned it will be impossible to get a restitution as their pleas will be we never appeared or any one else in our Favor to prove our innocency so that we shall suffer Imprisonment Loss of property and the ruin of our Familys for a Crime we are innocent. As the Vessels tryal commences on the 9th. of this month according to their protest (and as I believe you have never received any more than 2 Letters, you think we are set at Liberty long since) she will be undoubtedly condemned, but I have engaged a Counseller to attend if I hear nothing from you on wednessday). If no one be able to appear in our behalf beg you to do your utmost to release us to procure restitution of our Property and we shall ever be yours &c.   L. ASQUITH

N.B. The Letters sent to Morlaix were directed one to Paris the other to L'Orient and as we had part of the Articles of Alliance, have sent you in this the part of the Articles we had as translated by Monsiur Picrell L'aine (our agent that we first employd by some trifling Circumstances, since falling out we begin to Suspect his Prentended sincerity) are as follows.
Copy
Treaty of Friendship and Trade between France and the United States of America
Article 2nd.
The King of France and the United States Engaged Themselves Mutually to not grant any particular favor To others Nations in Concerning the trade and Navigation or they shall be common one to the other.
Article 4th.
The Subjects, Paple and habitants of the said United States and each one of the said shall not pay in the Ports, Roads, Islands Towns and other places other and greater Duties as the Nations which is the greatest favourised and the said Americans shall enjoy all rights Priviliges and exemptions What the trade concern so well as Navigation it be in the Passage from one port to one other in the said States in France and Europe or for all other parts of the World that may be from which the mentioned favourised Nations should enjoy.

Article 19th.

When the Subjects and habitants of france or the Subjects from the united States with their Vessel of War or Merchants shall be forced by Tempest by pursuit of enimies or by any other pressing Want or Nessesity to come in any Rivers, Bay, Roads from the said Nations, they shall be received and treated reciprocally with humanity and honesty and shall enjoy from all Friendship Protection and Assistance and it shall be permit to take Refreshment of Provisions and other Nessessary things for their Sub[sis]tance and for the mending of their Vessels, all things to be paid by Reasonable Price and they shall not be detained in any Manners and not prevent to go out from the said Ports or Roads When they shall will and please without hinderance or Opposition.

The articles mentioned here are word for word as the Translations run tho it is bad sence.

RC (DLC).

The 2 LETTERS TO DR. FRANKLIN AND 1 TO MR. JEFFERSON on the affair of the *William and Catherine* (see Adams to TJ, 4 Sep. 1785, note), have not been found. CAPT. ANTONY DE VILLE was doubtless the officer commanding at Roscoff who brought the matter to the attention of Ségur, minister of war, who in turn informed Vergennes of it on 23 Aug. 1785 (Arch. Aff. Etr., Corr. Pol., E.-U., xxx; Tr. in DLC). The TRANSLATIONS from the Treaty of 1778 not only made BAD SENCE but were hardly accurate (Hunter Miller, ed., *Treaties*, II, 3-18).

[1] This passage is keyed to a note at end of text, which reads: "When we reported in the Custom house we paid 10 Liv. 7s. ℔ our Clearance but the Officers never minded that."

[2] This passage is keyed to a note at end of text, which reads: "Is that I had forgot mentioning their Objections in regard of Tonnage, as I can protest that I had her according to the Bills of Sale. The Guager only measured her hold, and part of her Steerage from inside to inside. He never allowed any thing for the Cockpit Cabin Forecastle and above one half of the Steerage which almost contains one half the Vessel."

[3] This passage is keyed to a note at end of text, which reads: "Is that Capt. de Ville had a Copy of the Bills of Sail and one of the Protest. I suppose he has made away with them as he has the letters as they object to our Tonnage."

From Abigail Adams

DEAR SIR   London Septr. 6 1785

I cannot omit by this opportunity acquainting you that on Sunday the August packet arrived in which came Mr. Church and brought us Letters from our son to our no small joy. He arrived the 17 of july after a very tedious passage. He was however in good Health and Spirits. Mr. Adams has at Length received some Letters from the president, from Mr. Jay and a private Letter from

Mr. Gerry, together with some newspapers and journals of Congress. The papers contain nothing very material. Mr. Osgood, Mr. Walter Livingston and Mr. Arthur Lee are the commissioners of the Treasury. Mr. Lee was chosen a few days before the sailing of the packet and was just gone from New York. It is said that the commissioners will have a difficult task to bring order out of the confusion in which the late financier left the office. Mr. Rutledge had not accepted his appointment when the gentlemen wrote. Mr. Jay writes that about the 29 of May Lambe sent for the papers from Congress, that they were sent, and that he saild soon after.

They are very anxious in America with respect to the posts, especially since a reinforcement of troops have been sent out. The merchants say that the trade is worth annually 50.000 pounds sterling.

From the present movements here, there is no great prospect of obtaining them by fair means. *The prospect here,* is not the pleasantest in the World. But I must recollect this is to go by the post. Mr. A. is very buisy writing to New York as Mr. Storer is going out in a few days. He desires me to inform you that he would take any dispatches you may have provided you could trust them here. Mr. Storer was formerly private Secretary to Mr. Adams. I will tuck this in one corner of Mr. A's Letter. Yours &c.

RC (DLC); unsigned. Recorded in SJL as received 11 Sep. 1785. Since Adams' letter of 4 Sep. was also received on 11 Sep., it was presumably in "one corner of" it that the present letter was tucked.

To Geismar

DEAR SIR   Paris Sep. 6. 1785.

Your letter of March 28. which I received about a month after it's date, gave me a very real pleasure, as it assured me of an existence of which I valued, and of which I had been led to doubt. You are now too distant from America to be much interested in what passes there. From the London gazettes, and the papers copying them, you are led to suppose that all there is anarchy, discontent and civil war. Nothing however is less true. There are not on the face of the earth more tranquil governments than ours, nor a happier and more contented people. Their commerce has not as yet found the channels which their new relations with the world will offer to best advantage, and the old ones remain as yet unopened by new conventions. This occasions a stagnation in the sale of their produce, the only truth among all the circumstances published about them. Their hatred against Great Britain having lately received from that nation new cause and new aliment, has taken a new spring. Among the individuals of your acquaintance nothing remarkable has happened. No revolution in the happiness of any of them has taken place, except that of the loss of their only child to Mr. and Mrs. Walker, who however left them a grand-child for their solace, and your humble servant who remains with no other family than two daughters, the elder here (who was of your acquaintance), the younger in Virginia, but expected here the next summer. The character in which I am here at present confines me to this place and will confine me as long as I continue in Europe. How long this will be I cannot tell. I am now of an age which does not easily accomodate itself to new manners and new modes of living: and I am savage enough to prefer the woods, the wilds, and the independance of Monticello, to all the brilliant pleasures of this gay capital. I shall therefore rejoin myself to my native country with new attachments, with exaggerated esteem for it's advantages, for tho' there is less wealth there, there is more freedom, more ease and less misery. I should like it better however if it could tempt you once more to visit it: but that is not to be expected. Be this as it may, and whether fortune means to allow or deny me the pleasure of ever seeing you again, be assured that the worth which gave birth to my attachment, and which still animates it, will continue to keep it up while we both live and that it is with sincerity I subscribe myself, Dear Sir your friend & servant,   TH: JEFFERSON

PrC (DLC). Entry in SJPL reads: "Geismer. Baron. America. Small news."

From Lister Asquith

PLEASE YOUR EXCELLENCY SIR

St. Pauls Prison Sep. 7th. 1785

At last our unhappy sentence is passed, our Vessel and Cargo condem'd and we are condem'd to pay 6000 Livres, a sum it is impossible for us to raise being in a strange Country. Hope for the Almightys sake you will take our unfortunate cause in Hand. We are condem'd to the Gallies for a crime we are innocent of and our families now will perish for want of us. For gods sake do your utmost for us as we are so distressed here for the Thoughts of our poor Innocent Families and as we are ruined and our families starving, please to exert yourself as far as lies in your power to serve us and we shall never be able to express our thankfulness to you, so remain Your most obedient Servts., LISTER ASQUITH

Please to excuse bad writing and errors as I am so distracted. Please to direct the Letters to the care of Mr. Pecrel L'ainé Roscoff. For Christs sake consider our poor starving Families and the injustice of our Case, as they cannot prove any thing and we are condem'd for a crime we are innocent of. The Whole Affair I sent to you by Capt. De Ville. O what injustice. For gods sake Sir protect us from their Villainous usage if possible.

RC (DLC); endorsed. Recorded in SJL as received 11 Sep. from "St. Paul de Leon."

From Lister Asquith

St. Pol de Léon, 8 Sep. 1785. He wrote TJ the day before, with the news of their sentence by the farmers-general, and writes again in less agitation at the advice of Father John Mehegan. He begs TJ to intervene, for they have been in close confinement three weeks, are short of provisions, and are exceedingly anxious for their families. Encloses a petition of Father John "in our Favor as he sees our distress and the Injustice of their Sentence."

RC (DLC); 2 p. Dft (DLC); undated; with several practice words at foot of text, evidently made as Asquith attempted to compose his hand before preparing RC. The text of Dft differs from RC only in phraseology and in the absence of the postscript. The presence of both Dft and RC among TJ's Papers can be explained only on the ground that Asquith was so distraught that he sent both by mistake. Enclosure: Probably Asquith to Vergennes, 9 Sep. 1785, St. Pol de Léon, written in French by Mehegan and signed by Asquith (DLC: TJ Papers: 14: 2501-2), imploring Vergennes' protection and succor. There is also in DLC: TJ papers: 27: 4602-3 a letter from Asquith to John Paul Jones that was written about this time, addressed to him at L'Orient, and having at foot of its text a letter in Mehegan's hand asking his friend Jones ("whose portrait I always keep in my chamber") to intercede; neither of these is dated, but Asquith told Jones that they depended on him "and Mr. Jefferson for our relief" and that they had "been close confined these 3 Weeks." This letter, as shown by the postmarks and address, went to Brest, then to L'Orient, then to Paris, and was received and endorsed by TJ.

From G. K. van Hogendorp

DEAR SIR   Breda. Sept. 8. 1785.

It is but three days ago, that I received Your letter of the 29 July, which You committed to the care of Mr. William Short. Only by chance I met with Your friend at my mother's house in the Hague, where I was come from her country seat for a single day. Mr. Short, who visited me a moment before my departure, promised however, that if he should pass through Breda on his returning to Paris, he would inquire after me. I am, therefore, not quite destituted of the hope of thus cultivating his acquaintance; and whether I may see him again, or not, I am much obliged to You, my dear Sir, for having adressed to me a Gentleman of merit and talents and Your particular friend.

The Notes on Virginia, with a few lines on the first leave of the volume, I received three weeks ago, and intended to express my gratitude to You, and at the same time to communicate You some reflexions, as soon as I would have read them. This I have not done yet entirely, and therefore I beg leave to entertain You an other time more extensively on that subject. Now I'll restrain myself to the article of natural history only, which from its accuracy, and good reasoning, will please every reader. You perhaps recollect, dear Sir, that I told You once in Annapolis, I never read Paaw's philosophical researches respecting the Americans. I have got that book soon after my returning home, but impossible it was to me to peruse more than one third of it, so absurd did it appear to me. I conceive that on the borders of the Ocean, perhaps recently freed from the overflowing sea, the low lands of North America, on their first detection by european navigators, may have been more favorable to the breeding of Insects and serpents than of Quadrupeds, as all swampy lands are; but why is nature smaller, or rather less great, in the forming of one animal than of another? And now, after the metamorphosis of Your country, which settlements, as they always do, have rendered wholesome to men, and even dangerous to wild and offensive beasts, now, I say, is there any vestige remaining of Nature's unkindness towards man? Did not I see as great and good cattle in New-England, though less fatt, than in Holland? Don't You have among Your nation as strong, as hearty men, as they are in Europe? Do not Your horses grow better, when taken care of, and is not every natural production, in similar circumstances, generally speaking, the same with You as with us? Systems of that kind, however, though You oppose it with irresistible arms, are sometimes not to be eradicated by arguments, and time only is able to perform a change. Did You Sir, ever talk on that subject with Count Buffon, or any one of his Disciples? I should be very happy if You would inform me of the success of Your reasonings, and whether You expect a palinodia in a future edition of the great natural Historians immortal works.

The Code of laws Your friend will send me As I am now studying more particularly the civil law; that of a people understanding its rights, that which is built on common sense, rather than on authorities of former times, that which takes its origin from an enligthened nation (which You Surely allow the English to be), must be perculiarly interesting and worthy of my whole attention.

You are not ignorant, my dear Sir, of the accounts respecting Your country which we read in the english papers. There You are supposed ready to throw Yourself for protection into any European Prince's hands, or at least weary of a faint confederation, and resolved to bankrupcy. You may safely believe that from better information of Your circumstances a year ago, I don't give any faith to those reports; but, however, as they are so frequently repeated, and as my correspondents in America don't take a general survey of their situation I beg You to give me a short account of the remarkable events that have taken place in America since June 1784, and a sketch of Your present situation, particularly with respect to the confederacy and the national debt.

You tell me, for instance, that continental certificates are taken at the new land-office, which certificates I suppose to be valued according to the tables of depreciation. But then it is probable that however enormous Your debt may be, in proportion to Your revenue, and the annual surplus of the produce of America, it will be extinguished within some years. Do You have got already any information concerning the business of the land office, whether many lands are bought, and by whom? This selling of unsettled countries is so very important a business, and will influence so much the future state of their inhabitants, that no details however minute would appear tedious to me on that subject.

Did You read Dr. Prices advice to the Americans? I should think that he has sent it to you. I only perused it in a translation by Count Mirabeau, who added his reflexions to the Doctor's. It appears to me that both these gentlemen are enthousiasts, little informed of local circumstances, and forming a judgement on America rather from what they wish mankind to be, than from what it is. The reflexions however on the matter of foreign commerce have struck me, and though it is not the first time that the celebrated doctrine of power arising from foreign trade appeared to me to be contrary to the principles of good pilosophy, yet I fancy that in Your case it would be in a peculiar manner to misunderstand Your true interest, if You were to neglect agriculture and inland commerce for the sake of supporting an extensive navigation. If I might be so happy as to learn from You, my wise friend, which is the opinion of the best citizens among You, and to which system Yourself adhere; I should venture to communicate You my doubts, and some reflections, made on and since my voyage through a part of North America.

I am glad to learn that Virginia now avails herself of the peculiar advantages of her soil and situation; because as liberty promotes the availing one's self of every natural advantage, so this availing is a symptom of liberty, and may give us nearly the measure of its extension. My correspondant in London told me in the fall of the last year that almost the whole crop of virginian tobacco had passed through England and English hands before it came into France. This I can hardly think agreeable with the prosperity of Your state, which You mention, because in that case the profits of the English surely were considerable, and could not be so but to Your detriment.

As to the conduct of the English, whom You surely by derision call Your good friends, and who now, as You inform me, by their operations produce that union among the States, which was necessary in the course of the whole war to oppose them; I beg leave to know of what a nature these operations are, whether measures of private men or of government, why they are destructive of your wellfare, and in which way You will oppose their influence?

Don't be angry at my questioning You so much; it arises partly from my curiosity to know what will be the good or bad effects of so remarkable an event as Your resolution, and partly from a persuasion that few of those who brought about Your independency look deeper into the first causes, and foresee better the probable consequences of it, than You do.

We are more removed from the prospect of peace than You did suppose the 29 July when You wrote to me. We are now much stronger, Sir, as to good troops and a powerfull barreer of all the elements combined, than the Austrian forces in the Netherlands. The Emperor, because of the German League, dares not to Send a single man from his hereditary lands against our country. These are facts that I think nobody will doubt of who trusts his eyes. Therefore (a priori) it is to be Supposed, and I can't chuse but to expect, that the Emperor's extravagant claims will be entirely rejected.

I wish You, my dear Sir, a good health, which is all You want to be perfectly happy.

I have the honour to be with the highest esteem Dear Sir Your most obedient Servant,   G. K. van Hogendorp

RC (DLC); endorsed. Recorded in SJL as received 23 Sep. 1785 "by W. Short."

From William Short

The Hague, Friday
Septr. 9th. 1785

Dear Sir

On my Return from Amsterdam on Saturday last I met with a Letter here which arrived the same Day from Mr. Adams. The Baron de Thulemeier had also received his Answer from Berlin. His letter and that from Mr. Adams removed all the Difficulties except that of the Errata. As I had not inclosed a List of them at first to Mr. Adams he could say nothing on that Subject to me. Notwithstanding the Baron urged the unimportance of the Errata and seemed impatient to have them corrected and signed, I chose rather to await the Tuesday's Post, adding it was only two Days and that I should certainly at that Time have a Letter from you. As no Letter arrived and the Baron seemed to desire very much that the Affair should be completed, and above all as the English Part of the Treaty will correct the Errata of the French, I promised him that if he would await the Post of this Day I would undertake, in Case no Letter arrived from you, to correct the Errata and exchange the Treaties. To this I was the rather induced because he had agreed to accept the Originals which I had brought and to recieve and exchange them, notwithstanding this is the first Instance that has ever happened in the Prussian Cabinet. As this Concession on the Part of his Majesty seemed to have a Right to something on the other Side I did not think I could do less than accede to his Desire of despatching this Business; particularly as I knew it was your Desire it should be finished as soon as possible. No Letter therefore having arrived by this Day's Post I shall tomorrow agreeable to Engagement, meet with Mr. Dumas at the Baron de Thulemeier's to put the final Hand to it and on Sunday shall set out on my Route to Paris. Should you do me the Favor Sir to write to me, direct to *Bruxelles, poste restante.* I shall probably be there the Day Week that I set out from hence. It will give me great Pleasure to receive a Letter from you at that

Place, and I hope I shall hear that you approve my acceding to the Baron de Thulemeiers Sollicitations to finish this Business without waiting longer; as I assure you Sir, it is not without some Reluctance that [I] undertake it after having communicated to you a List of the Errata.

My Compliments for Colo. Humphries and I beg you to be persuaded of the sincere Affection & Regard with which I am yours, &c.,

W SHORT

RC (ViWC). Short wrote a similar letter to Adams, this date (MHi: AMT).

Short had written Adams on 5 Sep. that De Thulemeier had that moment received authorization from the Prussian court to receive the text of the treaty in French and English, but to give in exchange for it "an Exemplaire in French" only. He added that De Thulemeier "hopes we will be induced to accept in Exchange what alone he is authorized to offer. But this is no more than what the Baron offered to do at our first Interview so that his Powers on this Subject have not been enlarged . . . since his Arrival here. Thus circumstanced Sir I rather suppose it will be necessary to cede this Point although I shall do it with Reluctance and not without trying other Means as it seems to be desired by you to have the Treaty exchanged in the two Languages" (Short to Adams, 5 Sep. 1785, acknowledging Adams' of 30 Aug. 1785; MHi: AMT; see note to Short to TJ, 23 Aug. 1785). Short evidently did not report to TJ this limitation in De Thulemeier's instructions. Adams replied to Short's observations of the 5th: "I have received from Mr. Jefferson a copy of his letter to you of the 1st. inst. and agree fully with him in sentiment that we should agree to consider the French column as the Original if the Baron thinks himself bound to insist upon it, but if the practice of his Court will admit of the execution in the two languages, each to be considered as equally original, it would be very agreeable to me. I . . . agree that it will be necessary to cede the point, if the Baron cannot be persuaded to sign the Copy in both languages, upon your agreeing that the French shall be considered as the Original. I wish, however, to try the experiment; not urging it with too much

earnestness, nor persisting in it too long. I will not disguise from you, what I should advise you to reserve from others with some discretion, that, old as I am, I hope to live to see the day when the American language will be understood and respected in every Court in Europe—not from any dislike to the French or the London" (Adams to Short and Dumas, 11 Sep. 1785: MHi: AMT). Adams' interest in the problem of language was not a mere matter of diplomatic etiquette. As early as 1780 he had made the remarkable proposal that Congress establish an "American Academy for refining, improving, and ascertaining the English Language" (Adams to the president of Congress, 5 Sep. 1780; *Works*, ed. C. F. Adams, VII, 250). In the letter to Short and Dumas of 11 Sep. 1785, incidentally, Adams seems to have acquired the honor of being the first to employ the phrase "American language," heretofore accorded to Dr. William Thornton, who used it in his *Cadmus; or, a Treatise on the Elements of Written Language*, published in Philadelphia in 1793 (cited by H. L. Mencken, *Supplement I: The American Language*, 1945, p. 5, who points out that "American dialect" dates from 1740 and "American tongue" from 1789).

It was the arrival of TJ's letter of 1 Sep. 1785 to Short that enabled De Thulemeier to overcome the obstacle of his instructions—that is, the authorization to Short to regard the French column as the original (see Short to TJ, 11 Sep. 1785). The signed copy of the treaty retained for the United States bears at the head of each of the two texts the word "Original"; but this was probably a later addition, and when and by whose authority the designation was made is not clear.

From Patrick Henry

DEAR SIR   Richmd. Sept. 10th. 1785

I was honor'd with yours in the Spring, by which you inform me Mr. Heudon intended to come over to see Genl. Washington in person, by Means of which he would be better enabled to take the Likeness desired. I should have written you on the Receipt of yours, but as Mr. Heudons Arrival here was to be expected about the Time I received the Letter, I thought it needless to write on the Subject. I communicated the Affair to the Council, and they thought with me, that, as you and your much esteemed Colleague, on conferring with the Artist, could best determine on the Means for executing the Intentions of the Assembly, as to the Statue, your Arrangements with Mr. Heudon ought to be confirmed, if indeed any Confirmation from me be necessary.

I am very much obliged to you for the Hints respecting Mr. Alexander. They came very seasonably; and some important Transactions with him have been managed conformably to your Ideas.

A few Days past I got your Letter on the subject of the Arms, together with one from the Marquiss. The Bills have been procured and are sent away according to my promise to Mr. Barclay. I make no Doubt of their Arrival in Time, and of their being duly paid, as Mr. Robt. Morris the Drawer is acquainted with the purpose which this Money is drawn for by the State.

Sir Robt. Herries's proposals for supplying Tobacco to the French I have made known to our Merchants, in Hopes, as you wish, to stimulate them to something similar. But am not very sanguine in my Expectations from them, as they generally want that successfull Enterprize which is derived from sufficient Capital.

I am bound in Duty Sir to make you my best Acknowledgements, for the repeated Instances your Letters afford, of your Attention to the Interests of this State. And I am happy to find, that your Efforts to procure good Arms for our Militia are like to have Success.

Were it possible to establish Manufactures of Arms here in a short Time, something of that Kind would have been done. But from the high price of Labor, the Scarcity of Money, and other Difficultys it was thought best to purchase Arms from abroad for the present. I hope your Idea will be adopted eer very long.

With high Regard & Esteem I am dear sir your most obedient Servant,   P. HENRY

RC (MHi); endorsed: "Virginia Govr. of." Recorded in SJL as received 30 Dec. 1785 "by Houdon."

From Patrick Henry

Dear Sir   Richmond Sept. 10th. 1785

While I was writing to you about Matters of a public Nature I supposed you would be glad to know of such Incidents as cannot properly make a part of our official Communications. Indeed our present Tranquility scarcely affords an Anecdote interesting enough to relate; but I am happy in reflecting, that it is in such scarcity of News and Materials for Narration, that political Growth and Increase in Strength are experienced. There is however a certain Collision of Parts in our Body-politic which is no Doubt conducive to Prosperity. Of this we have some, but whether it be of the right Kind, or degree, I am not skilfull enough to say. I think however that we are as free from Faction, or party as any in the Union. A Matter which from its Importance and the Variety of Interests concerned, I always thought would endanger our Quiet, seems like to be accomplished in a good Humour: I mean the Separation of Kentuckie into a distinct Government. It has been in Agitation for some time, and within a few Days I've Seen a Copy of a Resolution unanimously passed at a Convention of Delegates there, for petitioning our next assembly for a Separation "injurious to neither and honorable to both parts of the State."

Very different is the Condition of No. Carolina. Her people settled on the western Waters, have assumed sovereign Power, and organized their Society into a Goverment similar to that prevalent in the neighbouring States. There are severe Bickerings between them and their Brethren eastward of the great Mountains. The new Society sent Wm. Cocke (perhaps you saw him when formerly a Delegate from Washington) to Congress to sollicit Admission into the Union. His Mission was fruitless, tho' he said the contrary as I am told. Where this affair will end, is hard to say. Perhaps it may turn out to be very interesting. They have about 5000 men able to bear Arms. Very few of their people are of Character apt to inspire public Confidence. The present poverty of the Inhabitants, and their future prospects will deter people generally from settling there especially if the threatned Confusions take place.

We have lately made a large payment to the foreign Creditors of Virga., and I please my self to think it will be an Evidence of our upright Intentions.

We have had a very dry summer. The Crops of Corn are in

general the most scanty of any for 20 years past, I think. If the Frosts are late, the Crop of Tobaco will be good. Our Wheat suffered much from an Insect called the black Bugg. Their Increase is prodigious, and their ravages from being confined to the Southern Countys last year, are become general, this.

We are much disappointed in our Expectations of French and Dutch Traders rivalling the British here. The latter engross the greatest share of our Trade, and was it not, that the Irish bid up for our Produce, the Scotch would soon be on their former Footing. I see no Way to place our Commerce in a better State, but discriminating by Taxes between our own and foreign Vessels and Goods. The Interuption of our west India Trade is severely felt by some. The numberless Difficultys attending our Voyages to Europe, are complained of by all. One would think this ought to make us manufacturers. And really I should not regret the Embarrassments at present on our Trade, if they had that Effect. But how could we pay Taxes? This puzzles me, and forces our people into that Kind of agriculture which if long persisted in seems to present a disagreable prospect. The State of Learning is much as you left it. A Desire of acquiring it prevails generally. The Means too difficult, and discouraging to many. The Necessity of it is universally admitted, and in several Instances have happen'd in which the Assembly have shewn a Desire to disseminate it.

The Foundations of our Capitol are laid and the Wall advancing so as to be above the Surface of the Ground a few Feet this Winter. The Building I believe will be the most magnificent in the 13 States by far, unless the Design is alter'd, or ill timed Frugality curtails the Execution. The Length is 148 feet—Breadth 118—with four elegant (not to say magnificent) Fronts. To one who has seen Paris this is nothing; but I give you the Description and I know your predilections will place it in a point equally pleasing with the Structures upon which Architecture hath lavished every thing beautifull and grand.

The annual Meeting of our Assembly is fixed to the 3d. Monday of October. Two principal points for Discussion are expected to be a general assessment for supporting Religion, and striking paper Money for paying our military Claimants. Both are delicate points. Much too will be said as to the State of our Commerce. But I suppose it will be refer'd to Congress to fix upon the general plan. I guess I've tired you because you see continually Matters more interesting than the dry Detail of little Things I give you.

If you will be so good as drop me in some leisure Hour the News with you it will be highly acceptable to Dear Sir Your affte. hble. Servant.,

P. HENRY

Pray give my Respects to Mr. Short.

RC (Lloyd W. Smith, Madison, N.J., 1946); at foot of letter: "(Private)"; endorsed. Recorded in SJL as received 30 Dec. 1785 "by Houdon."

From John Adams

DEAR SIR   Grosvr. Square 11th. Septemr. 1785.

In answer to your enquiry in your letter of the 4th. inst. I can only say that I knew Mr. Matzei at Paris and that he made long journeys. But in what stile he lived and at what expence he travelled I know not. He always made a genteel appearance without any unnecessary show, and kept good Company wherever he went. I observed this in Paris and heard of it in Holland. In Italy it could not be otherwise, for he is well known and esteemed there as I have always heard and particularly within these few days from the Genoese Ambassador and General Paoli; both of whom enquired of me, very respectfully, after Mr. Mazzei, at the Drawing Room, of their own motion. Knowing as you and I do how little way a thousand pounds go, in expences of living, if I were to guess at his expences, altho' he had not a house and train of Servants to maintain, nor a table that I know of, yet, considering the indispensible article of Cloaths, Carriage, Postage and Stationary, as well as the ordinary expences of Apartments, travelling and all the rest, I could not undertake to pay his way for a less Sum.

I am, dear Sir, Yrs: &c: &c.

FC (MHi: AMT); in an unidentified hand. Recorded in SJL as received 22 Sep. 1785.

From John Adams

DEAR SIR   Grosvenor Square Westminster Septr. 11. 1785.

In Answer to your Favour of September 4. I am sorry to inform you that I have not received one line from the Commissioners of the Treasury, nor from Congress, nor any of their Ministers, respecting the Interest due in France. It is possible Messieurs

Willinks and Van Staphorsts may, or possibly the orders may have been suspended to be sent by the Minister to the Hague, when they can find one who will venture to Europe under the present Regulations.

The System of having no Ministers in Europe has involved our Country in so many Inconveniences that I fancy it will go out of Fashion. It would be well to send Consuls, I think, who, upon Permission to trade, would serve without Salaries, if We cannot afford the salaries of Ministers. I am with great Respect, sir, your Friend and Servant, JOHN ADAMS

RC (DLC). FC (MHi: AMT); in an unidentified hand. Recorded in SJL as received 22 Sep. 1785.

To Gilles de Lavallée

SIR   Paris Sep. 11. 1785.

I received duly your favour of Aug. 14. It is not in my power to take on the account of Congress any part of the expences of your passage, having received no authority of that kind from them: nor indeed is the encouragement of emigrations among the objects with which they are charged. I fear that when you get to Portsmouth you will find difficulties in the winter season to go by water to any more Southern state. Your objects being the manufacture of wool and cotton, you will of course chuse to fix yourself where you can get both or one of these articles in plenty. The most and best wool is to be had in the middle states. They begin to make a little cotton in Maryland: they make a great deal in Virginia and all the states South of that. The price of clean cotton in Virginia is from 21 to 26 sols a pound, that is to say from a fifth to a fourth of a dollar. Genl. Washington being at the head of the great works carrying on towards clearing the Patowmac, I have no doubt but that that work will be completed. It will furnish great opportunities of using machines of all kinds. Perhaps you may find emploiment there for your skill in that way. Alexandria on the Patowmac will undoubtedly become a very great place. But Norfolk would be the best for Cotton manufactories. As you are a stranger, I mention such facts as I suppose may be useful to you. I wish you success & am Sir your very humble servt.,

TH: JEFFERSON

PrC (DLC).

To John Langdon

Dear Sir   Paris. Sep. 11. 1785.

Your Capt. Yeaton being here furnishes me an opportunity of paying the tribute of my congratulations on your appointment to the government of your state, which I do very sincerely. He gives me the grateful intelligence of your health and that of Mrs. Langdon. Anxious to promote your service, and beleiving he could do it by getting himself naturalized here and authorised to command your vessel, he came from Havre to Paris. But on making the best enquiries I could, it seemed that the time requisite to go through with this business would be much more than he could spare. He therefore declined it. I wish it were in my power to give you a hope that our commerce either with this country or it's islands was likely to be put on a better footing. But if it be altered at all, it will probably be for the worse. The regulations respecting their commerce are by no means sufficiently stable to be relied on. Europe is in quiet and likely to remain so. The affairs of the Emperor and Dutch are as good as settled, and no other cloud portends any immediate storm. You have heard much of American vessels taken by the Barbary pyrates. The Emperor of Marocco took one last winter (the brig Betsey from Philadelphia). He did not however reduce the crew to slavery nor confiscate the vessel or cargo. He has lately delivered up the crew on the sollicitation of the Spanish court. No other has ever been taken by them. There are indeed rumours of one having been lately taken by the Algerines. The fact is possible, as there is nothing to hinder their taking them but it is not as yet confirmed. I have little doubt but that we shall be able to place our commerce on a proper footing with the Barbary states this summer, and thus not only render our navigation to Portugal and Spain safe but open the Mediterranean as formerly. In spite of treaties, England is still our enemy. Her hatred is deep-rooted and cordial, and nothing is wanting with her but the power to wipe us and the land we live on out of existence. Her interest however is her ruling passion: and the late American measures have struck at that so vitally, and with an energy too of which she had thought us quite incapable, that a [pos]sibility seems to open of forming some arrangement with her. When they shall see decidedly that without it we shall suppress their commerce with us, they will be agitated by their avarice on one hand, and their hatred and their fear of us on the other. The result of this conflict of d[irty passions] is yet [to be] awaited. The body of the people of this country love us cordially. But ministers and merchants love nobody. The merchants here are endeavouring to exclude us from their islands. The ministers will be governed in it by political motives, and will do it, or not do it, as these shall appear to dictate, without love or hatred to any body. It were to be wished they were able to combine better the various circumstances which prove beyond a doubt that all the advantages of their colonies result in the end to the mother country. I pray you to present me in the most friendly terms to Mrs. Langdon and to be assured of the esteem with which I am, Your excellency's Most obedient & most humble servt.,   TH: JEFFERSON

PrC (DLC). MS slightly torn; missing words have been supplied in brackets from the printing in TJR, I, 313. Entry in SJL reads: "J. Langdon Presidt. of N. Hampsh. See copy"; entry in SJPL reads: "Langdon John. Engld. France."

To André Limozin

SIR   Paris Sep. 11. 1785.

According to the desire expressed in your letter by Capt. Yeaton I have enquired into the practicability of getting him naturalised here, and authorised to command his vessels, but the information given us, rendering it probable that more time would be consumed, in attending here till the objects could be obtained, than he chuses to spare, he declines pursuing it. I will beg permission to address to your care three or four trunks of books for some of my friends in Virginia. I shall send them in a few days, by water, as they would be too much rubbed were I to send them by land. I will pray you to keep them till some vessel shall be going from your port to James, York, or Ra[ppahann]ock rivers in Virginia. I should be obliged to you i[f you would be a]ble to inform me whenever there is [a vessel coming from or going to Vir]ginia, as I should frequ[ently have letters and parcels to send It will be] necessary for me always to [know to what port the] vessel would be bound. I have the honour [to be, Sir,] Your most obedient humble servt.,   TH: JEFFERSON

PrC (DLC); the lower right and left-hand corners of text are torn away; missing words have been supplied conjecturally, partly on the basis of TJ's reply.

Limozin's LETTER BY CAPTN. YEATON is missing. It was recorded in SJL as received 9 Sep. and was dated at Le Havre, 4 Sep. 1785.

To De Ponçins

I received three days ago the letter you did me the honour to write to me on the 2d of August. Congress have purchased a very considerable extent of country from the Indians, and have passed an Ordinance laying down rules for disposing of it. These admit only two considerations for granting lands: first, military service rendered during the late war: and secondly, money to be paid at the time of granting, for the purpose of discharging their national debt. They direct these lands to be sold at auction to him who will give most for them, but that, at any rate, they shall not be sold for less than a dollar an acre. However as they receive as money the certificates of public debt, and these can be bought for the half or fourth of their nominal value, the price of the lands is reduced in proportion. As Congress exercise their government by general rules only, I do not beleive they will grant lands to any individual for any other considerations than those mentioned in their ordinance. They have ordered the lands to be surveyed, and this work is now actually going on under the directions of their own geographer. They do not require information of the quality of the soil, because they will sell the lands faster than this could be obtained, and after they are sold it is the interest of the purchaser to examine for what the soil is proper. As ours is a country of husbandmen I make no doubt they will receive the book of which you write to me with pleasure and advantage. I have stated to you such facts as might enable you to decide for yourself how far that country presents advantages which might answer your views. It is proper for me to add that every thing relative to the sale and survey of these lands is out of the province of my duty. Supposing you might be desirous of receiving again the letters of Doctr. Franklin, I inclose them and have the honour to be with the greatest respect Sir Your most obedt. & most humble servt.,   Th: Jefferson

PrC (DLC). Entry in sjpl reads: "Ponçins, Marquis. American lands." Enclosures: The letters enclosed in De Ponçins to TJ, 29 Aug. 1785 (see note there). In referring to De Ponçins' letter of the 2d. of august, TJ evidently erred as he did on 8 Sep. in recording receipt of such a letter in sjl.

From William Short

DEAR SIR   The Hague Septr. 11th. 1785

You will be surprized by my Letter written on Friday Evening which mentioned that yours had not arrived. I waited until as late in the Evening as I could on Account of the Departure of the Post before I wrote. Some Time after that Mr. Dumas called to let me know he had just received the Letter which he presented me. I was exceedingly happy to find that it allowed us to pursue the Measures agreed on with the Baron, and yesterday Evening we put the finishing Hand to the Business. He has signed both of the Treaties which I brought, retained one and delivered me the other, which I shall have the Pleasure of putting into your Hands very soon, as I set out this Morning for Paris. The Post travelling faster than I can I have thought it best to give you the earliest Information I could of the Completion of this Affair, and of the Arrival of your Letter. Still it is to be observed that it could not have been given to the Post so early as you expected, since it was nine Days from its Date to its Arrival. Accept Sir my sincerest Wishes for your Happiness, and believe me yours, with the greatest Sincerity,

W SHORT

RC (ViWC). TJ's entry in SJL of its receipt under 19 Sep. reads in part: "(found in the streets, open)."

From Elbridge Gerry

MY DEAR SIR   New York 12th. Sepr. 1785

I intended by the last packet to have answered your Letter of the 11th. of May, for which I am much indebted to you: but was accidentally prevented by her having sailed the Day before I expected it. I cannot account for the Detention of your Letter by Colo. Le Mair: And will give you notice,* if the Commissioners' Letter by him to Congress, has not been received. Your Reasoning, respecting *Entrepots* corresponds with my own Ideas of the Subject: I cannot see any great Advantages from multiplying them in Times of peace: in War they may be more useful. With Respect to the commercial arrangements of the Court of France, in the West Indies, however favorably they may be veiwed by some, they affect our Fishery and have a direct Tendency to discourage it. A Duty on our Exports of Fish, applied as a Bounty to encourage theirs, is a Rule that has a two fold operation and has been very alarming. This I suppose was the Cause why an Act of Massachusetts which originated before I left the State, to retaliate british restrictions, has since my arrival here been extended to other Nations. With respect to the oyl Contract, it does not raise the Expectations of those who were to be at the Head of it, in this Quarter, so far as to engage them in an Adventure. At least Mr. Wadsworth &c. appear to be cool about it, whether to secure the oyl at a cheaper Rate or from Motives of Dislike, I am unable to determine. Be this as it may We are not the less obliged to our good Friend the Marquis, to whom pray present my affectionate Regards. The provision obtained in the Treaty with prussia, appears to me of great Importance. The advantages You mention and I think many others will result therefrom.

We have done very little in the present Congress. The Want of a full Representation has retarded all and prevented an adoption of the most important fœderal Measures. The Requisition labours exceedingly and I am apprehensive of an adjournment without compleating it. Congress appear to be in earnest respecting a Mint, which the Board of Treasury have under Consideration. They are to digest the several plans and reduce them to System. Mr. Jay is conducting the Negotiation with Mr. Gardoqui, the Spanish Encargado de negotios. Western posts in statu quo. General Howe is added to the Indian Commissioners and the Treaty is soon to be held: Colo. Monroe left us, to attend it on private Considerations. In short both Congress and the States seem to lie on their Oars, and this political Calm will soon produce I hope an Exertion that will be worthy of both. Congress have adopted the plan of conveying by the Stages, the Mail from N. Hampshire to Georgia and from this City to Albany. Inclosed is a paper containing the Correspondence between Governor Bowdoin and Capt. Stanhope, who commanded a british Frigate. It is not correct, but substantially the same. Congress have taken the Matter up and directed Mr. Adams to lay it before the King of G. Britain. Adeiu my dear Sir & be assured I am on every Occasion your affectionate Friend,

E. GERRY

* I am informed at Mr. Jays office the Letter was received.

RC (DLC). Recorded in SJL as received 16 Oct. 1785. Enclosure: Copy of the correspondence between James Bowdoin and Henry Stanhope, 1-4 Aug. 1785 (newspaper extract in DLC; see also JCC, XXIX, 637-47); the paper that Gerry sent has not been identified, but there is a clipping from an unidentified American newspaper in DLC: TJ Papers, 13: 235 containing the letters that passed between Stanhope and Bowdoin. Marbois also sent copies to Vergennes on 23 Aug. 1785 (Arch. Aff. Etr., Corr. Pol., E.-U., xxx; Tr in DLC). See Abigail Adams to TJ, 20 Dec. 1785 and 23 July 1786.

From Elizabeth Wayles Eppes

[*Eppington, Va., 13 Sep. 1785.* Recorded in SJL as received 19 Jan. 1786, "by Mr. Littlepage." Not found.]

From Mary Jefferson

DEAR PAPA   [ca. 13 Sep. 1785?]

I want to see you and sister Patsy, but you must come to Uncle Eppes's house.   POLLY JEFFERSON

MS not found. The text is taken from Randolph, *Domestic Life*, p. 104, where it is printed with two other un-dated letters from Mary Jefferson. Though there is no evidence to prove that this letter is the one without date which TJ recorded in SJL as received 19 Jan. 1786 "by Mr. Little-page," with letters from Elizabeth Wayles Eppes and Francis Eppes dated 13 and 14 Sep. 1785 respectively, the text printed above has been chosen as presumably the earliest of the three

(see also TJ to Francis Eppes, 24 Jan. 1786; Mary Jefferson to TJ, ca. 22 May 1786 and ca. 30 Mch. 1787).

This brief letter from seven year-old Mary must have been written after the Eppeses had received TJ's (missing) letter of 11 May to Francis Eppes, in which he evidently said much the same things about the dangers of the sea that he set forth in his letter of 30 Aug. 1785. Under these circumstances the letter's brevity takes on eloquent meaning.

To Lister Asquith

SIR   Paris Sep. 14. 1785.

Several of your letters have been received, and we have been occupied in endeavours to have you discharged: but these have been ineffectual. If our information be right, you are mistaken in supposing you are already condemned. The Farmers general tell us you are to be tried at Brest, and this trial may perhaps be a month hence. From that court you may appeal to the parliament of Rennes, and from that to the king in Council. They say that from the depositions sent to them there can be no doubt but that you came to smuggle, and that in that case the judgment of the law is a forfeiture of the vessel and cargo, a fine of a thousand livres on each of you and six year's condemnation to the gallies. These several appeals will be attended with considerable expence. They offer to discharge your persons and *vessel* (but not the cargo) on your paying two thousand livres and the costs already incurred, which are 3 or 400 more. You will therefore chuse whether to go through the trial or to compromise, and you are the best judge what may be the evidence for or against you. In either case I shall render you all the service I can. I will add that if you are disposed to have the matter tried, I am of opinion that, if found against you, there will be no danger of their sending you to the gallies: so that you may decide what course you will take without any bias from that fear. If you chuse to compromise, I will endeavor to have it done for you on the best terms we can. I fear they will abate little from the 2000 livres because the Capt. Deville whom you sent here fixed the matter by offering that sum, and has done you more harm than good. I shall be glad if you will desire your lawyer to make out a state of your case (which he may do in French) and send it to me. Write [me] also yourself a plain and full narration of your voiage, and the circumstances which have brought so small a vessel, with so small a cargo, from America into France. As far as we as yet know them, they are not in your favor. Inform me who you are and what papers you have on board. But do not state to me a single fact which is not true: for if I am led by your information to advance any thing which they shall prove to be untrue I will abandon your case from that moment: whereas, sending me a true state, I will make the best of it I can. Mr. Barclay the American consul will be here some few days yet. He will be, as he has already been, of much service to you if the information I ask both from yourself and your lawyer can come before his departure. I repeat my assurances of doing whatever I can for you, and am Sir Your very humble servt.,   TH: JEFFERSON

PrC (DLC). Entry in SJPL reads: "Asquith Lister. His case. Smuggler."

From Francis Eppes

[*Eppington, Va., 14 Sep. 1785*. Recorded in SJL as received 19 Jan. 1786, "by Mr. Littlepage." Not found, but see T.J.'s reply, 24 Jan. 1786.]

From John Jay

DR. SIR   New York 14th. September 1785

Your joint Letters of 11th. November and   December 1784 were received by Congress. I have had the Honor of receiving other joint ones of 9th. February, 13th April, 11th. May and 18th. June last, and also three from you Vizt. two of the 11th. May and one of the 17th. June last.

By the last Packet I had the Pleasure of writing two Letters to you of the 13th. August 1785, which I hope have come safe to your Hands.

As yet I have heard nothing of or from Captain Lamb, who was the Bearer of several important Papers relative to our Affairs with the Barbary States.

Your Correspondence with Mr. Adams doubtless furnishes you with ample Information relative to the Objects of his Legation. His Letters to me were dated at a Time when he had not yet entered on Business. His Reception is satisfactory, and I wish the Result of his Negociations may be equally so. In my Opinion we have little to expect from the liberal Policy of that Court. If we obtain Justice from them my Expectations will be fulfilled, but even of that I am not without my Doubts.

I wish it was in my Power to enter minutely into the Subjects of your Letters but it is not. They still remain with my Reports on some of them under the Consideration of Congress, so that at present I am not enabled to convey to you their Sentiments respecting those Matters.

At present they are employed in forming a Requisition for Supplies. When compleated you shall have a Copy of it.

The Affair of Longchamps is agreeably terminated. His most Christian Majesty will not persist in that Demand, and the Paper containing it has been returned to Mr. De Marbois in Consequence of a Conference I had with him on that Subject. I admire the Wisdom of the french Minister in forbearing to press this Point. It would have produced Discontent without answering any useful Purpose. I am sure he has gained more with us by this temperate and prudent Conduct than could possibly have been done by harsh and irritating Measures.

Governor Rutledge declines going to Holland, so that it is yet uncertain who will succeed Mr. Adams there.

The vacant seat at the Treasury Board has been given to Mr. A. Lee. That Board is now full and consists of Mr. Osgood, Mr. Walter Livingston and Mr. A. Lee.

A Court to decide the Controversy between Massachusetts and New York is to meet this Fall at Williamsburgh. It is much to be wished that all our Boundaries were adjusted; and that the Vigour of Government may abate the Rage for making new States out of Parcels of the old which prevails in some of them. North Carolina and this State suffer by such unauthorized Proceedings, and Massachusetts has her Fears. Our fœderal Government wants Power and is [in] many Respects inadequate to its Objects. Much is expected from the ensuing Sessions of the Legislatures; but for my Part I fear the Love of Popularity restrains many from promoting Measures which, though essential to the public Welfare, may not be pleasant to the many whose Views and Wishes are chiefly personal.

The Papers herewith enclosed are a Copy of a Letter to me from Mr. Shaw, and a Letter from me to His Excellency the President respecting it. Congress adopted the Opinion I expressed in the latter and referred it to me to take Order. As both Letters are particular and in Detail, it would be useless to repeat in this what you will find in them.

I have the Honor to be &c.,   JOHN JAY

FC (DNA: PCC, No. 121); at foot of text: "For the Letters alluded to in the above See book of American Letters Pages 281 and 429" (referring to Jay's files, DNA: PCC, No. 120). Recorded in SJL as received 19 Oct. 1785. Immediately following the entry in SJL for this letter and for that from Jay of 15 Sep., there is an entry under 19 Oct. reading as follows: "Do. [Mr. Jay's] 1. Sep. O.F.A. But there appears to be a line drawn through "1 Sep. O.F.A." and also there is no entry in the Journal of the Office of Foreign Affairs (DNA: PCC, No. 127) for a letter of 1 Sep. 1785 from Jay to TJ. TJ's entry in SJL and his acknowledgment of such a letter in his of 24 Dec.

1785 would therefore appear to be an error; TJ evidently confused his entry and acknowledgment with Jay's letter to Congress of 1 Sep. 1785, which was enclosed in the present letter. Enclosures: (1) Jay to Congress, 1 Sep. 1785 (JCC, XXIX, 673-4), recommending that a copy of Samuel Shaw's letter be sent to TJ and that he be requested to "express to the french Minister the Sense which Congress entertain of the friendly Offices and Civilities shewn by the french Officers in question" to the *Empress of China*. (2) Samuel Shaw to Jay, 19 May 1785, describing the voyage of the *Empress of China* (see TJ to Vergennes, 21 Oct. 1785).

To William Short

DEAR SIR   Paris Sep. 14. 1785.

Your letter of the 9th. came to hand yesterday. I wrote to you on the first instant, by the post which was to leave Paris the next day and should have arrived at the Hague on Tuesday the 6th. That you did not receive it then can have proceeded from no other cause than the infidelity of the post office in opening letters and detaining or suppressing them altogether. I receive very few which do not bear on them proofs of this infamy. The present miscarriage is of no other consequence than as it would have relieved you from the difficulties you were under. Should it have come to hand after the date of your letter you will have seen that it proposed the measures you adopted. We have little new here. You will find all the Americans whom you left here. We have heard of young Adams's arrival in America and Dr. Lee's appointment to be one of the Commissioners of the treasury. I am so doubtful of your receiving this letter that I shall add nothing more than assurances of the esteem with which I am Dear Sir your sincere friend & servant,

TH: JEFFERSON

PrC (DLC).

From John Adams

DEAR SIR   Grosvenor Square Septr. 15. 1785

I have received your Letter of the fourth instant by Colonel Franks, with a Project of a Letter to the Emperor of Morocco, and several other Papers.

I have had this Letter, fairly copied, with very few and very inconsiderable Alterations and have signed it. I have left room enough, at the Beginning, for you to insert, or leave Mr. Barclay to insert, the Emperors Titles and Address, which may be done, with the most certainty in Morocco.

By the Treaty we have with Holland, the States General have agreed, upon Requisition, to second our negotiations in the most favourable manner, by means of their Consuls. I would have prepared a Memorial and Requisition to that Purpose and have sent it to the Hague, But such a Memorial would publish to all the World Mr. Barclays Mission. I shall wait for your Advice, and if you think proper, I will still send a Memorial. But I am inclined to think We had better wait till We receive from Mr. Barclay in Morocco some account of his Prospects.

The best Argument Mr. Barclay can use, to obtain Treaties upon moderate Terms, is that We have absolutely as yet no ships in the Mediterranean Sea, and shall have none untill Treaties are made. That our Seamen will not go there, untill Treaties are made. That therefore the Algerines will have no Chance of taking any American Vessells, any where but in the Atlantic, and there they can expect to take but very few, at a vast Expence of Corsairs, and exposed to our Privateers and Frigates.

Treaties of Peace are very unpopular, with the People of Algiers. They say it is taking from them all the opportunities of making Profits by Prizes for the sake of inriching the Dey by Presents. The Probability then that our Trade would be more beneficial to the People, than the Few Prizes they would have a chance to make, by going at a vast Expence out of the Mediterranean and spreading themselves over the Ocean in quest of our ships, exposed to our Frigates and the Men of War of Portugal, &c. would be the best Reason for the Dey to use with the People. The common Argument is the Bombardments and Depredations with which their Ennemies threaten them by their Fleets and Squadrons, which commonly accompany the Embassy. Mr. Barclay will be very naked in this respect.

With great Respect, your most obedient   JOHN ADAMS

RC (DLC). FC (MHi: AMT). Recorded in SJL as received 22 Sep. 1785. Enclosures: Although Adams mentioned no enclosures as such, several documents relating to the mission of Barclay and Lamb accompanied the present letter (see under 11 Oct. 1785).

From Edward Bancroft

DEAR SIR   London 15th. Septr. 1785.

The bearer Mr. Barbauld, is just setting out for Paris, with his Lady, whose distinguished reputation and beautiful Poetical Publications (whilst Miss Aikin) cannot have been unknown to you, and I beg Leave to recommend him to your acquaintance and Civilities, persuaded that his great merits and Litterary Talent cannot fail of rendering this Introduction acceptable to you.

Mr. Barbauld will be so obliging as to deliver you a Packet which I have received from Mr. Adams, and I must beg leave to refer you to him for the little News here. Permit me to give you the trouble of making my best Compliments to Col. Humphreys and to assure you of the great Respect with which I have the honor to be Dear Sir Your most faithful & Devoted Humble Servant,

EDWD. BANCROFT

RC (DLC); endorsed. Recorded in SJL as received 17 May 1786, "by Barbaud."

The PACKET . . RECEIVED FROM MR. ADAMS presumably referred to that of 15 Sep. and its enclosures; if so, Bancroft—or Barbaud—must have changed his mind and turned the packet over to Franks, who delivered it to TJ on 22 Sep. 1785, whereas the present letter, together with Henley's of 15 Sep. 1785, was not delivered to TJ until 17 May 1786 "by Barnaud." If Adams' packet of 15 Sep. was in Bancroft's hands even temporarily its contents were almost certainly made available to the British secret intelligence.

From Samuel Henley

Rendlesham near Melton & Ipswich
15 Sepr. 1785.

DEAR SIR

I was happy to be informed by my friend Bradford that you were well, and have a thousand acknowledgements to make for your attentions to him, which he speaks of to me in the handsomest manner. I trust however that you will not repent of them, though they have encouraged me to introduce two other friends from this side the water. You have I doubt not read the Poems of Mrs. Barbauld (late Miss Aiken) and perhaps her other works. To say of her that she is the first Poetess that hath adorned the literature of England is but intimating the least part of her desert. No heart can possess more worth. Her husband has a most ungracious outside, but you will find him the verse within.

I am sorry to learn the fate of my books, prints &c., and exceedingly regret that no more of them fell into your hands. The pleasure I once took in them, made me feel the more pain for their loss, which however is in some measure alleviated by the consideration that some of them escaped the flames and are in the possession of a friend I so much respect.

Will you have the goodness to present my best compliments to Mrs. Jefferson if she be with you, or when you write to her? Mrs. Henley would be very happy to receive her in England, as I trust you are convinced would Dear Sir, Your most obliged and obedient servant,   S. HENLEY

RC (MHi); addressed to TJ at the "Cul de Sac Taitbout à Paris"; endorsed. Recorded in SJL as received 17 May 1786, "by Barbaud."

From John Jay

DR. SIR   New York 15th. September 1785

I herewith enclose a Letter for Count de Vergennes, and also a Copy of it for your Perusal and Information. Although certain Circumstances have left to Mr. De Marbois a less Share in the Confidence and Attachment of our People, than it was in his Power to have acquired, yet his Conduct as Chargé des Affaires having been unexceptionable, he merited and has received Commendation for it. He is still here, and until his Departure Mr. Otto will probably postpone entering on the Business of his Place. The Idea of Chevr. de la Luzerne's Return still prevails, and I think it would be useful that he should, because it is generally thought that his private Sentiments and Wishes are friendly to this Country. It is much in the Power of Ministers to cherish or diminish Harmony; and it is much to be wished that France may send none here who may be more disposed to blame than to approve. The Chevalier already possesses Rank and Character, and therefore is not exposed to Temptations to endeavour to raise himself by means of the first Step he may meet with whether clean or otherwise.

I am Dr. Sir &c., JOHN JAY

FC (DNA: PCC, No. 121). Recorded in SJL as received 19 Oct. 1785. Enclosure: Copy and RC of Jay to Vergennes, 6 Sep. 1785, acknowledging Vergennes' letter of 20 June 1785 informing him that "a Chargé des affaires has been named . . . during the Absence of Chevr. De la Luzerne." Jay's paragraph concerning Marbois reads: "In Justice to Mr. De Marbois, I ought to observe that the Manner in which he has filled the Place of his Majesty's Chargé des Affaires, not only corresponds with my Ideas of Propriety, but has given great satisfaction to Congress; who have directed me to mention it to your Excellency" (Arch. Aff. Etr., Corr. Pol., E.-U., xxx; Tr in DLC; DNA: PCC, No. 121).

Marbois' letters of 30 Aug. to Congress and to Jay announcing Otto's appointment as chargé d'affaires were submitted to Congress on 2 Sep. and Jay was thereupon directed to report. He did so by submitting drafts of two letters to Marbois, in the first of which he wrote: "The manner in which you have filled the place of his Majesty's Chargé des Affaires here has given them [Congress] great satisfaction, and I am ordered to mention this to Count de Vergennes" (JCC, XXIX, 675-8). Only a few days before TJ transmitted Jay's letter to Vergennes, that minister had received an anonymous letter signed "Union" and dated "United States 20th August 1785" asking for Marbois' recall (Arch. Aff. Etr., Corr. Pol., E.-U., xxx; Tr in DLC). Otto arrived on 25 Aug. 1785 and called on Jay the next morning. Jay, Otto wrote Vergennes, "m'a reçu avec sa reserve ordinaire; il m'a fait plusieurs questions sur le retour de M. Franklin et sur M. Jefferson." Otto touched land just at the moment "M. de Marbois alloit celebrer avec les Membres du Congrès et les personnes principales de l'Etat de New-york la fête du Roi. Il avoit rassemblé dans sa maison de campagne vis à vis de Newyork sur la Longue isle une societé nombreuse; l'arrivée du paquebot de S.M., les nouvelles de france qu'on attendoit depuis longtems et surtout l'annonce de l'avancement de M. de Marbois, auquel tout le monde prenoit le plus vif interêt augmenterent la gaieté et le contentement des Convives" (Otto to Vergennes, 26 Aug. 1785; Arch. Aff. Etr., Corr. Pol., E.-U., xxx; Tr in DLC). A few days later Otto had a long conversation with Jay, who seemed much more communicative than at the first interview. Jay began by praising Luzerne, who, he thought, had acted as a sort of mediator between the two nations and who knew better than anyone else how to reconcile "l'avantage de son souverain avec la prosperité de la republique près de laquelle il etoit accredité." Otto seized this opportunity "pour lui parler de M. Jefferson, mais il a detourné la conversation par des observations generales en me disant 'qu'il etoit beaucoup plus aisé de negocier dans une Monarchie que dans un pays republicain . . .'" (Otto to Vergennes, 30 Aug. 1785; same).

From John Adams

Grosvenor Square Septr. 16. 1785

At the desire of the Baron De Poellnitz, I do myself the Honour to introduce him to you. This Nobleman you know married a Daughter of the Earl of Bute once the Wife of Earl Piercy. They have lived some time in New York. He goes to France to meet his Lady who arrived there sometime since.

Coll. Franks will leave Us tomorrow. There are abroad so many infamous Fictions concerning the Captures made by the Algeriens, that I still hope the Report of their Advertizing American Vessells and Cargoes for sale, is without a better foundation. With great Esteem Your Friend and Servant, JOHN ADAMS

RC (DLC); endorsed. Recorded in SJL as received 2 Oct. 1785.

From James Wilkie

Marseilles, 16 Sep. 1785. Forwards enclosure received from "Consul Logie of Algiers"; since vessels are constantly going from Marseilles to Algiers, he offers TJ his services.

RC (MoSHi); 2 p.; endorsed. The enclosure has been identified from TJ's record in SJL of its receipt on 22 Sep. 1785, which reads in part: "Jas. Wilkie's inclosing former [i.e., Richard O'Bryen to TJ, 24 Aug. 1785]."

From John Adams

DEAR SIR Grosvenor Square 18 Sepr. 1785

Inclosed, you have in Confidence some Compliments. Give me in confidence your Opinion of them. Is there any thing said by me which I ought not to have said? Is there any expression exceptionable? Have I compromised myself or the public in any thing? more than ought to be—

The Custom of making a Speech is so settled, that not only, the Secretary of State and the Master of the Ceremonies, but some of the Foreign Ministers, took the pains to inform me it was indispensable; otherwise being sensible of the difficulty of being complaisant enough without being too much, I intended to have delivered my Credentials, without saying more, than that they were Credentials to his Majesty from the United States. Your Friend.

FC (MHi: AMT); unsigned. Recorded in SJL as received 22 Sep. 1785. Enclosures (DLC: TJ Papers, 12: 2133-4): Copies of Adams' address to George III, delivered on the occasion of his audience to present his credentials as minister to Great Britain, 1 June 1785; the King's reply; Adams' address to the Queen of 9 June and her reply.

It is puzzling that Adams should have waited so long to transmit these ceremonial addresses to TJ. He had already sent them, under an injunction of secrecy, to Jay in his letters of 2 and 10 June 1785 (*Dipl. Corr., 1783-1789*, II, 367-71, 376-8; the rough draft of the letter of 2 June, with a number of revisions in the speeches by Adams and by George III, is in MHi: AMT, Letter-book No. 21; the fair copy is in same, Letter-book No. 22). The texts of these addresses as printed in *Dipl.*

Corr., 1783-1789 and in Adams' *Works*, ed. C. F. Adams, VIII, 255-9, 265-6, are the same, but they vary in a number of particulars from those sent to TJ. As published, for example, the remarks of George III are quoted in part as follows: "I will be very frank with you. I was the last to consent to the separation; but the separation having been made, and having become inevitable, I have always said, as I say now, that I would be the first to meet the friendship of the United States as an independent Power." The text sent to TJ reads: "I will be very frank with you, Sir. I was the last to consent to the Seperation, but the seperation having been made and having become inevitable, I have always said as I say now, that I will be the last to disturb the Independence of the United States, or in any way to infringe upon their Rights."

From André Limozin

Le Havre, 18 Sep. 1785. Acknowledges TJ's letter of 11 Sep. by Capt. Yeaton and regrets that Yeaton did not succeed. Limozin will be happy to be of any service to TJ and to inform him of all ships passing between France and Virginia and the ports for which they are bound; he will also take care of the trunks as TJ requested.

RC (MHi); 3 p.; dated at "Havre de Grace." TJ's entry in SJL for its receipt under 20 Sep. 1785 reads in part: "(after I had written of this date)."

To John Adams

Sep. 19. 1785. Paris.

Lambe[1] *is arrived. He brings new full powers to us from Congress to appoint persons to negotiate with the Barbary states, but we are to sign the treaties. Lambe has not even a recommendation from them to us, but it seems clear that he would be approved by them. I told him of Mr. Barclay's appointment to Marocco and proposed Algiers to him. He agrees. A small alteration in the form of our dispatches will be necessary, and of course another courier shall be dispatched to you on the return of Colo. Franks, for your pleasure herein.*

RC (MHi: AMT); unsigned; partly in code, followed by a full text in an unidentified hand of the letter as decoded, labelled "Translation." Dft

(DLC); at head of text: "letter to Mr. Adams. All in cypher except the words lined." The texts of this translation and Dft are identical, except for minor variations of spelling and punctuation. Entry in SJPL reads: "Adams John. Lambe's arrival."

1 This and subsequent words in italics are written in code; the text presented here is the decoding accompanying RC in MHi, which has been verified so far as possible by the editors, employing the partly reconstructed Code No. 8.

From Lister Asquith

PLEASE YOUR EXCELLENCY

St Pauls Prison
Sept. 19th. 1785

I received your kind and exceptionable Letter which has relieved my mind of a great deal of trouble. I left Baltimore on the 20th. of June and got down to Hampton Roads and, finding that all Tobacco would answer better than Flour, discharged 50 Barrels of Flour and one Hdd. of Tobacco, it not being very good. But before our Cargo came on board we were drove out to sea by a heavy Gale of Wind and drove of the Coast without any clearance but that we had from Baltimore, and have sent you my Log Book which [gives] a true account of our Circumstances. Sir the reason of my coming in so small a Vessel was that having a law suit in England going on that was to be tryed very soon and no Vessels that were ready to sail that I thought could make so quick a Passage as myself, was determined to venture to England directly, as all my Estate almost in the World depended on that Suit as some of my relations had got Possession of it before Peace was proclaimed and are now trying to deprive me of it, because I was born in England and had been in the American service all the war and married to an American Lady and taken up arms against the Brittish. My wife was to sail in a short time after me for England and since my departure I never have had the least account. I am affraid that the Suit will be given against me by my Absence. As for my Expences it has cost me almost all the money I brought with me as they impose on me on the most barefaced manner charging us the most exorbitant prices for every thing. So that if I lose the Vessel and Cargo I am perhaps with my unhappy Family ruined, which thoughts are worse to me than Death because I have lost a Handsome fortune the last War. I believe the Judge of the High Court of Admiralty and a Lawyer Mr. Koch has begun a Suit at Brest in my Favor, for every person that saw our Vessel, even the Officer that drew out the Protest against me, owns that we were not fit to proceed farther for Want of Necessarys to save our lives and property, tho' he was obliged to do it to save his Bread tho' it was against his inclinations.

The register was taken out by Capt. Charls. Harrison (a Gentleman that I was taken with about four months before the peace was proclaimed in the Ship Jolly Tar belonging to Mr. Messieruer & Co. French Merchants Baltimore) for 21 Tons before I knew any thing of it, to save the Expences and port Charges in England as we pay double to what they do themselves on Account that we are Foreigners. But I can give my Affidavit that I bought her according to the Bill of Sale the Coppy of which was sent to you by Capt. De Ville. The guager did not measure only her Hold from inside to inside and not $\frac{1}{2}$ Her steerage. He allowed nothing for the Cocpit Cabin Forecastle and one half her steerage by what I saw him measure. I implore your utmost protection as I am so distressed and all my property I am affraid is lost in England. I hope you will do your utmost to forward the tryal on as soon as possible as we shall have nothing in a few days to live on, only their 3 Sols ℔ Day as our Cash is near out. I have wrote to our Lawyer at Brest and to the judge of the Admiralty to let you know what they think of it and to prosecute the suit with great dispatch, and beg you will help on the Suit as fast as possible as we have no other Friend to apply to but you and bring it to tryal as soon as possible, as I know we are innocent, and for us to be present as we can give the clearest reasons against all their false suppositions. As I am so distressed about my unhappy family who I suppose are in a Strange Country I beg you to get it brought to tryal as soon as you can. I suppose they will put the tryal off as long as they can and then turn it through several Courts of Justice, as Mr. Picrel L'Aine informs us, to keep us in Confinement and out of our property as Long as they can, as they are rich and able to keep puting it off by their influence. The Trial I wish it was to morrow as I know we are innocent and not the least evidence against us, as they only form bare suppositions. And I am determined to prosecute for all Costs damages and false imprisonment, for I believe it is, and am almost certain it is all I am worth in the World if I have lost the suit in England. And I have no friend but you in this Part to help me or advise and they have cost me all that I brought with me within a Trifle. And now I must make the Best I can of this Unfortunate Affair and your Protection in it we shall never be able to express our Gratitude to you for it. From your most obedient & humble Servt.,   LISTER ASQUITH

P.S. I cleared out from Baltimore and sailed the 11th. of June but run on shore at Smith's Point and sprung a leak. I returned to Baltimore and hove her down and stopd the Leak and Ship'd Capt. McNeel, as I was in a poor state of Health, and sailed again on the 20th. My register and original Bill of Sail I sent to Brest and have sent you the Log Book and Clearance, also 2 Letters from Mr. Hamer, Broker in Liverpool, for your inspection and my Coppy to him to insure the Vessel and Cargo I have lost. If it Lyes in your power to get our Vessel for us, we should be happy as we could one of us go to sea and settle our Business as we could and make some trifle and the other would be content to stay here.

RC (DLC). Recorded in SJL as received 25 Sep. 1785. Enclosure not found, but see TJ's statement of the case (TJ to Vergennes, 14 Nov. 1785) which was based on the log of the *William and Catherine*.

From John Banister, Jr.

Avignon, 19 Sep. 1785. Acknowledges receipt two days before of TJ's letter of 16 Aug.; advises that letters be directed to the care of "Mr. Teste banquier expeditionaire en cour de Rome Avignon." Since his last letter to TJ, he has suffered a very severe attack of "the ague and fever which together with the disorder in my bowels reduced me as low as it was possible"; he has no illusions concerning the rapidity or permanence of his recovery. He expects to remain at Avignon for the winter "more from a dislike . . . to changing place at present than from the satisfaction I enjoy in my situation." Asks TJ's advice regarding "the best seminary of Education at this time in Europe for the elevation of Youth"; his father hopes to send over his other son in the spring; from what he has heard, "Geneva is the most eligible."

RC (MHi); 4 p.; endorsed; at foot of text there is a slip attached with a variant address in TJ's hand: "Bannister chez Monsr. Deleutre Apothecaire place du change." TJ's record in SJL of receipt of this letter on 25 Sep. 1785 includes the address furnished by Banister in the letter. The differing address on the slip contains on its verso what appears to be the beginning of a letter from TJ: "Votre lettre de l'11me. Octobre ma chere Mad[ame]"; this letter of 11 Oct. [1785?] from TJ's unidentified correspondent has not been found, nor has his reply, if completed, been identified.

From Barré

EXCELLENCE   Lorient ce 19 Septembre [1785]

J'ose toujour esperer que vous voudrés bien ne pas oublier ce que vous m'avés fait L'honneur de me promettre. Le Général M'a demandé hier si vous m'aviés honnoré d'une Lettre depuis quelques mois. Je lui ai Répondu que oui. Mais comme vos Lettres sont en anglois et qu'il ne Le Sçait pas, il pourroit Soupçonner que je Cherche à me prévaloir de vos Bontés auprès de Lui pour Capter les Siennes. Et Rien au monde n'est peut être aussi dangereux que d'avoir tord vis avis de son chef. Je ne L'ai pas il est vray! Mais l'on ne peut empecher des Soupçons; la crainte d'être trompée est souvent La prémière Idée qui vient Contre un jeune homme. J'attend donc des Bontés de votre excellence L'éxecution des promesses qu'elle à bien voulu me faire au Sujet du portrait du Général Waginston. Ma Reconnaissance égallera la durée de celle de L'amérique pour La Grandeur de vos Entreprises.

J'ai L'honneur dêtre avec Respect Excellence Votre très Humble Et très Obeissant Serviteur,   BARRÉ

RC (DLC); at foot of letter: "Lieutenant des frégattes du Roi hotel de M. thévenard, Commande. de la marine, a Lorient"; endorsed. Recorded in SJL as received 25 Sep. 1785.

From William McNeill

[*St. Pol de Léon, 19? Sep. 1785*]. Acknowledges TJ's letter and states that he is the son of William McNeill of Boston. At the beginning of the war he built a ship there with Admiral Montague's permission, but "After She was bult admrill Graves tuck the Station and would not alow me to Lanch the Ship unless I Enterd hur in the Kings Survis which was much against my Will and was obliged to Sell hur on the Stocks." He then bought a brig in Salem and made several voyages; later, en route to Baltimore, he was captured by the *Otter* off Annapolis, taken to Dunmore at Quinn's Island, and kept in irons for two months. He escaped, went to Philadelphia, took command of the *Rattlesnake*, and cruised successfully off the Barbados; he returned home, volunteered in the Continental Army, "and under General Knox I had the honner to Ride the Genrals aide de camp German Town Battel." Several weeks later he was sent to the support of Fort Mifflin; when the *Vigilant* came up and the troops were withdrawn from the island, McNeill and sixteen others were left to destroy the works and burn the barracks. He spent the latter part of the war privateering. McNeill and his companions implore TJ's assistance, for they are strangers to France, their families are suffering from their unjust imprisonment, and their funds are almost exhausted. If their vessel were returned, one could go to England to settle their business, and the other would stay at Roscoff.

RC (DLC); 3 p.; without date; in Lister Asquith's hand. The letter is clearly in reply to TJ to Asquith, 14 Sep. 1785, and was probably written at the same time as Asquith's reply to TJ, 19 Sep. 1785.

From Nicolas & Jacob van Staphorst

We are honored with Your Excellency's esteemed Favor of 31 July and are much Obliged by the very particular and satisfactory Manner in which you have furnished your Opinion of the Value of the different species of Public Funds in America. The Settlement of the Concerns of Mess. De la Lande and Fynje in any other possible Way than by Acceding to Mr. Daniel Parker's Proposal presenting numberless difficulties, great delay and very considerable Losses, The Trustees have judged it to be for the General Advantage to enter into a Treaty with Mr. Parker, of which we forwarded Intelligence to the Honorable The Commissioners of the Board of Treasury of the United States of America ℔ inclosed Copy of Mess. W. & J. Willink and Our joint Letter on the Subject, Whereto we beg your Reference, entreating Your Excellency's Sentiments relative to our Proceedings in this Business.

We have now the Pleasure to communicate that the Trustees of the Estate of De la Lande and Fynje have agreed with Mr. Parker upon the principal Conditions on which that Gentleman is to take over all the remaining Goods and debts in America due to the society of Geyer, De la Lande and Fynje &c. so that there is not any thing of Consequence to be further argued except some Points of Regulation, Which are not of a Nature to endanger the Plan.

It is with sincere satisfaction We can assure you Mr. Parker's Conduct throughout has been manly, candid, and explicit, Which joined to the Idea we entertain of his Character And the Informations we have had of his past Situation and Circumstances, tranquilize us about his Intention and Ability to fulfill his Engagement And thereby terminate satisfactorily a Transaction attended with this very singular Circumstance: That at same time the Concerned in the Estate of de la Lande and Fynje will benefit in a very extensive degree By the Transfer to Mr. Parker, That Gentleman will reap considerable Advantages by being able to raise a large Sum of Money upon a deposit, so peculiarly situated that at present it would not admit of a Conversion into specie but thro' an enormous sacrifice.

Should your Excellency please to favor us with your Advice or any Hints you may judge necessary, They will be received and attended to with the greatest Attention. Having the Honor to be with

Sincere Respect and Regard Your Excellency's Most obdt. & very hble. Servs., NICS. & JACOB VAN STAPHORST

RC (DLC); endorsed. Enclosure: Copy of W. & J. Willink and N. & J. van Staphorst to commissioners of the treasury, without date, concerning the affairs of the estate of De la Lande & Fynje whose trusteeship they have assumed; they hope the commissioners will approve of Daniel Parker's proposal to take over from the estate all the goods shipped to America at their original prices and discharge the full value in twelve to fifteen years, depositing as collateral "Double the Amounts of the Goods in Continental Funds bearing an Interest of six ℗ Cent.," plus 5 per cent interest until the whole obligation is liquidated; they think almost all of the creditors in Europe will approve the plan and added: "We would hesitate more in case it appeared to be mysterious how Mr. Parker will make his Accounts, but this we think is clear to a Man who knows that from the present scarcity of Money the most solid Continental debts must necessarily sell in America with difficulty and under their real value and that probably this will change very much in the Twelve or Fifteen years after which Mr. Parker will be obliged to discharge his Bonds, and

Consequently he will at the same time have the command of the money proceeding from the sales and the Prospect of the Rise of his Stock. This Consideration makes us believe that his Proposal is fair and honest"; from "the many infamous Reports by the Way of England" concerning public and private business on the Continent, together with the failure of American houses in Europe, American credit had sunk below what it was during the war: "Now we beg you to consider what a new stroke it would receive in case Congress should decline to accept a Security for its own Engagements for double the Amount of a Debt due to it. . . . and on the Contrary What will be the Consequences of its Accepting the Proposals. It will persuade People here of the Solidity of the Union and the sacredness of their Engagements and May contribute to restore the American Credit, Which will operate advantageously upon any new Loans Congress may wish to raise when more favorable Junctures shall offer" (Tr. in DLC: TJ Papers, 17: 3059-60).

TJ's letter OF 31 JULY is dated 30 July in SJL, SJPL, and PrC.

To Mary Jefferson

MY DEAR POLLY   Paris Sep. 20. 1785.

I have not received a letter from you since I came to France. If you knew how much I love you and what pleasure the receipt of your letters gave me at Philadelphia, you would have written to me, or at least have told your aunt what to write, and her goodness would have induced her to take the trouble of writing it. I wish so much to see you that I have desired your uncle and aunt to send you to me. I know, my dear Polly, how sorry you will be, and ought to be, to leave them and your cousins but your [sister and m]yself cannot live without you, and after a while we will carry you back again to see your friends in Virginia. In the meantime you shall be taught here to play on the harpsichord, to draw, to dance, to read and talk French and such other things as will make you more worthy of the love of your friends. But above all things, by our care and love of you, we will teach you to love us more than you will do if you stay so far from us. I have had no opportunity since Colo. LeMaire went, to send you any thing: but when you come here you shall have as many dolls and playthings as you want for yourself, or to send to your cousins whenever you shall have opportunities. I hope you are a very good girl, that you love your uncle and aunt very much, and are very thankful to them for all their goodness to you; that you never suffer yourself to be angry with any body, that you give your playthings to those who want them, that you do whatever any body desires of you that is right, that you never tell stories, never beg for any thing, mind your book and your work when your aunt tells you, never play but when she permits you, nor go where she forbids you. Remember too as a constant charge not to go out without your bonnet because it will make you very ugly and then we should not love you so much. If you will always practise these lessons we shall continue to love you as we do now, and it is impossible to love you more. We shall hope to have you with us next summer, to find you a very good girl, and to [assure you of the truth] of our affection to you. Adieu my dear child! Your's affectionately,   TH: JEFFERSON

PrC (CLU); portions of MS worn, for which missing words have been supplied in brackets from text in Randolph, *Domestic Life*, p. 103-4; at foot of text "Polly Jefferson"; endorsed (presumably much later): "Jefferson Maria." Recorded in SJL as sent by "Mr. Fitzhugh."

To André Limozin

SIR   Paris Sep. 20. 1785.

I have lately received a letter from the Secretary for Foreign affairs in America, on the case of a Mr. Fortin, an American to whom an inheritance in the town of Havre has fallen some time ago. The party complains of delays in the recovery of his inheritance, and the Minister desires my enquiries into the cause of them, and that I will endeavor to obtain that dispatch which is an essential part of the justice due to every man. As I perceive by the papers sent me that Mr. Fortin is already much indebted to your friendly information and assistance, I will take the liberty of asking you to send me a state of his rights, of the particular circumstances on which he founds them, and those also on which his adversaries rest their defence, together with the cause of the delay which he experiences. My apology for the trouble I give you, will, I hope, be found, in the friendly dispositions you have already shewn to Mr. Fortin, and in the instructions which I have received on this subject. I have the honour to be with much respect Sir Your most obedient humble servant, TH: JEFFERSON

PrC (DLC). Entry in SJL reads: "added P. S. to Limozin acknoleging receipt of his of Sep. 11 [i.e., 18] and thanking him for friendly offers"; entry in SJPL reads: "Limozin Andrew. Fortin's case."

To James Madison, with Account Enclosed

DEAR SIR   Paris Sep. 20. 1785.

By Mr. Fitzhugh you will receive my letter of the 1'st inst. He is still here, and gives me an opportunity of again addressing you much sooner than I should have done but for the discovery of a great peice of inattention. In that letter I send you a detail of the cost of your books, and desire you to keep the amount in your hands, as if I had forgot that a part of it was in fact your own, as being a balance of what I had remained in your debt. I really did not attend to it in the moment of writing, and when it occurred to me, I revised my memorandum book from the time of our being in Philadelphia together, and stated our account from the beginning lest I should forget or mistake any part of it: I inclose you this state. You will always be so good as to let me know from time to time your advances for me. Correct with freedom all my proceedings for you, as in what I do I have no other desire than that of doing exactly what will be most pleasing to you.

I received this summer a letter from Messrs. Buchanan and Hay as directors of the public buildings desiring I would have drawn for them plans of sundry buildings, and in the first place of a Capitol. They fixed for their receiving this plan a day which was within one month of that on which their letter came to my hand. I engaged an Architect of capital abilities in this business. Much time was requisite, after the external form was agreed on, to make the internal distribution convenient for the three branches of government. This time was much lengthened by my avocations to other objects which I had no right to neglect. The plan however was settled. The gentlemen had sent me one which they had thought of. The one agreed on here is more convenient, more beautiful, gives more room and will not cost more than two thirds of what that would. We took for our model what is called the Maisonquarrèe of Nismes, one of the most beautiful, if not the most beautiful and precious morsel of architecture left us by antiquity. It was built by Caius and Lucius Caesar and repaired by Louis XIV. and has the suffrage of all the judges of architecture who have seen it, as yeilding to no one of the beautiful monuments of Greece, Rome, Palmyra and Balbec which late travellers have communicated to us. It is very simple, but it is noble beyond expression, and would have done honour to our country as presenting to travellers a morsel of taste in our infancy promising much for our maturer age. I have been much mortified with information which I received two days ago from Virginia that the first brick of the Capitol would be laid within a few days. But surely the delay of this peice of a summer would have been repaid by the savings in the plan preparing here, were we to value it's other superiorities as nothing. But how is a taste in this beautiful art to be formed in our countrymen, unless we avail ourselves of every occasion when public buildings are to be erected, of presenting to them models for their study and imitation? Pray try if you can effect the stopping of this work. I have written also to E. R. on the subject. The loss will be only of the laying the bricks already laid, or a part of them. The bricks themselves will do again for the interior walls, and one side wall and one end wall may remain as they will answer equally well for our plan. This loss is not to be weighed against the saving of money which will arise, against the comfort of laying out the public money for something honourable, the satisfaction of seeing an object and proof of national good taste, and the regret and mortification of erecting a monument of our barbarism which will be loaded with execrations as long as it shall endure. The plans are in good forwardness and I hope will be ready within three or four weeks. They could not be stopped now but on paying their whole price which will be considerable. If the Undertakers are afraid to undo what they have done, encourage them to it by a recommendation from the assembly. You see I am an enthusiast on the subject of the arts. But it is an enthusiasm of which I am not ashamed, as it's object is to improve the taste of my countrymen, to increase their reputation, to reconcile to them the respect of the world and procure them it's praise.

I shall send off your books, in two trunks, to Havre within two or three days to the care of Mr. Limozin, American agent there. I will advise you as soon as I know by what vessel he forwards them. Adieu. Your's affectionately,   TH: JEFFERSON

ENCLOSURE

J. Madison to Th: J. Dr.

			Dollars
1783. Nov.	5.	To paid Stockdon at Princeton	9.133
		Dr. Wiggins	2.333
		Laurence	4.533
	13.	to cash	86.666
			102.666

Cr.

			Dollars	
Nov.	2.	By cash	98.	
	12.	By do.	4.666	102.666

Dr.

1784.

		Dollars	
Apr. 6.	To paid Dudley (by Mr Maury) for a pr. spectacles	13.666	
	To my assumpsit to do. for a 2d. pr. spectacles	13.666	
	To my bill on the Treasurer of Virginia for	407.333	
	Balance in your favour	68.666	503.333

Cr.

1783. Nov.	22.	By cash at Philadelphia	170.	
	26.	By bill on the Treasurer of Virginia (given me at Annapolis)	333.333	503.333

Dr.

1784. May 25.	To pd. Aitken for Blair's lectures for you	4.666	
	Balance in your favor	77.666	82.333

Cr.

1784.	By balance as above	68.666	
	By my omission to pay Dudley for the 2d pr of spectacles ..	13.666	82.333

1784.[1]   J. Madison to Th: J.   Dr.

		₶	s
Sep. 1.	To amount of advances for books &c. as by acct. rendered this day	1154	13
	Testament politique d'Angleterre 12 mo.	2	10
	Memoires de Voltaire 12mo.	3	0
	Frederic le grand. 8vo.	4	0
		1164	3

RC (DLC: Madison Papers); endorsed at head of text: "Recd. Feby. 24. 1786." PrC (DLC: TJ Papers). Recorded in SJL as sent by "Mr. Fitzh[ugh]"; entry in SJPL reads: "Madison James. Private accounts. Capitol." Enclosure: TJ's account with Madison, 2 Nov. 1783 to 1 Sep. 1784 [i.e., 1785] (DLC: Madison Papers; in TJ's hand).

The information that TJ RECEIVED TWO DAYS AGO FROM VIRGINIA was in Currie's letter of 5 Aug. which arrived on 18 Sep. 1785.

¹ i.e., 1785.

To Edmund Randolph

DEAR SIR   Paris Sep. 20. 1785.

Being in your debt for ten volumes of Buffon, I have endeavored to find something that would be agreeable to you to receive in return. I therefore send you by way of Havre a dictionary of law Natural and municipal in 13. vols. 4to. called le Code de l'humanite. It is published by Felice, but written by him and several other authors of established reputation. It is an excellent work. I do not mean to say that it answers fully to it's title. That would have required fifty times the volume. It wants many articles which the title would induce us to seek in it. But the articles of which it does treat are well written. It is better than the voluminous dictionnaire diplomatique, and better also than the same branch of the Encyclopedie methodique. There has been nothing published here since I came of extraordinary merit. The Encyclopedie methodique which is coming out from time to time must be excepted from this. It is to be had at two guineas less than the subscription price. I shall be happy to send you any thing in this way which you may desire. French books are to be bought here for two thirds of what they can in England. English and Greek and Latin authors cost from 25. to 50. pr. cent more here than in England.

I received some time ago a letter from Messrs. Hay and Buchanan as directors of the publick buildings desiring I would have plans drawn for our public buildings and in the first place for the Capitol. I did not receive their letter till within a month of the time they had fixed on for receiving the drawings. Nevertheless I engaged an excellent architect to comply with their desire. It has taken much time to accomodate the External adopted, to the internal arrangement necessary for the three branches of government. However it is effected, on a plan which with a great deal of beauty and convenience within, unites an external form on the most perfect model of antiquity now existing. This is the Maison quarrée of Nismes built by Caius and Lucius Caesar and repaired by Louis XIV. which in the opinion of all who have seen it yeilds in beauty to no peice of architecture on earth. The gentlemen inclosed me a plan of which they had thought. The one preparing here will be more convenient, give more room, and cost but two thirds of that: and as a peice of architecture, doing honour to our country, will leave nothing to be desired. The plans will be ready soon. But two days ago I received a letter from Virginia informing me the first brick of the Capitol would be laid within a few days. This mortifies me extremely. The delay of this summer would have been amply repaid by the superiority and œconomy of the plan preparing here. Is it impossible to stop the work where it is? You will gain money by losing what is done, and general approbation instead of occasioning a regret which will endure as long as your building does. How is a taste for a chaste and good style of building to be formed in our countrymen unless we seize all occasions which the erection of public buildings offers, of presenting to them models for their imitation? Do, my dear Sir, exert your influence to stay the further progress of the work till you can receive these plans. You will only lose the price of laying what bricks are already laid, and of taking part of them asunder. They will do again for the inner walls. A plan for a prison will be sent at the same time.

Mazzei is here and in pressing distress for money. I have helped him as far as I have been able, but particular circumstances put it out of my power to do more. He is looking with anxiety to the arrival of every vessel in hopes of relief through your means. If he does not receive it soon it is difficult to foresee his fate.

The quiet which Europe enjoys at present leaves nothing to communicate to you in the political way. The Emperor and Dutch still differ about the quantum of money to be paid by the latter, they know not for what. Perhaps their internal convulsion will hasten them to a decision. France is improving her navy as if she was already in a naval war: yet I see no immediate prospect of her having occasion for it. England is not likely to offer war to any nation, unless perhaps to ours. This would cost us our whole shipping: but in every other respect we might flatter ourselves with success. But the most succesful war seldom pays for its losses. I shall be glad to hear from you when convenient & am with much esteem Dr. Sir Your friend & servant,   TH: JEFFERSON

P.S. Mazzei having desired me to write to Mr. Adams on the subject of the inclosed letter, has further desired me to transmit the letter to you.

PrC (DLC). Recorded in sjl as sent by "Mr. Fitzh[ugh]"; entry in sjpl reads: "Randolph Edmund. Books. Mazzie. Europe." Enclosure: Presumably a copy of Adams' reply of 11 Sep. to TJ's letter of 4 Sep. 1785 about Mazzei's style of living in Europe while agent of Virginia.

To James Buchanan

Dear Sir   Paris Sep. 22. 1785.

By my letter of Jan. 13. I took the liberty of praying you to send me Hayes's newspapers to the care of N. Jamieson of New York, by post if free, or otherwise by other opportunities. I have not yet received any: but pre[suming] on past experiences of your goodness I suppose some may [be] on the way. In the mean time experience proves to me that the French postage is exorbitant beyond conception. The Newyork papers of one month coming at the close of the month by the packet cost me 8. or 10. guineas a packet. I am therefore obliged to change my plan, by desiring all newspapers for me to be put under cover to Mr. Jay Secretary for foreign affairs at New York. Him I have desired to pack the whole in a box and direct to the Consul at l'Orient, sending them on the Packet as merchandize, in which way they will cost me livres only instead of guineas. I will pray you to have mine sent in this way to Mr. Jay and by post, as they will be free of American postage. Nothing new, all being quiet. I am with much esteem Dr. Sir Your most obdt. servt.,   Th: Jefferson

PrC (DLC); portions of MS worn and faded, for which missing words have been supplied conjecturally. Recorded in sjl as sent by "Mr. Fitzh[ugh]."

To Elizabeth Wayles Eppes

Dear Madam   Paris, Sept. 22d, 1785.

The Mr. Fitzhughs having staid here longer than they expected, I have (since writing my letter of Aug. 30, to Mr. Eppes) received one from Dr. Currie, of August 5, by which I have the happiness to learn you are all well, and my Poll also. Every information of this kind is like gaining another step, and seems to say we "have got so far safe." Would to God the great step was taken and taken safely; I mean that which is to place her on this side of the Atlantic. No event of your life has put it into your power to conceive how I feel when I reflect that such a child, and so dear to me, is to cross the ocean, is to be exposed to all the sufferings and risks, great and small, to which a situation on board a ship exposes every one. I drop my pen at the thought—but she must come. My affections would leave me balanced between the desire to have her with me, and the fear of exposing her; but my reason tells me the dangers are not great, and the advantages to her will be considerable.

I send by Mr. Fitzhugh some garden and flower seed and bulbs; the latter, I know, will fall in your department. I wish the opportunity had admitted the sending more, as well as some things for the children; but Mr. Fitzhugh being to pass a long road both here and in America, I could not ask it of him. Pray write to me, and write me long letters. Currie has sent me one worth a great deal for the details of small news it contains. I mention this as an example for you. You always know facts enough which would be interesting to me to fill sheets of paper. I pray you, then, to give yourself up to that kind of inspiration, and to scribble on as long as you recollect any thing unmentioned, without regarding whether your lines are straight or your letters even. Remember me affectionately to Mr. Skipwith, and to the little ones of both houses; kiss dear Polly for me, and encourage her for the journey. Accept assurances of unchangeable affection from, dear Madame, your sincere friend and servant,   TH. JEFFERSON

MS not found; text taken from Randolph, *Domestic Life*, p. 104-5. Recorded in SJL as sent by "Mr. Fitzh[ugh]."

To Neil Jamieson

DEAR SIR   Paris Sep. 22. 1785.

By a letter of Jan. 13. I took the liberty of requesting you to send me such of the New York newspapers as you thought best, by the French packet always. Since Mr. Jay's coming into office he is so kind as to do this regularly, so that I am able to save you that trouble as soon as the subscription expires which you entered into for me. A more important article is to pray you, whenever packets of newspapers for me from other parts of the continent come to your hands (as I had taken the liberty to direct), to be so good as to send them to Mr. Jay's office. I have desired him to pack newspapers for me all together in a box and to send them as merchandize directed to the Consul at l'Orient, instead of paying 8. or 10. guineas a packet as I do now for newspapers. They will then come for so many livres. Your favors of June 14, and Aug. 14. came safely to hand. There is nothing interesting here at present. Europe enjoys quiet. The English news you get as speedily almost as we do here. Accept assurances of the respect and esteem with which I am Dr. Sir Your most obedt. humble servt,

TH: JEFFERSON

PrC (MoSHi). Recorded in SJL as sent by "Mr. Fitzh[ugh]."

From André Limozin

[*Le Havre, ca. 22 Sep. 1785.*] Acknowledges TJ's letter of 20 Sep. Though he is busy and has not been well, he will have his old letters to his friend, Robert Morris, looked through and will send TJ copies of what he wrote on the question of Fortin's claim to an inheritance. Since the given name in the papers sent by Morris to support the claim is not the same as that in church records in France, Limozin thinks the claim will not be upheld.

His ship *Eolus*, Capt. Paon, will sail on 15 Oct. for Portsmouth "on her Ballast to take thither a Cargoe of Lumber for the Island of Tobago"; Limozin offers to send anything TJ wishes.

RC (MHi); 3 p.; without date; at foot of letter: "His Excellency Ths. Jefferson Esqre. Ambassador of the United States of America to the Court of Versailles Cul de Sac rüe Tetebout près la Comédie Italienne Paris." This is evidently the undated letter from Limozin which TJ recorded in SJL as received 25 Sep. 1785.

From Ferdinand Grand

Paris, 23 Sep. 1785. Thanks TJ for communicating the contents of Adams' letter on the payment of interest on the Dutch loan. Grand forwarded to Messrs. Willink & van Staphorst a letter from the Commissioners of the Treasury and asked them to notify him if it contained "an order to remit me against the Payment to be made in 9bre. to the Treasury . . . as I had been several times apply'd to, on this affair"; he will inform TJ. Acknowledges TJ's favor of this date; "I . . . shall conform myself to the contents."

RC (DLC); 2 p. TJ's letter to Grand of 23 Sep. has not been found, and none is recorded in SJL.

From William Stephens Smith

SIR   Potsdam 23d. Septr. 1785

I was so exceedingly hurried the few Days that I remained in London after the receipt of your polite Letter (preparing for this excurtion, to the Prussian Camp) that it was not in my power to assure you how much I thought myself honoured by your attention, and of my determination to avail myself of the opertunity of establishing a Corespondence where the returns would be so evidently in my favour. I shall leave this in the morning for Leipsic, Dresdé and Vienna, where after spending a few Days, I propose paying my respects to you at Paris, and will with pleasure take your commands to London, to which as the reviews are now finished, I shall hasten with all convenient expedition. I have the honor to be with great respect Your Excellency's most obedt. Humble Servt.,

W. S. SMITH

RC (MHi); endorsed. Entry in SJL under 23 Oct. 1785 reads in part: "recd. about this time."

To John Adams

DEAR SIR   Paris Sep. 24. 1785.

My letter of Sep. 19. written the morning after Mr. Lamb's arrival here, would inform you of that circumstance. I transmit you herewith copies of the papers he brought to us on the subject of the Barbary treaties. You will see by them that Congress has adopted the very plan which we were proposing to pursue. It will now go on under less danger of objection from the other parties. The receipt of these new papers therefore has rendered necessary no change in matter of substance in the dispatches we had prepared. But they render some formal changes necessary. For instance in our letter of credence for Mr. Barclay to the Emperor of Marocco, it becomes improper to enter into those explanations which seemed proper when that letter was drawn; because Congress in their letter enter into that explanation. In the letter to the Ct. de Vergennes it became proper to mention the new full powers received from Congress and which in some measure accord with the idea communicated by him to us from the M. de Castries. These and other formal alterations, which appeared necessary to me, I have made, leaving so much of the original draughts approved and amended by you as were not inconsistent with these alterations. I have therefore had them prepared fair to save you the trouble of copying; yet wherever you chuse to make alterations you will be so good as to make them; taking in that case the trouble of having new fair copies made out.

You will perceive by Mr. Jay's letter that Congress had not thought proper to give Mr. Lamb any appointment. I imagine they apprehended it might interfere with measures actually taken by us. Notwithstanding the perfect freedom which they are pleased to leave to us on his subject, I cannot feel myself clear of that bias which a presumption of their pleasure gives, and ought to give. I presume that Mr. Lamb met their approbation, because of the recommendations he carried from the Governor and state of Connecticut, because of his actual knowlege of the country and people of the states of Barbary, because of the detention of these letters from March to July, which considering their pressing nature would otherwise have been sent by other Americans who in the mean time have come from N. York to Paris; and because too of the information we received by Mr. Jarvis. These reasons are not strong enough to set aside our appointment of Mr. Barclay to Marocco: that I think should go on, as no man could be sent who would enjoy more the confidence of Congress. But they are strong enough to induce me to propose to you the appointment of Lamb to Algiers. He has followed for many years the Barbary trade and seems intimately acquainted with those states. I have not seen enough of him to judge of his abilities. He seems not deficient as far as I can see, and the footing on which he comes must furnish a presumption for what we do not see. We must say the same as to his integrity; we must rely for this on the recommendations he brings, as it is impossible for us to judge of this for ourselves. Yet it will be our duty to use such reasonable cautions as are in our power. Two occur to me. 1. To give him a clerk capable of assisting and attending to his proceedings and who, in case he thought any thing was going amiss, might give us information. 2. Not to give a credit on Van Staphorst and Willinck, but let his draughts be made on yourself, which with the knowlege you will have of his proceedings, will enable you to check them, if you are sensible of any abuse intended. This will give you trouble; but as I have never found you declining trouble when it is necessary, I venture to propose it. I hope it will not expose you to inconvenience as by instructing Lamb to insert in his draughts a proper usance you can in the mean time raise the money for them by drawing on Holland. I must inform you that Mr. Barclay wishes to be put on the same footing with Mr. Lamb as to this article and therefore I return you your letter of Credit on Van Staphorsts & co. As to the 1st. article there is great difficulty. There is no body at Paris fit for the undertaking who would be likely to accept of it. I mean there is no American, for I should be anxious to place a native in the trust. Perhaps you can send us one from London. There is a Mr. Randolph there from New York whom Mr. Barclay thinks might be relied on very firmly for integrity and capacity. He is there for his health: perhaps you can persuade him to go to Algiers in pursuit of it. If you cannot, I really know not what will be done. It is impossible to propose to Bancroft to go in a secondary capacity. Mr. Barclay and myself have thought of Cairnes at l'Orient as a dernier resort. But it is incertain, or rather improbable that he will undertake it. You will be pleased in the first place to consider of my proposition to send Lamb to Algiers, and in the next all the circumstances before detailed as consequences of that. The inclosed letter from Richard O'Bryan furnishes powerful motives for commencing, by some means or other, the treaty with Algiers more immediately than would be done if left on Mr. Barclay. You will perceive by that that two of our vessels with their crews and cargoes have been carried captive into that port. What is to be done as to those poor people? I am for hazarding the supplementory instruction to Lamb which accompanies these papers. Alter it or reject it as you please. You ask what I think of claiming the Dutch interposition. I doubt the fidelity of any interposition too much to desire it sincerely. Our letters to this court heretofore seemed to oblige us to communicate with them on the subject. If you think the Dutch would take amiss our not applying to them, I will join you in the application. Otherwise the fewer are apprised of our proceedings the better. To communicate them to the States of Holland is to communicate them to the whole world.[1]

Mr. Short returned last night and brought the Prussian treaty duly executed in English and French. We may[2] send it to Congress by the Mr. Fitzhughs going from hence. Will you draw and sign a short letter for that purpose? I send you a copy of a letter received from the M. Fayette. In the present unsettled state of American commerce, I had as lieve avoid all further treaties except with American powers. If Count Merci therefore does not propose the subject to me, I shall not to him, nor do more than decency requires if he does propose it. I am with great esteem Dr. Sir your most obedient humble servt.,   TH: JEFFERSON

RC (MHi: AMT). PrC (DLC). Tr (DNA: PCC, No. 87, 1); in Short's hand; at head of text: "Extract"; lacks final paragraph and signature.

Recorded in SJL as sent "by Colo. Franks"; entry in SJPL reads: "Adams J. Lambe. Barbary missions. Barclay and Randolph. O'Bryan. Short." Enclosures: Copy of O'Bryen to TJ, 24 Aug. 1785; Lafayette to TJ, 4 Sep. 1785; for a description of other enclosures see Adams and TJ to Barclay and Lamb, 11 Oct. 1785.

For the recommendation of Lamb by THE GOVERNOR AND STATE OF CONNECTICUT, see Abiel Foster to TJ, 26 Mch. 1785. The INFORMATION . . .

BY MR. JARVIS was set forth in TJ to Carmichael, 22 June 1785. MR. RANDOLPH, of course, was Paul R. Randall (see Adams to TJ, 2 Oct. 1785).

1 Text of Tr ends at this point.
2 "I will" deleted thoroughly in RC and less so in FC.

To John Adams

DEAR SIR   Paris Sep. 24. 1785.

I have received your favor of the 18th. inclosing your compliments on your presentation. The sentiments you therein expressed were such as were entertained in America till the Commercial proclamation, and such as would again return were a rational conduct to be adopted by Gr. Britain. I think therefore you by no means compromitted yourself or our country, nor expressed more than it would be our interest to encourage, if they were disposed to meet us. I am pleased however to see the answer of the king. It bears the marks of suddenness and surprize, and as he seems not to have had time for reflection we may suppose he was obliged to find his answer in the real sentiments of his heart, if that heart has any sentiment. I have no doubt however that it contains the real creed of an Englishman, and that the word which he has let escape is the true word of the ænigma, "The moment I see such sentiments as yours prevail and a disposition to give this country *the preference*, I will &c." All this I stedfastly beleive. But the condition is impossible. Our interest calls for a perfect equality in our conduct towards these two nations; but no preferences any where. If however circumstances should ever oblige us to shew a preference, a respect for our character, if we had no better motive, would decide to which it should be given. My letters from members of Congress render it doubtful whether they would not rather that full time should be given for the present disposition of America to mature itself and to produce a permanent improvement in the federal constitution, rather than, by removing the incentive, to prevent the improvement. It is certain that our commerce is in agonies at present, and that these would be relieved by opening the British ports in the W. Indies. It remains to consider whether a temporary continuance under these sufferings would be paid for by the amendment it is likely to produce. However I beleive there is no fear that Great Britain will puzzle us by leaving it in our choice to hasten or delay a treaty.

Is insurance made on Houdon's life? I am uneasy about it, lest we should hear of any accident. As yet there is no reason to doubt their safe passage. If the insurance is not made I will pray you to have it done immediately.

As I have not received any London newspapers as yet I am obliged to ask you what is done as to them, lest the delay should proceed from some obstacle to be removed. There is a Mr. Thompson at Dover who has proposed to me a method of getting them post free: but I have declined resorting to it till I should know in what train the matter is actually.

I have the honour to be with the most perfect esteem Dear Sir Your friend & servt.,   TH: JEFFERSON

RC (MHi: AMT); endorsed. PrC (DLC). Recorded in SJL as sent "by Colo. Franks"; entry in SJPL reads: "Adams J. His presentation. Commerce with Engld. Houdon."

The part of the reply of George III quoted by TJ does not conform precisely with the phraseology of the text as published or as preserved in the copy in DLC: TJ Papers, 12: 2133-4, which is presumably the text enclosed in Adams' letter of 18 Sep. The latter reads: ". . . the Moment I see such Language and sentiments as yours prevail, and a disposition to give this Country the preference, I will be the first to meet their Friendship and to say let the Circumstances of Language, Religion, and Blood have their natural and full Effect." The text as published reads: "The moment I see such sentiments and language as yours prevail, and a disposition to give to this country the preference, that moment I shall say, let the circumstances of language, religion, and blood have their natural and full effect" (Adams, *Works*, ed. C. F. Adams, VIII, 257). TJ evidently was copying from the former and inadvertently omitted the words "Language and."

To Ferdinand Grand

SIR   Paris Sep. 24. 1785.

I have appointed the bearer hereof, Mr. William Short, my Secretary. His salary as such will be the same which young Mr. Franklin received. I am therefore to ask the favor of you to pay it to him from time to time as it shall become due, and to debit the United States therewith. I have the honor to be with very great respect, Sir your most obedient and most humble servt.,

TH: JEFFERSON

PrC (DNA: PCC, No. 87, I); the month "Sep." is written in TJ's hand over the original date, "July." Another PrC (DLC: TJ Papers); without the correction in date and lacking part of the complimentary close and signature; follows on the same page the PrC of TJ to Short of this date. Tr (DNA: PCC, No. 107, I). Entry in SJPL reads: "Grand. Notification." A copy was later enclosed in TJ to John Jay, 6 Oct. 1785.

TJ's delay in dispatching this and its companion letter to Short, following, is explained by Short's absence during August and September as courier to London and The Hague (see TJ to John Adams, 28 July 1785).

To William Short

DEAR SIR   Paris Sep. 24. 1785.

Finding the assistance of a private Secretary necessary in my office I would wish you to accept of the appointment. In this case it will be necessary for you to abandon your plan of continuing at St. Germain's. I need not detail to you the ordinary business in which you will be engaged. That will open itself on you of course. But it is necessary for me particularly to authorize and instruct you, in case of any accident happening to myself, to take possession of whatever papers may be in my hands as Minister plenipotentiary for the United States at the court of Versailles, and to deliver them to the order of the Secretary for foreign affairs. I am not able to say with certainty what is the salary allowed: but Mr. Grand who paid young Mr. Franklin's, and who will pay yours also, will inform you. I think it was a thousand dollars a year. I must add that you are to expect this appointment to cease whenever Congress shall be pleased to countermand or supersede it by any other arrangement. I am with much esteem Dr. Sir your most obedient humble servt.,   TH: JEFFERSON

RC (DLC: Short Papers); the month "Sep." is written in TJ's hand over the original date, "July." PrC (DNA: PCC, No. 87, I); with the same date correction as in RC. Another PrC (DLC: TJ Papers); also redated and with faint or illegible passages restored in TJ's hand. Tr (DNA: PCC, No. 107, I). Recorded in SJL under this date; entry in SJPL reads: "Short Wm. App'nt. of Secretary." A copy was later enclosed in TJ to John Jay, 6 Oct. 1785.

To Abigail Adams

DEAR MADAM   Paris Sep. 25. 1785.

Mr. Short's return the night before last availed me of your favour of Aug. 12. I immediately ordered the shoes you desired which will be ready tomorrow. I am not certain whether this will be in time for the departure of Mr. Barclay or of Colo. Franks, for it is not yet decided which of them goes to London. I have also procured for you three plateaux de dessert with a silvered ballustrade round them, and four figures of Biscuit. The former cost

192ᵗ, the latter 12ᵗ each, making together 240 livres or 10. Louis. The merchant undertakes to send them by the way of Rouen through the hands of Mr. Garvey and to have them delivered in London. There will be some additional expences of packing, transportation and duties here. Those in England I imagine you can save. When I know the amount I will inform you of it, but there will be no occasion to remit it here. With respect to the figures I could only find three of those you named, matched in size. These were Minerva, Diana, and Apollo. I was obliged to add a fourth, unguided by your choice. They offered me a fine Venus; but I thought it out of taste to have two at table at the same time. Paris and Helen were presented. I conceived it would be cruel to remove them from their peculiar shrine. When they shall pass the Atlantic, it will be to sing a requiem over our freedom and happiness. At length a fine Mars was offered, calm, bold, his faulchion not drawn, but ready to be drawn. This will do, thinks I, for the table of the American Minister in London, where those whom it may concern may look and learn that though Wisdom is our guide, and the Song and Chase our supreme delight, yet we offer adoration to that tutelar god also who rocked the cradle of our birth, who has accepted our infant offerings, and has shewn himself the patron of our rights and avenger of our wrongs. The groupe then was closed, and your party formed. Envy and malice will never be quiet. I hear it already whispered to you that in admitting Minerva to your table I have departed from the principle which made me reject Venus: in plain English that I have paid a just respect to the daughter but failed to the mother. No Madam, my respect to both is sincere. Wisdom, I know, is social. She seeks her fellows. But Beauty is jealous, and illy bears the presence of a rival—but, Allons, let us turn over another leaf, and begin the next chapter. I receive by Mr. Short a budget of London papers. They teem with every horror of which human nature is capable. Assassinations, suicides, thefts, robberies, and, what is worse than assassination, theft, suicide or robbery, the blackest slanders! Indeed the man must be of rock, who can stand all this; to Mr. Adams it will be but one victory the more. It would have illy suited me. I do not love difficulties. I am fond of quiet, willing to do my duty, but irritable by slander and apt to be forced by it to abandon my post. These are weaknesses from which reason and your counsels will preserve Mr. Adams. I fancy it must be the quantity of animal food eaten by the English which renders their character insusceptible of civilisation. I suspect it is in their kitchens and not in their churches that their reformation must be worked, and that Missionaries of that description from hence would avail more than those who should endeavor to tame them by precepts of religion or philosophy. But what do the foolish printers of America mean by retailing all this stuff in our papers? As if it was not enough to be slandered by one's enemies without circulating the slanders among his friends also.

To shew you how willingly I shall ever receive and execute your commissions, I venture to impose one on you. From what I recollect of the diaper and damask we used to import from England I think they were better and cheaper than here. You are well acquainted with those of both countries. If you are of the same opinion I would trouble you to send me two sets of table cloths and napkins for 20 covers each, by Colo. Franks or Mr. Barclay who will bring them to me. But if you think they can be better got here I would rather avoid the trouble this commission will give. I inclose you a specimen of what is offered me at 100. livres for the table cloth and 12 napkins. I suppose that, of the same quality, a table cloth 2. aunes wide and 4. aunes long, and 20 napkins of 1. aune each, would cost 7. guineas.—I shall certainly charge the publick my house rent and court taxes. I shall do more. I shall charge my outfit. Without this I can never get out of debt. I think it will be allowed. Congress is too reasonable to expect, where no imprudent expences are incurred, none but those which are required by a decent respect to the mantle with which they cover the public servants, that such expences should be left as a burthen on our private fortunes. But when writing to you, I fancy myself at Auteuil, and chatter on till the last page of my paper awakes me from my reverie, and tells me it is time to assure you of the sincere respect and esteem with which I have the honour to be Dear Madam your most obedient & most humble servt.,

TH: JEFFERSON

P.S. The cask of wine at Auteuil, I take chearfully. I suppose the seller will apply to me for the price. Otherwise, as I do not know who he is, I shall not be able to find him out.

RC (MHi: AMT). PrC (DLC).

In MHi there is a receipted invoice from "Bazin Md. Rue des fossés St. Germain L'auxerois à Paris," dated 27 Sep. 1785 for "1 Service de 3. plateaux à Balustrade et perles de Cuivre argenté garnis de glaces," 192 livres; "4 figures divinites de porcelaine en Biscuit," 48 livres, &c., totalling 264tt.-17s.-6d. The receipt is dated 5 Jan. 1786.

From John Adams

DEAR SIR   Grosvenor Square Septr. 25. 1785.

The Bearer of this Letter Mr. Thomas Boylston, is one of the clearest and most solid Capitalists, that ever raised himself by private Commerce in North America. He seems to be desirous of assisting us, in introducing the knowledge and use of our white Sperma Cœti Oil, into France. His Judgment and Abilities to carry through whatever he undertakes may be depended on. Let me beg your Attention to him.

With great Esteem, I have the Honour to be, Sir your most obedient and most humble Servant,   JOHN ADAMS

RC (DLC). FC (MHi: AMT); in Adams' hand. Recorded in SJL as received 2 Nov. 1785.

On this same day Adams wrote letters introducing Boylston to Lafayette ("his Fortune and his Judgement is equal to any Thing he may propose relative to this Subject"), and on 28 Sep. he wrote similar introductions to Messrs. Coffin, Garvin, Grand, and Le Couteulx (MHi: AMT). In younger days Adams had called his distant kinsman "a perfect viper, a fiend, a Jew, a devil, but . . . orthodox in politics" (Adams, *Works*, ed. C. F. Adams, II, 179). In the last he seems to have been mistaken, for Boylston leaned toward loyalism and left Boston during the Revolution. On 13 Nov. 1785 Adams gave Lafay-ette a further characterization of Boylston: "The commerce of New England will follow their oil, wherever it may go and therefore I think it good policy, in the Controller General to take off the duty. . . . I hope that Mr. Boylston and Mr. Barrett will be able to compleat a Contract, with Monsieur Tourtille De Sangrain for the Illumination of your Cities. Boylston's Capital will enable him to do what he pleases, but you may depend upon it, he will do nothing but what is profitable. No man understands more intuitively, everything relating to these subjects, and no man is more attached to his Interest" (MHi: AMT). See also Adams' candid opinion of Boylston in his to TJ, 20 Dec. 1785.

To Francis Hopkinson

DEAR SIR   Paris. Sep. 25. 1785.

My last to you was of the 6th. of July. Since that I have received yours of July 23. I do not altogether despair of making something of your method of quilling, tho' as yet the prospect is not favourable. I applaud much your perseverance in improving this instrument and benefiting mankind almost in spite of their teeth. I mentioned to Piccini the improvement with which I am entrusted. He plays on the Pianoforte and therefore did not feel himself personally interested. I hope some better opportunity will yet fall in my way of doing it justice. I had almost decided, on his advice, to get a Pianoforte for my daughter. But your last letter pauses me, perhaps till I see it's effect.

Arts and Arms are alike asleep for the moment. Balooning indeed goes on. There are two artists in the neighborhood of Paris who seem to be advancing towards the desideratum in this business. They are able to rise and fall at will without expending their gaz, and to deflect 45.° from the course of the wind.

I desired you in my last to send the newspapers, notwithstanding the expence. I had then no idea of it. Some late instances have made me perfectly acquainted with it. I have therefore been obliged to adopt the following plan. To have my newspapers from the different states inclosed to the Office for foreign affairs, and to desire Mr. Jay to pack the whole in a box and send it by the packet as merchandize, directed to the American Consul at l'Orient who will forward it to me by the periodical waggons. In this way they will only cost me livres where they now cost guineas. I must pray you, just before the departure of every French packet, to send my papers on hand to Mr. Jay in this way. I do not know whether I am subject to American postage or not in general; but I think newspapers never are.—I have sometimes thought of sending a copy of my Notes to the Philosophical society as a tribute due to them: but this would seem as if I considered them as worth something, which I am conscious they are not. I will not ask you for your advice on this occasion because it is one of those on which no man is authorized to ask a sincere opinion. I shall therefore refer it to further thoughts. I am with very sincere esteem Dear Sir Your friend & servt.,   TH: JEFFERSON

PrC (DLC). Recorded in SJL as sent by "Mr. Fitzh[ugh]"; entry in SJPL reads: "Hopkinson Francis, Harpsichord. Baloon. Newspapers."
TWO ARTISTS IN THE NEIGHBORHOOD OF PARIS—referred to again in TJ to Ralph Izard, 26 Sept. 1785, as TWO PERSONS AT JAVEL, and in TJ to Charles Thomson, 8 Oct. 1785, as TWO

ARTISTS AT JAVEL—were Messrs Alban and Vallet, directors of the Manufacture de Javel, a chemical factory and laboratory sponsored by the Comte d'Artois, where numerous important experiments were conducted, including those relating to hydrogen gas for balloons; see L. V. Thiéry, *Guide des amateurs . . . à Paris*, 1787, II, 642-644.

To Lister Asquith

SIR   Paris Sep. 26. 1785.

I have received your letter of Sep. 19. with your Log-book and other papers. I now wait for the letter from your lawyer, as, till I know the real nature and state of your process it is impossible for me to judge what can be done for you here. As soon as I receive them you shall hear from me. In the mean time I supposed it would be a comfort to you to know that your papers were come safe to hand, and that I shall be attentive to do whatever circumstances will admit. I am Sir your very humble servt.

TH: JEFFERSON

PrC (DLC). Recorded in SJL as addressed to the "care Mr. Pecrel L'ainé."

To Thomas Barclay

Paris Sep. 26. 1785.

Colo. Franks has occasion for money to carry him to London. As we propose that all the money for this business shall be procured by draughts on Mr. Adams, will it not be better for you to draw on him at present for enough to cover the last journey of Colo. Franks, to defray the present one, to pay for the articles to be purchased here, the expences of the future journey Southwardly &c.? All this be pleased to decide on for yourself as you are the best judge of it. I am Dr. Sir Your's respectfully,

TH: JEFFERSON

RC (MHi: AMT); addressed: "A Monsieur Monsieur Barclay Consul des E. U. d'Amerique rue d'Orleans." Not recorded in SJL.

On 1 Oct. 1785 Barclay sent this letter to Adams: "You will see by the Inclosed Note from Mr. Jefferson what his sentiments are about the manner of drawing. I wrote to Mr. Grand a few days ago that I shou'd have occasion to Value on you in the Course of a Month for twelve or fifteen hundred pounds Sterling" (MHi: AMT).

To Ralph Izard

DEAR SIR
Paris Sep. 26. 1785.

I received a few days ago your favor of the 10th. of June and am to thank you for the trouble you have given yourself to procure me information on the subject of the commerce of your state. I pray you also to take the trouble of expressing my acknolegements to the Governor and Chamber of Commerce as well as to Mr. Hall for the very precise details on this subject with which they have been pleased to honour me. Your letter of last January, of which you make mention, never came to my hands. Of course the papers now received are the first and only ones which have come safe. The infidelities of the post-offices both of England and France are not unknown to you. The former is the most rascally because they retain one's letters, not chusing to take the trouble of copying them. The latter when they have taken copies, are so civil as to send the originals, re-sealed clumsily with a composition on which they have previously taken the impression of the seal. England shews no dispositions to enter into friendly connections with us. On the contrary their detention of our posts seems to be the speck which is to produce a storm. I judge that a war with America would be a popular war in England. Perhaps the situation of Ireland may deter the ministry from hastening it on. Peace is at length made between the emperor and Dutch. The terms are not published, but it is said he gets 10. millions of florins and the navigation of the Scheld not quite to Antwerp, and two forts. However this is not to be absolutely relied on. The league formed by the K. of Prussia against the Emperor is a most formidable obstacle to his ambitious designs. It has certainly defeated his views on Bavaria, and will render doubtful the election of his nephew to be king of the Romans. Matters are not yet settled between him and the Turk. In truth he undertakes too much. At home he has made some good regulations.

Your present pursuit being (the wisest of all) agriculture, I am not in a situation to be useful to it. You know that France is not the country most celebrated for this art. I went the other day to see a plough which was to be worked by a windlass, without horses or oxen. It was a poor affair. With a very troublesome apparatus, applicable only to a dead level, four men could do the work of two horses. There seems a possibility that the great desideratum in the use of the baloon may be obtained. There are two persons at Javel (opposite to Auteuil) who are pushing this matter. They are able to rise and fall at will without expending their gaz, and they can deflect 45°. from the course of the wind. This and better will do. I took the liberty of asking you to order me a Charlestown newspaper. The expence of French postage is so enormous that I have been obliged to desire that my newspapers from the different states may be sent to the office for foreign affairs at New York; and I have requested of Mr. Jay to have them always packed in a box and sent by the French packets as merchandize to the care of the American Consul at l'Orient, who will send them on by the periodical waggons. In this way they will cost me livres only where they now cost guineas. Will you permit me to add this to the trouble I had before given you of ordering the printer to send them under cover to Mr. Jay by such opportunities by water as occur from time to time. This request must go to the acts of your assembly also. I shall be on the watch to send you any thing which may appear here on the subjects of agriculture or the arts, which [may] be worth your perusal. I since[rely] congratulate Mrs. [Izar]d and yourself on the double accession to your family by marriage and a new birth. My daughter values much your remembrance of her and prays to have her respects presented to the ladies and yourself. In this I join her, and shall embrace with pleasure every opportunity of assuring you of the sincere esteem with which I have the honor to be Dear Sir Your most obedient and most humble servant,   TH: JEFFERSON

PrC (DLC); a few words obscured by blots have been supplied from the printing in Randall, *Life*, I, 324-6. Entry in SJPL reads: "Izard Ralph. Commerce of S.C. Post. O. England. Europe. Arts."

To John Stockdale

Paris Sep. 26. 1785.

Th: Jefferson will be obliged to Mr. Stockdale to send him by the bearer, Colo. Franks, the following plates of Cook's last voiage.
Plate.   1. The general map.
             36. Map of the N.W. coast of America and of the coast of Asia.
             53. Map of the entry of Norton and the streight of Bhering.
He means to put these maps into his American Atlas. Mr. Short is just arrived and brings the Parliamentary debates, Andrews's American war, Irish pamphlets &c. for which Mr. Jefferson thanks Mr. Stockdale. He will be obliged to him to continue sending him the Numbers of Andrews's book, and the Parliamentary debates in the same form hereafter. As to pamphlets he only wishes for those which relate to America, and which have also some degree of merit. He will be also obliged to him to add Baretti's Eng. and Span. dictionary to the books he desired him to send to Virginia.

PrC (DLC). Recorded in SJL under this date as addressed to Stockdale "opposite Burlington house Piccadilly."

To Nathaniel Tracy

DEAR SIR   Paris Sep. 26.

I wrote you on the 17th. Ult. by Mr. Derby. I then took the liberty of asking you to order me your best newspaper, to the care of Mr. Jamieson New York. Subsequent experience of the enormous expence of French postage on newspapers obliges me to a change of plan. I have desired my newspapers from the different states to be directed to me but sent to the office for foreign affairs under cover to Mr. Jay, of whom I have asked the favour to pack them altogether in a box, and to send them from time to time by the French packets as merchandize to the care of the American consul at l'Orient who will forward them by the periodical waggons, and thus I shall get them for livres where I now pay guineas. Will you be so kind as to direct the printer to whom you may have already given orders, to send them to Mr. Jay in this manner? The Emperor and Dutch have at length signed articles but they are not yet published. It is beleived the Emperor gets 10. million of florins, the navigation of the Scheld not quite to Antwerp, and two forts. Great Britain still holds off. We have hopes of quieting immediately the Barbary states; at least if we do not it will not be our fault. They had taken from us on the last of July three vessels in all, to wit the Emperor of Marocco one, which he has given up with the crew and cargo, and the Algerines two. One of these is the Maria from Boston. Nothing further new: for it

PrC (MoSHi); letter incomplete, consisting of one page only. Recorded in SJL under this date as sent by "Mr. Fitz[hugh]."

From George Washington

DEAR SIR   Mount Vernon 26th. Septr. 1785

I have had the honor to receive your favors of the 10th. and 17th. of July which were committed to the care of Mr. Houdon; but I have not yet had the pleasure to see that Gentleman. His Instruments and materials (Doctr. Franklin informs me) not being arrived at Havre when they Sailed, he was obliged to leave them, and is now employed in providing others at Philadelphia, with which he will proceed to this place as soon as they are ready. —I shall take great pleasure in shewing Mr. Houdon every civility and attention in my power during his stay in this Country, as I feel my self under personal obligations to you and Doctr. Franklin (as the State of Virginia have done me the honor to direct a statue to be erected to my Memory) for having entrusted the execution of it to so eminent an Artist, and so worthy a character.

I have the pleasure to inform you, that the subscriptions to the inland Navigations of the Rivers Potomack and James require no aid from Foreigners. The product of the first when the Books were exhibited at the General Meeting in May last, amounted to £40,300 Sterling, and is since nearly compleated to the full sum required by Law. That of the latter, at the General Meeting in August, were superabundant. The work of the former began the first of August and is progressing very well. The latter I am persuaded will do *more* than keep pace with it, as the difficulties are much less.

I have the further pleasure to inform you (and I should have done it long since, had I not supposed that your information would have been more full and perfect from some of your friends in the Assembly) that a resolution authorizing the Executive to appoint Commissioners to explore and report the best communication between the Waters of Elizabeth River and those of Albemarle passed last Session, That the Commissioners have proceeded to the survey, and have reported in favor of that which will pass through Drummonds pond to the Pasquetank; but what will be the result I am unable to inform you, as I find by some of the principal characters of No. Carolina (Members of Congress) who have called here, that jealousies prevail, and a powerful opposition will be given to any Water Communication between the two states, lest Virginia should derive the benefits arising from their Exports, &ca.

I am very happy to find that your sentiments respecting the interest the Assembly was pleased to give me in the two navigations of Potomack and James Rivers, coincide so well with my own. I never for a moment, entertained an idea of accepting. The difficulty which laboured in my Mind was how to refuse without giving offence. Ultimately I have it in contemplation to apply the profits arising from the Tolls to some public use. In this, if I knew how, I would meet the wishes of the Assembly; but if I am not able to get at these, my own inclination leads me to apply them to the establishment of two charity Schools, one on each river, for the Education and support of poor Children; especially the descendants of those who have fallen in defence of their Country.

I can say nothing decisively respecting the Western settlement of this state. The Inhabitants of Kentucke have held several Conventions, and have resolved to apply for a seperation. But what may be the final issue of it, is not for me, at this time, to inform you. Opinions as far as they have come to my knowledge, are diverse. I have uniformly given it as mine, to meet them upon their

own ground, draw the best line, and best terms we can of seperation, and part good friends. After the next Session of our Assembly
more may be discovered, and communicated, and if you should
not receive it through a better channel, I will have the honor to
inform you.

I am sorry I cannot give you full information respecting Captn.
Bushnels project for the destruction of shipping. No interesting
experiment having been made, and my memery being treacherous,
I may, in some measure, be mistaken in what I am about to relate.

Bushnel is a Man of great Mechanical powers, fertile of invention, and a master in execution. He came to me in 1776 recommended by Governor Trumbull (now dead) and other respectable
characters who were proselites to his plan. Although I wanted faith
myself, I furnished him with money, and other aids to carry it
into execution. He laboured for sometime ineffectually, and though
the advocates for his scheme continued sanguine he never did succeed. One accident or another was always intervening. I then
thought, and still think, that it was an effort of genius; but that a
combination of too many things were requisite, to expect much
success from the enterprise against an enemy, who are always upon
guard. That he had a Machine which was so contrived as to carry
a man under water at any depth he chose, and for a considerable
time and distance, with an apparatus charged with Powder which
he could fasten to a ships bottom or side and give fire to in any
given time (sufficient for him to retire) by means whereof a ship
could be blown up, or sunk, are facts which I believe admit of
little doubt. But then, where it was to operate against an enemy,
it is no easy matter to get a person hardy enough to encounter the
variety of dangers to which he must be exposed, 1. from the
novelty, 2. from the difficulty of conducting the Machine, and
governing it under Water on account of the Currents &ca. 3. the
consequent uncertainty of hitting the object of destination, without
rising frequently above water for fresh observation, which, when
near the Vessel, would expose the Adventurer to a discovery, and
almost to certain death. To these causes I always ascribed the
non-performance of his plan, as he wanted nothing that I could
furnish to secure the success of it. This to the best of my recollection is a true state of the case. But Humphreys, if I mistake not,
being one of the proselites, will be able to give you a more perfect
account of it than I have done. With the most perfect esteem &
regard I have the honor to be Dear Sir Yr. Most Obedt. Servt.,

G: WASHINGTON

RC (DLC: TJ Papers). FC (DLC: Washington Papers). Recorded in SJL as received 30 Dec. 1785, "by Houdon." The text of FC differs considerably in phraseology from that of RC.

To James Currie

DEAR SIR   Paris Sep. 27. 1785.

Your favor of Aug. 5. came to hand on the 18th. inst. and I mark well what you say, 'that my letters shall be punctually answered.' This is encouraging, and the more so, as it proves to you that in sending your letters in time to arrive at New York the middle of the month when the French packet sails they get to hand very speedily. The last was but six weeks from you to me. I thank you again and again for the details it contains, these being precisely of the nature I would wish. Of political correspondents I can find enough. But I can persuade nobody to beleive that the small facts which they see passing daily under their eyes are precious to me at this distance: much more interesting to the heart than events of higher rank. Fancy to yourself a being who is withdrawn from his connections of blood, of marriage, of friendship, of acquaintance in all their gradations, who for years should hear nothing of what has passed among them, who returns again to see them and finds the one half dead. This strikes him like a pestilence sweeping off the half of mankind. Events which had they come to him one by one and in detail he would have weathered as other people do, when presented to his mind all at once are overwhelming. Continue then to give me facts, little facts, such as you think every one imagines beneath notice, and your letters will be the most precious to me. They will place me in imagination in my own country, and they will place me where I am happiest: but what shall I give you in return? Political events are scarcely interesting to a man who looks on them from high ground. There is always war in one place, revolution in another, pestilence in a third interspersed with spots of quiet. These chequers shift places, but they do not vanish; so that to an eye which extends itself over the whole earth there is always an uniformity of prospect. For the moment, Europe is clear of war. The Emperor and Dutch have signed articles. These are not published: but it is beleived the Emperor gets 10. millions of florins, the navigation of the Scheld to Saptinghen, and two forts; so that your conjecture is verified and the Dutch actually pay the piper.

The league formed in the Germanic body by the K. of Prussia is likely to circumscribe the ambitious views of the Emperor on that side, and there seems to be no issue for them but on the side of the Turk. Their demarcation does not advance. It is a pity the emperor would not confine himself to internal regulation. In that way he has done much good. One would think it not so difficult to discover that the improvement of the country we possess is the surest means of increasing our wealth and power. This too promotes the happiness of mankind, while the others destroy it, and are always incertain of their object. England seems not to permit our friendship to enter into her political calculations as an article of any value. Her endeavor is not how to recover our affections or to bind us to her by alliance, but by what new experiments she may keep up an existence without us. Thus leaving us to carry our full weight, present and future, into the scale of her enemy, and seeming to prefer our enmity to our neutrality. The Barbary corsairs have committed depredations on us. The Emperor of Marocco took a vessel last winter, which he has since restored with the crew and cargo. The Algerines took two vessels in July. These are the only captures which were known of at Algiers on the 24th. of Aug. I mention this because the English papers would make the world beleive we have lost an infinite number. I hope soon to be able to inform our countrymen that these dangers are ceased. There is little new to communicate in the arts and sciences. The great desideratum which is to render the discovery of the baloon useful, is not absolutely desperate. There are two artists at Javel, about 4. miles from here, who are able to rise and fall at will without expending their gaz, and to deflect 45°. from the course of the wind. The investigations of air and fire which have latterly so much occupied the Chymists, have not presented any thing very interesting for some time past. I send you four books, Roland, Sigaud de la fond, Metherie, and Scheele, which will put you in possession of whatever has been discovered as yet on that subject. They are packed in a trunk directed to J. Madison of Orange which will be carried to Richmond. They are in French, which you say you do not understand well. You lose infinitely by this, as you may be assured that the publications in that language at present far exceed those of the English in science. With respect to the Encyclopedie, it is impossible for me to judge whether to send it to you or not, as I do not know your degree of knowledge in the language nor your intentions as to increasing it. Of this you must decide for yourself and instruct me accordingly. I was unlucky as to the partridges, pheasants, hares and rabbits which I had ordered to Virginia. The vessel in which I came over was to have returned to Virginia, and to Warwick. I knew I could rely on the captain's care. A fellow passenger undertook to provide them. He did so. But the destination of the vessel was changed, and the poor colonists all died while my friend was looking out for another conveyance. If I can be useful to your circulating library, the members may be assured of my zealous services. All books except English, Latin and Greek, are bought here for about two thirds of what they cost in England. They had better distribute their invoices accordingly. I must trouble you to present assurances of my friendship to Mr. and Mrs. Randolph of Tuckahoe, Mr. Cary, and their families. My attachments to them are sincere: I wish I could render them useful to them. Tell McLurg I shall enjoy a very real pleasure whenever he shall carry his intentions of writing to me into execution; and that there is no one who more fervently wishes him well. Accept yourself assurances of the esteem with which I am Dear Sir Your friend & servant,   TH: JEFFERSON

PrC (DLC).

From Dolomieu

[*Saintes, 27 Sep. 1785.* Recorded in SJL as received 4 Oct. 1785. Not found; but see TJ to Adams and to Dolomieu, 5 Oct. 1785.]

From Lister Asquith

St. Pol de Léon, 28 Sep. 1785. "I am now convinced of the Villiany of the People we have here to deal with and beg in the name of God your protection and assistance." After believing that Picrel had engaged a lawyer and paid him, they now find that the lawyer demands twelve guineas to take the case, and that "Picrel has deceived us the whole time and had a design himself on the Vessel. As we are well informed that he says he will buy her." They have written to Brest to learn whether the lawyer will proceed with the suit, though they have only three guineas left.

RC (DLC); 2 p.

From C. W. F. Dumas

MONSIEUR   Lahaie 28 7br. 1785

Quoiqu'il me fût plus commode de tirer immédiatement sur
Messrs. Wm. & Jn. Willink, Nic. & Jb. van Staphorst, le modique
salaire provisionnel, de 225 Louis d'or annuels, qui m'est alloué en
attendant que le Congrès, selon des promesses souvent réitérées,
veuille enfin me faire un meilleur sort; cependant, comme je l'ai
toujours tiré sur la Légation Américaine à Paris, j'ai cru, de peur
de confusion dans les comptes des Etats-Unis, devoir, sans rien
innover de mon chef, continuer sur le même pied, en tirant sur
Votre Excellence les £2700 tournois du second semestre de mon
salaire de cette annee 1785, espérant que Votre Excellence voudra
bien, comme ci-devant Mr. Franklin, ordonner que tout honneur
y soit fait.

Un Mr. Moses Tandy, Virginien, disant être connu de Votre
Excellence et produisant quelques documens passables, a paru
chez moi dans un triste état. Je lui ai donné selon mon pouvoir, que
je lui ait dit très borné, le secours et passeport qu'il me demandoit.
Je viens d'apprendre qu'il mene à Amsterdam une vie crapuleuse
et libertine; et je lui ai fait parvenir le conseil amical de craindre
la police, et de se rembarquer promptement pour l'Amérique. Il
paroit d'une famille honnête, et est associé de Mr. Watson, qui l'a
muni d'un pouvoir ou procure, dont il paroit se montrer indigne.

J'espere que Mr. Short est de retour en bonne santé, et que la
besogne que nous avons faite ici a eu votre approbation, et celle
de Mr. Adams.

Maintenant, que la derniere main va être mise à la paix, j'espere
de pouvoir bientôt recommencer à faire passer mes Lettres pour
le Congrès par la route d'ici à Paris, et sous les yeux de Votre
Excellence. Car, instruit à fond du secret de la république, j'ai
dû promettre de ne point l'exposer jusque là sur cette route.

Je suis avec grand respect, De Votre Excellence, le très-humble
et très-obeissant serviteur,   C. W. F. DUMAS

RC (DLC); addressed to TJ at
Paris; postmarked and endorsed. FC
(Dumas Letter Book, Rijksarchief, The
Hague; photostats in DLC). Recorded
in SJL as received 2 Oct. 1785.
MOSES TANDY of Alexandria had
been soliciting Dumas' aid for some
weeks. Dumas wrote Adams that Tandy, the handsomest man he had seen
in all his life, had presented himself
in "l'équipage la plus disgracié," except for a gold sword and his head
which was "bien accomodée." Tandy
had told Dumas that he was known
to TJ and asked for a passport and an
advance for expenses in order to go to
London. Dumas had given him eight
florins and a passport, directing him
to Adams, and Tandy said that he
would leave the next day by packet

(Dumas to Adams, 19 Aug. 1785; MHi: AMT). Evidently he did not take the packet, but he eventually returned to Virginia (Hening, XIII, 622; CVSP, VI, 231). See TJ to Dumas, 4 Oct. 1785.

From Francis Hopkinson

DEAR SIR   Philada. 28th. Sepr. 1785

Your Favour of the 6th. July was handed to me by our mutual friend Dr. Franklin, as also were four Volumes of the Bibliothèque Œconomique, and your Notes on Virginia for which I heartily thank you. I shall be careful to observe your Instruction in the blank Leaf of your Notes. I hope you will continue to send me the Bibliothèque Œconomique, as I have found much valuable Entertainment in them. You will oblige me greatly by taking up my Encyclopedie as they come out, Dr. Franklin having made no Provision for that purpose as I understand. He has many Volumes for me but I know not when I shall have the Pleasure of seeing them, as all his Library was left behind. I send herewith another Package of news papers which is the third I have forwarded. You will see by them that party Politics run high and the Fever heightens as the general Election approaches. We are divided distinctly into two Parties under the Names of the *Constitutionalists* and the *Republicans*. The Republicans are those who wish to have two Branches of Legislation. The Constitutionalists wish to have but one, especially since they are in Power and have the Management of it. They have endeavour'd to support their Influence by removing out of the Way with a high hand all Institutions that are thought not to be in their Interests. They some Time ago took the Colledge out of the hands of the Legal Trustees and have lately most arbitrarily retracted and annull'd the Charter of the national Bank, because they hated Mr. Morris personally and because the Directors were not under their Influence. There will probably be a tight Struggle next Month for Power. The Contest will be for a Ride in the One-horse Chaise. It is agreed by all that Dr. Franklin is to be President of the State, and he seems willing to accept the Charge. But, in our Constitution, two or three leading Members of the House drive the political Coach. The President is the Footman and the Chief Justice rides in the Body of the Carriage, and the *People* run whooping and hallowing along side, choak'd with Dust and bespatter'd with Mire.

Mr. Rittenhouse is just returned from the Western Country.

He has been over the Ohio and made many philosophical observations which he will commit to writing. I shall inform him of this opportunity and he will probably write to you.

I am sorry my Improvement in Quilling a Harpsichord has cost you so much Trouble. I resign any Expectations from that Source. I have since made a further and more important Improvement. I have long suspected that the Quill did not draw the full Power of Tone from Strings so long and so advantageously stretchd and on Experiment find my Conjecture was right. My Harpsichord has not now got a single Quill in it, and for Richness of Tone and the Body or Quantity of Sound it yields, exceeds any Instrument of the kind I ever heard. The enclosed Model will give you a full Idea of this Contrivance and save the Trouble of Descriptions. My Harpsichord is at present furnished thus. The first Unison with sole-Leather, well rubb'd with black-Lead, the Second Unison, a kind of soft Morocco Leather, for the Piano of the Instrument, and the Octave with wooden Tongues polish'd with black Lead, for giving Vivacity to the whole. All mounted on Springs, according to the Model. I say nothing as to the admirable Result. Let Experiment determine. I have also discovered a simple Contrivance for assisting a Vessel in sailing, or a Waggon in the Draught, but as I have not yet exhibited it to our Philosophical Society, I must defer sending you an Account of it till another opportunity. Once more, I have made an Ointment for greasing the wheels of Carriages and the moving Parts of mills or other machines. It is Gum Elastic dissolved in Oil and made pretty thick with powder'd black-Lead. I have not Time to give you the Reasons why this is an advantageous Ointment. Let the Experiment be tried. The only Disadvantage I fear is the Expence.

You will oblige me much by sending me Two or three sets of best Crayons or Pastels and charge me with the Cost. They are to be had good à L'Iris Rue de Gévres par le bout du Pont Notre-Dame, la Boutique en face du Passage du Quai de Gévres, à Coté du café. If you can add a few Pieces of good black and white Chalk, so much the better. I do not mean sized Chalk as in the Case of Stradling versus Stiles.

My Mother is much obliged by Miss Jeffersons kind Letter. She would probably answer it by this Conveyance, but she is at present at Baltimore.

I cannot say I have nothing to add; but I am rather in Haste. Your truly affectionate & obliged Friend,   FRAS. HOPKINSON

RC (DLC); endorsed. Recorded in SJL as received 18 Jan. 1786, "by the [. . .] and post." The model intended to be enclosed was not in the letter when it was received (see TJ to Hopkinson, 26 Jan. 1786; see also Sonneck, *Francis Hopkinson*, Washington, D.C., 1905, p. 71).

MISS JEFFERSONS KIND LETTER (missing) was enclosed in TJ to Hopkinson, 6 July 1785. Hopkinson's apparently casual comment on *Notes on Virginia* may be explained by the fact that he had already read the MS. This is proved by a three-page set of "Notes on Mr. Jefferson's Acct. of Virginia" found in the Hopkinson Papers (PHi). These notes are undated but internal evidence shows that their page references are keyed to the pages of the MS and that TJ altered the MS in some particulars after receiving Hopkinson's observations; they must, therefore, have been written before TJ left for France.

To the Governor of Virginia

SIR   Paris Sep. 28. 1785.

The house of LaVal & Wilfelsheim have lately protested Mr. Morris's bills. I should not venture to say they have stopped paiment altogether; but it is something so like that that those who have bills on them may count on their being protested. They stopped their paiments on Saturday last. Their creditors are endeavoring to boulster up LaVal, but I doubt whether American demands will receive the benefit of this. As I find by a letter from the honourable Mr. Beverley Randolph that you rely for the arms ordered here on bills of Mr. Morris and these may probably be drawn on this house, and as it may also have happened that you have taken bills of Alexander on them, I thought it my duty to give you the earliest notice possible of this, by sending copies of this letter to the several seaports to be forwarded to you. The arms will be got so much better for ready money, and can be prepared in so short a time that we think it best not to call for them but with the money in hand.

I have the honour to be with due respect your Excellency's most obedt. humble servt.,   TH: JEFFERSON

P.S. Mr. Barclay leaves France in a few days.

RC (MB). PrC (MoSHi). Recorded in SJL as sent "via Bourd. Nantes. l'Orient. London." The "letter from . . . Mr. Beverly Randolph" was probably not to TJ but to Barclay.

To André Limozin

Sir   Paris Sep. 28. 1785.

I have taken the liberty to send this day to your address 3 trunks and a box, all of them containing books and nothing else. They are all marked L.S. They are directed as follows.

The box. Edmund Randolph. Richmond. Virginia.

The two largest trunks. James Madison. Orange. To the care
of James Buchanan. Richmond.

The smallest trunk. James Madison. Williamsburgh. Virginia. By which you will perceive the three first parcels are destined for Richmond on James River in Virginia, and the last for Williamsburgh. If your vessel goes to Portsmouth, there will be daily opportunities of sending them from thence to their respective destinations. There are two gentlemen, Virginians, here who think of taking the opportunity of your ship Eolus to return to their own country. If so, they will be able to attend to my packages. I happened to be out today when my servant sent off these packages; and instead of his paying the charges he has left them unpaid, by which means they will be demanded of you. When I came in, the waggon was set out. You will therefore be so good as to pay the charges, which are 39^{tt}-18 to the Douaine and 27^{tt}-12 for carrying them, which I will repay you together with the freight to Virginia, on your draught if you will be pleased to draw on me, or otherwise I will send it to you by the gentlemen abovementioned. I have the honour to be,

PrC (MHi); lacks part of complimentary close and signature, which in RC would have been carried over to second page.

From David Rittenhouse

Dear Sir   Philadelphia Sepr. 28th. 1785

That I have so long delayed acknowledging your favours has been owing to my absence from home. Two Summers past I have been employed in determining the Boundary of Pennsylvania. In 1784. Observations were continued for near 3 months on the Eclipses of Jupiters Satellites, on the Banks of the Delaware and near the Ohio. The result gave 53,225 Miles to a degree of Longitude in Latitude 39.° 43.′ 18.″, something less than we had reason to Expect from former measurements of Degrees of Latitude.

The Autumn of 84 and Summer of 85 I have spent in assisting to carry on the remainder of the Southern and the Western Boundary of this State. This last being one Straight Meridian Line is certainly the most grand and beautiful Vista in the World. In these Excursions I have not been inattentive, so far as my Situation wou'd permit, to the natural Curiosities of that Country, and I wish to give you some account of them when I can find leisure for the purpose.

You have greatly obliged me by the Books you have sent. Each of the Connoissance Des Temps contains many things Curious and useful. 'Tis a pity they are not more correctly printed. But the Notes on Virginia are an inestimable Treasure. I have just received the Book and have not yet read it with that attention I mean to bestow on it. Nothing has hitherto occurred to me in it contrary to my own Philosophical notions, except that of Stones growing in imitation of Shells without real animal Shells to give them that form. The Petrifications I have collected on the Allegany Mountains and beyond them seem to me sufficient to induce you to give up that opinion. But I may be mistaken. What has with me the greatest weight is that abundance of the Shells and Bones thus found lodged in Solid Stone are still real Shells and Bones, as not only their appearance but their taste and smell when heated sufficiently evince. I must beg a continuance of your favours and that you will inform me how I may reimburse the Expence you have been at on my account. Mrs. Rittenhouse's Compliments and mine to Miss Jefferson. I hope she is very happy, nay I am sure she must be so under the care of such a parent. Dear Sir, your most sincere friend and Humbl Servt.,   DAVD. RITTENHOUSE

RC (DLC); endorsed. Recorded in SJL as received 18 Jan. 1786, "by the [. . .] & post."

From William Carmichael

SIR   Madrid 29th. September 1785

Having been in daily expectation to have the honor to hear from your Excellency, agreable to the contents of your last Letter, I have perhaps been led to a longer silence, than I wished or may be consonant to your Ideas of our respective Situations. A Letter from Mr. Barclay perhaps has contributed to my Error. Since Writing to you Mr. Harrison of Cadiz has transmitted me the Inclosed Letters from Algiers. Intreat your Excellency to lay them le Cachet de leurs armes, / aux lieux de leur domicile / respectif, ainsi qu'il sera / exprimé ci dessous.

F. g. de Thulemeier, a la Haye le 10. September. / 1785.

their Seals at the places / of their respective residences / and at the dates expressed / under their several / signatures.

Th. Jefferson
Paris. July 28. 1785.

B. Franklin
Passy, July 9. 1785.

John Adams.
London. August 5. 1785.

Final page of the Definitive Treaty between the
United States and Prussia. (See p. xxix.)

Nous THOMAS JEFFERSON,

Ecuyer, Miniftre Plénipotentiaire des Etats-Unis d'Amérique, près Sa Majefté Très-Chrétienne,

PRIONS tous ceux qui font à prier de vouloir laiffer furement & librement paffer *le Sieur John Lamb citoyen des etats Unis d'Amerique avec son domestique* — sans *leur* donner ni permettre qu'il *leur* foit donné aucun empéchement, mais au contraire de *leur* accorder toutes fortes d'aide & d'affiftance, comme nous ferions en pareil cas, pour tous ceux qui nous feroient recommandés.

EN FOI DE QUOI nous *leur* avons délivré le préfent Paffeport, valable pour *deux ans* —— figné de notre main, & au bas duquel eft l'empreinte de nos Armes.

DONNÉ à Paris, en notre Hôtel, le *cinquieme novembre l'an* mil fept cent quatre-vingt-*cinq*

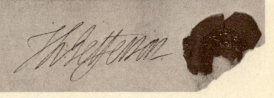

Passport for John Lamb. (See p. xxix.)

before Mr. Adams and to send copies to Congress. Not having instructions from Congress, indeed not having any direct Intelligence from that Body for several Months, I could take no part *officially* in our actual situation with Algiers. I have therefore confined myself to general expressions with this Ministry and have found in his Excellency the Ct. de Florida Blanca the same Liberality of thinking and the same desire to serve us as he evinced in the Affaires of Morrocco. I have endeavoured to conciliate the good will of *Persons* who may be useful to us in that part of the world, without compromising in any manner the Dignity of the United States. Without having the honor to be personally known to you, I cannot refrain from avowing to your Excellency that the neglect which I experience not only is prejudicial to our general Interests, but Affects me to a degree that at times renders me incapable of making any other reflections than those which My personal Situation impresses upon me; and to the sensations to which these reflections give rise I impute the bilious disorders to which I am Subject. I beg you to excuse this digression.

I *cannot enter into details*. The peace with Algiers will be concluded. Naples will as I am informed be included, and *possibly* Portugal. The Minister of Prussia has notified to this Court the Treaty concluded between the German Princes of which the King of Prussia is the cheif: The answer, which I have seen, from this Court, I think expresses an approbation of the principles on which the Treaty is founded. I regret that I have not proper means of conveying to you many incidents, which confirmed by your own Observation might at least be amusing, if not usefull. Until I can have that satisfaction, I must finish with assurances of the great regard and respect With Which I have the honor to be Your Excys. Most Obedt. & Most Humble Sert.,   WM. CARMICHAEL

RC (DLC). Recorded in SJL as received 15 Oct. 1785. Enclosures not identified.

To Richard O'Bryen

SIR   Paris Sep. 29. 1785.

I have received your letter and shall exert myself for you. Be assured of hearing from me soon: but say nothing to any body except what may be necessary to comfort your companions. I add no more, because the fate of this letter is incertain. I am Sir Your very humble servant,   TH: JEFFERSON

PrC (DLC). Entry in sJPL reads: "O'Brien Richd. Captives." Enclosed in the following letter.

To James Wilkie

[*Paris*, *29 Sep. 1785*. Entry in sJL reads: "Jas. Wilkie. Inclosing the preceding and praying to send it under cover to Eng. or Fr. Consul as he thinks best." Not found. Enclosure: TJ to Richard O'Bryen of this date.]

To Charles Bellini

DEAR SIR   Paris Sep. 30. 1785.

Your estimable favour covering a letter to Mr. Mazzei came to hand on the 26th. inst. The letter to Mr. Mazzei was put into his hands in the same moment, as he happened to be present. I leave to him to convey to you all his complaints, as it will be more agreeable to me to express to you the satisfaction I received on being informed of your perfect health. Tho' I could not receive the same pleasing news of Mrs. Bellini, yet the philosophy with which I am told she bears the loss of health is a testimony the more how much she deserved the esteem I bear her.—Behold me at length on the vaunted scene of Europe! It is not necessary for your information that I should enter into details concerning it. But you are perhaps curious to know how this new scene has struck a savage of the mountains of America. Not advantageously I assure you. I find the general fate of humanity here most deplorable. The truth of Voltaire's observation offers itself perpetually, that every man here must be either the hammer or the anvil. It is a true picture of that country to which they say we shall pass hereafter, and where we are to see god and his angels in splendor, and crouds of the damned trampled under their feet. While the great mass of the people are thus suffering under physical and moral oppression, I have endeavored to examine more nearly the condition of the great, to appreciate the true value of the circumstances in their situation which dazzle the bulk of the spectators, and especially to compare it with that degree of happiness which is enjoyed in America by every class of people. Intrigues of love occupy the younger, and those of ambition the more elderly part of the great. Conjugal love having no existence among them, domestic happiness, of which that is the basis, is utterly unknown. In lieu of this are substituted pursuits which nourish and invigorate all our bad passions, and which offer only moments of extasy amidst days and months of restlessness and torment. Much, very much inferior this to the tranquil permanent felicity with which domestic society in America blesses most of it's inhabitants, leaving them to follow steadily those pursuits which health and reason approve, and rendering truly delicious the intervals of these pursuits. In science, the mass of people is two centuries behind ours, their literati half a dozen years before us. Books, really good, acquire just reputation in that time, and so become known to us and communicate to us all their advances in knowlege. Is not this delay compensated by our being placed out of the reach of that swarm of nonsense which issues daily from a thousand presses and perishes almost in issuing? With respect to what are termed polite manners, without sacrificing too much the sincerity of language, I would wish [my] countrymen to adopt just so much of European politeness as to be ready [to] make all those little sacrifices of self which really render European manners amiable, and relieve society from the disagreeable scenes to which rudeness often exposes it. Here it seems that a man might pass a life without encountering a single rudeness. In the pleasures of the table they are far before us, because with good taste they unite temperance. They do not terminate the most sociable meals by transforming themselves into brutes. I have never yet seen a man drunk in France, even among the lowest of the people. Were I to proceed to tell you how much I enjoy their architecture, sculpture, painting, music, I should want words. It is in these arts they shine. The last of them particularly is an enjoiment, the deprivation of which with us cannot be calculated. I am almost ready to say it is the only thing which from my heart I envy them, and which in spight of all the authority of the decalogue I do covet.—But I am running on in an estimate of things infinitely better known to you than to me, and which will only serve to convince you that I have brought with me all the prejudices of country, habit and age. But whatever I may allow to be charged to me as prejudice, in every other instance, I have one sentiment at least founded on reality: it is that of the perfect esteem which your merit and that of Mrs. Bellini have produced, and which will for ever enable me to assure you of the sincere regard with which I am Dear Sir Your friend & servant,

TH: JEFFERSON

PrC (DLC). Recorded in SJL as sent by "Mr. Fitz[hugh]"; entry in SJPL reads: "Bellini Carlo. My view of Europe."

From William Carmichael

MY DEAR SIR   Madrid 30th. Septr. 1785

Your reputation or my supposed Influence with you or both, joined to my desire of contributing to the pleasure of those who entertain such an Idea, Induce me to take the Liberty of presenting to your acquaintance the Marquis de Trotti, a young Nobleman from Milan who is not less distinguished for his desire of Information and Instruction than from his birth and amiable qualities. I have had the Pleasure of being often with him during his residence here. He has relatives of the highest rank and Consideration in this Country, particular the Marquis de Santa Cruz Grande Maitre du Pallais, from whom I have received and continue to receive Many civilities. The Marquis is accompanied by a Friend with whose conversation, I flatter myself you will be pleased, for to great urbanity of Manners, He joins much Instruction. I have the honor to be With great respect & regard Yr. Excys. Most Obliged & Affectionate Hble. Sert.,   WM. CARMICHAEL

RC (DLC); endorsed.

From André Limozin

MOST HONORED SIR   [ca. 30 Sep. 1785]

I shall take a particular Care in forwarding by my Ship Eolus Captn. Paon your Box and three trunks according to the direction you give me: my ship is to sail on the 5th. Instant if wind and weather permitt it. I wish therefore that the two Virginia's Gentlemen you mentionn may have left Paris before this reach you.

I have the Honor to acquaint you that the French Ship La Diligence de Cadix Cap. J. Bte. La Rocque is put up to sail for Philadelphia the 15th. instant. If you have any Commands for her I beg you would not Spare me. She is consignd to me.

I have the Honor to be with the highest regard your Excellency's Most obedient & very Humble Servant,   ANDRE. LIMOZIN

I shall do my self the Honor to apply again to your Excellency in a few days.

RC (MHi); without date; at foot of first page, addressed to TJ in part "en son Hotel a la Grille de Chaillot Paris"; endorsed. The letter is clearly in reply to TJ's of 28 Sep., and it is probably the undated letter from Limozin which TJ recorded in SJL as received 2 Oct. 1785.

From Benjamin Franklin

SIR   Philada. Oct. 1. 1785.

I wrote to you by a former Opportunity, to acquaint you with our safe Arrival. Mr. Houdon, who had been much perplex'd by the Accident of leaving his Things behind him, has found here the Tools and Materials he wanted, and set out last Wednesday for General Washington's. My Grandson went the Day after to New York, where the Congress are still sitting, and likely to sit the Year out, having as I am told much Business, and finding it very difficult to agree upon the Mode of the Requisition. In general the Affairs of our Country seem to be in good Train: the last Harvest good, our own Produce high, foreign Supplies, both European and West Indian low: We have indeed some Party Wranglings; but no free Country was ever without them; and I do not think they are likely to produce any considerable bad Conse-quences. Mr. Houdon has been furnish'd here with the Value of Twenty-four Hundred Livres, for his Occasions, for which he has drawn on you in my favour. I find myself the better for my Voyage, and I hope you continue well; being, with sincere Esteem, Sir, Your most obedient & most Humble Servant, B. FRANKLIN

RC (CtY). Recorded in SJL as received 12 Dec. 1785.
Franklin's letter BY A FORMER OPPORTUNITY has not been found. On 24 Oct. Houdon issued a thirty-day draft on TJ, payable to Franklin for 3600 livres (PPAP: Franklin Papers).

From John Adams

DEAR SIR   Grosvenor Square Oct. 2. 1785.

Coll. Franks arrived Yesterday afternoon, with your Favour of Septr. 24.—I have signed all the Papers as you sent them, not perceiving any Alteration necessary. I am afraid, that our Agent to Algiers going without any military Power will not succeed; as the Danger of having their Town bombarded, or their Vessells taken, is the Principal Argument which the Dey has to use with the People, to reconcile them to a Peace. However We must try the Experiment. I have received a Letter from Mr. Stephen Sayre, dated N. York 25. Aug. inclosing another of 23. of Aug. signed by Messrs. Gerry, King, Hardy, Monroe, and Grayson recommending strongly Mr. Sayre to you and me, to be employed as Agent to Morocco, Algiers and the other Powers, and inclosing another Letter to you, probably to the same Effect. This Letter I now inclose to you. It is but a day or two that these Letters have been received by me. Franks is gone to see if Mr. Randolph[1] can be prevailed on to go. If he cannot, will you join Sayre with Lamb? If you will, insert his Name in the Papers. Mr. Lamb will meet Mr. Sayre at Madrid, where I suppose he now is. But if he is not, Lamb must not wait for him a Moment. I should very readily undertake the Trouble, of having Bills drawn upon me, both by Mr. Barclay and Mr. Lamb, if the good of the service could be promoted by it. But you are sensible there must be a Loss, in transferring Money, from Amsterdam to London: Yet the Advantage may ballance it.

You are diffident of Interpositions: but it is possible We may carry this too far. I think Mr. Barclay and Mr. Lamb would do well, to visit all the foreign Consulls, every one of whom will I am persuaded, shew them Civilities, and do nothing at all to obstruct their negotiations. They will not dare to do it, without orders, and no Cabinet in Europe I verily believe, would venture to give such orders. It will not be from Governments, that We shall receive opposition. Agents of Insurance offices in London or of Merchants trading in Fish &c. in the Mediterranean, may stimulate the Corsairs by exaggerated Representations of our Wealth and the Riches of our Prizes, but that is all. As nothing can be more hostile to the United States, than any Endeavours to embarrass, obstruct or counteract them in their Endeavours to form Treaties of Peace with the Barbary Powers, I wish you would impress it upon Mr. Barclay and Mr. Lamb, to be attentive to this, and obtain Proofs; and if the Consul or Agent of any foreign Power should be found and proved to do any Thing against Us, that they transmit to Us the earliest account of it with the Evidence. Congress would no doubt order a formal Complaint to be made against him to his Court, and in this way he would be held up publicly to the Execrations of all Mankind, and probably be punished by his Master.

Oct. 5 [i.e., 6] We have prevailed upon John[2] Randal Esqr. to go with Mr. Lamb, so that Sayre I suppose must be out of the Question, especially as We know not that he is arrived in Europe. I should think that much time may be saved, by Mr. Lambs going directly to Marseilles, and from thence over to Algiers but if you think there will be a greater Advantage, in seeing the Algerine Envoy at Madrid, or the Comte de Spilly, if he negotiated the late Treaty for Spain, I shall submit entirely to your better Judgment.

As our Commission authorizes us, I suppose it will be construed that it requires us to constitute the Agents by Writing under our Hands and Seals: I have accordingly made out four Commissions, which if you approve you will sign and seal, as I have done. I have written Letters to Mr. Barclay and Mr. Lamb authorizing them to draw upon me. These Letters you will please to sign, as the signature of both of us will be necessary. You will be so good as to write also to Messrs. Wilhem and Jan Willink and Nicholas & Jacob Vanstaphorst of Amsterdam, giving your Approbation and Consent to their Paying the Bills to be drawn upon me by Barclay and Lamb, otherwise they may think my Authority alone, imperfect.

I am Sir your most obedient and humble Servant,

JOHN ADAMS

RC (DLC); endorsed in Adams' hand: "Letter to Mr. Jefferson Oct. 6. 1785." FC (MHi: AMT). Recorded in SJL as received 10 Oct. 1785. Enclosures: Stephen Sayre to Adams, 25 Aug. 1785; Commissions, letters of credence, instructions, &c. to Barclay and Lamb (see Adams and TJ to Barclay and Lamb, 11 Oct. 1785); Commissioners to Vergennes, 11 Oct. 1785; Commissioners to Jay, 11 Oct. 1785.

[1] FC reads "Randall," which, of course, is correct. Adams was misled by TJ's letter of 24 Sep. wherein he had referred to "a Mr. Randolph . . . from New York."
[2] FC reads "Paul," which is correct.

To Barré

SIR   Paris Oct. 2. 1785.

I am now to acknolege the receipt of your favour of Sep. 19. I think I informed you that when I proposed to Wright to draw the picture of Genl. Washington for me, he would not agree to do it until I promised him that no copy should be taken till he should have had time to send another, which he had just drawn, to his mother in London and she also time to have an engraving made from it and stamps taken. This was in May 1784. In a letter of Jan. 13. 1785 I wrote to Mr. Hopkinson of Philadelphia praying him to ask of Wright if I was yet at liberty to permit copies to be taken from the picture drawn by him. Mr. Hopkinson in a letter, written immediately after the receipt of mine, tells me he has not yet seen Wright, but will take care to get me an answer. Nevertheless I have received as yet no answer, tho' Mr. Hopkinson wrote me a letter a month after that. A gentleman lately from London who saw Mrs. Wright there, assures me that she has never received the picture which her son was to send her, which induces a presumption that he has declined sending it. Should I not ere long receive an answer from Mr. Hopkinson I shall think myself at liberty to suffer copies to be taken, and will certainly give the first notice to Monsieur Thevenot [Thévénard], repeating, what I before mentioned, that if he would prefer a copy from Peale's drawing, which I also have, he may have that taken immediately. I shall seize with pleasure the first moment of obliging Monsieur de Thevenot as well on account of his general merit and rank, as of the particular friendly dispositions which he bears towards my countrymen, testimonies of which I receive from those of them who come from L'Orient. I have the honour to be Sir Your most obedient humble servt.,   TH: JEFFERSON

PrC (DLC). Entry in SJL reads: "Barré lt. des fregates du roi à l'hotel de Mr. Thevenot Commandt. de la marine à L'Orient." Hopkinson's letter saying that he had not yet seen Wright was that of 20 Apr. 1785, and the next that he wrote was not A MONTH AFTER THAT, but three months—that is, on 23 July 1785.

To the Rev. James Madison

DEAR SIR   Paris Oct. 2. 1785.

I have duly received your favor of April 10. by Mr. Mazzei. You therein speak of a new method of raising water by steam which you suppose will come into general use. I know of no new method of that kind and suppose (as you say that the account you have received of it is very imperfect) that some person has represented to you as new a fire engine erected at Paris and which supplies the greater part of the town with water. But this is nothing more than the fire engine you have seen described in the books of Hydraulics and particularly in the dictionary of arts and sciences published in 8vo. by Owen, the idea of which was first taken from Papin's digester. It would have been better called the Steam engine. The force of the steam of water you know is immense. In this engine it is made to exert itself towards the working of pumps. That of Paris is I believe the largest known, raising 400,000 cubic feet (French) of water in 24 hours: or rather, I should have said, *those* of Paris, for there are two under one roof, each raising that quantity.

The Abbé Rochon not living at Paris, I have not had an opportunity of seeing him and of asking him the questions you desire relative to the Chrystal of which I wrote you. I shall avail myself of the earliest opportunity I can of doing it.—I shall chearfully execute your commands as to the Encyclopedie when I receive them. The price will be only 30. guineas. About half the work is out. The volumes of your Buffon which are spoiled can be replaced here.

I expect that this letter will be carried by the Mr. Fitzhughs in a ship from Havre to Portsmouth. I have therefore sent to Havre some books which I expected would be acceptable to you. These are the Bibliotheque physico-œconomique which will give you most of the late improvements in the arts; the Connoissance des tems for 1786. and 1787. which is as late as they are published, and some peices on air and fire wherein you will find all the discoveries hitherto made on these subjects. These books are made into a packet with your address on them and are put into a trunk wherein is a small packet for Mr. Wythe, another for Mr. Page, and a parcel of books without direction for Peter Carr. I have taken the liberty of directing the trunk to you as the surest means of it's getting safe. I pay the freight of it here, so that there will be no new demands but for the transportation from the ships side to Wmsburg. which I will pray you to pay, and as much the greatest part is for my nephew I will take care to repay it to you.

In the last volume of the Connoissance des tems you will find the tables for the planet Herschel. It is a curious circumstance that this planet was seen 30 years ago by Mayer, and supposed by him to be a fixed star. He accordingly determined a place for it in his catalogue of the Zodiacal stars, making it the 964th. of that catalogue. Bode of Berlin observed in 1781 that this star was missing. Subsequent calculations of the motion of the planet Herschel shew that it must have been, at the time of Mayer's observation, where he had placed his 964th. star.

Herschell has pushed his discoveries of double stars now to upwards of 900. being twice the number of those communicated in the Philosophical transactions. You have probably seen that a Mr. Pigott had discovered periodical variations of light in the star Algol. He has observed the same in the η of Antinous, and makes the period of variation 7D. 4H. 30′, the duration of the increase 63.H. and of the decrease 36H. What are we to conclude from this? That there are suns which have their orbits of revolution too? But this would suppose a wonderful harmony in their planets, and present a new scene where the attracting powers should be without and not within the orbit. The motion of our sun would be a miniature of this. But this must be left to you Astronomers.

We were told some time ago of a cheap method of extricating inflammable air from pit-coal. This would facilitate the experiments with baloons. Two artists are employing themselves in the means of directing their course. They can ascend and descend at will without expending their gaz, and have been able to deflect from the course of the wind 45°.

I went sometime ago to see a machine which offers something new. A man had applied to a light boat a very large screw, the thread of which was a thin plate two feet broad applied by it's edge spirally round a small axis. It somewhat resembled a bottle brush if you will suppose the hairs of the bottle brush joining together and forming a spiral plane. This, turned on it's axis in the air, carried the vessel across the Seine. It is in fact a screw which takes hold of the air and draws itself along by it: losing indeed much of it's effort by the yeilding nature of the body it lays hold of to pull itself on by. I think it may be applied in the water with much greater effect and to very useful purposes. Perhaps it may be used also for the baloon.

It is impossible but you must have heard long ago of the machine for copying letters at a single stroke, as we had received them in America before I left it. I have written a long letter to my nephew, in whose education I feel myself extremely interested. I shall rely much on your friendship for conducting him in the plan I mark out for him, and for guarding him against those shoals on which youth sometimes shipwreck. I trouble you to present to Mr. Wythe my affectionate remembrance of him and am with very great esteem Dear Sir Your friend & servant, TH: JEFFERSON

PrC (DLC); at foot of letter: "Jas. Madison, W. & M. college." Recorded in SJL as sent by "Mr. Fitzh[ugh]"; entry in SJPL reads: "Madison Bishop. Books. Arts. Herschel. Bode."

A FIRE ENGINE . . . WHICH SUPPLIES THE GREATER PART OF THE TOWN WITH WATER refers to the "pompes à feu" of the Compagnie des Eaux de Paris. For a description of this water distribution system, managed by Messrs Perrier frères, see L. V. Thiéry, *Guide des amateurs . . . à Paris*, 1787, I, 47-51. TJ's water supply at the Hôtel de Langeac came from this system; his account book records annual payments of 50f. to Perrier, 10 July 1786, 10 July 1787, 22 Nov. 1788. The pieces ON AIR AND FIRE were doubtless the same as those mentioned in TJ to Currie, 27 Sep. 1785.

TJ's suggestion that the screw propeller MAY BE USED ALSO FOR THE BALOON was evidently one of the earliest to embrace the idea. Milbank, *First Century of Flight in America*, Princeton, 1943, p. 75, says that Rufus Porter in *Scientific American* for 18 Sep. 1845 describes a flying machine with a large screw propeller, and comments that "Porter was not, however, the first American to have conceived of an aerostat driven by propeller. Francis Hopkinson had proposed the idea to Franklin in 1784, while Thomas Jefferson in a letter to James Madison in 1785 had suggested what was tantamount to the same thing."

From John Adams

DEAR SIR   Grosvenor Square Oct. 3. 1785

You have undoubtedly hit upon, the true Word of the Riddle. Yet there was no riddle, nor any clear meaning. It is impossible for any Country to give to another, more decided Proofs of Preference, than our thoughtless Merchants have since the Peace given to this, in matters of Commerce. He had seen this Preference sufficiently prevail. This alone then could not be his Meaning. If he meant a political Preference, an Alliance, such as¹ Hartley was perpetually harping upon, he will wait till Doomsday, and it will never come. We ought to have no Prefferences nor Partialities. But this must be understood upon Condition, that this Country uses us, as well as France. If she does not, I am for giving France the Preference. I would wait with Patience and give full Time to deliberate, but if finally this Court will not act a reasonable and equitable Part, I would enter into still closer and stronger connections with France, both commercial and political. I would enter into Treaty, that certain French Manufactures should pay in the U.S. but half or a quarter of the Duties imposed upon English. French ships should have priviledges from which English should be excluded, and I would enter into an Alliance, offensive and defensive. But more of this hereafter.

I went out, eight days ago, to Dr. Price to get him to have the Insurance done.

October 5. Dr. Price called upon me this morning, but had unfortunately wholly forgot the Insurance on Heudon's Life. But I gave him an extract of your Letter to me, and promised to pay the Money for the Premium at any Moment. I am afraid that Certificates of Heudons State of Health will be required, and the Noise of Algerine Captures may startle the Insurers. The Doctor However will get it done if he can, and as low as possible.

I went to Stockdale with your Letter. He says he sent some News

Papers by Mr. Short and by a Friend since, and will send by Franks. He applied to the office, he says in Cleaveland Row but could not get them sent that way. But he will call on the Duke of Dorsett, and get his Permission. If your Correspondent at Dover however can convey them to you free of Postage you had better agree with him. But after all your surest way would be to apply to the Comte de Vergennes, or Mr. Gennet, the Premier Comis du Bureau des Interpretes. In any other way your Papers will be liable to frequent Interruptions. I found that the only sure way, in the year 1780, after many fruitless Projects and Endeavours for several months.

Yours affectionately, JOHN ADAMS

RC (DLC); endorsed in Adams' hand: "Letter to Mr. Jefferson. Oct. 3. 1785." FC (MHi: AMT). Recorded in sjl as received 10 Oct. 1785.

The extract of TJ's letter that Adams gave to Houdon was probably taken from that of 10 Aug.; see TJ to Adams, 7 July and 24 Sep. 1785. TJ's

CORRESPONDENT AT DOVER was Thomas Thompson; see Thompson to TJ, 12 and 22 Aug.; and TJ to Thompson, 17 Aug. 1785.

[1] Two words are deleted in RC at this point. They appear to be "one Minister."

From Lister Asquith

St. Pol de Léon, 3 Oct. 1785. Asquith has received from Picrel a copy of a letter from "Mr. Maisoneiuve Floch Procureiur of Brest," the lawyer engaged earlier by Picrel, who agrees now to take the case if Asquith advances him ten guineas, though he has already received three. Asquith is doubtful whether his last three guineas will satisfy. He had instructed Floch to write TJ a state of their case and now asks TJ to write to him to learn whether he will proceed. Picrel thinks they will have little success in Brest; "we must depend on your strong solicitations with the Ministers and the Crown, who will no doubt they think assist us. But I believe this is only a Story raised by Mr. Picrel to get us to drop it." Expected "humain treatment and assistance" when he landed in France. "If you are the Gentleman who was Governor of Virginia perhaps you may have [heard] of me as I used part of the War to sail in Col. Parker's & Co. and Col. Godwins & Co. Smithfield Pagan Creek but was drove from there by Arnold and lost almost all I had by that Villian." Asquith recounts to TJ two reports of the farmers'-general false imprisonment and coercion of strangers to France, one of which "happend . . . in the very same circumstances we are in." The farmers-general finally lost the case after confining the accused for eleven months and after it was tried five times "because the Merchants were able to stand them," though generally "they are so Strong that few are able to stand a Law suit with them."

RC (DLC); 4 p.; addressed and endorsed. Recorded in sjl as received 9 Oct. 1785.

From James Madison

In pursuance of the plan intimated in my last I came to this City about three weeks ago, from which I continued my trip to New York. I returned last night and in a day or two shall start for Virginia. Col. Monroe had left Philada. a few days before I reached it, on his way to a treaty to be held with the Indians about the end of this month on the Wabash. If a visit to the Eastern States had been his choice, short as the time would have proved, I should have made an effort to attend him. As it is I must postpone that gratification, with a purpose however of embracing it on the first convenient opportunity. Your favour of the 11 May by Monsr. Doradour inclosing your Cypher arrived in Virga. after I left it, and was sent after me to this place. Your notes which accompanied it, remained behind, and consequently I can only now say on that subject, that I shall obey your request on my return, which my call to Richmond will give me an early opportunity of doing. During my stay at New York I had several conversations with the Virga. Delegates, but with few others, on the affairs of the Confederacy. I find with much regret that these are as yet little redeemed from the confusion which has so long mortified the friends to our national honor and prosperity. Congress have kept the Vessel from sinking, but it has been by standing constantly at the pump, not by stopping the leaks which have endangered her. All their efforts for the latter purpose have been frustrated by the selfishness or perverseness of some part or other of their constituents. The desiderata most strongly urged by our past experience and our present situation are 1. a final discrimination between such of the unauthorised expences of the States, as ought to be added to the common debt, and such as ought not; 2. a constitutional apportionment of the common debt, either by a valuation of the land, or a change of the article which requires it; 3. a recognition by the States of the authority of Congress to enforce payment of their respective quotas; 4. a grant to Congress of an adequate power over trade. It is evident to me that the first object will never be effected in Congress, because it requires in those who are to decide it the spirit of impartial judges, whilst the spirit of those who compose Congress is rather that of advocates for the respective interests of their constituents. If this business were referred to a Commission filled by a member chosen by Congress out of each

State, and sworn to impartiality, I should have hopes of seeing an end of it. The 2d. object affords less ground of hope. The execution of the 8th. art. of Confederation is generally held impracticable, and R. Island, if no other State, has put its veto on the proposed alteration of it. Until the 3d. object can be obtained the Requisitions of Congress will continue to be mere calls for voluntary contributions, which every State will be tempted to evade, by the uniform experience that those States have come off best which have done so most. The present plan of federal Government reverses the first principle of all Government. It punishes not the evildoers, but those that do well. It may be considered I think as a fortunate circumstance for the U.S. that the use of coercion, or such provision as would render the use of it unnecessary, might be made at little expence and perfect safety. A single frigate under the orders of Congress could make it the interest of any one of the Atlantic States to pay its just Quota. With regard to such of the Ultramontane States, as depend on the trade of the Mississippi, as small a force would have the same effect; whilst the residue trading thro' the Atlantic States might be wrought upon by means more indirect indeed, but perhaps sufficiently effectual. The fate of the 4th. object is still suspended. The Recommendations of Congress on this subject past before your departure, have been positively complied with by few of the States I believe; but I do not learn that they have been rejected by any. A proposition has been agitated in Congress, and will I am told be revived, asking from the States a general and permanent authority to regulate trade, with a proviso that it shall in no case be exercised without the assent of *eleven* States in Congress. The Middle States favor the measure, the Eastern are Zealous for it, the Southern are divided. Of[1] the *Virginia delegation* the *president*[2] *is* an *inflexible adversary, Grayson unfriendly* and *Monroe* and *Hardy warm on the opposite side.* If the proposition should pass Congress its fate will depend much on the reception it may find in Virga. and this will depend much on the part which may be taken by a few members of the Legislature. The prospect of its being levelled against G. Britain will be most likely to give it popularity. In this suspence of a general provision for our commercial interests, the more suffering States are seeking relief from partial efforts which are less likely to obtain it than to drive their trade into other channels, and to kindle heartburnings on all sides. Massachussetts made the beginning. Penna. has followed with a catalogue of duties on foreign goods and tonnage, which could scarcely be enforced against the smuggler, if N. Jersey, Delaware and Maryland were to cooperate with her. The avowed object of these duties is to encourage domestic manufactures, and prevent the exportation of coin to pay for foreign. The Legislature had previously repealed the incorporation of the bank, as the cause of the latter and a great many other evils. S. Carolina I am told is deliberating on the distresses of her commerce and will probably concur in some general plan, with a proviso, no doubt against any restraint from importing slaves, of which they have received from Africa since the peace about twelve thousand. She is also deliberating on the emission of paper money, and it is expected she will legalize a suspension of Judicial proceedings which has been already effected by popular combinations. The pretext for these measures is the want of specie occasioned by the unfavorable balance of trade.—Your introduction of Mr. T. Franklin has been presented to me. The arrival of his grandfather has produced an emulation among the different parties here in doing homage to his character. He will be unanimously chosen president of the State, and will either restore to it an unexpected quiet or lose his own. It appears from his answer to some applications that he will not decline the appointment.—On my journey I called at Mount Vernon and had the pleasure of finding the General in perfect health. He had just returned from a trip up the Potowmac. He grows more and more sanguine, as he examines further into the practicability of opening its navigation. The subscriptions are compleated within a few shares, and the work is already begun at some of the lesser obstructions. It is overlooked by Rhumsey the inventor of the boats which I have in former letters mentioned to you. He has not yet disclosed his secret. He had of late nearly finished a boat of proper size which he meant to have exhibited, but the house which contained it and materials for others was consumed by fire. He assured the General that the enlargement of his machinery did not lessen the prospect of utility afforded by the miniature experiments. The General declines the shares voted him by the assembly, but does not mean to withdraw the money from the object which it is to aid, and will even appropriate the future tolls I believe to some useful public establishment if any such can be devised that will both please himself and be likely to please the State. This is accompanied by a letter from our amiable friend Mrs. Trist to Miss Patsy. She got back safe to her friends in Augst. and is as well as she has generally been, but her chearfulness seems to be rendered less uniform than it once was by the scenes of adversity through which[3] fortune has led her. Mrs. House is well and charges me not to omit her respectful and affectionate compliments to you.

I remain Dr. Sir Yrs   J. M.

RC (DLC: Madison Papers); endorsed; partly in code, with interlineal decoding by TJ. Recorded in SJL as received 30 Dec. 1785 "by Houdon." Enclosure: Eliza House Trist's letter to Martha Jefferson has not been found.

[1] This and subsequent words in italics are written in code and were decoded interlineally by TJ; his decoding has been verified by the editors, employing Code No. 9.

[2] This word is keyed by asterisk to a marginal note in Madison's hand (probably made after TJ's death) which reads: "R. H. Lee."

[3] Madison deleted two words at this point, which appear to be "her dreadful." It cannot be determined whether this deletion was made at the time the letter was written or many years later when Madison received his letters back from TJ's estate.

To C. W. F. Dumas

SIR   Paris. Oct. 4. 1785.

I received yesterday your favour of Sep. 28. and shall take care that your bill be honoured. I propose to write to the Commissioners of the Treasury to direct in what manner the salaries of the public servants and other money demands shall be paid. Dr. Franklin had of course a general direction of the funds here. Circumstances rendered this necessary. These have now changed, insomuch that it will be practicable for the Commissioners themselves to undertake that direction; and it will relieve me from a task very foreign to my talents and to the regular duties of my office. In the mean time I continue to advise the paiment of monies by their banker here as my predecessor had done to prevent the public service from suffering.

I know very well the father of the Mr. Tandy whom you mention. He is a worthy farmer of Virginia, not rich, but easy in his circumstances. I have understood from different quarters that the son, Moses Tandy, is actually become mad. But whether mad, or only dissipated, the most friendly and humane thing which could be done for him would be to prevail on him to go back to his own country. If you can have influence enough on him to effect this, I should be very glad of it for the sake of his parents. I am with much respect Sir your most obedient humble servant,

TH: JEFFERSON

P.S. I must not omit to assure you of my perfect approbation of your proceedings in the business referred to yourself and Mr. Short.

RC (CtY). MS slightly torn; portions of two missing words have been supplied from PrC in DLC. Though dated 4 Oct., the letter was not correctly posted until the 8th, having been misdirected under cover to André Limozin and returned by him to TJ (see Limozin to TJ, 6 Oct. and TJ to Limozin, 8 Oct. 1785).

From C. W. F. Dumas

Lahaie 4e. Oct. 1785

En confirmant à Votre Excellence ma Lettre du 28 7bre. que Messrs. Nic. & Jb. van Staphorst vous auront acheminée, et sur laquelle j'espere que Votre Excellence voudra bien me faire prompte et favorable réponse, celle-ci est pour prendre la Liberté de vous adresser, Monsieur, l'incluse pour notre Ami le Colonel Senf, avec prière de vouloir bien la lui remettre. Elle en contient une pour S. E. Mr. Rutledge, notre nouveau Ministre, à qui le Colonel m'a promis de la remettre, et à qui il est naturel et convenable que je m'empresse de présenter mon Zele constant pour le service des Etats-Unis, et celui pour lui être personnellement utile et agreable. Je repete que je n'attends que la Signature finale de la paix avec l'Empereur et de l'Alliance avec la France, auxquelles j'ai la satisfaction d'avoir pu grandement et intimement coopérer, pour recommencer à faire passer mes Dépeches par la voie de France, et par conséquent sous les yeux de Votre Excellence de qui je suis &c.

FC (Dumas Letter Book, Rijksarchief, The Hague—photostats in DLC). Recorded in SJL as received 9 Oct. 1785. Enclosures: Dumas to John Christian Senf and to John Rutledge, 4 Oct. 1785 (Dumas Letter Book).

From André Limozin

Le Havre, 4 Oct. 1785. Encloses copy of his letter to Joseph Fortin concerning his inheritance rights to the "Estate to which he would be entitled had his Father not alterd his Christen name when he landed in America"; also copies of the church register and notice of property sale. It will be evident to TJ that Fortin's claim cannot be pressed "as long as he will call him self son of Joseph Fortin as he does by the Vouchers he sent me, because none of the Family of the deceasd Fortin who left that Estate was calld Joseph."

RC (DNA: PCC, No. 87, I); 2 p.; at foot of first page, in part: "en son Hotel a la Grille de Chaillot Paris." Tr (DNA: PCC, No. 107, I). Recorded in SJL as received 6 Oct. 1785. Enclosures (DLC): Copies of baptismal certificate of Jean Baptiste Fortin, dated 29 Dec. 1719; notice of sale of the property of Jean Fortin, dated 30 Nov. 1732; and Limozin to Joseph Fortin, 11 Oct. 1782, in which he said: "I have had a Copy drawn of the Birth and Names of all the Fortins, I have got all the Papers you sent me Translated by a Sworn Broker, or Interpreter: that cost 50 Livers besides Postage, and it grieves me mostly that you will find no benefit neither by the expences I have made, nor by the troubles you have had to procure so many Papers, to send them to me, nevertheless if you can get all the Papers altered in mentionning the home of your late Father John, instead of Joseph, I am in good hopes yet to succeed. . . . I have been prudent enough to not shew to any Body the Papers you sent me, nor to make any application to Justice, to Claim the Estate. . . . I [am] really astonished to hear that you had drawn on me already Ten thousand Livers on Account of that expected Estate. Your draft is returned with Protest. . . ."

To André Limozin

SIR   Paris Oct. 4. 1785.

I received yesterday your favour informing me that your Ship Eolus would sail on the 5th. inst. As you had expected she would not sail till the 15th. when you wrote me before, I had so informed the two Mr. Fitzhughs, two gentlemen of Virginia who wished to go in her. When I received your letter yesterday therefore, the warning to them was too short to get ready. Of consequence they have concluded to go in the ship bound for Philadelphia which you say will sail the 15th. They will leave Paris the 10th. for Havre. Still I wish that my trunks and box should go in the vessel bound for Portsmouth. But it will be necessary to give to the Captain those instructions that I had intended for Mr. Fitzhugh, that is to say, to send the smallest trunk to Williamsburgh and the other two and the box to Richmond. As the Captain is probably unacquainted with the communications of that country, it will be necessary to caution him particularly not to send all the packages together to Williamsburgh under any expectation of their being forwarded from thence to Richmond. There is no conveyance between Williamsburgh and Richmond, and there are almost daily conveyances from Portsmouth to both those places. I have the honour to be with much respect Sir Your most obedient humble servant,

TH: JEFFERSON

PrC (MHi). Though dated 4 Oct., the letter actually reached Limozin as an enclosure to TJ's later letter of the 8th, having been first misdirected under cover to C. W. F. Dumas, in error for TJ's to Dumas of 4 Oct. (see Limozin to TJ, 6 Oct.; TJ to Limozin, 8 Oct. 1785).

To John Adams

Sir   Paris Oct. 5. 1785.

The Chevalier Dolomieu of the order of Malta, who served in the army of Count Rochambeau in America being to pass into England, I take the liberty of introducing him to you. An acquaintance with him in America enables me to assure you of his merit; his politeness and good understanding will of themselves recommend him to your esteem.

I have the honour to be with the highest respect Sir Your most obedient & most humble servt.,   Th: Jefferson

RC (Mrs. Ellen Barbour Glines, Puerto Rico; deposited in Ct, 1946); without indication of addressee; at foot of letter in another hand: "de la hay street. near great george Street. Westminster No. 5." Entry in sjl under this date reads: "Cheval. Dolomieu. Inclosing introductory letter to J. Adams." This covering letter to Dolomieu has not been found.

To Benjamin Franklin

Sir   Paris Oct. 5. 1785.

A Vessel sailing from Havre to Philadelphia furnishes the Mr. Fitzhughs with a passage to that place. To them therefore I confide a number of letters and packets which I have received for you from sundry quarters and which, I doubt not, they will deliver safe. Among these is one from Mr. Du Plessis. On receipt of your letter, in answer to the one I had written you on the subject of his memorial, I sent to Mr. La Motte, Mr. Chaumont and wherever else I thought there was a probability of finding out Du Plessis's address. But all in vain. I meant to have examined his memoir, as you desired, and to have had it copied. Lately he came and brought it with him, copied by himself. He desired me to read it and inclose it to you, which I have done.

We have no public news worth communicating to you but the signing of preliminaries between the emperor and Dutch. The question is then with whom the emperor will pick the next quarrel. Our treaty with Prussia goes by this conveyance. But it is not to be spoken of till a convenient time is allowed for exchanging ratifications. Science offers nothing new since your departure, nor no new publication worth your notice. All your friends here are well. Those in England have carried you captive to Algiers. They have published a letter as if written by Truxen the 20th of Aug.

from Algiers, stating the circumstances of the capture, and that you bore your slavery to admiration. I happened to receive a letter from Algiers dated Aug. 24. informing me that two vessels were then there taken from us, and naming the vessels and captains. This was a satisfactory proof to us that you were not there. The fact being so, we would have gladly dispenced with the proof, as the situation of our countrymen there was described as very distressing.—Were I to mention all those who make enquiries after you there would be no end to my letter. I cannot however pass over those of the good old Countess d'Hoditot, with whom I dined on Saturday at Sanois. They were very affectionate. I hope you have had a good passage. Your essay in crossing the channel gave us great hopes you would experience little inconvenience in the rest of the voiage. My wishes place you in the bosom of your friends, in good health, and with a wellgrounded prospect of preserving it long for your own sake, for theirs, and that of the world. I am with the sincerest attachment & respect Dear Sir Your most obedient & most humble servant, TH: J[EFFERSON]

PrC (DLC); part of signature torn away. Recorded in SJL as sent "by Mr. Fitzhugh"; entry in SJPL reads: "Franklin Dr. Du Plash's, his voyage and friends." Enclosures not identified.

From David Hartley

MY DEAR SIR   London October 5 1785

I return you many thanks for the favours of yours which I received by Col. Franks. You will make me very happy by the continuance of your correspondences and the longer your letters are the better, more especially if you will not expect long letters from me in return. In my situation I must hear and be silent. My lesson is from Hamlet: *You never shall—with arms encumbred thus, or thus, head shake, or by pronouncing of some doubtfull Phrase; as well, we know, or we could an if we would* &c. But I can most sincerely sum up all that I have or ever can have to say; viz. That I ever have and ever will, to the utmost of my power, endeavour to promote political and commercial amity between our two Countries. I do not think myself so unreasonable, as the proposition in itself might give out in desiring to be the recipient of all informations and sentiments respecting the state of our two Countries, without making return in kind. I am very covetous to fill my budget with all possible information, for chances of being enabled at any time hereafter to promote some substantial good between your country and mine, an occasion which I should at any time most ardently seize, if ever such a lot should fall to my share. I must keep my thoughts to myself, unless I were to be called upon. This discretion constitutes all the difference of acting in season or out of season, which in cases of importance is most important.— *Verbum sapienti.*

I have always understood the law of Consuls to be as you express it, and I take for granted when Mr. Temple declares his Commission in America, that Congress will give him the reasons of their proceedings, whatever they may be. That would contribute to a conciliatory understanding between us. As to the English newspapers you must not lay much stress upon them. Every one writes and prints what he thinks proper, and whatever may suit either his passion or his interest. There are many persons who are now tacitly reproached, with their former dispositions towards America, during the war. Some allowance of temper should be made. An English proverb says Losers have a right to complain. After a storm the waves will continue to roll for some time. I do not doubt but time will abate regrets, and restore Amity between our Countries.—I have received a letter from Mr. Jay and have put Mr. Upton's affair into a good train. Pray remember me whenever you write to Mr. Adams or have any safe opportunity. My best wishes for health and happiness attend yourself and family. Pray give my best compliments to Mr. Humphreys. I am Dr. Sir with very sincere respect Yours &c.,   D HARTLEY

RC (DLC); endorsed. Recorded in SJL as received 10 Oct. 1785.

From John Paul Jones

SIR   Paris Oct. 5th. 1785

The following is the best Information I am able to give you in Compliance with the Letter dated at Paris the 3d. of August 1785 which you did me the Honor to address to me at L'orient.

The Boussole and the Astrolabe, two Gaberts [gabares] of 600 Tons each, sheathed with Copper, and equipped in the best Manner, sailed from Brest the 1st. of August 1785, under the Command of Messrs. de la Perouse and the Viscount de Langle, Captains in the royal Navy. They had on Board a great Variety of Trees, Plants and Seeds that suit the Climate of France; Manufactures in Linen, Woolen, and Cotton and in Iron and Copper &c.; Mechanical Tools of all Sorts; A great Quantity of Trinkets and Toys; Ploughs and all Sorts of Utensils and Implements for Agriculture; And a Quantity of unwrought Iron. Each Ship had on board a large Shallop in Frames and a Million of French Livres in the Coins of different Nations. Each Ship had also on board twenty one Soldiers, draughted from the two Regiments at Brest; all of whom were either Mechanics or Farmers. They had on board no Women; nor any Animals except such as appeared to be destined for the Refreshment of the Crews. The Crew of each Ship is one hundred Men, including Officers and Men of Genius.

The King himself planned the Expedition, and made out all the Detail with his own Hand, before he spoke a Word of it to any Person. His Majesty defrays the Expence out of his private Coffer, and is his own Minister in every Thing that regards the Operations of his Plan. There is no Doubt but the perfectioning the Geography of the Southern Hemisphere is one of his Majesty's Objects in View: and it is not difficult to percieve that he has others equally worthy the Attention of a great Prince; one of which may be to extend the Commerce of his Subjects by Establishing Factories at a future Day, for the Fur Trade on the North West Coast of America; and another to establish Colonies in New Holland, after having well explored the Coast, and made Experiments on the Soil of that vast Island, which is situated in so happy a Climate, and so contiguous to the Establishments of France in the East Indies.

I am Sir, with great Respect your most obedient & most humble Servant,   J. P. JONES

Tr (DNA: PCC, No. 87, 1); in Short's hand, with Jones's signature in TJ's hand. In DNA: PCC, No. 87, 1 and No. 107, 1 are lists in Short's hand of the officers and specialists on board the *Boussole* and the *Astrolabe*. A copy of the covering letter was enclosed in TJ to John Jay 6 Oct. 1785.

To Samuel Osgood

DEAR SIR   Paris Oct. 5. 1785.

It was with very sincere pleasure I heard of your appointment to the board of treasury, as well from the hope it might not be disagreeable to yourself, as from the confidence it's administration would be wise. I heartily wish the states may by their contributions enable you to reestablish a credit which cannot be lower than at present to exist at all. This is partly owing to their real deficiencies, and partly to the lies propagated by the London papers, which probably are paid for by the minister to reconcile the people to the loss of us. Unluckily, it indisposes them at the same time to form rational connections with us. Should this produce the amendment of our federal constitution, of which your papers give us hopes, we shall receive a permanent indemnification for a temporary loss.—All things here promise an arrangement between the Emperor and Dutch. Their ministers have signed preliminary articles, some of which however leave room for further cavil. The Dutch pay 10. million of florins, yeild some forts and territory, and the navigation of the Scheldt to Saftigen. Till our treaty with England is fully executed it is desireable to us that all the world should be in peace. That done, their wars would do us little harm.

I find myself under difficulties here which I will take the liberty of explaining to you as a friend. Mr. Carmichael lately drew a bill on Mr. Grand for 4000^{tt}, I suppose for his salary. Mr. Grand said he was not used to accept draughts but by the desire of Dr. Franklin, and rested it on me to say whether this bill should be paid or not. I thought it improper that the credit of so confidential a person as Mr. Carmichael should be affected by a refusal, and therefore advised paiment. Mr. Dumas has drawn on me for 2700.^{tt} his half year's salary, informing me he always drew on Dr. Franklin. I shall advise the paiment. I have had loan office bills drawn on the Commissioners of the U.S. presented to me. My answer has been 'These are very old bills. Had they been presented while those gentlemen were in Europe they would have been paid. You have kept them up till Doctor Franklin, the last of them, has returned to America. You must therefore send them there and they will be paid. I am not the Drawee described in the bill.' It is impossible for me to meddle with these bills. The gentlemen who had been familiar with them from the beginning, who kept books of them and knew well the form of these books, often paid bills twice. But how can I interfere with them who have not a scrip of a pen on their subject, who never saw a book relating to them, and who, if I had the books, should much oftener be bewildered in the labyrinth than the gentlemen who have kept them? I think it therefore most adviseable that what bills remain out should be sent back to America for paiment, and therefore advise Mr. Barclay to return thither all the books and papers relative to them.

There is the proper and ultimate deposit of all records of this nature. All these articles are very foreign to my talents, and foreign also as I conceive to the nature of my duties. Dr. Franklin was obliged to meddle with them from the circumstances which existed. But these having ceased, I suppose it practicable for your board to direct the administration of your monies here in every circumstance. It is only necessary for me to draw my own allowances, and to order paiment for services done by others by my direction and within the immediate line of my office, such as paying couriers, postage, and other extraordinary services which must rest on my discretion and at my risk if disapproved by Congress. I will thank you for your advice on this subject, and if you think a resolution of your board necessary I will pray you to send me such a one, and that it may relieve me from all concerns with the money of the U.S. other than those I have just spoken of. I do not mean by this to testify a disposition to render no service but what is rigorously within my duty. I am the farthest in the world from this. It is a question I never shall ask myself, nothing making me more happy than to render any service in my power, of whatever description. But I wish only to be excused from intermeddling in business in which I have no skill and should do more harm than good.

Congress were pleased to order me an advance of two quarters salary. At that time I supposed that I might refund it, or spare so much upon my expences, by the time the third quarter became due. Probably they might expect the same. But it has been impossible. The expences of my Outfit, tho' I have taken it up on a scale as small as could be admitted have been very far beyond what I had conceived. I have therefore not only been unable to refund the advance ordered, but been obliged to go beyond it. I wished to have avoided so much as was occasioned by the purchase of furniture. But those who hire furniture asked me 40. pr. cent a year for the use of it. It was better to buy therefore, and this article, clothes, carriage &c. have amounted to considerably more than the advance ordered. Perhaps it may be thought reasonable to allow me an outfit. The usage of every other nation has established this, and reason really pleads for it. I do not wish to make a shilling, but only to be defrayed and in a moderate style. On the most moderate which the reputation or interest of those I serve would admit, it will take me several years to reduce the advances for my outfit.—I mention this to enable you to understand the necessities which have obliged me to call for more money than probably was expected, and understanding them to explain them to others. Being perfectly disposed to conform myself decisively to what shall be thought proper, you cannot oblige me more than by communicating to me your sentiments hereon, which I shall receive as those of a friend and govern myself accordingly. I am with the most perfect esteem Dr. Sir your friend & servt.,   TH: JEFFERSON

RC (NHi). PrC (DLC). Recorded in SJL as sent "by Mr. Fitzhugh"; entry in SJPL reads: "Osgood Samuel. Our finances."

In DLC: TJ Papers, 17: 2900 there is a paper in TJ's hand summarizing various resolutions of Congress from 1779 to 1785 affecting salaries and contingent expenses of ministers: (1) 6 Aug. 1779, salary to commence from time of leaving place of abode and to be continued for three months after notice of recall: (2) 4 Oct. 1779, salary fixed at £2,500 sterling; (3) 16 May 1783, couriers and postage allowed among contingencies; (4) 7 May 1784, salary of minister "shall not exceed 9000 Dollars per annum" beginning 1 Aug. 1784; (5) 22 July 1785, Dana allowed traveling expenses. These memoranda were probably made in the autumn of 1785 and the following calculation, which was certainly made after 5 Sep. 1785 when TJ negotiated a lease for the Hôtel de Langeac, was also evidently made about this time and was no doubt in his mind when he spoke of requiring SEVERAL YEARS TO REDUCE THE ADVANCES FOR MY OUTFIT:

		Actual		Reformed to	
		Monthly	Yearly	Monthly	Yearly
"Carriage		200	2400	195	2340
Dress		100	1200	70	840
Washing		50	600	50	600
Houserent		625	7500	625	7500
Servants.	Wages	3315[1]	4200	283	3816
	Dress	35		35	
Hôtel exp.	Wood	135		100	
	Wine	155	15,000	80	13,320
	Trait.	520		510	
	Resid.	440		420	
Patsy		350	4,200	350	4,200
Contingencies		400	4,800	400	4,800
Household furn.		50	600	42	504
Books		100	1200	50	600
[A]ids to Amer.		100	1200	100	1200
[R]esidy. acqns.		25	300	25	300
		3600	43,200	3335	40,020

Etrennes
47,250
40,020

7,230 of the advance may be replaced annually"

(MS in TJ's hand; owned by Oliver R. Barrett, Chicago, 1948). The fact that TJ felt obliged to reduce his book purchases by half in order to repay the advance and to meet expenses is an indication of the urgency of his need.

[1] Thus in MS; the figure should be 315. TJ may have started to write the figure in the wrong column, then omitted erasing the first "3."

To John Jay

My letter of Aug. 30. acknowleged the receipt of yours of July 13. Since that I have received your letter of Aug. 13. inclosing a correspondence between the M. de la Fayette and Monsr. de Calonne, and another of the same date inclosing the papers in Fortin's case. I immediately wrote to Mr. Limozin at Havre desiring he would send me a state of the case, and inform me what were the difficulties which suspended it's decision. He has promised me by letter to do this as soon as possible, and I shall not fail in attention to it.

The emperor and Dutch have signed preliminaries, which are now made public. You will see them in the papers which accompany this. They still leave a good deal to discussion. However it is probable they will end in peace. The party in Holland possessed actually of the sovereignty wish for peace that they may push their designs on the Stadthoulderate. This country wishes for peace because their finances need arrangement. The Bavarian exchange has produced to public view that jealousy and rancour between the courts of Vienna and Berlin which existed before, tho' it was smothered. This will appear by the declarations of the two courts. The demarcation between the Emperor and Turk does not advance. Still however I suppose neither of those two germs of war likely to open soon. I consider the conduct of France as the best evidence of this. If she had apprehended a war from either of those quarters she would not have been so anxious to leave the emperor one enemy the less by placing him at peace with the Dutch. While she is exerting all her powers to preserve peace by land, and making no preparation which indicates a fear of it's being disturbed in that quarter, she is pushing her naval preparations with a spirit unexampled in time of peace. By the opening of the next spring she will have eighty ships of 74 guns and upwards ready for sea at a moment's warning, and the further constructions proposed will probably within two years raise the number to an hundred. New regulations have been made too for perfecting the classification of their seamen, an institution which dividing all the seamen of the nation into classes, subjects them to tours of duty by rotation, and enables them at all times to man their ships. Their works for rendering Cherburg a harbour for their vessels of war, and Dunkirk for frigates and privateers leave now little doubt of success. It is impossible that these preparations can have in view any other nation but the English. Of course they shew a greater diffidence of their peace with them than with any other power.

I mentioned to you in my letter of Aug. 14. that I had desired Capt. J. P. Jones to enquire into the circumstances of Peyrouse's expedition. I have now the honour of inclosing you copies of my letter to him, and of his answer. He refuses to accept of any indemnification for his expences, which is an additional proof of his disinterested spirit and of his devotion to the service of America. The circumstances are obvious which indicate an intention to settle factories, and not colonies at least for the present. However nothing shews for what place they are destined. The conjectures are divided between New Holland and the North-west coast of America.

According to what I mentioned in my letter of Aug. 30. I have appointed Mr. Short my secretary here. I inclose to you copies of my letters to him and Mr. Grand which will shew to Congress that he stands altogether at their pleasure. I mention this circumstance that if it meets with their disapprobation they may have the goodness to signify it immediately: as I should otherwise conclude that they do not disapprove it. I shall be ready to conform myself to what would be most agreeable to them.

This will be accompanied by the gazettes of France and Leyden to the present date.

I have the honour to be with sentiments of the highest esteem & respect, Sir your most obedient & most humble servant,

TH: JEFFERSON

RC (DNA: PCC, No. 87, i). PrC (DLC). Tr (DNA: PCC, No. 107, i). Recorded in SJL as sent "by Mr. Fitzhugh"; entry in SJPL reads: "Jay John. Fortin. Europe. Cherburg. Brest navy. Peyrouse. Short." Enclosures (same): Copies of TJ to John Paul Jones, 3 Aug. 1785; Jones's reply, 5 Oct.; and TJ to Ferdinand Grand and to William Short, 24 Sep. 1785.

From André Limozin

[*Le Havre, 6? Oct. 1785.* Entry in SJL for receipt on 8 Oct. 1785 reads: "Limozin's. Re-inclosing letter intended for Dumas." Not found; the date has been assigned from the postscript to TJ to Limozin, 8 Oct. Enclosure: TJ to C. W. F. Dumas, 4 Oct. 1785.]

From Abigail Adams

Your very polite favour was handed me by Colo. Franks. I am much obliged to you for the execution of the several commissions I troubled you with. Be assured sir that I felt myself Honourd by your commands, tho I have only in part executed them. For I could not find at any store table Cloths of the dimensions you directed. The width is as you wisht, but they assure me that four yds. and three quarters are the largest size ever used here which will cover a table for 18 persons. To these Cloths there are only 18 Napkins, and to the smaller size only twelve. I was the more ready to credit what they said, knowing that I had been obliged to have a set of tables made on purpose for me in order to dine 16 or 18 persons. These rooms in general are not calculated to hold more and it is only upon extraordinary occasions that you meet with that number at the tables here. The Marquis of Carmarthan who occasionally dines the Foreign ministers, and has a House found him by his Majesty, cannot entertain more than 15 at once, and upon their Majesties Birth days, he is obliged to dine his company at his Fathers the Duke of Leeds's. The person where I bought the Cloth offerd to have any size made, that I wisht for, and agreed to take eight pounds ten shillings for 20 Napkins and a cloth 5 yds. long. I gave Seven for this which I send, and shall wait your further directions. I took the precaution of having them made and marked to Secure them against the custom House, and hope they will meet your approbation. I think them finer than the pattern, but it is difficult judging by so small a Scrap. I have also bought you two pairs of Nut crackers for which I gave four Shillings. We [find them so?] convenient that I thought they would be equally so to [you. The]re is the article of Irish linen which is much Superiour here to any that is to be had in France, and cheeper I think. If you have occasion for any you will be so good as to let me know. It cannot easily pass without being made. But that could be easily done. Only by sending a measure, at the rate of 3 Shilling and six pence per yd. by the peice, the best is to be had. As we are still in your debt, the remainder of the money shall be remitted you or expended here as you direct. Mr. Adams supposed there might be something of a balance due to him in the settlement of a private account with Mr. Barclay, which he has orderd paid to you. He will also pay the money here for the insurence of Mr. Hudons

Life, by which means whatever remains due to you can be easily settled.

Haveing finishd the article of Business, I am totally foild at that of Compliment. Sure the air of France, conspired with the Native politeness and Complasance of the writer to usher into the World Such an assemblage of fine things. I shall value the warrior Deity the more for having been your choise, and he cannot fail being in taste in a Nation which has given us such proofs of their Hostility; forgiveness of injuries is no part of their Character, and scarcly a day passes without a Boxing match; even in this Square which is calld the polite and Court end of the city, my feelings have been repeatedly shock'd to see Lads not more than ten years old striped and fighting untill the Blood flow'd from every part, enclosed by a circle who were claping and applauding the conquerer, stimulating them to continue the fight, and forceing every person from the circle who attempted to prevent it. Bred up with such tempers and principals, who can wonder at the licentiousness of their Manners, and the abuse of their pens. Their arrows do not wound, they rebound and fall harmless [. . .] but amidst their boasted freedom of the press, one must bribe [. . .] to get a paragraph inserted in favour of America, or her Friends. Our Country has no money to spair for such purposes; and must rest upon her own virtue and Magnimimity. So we may too late convince this Nation that the Treasure which they knew not how to value, has irrecoverably past into the possession of those who were possest of more policy and wisdom.

I wish I might flatter myself with the hope of seeing you here this winter. You would find a most cordial welcome from your American Friends, as well as from some very distinguishd literary Characters of this Nation.

My best regards to Miss Jefferson, to Col. Humphries, to Mr. Short, or any other Friends or acquaintance who may inquire after Your Friend and humble Servant,   A ADAMS

My daughter presents her respectfull regards to you and compliments to the rest of the Gentlemen.

RC (DLC); addressed. MS is torn at the upper right corner; missing words have been conjecturally supplied. Recorded in SJL as received 10 Oct. 1785.

From Froullé

MONSIEUR Paris le: 7: 8bre. 1785.

Jai reflechi sur L'honneur de vôtre proposition, et calculé à combien me reviendroit L'ouvrage de Monsieur vôtre ami. En suposant qu'il produise 36 feuille D'impression à 36.ᵗ par feuille cela formeroit une somme de 1296.ᵗ

Pour la traduction à 24.ᵗ la feuille 864

2160ᵗ

Pour papier et Impression tiré à
trois mil Exemplaires; au moins à raison
de 84ᵗ La feuille forme une somme De 3024

5184

faux frais de Manutention 300

Total de depence 5484ᵗ

Les trois mil exemplaires vendu à raison de 3.ᵗ 10s. c'est L'Evaluation que je puis en faire, à raison qu'il faut en soustraire la remise qui est d'usage au Libraire de Province et autres. Je dis donc que 3000 Exemplaires vendu à raison de 3.ᵗ 10s. ne peuvent produire que 10500ᵗ. Sur ce, j'ai touts les Risques à courir: 1º. L'incertitude du débit; 2º. La crainte d'une autre traduction; 3º. L'inconvenient de La perte enver le Libraire de Province; 4ᵗº. Celui de la contrefaction, aussitot que je l'aurez mis au jour. Sur ce Monsieur je ne vous fait aucune exageration, je ne parle qu'àpres Les experiences que j'ai eprouves dans le commerce.

Vous voyez donc Monsieur que L'offre de Payer 900ᵗ à L'auteur, un an apres que L'ouvrage aura paru, est une offre raisonnable: ou si mieux aimé je le ferez à moitier frais, et moitier benefice. Sur ce Monsieur, je ne vous demande que la préference, vous priant de me croire avec le plus profond respect Monsieur Vôtre tres umble et tres obeissant serviteur, FROULLÉ

Mon epouse etant absente, m'enpeche de pouvoir vous porter ma reponse, et je ne pourai avoir L'honneur de Passer ches vous que Dimanche le matin.

J'ai ecrit à Londre pour Les deffets du Catesby.

RC (DLC). LES DEFFETS [dèfets] DU CATESBY: TJ acquired a copy of the first edition of Mark Catesby's *The Natural History* of *Carolina*, which he later exchanged with Froullé for a copy of the second edition (Sowerby No. 1027). VÔTRE AMI was, of course, David Ramsay.

From John Mehegan

St. Pol de Léon, 7 Oct. 1785. Asks TJ to intervene in behalf of Lister Asquith and the other prisoners. They are suffering from insufficient food, the cold of the prison, and have almost no funds with which to pay for their defense, "the people in whom they confided, having got all the money they had, three poor guineas excepted." Officers and everyone who saw their condition upon landing at Roscoff acknowledges that they were in desperate circumstances and that "they must either perish at sea . . . or come into this place." Without "the least circumstantial proof against them," they are confined "the same as criminals" and are now deserted by those "who came to get what they could from them." Sends his regards to John Paul Jones.

RC (DNA: PCC, No. 87, i); 2 p.; signed "John Mehegan Carmelite fryar"; without indication of addressee. Tr (DNA: PCC, No. 107, i). Recorded in SJL as received 19 Oct. 1785.

From John Paul Jones

SIR   Paris, October 8th, 1785.

As The Baron de Waltersdorff does not return here, as was expected, and I wish to apply, without farther loss of time to the Court of Denmark, for a compensation for the prizes taken by the squadron I commanded in Europe, and given up to the British, by the people in authority at Bergen in Norway; if you approve it, I will assign the powers I received, for that business from Congress, to my friend Dr. Bancroft in London. You will oblige me therefore, if you will write to Mr. Adams, requesting him to support Dr. Bancroft's application through the Danish minister in London. I am, with great respect and esteem, &c.

MS not found; text from Sherburne, *John Paul Jones*, p. 269-70.

To John Paul Jones

SIR   Paris Oct. 8. 1785.

I think the method you propose for applying to the court of Denmark for the compensation due for the prizes taken by the squadron you commanded in Europe, is a proper one: therefore I will undertake to write to Mr. Adams on the subject, and have no doubt he will support Doctr. Bancroft in his sollicitations to the Danish minister at London for this purpose.

I have the honour to be with the highest respect Sir Your most obedt. humble servt.,   TH: JEFFERSON

PrC (DLC). Entry in SJPL reads: "Jones J. Paul. Danish affair." See TJ to Adams, 11 Oct. 1785, note.

To André Limozin

SIR   Paris Oct. 8. 1785.

I am to thank you for the receipt of your favor of the 4th. inst. but am obliged to trouble you further, to inform me whether any suit was ever commenced for Mr. Fortin to recover the estate fallen to him? If a suit was commenced, whether it has been decided, and what was the decision? Or if not decided, for what cause it is suspended, and when will it probably come to decision? I am sorry to be so troublesome to you, but my instructions render it a duty.

I took the liberty two days ago of sending by the Diligence to your care a box addressed to Mr. Charles Thomson secretary of Congress. I wish it to go by the vessel bound for Philadelphia. I would be obliged to you to ask the favor (in my name) of Colo. Senf to take charge of it and to deliver it to Mr. Thomson whom he will see in New York. I have the honour to be with great respect Sir Your most obedient humble servt.,   TH: JEFFERSON

P.S. Your favor of the 6th. came to hand in time to enable me to withdraw from the post office the inclosed letter intended for you but by mistake directed to another while his was put under your address. I thank you for the speedy return of it which enabled me to correct the error.

PrC (MHi). Enclosure: TJ to Limozin, 4 Oct. 1785. The letter returned by Limozin was TJ's to Dumas, 4 Oct. 1785, which had been erroneously addressed to Limozin.

To Charles Thomson

DEAR SIR   Paris Oct. 8. 1785.

The last letter received from you was of Mar. 6. Since that I have written one to you of June 21. by Mr. Otto, and another of July 14. by Mr. Houdon. In yours of Mar. you express a wish of an opportunity of getting the Cylinder lamp. Colo. Senf going to

America furnishes me an opportunity of sending you one, which you must do me the favor to accept. There is but one critical circumstance in the management of it; that is the length of the wick above the top of the cylinder. If raised too high it fills the room with smoke. If not high enough it will not yeild it's due light. The true medium is where it first ceases to give a sensible smoke in the room. Two or three experiments will set you to rights in this. I send some spare wicks, and a set of spare glasses.

The Emperor and Dutch have signed preliminaries. You will see them in the papers sent to Mr. Jay.—Two artists at Javel, about 4 miles hence, are pursuing the art of directing the baloon. They ascend and descend at will, without expending their gaz, and they can deflect 45°. from the course of the wind when it is not very strong. We may certainly expect that this desideratum will be found. As the birds and fish prove that the means exist, we may count on human ingenuity for it's discovery. I am with very great esteem Dear Sir Your friend & servant,   TH: JEFFERSON

RC (PHi). PrC (DLC). Recorded in SJL as sent "With a lamp. By Mr. Fitzhugh"; entry in SJPL reads: "Thomson Charles. Cylinder lamp. Europe. Baloon."

TJ later sent Thomson an English lamp; a note by John Fanning Watson, the Philadelphia historian, is attached to the present letter and reads: "The annexed Letter of Mr. Jefferson to Chs. Thomson Esqre. was made a gift to J. F. Watson with the *Lamp* referred to therein, by John Thomson Esqre. (his nephew) in 1825. Another letter from Mr. Jefferson to Mr. Thomson dated *London* April 22, 1786 thus writes to wit: 'In your former letters you expressed a wish to have one of the Newly invented Lamps. I find them made *here* much better than at Paris, and take the liberty of asking you to accept of one which will accompany this letter. It is found that any tolerable oil may be used in them. Spermaceti is best of the cheap Kind.' [Note the Argand Lamp, such as is here spoken of was Patented I find in the year 1784.]—But *this* Lamp which I have as above referred to was made in London by Mr. Meigs a nominal Quaker of Cow-cross. I lately saw in business in Philada. a man who was then his apprentice when this identical Lamp was made and was very glad to see it. Meigs managed to Evade the Patent. Argand had been a shoemaker and made his first cylinder of leather. J. F. W. 1826." For a description and illustration of different types of the Argand lamp, see F. W. Robins, *The Story of the Lamp*, 1939, p. 112-14; plate XXIV.

From James Warren

Milton, 9 Oct. 1785. Though they were only briefly acquainted in Boston, Warren writes to TJ concerning his son, Winslow Warren. The latter, "encourag'd by the principal Members of Congress," established himself at Lisbon over a year before, in anticipation of an appointment as consul in Portugal. Though consular appointments had been postponed until treaties of commerce were concluded, it now appears that Congress will "probably adopt a Report made by the Minister for Foreign Affairs, to make the Ministers abroad Consuls General, with the Power of Appointment to the several Ports, within their respective Departments." In that event, the choice for Portugal will be TJ's, and Warren asks that it be given to his son. Since the "partiality of a Father might be suspected on such an Occasion," he refers TJ to "others, who know him, for his Merits and Qualifications. . . . I shall only say that he has been much Abroad, in England, Holland and France, especially the last, and speaks the French Language fluently, and that the Countenance and Encouragement, he has receiv'd from many Members of Congress, particularly from all those of this State, is a strong Evidence in his Favor." Portuguese-American trade suffers from the absence of a consul there. "If the Office should not be very Lucrative, it would give him Consequence, and Support, and prevent that Injury, to the Feelings of a Young Man of Spirit, and Sensibility, which would arise from a Disappointment, in a matter so long and so generally expected. I will only add that I have had a considerable Share (for an Individual) in the American Revolution, without deriving yet any Personal Advantage to myself or Family."

RC (MHi); 2p.; in a clerk's hand, signed by Warren; endorsed. Recorded in SJL as received 6 Dec. 1785.

Though Warren did not mention Adams in his letter, he must have anticipated that TJ would think of Adams as being among the OTHERS WHO KNOW HIM. Warren had already written Adams on 6 Oct. 1785 saying that his son "went to Lisbon with great and well founded expectations of being appointed the consul there and still remains there with such Expectations. Congress have delayed the Appointment until a Commercial Treaty should be formed. By a letter from my Friend Gerry last Evening I am informed they now have it in Contemplation and probably will appoint the foreign Ministers Consul General and leave the appointment to the several Ports with them and that Lisbon will fall into the department of Mr. Jefferson. Will you write to him, and use your influence to gratify me in the acquisition of this small favor" (MHi: AMT). In acknowledging Warren's letter, Adams wrote: "I had before written very fully to Mr. Jay, a recommendation of your son to be consul of Lisbon, and desired him to communicate it to the Members of Congress. I will also write to Mr. Jefferson, and wish very heartily that he may be appointed" (Adams to Warren, 12 Dec. 1785, same). See Adams to TJ, 13 Dec. 1785.

From John Adams

[*London, 10 Oct. 1785*. Entry in SJL for 15 Oct. 1785 reads: "Mr. Adams. Oct. 10. Inclosing letter to Mr. Grand." Not found. Enclosure: Evidently a copy of Willem & Jan Willink and Nicolas & Jacob van Staphorst to Ferdinand Grand, 6 Oct. 1785; another copy was sent to TJ by Grand as enclosure to his letter of 10 Oct. 1785 (see note there and TJ to Adams, 18 Oct. 1785).]

From James Bowdoin

Sir   Boston October 10th. 1785

I have lately understood that Congress have under consideration a report of their Minister for foreign affairs, relative to the appointment of Consuls in several parts of Europe; and that the appointment is to be made by the Ministers Plenipotentiary from the United States: the power of each Minister in this respect to be exercised within a certain district; and that your Excellency's district includes Lisbon.

A friend of yours in this neighbourhood, and a distinguished one in the American Cause, General Warren of Milton, has a Son at Lisbon, Mr. Winslow Warren, whom I take the liberty of recommending to your friendship.

He is settled at Lisbon in the mercantile line, for which he has been qualifying himself by visiting several parts of Europe to gain a knowledge of its trade and manufactures; and which, with such a knowledge your Excellency will probably think, is no disrecommendation of him to the Office of Consul.

He would esteem himself honoured by your Commission; and I doubt not, would execute the business of it to your acceptance, and to the acceptance of the United States.

I have the honour to be, With the most perfect Esteem, Sir, Your Excellency's Most Obedient Humble Servant,

James Bowdoin

RC (DLC); in a clerk's hand, signed by Bowdoin; endorsed: "Bowdoin Govr." Recorded in SJL as received 6 Dec. 1785.

From Ferdinand Grand

10 Oct. [*1785*]. Encloses a letter received this date from Amsterdam, "d'après laquelle il ne paroit pas qu'il y ait des ordres des Commissaires."

RC (DLC); 2 p.; in French; addressed to TJ in Paris at the "Cul de Sac Thaitbout"; endorsed. Enclosure (DLC): Copy of Willem & Jan Willink and Nicolas & Jacob van Staphorst to Grand, 6 Oct. 1785, informing him that they have not yet received instructions from the Commissioners of the Treasury to make available "au moins d'une partie des fonds que le Congrès pouroit avoir besoin pour satisfaire leurs engagemens avec le Tresor Royal"; but advising him that he will be notified as soon as orders arrive.

To Abigail Adams

Paris Oct. 11. 1785.

Your favor of the 7th. was put into my hands the last night and as I received at the same time dispatches from Mr. Adams which occasion a great deal to be done for Congress to be sent by the Mr. Fitzhughs who set out tomorrow morning for Philadelphia as Mr. Preston the bearer of this does for London, I have only time to thank you for your kind attention to my commission and your offer of new service. Your information as to the shirt linen draws a new scene of trouble on you. You had better have held your tongue about it: but as it is, you must submit to what cannot now be prevented and take better care hereafter. You will think it some apology for my asking you to order me a dozen shirts of the quality of the one sent, when I assure you they made me pay for it here 10 livres and a half the aune, which is at the rate of 6/6 sterl. the yard. I will pray you to chuse me linen as nearly as possible of the same quality because it will enable me to judge of the comparative prices of the two countries. There will probably be Americans coming over from London here in the course of the winter who will be so kind as to bring the shirts to me, which being ready made will escape the custom houses. I will not add to your trouble that of a long apology. You shall find it in the readiness and zeal with which I shall always serve you. But I find that with your friends you are a very bad accountant, for after purchasing the table linen, and mentioning the insurance money on Houdon's life, you talk of what will still remain due to me. The truth is that without this new commission I should have been enormously in your debt. My present hurry does not permit me to state the particulars, but I will prove it to you by the first opportunity. And as to the balance which will be due from me to Mr. Adams should he have no occasion of laying it out here immediately I will transmit it by some safe hand. I have not yet seen the table linen you were so kind as to buy for me, but I am sure it is good. The merchant here promises to shew me some of a new supply he has, which will enable me to judge somewhat of the two manufactures and prices. The difference must be considerable tho' to induce me to trouble you. Be so good as to present my respects to Miss Adams and to accept assurances of the esteem and respect with which I have the honour to be Dear Madam Your most obedient & most humble servt.,   TH: JEFFERSON

RC (MHi: AMT). PrC (DLC). Recorded in SJL as sent "by Mr. Preston." This letter was temporarily lost; see John Adams to TJ, 24 Oct. 1785; Abigail Adams to TJ, 25 Oct. 1785. Preston evidently carried with him one of TJ's shirts, referred to here as THE ONE SENT.

To John Adams

DEAR SIR   Paris Oct. 11. 1785.

Colo. Franks and Mr. Randolph [Randall] arrived last night. This enables me to send copies of all the Barbary papers to Congress by the Mr. Fitzhughs, together with the Prussian treaty. They wait till tomorrow for this purpose.

Considering the treaty with Portugal as among the most important to the U.S. I some time ago took occasion at Versailles to ask the Portuguese Ambassador if he had yet received an answer from his court on the subject of our treaty. He said not, but that he would write again. His Secretaire d'Ambassade called on me two days ago and translated into French as follows a paragraph of a letter from his minister to the Ambassador. 'Relativement à ce que V. E. nous a fait part de ce qu'elle avoit parlé avec le ministre de l'Amerique, cette puissance doit etre dejà persuadée par d'effets la maniere dont ses vaisseaux ont eté accueillis içi: et par consequence sa majesté auroit beaucoup de satisfaction à entretenir une parfaite harmonie et bonne correspondence entre[1] les memes etats unis. Mais il seroit à propos de commencer par la nomination reciproque des deux parties des personnes qui, au moins avec la caractere d'Agens, informeroient reciproquement leurs constituents de ce qui pourroit conduire à la connoissance des interets des deux nations sans prejudice de l'un ou de l'autre. C'est le premier pas qu'il paroit convenable de donner pour conduire à la fin proposée.' By this I suppose they will prefer proceeding as Spain has done, and that we may consider it as definitive of our commission to them. I communicate it to Congress that they may take such other measures for leading on a negotiation as they may think proper.

You know that the 3d. article of instructions of Oct. 29. 1783. to the Ministers for negotiating peace, directed them to negociate the claim for the prizes taken by the Alliance and sent in to Bergen, but delivered up by the court of Denmark: you recollect also that this has been deferred in order to be taken up with the general negotiation for an alliance. Capt. Jones desiring to go to America proposed to me that he should leave the sollicitation of this matter in the hands of Doctor Bancroft, and to ask you to negotiate it through the minister of Denmark at London. The delay of Baron Waltersdorf is one reason for this. Your better acquaintance with the subject is a second. The Danish minister here being absent is a third: and a fourth and more conclusive one is that, having never acted as one of the commissioners for negotiating the peace I feel an impropriety in meddling with it at all, and much more to become the principal agent. I therefore told Capt. Jones I would sollicit your care of this business. I beleive he writes to you on the subject. Mr. Barclay sets out in two or three days. Lamb will follow as soon as the papers can be got from this ministry. Having no news, I shall only add assurances of the esteem with which I am Dear Sir Your friend & servant,   TH: JEFFERSON

RC (MHi: AMT); endorsed. PrC (DLC). Recorded in SJL as sent "by Mr. Preston."

TJ was mistaken in thinking that HE WRITES TO YOU ON THE SUBJECT: Jones wrote instead to Dr. Edward Bancroft. As Jones later explained to Adams: "On the 8th of October last Mr. Jefferson wrote me a Letter approving a proposition I had made to him that I should deputize Dr. Bancroft to sollicit the Court of Denmark, through the Danish Minister at London, for the Compensation due for the Prizes made by the Squadron I commanded in Europe and given up to the British by the Danish Government, in the year 1779 in the port of Bergen in Norway. Mr. Jefferson was also so obliging as to undertake to write to you on the subject and to pray you to support Dr. Bancroft's application." In consequence of this, Jones added, he wrote to Bancroft on 11 Oct. 1785 enclosing all of the necessary papers. Jones enclosed a copy of his letter to Bancroft and

added: "I shall esteem myself personally and particularly obliged by the kind support you are pleased to give Dr. Bancroft's application" (Jones to Adams, 6 Jan. 1786; MHi: AMT; copies of the letter to Bancroft and of all the documents enclosed therein are in same; these included the resolution of Congress of 1 Nov. 1783; Franklin's authorization of 16 Dec. 1783; and Franklin's letter to Jones of 21 July 1785, Le Havre, stating that he had rejected the offer made by Walterstorff in behalf of the King of Denmark of £10,000 sterling as he conceived it was too small a sum, "they [the prizes] having been valued to me at fifty thousand pounds"). See Sherburne, *John Paul Jones*, p. 248-9, 250; Jones to TJ, 9 Aug. 1786.

[1] This word is underscored in both RC and PrC, and in the latter is keyed by underscoring to a marginal note in TJ's hand which reads: "qu. *avec.*" See TJ to Jay, 11 Oct. 1785.

To Elbridge Gerry

DEAR SIR   Paris Oct. 11. 1785.

I received last night the letter signed by yourself and the other gentlemen delegates of Massachusets and Virginia, recommending Mr. Sayre for the Barbary negotiations. As that was the first moment of it's suggestion to me, you will perceive by my letter of this day to Mr. Jay that the business was already established in other hands, as your letter came at the same time with the papers actually signed by Mr. Adams for Messrs. Barclay and Lamb, according to arrangements previously taken between us. I should with great satisfaction have acceded to the recommendation in the letter: not indeed as to Marocco, because no better man than Mr. Barclay could have been substituted; but as to the other who is less known to me. However I hope well of him, and rely considerably on the aid he will receive from his secretary Mr. Randolph [Randall] who bears a very good character. I suppose Mr. Adams entitled to the same just apology as matters were settled otherwise before he probably received your letter. I pray you to communicate this to the other gentlemen of your and our delegation as my justification.

The peace made between the Emperor and Dutch leaves Europe quiet for this campaign. As yet we do not know where the storm, dissipated for the moment, will gather again. Probably over Bavaria or Turkey. But this will be for another year.

When our instructions were made out, they were conceived on a general scale, and supposed that all the European nations would be disposed to form a commercial connection with us. It is evident however that a very different degree of importance was annexed to these different states. Spain, Portugal, England, and France was most important. Holland, Sweden, Denmark in a midling degree. The others still less so. Spain treats in another line. Portugal is disposed to do the same. England will not treat at all, nor will France probably add to her former treaty. Failing in the execution of these our capital objects, it has appeared to me that the pushing the treaties with the lesser powers might do us more harm than good, by hampering the measures the states may find it necessary to take for securing those commercial interests by separate measures which are refused to be done here in concert. I have understood through various channels that the members of Congress wished a change in our instructions. I have, in my letter to Mr. Jay of this date, mentioned the present situation and aspect of these treaties, for their information.

My letter of the 6th. inst. to Mr. Jay having communicated what little there is new here, I have only to add assurances of the sincere esteem with which I have the honor to be Dear Sir Your friend and servt., TH: JEFFERSON

PrC (DLC). Recorded in SJL as sent "by Mr. Fitzhugh."

American Commissioners to John Jay

DEAR SIR

We have the Honour to transmit to Congress, by Mr. Fitzhughs, the Treaty between the United States and the King of Prussia, Signed Seperately by your Ministers at the several Places of their Residence, and by the Baron De Thulemeier at the Hague, in English and French and exchanged at the Hague in Presence of Mr. Short and Mr. Dumas. As this Treaty may be of considerable Importance to the United States, and will certainly promote their Reputation, it is to be wished, that the Ratifications may be exchanged, and the Publication made as soon as possible. The Admission of our Privateers into the Prussian Ports, by a Treaty Signed at the moment of the Negotiation of the League, in which Brandenburg and Hanover are Parties is a little remarkable. It certainly merits the Consideration of Congress and the States. With great Respect We have the Honour to be, Sir your most obedient and most humble servants,

London Octr. 2. 1785   JOHN ADAMS
Paris Octob. 11. 1785.   TH: JEFFERSON

RC (DNA: PCC No. 86); in Adams' hand, signed by Adams and TJ; docketed: "Referred to Report 9 Feby: 1786." FC (DNA: PCC No. 116); in the hand of Humphreys; at head of text: "9th. Report to Congress addressed to Mr. Jay Secretary of foreign Affairs." TJ had asked Adams to draft this letter and it accompanied Adams' to TJ of 2 Oct. 1785. The Treaty with Prussia which the Fitzhughs carried to America is in DNA; the final page bearing the signatures is reproduced in this volume. The instrument of ratification, which recited both the French and English texts, was adopted by Congress on 17 May 1786 (JCC, XXX, 110-12, 268-85). The Prussian instrument of ratification recited only the French text. De Thulemeier notified both Adams and TJ on the very day that the present letter was written that the Treaty had already been ratified by the Prussian court (see De Thulemeier to TJ, 11 Oct.). The treaty was evidently never proclaimed formally (Hunter Miller, ed., *Treaties of the United States*, II, 184).

To John Jay

SIR   Paris Oct. 11. 1785.

In my letter of Aug. 14. I had the honor of expressing to you the uneasiness I felt at the delay of the instructions on the subject of the Barbary treaties of which Mr. Lamb was the bearer, and of informing you that I had proposed to Mr. Adams that if he did not arrive either in the French or English packets then expected, we should send some person to negotiate these treaties. As he did not arrive in those packets, and I found Mr. Barclay was willing to undertake the negotiations I wrote to Mr. Adams (who had concurred in the proposition made him) informing him that Mr. Barclay would go, and proposing papers for our immediate signature. The day before the return of the Courier Mr. Lamb arrived, with our instructions, the letters of credence, &c. inclosed in yours of March 11. 1785. Just about the same time came to hand the letter No. 1. informing me that two American vessels were actually taken and carried in to Algiers, and leaving no further doubt that that power was exercising hostilities against us in the Atlantic. The conduct of the Emperor of Marocco had been such as forbade us to postpone his treaty to that with Algiers. But the commencement of hostilities by the latter and their known activity, pressed the necessity of immediate propositions to them. It was therefore thought best, while Mr. Barclay should be proceeding with the Emperor of Marocco, that some other agent should go to Algiers. We had few subjects to chuse out of. Mr. Lambe's knowlege of the country, of it's inhabitants, of their manner of transacting business, the recommendations from his state to Congress of his fitness for this emploiment, and other information founding a presumption that he would be approved, occasioned our concluding to send him to Algiers. The giving him proper authorities, and new ones to Mr. Barclay conformable to our own new powers, was the subject of a new courier between Mr. Adams and myself. He returned last night, and I have the honour of inclosing you copies of all the papers we furnish those gentlemen with, which will possess Congress fully of our proceedings herein. They are numbered from 2. to 10. inclusive. The supplementory instruction to Mr. Lamb No. 5. must rest for justification on the emergency of the case. The motives which lead to it must be found in the feelings of the human heart, in a partiality for those sufferers who are of our own country, and in the obligations of every government to yeild protection to their citizens as the consideration for their obedience. It will be a comfort to know that Congress does not disapprove of this step.

Considering the treaty with Portugal among the most interesting to the United states, I some time ago took occasion at Versailles to ask of the Portuguese Ambassador if he had yet received from his court an answer to our letter. He told me he had not, but that he would make it the subject of another letter. Two days ago his

Secretaire d'Ambassade called on me with a letter from his minister to the Ambassador, in which was the following paragraph as he translated it to me and I committed it to writing from his mouth. 'Relativement à ce que votre Excellence nous a fait part de ce qu'elle avoit parlé avec le ministre de l'Amerique, cette puissance doit etre dejà persuadée par d'effets [de] la maniere dont ses vaisseaux ont eté accueillis ici: et par consequence sa majeste auroit beaucoup de satisfaction à entretenir une parfaite harmonie et bonne correspondence *entre*[1] les memes etats unis. Mais il seroit à propos de commencer par la nomination reciproque des deux parties des personnes qui, au moins avec la caractere d'Agens, informeroient reciproquement leurs constituents de ce qui pourroit conduire à la connoissance des interets des deux nations, sans prejudice de l'un ou de l'autre. C'est le premier pas qu'il paroit convenable de donner pour conduire à la fin proposée.' By this it would seem that this power is more disposed to pursue a tract of negociation similar to that which Spain has done. I consider this answer as definitive of all further measures under our commission to Portugal. That to Spain was superseded by proceedings in another line. That to Prussia is concluded by actual treaty; to Tuscany will probably be so; and perhaps to Denmark. And these I believe will be the sum of the effects of our commissions for making treaties of alliance. England shews no disposition to treat. France, should her ministers be able to keep the ground of the arret of August 1784. against the clamours of her merchants, and should they be disposed hereafter to give us more, it is not probable she will bind herself to it by treaty, but keep her regulations dependant on her own will. Sweden will establish a free port at St. Bartholomew's, which perhaps will render any new engagements on our part unnecessary. Holland is so immoveable in her system of colony administration, that as propositions to her on that subject would be desperate, they had better not be made. You will perceive by the letter No. 11. from the M. de la fayette that there is a possibility of an overture from the Emperor. A hint from the Chargé des affaires of Naples lately, has induced me to suppose something of the same kind from thence. But the advanced period of our commissions now offers good cause for avoiding to begin what probably cannot be terminated during their continuance; and with respect to these two and all other powers not before mentioned, I doubt whether the advantages to be derived from treaties with them may countervail the additional embarrasments they may impose on the states when they shall proceed to make those commercial arrangements necessary to counteract the designs of the British cabinet. I repeat it therefore that the conclusion of the treaty with Prussia and the probability of others with Denmark, Tuscany and the Barbary states may be expected to wind up the proceedings of the general commissions. I think that in possible events it may be advantageous to us, by treaties with Prussia, Denmark and Tuscany to have secured ports in the Northern and Mediterranean seas. I have the honor to be with sentiments of the highest respect and esteem, Sir, your most obedient & most humble servant, TH: JEFFERSON

RC (DNA: PCC, No. 87, i). PrC (DLC). Tr (DNA: PCC, No. 107, i). Tr (DNA: PCC, No. 117); an unreliable copy. Recorded in SJL as sent "by Mr. Fitzhugh"; this entry has a later notation in TJ's hand: "[copy lost or mislaid. State of negociations]." Enclosures: No. 1: Richard O'Bryen to TJ, 24 Aug. 1785; Nos. 2-10: copies of the various documents furnished to Barclay and Lamb, printed below, 11 Oct. 1785; No. 11: Lafayette to TJ, 4 Sep. 1785.

TJ's enclosure No. 8 was the Commissioners' letter to Vergennes, 11 Oct. 1785. According to the present letter, copies of the appeal to Vergennes were included among the COPIES OF ALL THE PAPERS WE FURNISH Barclay and Lamb.

This was evidently a mistake, for there is no indication that such a copy was prepared for the agents, or needed to be. TJ and Humphreys were exceedingly busy executing documents and making copies on 11 Oct. in order to be able to hand the letter to Jay and its enclosures to the Fitzhugh brothers, and this haste may account for the reference to enclosure No. 8. For Jay's report on this letter and its enclosures, see Jay to Congress, 11 May 1786 (JCC, XXX, 259-62).

1 This word is keyed by underscoring to a marginal note in TJ's hand which reads: "qu. avec." See TJ to Adams, 11 Oct. 1785.

Documents Pertaining to the Mission of Barclay and Lamb to the Barbary States

I. COMMISSION
II. INSTRUCTIONS
III. SUPPLEMENTARY INSTRUCTIONS TO JOHN LAMB
IV. JEFFERSON'S "HEADS FOR A LETTER"
V. AMERICAN COMMISSIONERS TO THE EMPEROR OF MOROCCO
VI. HEADS OF INQUIRY
VII. LETTER OF CREDIT
VIII. AMERICAN COMMISSIONERS TO WILLIAM CARMICHAEL
IX. PROJET OF A TREATY WITH THE BARBARY STATES

EDITORIAL NOTE

The documents in this group were prepared by Adams and Jefferson during September and early October. Each of the agents was furnished with a full set of the documents, their texts varying in respect to names of persons and countries, sums of money, and other particulars. In addition to the increased paper work resulting from their separation, Adams and Jefferson were obliged to make revisions in some of the documents and to draft supplementary instructions to Lamb owing to his tardy arrival and to the news contained in Richard O'Bryen's letter of 24 Aug. Franks arrived back in Paris on 10 Oct. with the various documents signed by Adams, and Jefferson and Humphreys must have put in long hours the next day executing the texts of all documents for the agents and making copies so that these could be carried to America by the Fitzhugh brothers, who delayed their departure to the 12th for this purpose. The pressure and haste under which these various texts were prepared must account for Jefferson's evidently mistaken indication in his letter to Jay of 11 Oct. 1785 that a copy of the Commissioners' letter to Vergennes had been furnished to each of the agents. But this urgency was to no avail: the Fitzhugh brothers did not leave French soil for several weeks.

"Mr. Jefferson and I," John Adams wrote to Stephen Higginson on 4 Oct. 1785, "are sending Mr. Barclay to Morroco and Mr. Lamb to Algiers. . . . We shall have numberless difficulties, much Time I fear will be required; and our Presents not rich enough. The difficulties attending all our operations in Europe are so numerous and tedious that it is enough to tire the Patience of Job. We must now send Agents for the Redemption of Captives as well as to Treat. Captain Stevens in a Vessel of Mr. Fosters, and Capt. Obrien in one of the Rivins of Philadelphia are taken and Carried into Algiers, at least if the spirit of Forgery has not gone so far as to Counterfeit Letters both to me and Mr. Jefferson which have great appearance of Authenticity. As long ago as 1778 I engaged earnestly in the Business of Treating with the Barbary Powers: but Dr. Franklin's opinion allways was that the Freedom of the Navigation of the Mediterranean was not worthy the Presents, and everything allways withered more or less that Dr. Franklin blasted" (MHi: AMT).

For Jefferson's later review of the negotiations with the Barbary states, see under 28 Dec. 1790.

I. Commission

To all to whom these Presents shall come or, may be made known.

Whereas the United States of America in Congress Assembled, reposing special trust and confidence in the integrity, prudence and ability of their trusty and well-beloved the Honble. John Adams late one of their Ministers Plenipotentiary for negotiating a peace, and heretofore a Delegate in Congress from the State of Massachusetts and chief Justice of the Said State: the Honble. Doctr. Benjamin Franklin their Minister Plenipotentiary at the court of Versailles and late another of their Ministers Plenipotentiary for negotiating a peace: and the Honble. Thomas Jefferson a Delegate in Congress from the State of Virginia and late Governor of the said State, did by their Commission under the seal of the United States and the signature of their then President, bearing date the twelfth day of May in the year of our Lord Christ one thousand seven hundred and eighty four, constitute and appoint the said John Adams, Benjamin Franklin and Thomas Jefferson their Ministers Plenipotentiary, giving to them or a majority of them full powers and authority for the said United States and in their name to confer, treat and negotiate with the Ambassador, Minister or Commissioner of His Majesty the Emperor of Morocco, vested with full and sufficient powers of and concerning a Treaty of Amity and Commerce as the case might be, to make and receive propositions for such a Treaty, and to conclude and sign the same transmitting it to the United States in Congress Assembled, for their final ratification. And as it might so happen that the great and various affairs which the said United States had committed to the care and management of their said Ministers Plenipotentiary, might not admit of their meeting the Minister or Commissioner which His Majesty the Emperor of Morocco might appoint to treat with them, of and concerning such Treaty, at a time and place that might otherwise be most convenient. Therefore The said United States in Congress Assembled, did on the eleventh day of March in the year of our Lord Christ one thousand seven hundred and eighty five, by their Commission under their seal and the signature of their President, authorize and empower their said three Ministers Plenipotentiary and the majority of them, by writing under their hands and seals to appoint and employ, and at pleasure to remove, such Agent in the said business as they or the majority of them might think proper, which said Agent should have authority under directions and instructions of their said Ministers, to commence and prosecute negotiations and conferences for the said Treaty, with such person or persons on the part of His Majesty the Emperor of Morocco as to their said Ministers or the majority of them should appear proper. Provided always that the Treaty in question should be signed by the said Ministers, but that preliminary articles thereto, might if previously approved by their said Ministers, or the majority of them be signed by the said Agent. And whereas Dr. Benjamin Franklin one of the Ministers Plenipotentiary aforesaid is since returned to America.

Now know ye, that we John Adams Minister Plenipotentiary of the United States of America at the court of Great Britain and Thomas Jefferson Minister Plenipotentiary of the said States at the court of France, two of the Ministers Plenipotentiary aforesaid and a majority of them, reposing special trust and confidence in the integrity, prudence and ability of the Honble. Thomas Barclay Esqr. Consul General of the United States in France, have constituted, appointed and employed, and do by these presents constitute appoint and employ him the said Thomas Barclay, as Agent in the business aforesaid, hereby giving him full authority under our direction and instructions, to commence and prosecute negotiations and conferences for the said Treaty with such person or persons on the part of the Emperor of Morocco, as His Majesty shall appoint and empower for that purpose. Provided always that the Treaty in question shall be signed by us, but that preliminary articles thereto may if previously approved by us, be signed by the said Agent.

In testimony whereof we have hereto set our hands and seals.

London Octr. 5. 1785   JOHN ADAMS
Paris 11 October 1785   TH: JEFFERSON

Tr (DNA: PCC, No. 87, I); in David Humphreys' hand; at foot of text: "N.B. The Commission to John Lamb Esqr. Agent to the Dey and Government of Algiers is of the same tenor and date." Dft (MHi: AMT); in Adams' hand, signed by him and dated "London Oct.   1785." Tr (DNA: PCC, No. 107, I); at head of text: "No. 2." A copy accompanied TJ's letter to Jay of 11 Oct. 1785 as its second enclosure. In DNA: PCC, No. 117, p. 22-6, is a copy of the commission to John Lamb to treat with the "most illustrious, Lords, and governors of the City and Kingdom of Tripoly," which records only Adams' signature and dating. Aside from its numerous obvious omissions and inaccuracies, that text and the Dft and Tr of Barclay's commission differ only in the substitutions appropriate to the title of the court and to Lamb as agent.

In his letter of 2 Oct. 1785 Adams said that he had made out four commissions. In addition to the above, these included one to Lamb for Algiers, one to Lamb for Tripoli, and one, probably to Lamb also, for Tunis.

II. Instructions

Congress having been pleased to invest us with full powers for entering into treaty of Amity and Alliance with the Emperor of Morocco,[1] and it being impracticable for us to attend his court in person and equally impracticable on account of our seperate stations to receive a Minister from him, we have concluded to effect our object by the intervention of a confidential person. We concur in wishing to avail the United States of your talents in the execution of this business, and therefore furnish you with a letter to the Emperor of Morocco to give a due credit to your transactions with him.

We advise you to proceed by the way of Madrid, where you will have opportunities of deriving many lights from Mr. Carmichael, through whom many communications with the court of Morocco have already passed.[2] From thence you will proceed by such rout as you shall think best to the court of the Emperor.

You will present to him our letter with the copy of our full powers, with which you are furnished, at such time or times, and in such manner as you shall think best.

As the negociation and conclusion of a treaty may be a work of time you will endeavour in the first place to procure an immediate suspension of hostilities.[3] You will proceed to negotiate with his Minister the terms of a treaty of Amity and Commerce as nearly as possible conformed to the draught we give you: Where alterations which in your opinion shall not be of great importance shall be urged by the other party, you are at liberty to agree to them: where they shall be of great importance, and such as you think should be rejected, you will reject them: but where they are

[613]

of great importance, and you think they may be accepted, you will ask time to take our advice, and you will advise with us accordingly by letter or by courier as you shall think best. When the articles shall all be agreed you will [sign them in a preliminary form and send them to us] by some proper person for [definitive execution.][4]

The whole expences of this treaty, including as well the expences of all persons employed about it as the presents to the Emperor and his servants, must not exceed 20,000[5] Dollars and we urge you to use your best endeavours to bring them as much below that sum as you possibly can. And to this end, we leave it to your discretion to represent to His Majesty or to his Ministers, if it may be done with safety, the particular circumstances of the United States just emerging from a long and distressing war with one of the most powerful nations of Europe, which we hope may be an apology if our Presents should not be so splendid as those of older and abler nations.[6] As custom may have rendered some presents necessary in the beginning or progress of this business, and before it is concluded or even in a way to be concluded, we authorize you to conform to the custom; confiding in your discretion to hazard as little as possible before a certainty of the event, and to provide that your engagements shall become binding only on the definitive execution of the treaty.[7] We trust to you also to procure the best information in what form and to what persons these presents should be made, and to make them accordingly.

The difference between the customs of that and other Courts, the difficulty of obtaining a knowledge of those Customs but on the spot and our great confidence in your discretion, induce Us to leave to that all other Circumstances relative to the object of your Mission. It will be necessary for you to take a Secretary well skilled in the French language to aid you in your business, and to take charge of your papers in case of any accident to yourself. We think you may allow him 150[8] Guineas a year, besides his expences for travelling and subsistence. We engage to furnish your own expences according to the respectability of the character with which you are invested; but, as to the allowance for your trouble, we wish to leave it to Congress.

We annex hereto sundry heads of enquiry which We wish you to make, and to give us thereon the best information you shall be able to obtain. We desire you to correspond with us by every opportunity which you think should be trusted; giving us from time to time an account of your proceedings and prospects[9] by the

way of Holland under cover to Mr. Dumas at the Hague or Messrs. Willincks of Amsterdam; by the way of England, to Uriah Forrest Esqr.; by way of France to Mr. Grand Paris; and to Mr. Carmichael by way of Spain. We wish you a pleasant Journey and happy Success, being with great Esteem your Friends and Servants.[10]   [London, 2? Oct. 1785   JOHN ADAMS][11]
        [Paris Octr. 11. 1785.   TH: JEFFERSON][12]

Tr (DNA: PCC, No. 87, 1); in Humphreys' hand; without dates or signatures; at head of text: "Instructions to Thomas Barclay Esqr."; in margin of last page in TJ's hand: "No. 3."; at foot of text in part: "N.B. The Instructions to Mr. Lamb are the same, except in the style of the court," followed by two other substitutions, which are noted below, for the text of the instructions to Lamb. Tr (DNA: PCC, No. 107, 1). FC (DNA: PCC, No. 117); an unreliable copy; records in a clerk's hand Adams' signature with his earlier dating of "London Septr. 15 1785" and, in Humphreys' hand, TJ's signature and dating of "Paris Octr. 11. 1785." 1st Dft (MHi: AMT); in TJ's hand, with several additions in Adams' hand. PrC (DLC). Tr (DNA: RG 59); in Humphreys' hand, with two corrections by TJ and endorsed by him. 2d Dft (DNA: PCC, No. 91, 1); a fair copy of 1st Dft in the hand of a clerk in Adams' office, with several additions by Adams and later alterations by TJ; at head of text: "Instructions to Thomas Barclay Esqr:"; dated at foot of letter by Adams "London Septr. 15. 1785" and signed by him. In DNA: PCC, No. 98, p. 280-81, there is an undated memorandum in TJ's hand supplementing 2d Dft (apparently for the clerk), which lists the substitutions to be made for the instructions to Lamb.

The 1st Dft was sent by TJ to Adams with his first letter of 4 Sep. Adams made some additions, had a fair copy drawn off (2d Dft), added the complimentary close, and signed it on the 15th, intending it to serve (after being signed by TJ) as the official instructions to be handed to Barclay. This copy TJ received on 22 Sep., but, because of new circumstances, he altered it to provide for (1) negotiations for immediate cessation of Barbary hostilities; (2) the preliminary signing of treaties of amity of commerce and their return to the

Commissioners for definitive execution; and (3) the treaties to become effective only upon definitive execution. This text (the missing RC) he returned to Adams, who signed it probably on 1 or 2 Oct. when he signed the other revised papers. The same procedure, of course, was followed with respect to the text of instructions for Lamb, since they were identical save for the "style of the court." In MHi: AMT there is an undated memorandum in Adams' hand labelled "farther Instructions to Mr. Barclay," which directs him, after concluding the treaty with Morocco, to proceed to Algiers, Tunis, and Tripoli for negotiations with those states and to limit all expenses to $80,000. Presumably this was drawn up by Adams at the same time as his revision of TJ's 1st Dft of Barclay's instructions, but was never given to Barclay because its need was obviated by the long-awaited arrival of Lamb who was designated agent to treat with Algiers, &c.

[1] TJ's memorandum for the copyist preparing Lamb's instructions directs that throughout the text the words "the Dey and government of Algiers" should be substituted for "the Emperor of Marocco" and "in like manner for 'him' 'his' &c. use 'them' 'their' &c."

[2] As directed by TJ's memorandum and explained in the note appended to Tr the words "through whom . . . already passed" were omitted from Lamb's instructions and the following inserted: "and from the Minister from Algiers to the Court of Madrid and the Count d'Espilly lately arrived there from Algiers who doubtless are persons of information and credit with that government" (this was not mentioned of course in either Dft). Adams hesitantly questioned the specification in his letter of 2-6 Oct. 1785: "I should think that much time may be saved, by Mr. Lamb's going directly to Marseilles, and from thence over to Algiers but if you think there will be a greater

advantage, in seeing the Algerine Envoy at Madrid, or the Comte de Spilly, if he negotiated the late Treaty for Spain, I shall submit entirely to your better Judgment."

3 This sentence is not in 1st Dft, but was inserted by TJ in 2d Dft.

4 Instead of the words "you will sign . . . execution," 1st Dft reads: "you will send them to us by some proper person, for our signature." The words enclosed in square brackets (supplied) were inserted in 2d Dft by TJ.

5 This figure is keyed to a note at the end of text which records the substitution of "40,000" made in the instructions to Lamb, as directed by TJ's memorandum.

6 This sentence was inserted in 1st Dft by Adams.

7 The words "and to provide . . . the treaty" are not in 1st Dft but were inserted by TJ in 2d Dft.

8 Left blank in 1st Dft, this figure was inserted in 2d Dft by Adams as his choice of the allowance suggested by

TJ in his first letter of 4 Sep. 1785, "between 100 and 150 guineas."

9 1st Dft ends at this point. The next words "by the way of Holland . . . England" were inserted in 1st Dft by Adams, with the additional words "France or Spain"; the passage was then altered in 2d Dft to read as in text above.

10 The complimentary close was added in 2d Dft by Adams.

11 The dating and signature by Adams of Barclay's and Lamb's missing RC have been assigned in brackets from the known dates of his signing the other final papers printed herewith (see also Adams to TJ, 2 Oct. 1785). 2d Dft is signed by him with his earlier date of "London Septr. 15. 1785"; FC is similar in this respect to 2d Dft.

12 TJ's signature and dating of missing RC have been supplied here in brackets from FC and from the known dates of his signing the other final papers printed herewith.

III. Supplementary Instructions to John Lamb

We have received information that two American vessels, the Dauphin from Philadelphia and the Maria from Boston with their crews and cargoes have lately been taken by the Algerines off the coast of Portugal and that the crews are reduced to slavery. Our full powers to that State being for the general purpose only of concluding a treaty of Amity and Commerce, the redemption of our citizens made captive before the conclusion of such treaty may not be thought comprehended within those powers. Nevertheless as the misfortune of these our countrymen has not been produced by any fault or folly of theirs, as their situation would illy admit the delay of our asking and receiving the pleasure of Congress on their subject, and as we presume strongly that it would be the will of Congress that they should be redeemed from their present calamitous condition, we think ourselves bound, in so distant a situation, and where the emergency of the case is so great, to act according to what we think would be the desire of Congress, and to trust to their goodness and the purity of our own motives for our justification.

We therefore authorize you to treat for the emancipation of the crews of the said vessels and of any others which have been or may be taken by the same power before the cessation of hostilities which we expect you to effect, administering in the mean time such necessary aids as their situation may require. In negotiating this special treaty you are to consider yourself as acting for the masters of the vessels as well as for the United States, and you will agree to no terms which they shall not approve. You will take from them their obligations, each for his crew separately, binding themselves and their owners to indemnify the United States for the monies which shall be paid for their redemption, subsistence, transportation to their own country and other charges incurred, if the Congress shall be of opinion that such indemnification should be required, transmitting to us such special treaty for our definitive execution. You will also adopt the best measures you can for returning the citizens you shall redeem to their own country. As we require a transmission of this treaty before its definitive conclusion, it is the less necessary for us to speak of the sum which you may venture to engage. We do not expect to redeem our captives for less than 100 Dollars a head, and we should be fearful to go beyond the double of that sum. However we trust much in your discretion and good management for obtaining them on terms still better than these if possible.

London Octr. 1. 1785.   JOHN ADAMS
Paris Octr. 11. 1785.   TH: JEFFERSON

RC (Albert Doezema, Grand Rapids, Mich., 1948); in Humphreys' hand, signed and dated by Adams and TJ. Dft (DNA: PCC, No. 98); in TJ's hand; undated but drafted 22-24 Sep.; at head of text: "Supplementory Instruction for Mr. Lambe." Tr (DNA: PCC, No. 87, 1); also in Humphreys' hand; without dates or signatures. Tr (DNA: PCC, No. 107, 1); at head of text: "No. 5." FC (DNA: PCC, No. 117); an unreliable copy.

IV. Jefferson's "Heads for a letter"

That the U.S. of America heretofore connected in government with Great Britain, had found it necessary for their happiness to separate from her, and to assume an Independant station.

That, consisting of a number of separate states, they had confederated together and placed the sovereignty of the whole, in matters relating to foreign nations, in a body[1] consisting of delegates from every state, and called the Congress of the U.S.

That Great Britain had solemnly confirmed their separation and acknoleged their independance.

[617]

That after the conclusion of the peace which terminated the war in which[2] they had been engaged for the establishment of their independance, the first attentions of Congress were necessarily engrossed by the re-establishment of order and regular government.

That they had as soon as possible turned their attention to foreign nations, and, desirous of entering into amity and commerce with them, had been pleased to appoint us with Doctr. B. F. to execute such treaties for this purpose as should be agreed on by such nations with us or any two of us.

That Doctr. F. having found it necessary to return to America, the execution of these several commissions had devolved on us.

That being placed as Minister plenipotentiary for the U.S. at the courts of————this circumstance[3] with the commissions with which we are charged for entering into treaties with various other nations, put it out of our power to attend at the other courts in person, and oblige us to negotiate by the intervention of confidential persons.

That respecting the friendly dispositions shewn by his majesty the Emperor of Morocco towards the U.S. and in compliance with their[4] desire of forming a connection with a sovereign so renowned for his power, his wisdom and his justice, we had embraced the first moment possible, of assuring him of these the sentiments of our country and of ourselves and of expressing to him our wishes to enter into a connection of friendship and commerce with him.

That for this purpose we had commissioned the bearer hereof T.B. a person in the highest confidence of the Congress of the U.S. and as such having been several years and still being their Consul general with our great and good friend and ally the king of France, to arrange with his majesty the Emperor, those conditions which it might be advantageous for both nations to adopt for the regulation of their commerce and their mutual conduct towards each other.

That we deliver to him a copy of the full powers with which we are invested to conclude a treaty with his majesty, which copy he is instructed to present to his majesty.

That tho' by these we are not authorized to delegate to him the power of ultimately signing the treaty, yet such is our reliance on his wisdom, his integrity and his attention to the instructions with which he is charged that we assure his majesty that the conditions which he shall arrange and send to us, shall be returned with our signature in order to receive that of the person whom his majesty shall commission for the same purpose.[5]

MS (MHi: AMT); in TJ's hand; undated; at head of text: "Heads for a letter to the Emperor of Marocco." PrC (DLC). Tr (DNA: PCC, No. 91, I); in Humphreys' hand, with one alteration by TJ. Tr (MHi: AMT); in the form of a letter, with appropriate changes, partly in Adams' hand and partly in his clerk's hand; without date. MS was enclosed in TJ's first letter to Adams of 4 Sep. 1785.

The text of "Heads for a letter" and of the letter itself (Document v) should be compared with the "Draft of a Letter from Congress to the Emperor of Morocco" that Jay prepared and, with Congress' approval, transmitted to the Commissioners in his letter of 11 Mch. 1785 (printed in JCC, XXVIII, 143-5).

[1] Adams changed this in Tr in MHi to read: "an Assembly."

[2] Tr in MHi reads instead: "the distressing War of Eight Years, in which. . . ."

[3] Tr in MHi reads: "One of us, being placed as Minister from the U:S: at the Court of G:B: and the other at the Court of France [these] Circumstances, together with. . . ."

[4] This and the preceding four words are not in PrC; they were interlined by TJ in MS and Tr in DNA.

[5] The following complimentary close is in Tr in MHi: "With the most profound respect, & our best wishes for the health, happiness, prosperity & glory of Yr. Imperial Majesty we have the honor of subscribing ourselves, Yr. Majesty's Most Obdt. Most Hume. Servts.,   J:A T.J."

V. American Commissioners to the Emperor of Morocco

The Congress of the United States of America after the conclusion of that war which established their freedom and independance, and after the cares which were first necessary for the restoration of order and regular government, turned their attention in the first moment possible to the connections which it would be proper to form with the nations on this side the Atlantic for the maintenance of friendship and improvement of commerce with them. They therefore on the twelfth day of May[1] in the last year thought proper to appoint us with Doctr. Benjn. Franklin their Ministers Plenipotentiary to negotiate and to conclude such treaties of Amity and Commerce as should be agreed on with those nations. The variety of the commissions of this nature with which we were charged rendered impracticable our attending in person at the several courts to which they were addressed, and required that we should execute them by the intervention of confidential persons to be sent to those courts. Congress sensible of this have been pleased by other full powers bearing date the 11th. day of March last to give to the same Ministers or a majority of them authority to appoint such Agents for the purpose of negotiating these treaties under our instruction, of bringing them to maturity and of signing them in a preliminary form, referring them to us for definitive execution, as by the full powers, a copy of which we have the honour of transmitting herewith to your Majesty,[2] will more particularly appear. Doctr. Franklin our collegue having found it necessary to return to America, the execution of these full powers has devolved on us alone. As the circumstances before explained put it out of our power to have the honour of presenting ourselves in person at the court of your Majesty, so others supervened which rendered impracticable our meeting at any other place such minister as your Majesty might condescend to authorize to treat with us on the subjects with which we were charged: one of us being placed as Minister Plenipotentiary for the United States at the court of Great Britain and the other in the same character at the court of France. We have therefore adopted the only remaining method that of sending a confidential Agent according to the authority given us, [to testify to your Majesty our high respect and gratitude for the friendly disposition you have manifested to the U.S. to assure you of the desire of our country to form a connection with a Sovereign so renowned for his power, his wisdom and his justice, and][3] to concert with such Minister as your Majesty shall think proper to appoint those conditions which will be most advantageous for both nations to adopt for the regulation of their commerce and of their mutual conduct towards each other. The person whom we charge with this high mission is Thomas Barclay Esqr., possessing in the highest degree the confidence of the U.S. and as such having been several years and still being their Consul General with our great and good Friend and Ally the King of France. Although our full powers reserve to us the ultimate signature of the Treaty to be established yet such is our reliance on the wisdom and integrity of Mr. Barclay that we assure your Majesty you may have full faith in whatever he shall agree to, and that the same when sent to us will be returned with our signature in order to receive that of the person whom your Majesty shall commission for the same purpose.[4]

With the most profound respect and our best wishes for the health, happiness, prosperity and glory of your Imperial Majesty We have the honor to subscribe ourselves Your Majesty's Most Obedient Most hble. Servants.

Tr (DNA: PCC, No. 87, I); in Humphreys' hand; without dates or signatures; at foot of text is a note pointing out the variations in the text of the letter for Lamb to the Dey of Algiers. Tr (DNA: PCC, No. 107, I); at head of letter: "No. 7." FC (DNA: PCC, No. 117); lacks the note appended to Tr. Dft (DNA: PCC, No. 107, II); in TJ's hand; undated; written on a leaf endorsed on verso by Adams: "Letter to Mr. Jefferson concerng. Money." In DNA: PCC, No. 98 there is an undated memorandum in TJ's hand which supplements Dft and instructs the copyist regarding substitutions to be made in preparing the letter to the Dey of Algiers; at end of text is a note by the clerk. A copy was sent by TJ to John Jay as the seventh enclosure to his letter of 11 Oct. 1785. As TJ wrote Adams on 27 Dec. 1785, the intended enclosures, the copies of their "full powers," (see Jay to the Commissioners, 11 Mch. 1785).

¹ The date and month were left blank in Dft and filled in by Humphreys.

² TJ's memorandum for the clerk contained the following instruction: "in the letter to Algiers wherever the term *Your Majesty* is used, leave a blank."

³ The passage in square brackets (thus in Dft) was omitted from the letter to Algiers, as directed by TJ's memorandum.

⁴ According to TJ's memorandum, the following passage was substituted in the letter to Algiers for the words "Thomas Barclay Esqr." and the remainder of the paragraph: " '
Lamb esquire a citizen of the U.S. in whose wisdom and integrity we have so high confidence that tho our full powers reserve to us the ultimate signature of the treaty to be established, yet we may venture to assure
that we will ratify and confirm definitively whatever preliminary conditions he shall agree and transmit to us for that purpose.' " The note at end of Tr agrees with this except for a few minor differences of phrasing and the insertion of Lamb's given name in the first blank.

VI. Heads of Inquiry

1. Commerce. What are the articles of their export and import? What articles of American produce might find a market in Algiers¹ and at what prices?² Whether rice, flour, tobacco, furs, ready built ships, fish, oil, tar, turpintine, ship timber &c. and whether any of these articles would hereafter be acceptable as presents?² What duties are levied by them on exports and imports? Do all nations pay the same, or what nations are favoured and how far? Are they their own carriers or who carries for them? Do they trade themselves to other countries, or are they merely passive? What manufactures or productions of this Country would be convenient in America, and at what prices?²

2. Ports. What are their principal ports, what depth of water into them, what works of defence protect these ports?

3. Naval force. How many armed vessels have they, of what kind and force? What is the constitution of their naval force? What resources for encreasing their navy? What number of seamen, their cruizing grounds, and season of cruizing?

4. Prisoners. What is their condition and treatment, at what price are they ordinarily redeemed and how? Do they pay respect to the treaties they make? *Land forces*, their numbers, constitution and respectability? *Revenues*, their amount?³

[621]

5. Language. What language is spoken and what European language is most understood?

6. Government. What is their connection with the Ottoman Porte? Is there any dependance or subordination to it acknowledged, and what degree of power or influence has it?

7. Religion. By what principle of their religion is it that they consider all Christian Powers as their enemies, until they become friends by Treaties?

8. Captures. What captures have been made of ships or citizens of the United States, and any other nation? What nation are they now at war with?[4]

London Octr. 1. 1785   JOHN ADAMS

Paris Octr. 11. 1785.   TH: JEFFERSON

RC (Albert Doezema, Grand Rapids, Mich., 1948); in Humphreys' hand, signed and dated by Adams and by TJ; at head of text: "Heads of enquiry for Mr. Lamb at Algiers." Dft (MHi: AMT); in TJ's hand, with additions by Adams; undated; at head of text: "Heads of enquiry for Mr. Barclay, as to Marocco [and in Adams' hand:] Algiers, Tunis &c." PrC (DLC). Tr (DNA: PCC, No. 87, I); in Humphreys' hand; without dates or signatures; at foot of text: "N. B. Similar heads of enquiry were given to Mr. Lamb." Tr (DNA: PCC, No. 107, I); at head of text: "No. 4." FC (DNA: PCC, No. 117); records Adams' signature and dating, "Grosvenor Square London Sept. 12 1785," and TJ's, "Paris Octr. 11 1785."

[1] Barclay's text reads instead: "Morocco, Algiers, Tunis, Tripoli &c."

[2] This query was added to Dft by Adams; it is not in PrC.

[3] At this point in Dft is the following query in TJ's hand which is not in any other copy except PrC: "Coins. What coins pass there and at what rates?"

[4] This and the preceding three queries were added to Dft by Adams; they are not in PrC.

VII. Letter of Credit

Grovenor Square

Westminster Octr. 6. 1785.

The United States of America in Congress Assembled on the 14th. day of Febry. last resolved, that the Ministers of the United States who are directed to form Treaties with the Emperor of Morocco and the Regencies of Algiers Tunis and Tripoli be empowered to apply any Money in Europe belonging to the United States to that use: As you are appointed to proceed to Morocco[1] as Agent for forming such Treaty with the Emperor you are hereby authorized and empowered to draw Bills of Exchange to the amount of a sum not exceeding twenty[2] thousand Dollars, at one or two usances, upon "John Adams Esqr. Minister Plenipotentiary

[622]

of the United States of America at the court of Great Britain, residing in Grosvenor Square, at the corner between Duke Street and Brook Street," who will regularly accept and pay the same either at the house of R. & C. Pullen in London or of Wilhem & Jan Willink & Nicholas & Jacob Staphorsts at Amsterdam.[3] Your Bills are however to be always accompanied with a letter of Advice in your own hand writing to Mr. Adams, a duplicate of which you will also send by some other conveyance.[4] With great respect We have the honour to be Sir Your affectionate friends & humble Servants,

Grosvenor Square London Octr. 6. 1785.   JOHN ADAMS
Paris Octr. 11. 1785   TH: JEFFERSON

Tr (DNA: PCC, No. 87, i); in Humphreys' hand; at foot of letter: "The Honble. Thos. Barclay Esqr. Agent to the Emperor of Morocco," followed by a note indicating the substitutions made in the letter for Lamb, agent to Algiers. Tr (DNA: PCC, No. 107, i); at head of text: "No. 6." Tr (DNA: PCC, No. 91, ii); in Humphreys' hand; at foot of letter: "Mr. John Lamb," followed by a note which quotes the variant portion of Barclay's letter. FC (DNA: PCC, No. 117); an imperfect text.

These letters of credit to Barclay and Lamb were drawn by Adams and enclosed in his of 2 Oct. 1785; he had previously authorized Barclay to draw directly upon the Holland bankers, but with Lamb's arrival this different method was arranged for both (Adams to TJ, 15 Sep.; TJ to Adams, 24 Sep.; Adams to W. & J. Willink

and N. & J. van Staphorst, 12 Sep. 1785, MHi: AMT; N. & J. van Staphorst to TJ, 20 Oct. 1785, note).

[1] Lamb's letter reads: "Algiers."
[2] Lamb's letter reads: "Forty."
[3] At this point Lamb's letter reads: "as you shall find most for the interest of the U.S."; this variation is not recorded in the note appended to Barclay's letter.
[4] Instead of the words "in your own hand . . . conveyance," Lamb's letter reads: "and as your hand writing is wholly unknown to Mr. Adams, these letters of advice are always to be in the hand writing of Paul R. Randal Esqr. who accompanies you, whose hand writing is left in the custody of Mr. Adams as a check and a proof by comparison. The letters however are to be subscribed by you."

VIII. American Commissioners to William Carmichael

SIR

Mr. Barclay will deliver you this letter in his way to Morocco.

We have appointed him to this negotiation in hopes of obtaining the friendship of that State to our country, and of opening by that means the commerce of the Mediterranean, an object of sufficient importance to induce him to accept of the trust.

We recommend him and Colo. Franks who goes with him to your attention and assistance, and we particularly desire you to interest the court of Spain in his favour if you think it practicable. Your success upon many occasions with the Spanish Ministers, gives us hopes that you may obtain for him, Instructions or Letters to Spanish Consuls or other Gentlemen which may contribute both to the comfort of his travels and the success of his Mission.

Any Dispatches, for us, which he may convey to you, your own just sense of the importance of them will induce you to transmit to us with all possible care.

We are informed of the friendly attention of the court of Madrid to the case of our fellow citizens late in captivity as well as on many other occasions, and if you think it will not be taken amiss, you will oblige us by expressing our grateful sense of it wherever you think proper.

With great esteem We have the honour to be Sir Your Most obedt. & Most humble Servts.,

London Septr. 12 1785   JOHN ADAMS
TH: JEFFERSON

Tr (DNA: PCC, No. 87, I); in Humphreys' hand; with only Adams' dating; at foot of letter: "Mr. Carmichael Chargé des Affairs of the United States of America at the court of Madrid" and "(N.B. A similar letter was given to Mr. Lamb)." Tr

(DNA: PCC, No. 107, I); at head of text: "No. 9." The text of the letter to Lamb must obviously have substituted his own name for Barclay's, Algiers for Morocco, and Randall for Franks.

IX. Projet of a Treaty with the Barbary States

See Jefferson's Draft of a Treaty, printed above as enclosure to TJ to Adams, 6 Aug. 1785, to which the texts provided Barclay and Lamb on 11 Oct. are identical, except for Article 17. That article reads: "The subjects or citizens of either party may frequent the coasts and countries of the other, and reside and trade there in all sorts of produce, manufactures and merchandize, the purchase and sale of which shall be free to all persons of every discription unembarrassed by monopoly, paying no greater duties than the most favoured nation pay; and they shall enjoy all the rights privileges and exemptions in navigation and commerce which the subjects of the most favoured nation enjoy. They shall also be free to pass and repass with their merchandize within the territories of the other without being obliged to obtain passports."

Tr (DNA: PCC, No. 87, I); in Humphreys' hand; without date. FC (DNA: PCC, No. 116); an imperfect copy. See Adams to TJ, 18 Aug. 1785.

From André Limozin

Le Havre, 11 Oct. 1785. Acknowledges TJ's letters of the 8th. He had never begun legal action on Fortin's claim; use of the vouchers furnished under the name of Joseph would surely have defeated it and prevented him thereafter from any right to the estate, since "none of the deceasd Fortin's family who left the Estate were calld Joseph, but . . . there is one missing calld Jean Baptiste." Fortin's only recourse is to provide new vouchers under that name.

RC (DNA: PCC, No. 87, I); 2 p.; addressed at foot of first page to TJ in part: "en son Hotel a la Grille de Chaillot a Paris." Tr (DNA: PCC, No. 107, I).

From André Limozin

⟦*Le Havre, 11 Oct. 1785.* Recorded in SJL as received 13 Oct. 1785 with Limozin's other letter of this date. Not found.⟧

From De Thulemeier

The Hague, 11 Oct. 1785. Informs TJ of his receipt of the Ratification of the treaty by his government; as soon as Congress' ratification shall come to TJ, he will arrange with him for the proper exchange. Asks to be remembered to Short and is conscious of his obligation to TJ for their acquaintance. "Mr. Schort me paroît aussi distingué par ses connoissances et ses lumières que par sa dextérité à manier les affaires." Encloses a letter to be forwarded to Baltimore from a merchant of Silesia.

RC (DNA: PCC, No. 87, I); 1 p.; in French; in a clerk's hand, with last phrase of complimentary close and signature in De Thulemeier's hand; accompanied by an English translation labelled at head of text: "No. 7." Tr (DNA: PCC, No. 107, I); with an English translation. Recorded in SJL as received 15 Oct. 1785. Enclosure not identified.

On this date De Thulemeier wrote John Adams a similar letter, to which Adams replied somewhat optimistically that the treaty had already been dis-patched to America (it actually remained in France with the Fitzhughs for another month) and that the instrument of ratification might be expected in three months (it was nearer ten). "As soon as it arrives," he added, "you will be made acquainted with it either by Mr. Jefferson or me, and then we may proceed to the Exchange in such a manner as may be agreed upon as most convenient to both parties" (Adams to De Thulemeier, 4 Nov. 1785; MHi: AMT).

American Commissioners to Vergennes

Sir

The friendly dispositions which his Majesty has been pleased to shew to the United States of America on every occasion, as well as

[625]

the assurances given them in the 8th. Article of the treaty of Amity and Commerce that he would employ his good offices and interposition with the powers on the coast of Barbary to provide for the safety of the Citizens of the United States, their vessels and effects encouraged us to address you our letter of March 28th. on that subject. To this you were pleased to favour us with an answer on the 28th. of April enclosing the sentiments of His Excellency the Maal. de Castries on the same subject and confirming our expectations of His Majesty's good offices whensoever we should be efficaciously prepared to enter into negotiation with those States. As circumstances rendered impracticable our proceeding in person to that court, Congress have been pleased to invest us with other full powers authorizing us to substitute agents to proceed thither for the purpose of negotiating and maturing the terms of treaty and of signing them in a preliminary form but requiring their definitive execution by us. They have also permitted and enabled us to comply with those demands to which other nations are in the habit of submitting. In consequence of these powers we have appointed Thomas Barclay, Esqr., agent to the court of Morocco and John Lamb Esqr., to the Government of Algiers who will immediately proceed to their respective destinations for the purpose of negotiating treaties of Amity and Commerce with those two powers. It remained for us to apprise your Excellency of these transactions, and to beg leave through you to represent to His Majesty that being now fully vested with the powers requisite for carrying these negotiations into effect, and enabled to comply with such moderate demands as actual circumstances give us reason to expect, the moment is arrived in which his powerful influence with those States may be interposed to our great benefit. And to pray that he will interpose it either by direct address to those powers, or through the medium of his Ministers, Consuls or Agents residing there, or in such other manner as His Majesty shall judge most consistent with his honour and most likely to avail the United States of his efficacious aid.

We have the honour to be with sentiments of the most profound respect Your Excellency's Most obedient and Most humble Servants,   London Octr. 1. 1785. John Adams

Paris Octr. 11. 1785. Th: Jefferson

RC (Arch. Aff. Etr., Corr. Pol., E.-U., xxx; Tr in DLC); in Humphreys' hand, signed and dated by Adams and by TJ; accompanied by a French translation. Dft (DNA: PCC, No. 98); in TJ's hand; undated. Tr (DNA: PCC, No. 87, 1); undated. Tr (DNA: PCC, No. 107, 1); at head of text: "No.

8." FC (DNA: PCC, No. 117); an unreliable copy. In MHi: AMT there is an earlier draft in Adams' hand, signed and dated "London Septr. 15. 1785," which, having been drawn up before Lamb's arrival in Paris with Congress' instructions to the American Commissioners of 11 Mch. 1785, differs considerably from TJ's Dft. A copy of the letter was sent to Jay in TJ's letter of 11 Oct. 1785; see note there.

To Lister Asquith

SIR   Paris Octob. 12. 1785.

I have received your letters of Sep. 28. and Octob. 3. but no information is yet received from your lawyer, so that I am utterly uninformed of the nature of the process instituted against you, and the court in which it is depending. Till I receive this I am unable to obtain advice how to interfere for your relief. That you may not suffer for want of money, I will advance for you what may be necessary to engage a lawyer, and a livre a day a head for the support of yourself and those with you, for which I shall expect yourself and your captain to make yourselves accountable. Draw bills on me for these purposes from time to time and Messrs. Desbordes, merchants at Brest, will give you money for them. I have written to these gentlemen to pray them to advise you what to do for your defence, to engage a good lawyer for you, and to desire him immediately to send me such information as may enable me to judge whether I can do any thing for your relief. I am Sir Your most obedient humble servant,   TH: JEFFERSON

P.S. Send me the number and names of those with you and of what country they are.

PrC (DLC). Enclosed in TJ to Borgnis Desbordes, Frères, 12 Oct. 1785.

To Borgnis Desbordes, Frères

SIR   Paris Octob. 12. 1785.

There are in the prison of St. Pol de leon six or seven citizens of the United states of America, charged with having attempted a contraband of tobacco, but, as they say themselves, forced into that port by stress of weather. I beleive that they are innocent. Their situation is described to me as deplorable as should be that of men proved guilty of the worst of crimes. They are in close jail, allowed three sous a day only, and unable to speak a word of the language of the country. I hope their distress, which it is my duty to relieve, and the recommendation of Mr. Barclay to address myself to you will apologize for the liberty I take of asking you to advise them what to do for their defence, to engage some good lawyer for them, and to pass to them the pecuniary reliefs necessary. I write to Mr. Lister Asquith the owner of the vessel, that he may draw bills on me from time to time for a livre a day for every person of them, and for what may be necessary to engage a lawyer for him. I will pray the favor of you to furnish him money for his bills drawn on me for these purposes which I will pay on sight. You will judge if he should go beyond this allowance and be so good as to reject the surplus. I must desire his lawyer in the first moment to send me a state of their case, in what court their process is, and when it is likely to be decided. I hope the circumstances of the case will excuse the freedom I take, and I have the honor to be.

PrC (DLC); lacks part of complimentary close and signature; on verso: "Messrs. Desbordes freres negociants à Brest." Enclosure: TJ to Lister Asquith, 12 Oct. 1785, preceding.

To Froullé

12me. Octobre 1785.

[J'accepte] Monsieur, de votre proposition [de donner] à Monsieur Ramsay pour [son] histoire de la revolution de la Caroline [du Sud] neuf cents livres paiables un [an] après l'impression. Je vous envoye [328] pages de l'ouvrage, et j'enverrai [le] reste aussitot que je la recevrai.

J'ai l'honneur d'etre avec beaucoup de respect, Monsr. votre tres obeissant serviteur, TH JEFFERSON

PrC (ViWC). The left-hand edge of MS is badly crumpled and worn; missing words have been supplied conjecturally. Not recorded in SJL.

From Froullé

a Paris le 12. 8bre. 1785

Je sousigné, Reconnois avoir reçu de Monsieur de Chefersone, trois cent vingt huite pages d'impression histoire de la Revolution de la Caroline du Sud, par Monsieur Ramsay, en anglois, pour lequel je suis convenu de Payer une somme de neuf cent

Livres un an apres que L'ouvrage aura été mis au jour en francois, la suite du dit ouvrage me devant etre fournie par Monsieur de Chefersone.   FROULLÉ

Je remet à votre domestique de L'esprit par Helvetius. J'ignore si touts ces oeuvres sont de ce format: Je [sais?] qu'elle Existe En in 8to. 5 vol. Si je puis les trouver je vous les enverez avec les autres demandé demain ou vendredy au plus tard.

Il ny a point de Dictionnaire de Beaumard in 12 mais bien en grand in 8to. et petit 8to., 9 vs. chacun. Il n'a point donné celui de chymie, c'est Mr. Macquer qui a fait cet ouvrage. Il y a 4 vol. petit 8to.

RC (ViWC); addressed: "A Son Exelence Monsieur de chefersone Mynistre Plenipotentiaire des Etats unis de L'amerique En son hotel a Paris." Inserted after the signature are later notations in the hands of both Froullé and TJ recording subsequent deliveries of portions of the book: in Froullé's hand: "du 11 9bre. recu les pages 25 à 144 du tome deuxieme," and in TJ's: "Dec. 14. 1785. delivd. from Vol. 1. pa. 329. to Vol. 2. pa. 24. inclusive. Jan. 20. 1786. sent Vol. 2 pa. v—xx and 305—440 and 545—574. being the end." See Ramsay to TJ, 11 Dec. 1785 and 3 May 1786; TJ to Ramsay, 26 Jan. 1786.

To David Ramsay

SIR   Paris Oct. 12. 1785.

The Mr. Fitzhughs the bearers of this letter being on the point of setting out, I have only time to inform you that after trying many booksellers and receiving a variety of propositions the best offer is of 900 livres for your book, paiable 12 months after the printing of it here shall be completed. The M. de Chastellux thinks it best to accept of this, I shall therefore do it this day. I should have been pleased to have obtained terms somewhat more like reason, but it could not be done. Being only a translation, others have a right to translate also and to sell in competition with the first. I have the honor to be with the greatest respect Sir Your most obedient humble servt.,   TH: JEFFERSON

PrC (DLC).

To Nicolas & Jacob van Staphorst

GENTLEMEN   Paris Oct. 12. 1785.

The receipt of your favor of Sep. 19. should not have been so long unacknoleged but that I have been peculiarly and very closely engaged ever since it came to hand.

With respect to the expediency of the arrangement you propose to take with Mr. Parker I must observe to you that it would be altogether out of my province to give an official opinion for your direction. These transactions appurtain altogether to the Commissioners of the treasury to whom you have very properly written on the occasion. I shall always be willing however to apprize you of any facts I may be acquainted with and which might enable you to proceed with more certainty, and even to give my private opinion where I am acquainted with the subject, leaving you the most perfect liberty to give it what weight you should think proper. In the present case I cannot give even a private opinion, because I am not told what are precisely the securities offered by Mr. Parker. So various are the securities of the United states that unless they are precisely described by their dates, consideration and other material circumstances, no man on earth can say what they are worth. One fact however is certain that all debts of any considerable amount contracted by the U.S. while their paper money existed, are subject to a deduction, and not paiable at any fixed period. I think I may venture to say also that there are no debts of the U.S. 'on the same footing with the money loaned by Holland' except those due to the kings of France and Spain. However I hope you will soon receive the answer of the Commissioners which alone can decide authoritatively what is to be done.

Congress have thought proper to entrust to Mr. Adams and myself a certain business which may eventually call for great advances of money: perhaps four hundred thousand livres or upwards. They have authorised us to draw for this on their funds in Holland. The separate situation of Mr. Adams and my self rendering joint draughts inconvenient we have agreed that they shall be made by him alone. You will be pleased therefore to give the same credit to these bills drawn by him as if they were also subscribed by me.[1]

I have the honor to be with high respect Gentlemen Your most obedient & most humble servant, TH: JEFFERSON

PrC (DLC). Tr (DNA: PCC, No. 87, 1); in Short's hand. Tr (DNA: PCC, No. 107, 1); in a clerk's hand.

[1] This paragraph is omitted from both Tr.

To Vergennes

SIR   Paris Octr. 12th. 1785.

In the enclosed letter Mr. Adams and myself have the honor to
inform your Excellency of the measures ultimately taken for procuring arrangements between the United States of America and
the States of Barbary, and to ask his Majesty's interposition.[1] To
the information therein contained it is necessary for me to add that
Mr. Barclay who is charged with the commission to Morocco will
set out in two or three days; and that Mr. Lamb, charged with the
commission to Algiers, waits to be the bearer of such letters as
you may think necessary for manifesting the interest his Majesty
will be so good as to take in these negotiations. Having received
these he will follow Mr. Barclay proposing to overtake him in the
road to Madrid. There they will separate. Letters of protection
for their persons, effects, vessels and attendants during their passage to and from Africa and their stay there seem to be the first
requisite; to which such others will be added for procuring favorable dispositions on the part of those powers as you shall think
proper to honor[2] them with.

I have the honor to be With Sentiments of the most profound
esteem and respect Your Excellency's Most obedient & Most humble
Servant,   TH: JEFFERSON

RC (Arch. Aff. Etr., Corr. Pol., E.-U., xxx); in Humphreys' hand; at head of text: "M. De R[ayneval]"; accompanied by French translation, with a note at head of text which reads: "Envoyé copie de cette Lettre et de celle y jointe du 1er. 8bre. a M. le Maal. de Castries le 18. 8bre. 1785." Dft (DNA: PCC, No. 98). FC (DNA: PCC, No. 117). Not recorded in SJL, but TJ may have had the present letter in mind, mistakenly, when he made the follow-

ing entry under 21 Oct. 1785: "C. de Vergennes, s.c. (copy lost or mislaid. Barbary affairs)." Enclosure: Adams and TJ to Vergennes, 11 Oct. 1785.

[1] TJ first wrote in Dft ". . . to ask the aid of his Majesty's mediation" and then altered the phrase to read as above.
[2] This word interlined in Dft in substitution for "favor," deleted.

To G. K. van Hogendorp

DEAR SIR   Paris Oct. 13. 1785.

Having been much engaged lately, I have been unable sooner
to acknolege the receipt of your favor of Sep. 8. What you are
pleased to say on the subject of my Notes is more than they deserve.
The condition in which you first saw them would prove to you
how hastily they had been originally written; as you may remem-

ber the numerous insertions I had made in them from time to time, when I could find a moment for turning to them from other occupations. I have never yet seen Monsr. de Buffon. He has been in the country all the summer. I sent him a copy of the book, and I have only heard his sentiments on one particular of it, that of the identity of the Mammoth and Elephant. As to this he retains his opinion that they are the same.—If you had formed any considerable expectations from our Revised code of laws you will be much disappointed. It contains not more than three or four laws which could strike the attention of a foreigner. Had it been a digest of all our laws, it would not have been comprehensible or instructive but to a native. But it is still less so, as it digests only the British statutes and our own acts of assembly, which are but a supplementory part of our law. The great basis of it is anterior to the date of the Magna charta, which is the oldest statute extant. The only merit of this work is that it may remove from our book shelves about twenty folio volumes of statutes, retaining all the parts of them which either their own merit or the established system of laws required.

You ask me what are those operations of the British nation which are likely to befriend us, and how they will produce this effect? The British government, as you may naturally suppose, have it much at heart to reconcile their nation to the loss of America. This is essential to the repose, perhaps even to the safety of the king and his ministers. The most effectual engines for this purpose are the public papers. You know well that that government always kept a kind of standing army of newswriters who without any regard to truth, or to what should be like truth, invented and put into the papers whatever might serve the minister. This suffices with the mass of the people who have no means of distinguishing the false from the true paragraphs of a newspaper. When forced to acknolege our independance they were forced to redouble their efforts to keep the nation quiet. Instead of a few of the papers formerly engaged, they now engaged every one. No paper therefore comes out without a dose of paragraphs against America. These are calculated for a secondary purpose also, that of preventing the emigrations of their people to America. They dwell very much on American bankruptcies. To explain these would require a long detail, but would shew you that nine tenths of these bankruptcies are truly English bankruptcies in no wise chargeable on America. However they have produced effects the most desireable of all others for us. They have destroyed our credit, and thus checked our disposition to luxury; and forcing our merchants to buy no more than they have ready money to pay for, they force them to go to those markets where that ready money will buy most. Thus you see they check our luxury, they force us to connect ourselves with all the world, and they prevent foreign emigrations to our country all of which I consider as advantageous to us. They are doing us another good turn. They attempt without disguise to possess themselves of the carriage of our produce, and to prohibit our own vessels from participating of it. This has raised a general indignation in America. The states see however that their constitutions have provided no means of counteracting it. They are therefore beginning to vest Congress with the absolute power of regulating their commerce, only reserving all revenue arising from it to the state in which it is levied. This will consolidate our federal building very much, and for this we shall be indebted to the British.

You ask what I think on the expediency of encouraging our states to be commercial? Were I to indulge my own theory, I should wish them to practice neither commerce nor navigation, but to stand with respect to Europe precisely on the footing of China. We should thus avoid wars, and all our citizens would be husbandmen. Whenever indeed our numbers should so increase as that our produce would overstock the markets of those nations who should come to seek it, the farmers must either employ the surplus of their time in manufactures, or the surplus of our hands must be employed in manufactures, or in navigation. But that day would, I think be distant, and we should long keep our workmen in Europe, while Europe should be drawing rough materials and even subsistence from America. But this is theory only, and a theory which the servants of America are not at liberty to follow. Our people have a decided taste for navigation and commerce. They take this from their mother country: and their servants are in duty bound to calculate all their measures on this datum: we wish to do it by throwing open all the doors of commerce and knocking off it's shackles. But as this cannot be done for others, unless they will do it to us, and there is no great probability that Europe will do this, I suppose we shall be obliged to adopt a system which may shackle them in our ports as they do us in theirs.

With respect to the sale of our lands, that cannot begin till a considerable portion shall have been surveyed. They cannot begin to survey till the fall of the leaf of this year, nor to sell probably till the ensuing spring. So that it will be yet a twelvemonth before we shall be able to judge of the efficacy of our land office to sink our national debt. It is made a fundamental that the proceeds shall be solely and sacredly applied as a sinking fund to discharge the capital only of the debt.

It is true that the tobaccos of Virginia go almost entirely to England. The reason is that they owe a great debt there which they are paying as fast as they can. I think I have now answered your several queries, and shall be happy to receive your reflections on the same subjects, and at all times to hear of your welfare and to give you assurances of the esteem with which I have the honor to be Dear Sir your most obedient & most humble servant,

TH: JEFFERSON

RC (Rijksarchief, The Hague). PrC (DLC).

To Samuel Henley

DEAR SIR   Paris Oct. 14. 1785

This is accompanied by the copy of a letter I did myself the pleasure of writing you in March last. I sent it by a gentleman going to London who promised to endeavor to find you out. He brought it back to me with an assurance that he had been unable to learn the place of your residence. I gave it to another who went soon after to London: and as he did not return it to me I flattered myself it had got safely to your hands. I first learned the contrary by your favor of July 18. by Mr. Bradford. I should have sent this answer by him but he told me his return would be circuitous and occupy much time, and that, having now your address, a letter by post would go safely.

My residence here being now likely to be of longer continuance than I had expected when I wrote the preceding letter, it is become less probable that you would prefer receiving the books therein mentioned to the money. However of this you are still the judge. Should you chuse the money, I will either pay your bill on me, or I will take some opportunity by a safe hand to remit it to any person in London whom you will be so good as to point out to me.

Mr. Bradford was the first person I had met with able to give me any news of you since you left Virginia. I am happy to hear by him that you are agreeably situated. I am here with one daughter having left another in America, being all the family now remaining to me. I should be glad to hear that Mr. Gwatkin has also succeeded to his mind.

You have been so long from Virginia, that an account of recent events would be scarcely intelligable to you without a knowlege of what has preceded them. You know, doubtless of the removal of the seat of government to Richmond. This has made of Williamsburgh a mere academical village, disfigured by the burning of the president's house the palace and some others of smaller note. We have new modelled the institution of the college, having suppressed the two divinity schools and the grammar school, and substituted in their places a professorship of law (Mr. Wythe) another of Medecine, anatomy, chemistry and surgery (McLurg) and a third of Modern languages, (Bellini). We were confined by the charter to six professorships and the legislature had not leisure at that time to change the constitution of the college fundamentally. The alteration has proved very succesful. They have now ordinarily about 80. students. I shall hope the pleasure of hearing from you, & am with great esteem Dr. Sir Your most obedient humble servt., TH: JEFFERSON

PrC (DLC). Entry in SJL under this date reads: "S. Henley at Rendlesham near Melton and Ipswich in Suffolk." Enclosure: Copy of TJ to Henley, 3 Mch. 1785.

To John Banister, Jr.

DEAR SIR   Paris Oct. 15. 1785.

I should sooner have answered the paragraph in your favor of Sep. 19. respecting the best seminary for the education of youth in Europe, but that it was necessary for me to make enquiries on the subject. The result of these has been to consider the competition as resting between Geneva and Rome. They are equally cheap, and probably are equal in the course of education pursued. The advantage of Geneva is that students acquire there the habits of speaking French. The advantages of Rome are the acquiring a local knowlege of a spot so classical and so celebrated; the acquiring the true pronuntiation of the Latin language; the acquiring a just taste in the fine arts, more particularly those of painting, sculpture, Architecture, and Music; a familiarity with those objects and processes of agriculture which experience has shewn best adapted to a climate like ours; and lastly the advantage of a fine climate for health. It is probable too that by being boarded in a French family the habit of speaking that language may be obtained. I do not count on any advantage to be derived in Geneva from a familiar acquaintance with the principles of it's government. The late revolution has rendered it a tyrannical aristocracy more likely to give ill than good ideas to an American. I think the balance in favor of Rome. Pisa is sometimes spoken of as a place of education. But it does not offer the 1st. and 3d. of the advantages of Rome. But why send an American youth to Europe for education? What are the objects of an useful American education? Classical knowlege, modern languages and chiefly French, Spanish, and Italian; Mathematics; Natural philosophy; Natural History; Civil History; Ethics. In Natural philosophy I mean to include Chemistry and Agriculture, and in Natural history to include Botany as well as the other branches of those departments. It is true that the habit of speaking the modern languages cannot be so well acquired in America, but every other article can be as well acquired at William and Mary College as at any place in Europe. When College education is done with and a young man is to prepare himself for public life, he must cast his eyes (for America) either on Law or Physic. For the former where can he apply so advantageously as to Mr. Wythe? For the latter he must come to Europe; the medical class of students therefore is the only one which need come to Europe. Let us view the disadvantages of sending a youth to Europe. To enumerate them all would require a volume. I will select a few. If he goes to England he learns drinking, horse-racing and boxing. These are the peculiarities of English education. The following circumstances are common to education in that and the other countries of Europe. He acquires a fondness for European luxury and dissipation and a contempt for the simplicity of his own country; he is fascinated with the privileges of the European aristocrats, and sees with abhorrence the lovely equality which the poor enjoys with the rich in his own country: he contracts a partiality for aristocracy or monarchy; he forms foreign friendships which will never be useful to him, and loses the season of life for forming in his own country those friendships which of all others are the most faithful and permanent: he is led by the strongest of all the human passions into a spirit for female intrigue destructive of his own and others happiness, or a passion for whores destructive of his health, and in both cases learns to consider fidelity to the marriage bed as an ungentlemanly practice and inconsistent with happiness: he recollects the voluptuary dress and arts of the European women and pities and despises the chaste affections and simplicity of those of his own country; he retains thro' life a fond recollection and a hankering after those places which were the scenes of his first pleasures and of his first connections; he returns to his own country, a foreigner, unacquainted with the practices of domestic œconomy necessary to preserve him from ruin; speaking and writing his native tongue as a foreigner, and therefore unqualified to obtain those distinctions which eloquence of the pen and tongue ensures in a free country; for I would observe to you that what is called style in writing or speaking is formed very early in life while the imagination is warm, and impressions are permanent. I am of opinion that there never was an instance of a man's writing or speaking his native tongue with elegance who passed from 15. to 20. years of age out of the country where it was spoken. Thus no instance exists of a person writing two languages perfectly. That will always appear to be his native language which was most familiar to him in his youth. It appears to me then that an American coming to Europe for education loses in his knowlege, in his morals, in his health, in his habits, and in his happiness. I had entertained only doubts on this head before I came to Europe: what I see and hear since I come here proves more than I had even suspected. Cast your eye over America: who are the men of most learning, of most eloquence, most beloved by their country and most trusted and promoted by them? They are those who have been educated among them, and whose manners, morals and habits are perfectly homogeneous with those of the country.—Did you expect by so short a question to draw such a sermon on yourself? I dare say you did not. But the consequences of foreign education are alarming to me as an American. I sin therefore through zeal whenever I enter on the subject. You are sufficiently American to pardon me for it. Let me hear of your health and be assured of the esteem with which I am Dear Sir Your friend & servant,

Th: Jefferson

RC (DLC: Shippen Papers, 1); slightly mutilated in third and fourth pages; missing words supplied from PrC (DLC).

In DLC: TJ Papers, 234: 41840 there is a single leaf, written on both sides, that carries the endorsement: "on sending American youth to Europe." This is an outline of what may have been intended as an essay on France. This outline, which TJ may have drawn up about this time for later elaboration, reads:

"Government. Pure Despotism
  Powers of king. Legislative—registg. of parl.
       Executive. Military
           Lettres de cachet
           Printing.

Aristocracy. Oppressions
           Pensions, &c.
Finances. Abuses in
           Unproductive of revenue
Judiciary. Venality
           Protections
                Effects of these on commerce
                Grand seigneurs never pay
                Poor man not venture to force them
                Others therefore pay higher price.
Commerce affected by preceding circumstances
              by internal duties
              by difficulties at bureaux
              by unwritten agreement
              by taste for pleasure
Manufactures.   Silks, cloths, linen, household furniture, bijouterie & [montres?]
              looking glass, books
Productions.   Wine, oil, fruits, brandy, marble plaister
Fine arts.   Painting, statuary, architecture.
              Music, poetry, gardening.
Science
Society   Love
              Friendship
              Charity
              Religion
              Children
              Dogs
              Theatres
              Concerts
              Balls
              Meals
              Talkativeness
              Sexes have changed business
              Convents
Paris.   Streets. No trottoirs. Lighted. Sewers.
              Buildings. Portes cocheres. Courts. Little houses. Gardens.
              ⟨*Littlehouses*⟩
              ⟨*Sewers*⟩
              Police
              Filles de joie
              Fiacres
              ⟨*Lamps*⟩
              Public gardens
The country.   Soil
              Climate. Compare with America
              Agriculture
                Inclosures
                Animals. Horses
                    Cattle
                    Mules
                    Asses."

From André Limozin

MOST HONORED SIR   Havre de Grace 16th. october 1785

You will find here annexed three Bills of Lading for the Box and three Trunks of Books you have sent me for Virginia, and which I have shipp'd on board the Eolus Le Paon Master. That Ship is saild this Morning and as she is consignd in Portsmouth to Mr. Thoms. Brown, I have desird him to forward these Books as directed by the bills of Lading. I have the Honor to be with the highest regard your Excellency's Most obedient & very Humble Servant, ANDRE LIMOZIN

RC (MHi); addressed to TJ in part: "en son Hotel a la Grille de Chaillot Paris"; endorsed. Not recorded in SJL. Enclosures not found.

To De Thulemeier

SIR   Paris Octob. 16. 1785.

I am to acknolege the receipt of the letter of the 11th. inst. with which you have honored me, and wherein you are pleased to inform me of the ratification by his Prussian majesty of the treaty of Amity and Commerce between him and the United States of America. On our part the earliest opportunity was embraced of forwarding it to Congress. It goes by a vessel sailing about this time from Havre. I shall with great pleasure communicate to you it's ratification by Congress in the first moment in which it shall become known to me, and concur in the measures necessary for exchanging the ratifications.

I shall take the greatest care to forward the letter you are pleased to enclose for Baltimore according to it's address.

I have the honour to be with sentiments of the highest respect & esteem Sir Your most obedient and most humble servant,

TH: JEFFERSON

PrC (DLC). Tr (DNA: PCC, No. 87, I); in Short's hand. Tr (DNA: PCC, No. 107, I).

From Lister Asquith

St. Pol de Léon, 17 Oct. 1785. He has heard nothing from Floch himself but learns he can do nothing until he receives the prisoners' papers, which were sent to him and the judge of the Court of Admiralty several weeks before. Asquith also learned from Father John Mehegan that the case will be settled at Paris by Vergennes and Calonne; the prisoners would surely have lost it at Brest "as the Very Lawyers Mr. Picrel had employed were pensioners to the Farmers." The "Captain General" told the priest "it was our own Fault that we were confined here and if we had given him half the Money that we had gave to others he would have wrote to the Farmers in our favor that we were in great Distress when we came in and not fit to stand the sea any longer . . . and he believed we did not intend to Smuggle any thing, but as we had employed others and not him he had sent us to Prison and seized every thing to secure himself." They are grateful to TJ for arranging for the transfer of the case from Brest to Paris.

RC (DLC); 2 p. Recorded in SJL as received 23 Oct. 1785.

From James Currie

Sir   Richmond. Octr. 17th. 1785.

Tho I have nothing to write which can either amuse or instruct, yet I cannot let slip this Opportunity of doing myself the honor to trouble your Excellency with a few lines by my friend Captn. Lewis Little Page with whom I had the pleasure to become lately acquainted and who I confess has both pleased and instructed me. His na'al [natural] Genius, and Career hitherto both Political and military you very probably may have become acquainted with. If I am not exceedingly mistaken the Impressions he must make wherever he goes must be in his favor and from sundry European letters, wrote by very Elevated and Respectable Characters from thence in his favor to the Sovereigns, the Congress of this his native Country, in the strongest terms of praise and the highest recommendation of him to their particular attention, I am fully convinced he is amply deserving of them, and has Genius and talents which when fully matured, and properly applied cannot fail one day or other to render him an Ornament to Society, and a most valuable Accquisition to this or any other Country where his Starrs may lead him. Well knowing your respect for merit wherever (or in whomever) found and Patronage for Genius; as a young gentleman possessed of both in a very considerable degree I take the liberty to recommend him to your Excellencys particular attention, which I am conscious you will (from my knowledge of you) have particular pleasure in rendring; after becoming accquainted with the qualities of his head and heart. Here I'll stop this Subject.

My Last letter which was confided to the care of Mr. Neil Jameison of New York, was to be sent by the June Packet, which I hope you have received. I wrote Mr. Short by same Opportunity. I therein mentioned my having received the Phosphoretick Matches, the Balloon treatise and the Animal Magnetism &c. &c. by Coll. Le Maire who by the by I have seldom seen. Mr. Eppes has shown him many Civilities to my knowledge. I desired, as my particular friend you Would send me the Encyclopedia, if you thought proper, tho Came in the French language. It might divert my mind from play which has hitherto been my Bane and which I have altogether left off except Chess, wishing to accquire some knowledge in that in Expectation of having the pleasure of one day or other seeing you here and being further instructed by you in it. Short, I suppose by this time is become such an adept as not to make one false move in this Science. I mentioned in my last our having had a religious convention of which a Lawyer and Layman, I believe, was the prime Mover. The Other Religionists are damned ma[d?] at the Establishment and Anathematise the Assembly, and their Elect which they attempt to prove are not those of God. I don't care who preach or pray. Blairs Sermons I have read with pleasure and profit I hope [. . .] as to [. . .]. I am once more, warned to be on my guard.

The Situation of our Capitol is a contracted one as I before mentioned.

The Congress seldom reaches our Ears. The General Court is now sitting here and the Gentlemen of the law increase very fast at its Barr. John Mercer Esqr.—this is his 2d. Court there. I expect Munroe and Hardy soon &c. &c. The Votaries are numerous, but I believe 3 or 4 of them receive and have appetites sufficient to devour all the Loaves and Fishes. I cant help thinking we have too much Litigation and Law Suits here, to become a flourishing people till some Change in that and many other respects, takes place. We are fast Verging to Individual and Universal Bankruptcy. As a Commercial people, our Exports bear no proportion to our imports. Our Taxes are heavy, our Extravagance Unequalled in so young a Country. E.G. at Fredericksburg t'other day 40 new (and Elegant) Chariots appeard on the Turf in addition to what served them last year, on the same or similar Occasion. Every thing is in proportion. We astonish strangers and all Our Own natives who have been absent some time and just returned from Europe. Some Intelligence communicated by you in a letter to Our Executive, regarding Sir R. Herries's contract with the Farmers General of France made its appearance in Our publick papers t'other day with what degree of policy, delicacy or Prudence I leave you to judge. The General Assembly have met to day. Not enough to make a house. The late Governor Harrison was nonelect in Chas. City last Election of Delegates there, but went over to Surry, where he found Means to be Elected. It is expected his election will be Canvassed, and disputed by Mr. Tyler (the present Speaker of the house) as Illegal. Each have their Partizans and are Candidates for the Chair and have already had a good deal of Bickering which has impressed me with the Idea, Emolument is as much their Object as Patriotism or the honor of the place. Perhaps I am mistaken. McClurg is a Councillor here. Indolent as a Physician, Often in at the Death on account of his being so often called when the last offices of humanity are only wanting to close the Scene, his talents are great, and in that line have met with too little patronage from his Countrymen hitherto. I hope the Scales will fall from their Eyes before old age unfitts him for business—for his family's sake I sincerely wish it.

Your friend Mr. Maddison has been spoke of by some for the Chair of the House of Delegates.

We have had a very dry Summer, short Crops both of Corn and Tobacco, Wheat tolerably good, no demand hardly for this last; Tobacco fallen and falling—1 guinea here to day. At Petersburg 26/ sh. ℔ Ct. The Corn is not more than sufficient for our own consumption. Heavy taxes, Extravagance, and dissipation; direfull prospects. The Assembly speak of Striking paper money. Whether sound policy directs the measure (if it takes place) or Sympathy for peculiar situations and circumstances directs the measure I know not nor pretend to say, but One thing is certain, it will certainly continue the delusion we are under in regard to our own Finances, and procrastinate the period when we ought and from dire necessity must live in every respect more conformable to our Situation as an infant Republick.

Have you seen or read Lord Sheffield's Pamphlett upon the Commerce of Great B. and America before, during and since the war; their Connexion and relation to one another as Commercial Countries, and with others in Europe. He seems to have been well informed upon the Subjects of which he writes and accounts to me very plainly what are the Efficient causes of Sir. R. Herries's Tobacco Contract with the Farmers General of France &c. &c. and as we manage matters here, has it more in his power perhaps to fullfill it than any man we can oppose him with as a Candidate or a competitor with him, on equal terms, in that business. Pardon (if you please Sir) this crude congestion of Ideas and Expressions as here wrote down; my entire Confidence in your lenity to my Ignorance in political matters and the politeness and friendship

I have invariably experienced at your hand, have led me on to be thus prolix tho desultory. Here I'll drop the matter.

In regard to myself the less I say perhaps the better. Having recovered from a dangerous illness last year I began the Old Routine of medical drudgery, only contracting my distant rides to shorter spaces. I have fallen into the rage for building houses, which has prevailed here. Among other houses of wood, I have built one of Brick, with 26 apartments, including Kitchen and Cellar under one roof, from which I expect to reap some profit. It is intended for a large Inn or Tavern; your friend Mr. D. Ross and myself have lately purchased ⅔ds. of the late Mr. DuVals Coal Pitts, North and South of Jas. River, and intend to begin to Work them the ensuing Xmas; if found to answer Our Expectations upon trial will continue to work them to some Extent. I now begin to wish, we Would burn our Own Coal in preference to that Imported and use our Own Iron Work, and manufactures of every kind, that our Situation allows us to make, in preference to that for which we are obliged to pay foreigners for, who send the Circulating medium to other Countries. Interest and Policy go hand and hand in this, with I must Confess—enough of this.

Your friends at Eppington and elsewhere in this country are all well as far as I know. I hope and very sincerely wish your Own health and Spirits have returned to you and that ere long, unless your interest and inclination forbid it, to have the pleasure to see you in this Country. Be that as it will or may I beg to have the honor of a letter from you as often as agreeable to yourself. It will always give me much pleasure to hear from you and of your wellfare. I hope [the t]erms of seeming freedom which runs thro this letter from a man in so obscure life as I am to a Character in so a deservedly elevated situation as your Excellency now stands, will be taken in good part and as it is really meant, being wrote in the openess and unreservedness of my heart as from one friend to another, forgetting the Dissimilarity of our stations &c. &c. in life altogether. Buchanan or Hay will write you by this Opportunity. D. Ross spoke of it, but is now up the Country. I beg leave to conclude this epistle with tenders of my best Respects to Miss Jefferson, and friendly regards to Mr. Short (to whom I intend writing a few lines) and with assurances to you Sir that it will ever afford me real pleasure to render you any Service in my power or attend to the smallest of your commands here or elsewhere; and that nothing which concerns you in any respect whatever is to me a matter of indifference.

I have the honor to Subscribe myself Your Excellency's most devoted and Obdt. H. Serv.,   JAMES CURRIE

Octr. 20th. 1785

P.S. Since writing the within, I recollect the publication in our paper was extracted from that of Maryland and did not originate here; therefore it is not a child of ours (I mean communication of Sir R. Herries's Tobacco Contract) and was further informed yesterday at Petersburg that Mssrs. Morris and Alexander have obtained it and Sir R. H.'s proposals were not accepted. Mr. Ross is now with me and intends doing himself the honor of writing your Excellency by this opportunity.   J CURRIE

RC (DLC); endorsed. Recorded in SJL as received 19 Jan. 1786, "by Mr. Littlepage." A letter from Currie to Short, 17 Oct. 1785, was enclosed in this (DLC: Short Papers).

I EXPECT MUNROE AND HARDY SOON: Samuel Hardy died on the day that Currie wrote these words.

From Archibald Stuart

DR. SIR   Richmond Octr. 17th. 1785

This is the third Letter which I have written to you since Your Departure from America, and I ascribe the silence which you have observed to the Accidents to which Letters in so long a passage are liable or to Your attentions to the Affairs of the publick.

I have already given you all the News even the most minute occurrences in the neighbourhood of Monticello and at present the subject seems exhausted.—I shall with pleasure now inform you that the companies under the "Acts for improveing and extending the navigation of James and Potowmack Rivers" have more than compleated the Subscriptions for that purpose. They were not authorized to exceed the sum of one hundred thousand dollars for each River. The Potowmack Company had their subscriptions first compleated and have at present upwards of one hundred hands employed in blowing Rocks &c. The James River Company have advertised their Intentions of letting the Business to proper undertakers who I am afraid cannot be had. Commissioners have been appointed to survey these Rivers and make Report how far they may be made navigable, at what expence, and how near this navigation will approach to the navigation of the Western Waters.

The Commissioners for James River have made a favorable report. They are of Opinion that the River may be rendered navigable One hundred miles beyond the Great Mountain to the mouth of Dunlaps Creek and that a good waggon Road may be had from thence to Meadow Creek which Runs into the Kanhawa below the great falls and that the portage by land will be about sixty miles. In consequence of these Prospects Lands on the River and those adjacent have risen fifty percent in their Value.

About twelve months past Specie was so plenty in this State that some merchants were of Opinion that commerce might be injured by it. At present it has almost disappeared, whether it is that our Imports exceed in value our Exports or that the price of Tobacco has been so high as to make it necessary for the Merchants to make remittances in Specie Or whatever may be the Cause I am afraid it will be difficult to collect the Revenue of the ensuing Year. It is certain that Extravagance and dissipation has seized all Ranks of People. It has become fashionable to import even Hay from the Northern States and Coffins from Europe. Coal, Iron and Castings are imported which ought if encouraged to be articles of Export shortly. Our assembly sits but Once in the Year and this is the first day in the Session for the Present year. As I am still a member I shall attempt some Regulations on the Last subject which I have mentioned, instead of emitting paper money which Our politicians from mistaking the Ground of our complaints will propose.

The Revenue last year was punctually collected and amounted to three hundred thousand pounds by which means it was in Our power to discharge fifty thousand pounds of the principal of Our national Debt. Great uniformity in Our finances has been observed for two years past and Publick credit is rising very fast, and would continue so to do were it not for the Apprehensions of paper money and the changeableness of Our Assembly. Competitions for seats in the house run higher than ever they Did under the Old government. The people begin to feel their power and I am afraid have not wisdom enough to make a proper use of it, and we are able to draw but little aid from the Senate. That Body continues to be contemptible in point of Capacity. They have not sufficient confidence in themselves to Oppose the voice of the Delegates upon any Occasion. I entertain sanguine hopes of Placing Our friend Madison in the Chair this Session. It is surely the just reward of his merit and ability. These qualifications have rendered him almost absolute in the House of Delegates. Although I am an Enemy to absolute Governments generally speaking, yet I cheerfully submit to his Authority and admire him as One of the brightest Ornaments of this Country.

He had influence enough last Octr. session to Pass a Bill which you and Mr. Pendleton formerly Drew Establishing Courts of Assize which is certainly a Capital improvement in the Jurisprudence of this Country. County court clerks and attorneys, magistrates and Debtors are all Opposed to the Measure but I am in hopes it will remain unshaken. It is to take place in Feby. next. A separation Betwixt the eastern and western parts of this state will be Proposed this Assembly and will certainly take place as far as depends upon the Assembly. I am told the western People wish to be admitted into the fœderal Government in which I think them very unwise. The Interests of that Country and the Atlantick States Will certainly interfere. Independant of the Atlantick States they may in time pursue their Interest in Opposition to the Present claim of Spain and from their situation remain secure from the United efforts of Spain and her colonies. This they will not be permitted to do if the Atlantick States are responsible for their Conduct, who by the Bye are interested in locking up the Mississippi from those people. Spain can chastise the Atlantick States with a few vessels While the Best appointed Army I am told (unless they had a passport through this Country) could never Reach the falls of Ohio.

I was informed yesterday evening that Proposals would be made to the Farmers general of France By David Ross, Thos. Pleasants, and Nelson, Heron and Co., One of the best established houses in Virga., to supply them with Tobacco Directly from this State upon better terms than they can procure it at present. They wish the Business should be carried on in American and french Bottoms only. The Americans and french appear to be an infatuated people to allow the British to interfere in that Trade which they cannot have the smallest claim to. Ross and Pleasants you know to be upright and valuable Citizens and I will take the liberty to inform you that Alexr. Nelson who is at the Head of his house is a man of unsullied Reputation and perhaps in point of capacity for Business is inferior to no man Except Ross. If you could promote this Application you would serve three worthy Characters, and your Country at large.

My Dear Sir you must Excuse the effects of haste which are

discoverable in this letter as I have scarcely time to read it over, being obliged to attend to a Cause to Day in the General Court.

Pray make my Compliments to Miss Patsey and Mr. Short who are my only acquaintances in France and be assured that I am with great sincerity Yr. most Obt. H. Sevt.,   ARCHD. STUART

RC (DLC); endorsed. Recorded in SJL as received 23 Jan. 1786. Stuart's two other letters WRITTEN . . . SINCE YOUR DEPARTURE FROM AMERICA have not been found and may have been intercepted.

To John Adams

DEAR SIR   Paris Oct. 18. 1785.

Your letter of the 10th. came safely to hand and I delivered the one therein inclosed to Mr. Grand. It was a duplicate of one he had before received. You will have heard of the safe arrival of Doctr. Franklin in America. Strange we do not hear of that of Otto and Doradour. If you know of the safe arrival of the packet in which they went, pray communicate it to me, as Madame de Doradour, who is ill in Auvergne, is greatly uneasy for her husband. Our dispatches to the Westward are all gone. Those to the Southward will go this week. This goes by post which will account for it's laconicism. I must however add my respects to the ladies and assurances to yourself of the esteem with which I am Dear Sir Your most obedient humble servt.,   TH: JEFFERSON

RC (MHi: AMT); endorsed in part: "Answered 1 Nov. 1785." PrC (DLC). TJ's entry in SJL under 16 Oct. 1785 probably refers to this letter.

From Borgnis Desbordes, Frères

[18? Oct. 1785.] They acknowledge TJ's letter of 12 Oct. and will be happy to serve him. His letter has been forwarded to J. Diot & Cie. at Morlaix, who live not far from St. Pol de Léon. Desbordes have asked Diot & Cie. to inform themselves completely of the situation of Lister Asquith and the other prisoners "pour les déffandre avec tout Le zele possible" and to give Asquith TJ's letter and all the help he had prescribed. Diot & Cie. will keep TJ informed and advise him. Desbordes ask TJ to communicate the next time in French.

RC (DLC); 2 p.; in French; undated; endorsed: "Desbordes." Recorded in SJL as received on 25 Oct. 1785 (see Asquith to TJ, 23 Oct. 1785).

From James Buchanan and William Hay

Your favour of the 15th. June came duely to hand, and we return you our warmest acknowledgements for undertaking in so obliging a manner to aid the Directors of the public buildings in procuring plans and estimates.

Your ideas upon the subject are perfectly corresponding to those of the Directors, respecting the stile and Ornaments proper for such a work, and we trust the plans will be designed in conformity thereto. We are sorry we did not sollicit your aid in the business at an earlier day, for, from the anxiety of the Public to have the work begun, we have been obliged to carry it on so far, that we may be embarrassed when we are favoured with a more perfect plan from you. As we expect to hear from you, and perhaps receive the plans before this can reach you, we deem it proper to inform you what has been done, that you may judge how far we shall be able to adopt the plan you transmit us. The foundation of the Capitol is laid, of the following demensions, 148 by 118 feet, in which are about 400M bricks; the Center of the building of 75 by 35 to be lighted from above, is designed for the Delegates; the rest is divided in such a manner as to answer every purpose directed by the Assembly; the foundation of the four porticos are not laid, tho' the end and side walls are contrived to receive them. The present plan differs from the One transmitted you, only in the arrangement, and we hope we shall be able to avail ourselves of your assistance without incurring much expence. As we are fully satisfied no expence unnecessarily will be imposed through you, we will chearfully answer your draught for the amount. We have the Honor to be with great respect Sir Your most Obedt. Servants,

JAMES BUCHANAN
WM. HAY

RC (DLC); in Buchanan's hand, signed by him and Hay; endorsed: "Hay. Wm." Recorded in sjl as received 19 Jan. 1786 from "Hay Wm. . . . by Mr. Littlepage."

To William Carmichael

Your favour of the 29. Sep. came safely to hand: the constant expectation of the departure of the persons whom I formerly gave you reason to expect has prevented my writing as it has done yours. They will probably leave this in a week, but their route will be circuitous and attended with delays. Between the middle and last of November they may be with you. By them you will receive a cypher by which you may communicate with Mr. Adams and my self. I should have sent it by Baron Dreyer the Danish minister, but I then expected our own conveyance would have been quicker. Having mentioned this gentleman, give me leave to recommend him to your acquaintance. He is plain, sensible and open: he speaks English well, and had he been to remain here I should have cultivated his acquaintance much. Be so good as to present me very respectfully to him. This being to go by post I shall only add the few articles of general American news by the last packet. Doctr. Franklin arrived in good health at Philadelphia the 15th. ult., and was received amidst the acclamations of an immense crowd. No late event has produced greater demonstrations of joy. It is doubted whether Congress will adjourn this summer; but they are so thin they do not undertake important business. Our Western posts in statu quo.

I have the honour to be, with great esteem, dear Sir, your friend and servant, TH: JEFFERSON

PrC (DLC); MS is considerably faded; about thirty illegible or missing words have been verified or supplied from text in TJR, I, 347-8.

From Madame d'Houdetot

SIR   Sanoy [Sannois] 18th. Octre. 1785

I am Greatly Indebted to you for Your Polite attention in Sending me so early the News of our Dear and Venerable Doctor's happy and safe arrival in his own country. He is become Respectable To all Nations and Peculiarly dear to his own, as well as To his Numerous Friends and acquaintances. You have Reliev'd me from a Great Load of uneasiness, and afforded me at the Same Time a most heartfelt Joy. Your Elegant account of the Reception he has meet with at Phia. has Moved me unto Tears.

Antiquity Itself do not afford a more pleasing Spectacle. This happy event seems to Justify a Super Intending Providence, which hath Crowned Virtue with a most Valuable Reward. As long as I live I shall unite the homage I owe this Great man, To that of the Two Continents. His Knowledge has been Immensely usefull To both, and his Virtue Singularly so To his own. We are Now Waiting for another Spectacle, which will not be less Interesting. I Mean the Meeting of the Doctor with Your Great and Immortal Washington. May those Two Great Men, the admiration of Future Ages, the Pride of our own, contribute To Crown that Work, To the completion of which they have so much Contributed; may they have Wisdom and Influence Enough to Prop and Consolidate your New Legislations and Permanently Establish the Seeds of that union without which Your States can be neither happy nor Lasting.

You'll Easily Forgive me those Sentiments when You Reflect on the Peculiar Esteem and admiration I have for those Two Great Men, on my Particular and unfeign'd Love for Doctor Franklin, on my Sincere attachement for the American Nation, become so Interesting in our days.

Accept the Respect & Esteem where with I subscribe myself Sir Your Very Humble Servt.,

SOPHIE DE LALIVE CTESE D'HOUDETOT

When will you Come to Sanoy again. I shall Expect you the first fair day with Col. Humphreys.

RC (DLC); at foot of first page: "His Excellency Thos. Jefferson Esqr." Recorded in SJL as received 19 Oct. 1785.

The FIRST FAIR DAY was evidently Sunday, 23 Oct., for TJ's Account Book shows that on that day he "lost at lotto at Sanois 18s."

From David Ross and Other Virginia Merchants

SIR   Richmond, the 18th. October 1785

His Excellency Governour Henry, having been pleased to communicate to us, an extract from your Letter to him, in respect to Supplying the Farmers-General of France with a quantity of Tobacco immediately from this State, and requested our Sentiments thereon; we have informed him that we believe no Merchants of Credit here, would at present enter into a Contract, as the fluctuating prices of Tobacco since peace, would make such a Contract very Hazardous, and Might be Injurious to one, or the other of the Contracting parties, and therefore it would be More eligible for them to obtain their supplies by a purchase on Commission, untill the trade became more settled; and we have taken the Liberty of offering our Services for that purpose. As you are well acquainted with our Situation, as also with our General Knowledge of the Country, and experience in its Commerce, so you are a proper Judge of our abilities to transact this business, and we would fain hope that you will render us such Services therein as may be in your power. And here it may not be amiss to observe that Norfolk from its Central and Convenient Situation to the Great Rivers of the Chesapeak, will be the proper place for shipping the greater part of the Tobacco, and in order to give proper efficacy and despatch to this business one of us would reside there, while the others would take such stations upon the Several Rivers as would give us every possible advantage in purchasing the Tobacco, and in procuring an exit for the Manufactures of France. If this business was principally Committed to us, we would Immediately erect Warehouses at Norfolk to contain fifteen hundred hhds. of Tobacco with a Wharf, on long side of which a ship of any burthen Might load, which would give Such despatch to the business, that it would greatly lessen the freights of the Tobacco.

Tho' we have for the above reasons declined to make any overtures towards a Contract, yet, if you should find that the Farmers prefer obtaining their supplies by Contract, we should be glad to be fully informed thereof and the prices that they would probably give, as when the Trade has acquired more Solidity it might be equally agreeable to enter into such engagements with them.

We have the Honour to be With great Respect, Your obliged, & Most ob Hble Sts.,

DAVID ROSS

NELSON, HERON, & CO.

THOMAS PLEASANTS JR.

RC (ViWC); in Ross' hand. Recorded in SJL as received 19 Jan. 1786 "by Mr. Littlepage."

The EXTRACT FROM YOUR LETTER that Henry communicated to Ross and his associates was from that of 16 June 1785 and its enclosure; see Henry to TJ, 10 Sep. 1785. On 18 Oct. Ross and his group wrote to Henry, thanked him for communicating the information from TJ, acknowledged that it would be more to the advantage of both countries that "the Tobacco should go immediately from the place of its growth, than that it should be procured thro' any other, more circuitous channel," but stated that "in the present Situation of the trade of this Country, it would be difficult, perhaps Impracticable, for any Merchants here to enter into an extensive Contract for this article, and give such Guarantee for its performance as would be required. Indeed, while the trade Continues so unsettled, such a Contract would be very hazardous, and might be very prejudicial, to one or the other of the Contracting parties, and therefore untill the trade becomes more settled, and a proper Confidence Established between the two Countries, it will perhaps be better for the Farmers General to purchase the Tobacco here upon Commission, which we would gladly undertake, and being well known to your Excellency, and no Strangers to Mr. Jefferson, you will be Competent Judges of our ability to transact the business.—Having no Correspondents in France, and it being as we Conceive improper to communicate the Subject to any Merchants of G Britain, whose interest it is to Counteract the Measure, we Could not give that assurance in Europe, which the Farmers General might perhaps require, but we could give to the Consul General of France, or to the Ambassadour from that Court, undoubted Security here for a full and faithful performance of the trusts Committed to us.—The following are among the advantages that would result from the Farmers General making their purchases here: it would open an immediate intercourse between the two Countries, and the Ships Necessarily employed in Carrying the Tobacco, will afford an opportunity of Importing the Manufactures of France at a very Moderate freight, at the same time that the bills drawn for the Tobacco, would facilitate the remittances; which are Circumstances that would greatly Contribute to encourage the Consumption of French Manufactures in this Country, and it would give to French, and American Ships the Exclusive right of Carrying this Valuable article of Commerce to market, which would greatly tend to Strengthen the Union and Friendship between the two Countries" (Ross, Nelson, Heron & Co., and Pleasants to Henry, 18 Oct. 1785; ViWC).

In this letter Ross and his group transmitted to Henry the conditions upon which they would be willing to undertake the business, requesting that, if these conditions met Henry's approval, he "transmit them to Mr. Jefferson, with such observations thereon, as you may think proper, in order that they may be laid before the Farmers General." The proposals, signed by Ross, Nelson, Heron & Co., and Pleasants at Richmond on the same day, read as follows: "We the subscribers, Merchants in Virginia, will undertake to purchase annually, on the lowest terms at the different Markets in this State and Maryland, any quantity and quality of Tobacco that the Farmers General of France think proper to Order; and ship it for such Ports in France as they may direct, on the most moderate Freight and charges, at a Commission of two and a half ₩ Cent. for our trouble.—And to enable us to take advantage of the proper seasons for the purchase of Tobacco, it will be necessary that the Farmers General make an advance of Money; we wou'd therefore require a Credit upon which we might draw for the Amount of one fifth part of the Annual order; and

after each shipment, that we have liberty to draw for the amount of such shipment, (Bills of Loading going before, or accompanying advice thereof) to enable us to prepare for the next ships without incurring the expence of Demurage.—And to facilitate the negociation of our Bills, it will be necessary that the above Credit be Lodged in good Banking Houses in London, Amsterdam, and Paris, and that it may be optional in us to draw on either we may find most convenient.—Seperate Invoices of the Tobacco, with the cost and charges of the Cargo shall be furnished by each ship; and on fulfilling each Order or once in every Year, a fair and regular state of the whole transactions shall be laid before the Farmers General for their Inspection.—Actuated by a desire of promoting the Intrest of both countries, and as much as in our power, encouraging a commercial intercourse between them, on terms of Mutual advantage, we wou'd farther propose that this business be confined to French and American ships; and we will to the utmost of our power, encourage and facilitate the Importation of the Produce and Manufactures of France, by return of these ships.—Shou'd the above propositions be acceptable to the Farmers General, they will please signify their acquiescence, with the time they wish this business to commence, to his Excellency Thomas Jefferson Esqr. who will do us the honor to receive and forward the same to Governor Henry for us; and we are ready to give the Consul of France, or any person the Farmers General may appoint, such Guarantee in America as they may deem necessary, for the true and faithful performance of what we undertake" (in Ross' hand; endorsed by TJ; MS in ViWC).

This proposal was forwarded to TJ by Patrick Henry, but there is uncertainty as to the date of the covering letter. In his reply to Henry of 24 Jan. 1786, TJ acknowledged Henry's of 14 Oct. 1785, and in SJL under date of 19 Jan. 1786 TJ also recorded a letter from Henry of 14 Oct. No such letter has been found, and none of that date is recorded in the Executive Letter Book in Vi. See also Ross to TJ, 22 Oct. and Pleasants to TJ, 24 Oct. 1785. It is probable that Henry's letter was dated 19 or 24 and that TJ misread it; certainly, as a covering letter for proposals dated 18 Oct., it could not have been written on 14 Oct. In any case, Henry's covering letter, whatever its date, has not been found.

See Short to TJ, 7 Aug. 1786, in which he reported that Ross' "Credit here [London] is absolutely wrecked, his Debts selling at a considerable Discount and in the Hands of Trustees."

From Abigail Adams

DEAR SIR   London October 19 1785

Mr. Fox a young gentleman from Philadelphia who came recommended by Dr. Rush to Mr. Adams, will have the Honour of delivering you this Letter. We requested him to call upon Mr. Stockdale for your papers &c.

Mr. Adams is unwell, and will not be able to write you by this opportunity. I am to acquaint you sir that Dr. Price has transacted the business respecting Mr. Hudon. The Money is paid, but the policy is not quite ready but the Doctor has promised that it shall be sent in a few days, when it will be forwarded to you.

In your English papers you will find an extract of a Letter from Nova Scotia, representing the abuse said to be received by a Captain Stanhope at Boston, the commander of the Mercury. The account is as false—if it was not too rough a term for a Lady to use, I would say false as Hell, but I will substitute, one not less expresive and say, false as the English.

The real fact is this. One Jesse Dumbar, a native of Massachusetts, and an inhabitant of a Town near Boston and one Isaac Lorthrope were during the War taken prisoners and from one ship to an other were finally turnd over to this Captain Stanhope, commander of the Mercury, who abused him and the rest of the prisoners, frequently whiping them and calling them Rebels. The ship going to Antigua to refit, he put all the prisoners into Jail and orderd poor Jesse a dozen lashes for refusing duty on Board his ship. This Mr. Dumbar felt as an indignity and contrary to the Law of Nations. Peace soon taking place Jesse returnd Home, but when Stanhope came to Boston, it quickened Jesses remembrance and he with his fellow sufferer went to Boston and according to his deposition, hearing that Captain Stanhope was walking on the Mall, he went theither at noon day and going up to the Captain asked him if he knew him, and rememberd whiping him on Board his ship. Having no weapon in his hand, he struck at him with his fist, upon which Captain Stanhope stept back and drew his sword. The people immediately interposed and gaurded Stanhope to Mr.

Mortens door, Dumbar and his comrade following him, and at Mr. Mortens door he again attempted to seize him, but then the high sheriff interposed and prevented further mischief, after which they all went to their several homes. This Mr. Stanhope calls assassination and complains that the *News papers* abuse him. He wrote a Letter to the Govenour demanding protection. The Govenour replied by telling him that if he had been injured the Law was open to him and would redress him upon which he wrote a very impudent abusive Letter to Mr. Bowdoin, so much so that Mr. Bowdoin thought proper to lay the whole correspondence before Congress, and Congress past some resolves in consequence and have transmitted them with copies of the Letters to be laid before Mr. Stanhopes master.

Dumbars Deposition was comunicated in a private Letter by Mr. Bowdoin himself to Mr. Adams, so that no publick use can be made of it, but the Govenour was sensible that without it the Truth would not be known.

Is Col. Smith in Paris? Or have we lost him? Or is he so mortified at the king of Prussias refusing him admittance to his Reviews, that he cannot shew himself here again? This is an other English Truth, which they are industriously Circulating. I have had, however, the pleasure of contradicting the story in the most positive terms, as Col. Smith had enclosed us the copy of his own Letter and the answer of his Majesty, which was written with his own hand. How mean and contemptable does this Nation render itself?

Col. Franks I hope had the good fortune to carry your things safely to you, and that they will prove so agreeable as to induce you to honour again with your commands Your Friend & Humble Servant,   ABIGAIL ADAMS

Compliments to the Gentlemen of your family and love to Miss Jefferson. Mr. Rutledge has refused going to Holland. I fancy foreign embassies upon the present terms are no very tempting objects.

RC (DLC); addressed: "His Excellency Thomas Jefferson Esqr. Minister Plenipotentiary from the United States of America. Paris—favour'd by Mr. Fox"; endorsed. Recorded in SJL as received 1 Nov. 1785.

On Samuel FOX, see Rush to TJ, 16 June 1785. The resolves PAST BY CONGRESS, together with the correspondence between Captain Stanhope of the *Mercury* and Gov. Bowdoin, are printed in JCC, XXIX, 637-41. See TJ's account of the Stanhope affair, printed under 1 Nov. 1785. Copies of Smith's OWN LETTER AND THE ANSWER OF HIS MAJESTY were enclosed in his to Adams, Berlin, 5 Sep. 1785; the answer of Frederick the Great giving Smith permission to attend the manoeuvres is dated 4 Sep.

From Nicolas & Jacob van Staphorst

Amsterdam 20 October 1785

We are honored by Your Excellency's ever respected Favor of 12 Instant, obliging us much by your useful Information and your Readiness to serve us. We request Your Excellency to be assured We entertain a high Sense of Your Condesendsion, And shall ever esteem ourselves happy to evince it all in our Power.

His Excellency John Adams Esqr. has already transmitted to Messrs. W. & J. Willink and ourselves, an attested Copy of the Resolve of Congress of 15 February last, appropriating a Sum not exceeding Eighty Thousand Dollars out of the Loans borrowed in Holland or from any other Monies belonging to the United States, to the Disposal of the Ministers of the United States in Europe, vested with Powers to form Treaties with the Barbary States; In consequence of which We hold said Amount subject to the Orders of His Excellency John Adams Esqr. Which we are pleased to find is conformable to Your Excellency's desire, And we beg leave to congratulate You sincerely on the Prospect of an Arrangement essentially necessary to the Prosperity of the Commerce of America, to which we are unalterably attached.

The Assignees of the Estate of Messrs. De la Lande and Fynje have closed with Mr. Daniel Parker, for his Assumption of the remaining Property in America of Geyer, De la Lande and Fynje, payable by a Security in Funds of the United States denominated the Liquidated Debt, The Nature of which may be learned by the Resolve of Congress of 27 April 1784 Upon Resumption of the Consideration of the Report of the Grand Committee appointed to prepare and report to Congress, the Arrears of Interest on the National Debt, together with the Expences of the Year 1784, from the First to the last day thereof inclusive, And a Requisition of Money on the States for discharging the same; We entreat Your Excellency's Reference to the above Resolve and Consequent Opinion upon that species of Debts of the United States denominated therein the Liquidated Debt, Which will be an additional Favor conferred on those, Who have the Honor to be with utmost Respect Your Excellency's Most Obedient and very humble Servants,   NIC: & JACOB VAN STAPHORST

RC (DLC); in a clerk's hand, with the signature of the firm; addressed: "A Son Excellence Thomas Jefferson Ecuyer Ministre Plenipotentiaire des Etats-Unis de l'Amerique auprès de Sa Majesté Tres Chretienne à Paris"; endorsed. Recorded in SJL as received 24 Oct. 1785.

The RESOLVE OF CONGRESS OF 15 FEBRUARY LAST was, of course, that of 14 Feb. 1785 (JCC, XXVIII, 65-6). Adams had written W. & J. Willink and N. & J. van Staphorst on 6 Oct.: "On the other leaf of this sheet you have copy of a resolution of Congress. . . . Please hold this money in readiness to be transmitted to London as I shall have occasion for it to pay bills of exchange to be drawn upon me which I shall accept payable at the house of Messrs. C. and R. Pullen in London or at your firm in Amsterdam as occasion may be. I shall have time to give you advice from time to time, as the bills will be drawn at one or two usances marked and double underscored 'secret and confidential' " (MHi: AMT).

To Vergennes

SIR   Paris Oct. 21. 1785.

I have the honour of inclosing to your Excellency a report[1] of the voiage of an American ship, the first which has gone to China. The circumstance which induces Congress to direct this communication is the very friendly conduct of the Consul of his Majesty at Macao, and of the Commanders and other officers of the French vessels in those seas. It has been with singular satisfaction that Congress have seen these added to the many other proofs of the cordiality of this nation towards our citizens. It is the more pleasing when it appears in the officers of government because it is then viewed as an emanation of the spirit of the government. It would be an additional gratification to Congress, in this particular instance, should any occasion arise of notifying those officers that their conduct has been justly represented to your Excellency on the part of the United States, and has met your approbation. Nothing will be wanting on our part to foster corresponding dispositions in our citizens, and we hope that proofs of their actual existence have appeared and will appear whenever occasion shall offer. A sincere affection between the two people is the broadest basis on which their peace can be built.

It will always be among the most pleasing functions of my office when I am made the channel of communicating the friendly sentiments of the two governments. It is additionally so as it gives me an opportunity of assuring your Excellency of the high respect and esteem with which I have the honour to be your Excellency's most obedient and most humble servant,   TH: JEFFERSON

RC (Arch. Aff. Etr., Corr. Pol., E.-U., XXX; endorsed at head of text: "M. De R[ayneval]"; accompanied by a French translation endorsed at head of text: "Envoyé copie de cette Lettre et de la pièce y jointe à M. le Maal. de Castries le 8. 9bre. 1785." PrC (DLC); MS faded; date later incorrectly restored by TJ as: "Oct. 11. 1785." Tr (DNA: PCC, No. 87, I, and No. 107, I); in Short's hand, similarly misdated. The entry in SJL under 11 Oct. 1785 is also evidently a misdated reference to the present letter. Enclosure: Samuel

Shaw to Jay, 19 May 1785 (Arch. Aff. Etr., Corr. Pol., E.-U., xxx; endorsed at head of text: "Joint à la lettre de M. Jefferson du 21. 8bre. 1785"). See Jay to TJ, 14 Sep. 1785.

Jay had recommended that Shaw's account of the *Empress of China* be transmitted to TJ with instructions "to express to the french Minister the Sense which Congress entertain of the friendly Offices and Civilities shewn by the french Officers . . . to that american Ship; to request the Favor of him to signify the same to them and to assure his most Christian Majesty that the People of the United States will on their part be happy in Opportunities of acknowledging these pleasing Acts of Kindness, and of cultivating and continuing the same spirit of Friend-

ship, which has hitherto so happily subsisted between the two Nations" (Jay to president of Congress, 1 Sep. 1785; JCC, XXIX, 673-4). An account of the voyage of the *Empress of China* had appeared in the *Mercure de France*, 30 July 1785. Shaw's letter is printed in *Dipl. Corr., 1783-89*, III, 761-5. In DLC: TJ Papers, 14: 2464 there is a copy of *The New-York Daily Advertiser* for 2 Sep. 1785 which includes Shaw's letter in full, prefaced by comments on Shaw's service in the American Revolution; this text has a few corrections in TJ's hand, presumably made after a comparison with the text sent by Jay.

1 This word is keyed to a marginal note in RC which reads: "du 19 Mai."

To D'Aranda

SIR   Paris October 22. 1785.

The friendly dispositions which the court of Madrid have been pleased to shew towards us in our affairs relative to the Barbary powers induce me to trouble you with an application on that subject. We are about sending persons to Marocco and Algiers to form arrangements with those powers. They will go by the way of Madrid. I ask the favour of your Excellency's passports for them. It would increase their value much if they could protect those persons from having their baggage searched. The one going to Marocco takes with him about a thousand guineas worth of watches, rings, and other things of that nature: he who goes to Algiers takes about a fourth of that value. I pledge myself that these, with their necessary clothes will constitute the whole of their baggage, and that these are neither to be sold nor left in Spain. The duties to which these things would be subject are of no consideration with us. It is to avoid the delays, the difficulties and even the losses which may accrue from the examination of small and precious things on the road. Two separate passports will be acceptable; the one for Thomas Barclay and David S. Franks and their servants, the other for John Lamb and Randall and their servants. We propose to keep these transactions as much as we can from the eyes of the public. I have the honour to be with the highest respect and esteem Your Excellency's Most obedient and most humble servant,   TH: JEFFERSON

PrC (DLC).

From D'Aranda

MONSIEUR   Paris ce 22 Octre. 1785

A la Lettre que vous m'avèz fait l'honneur de m'ecrire en datte d'aujourd'huy, j'ai celui de vous dire en réponse; que quoique je puisse donner de Passeports pour l'interieur de l'Espagne aux personnes indiquées dans votre Lettre, je n'ai cependant pas la faculté de leur en donner pour empecher la visite des èffets dont elles en seroient Chargées, qu'à coup sur seroient visitées malgre mon Passeport dans les frontieres d'Espagne. Je suis d'avis, que vous Monsieur écriviez en droiture au representant des Etats Unis à Madrid à fin qu'il demande à ma Cour les Passeports dont il est question; soyèz en bien assuré, que vû le motif elle ne les refusera pas, de même que tout ce qui peut étre agreable aux Etats Unies. Je suis reèllement peiné de ne pas me trouver à même de vous etre utile en cette occasion. Je saisirai avec empressement toutes celles qui se presenteront pour vous temoigner la parfaite Consideration avec la qu'elle j'ai l'honneur d'Etre Monsieur Votre tres hue. et très obeist. serviteur,   LE COMTE D'ARANDA

RC (DLC); in a clerk's hand, signed by D'Aranda; endorsed. Recorded in SJL as received 22 Oct. 1785.

To Ferdinand Grand

SIR   Paris Oct. 22. 1785.

You spoke to me some days ago on the subject of the bills which Mr. Barclay might have occasion to draw on Mr. Adams. I informed you they were good and would assuredly be paid. I ought to have added that a Mr. Lambe would have bills to negociate on Mr. Adams which would be drawn in the name of a Mr. Randall. These will be equally good, the whole being for the service of the United states in a matter referred to the direction of Mr. Adams and myself. I mention it at this moment because I beleive Mr. Lambe has occasion to-day to negotiate a bill of this kind of three or four hundred guineas, which I advised him to offer to you. I have the honour to be with much esteem Sir Your most obedient humble servt.,   TH: JEFFERSON

PrC (DLC).

From David Ross

I Expect this letter will be delivered to You by Capt. Lewis Littlepage who has been here for some time on a visit to his friends. As You are not a stranger to this Young Gentleman's character and extraordinary talents it would be superflous in me to say any thing in his favour. This Country at present furnishes nothing remarkable or very interesting to strangers but to you perhaps more trivial Circumstances may not be unacceptable. After the Peace the large importations of Merchandize and the advanced prices in ready Money for our produce Created a Considerable bustle and gave an appearance of business to our several Towns on Navigations. Rents rose exceedingly which encouraged building and this place as well as many others are exceedingly increased.

At present the price of our Staple is reduced to 25/. Money much scarce and a Considerable difficulty apprehended in paying Public and private debts this Year.

Our Assembly are now met tho' not a sufficient number to make House. It is expected by some there will be a large Emission of paper money in order to pay off our Domestic Creditors and thereby stop the interest. This scheme will no doubt meet with considerable opposition. It seems to be the design of the Present members to repeal the Law passed last session for Circuit Courts. I suppose you have heard that the Kentuckey Country are about to seperate from us and form them selves into an independent State. Messrs. George Mutter and Harry Innes are just arrived from that Country as Commissioners to treat upon that business. Some parts of North Carolina have also formed themselves into a New State but they are not recognized by Congress nor have they obtain'd the Permission of the Parent State. The Kentuckey people have hitherto Conducted their measures with great Moderation and respect. The long talkt of and much wisht for improvement of the Navigation of James River and Powtmk. is actually begun under the Auspices of Genl. Washington.

Commissioners have viewd James River from Lynch's ferry upwards and in the dry weather this summer they went up with two large Canoes through the great mountain Falls to Fort Young about 120 Miles from Lynch's ferry. They say the Navigation through the Mountain will be at a small expence made as good as the Seven Islands or Goolsby's falls, and from the mountain up to Fort Young the Navigation is good. They found the distance from Fort Young to the Navigable part of Green Briar 26 miles. Their intention was to explore that river to the Great Canaway and from thence to the Rapids but the Indians having done some mischief about that time they could not procure proper hands and Canoes and Can only report from the information of others that the navigation down to the Falls of the Canaway is pretty good. Commissioners are appointed to make a similar survey of Powtmk. River but they have not yet proceeded on the business. 'Tis also in Contemplation to make a navigable Cut from Nansamund river through the dismal swamp to a place Call'd the plank bridge on a branch of Perquimans. These great improvements of such Public Utility must give You real satisfaction and I fondly hope we shall soon lay the foundation for establishing some usefull Manufactures. Whilst we continue to export the Raw produce of our soil and import almost every thing we use, we must be poor and dependent. I am sure you have many anxious thoughts for the prosperity of Your Country and I am also sure any hints you may be pleased to give to men of influence here would be attended with happy effects. A few days ago I was Consulted on Sir Robert Herries's offer of supplying the Farmers General with Tobacco. I have heard his offer was rejected and that Messrs. Morris of Philadelphia and Alexander of this place have either got the Contract or the Agency of their Purchases here. 'Tis thought probable they are fixt for the present and that the Agency of those Gentlemen may give satisfaction. Should they not, or should they divide or extend the Agency I have subscribed to some propositions that will Pass through Governor Henry to you. At the same time have little expectations that Men so little known can succede in such business.

This last season has been very unfavorable for Corn and Tobacco. There will be a real scarcity of the former. Of the latter, from the vast preparations that were made, there will after all the disasters that have happened to it be enough or too much made for the Consumption. A small black bug little known till the year 82 and 83 has entirely ruined the Crops of Wheat in the Counties south of James River untill You approach the Mountains, and flour for the use of Private families in the interior Counties is a Considerable article of Commerce at our sea Ports. I hope this troublesome insect

is on the decline. I shall only add that I am with great respect
Your Mo ob Servt.,   DAVID ROSS

RC (DLC); endorsed. Recorded in SJL as received 19 Jan. 1786, "by Mr. Littlepage." See Ross and others to TJ, 18 Oct. 1785, note.

From Lister Asquith

St. Pauls Prison Oct. 23rd. 1784 [i.e., 1785]
PLEASE YOUR EXCELLENCY SIR

I received your kind and exceptionable Letter yesterday by Mr.
Diot which gives me great Satisfaction to find he has Orders to
assist us when in such great Distress for want of Provisions, which
Favors we are not able to express our thanks for. The Circumstances that occurred since our arrival are: On our arrival in the
Isle of Bas Roads the Officers came on board and I reported to them
the Cargo we had in and immediately went on Shore with a sick
man that I expected hourly would die. And hearing one Thos.
Martin spoke English and did Business, applyed to him and he
went with me to Mr. Picrels, but as he was not at home immediately
went with me to the admiralty Office and we protested the real
state of our Case and reported to him the Vessel by the Register.
But he told me that if she was no more than What the Register was
for she would be seized and I having the Bills of Sale of her by
me, I told him the Case and reported her by the Bill of Sale and
went to the Custom House and reported the Vessel and Cargo.
There we received a Clearance and paid him 10 Liv. 7s. for it.
The Captain General desired me to go with them on board where
they instantly Tore off the Tarpaulins, got the Keys and opened
the Hatchways and examined her, got up her anchor and Brought
her into the harbor, and set Centinels over us not to let us walk over
half the Pier. They sent for a Guager from Morlaix who measured
her hold from inside to inside and about one half her Steerage but
allowed nothing for her forecastle Cabin Cockpit and above one half
her Steerage which contain near one half the Vessel. Took the
tobacco out and weighed it 6487 lb. and the Loose Tobacco they
put in Casks which they provided for it and put it in their own
Stores and 5 Days after sent it with us to Landivisiau and weighed
it there when it had lost 84 lb. Left it there and sent us back to
St. Pauls Prison. During the time we were at Roscoff the Captain
General came almost every night to us to desire us to sign his

Papers which he was writing but as we did not understand French we always refused. We got Mr. Picrel to employ a Lawyer for us at Brest and advanced him 10 Guineas but thinking Mr. Picrel would want more help was going to employ another besides which affronted him so much that he returned us 7 Guineas, discharged his lawyer and sent to him for all the Papers back unknown to us. Keept 3 Guineas he said to pay the Lawyer but Mr. Delsal of Brest informed me that he only paid the Lawyer 11 Liv. 10 and had keept the rest. I wrote to Mr. Floch and the Judge of the Admiralty and implored they would take the Cause in hand and sent the Judge the Register, Bill of Sale, and our protest at the Admiralty Office and to Mr. Floch the Custom House Clearance and am sorry to find Mr. Floch was so ungenerous as not to let you know the State of our Cause. But as I was not able to advance him money, he had not the Humanity to write to you, being obliged to use the 3 Guineas that I keept for him for provision by reason of the small allowance and the Coldness of the Prison we are confined in. Mr. Diot has been here and as his Brother lives at Roscoff he will advance us the Money you are pleased to allow us advance weekley. As the Accounts being so small it will be perhaps Troublesome to Mess. Desbordes so that I shall draw on them once a Month for the sum. The paple on board are 4 Beside the Master and myself, Wm. Thomson born in Salem, William Neely, Carpenter Philadelphia, Robt. Andersen Baltimore, Wm. Fowler passenger Ireland who are all on board. Hope as soon as you hear the State of the Process you will use your utmost exertion to help us as soon as possible and we shall ever remain, Your most obedient & humble Servts.,   LISTER ASQUITH

RC (DLC); 4 p.; dated incorrectly "1784"; endorsed. Recorded in SJL as received 4 Nov. 1785. On 23 Oct. Asquith gave to Diot & Cie. a receipt for "Forty Eight Livres for 8 Days Pay at 1 Livres ⅌ Day each . . . in Consequence of Mr. Jeffersons Order" (DLC: TJ Papers, 14: 2673).

From James Bowdoin

SIR   Boston October 23d. 1785.

Proposals having been made by the Marquis de Lafayette for a Commercial Establishment between this Country and France; I beg Leave to recommend to your Excellency's Patronage and good Offices Mr. Nathl. Barrett, the Gentleman to whose Care the

Merchants here, Confiding in his Integrity and Judgment, have Committed the Negotiation.

The Object, the admission of American Oil into France, for their manufactures, is very important, and must if Obtained, prove extensively beneficial.

Monsr. Sangrain has suggested the Expediency of a Company for this purpose, but the State of Trade, and the usual mode of conducting it here, do not admit of such a plan.

It is Mr. Barrett's design to procure, if practicable, an Extension of the same benefits to individuals, as are offered to a Company.

If he succeeds, I apprehend the advantages would, in that case, be as great to the People and Goverment of France, as in the Way proposed.

As your attention to this business, and Influence for effecting it, may be of substantial Service to this Commonwealth, and the United States in general, I make no doubt it will give you real pleasure to have an opportunity of Exerting them for so important a purpose.

I have the honour to be, with Sentiments of the most perfect Esteem Sir, Your Excellency's Most Obedt. & very humbl. Servt.,

JAMES BOWDOIN

RC (DLC); in a clerk's hand, signed by Bowdoin. Recorded in SJL as received 6 Dec. 1785.

MONSR. SANGRAIN: Tourtille de Sangrain; concerning Sangrain and the street lighting of French cities, see Jean Bouchary, *Les Compagnies financières à Paris à la fin du XVIIIe siecle*, III, 59-77, "La Compagnie des illuminations de Paris et autres villes," Paris, 1942.

From John Adams

DEAR SIR   Grosvenor Square Octr. 24. 1785

Mr. Preston arrived here, two days ago, but had lost his Letters. I hope he had none of Consequence. He dont remember he had any for me. He tells me from you, that the Doctor is arrived at Philadelphia which I am glad to hear, and those oracles of Truth the English Newspapers tell us, he had an honourable Reception, which I should not however have doubted, if I had not any such respectable Authority for it.

The Insurance is made upon Houdons Life for Six Months from the 12 of October. I have paid Thirty two Pounds Eleven shillings Premium and Charges, which you will please to give me Credit for. I could not persuade them to look back, as they say, they never ensure but for the future and from the date of the Policy. I suppose it will be safest to keep the Receipt and Policy here, for fear of Accidents.

I begin to be uneasy about our Funds. The Draughts upon Willinks & Co. and the Expences of the Negotiations in Barbary, will exhaust the little that remains, and unless we have fresh supplies, we shall all be obliged to embark, in the first ships We can find before next March, for Want of bread. I hope you will press this subject in your Letters to America. Rutledge declines, and you will not wonder at it. I dont believe Congress will find any other Man, who will venture abroad upon the present Plan. The Doctor was lucky to get out of the Scrape, in Season. You and I shall soon wish ourselves at home too.

I have a Letter from Thulemeier, that he has received from the King a Ratification of the Treaty, and is ready to exchange it. I hope you will request of Congress a prompt Ratification on their Part, that one affair at least may be finished. I see no comfortable hopes here. We hold Conferences upon Conferences, but the Ministers either have no Plan or they button it up, closer than their Waistcoats. The thirteen States must each pass a Navigation Act, and heavy Duties upon all British Merchandizes, so as to give a clear Advantage to their own and the Manufactures of France and Germany, Prussia and Russia, or we shall be a long time weak and poor.

This will be delivered you by Dr. Rodgers a Son of Dr. Rodgers of New York a young Gentleman of Merit.

I am Sir with the greatest Esteem your Friend & Sert.,

JOHN ADAMS

RC (DLC); endorsed. FC (MHi: AMT); in the hand of Miss Abigail Adams. Recorded in SJL as received 2 Nov. 1785, "by Dr. Rogers." For the INSURANCE . . . MADE UPON HOUDONS LIFE, see the receipt for premium and charges issued on 12 Oct. 1785 by The Society for Equitable Assurances on Lives and Survivorships, reproduced in this volume. This receipt was transmitted to Adams by Dr. Richard Price, who informed him that it "Secures the Assurance of M.

Houdon's life from the day on which it is dated. The Policy itself will be ready in a few days. The whole expense being 31 guineas, Dr. Price is indebted to Mr. Adams 2 guineas" (Price to Adams, 16 Oct. 1785; MHi: AMT). PRESTON had carried TJ's letter to Adams of 11 Oct.; see Abigail Adams to TJ, 25 Oct., and Adams to TJ, 4 Nov. 1785. The LETTER FROM THULEMEIER was similar to that written by him to TJ, 11 Oct. 1785, and was dated the same day (MHi: AMT).

From William Carmichael

DEAR SIR   Madrid 24 October 1785

I have waited with much impatience to learn the Issue of the propositions your Excellency was pleased to advise me you had made to our Minister at London respecting our Affairs with the Powers of Barbary. In continual Expectation of receiving letters on this Subject, I have deferred writing. Indeed without a safer method of communicating my sentiments on this and other subjects, I must deprive myself of that confidential correspondence, which it is much my inclination as it is my Duty to entertain with those employed by congress and particularly with you who have given me more Information than I have received by Official Correspondence during the time that I have remained here Alone. On the 22d. Inst. I received the *Inclosed Letter*, which I entreat your Excellency to forward to America. I have taken every measure in my power by *insinuation* to put things in a good Train. I repeat that we may rely on the good Offices of this court, should it terminate its negotiations to its Satisfaction, which I presume will be the case Altho' the Ministers of the Northeren powers assert the Contrary. I inclose you also a circular Letter sent by his Moroccan Majesty to the European Consuls on which I shall make no Observations. The Bank of St. Charles has just published an account of their proceedings in the year 1784. As its actions make much noise in Europe I shall be glad to know the sentiments of the Parisians thereon. I find that Denmark has declined acceeding to the German Ligue of which the King of Prussia is the Cheif. But these Affairs you will know much better than Myself.

The Notification of the principles which gave rise to this Treaty (As I am Assured by the Prussian Minister) was well received by this Court. I beg your Excellency to favor me as often as possible with your Advice and to beleive me with great respect & regard Your Obliged and Most Hble. Sert.,   WM. CARMICHAEL

RC (DLC). Recorded in SJL as received 9 Nov. 1785. Enclosures (DLC): (1) Isaac Stephens to Carmichael, "American Embisendore Madrid," dated at Algiers, 15 Oct. 1785; endorsed by Carmichael: "Captn. Stephens Algiers 16th Oct. 1785 Recd. 22d. . . . Ansd. 24th." informing him that he had received Carmichael's of 22 Sep., which he "thought . . . the greatest honour Ever Don me in my Life"; he and his people, as well as Captain O'Bryen and his crew, were being well provided for; and that "the holl Number of americans hear Now is Twenty one But as the Crusers all Saild Two Days before the Counts arivel We Expect more in but God send Not for what the King Dont Take they are sold out Like horses in the West Indies and if the Spanyards make Peace it will com Very Dear to america for they must be at war with Som Nations the sooner america maks Peace I think the Easer it may be Don." (2) A copy of a circular letter from Francesco Chiappe to the consuls in Tangier, dated Morocco, 4 Sep. 1785; informing them of peace negotiations between Spain and Algiers and warning that if these negotiations should fail, Morocco would impose a blockade on the ports of Algiers, would make prizes of the vessels of any Christian nation attempting to enter such ports, and would declare war upon any nation whose vessels disregarded this warning.

From Thomas Pleasants, Jr.

SIR   Raleigh the 24th. Oct. 1785

Having been favoured with an extract from Your Letter to Governour Henry, in respect to supplying the Farmers-General of France with Tobacco, I have joined my friend Mr. David Ross, and Messrs. Nelson & Co. in an Answer thereto, which will be transmitted to you by the Governour, from which you will observe that in the present situation of the Trade and Circumstances of this Country, that we thought a Contract ineligible, and therefore proposed doing the business upon Commission.

Messrs. William Alexander & Co. appear here at present as the Agents of the Farmers General. You are acquainted with Mr. Alexander, and perhaps no Stranger to the Circumstances, but who his Connections are, or whether they purchase on Commission, or not, is uncertain.

You are also acquainted with Mr. Ross and may perhaps think that his knowledge and Experience in the Commerce of this Country, and general acquaintance with almost every man in it, better qualifies him to Conduct this business to advantage, to introduce the products and Manufactures of France into this Country and to promote a Commercial Intercourse between them, than a Stranger. If so, you will on some Suitable occasion represent the Matters to the Farmers General, and take such Measures therein, as to you may appear proper.

Tobacco is a Most Valuable article of our Commerce, and if properly Managed will be a great Source of Material Wealth. But the advantage will be lost, if the Merchants of another Country engross the Trade. In our present Infant State, it would have been temerity in us to have entered into a Contract for Tobacco. If known the Merchants of G. Britain would have Counteracted it, and from their great Resources and abilities, would in all probability have effected our Ruin. They are endeavouring to secure this branch of our Commerce to themselves. All their measures are directed to this end, and hitherto every thing has favoured their design. The proposal from Sir Robert Herries to the Farmers General, has I concieve originated with them, and the loss of One hundred thousand pounds would be of Little Consequence to them, when Compared with the great and permanent Advantages that would arise from getting the Tobacco trade into their own hands, which a Contract once obtained, would perhaps forever Secure. Every port of this Country is filled with British Goods and British Factors, which affords every excitement to Luxury and Extravagance, and unless some immediate measures are taken to check the present torrent of dissipation, and Regulate the Trade so as to place the Merchant Citizens, upon a better footing, there will not be in Virginia a Merchant unconnected with G. Britain, or a Single ship owned here, so that the whole advantages of the trade will be lost to this Country—in which Case, as an Independent people, it would better that we had no Commerce at all. But the Legislature will see the Necessity of taking up this Subject, and I hope will prohibit the Importation of many articles, impose heavy duties upon some, and encourage the Manufacture of other articles, particularly all those Necessary for the Internal security, strength, and defence of the State, and give to her Merchants some exclusive rights. In which hope I shall at present drop this Subject, and with sentiments of real Regard Remain Your friend, and Mo Ob. Hble St.,   THOMAS PLEASANTS JR.

RC (MoSHi); endorsed. Recorded in SJL as received 19 Jan. 1786, "by Mr. Littlepage." See note to Ross and others to TJ, 18 Oct. 1785.

From Richard Price

DEAR SIR   Newington Green Oct. 24th. 1785

Dr. Rogers, the bearer of this, is the Son of Dr. Rogers of New York. He has been for some time in this country studying Physick; and he intends, I find, to spend this winter at Paris with a view to farther improvement. I cannot help taking the opportunity which he offers me to convey to you a few lines to acknowledge the receipt of the letter with which I was favoured in August last, and to return you my thanks for it. The account you give of the prevailing Sentiments in the United States with respect to the Negro Slavery, and of the probability of its abolition in all the States except the *Carolinas* and *Georgia*, has comforted me much. It agrees with an account which I have had from Mr. Laurens, who at the same time tells me that in his own State he has the whole country against him. You do me much honour by the wish you express that I would address an exhortation on this Subject to the young persons under preparation for public life in the College of Willm. and Mary at Williamsburgh. But I cannot think of writing again on any political subject. What I have done in this way has been a deviation from the line of my profession to which I was drawn by the American war. Divinity and Morals will probably occupy me entirely during the remainder of a life now pretty far spent. My heart is impressed with a conviction of the importance of the Sentiments I have address'd to the united States; but I must now leave these Sentiments to make their way for themselves, and to be approved or rejected just as events and the judgments of those who may consider them shall determine. It is a very happy circumstance for *Virginia* that its young men are under the tuition of so wise and virtuous a man as you say Mr. Wythe is. Young men are the hope of every state; and nothing can be of so much consequence to a state as the principles they imbibe and the direction they are under. Able and liberal and virtuous tutors in all the colleges of America would infallibly make it in time such a seat of liberty, peace and science as I wish to see it.

I find myself very happy in the the conversation and friendship of Mr. Adams. I have lately managed for him the Assurance of Mr. Houdon's life, but of this he will himself give you an account.

I see with pain the disagreeable turn which affairs are likely to take between this country and yours. I am grieved for the prejudices by which we are governed. From an opinion of the necessity of maintaining our Navigation laws against America, and that its interest together with the weakness of the federal government will always secure the admission of our exports, we are taking the way to lose the friendship and the trade of a world rapidly increasing and to throw its whole weight into the scale of France. Such is our policy. I have given my opinion of it; but without the hope of being regarded. The United States, however, may be gainers by this policy if it puts them upon strengthening their federal government; and if also it should check their rage for trade, detach them from their slavery to foreign tinsel, and render them more independent by causing them to seek all they want within themselves.

We are, at present, much encouraged here by the rapid rise of our Stocks; and the influx of money occasioned by a turn of exchange in our favour which has hardly been ever known in an equal degree.

Accept, Sir, of the repetition of my assurances that I am with all the best wishes and particular respect, your obliged and very obedt. and humble Servt.,   RICHD: PRICE

Dr. Rogers will be made happy by any notice you may take of him.

RC (DLC). Recorded in SJL as received 2 Nov. 1785, "by Dr. Rogers."

From Abigail Adams

SIR   London october 25 1785

I should not so soon have ventured to interrupt your more important avocations by an other Scrible, having writen you a few Days since, if it was not to inform you of the loss of your Letters by Mr. Preston. He says that when he landed at Dover, he was very sick, and that he could not accompany his trunk to the custom House, into which for *Security* he had put his Letters. But upon his arrival here he found he had lost them; so that unless your Letter should contain any thing for the English newspapers I fear I shall never know its contents. The gentleman deliverd me a little bundle, by the contents of which I conjecture What you design, but must request you to repeat your orders by the first opportunity, that I may have the pleasure of punctually fulfilling them.

A Dr. Rogers from America will convey this to you with the Newspapers in which you will see the Letters I mentiond in my last between Governour Bowdoin and Captain Stanhope. Lord George Gordon appears to interest himself in behalf of his American Friends, as he stiles them, but neither his Lordships Friendship or enmity are to be coveted.

Mr. Adams writes you by this opportunity. I have directed a Letter to Mr. Williamos to be left in your care. Am very sorry to hear of his ill state of Health.

We hear nothing yet of Col. Smith, know not where he is, as we find by the Gentlemen last arrived that he is not at Paris. I am sir with Sentiments of respect & esteem Your &c,   AA

RC (DLC); endorsed: "Mrs. Adams." Recorded in SJL as received 2 Nov. 1785, "by Dr. Rogers." The LITTLE BUNDLE was evidently the shirt that TJ sent by Preston as a model of the others that he had asked Mrs. Adams to obtain for him (see TJ to Abigail Adams, 11 Oct. 1785). The LETTER TO MR. WILLIAMOS was probably carried by Rodgers; Mrs. Adams may have learned of Williamos' illness through Preston.

To William Carmichael

DEAR SIR   Paris Oct. 25. 1785.

I did myself the honour of writing to you on the 18th. inst. Since that date it has become probable that Mr. Lamb and Mr. Randall will set out for Madrid before Mr. Barclay will be ready. You will probably see them between the middle and last of November. I took the liberty of solliciting Count d'Aranda for passports for these gentlemen, which might protect their baggage from being searched. At that time I thought they would be necessary for Lamb as well as Mr. Barclay, supposing he would buy some trinkets here. But he does not. Mr. Barclay however will carry a thousand guineas worth to be given in presents at the place of his destination. Things small and precious are liable to loss on being searched on the road. Ct. d'Aranda however could not give passports which would protect from search, but advised me to write to you to try to obtain them from the court. I am therefore to pray you to ask for a passport for Mr. Thomas Barclay and Colo. David S. Franks and their servants, which may prevent their being searched. You may safely assure the minister that these gentlemen take nothing but their necessary baggage and the objects abovementioned, and that none of these will be sold or left in the kingdom. Be pleased to lodge the passport in the post office at Bayonne, directed to Mr. Barclay at Bayonne *poste restante*. I am with the greatest esteem Dear Sir Your most obedient humble servt.,   TH: JEFFERSON

PrC (DLC).

From Thomas Cushing

SIR   Boston Octobr. 25. 1785

Mr. Nathll. Barrett, A Gentleman of a very respectable Family and of good Character will deliver Your Excellency this Letter. He goes to France upon Bussiness, which the Merchants here, confiding in his wisdom and Integrity, have committed to his Care: His Excellency Governor Bowdoin having wrote you particularly upon this Subject renders it needless for me to Enlarge. Permit me, Sir, to Introduce Mr. Barrett to Your Acquaintance and to Reccommend him to your kind attention and Patronage. The Bussiness he goes upon is Important and, if he meets with Success, may be of very great Service to this Commonwealth as well as to the United

States in General. I doubt not, therefore, it will readily meet with your Countenance and Support.

I have the Honour to be with Sentiments of the greatest respect and Esteem Your most Obedient humble Servt,

THOMAS CUSHING

RC (DLC); endorsed: "Cushing Govr." Recorded in SJL as received 6 Dec. 1785.

From Francis Hopkinson

DEAR FRIEND   Philada. Octr. 25th. 1785

It is not long since I wrote to you and forwarded another Package (I think the third) of our news Papers, and at the same time sent you a Model of my last Improvement in the Harpsichord. The effect produced by furnishing an Instrument in that way is truly astonishing. I have discovered the Reason. It causes the Instrument to sound the Octave below the Tones produced by the Quill. The full Tone of the Harpsichord has never yet been drawn forth. The Quill on Account of it's Substance and the Smalness of it's Contact with the String, being only in a Point (because the Back of a Quill is a Portion of a Circle) has not been sufficient to put the String in a uniform Vibration thro'out it's whole length. It vibrates in two halves, and those halves vibrate in contrary Directions, so that the Tone produced will be only the Octave above that of the whole String. My Method draws forth the full clear and genuine Tone.

This will be delivered to you by Mr. Hudon, the Artist who came over to make a Model for a Statue of Gl. Washington. I yesterday saw the Head he has model'd of that great Man. I am charmed with it. He is certainly a most capital Artist. There is no looking at this Bust without Admiration and Delight. The noble Air, sublime Expression and faithful Likeness evince the Hand of a Master. You will be charmed with it. Mr. Hudon having executed the Purpose of his Voyage is impatient to return. I should have been happy in a further Acquaintance with him, for I not only admire the Artist but love the Man. As he had given me so much Pleasure I endeavoured to please him also in my Way. I played for him on my Harpsichord as well as I could. He was surprised at the Effect of the Instrument. I wish you would ask him what he thought of it.

This Month has brought about a Revolution in our State politics. There was a very great Struggle between the two Parties called Constitutionalists and Republicans at the late Election. The Constitutionalists are those who lately governed under the Auspices, indeed absolute Influence of George Bryan and Mr. McKean. They have been defeated and our present City members are of the Republican Party, viz. Mr. Rob. Morris, George Clymer, Ths: Fitzimmons &c. &c. I cannot enter into a Detail of the arbitrary measures of the late Administration. One of their last Manœuvres was to demolish the Bank, and they had passed a Law retracting the Charter which was to have taken Effect in March next. But I hope our State will now be governed with more Dignity and Justice.— Dr. Franklin President. I wish you would send me two double Sets of Crayons of the best kind and half a Dozen good black lead Pencils, and charge me with the Costs, which will not be great.

I have only Time to add that I am as ever Your affectionate & faithful friend, FRAS. HOPKINSON

I enclose another Model lest the former should not get to hand.

RC (DLC); endorsed. Recorded in SJL as received 30 Dec. 1785, "by Houdon." The enclosed MODEL has not been found.

From William Wenman Seward

SR. London 25th. Octr. 1785

By direction of an Associated company of Irish Merchants here, who have honour'd me with the Office of their Secretary, I am to congratulate you in their Names, on your appointment to the honourable Station you now hold under the United-states of America, at the Court of France.

It is with much concern the Gentlemen, by whose Authority I write, observe a settled determination in Great-Britain to prevent as far as possible that unrestrain'd commercial Intercourse, which they think should, (and would be beneficial to both Countries to have) subsist, between Ireland and America.

United here (tho' in a private manner) for certain purposes of general advantage to their Native Country, they find by an attention to the proceedings of the Ministry, that notwithstanding the state of the commercial propositions, (so well known) in the Irish House of Commons; the Trade, Rights, and Liberty of that country have been again attack'd, by the tenor of an Act of Parliament passed in the British Parliament, at the close of it's last Session, commonly call'd "A Tobacco Bill," the nature of which they presume you are not wholy unacquainted with.

Desirous of a correspondence with, and Trading connection between your Country and theirs, they have propos'd establishing a Company on their behalf in Ireland, to receive from America such Comodities as her Merchants may choose to export to that Country, by way of Exchange for such Articles as Ireland affords, in return.

On this Head I took the liberty of writeing (by directions as I now do) to Congress about six weeks since: and as we conceive it must be proper to acquaint you also with what has been done, and with the intelligence we receive of what is intended; I am to mention further there is good grounds to assert, that England intends equipping a Fleet, to be station'd along the Western Ocean, to intercept the Vessels (if any) which may be destin'd to Trade from America to Ireland: I speak as to American bottoms only. What pretext may be adopted for this proceeding we can not so well now determine, but many Vessels have been actualy fitted out, for this busieness.

Anxious how'er, from Public principles, that Ireland and America, should be still connected; (their Interests appearing now to require that connection) We have thought it not improper to suggest to you, how far Ostend might not be made a convenient place of security for conveying the Commerce of the two Countrys to each. And therefore we submit that point to your consideration, should you be of the same opinion with the Gentlemen for whom I write as to the Importance of Trade between your Country and theirs.

If such may be the case, they should be happy in receiving your Advice and assistance upon the occasion, and they will communicate such further information as may from time to time be requisite upon the subject. With every Apology for the liberty thus taken permit me both on their account and my own to subscribe myself with great respect Sr. Yr. most obedt. very humble Servt.,

Wm: Wenman Seward
Sec. Asso. Ir: Mer:

P.S. We have been indebted to Mrs. Wright of Cockspur street for the present opportunity of forwarding this. Any Answer or observations you may please to make in return directed to me (74 Haymarket, London) will be received with pleasure.

RC (ViWC); endorsed. Recorded in SJL as received 2 Nov. 1785. Seward's letter TO CONGRESS ABOUT SIX WEEKS SINCE was read on 24 Nov.

1785, "put under injunction of Secresy," and referred to Jay (JCC, XXIX, 885; DNA: PCC, No. 78). Jay evidently made no report on the subject. It may have been Seward's letter to Congress that William Grayson had in mind when he wrote to Monroe on 28 Nov. 1785: "There is some important foreign intelligence but which I cannot communicate without a cypher" (Burnett, *Letters of Members*, VIII, No. 289). This supposition is supported by the remark Grayson made in a letter to Madison the same day that Congress had received "not a word from Europe officially" (same, No. 290).

To Nicolas & Jacob van Staphorst

GENTLEMEN   Paris Oct. 25. 1785.

I received yesterday your favor of the 20th. inst. In order to give you the information you desire on the subject of the *Liquidated* debts of the United states, and the comparative footing on which they stand, I must observe to you that the first and great division of our federal debt is into 1. Foreign, and 2. Domestic. The Foreign debt comprehends 1. The loan from the government of Spain. 2. The loans from the government of France and from the Farmers general. 3. The loans negotiated in Holland by order of Congress. This branch of our debt stands absolutely singular: no man in the United states having ever supposed that Congress or their legislatures can in any wise modify or alter it. They justly view the United states as the one party and the lenders as the other and that the consent of both would be requisite were any modification to be proposed. But with respect to the Domestic debt, they consider Congress as representing both the borrowers and lenders, and that the modifications which have taken place in this, have been necessary to do justice between the two parties, and that they flowed properly from Congress as their mutual umpire. The Domestic debt comprehends 1. The army debt. 2. The Loan office debt. 3. The liquidated debt, and 4. the unliquidated debt. The 1st. term includes debts to the officers and souldiers for pay, bounty and subsistence. The 2d. term means monies put into the loan office of the United states. The 3d. comprehends all debts contracted by Quartermasters, Commissaries, and others duly authorised to procure supplies for the army, and which have been liquidated (that is, settled) by Commissioners appointed under the resolution of Congress of June 12. 1780. or by the officer who made the contract. The 4th. comprehends the whole mass of debts described in the preceding article which have not yet been liquidated. These are in a course of liquidation, and are passing over daily into the 3d. class. The debts of this 3d. class, that is the liquidated debt is the object of your enquiry. No time is fixed for the paiment of it, no fund as yet determined, nor any firm provision for the interest in the mean time. The consequence is that the certificates of these debts sell greatly below par. When I left America they could be bought for from 2/6 to 15/ in the pound: this difference proceeding from the circumstance of some states having provided for paying the interest on those due in their own state, which others had not. Hence an opinion had arisen with some, and propositions had even been made in the legislatures for paying off the principal of these debts with what they had cost the holder and interest on that. This opinion is far from being general, and I am of opinion will not prevail. But it is among possible events. I have been thus particular that you might be able to judge not only in the present case, but also in others, should any attempts be made to speculate in your city on these papers. It is a business in which foreigners will be in great danger of being duped. It is a science which bids defiance to the powers of reason. To understand it, a man must not only be on the spot and be perfectly possessed of all the circumstances relative to every species of these papers, but he must have that dexterity which the habit of buying and selling them alone gives. The brokers of these certificates are few in number, and any other person venturing to deal with them engages in a very unequal contest.

I have the honor to be with the highest respect, Gentlemen Your most obedient humble servant,   TH: JEFFERSON

PrC (DLC). Tr (DNA: PCC, No. 87, I); in Short's hand; docketed: "Referred 28 March 1785." Tr (DNA: PCC, No. 107, I).

From Philip Mazzei

MY VERY DEAR SIR   Paris 26 Oct. 1785 Wednesday night

Since you had said the day before yesterday that you would not go to Fontainebleau today unless the weather was good and since it rained yesterday all day without any sign of change in the near future I hoped to see you after dinner at Chaillot and I have learned with great sorrow that I shall have to leave for Holland without seeing you.

Monday evening after we parted I went to Mr. Meyer's house and took him with me to Williamos' to have him meet him. The thing went marvelously well; Williamos took great pleasure in conversing with this semi-countryman and he asked him to come back to see him. Meyer assumed the obligation to give him two écus every two days and he will begin Friday. I had given him two on Saturday as I told you and two I gave him on Monday when I went to see him with Meyer, but this evening I gave him nothing, because I learned from him himself that he has received a louis and a half from Mr. Barclay today, and that out of that sum he must pay only fifteen lire for some small purchases that he has made in the neighborhood. In addition I asked him whether he was in need and he himself replied no. As for the louis that I paid out I have an understanding with Meyer to whom your Excellency can pay it together with what additional sum he will give Williamos. On your return it will be well for you to see him and tell him to do (if you think it appropriate) as I have done, that is to give him the two écus every two days when he is in need and to give him nothing when he receives assistance from other quarters. Last night he was much better and from what I've been told the doctor hopes to bring him around.

I enclose herewith the note for the fifty louis and I am taking the liberty of taking with me the papers that you lent me which are so important to you. I take this liberty because I have great hopes of being able to have a copy made for myself in the office of the Van Staphorst brothers; because in my hand they are just as safe as if they were in your study and because I must return so soon that there is no likelihood that you could need them in the interval.

I should be much obliged to you if you would take the trouble to reply on the subject of this letter and to send me the reply *chez Messrs. Nicholas & Jacob Van Staphorst à Amsterdam.*

At my death I shall probably leave what little I shall have on me, that is, clothing, watch, &c. to those who attend me at that time. In my will, which I wish to make immediately, I shall dispose of the two lots in Richmond, of my money *in the loan office,* the military certificates, Colle, and the asses if I succeed in sending them to Virginia and in establishing title to them. My only definite and legitimate debts will probably be with the Van Staphorst brothers or with some other house which may take their place. Therefore the only trouble for my executor will be to safeguard the rights of my creditors and those to whom I shall leave the remainder, particularly against the claims of the scoundrelly Petronilla, indeed of her alone because I cannot see that any can arise from any other quarter. I should like to know if your Excellency will do me the favor to accept this responsibility in which case you would relieve me of a worry which weighs upon me. I should like to know also whether it is necessary to mention in the will the power of attorney given to Ed. Randolph and Mr. Blair or whether the said power of attorney ceases with my life.

I should very much like you to have the kindness to put in writing for me the formula for making a second mortgage in such a way that I may be sure of avoiding mistakes which might prejudice my creditors when my soul is dead and my body dissolved.

To avoid my wife's being entitled to half of the money in the Virginia bonds, or the military certificates, could I not mortgage the interest for a given sum or for a certain number of years to those persons to whom I should want to leave it?

If you will be kind enough to reply to me concerning everything, you will do me the greatest favor; and I now pass to a subject about which it would not be well to reply in writing.

After my return to Virginia I came to know better than I had known before that being born in a foreign country and not being wealthy tend to exclude one from those occupations reputed to be honorable and in which the zealous and active citizen can be useful to his country even though he have but mediocre ability. The persuasion that I could be useful, the desire to be so, my active nature and that sort of ambition which to me seems praiseworthy, do not permit me to see myself neglected without grave and continuous unhappiness. Men cannot change themselves as regards their innermost feelings even though they may be the absolute masters of their actions. If I could render some service in Europe so as to become honorably known in America the scene would doubtless change; and I am convinced that your Excellency and Mr. Adams could without difficulty open the path for me to do so if you would write what you know of me concerning my zeal (not for the trees or the rivers or for the land of America but for the asylum of liberty), the confidence that may be had concerning my honesty, about my connections which are perhaps still a great support for success in business, and of my knowledge of the world, particularly of those quarters where our wise compatriots probably would have need of charting a new course. I do not think it would be indelicate to mention to Mr. Adams, when you write to him about other matters, my desires and hopes, and to ask him for his opinion. Both of you know very well that every instrument has a particular use, and that many of the most learned and judicious men are not as capable of conducting an affair as one of mediocre ability who has a first-hand knowledge of the particulars.

Speaking of financial matters I ought to have asked you also to show me the method to keep from losing title to the asses if I succeed in sending them in my name or in the name of someone else and if it should happen that an heir of the person who appeared to be the owner should claim the title.

Pardon the inconvenience of such a long hodge-podge. I beg you to favor me with the information I need as soon as possible, honor me with your commands, and believe me invariably with the highest esteem, your most humble servant, most obliging and most affectionate friend,   FILIPPO MAZZEI

I have informed the M. de la Fayette of your present address. I beg you to send the letter to Mr. Adams by the first opportunity, and if you think he is able to send the other 3 to America first, pray send him those also.

RC (DLC); in Italian; endorsed. Not recorded in SJL. The enclosed note "for the fifty louis" has not been found; it was probably in acknowledgement of the 600 francs that, according to an entry in the Account Book for 22 Oct. 1785, TJ had lent Mazzei. The enclosed letter to John Adams was evidently that of 29 Oct. 1785 (MHi: AMT); see note below. The three other letters destined for America have not been identified.

The nature of the papers THAT YOU LENT ME WHICH ARE SO IMPORTANT TO YOU is not precisely known, but some are identified in Mazzei's letter to TJ of 6 Feb. 1786. Mazzei evidently took these with him in the hope of persuading Luzac, publisher of the Gazette de Leide to use them as counter-propaganda. Lafayette's return from the Prussian maneuvers was no doubt Mazzei's immediate stimulus in this direction. In his letter to Adams of 29 Oct. Mazzei wrote: "The Marquis de la Fayette is just returned from Germany, where he has been in the way of observing, that the many lies and exaggerations which are everywhere spread to our disadvantage must be injurious to our national honor, if we neglect contradicting them, as we have done hitherto with too much indulgence." He added that Lafayette had written to friends in Congress proposing to maintain a printer in behalf of American interest and urging them "not to mind a certain sum of money which can

hardly be better employed." Mazzei thought the newspapers had not done as much harm as the writings of "the untrue and partial Abbé Raynal and the good natured and uninformed Abbé de Mably. The first is an Angloman and the second has written for the mere sake of writing, probably in his dotage, without knowing what he was about." He also asked Adams whether he had authority to contradict the assertion of Abbé Mably "that you desired him to write on the several constitutions of the United States" (Mazzei to Adams, 29 Oct. 1785; MHi: AMT). "When I first came to Europe," Adams replied, ". . . my Indignation was roused, at the shameless falshoods which were continually propagated and I took a great deal of pains to have them contradicted, but I have long since found it an Augean stable. The Truth is, that this impudence is encouraged in France, almost as much, and in Germany still more, than in England. The real motive is to discourage Emigrations. One half of Germany and more than half of England, Scotland and Ireland would be soon on tiptoe and no inconsiderable Part of France—to fly to America for relief from that intollerable Load which they now carry on their shoulders, if they knew the true state of facts in America. The English Ministers and the whole Hierarchy of their Dependents are aware of this, and there is an incredible

Number of Persons constantly employed in preparing Paragraphs to represent the United States to be in a state of Anarchy and Misery. . . . You may contradict them to Eternity to no Purpose. Everything you insert will only occasion ten more lies to be made and your truths will be disbelieved and all the lies credited. . . . I don't believe you will do any good by entering into the Fracasseries of the Men of Letters in France. De Mably was as honest a Man and as Independent a Spirit as you will find among them" (Adams to Mazzei, 15 Dec. 1785; MHi: AMT). Mazzei yielded no ground in his reply: "As to News-papers, I beg leave to transcribe for your perusal the conclusion of a paragraph, which Marquis de la Fayette, to contradict a false assertion in which he had been named, sent to several Gazeteers in various parts of Europe, and was by them faithfully inserted. 'C'est une occasion d'avertir Messrs. les Gazetiers Européens que toutes les lamentations qu'ils reçoivent sur la prétendue Anarchie, corruption, et détrêsse des Américains n'ont en général d'autre but que de combattre à couvert les Etats Unis, les idées de liberté, et surtout l'esprit d'Emigration.' The publishing of such a paragraph, and others which at different times have been sent to several printers by Mr. Jefferson or myself, show most clearly that the printers are not all bribed, or controuled by the Governments they live under, at least on affairs relative to America. Some of them are; but that being known, they are not much credited. The harm is done by those who, although they would be glad to furnish their readers with true American accounts, are obliged to copy them from English papers, for want of a better information. Even the great Republican Luzac has found it necessary to do the same, not to appear negligent or partial in our favor, though he did not credit himself such things as his business, or rather his duty as a gazeteer, obliged him to insert in his gazette. . . . National honor has been my first inducement to undertake the confutation of the mistakes, follies, indiscretions and falsities of certain writers. . . . As to Buffon, who has been unwillingly induced into error . . . I shall refer my reader to the *Annotations on the State of Virginia*, wherein Mr. Jefferson has confuted him most masterly and completely. I will prove that Abbé Raynal is a willful lyer; and as to Mably, I have already brought to a geometrical demonstration his ignorance of our Constitutions and Codes of Laws. . . . He proves nothing, and teaches nothing if we except a few wrong, silly, and overbearing principles of Government. The stile is the only thing of his writings, that may be of some service in certain diseases, as it operates quicker than Laudanum. I defy the whole Corps of his friends to point out, *in any one of his whole works*, a single good part of his own, or any matter whatsoever properly discussed and thoroughly digested" (Mazzei to Adams, 23 Jan. 1786; MHi: AMT). This was scarcely convincing to Adams on either point—Mably's *Observations upon the Government and Laws of the United States* had been written in the form of letters addressed to Adams, who had once expressed great pleasure at seeing "the pens of a De Mably, a Raynal, a Cerisier, a Price, turned to the subject of government" (Adams to Cerisier, 22 Feb. 1784; *Works*, ed. C. F. Adams, IX, 522-3)—but it provides additional information as to the extent to which TJ, as well as Lafayette and Mazzei, sought to counteract hostile accounts in the European press. See Vol. 7: 540-5; TJ's account of the Stanhope affair, printed under 1 Nov. 1785; and note to Mazzei to TJ, 6 Feb. 1786.

The SCOUNDRELLY PETRONILLA was Mazzei's wife, from whom he had expressed the intention of obtaining a divorce "as soon as in our republic we shall have wise and sacred laws authorizing the dissolution of matrimonial ties" (quoted by Marraro, WMQ, 3rd ser., I [1944], 378, note 8). It was evidently at TJ's request—perhaps made during their conversation MONDAY EVENING—that MEYER ASSUMED THE OBLIGATION when he and Mazzei discussed Williamos' situation. On his return from Fontainebleau, TJ, according to an entry in his Account Book under 8 Nov. 1785, "gave Mayer for support of Williamos 120f." See note to TJ to Williamos, 7 July 1785.

From Nicolas & Jacob van Staphorst

[*Amsterdam, 27 Oct. 1785.* Recorded in SJL as received 1 Nov. 1785. Not found.]

From Vergennes

A Fontainebleau le 27. 8bre. 1785.

J'ai reçu, Monsieur, la lettre que vous m'avez fait l'honneur de m'écrire le 12. de ce mois ainsi que celle de Mr. Adams. Je les ai communiquées à Mr. le Maal. de Castries, et ce Ministre vient de m'adresser deux lettres de recommandation pour MM. Barklay et Lamb; l'une est pour notre Consul à Alger et l'autre pour notre Vice-Consul à Salé; vous les trouverez ci-jointes avec deux passeports. Vous devez être persuadé, Monsieur, que ces deux Officiers rendront à vos délégués tous les bons Offices qui pourront dépendre d'eux.

J'ai l'honneur d'être très sincerement Monsieur, votre très humble et très obéissant serviteur, DE VERGENNES

RC (DLC). FC (Arch. Aff. Etr., Corr. Pol., E.-U., xxx; Tr in DLC). Enclosures: (1) Letters to the French consul at Algiers and to the vice-consul at Salee; not found. (2) Passports for Barclay and Lamb. A copy of the passport for "le Sieur Thomas Barkley Agent des Etats Unis . . . près l'Empereur de Maroc" is in DNA: PCC, No. 117. It enjoined all French civil and military officers to give him "toute l'aide et l'assistance dont il pourra avoir besoin sans souffrir qu'il lui soit fait aucun trouble ni empechement . . . aussi, en cas de besoin toute faveur et protection"; signed by Castries for the king, at Fontainebleau, 23 Oct. 1785. Recorded in SJL as received on 1 Nov. 1785.

From Castries

Fontainebleau, 28 Oct. 1785. Sends certified copies of two receipts given by John Paul Jones to the treasurer of marine at L'Orient for payment of the shares of prizes claimed by U.S. citizens—105,185^{tt} 3s. 6d. for the crew of the *Alliance* and 75,853^{tt} 18s. 4d., including Jones' own shares as well as those of the Americans of the *Bon Homme Richard* and the *Pallas*.

RC (DLC); 1 p.; in French; in clerk's hand, signed by Castries; at head of text: "*Invalides*. [On] lui adresse les copies des recus qui constatent les sommes que Mr. Jones a touché." Tr (DNA: PCC, No. 87, I); in Short's hand, accompanied by English translation. Tr (DNA: PCC, No. 107, I); also with an English translation. Recorded in SJL as received 1 Nov. 1785. Enclosures (DLC): (1) Copy, certified by Gratien de Comorre, treasurer of marine at L'Orient, of John Paul Jones' receipts of 18 Aug. and 5 Sep. 1785. Copies with translations are also in DNA: PCC, No. 87, I, and No. 107, I.

To James Madison

Dear Sir   Fontainebleau Oct. 28. 1785.

Seven o'clock, and retired to my fireside, I have determined to enter into conversation with you; this is a village of about 5,000[1] inhabitants when the court is not here and 20,000 when they are, occupying a valley thro' which runs a brook, and on each side of it a ridge of small mountains most of which are naked rock. The king comes here in the fall always, to hunt. His court attend him, as do also the foreign diplomatic corps. But as this is not indispensably required, and my finances do not admit the expence of a continued residence here, I propose to come occasionally to attend the king's levees, returning again to Paris, distant 40 miles. This being the first trip, I set out yesterday morning to take a view of the place. For this purpose I shaped my course towards the highest of the mountains in sight, to the top of which was about a league. As soon as I had got clear of the town I fell in with a poor woman walking at the same rate with myself and going the same course. Wishing to know the condition of the labouring poor I entered into conversation with her, which I began by enquiries for the path which would lead me into the mountain: and thence proceeded to enquiries into her vocation, condition and circumstance. She told me she was a day labourer, at 8. sous or 4 d. sterling the day; that she had two children to maintain, and to pay a rent of 30 livres for her house (which would consume the hire of 75 days), that often she could get no emploiment, and of course was without bread. As we had walked together near a mile and she had so far served me as a guide, I gave her, on parting 24 sous. She burst into tears of a gratitude which I could perceive was unfeigned, because she was unable to utter a word. She had probably never before received so great an aid. This little attendrissement, with the solitude of my walk led me into a train of reflections on that unequal division of property which occasions the numberless instances of wretchedness which I had observed in this country and is to be observed all over Europe. The property of this country is absolutely concentered in a very few hands, having revenues of from half a million of guineas a year downwards. These employ the flower of the country as servants, some of them having as many as 200 domestics, not labouring. They employ also a great number of manufacturers, and tradesmen, and lastly the class of labouring husbandmen. But after all these comes the most numerous of all the classes, that is, the

poor who cannot find work. I asked myself what could be the reason that so many should be permitted to beg who are willing to
work, in a country where there is a very considerable proportion
of uncultivated lands? These lands are kept idle mostly for the sake
of game. It should seem then that it must be because of the enormous wealth of the proprietors which places them above attention
to the increase of their revenues by permitting these lands to be
laboured. I am conscious that an equal division of property is impracticable. But the consequences of this enormous inequality producing so much misery to the bulk of mankind, legislators cannot
invent too many devices for subdividing property, only taking care
to let their subdivisions go hand in hand with the natural affections
of the human mind. The descent of property of every kind therefore to all the children, or to all the brothers and sisters, or other
relations in equal degree is a politic measure, and a practicable one.
Another means of silently lessening the inequality of property is
to exempt all from taxation below a certain point, and to tax the
higher portions of property in geometrical progression as they
rise. Whenever there is in any country, uncultivated lands and
unemployed poor, it is clear that the laws of property have been so
far extended as to violate natural right. The earth is given as a
common stock for man to labour and live on. If, for the encouragement of industry we allow it to be appropriated, we must take
care that other employment be furnished to those excluded from
the appropriation. If we do not the fundamental right to labour the
earth returns to the unemployed. It is too soon yet in our country to
say that every man who cannot find employment but who can find
uncultivated land, shall be at liberty to cultivate it, paying a moderate rent. But it is not too soon to provide by every possible means
that as few as possible shall be without a little portion of land. The
small landholders are the most precious part of a state.—The next
object which struck my attention in my walk was the deer with
which the wood abounded. They were of the kind called 'Cerfs'
and are certainly of the same species with ours. They are blackish
indeed under the belly, and not white as ours, and they are more
of the chesnut red: but these are such small differences as would
be sure to happen in two races from the same stock, breeding
separately a number of ages.—Their hares are totally different
from the animal we call by that name: but their rabbet is almost
exactly like him. The only difference is in their manners; the land
on which I walked for some time being absolutely reduced to a

honeycomb by their burrowing. I think there is no instance of ours burrowing.—After descending the hill again I saw a man cutting fern. I went to him under the pretence of asking the shortest road to the town, and afterwards asked for what use he was cutting fern. He told me that this part of the country furnished a great deal of fruit to Paris. That when packed in straw it acquired an ill taste, but that dry fern preserved it perfectly without communicating any taste at all. I treasured this observation for the preservation of my apples on my return to my own country. They have no apple here to compare with our Newtown pipping. They have nothing which deserves the name of a peach; there being not sun enough to ripen the plumbpeach and the best of their soft peaches being like our autumn peaches. Their cherries and strawberries are fair, but I think less flavoured. Their plumbs[2] I think are better; so also the gooseberries, and the pears infinitely beyond any thing we possess. They have no grape better than our sweet-water. But they have a succession of as good from very early in the summer till frost. I am tomorrow to go to Mr. Malsherbes (an uncle of the Chevalr. Luzerne's) about 7. leagues from hence, who is the most curious man in France as to his trees. He is making for me a collection of the vines from which the Burgundy, Champagne, Bourdeaux, Frontignac, and other the most valuable wines of this country are made. Another gentleman is collecting for me the best eating grapes, including what we call the raisin. I propose also to endeavor to colonize their hare, rabbet, red and grey partridge, pheasants of different kinds, and some other birds. But I find that I am wandering beyond the limits of my walk and will therefore bid you Adieu. Yours affectionately,   TH: JEFFERSON

RC (DLC: Madison Papers); endorsed. PrC (DLC); torn in lower right hand corner of first leaf, so that a few words are missing.

[1] This figure interlined in substitution for "10,000," which TJ completely deleted in RC and partially in PrC. After this was done, he interlined the words "when the court is not here and 20,000 when they are."

[2] In RC TJ interlined, and then deleted, the words "and raspberries." This was not done in PrC.

From Richard Henry Lee

DEAR SIR   New York October the 29. 1785

My ill state of health having compelled me to look for benefit from the medical springs lately discovered in the vicinity of Philadelphia, I there received the letter that you did me the honor to write me on the 12th. of July. But tho Mr. Houdon arrived there with Dr. Franklin when I was in the city, the former of these gentlemen did not deliver your letter to me but it found me thro the medium of the Post. I have not yet seen Mr. Houdon, nor has he been in any manner before Congress that I know of. He went immediately after his landing to General Washington, from whence I understand that he returned to this City a day or two ago, but I have not yet seen him. Your request, independent of his singular merit, will secure him every civility and service in my power. I think that you have cause, from your statement, to complain of the remissness of your Correspondents. Were I not prevented by the unhappy state of my health, most certainly I should be more attentive to gratify you in a way that certainly must be very agreeable to you, sequestered as you are from your own Country. I think that we have reason to suppose that the requisition of this year (which with the plan for surveying and selling part of the Western lands I have now the honor to enclose you) will produce at least a sufficiency to pay with credit the interest of our foreign debt and to support the expences of the federal government. The unliquidated state of the domestic debt, and the unequal business of the facilities may perhaps obstruct for the present, the payment of the domestic interest. I understand the displeasure of the Commissioners of the Treasury arose from Mr. Grand's failing to comply with orders given him to pay the interest due to the Crown of France which has created uneasiness and doubt of our punctuality where these would not have existed had Mr. Grand not undertaken to pay himself instead of the Government. However, I suppose that the Commissioners will take care to make good the payments omitted by Mr. Grand to have been made to Government. Vermont remains as it was, and we have heard nothing lately concerning Franklin. The Virginia Assembly are agreed, so far as I know, to indulge Kentucky provided it shall be agreeable to the U. States to receive them into the Confederacy so that they may for every purpose be a part of the general system. A proposition is depending before Congress to declare the sense of the Union against all future dismemberments without the consent of the State to be dismemberd and of the United States. Concerning your idea of packets I have spoken to some Members. The expence alarms, and they seem rather to approve of sending on occasion a Courier in the packets as they now are. But since a plan has lately been adopted for sending the Mails by Stages instead of Post Riders, which will not only quicken communication greatly, but very much increase the Post

Office Revenue, I hope that Packets as well as Cross Posts may e'er long be supported. We have lost poor Hardy who dyed here after some weeks illness. The Surveyors are now at work (under the Ordinance) N. West of Ohio, and a Treaty with the Western Indians is holding at Great Miami. Our Assembly is now in Session, but we have not heard whether Harrison or Tyler has got the Chair, but certainly the contest will have been warm and pretty equal. My Presidential year ends in 9 days, after which I shall return to Virginia for some months at least; my return to Congress will depend on the state of my health which is better indeed, but far yet from being as I wish it. Let me be where I will I shall always be happy to hear from you and to give you the news of our Country such as it may be. My brother Arthur Lee being resident here as one of the Commissioners of the Treasury of the U. States, will receive your letters for me and forward them to Virginia. I shall esteem it a very particular favor if you will be so good as send me one of the newly invented Philosophical Lamps which I understand to be handsome, useful, and œconomical employing a small quantity of oil to great advantage in giving light. I will either thankfully repay the cost to your order in Virginia, or remit it to you in France thro the medium of my Brother Arthur from this place. I suppose that you may contrive it by one of the french packets to my brothers care in this City. And it will add to the favor if you accompany the Machine with a description of its use.

I am dear Sir, with sentiments of the sincerest esteem and regard, your most obedient and very humble servant,

RICHARD HENRY LEE

P.S. Remember me if you please to Mr. Short and tell him that I answerd immediately the only letter that I have had the pleasure to receive from him. R. H. LEE

RC (DLC); endorsed. Recorded in SJL as received 18 Jan. 1786. Enclosures: Copies of Congress' report on requisitions for 1785, 27 Sep. 1785 (printed broadside listed in JCC, XXIX, 928, No. 498; text printed in full at p. 765-71) and of the Ordinance for ascertaining the mode of disposing of lands in the Western Territory, 20 May 1785 (printed broadside listed in JCC, XXIX, 923, No. 478; text printed in full in JCC, XXVIII, 375-81).

From Vergennes

À Fontainebleau le 30. 8bre. 1785.

J'ai reçu, Monsieur, la lettre que vous m'avez fait l'honneur de m'ecrire le 21. de ce mois, ainsi que celle qui m'étoit adressée de la part du Sr. Samuel Shaw.

Je me suis fait un devoir, Monsieur, de rendre compte au Roi des prévenances que Ses Officiers ont faites à ceux qui commandoient le navire américain qui a été à la Chine; Sa Majesté a apris avec une véritable satisfaction que les premiers aient conformé leur conduite aux instructions qu'Elle leur avoit fait adresser, et Elle vous charge d'assurer le Congrès que dans toutes les occasions qui se présenteront, Elle s'empressera de manifester son affection et son amitié pour les Etats-unis, et l'interêt bien sincere qu'Elle prend à leur prospérité.

Mais le Roi m'a ordonné en même tems, Monsieur, de vous observer combien peu on a égard en Amérique à la règle de la réciprocité, et combien on y est disposé à s'écarter des principes qui ont servi de baze aux liens qui subsistent entr' Elle et les Etats-unis. Nous sommes informés en effet, Monsieur, que dans plusieurs Etats on a fait des réglements de navigation et de commerce nuisibles au commerce françois et contraires même à l'essence du traité du 6. fevrier 1776.[1] Le Congrès est trop éclairé pour ne pas sentir combien ces procédés doivent nous affecter, et il est trop sage et trop prévoyant pour n'être pas pénétré de la nécessité de maintenir[2] les choses dans l'état de réciprocité où elles ont été depuis que la France est l'alliée des Etats-unis; sans cette précaution il est impossible que le commerce mutuel des deux nations puisse prospérer et même subsister, et le Roi se trouvera Forcé, malgré lui, de chercher des expédients propres à mettre les choses dans une parfaite égalité.[3]

J'ai l'honneur d'être très-sincèrement Monsieur, votre très-humble et très-obéissant Serviteur,   DeVergennes

RC (DLC); in a clerk's hand, signed by Vergennes. Dft (Arch. Aff. Etr., Corr. Pol., E.-U., xxx); in Vergennes' hand, with marginalia in a clerk's hand; at head of text: "Envoyé copie à M. de Castries le 8 9bre. 1785"; opposite second paragraph: "satisfaction avec laquelle le Roi a apris les prevenances que ses officiers ont marquées à ceux qui commandoient le Navire américain qui a été à la Chine"; opposite third paragraph: "plaintes sur quelques reglements de navigation et de commerce faits par plusieurs Etats, et qui sont nuisibles au commerce de france." Tr (DNA: PCC, Nos. 87, 1, and 107, 1); accompanied by English translations.

Vergennes seized the opportunity afforded by TJ's letter of 21 Oct. to make the present protest against the navigation Acts of Massachusetts and New Hampshire, and reported to Castries what he had done (8 Nov. 1785, Arch. Aff. Etr., Corr. Pol., E.-U., xxx; Tr in DLC).

[1] Thus in RC and Dft; both Tr read, correctly, "1778."
[2] The passage "il est trop sage . . . maintenir" is interlined in Dft in substitution for the following deleted passage: "pour ne pas employer tous les moyens qui peuvent etre en son pouvoir pour faire retablir."
[3] The following words were deleted in Dft: "en faisant à l'egard des américains des règlements analogues a ceux qu'ils ont adoptés ou pourront adopter dans la suite à l'egard de la france."

From Thomas Elder

HOND. SIR   [Edinburgh, ca. Oct. 1785]

Dr. Lyons being just about to Step aboard a Ship bound to Amsterdam, on his way to Paris, have embraced so favourable an opportunity of droping you a few lines. If his departure had not been so sudden I should have wrote more at large.—I suppose you have been informed of Colo. Randolphs two Sons being at the University of this place in pursuit of those branches of Literature to be acquired here, and likewise that it will merit your attention how they are like to Succeed. With regard to Tom I think he bids fair for becoming a Worthy and Virtuous Character, and whose conduct even at his early period of life denounce both the Scholar and the Gentleman. But it is to be feared that the Stamina of his constitution are not vigorous enough for those exertions necessary for making the most distinguished figure in life. His brother is one of those easy characters neither too much elevated by prosperity nor depress'd by adversity. When he applies he is equal to the general run of boys, but it is not so easy for him to fix his attention on any Subject for a due length of time. He is looked upon here as a good natured facetious fellow, who studies mankind more than his brother.—Their Cousin Archie Randolph is a young man of an open, generous and candid turn of Mind, which if carried too far and not properly under the regulation of sound judgment may lay him open to the artful and designing. It is a pity that love of dress and of those accomplishments which are only exterior should be so often incompatable with those real improvements of mind most worthy of pursuit. Should take it kind if you can spare a few minutes in droping them a little of your good council, which no doubt in regard to the respectability of your character will have due weight with them. If Tom Randolphs health is not better established by the return of the Spring he is advised to try the climate of France, and should be glad of your opinion on that head. By late letters from Virginia, Colo. Cary and Colo. Randolph enjoy their usual State of health. From a letter dated Boston from Mrs. Randolph we find that she is on the mending hand, and likely to have a compleat recovery. And have the honour to be Sir wt. great respect your very obedt. humble servt.,   THOS. ELDER

RC (MHi); without date; addressed to TJ at Paris; endorsed. Noted in SJL as received 15 Nov. 1785; entry reads: "Thos. Elder. without date of time or place. by Lyon." The entry in SJL for TJ's reply of 25 Nov. shows that Elder wrote from "Mrs. Millar's. George's square. Edinburgh."

Preliminary indexes will be issued periodically for groups of volumes. A comprehensive index of persons, places, subjects, etc., arranged in a single consolidated sequence, will be issued at the conclusion of the series.

THE PAPERS OF THOMAS JEFFERSON is composed in Monticello, a type specially designed by the Mergenthaler Linotype Company for this series. Monticello is based on a type design originally developed by Binny & Ronaldson, the first successful typefounding company in America. It is considered historically appropriate here because it was used extensively in American printing during the last thirty years of Jefferson's life, 1796 to 1826; and because Jefferson himself expressed cordial approval of Binny & Ronaldson types.

✧

Composed and printed by Princeton University Press. Illustrations are reproduced in collotype by Meriden Gravure Company, Meriden, Connecticut. Paper for the series is made by W. C. Hamilton & Sons, at Miquon, Pennsylvania; cloth for the series is made by Holliston Mills, Inc., Norwood, Massachusetts. Bound by the J. C. Valentine Company, New York.

DESIGNED BY P. J. CONKWRIGHT